Magna Carta

ITS ROLE IN THE MAKING OF THE
ENGLISH CONSTITUTION
1300–1629

Old London Bridge

From Gordon Home's *Old London Bridge* (John Lane the Bodley Head Ltd.)

Magna Carta

ITS ROLE IN THE MAKING OF THE ENGLISH CONSTITUTION
1300–1629

by

FAITH THOMPSON

1972
OCTAGON BOOKS
New York

Copyright 1948 by the University of Minnesota

Reprinted 1972
by special arrangement with The University of Minnesota Press

OCTAGON BOOKS
A Division of Farrar, Straus & Giroux, Inc.
19 Union Square West
New York, N. Y. 10003

342,42
T471m

Library of Congress Catalog Card Number: 70-159233

ISBN 0-374-97870-0

Manufactured by Braun-Brumfield, Inc.
Ann Arbor, Michigan

Printed in the. United States of America

026661

✾ PREFACE ✾

Magna Carta is well called the oldest of "liberty documents." It has come to serve as the prototype of all bills of rights, a symbol, a slogan that comes readily to the tongue of a public speaker. Its history, in these days when human progress seems to depend on the success of a world charter, may seem of mere antiquarian interest. Yet the *New York Times* of January 11, 1946, saw fit to devote nearly a column to a description of the ceremony in which Dr. Luther H. Evans, Librarian of Congress, handed to his majesty's minister, John Balfour, one of the original parchment copies of the Great Charter for return to the Dean and Chapter of Lincoln Cathedral.

Of the Charter, during its stay in the United States, Dr. Evans said: "Fifteen million Americans have made pilgrimage to see it; American arms have been its guard." Mr. Balfour termed the Charter the "forefather" of the British and American bills of rights, the American Habeas Corpus Act, and the Declaration of Independence. "The Federal Constitution of the United States," Mr. Balfour said, "contained many of its provisions and even some of its actual words; and this in turn has been the model for many constitutions in many lands. The line of descent extends to our time and we can, without flight of fancy, trace as an authentic offspring the preamble to the Charter of the United Nations. Here is a lineage without equal in human history. For this we honor the Great Charter, and for this, not as Britons or as Americans, but as members of the whole brotherhood of free peoples, we give our thanks to the Librarians of Congress for the care with which during these momentous years, they have guarded a document that is beyond replacement and above price. Magna Carta is not the private property of the British people. It belongs equally to you and to all who at any time and in any land have fought for freedom under the law."

In the words of Professor A. B. White: "Today we study its history, yesterday it was our political Bible. If it became something of a myth few would question that the myth has been beneficent—and still is."

It was through Professor White that my interest in Magna Carta history was first awakened while preparing under his direction at the University of Minnesota a doctoral dissertation, published as *The First Century of Magna Carta*. These studies attempt to trace through three more centuries the varied uses and increasingly significant interpretations of the famous document. It is a pleasure to express to Professor White my gratitude for his continued interest and stimulating suggestions, and for reading parts of the manuscript.

v

The opportunity to use valuable sources available only in England was made possible by a Guggenheim Fellowship for the year 1938–39. For this I express hearty thanks to the foundation, as well as to the Graduate School of the University of Minnesota for a grant-in-aid for a research assistant. I am indebted to Mr. Pulling of the Harvard Law Library, and to Professor Bade and Miss Caroline Brede of the University of Minnesota Law Library, for permission and aid in using their remarkable collections of early printed law books. Acknowledgment is also due the Treasurer and Masters of the Bench of the Inner Temple for permission to use certain Inner Temple Library manuscripts. Professors Wallace Notestein and Hartley Simpson of Yale University generously made available their transcripts of unpublished parliamentary diaries for 1624, 1626, and 1628. To them and to Professor D. H. Willson and other colleagues and friends I am indebted for helpful suggestions, and especially to Professor C. C. Crawford of the University of Kansas for introducing me to the Tudor lawyers and their works.

F. T.

❧ LIST OF ABBREVIATED TITLES ❧

Cal. Close Rolls. Calendar of Close Rolls.
Cal. Letter Books. Calendar of Letter Books of the City of London.
Cal. Pat. Rolls. Calendar of Patent Rolls.
Cal. S. P. Calendar of State Papers, Domestic.
C. J. Journals of the House of Commons.
Cott. MSS. Cottonian Manuscripts.
D.N.B. The Dictionary of National Biography.
Gardiner. S. R. Gardiner, *History of England from the Accession of James I to the Outbreak of the Civil War.*
Harl. MSS. Harleian Manuscripts.
Holdsworth. Sir William S. Holdsworth, *A History of English Law.* (Other works of this author are cited in full.)
King's Bench Rolls. Select Cases in the Court of King's Bench.
L. J. Journals of the House of Lords.
Lansd. MSS. Lansdowne Manuscripts.
McKechnie. William Sharp McKechnie, *Magna Carta, A Commentary on the Great Charter of King John.*
Mass. MSS. Manuscripts in Massachusetts Historical Society Library.
Parl. Writs. Parliamentary Writs and Writs of Military Summons (Francis Palgrave, editor).
Pollock and Maitland. Sir Frederick Pollock and F. W. Maitland, *The History of English Law before the Time of Edward I.*
Rot. Parl. Rotuli Parliamentorum.
S. R. Statutes of the Realm.
Select Charters. Select Charters of English Constitutional History (William Stubbs, editor).
State Trials. T. B. and T. J. Howell, *Complete Collection of State Trials.*
Stowe MSS. Stowe Manuscripts.
Wilkins. *Concilia Magnae Britanniae et Hiberniae* (David Wilkins, editor).
Y. B. Year Books.

❖ TABLE OF CONTENTS ❖

LIST OF ABBREVIATED TITLES vii

INTRODUCTION 3

PART I. THE LATER MIDDLE AGES

I. PARLIAMENTARY CONFIRMATIONS AND SUPPLEMENTARY
STATUTES 9

II. MAGNA CARTA IN THE PLEA ROLLS AND YEAR BOOKS 33

III. MAGNA CARTA AND LIBERTY OF THE SUBJECT 68

IV. MAGNA CARTA AND SPECIAL INTERESTS: THE CITY OF LONDON . . 100

V. MAGNA CARTA AND SPECIAL INTERESTS: THE ENGLISH CHURCH . 121

PART II. THE TUDOR PERIOD

VI. MAGNA CARTA AND THE PRINTERS AND CHRONICLERS 139

VII. THE LAWYERS AND MAGNA CARTA 167

VIII. THE PURITANS AND MAGNA CARTA 197

PART III. THE EARLY STUART PERIOD

IX. SCHOLARSHIP AND CONTROVERSY INTENSIFY 233

X. CHAPTER 29 IN COURTS AND INNS OF COURT 268

XI. A DECADE OF PARLIAMENTS, 1621–1629 294

XII. COKE'S COMMENTARIES: SUMMATION OF THREE CENTURIES . . 354

APPENDIXES 377

BIBLIOGRAPHY 398

INDEX 406

ix

LIST OF ILLUSTRATIONS

OLD LONDON BRIDGE . . . . *frontispiece*

TITLE PAGE OF BERTHELET'S EDITION OF THE STATUTES, 1531 . . . 35

RESTORATION OF THE ANCIENT THOROUGHFARE FROM WESTMINSTER
TO LONDON 114

KING JOHN—A WOODCUT FROM JOHN RASTELL'S *The Pastyme of
People* 157

MIDDLE TEMPLE HALL . . . . *facing* 286

SIR EDWARD COKE 316

Magna Carta

ITS ROLE IN THE MAKING OF THE
ENGLISH CONSTITUTION
1300–1629

❖ INTRODUCTION ❖

A study of the first century of Magna Carta served to indicate why it persisted as a document and entered upon its long career of endurance and fame, but the period set was an arbitrary one. It became obvious to the researcher that the lines of interest uncovered did not cease with the death of Edward I; that the Charter was never entirely eclipsed in the later Middle Ages or even in the Tudor period; that its reinterpretation in the early Stuart period was not something undertaken *de novo,* an abrupt and novel phenomenon. The statesmen who transformed a charter of feudal "liberties" into a charter of "liberty of the subject" were using a document with a long history behind it, its reputation already partly made in plea rolls and Year Books, parliament and statute rolls, law treatises and even chronicles.

These chapters, then, undertake to carry on the story from the close of the reign of Edward I to the death of Sir Edward Coke. The parliament which framed the Petition of Right had been abruptly dissolved in 1629, and Sir Edward was putting the finishing touches on his *Second Institute* at about the same time. To be sure, there is not any good stopping place in the story. It remained for Hampden's counsel in the *ship-money case* to restore to use certain clauses of John's Charter and for the Long Parliament (1641) to authorize the printing of Coke's treatise and to embody the spirit of chapter 29 in some of its definitive statutes. Lilburne and the radicals were to do some novel things with the Great Charter in the 1640's. It was the subject of a reading in the Inns of Court in Charles II's reign and continued to be cited in the courts, and in the eighteenth century it elicited another great commentary, that of Blackstone. Nevertheless, by 1629 the initial work of revival, reinterpretation, and publicization had been accomplished.

It need hardly be said that this book does not claim to be exhaustive. To collect from three centuries of sources all the instances, so ubiquitous yet so illusive, of the citing of Magna Carta would be an almost hopeless task. Every reader who is a specialist in a given period or class of sources will no doubt be able to call to mind instances which the present writer has missed.

What has been attempted here is (1) for the most active periods of Charter history to explore and exploit a great variety of sources; (2) for

3

the relatively inactive periods, to examine only the most likely sources. These are described *passim* in succeeding chapters. Of course, secondary accounts have been freely drawn upon, especially the important contributions of Professors McKechnie, Holdsworth, and McIlwain.

From the very nature of the subject the reader may find at times that he is getting more background than foreground, but it is hoped that these studies will serve to elucidate and illuminate several aspects of English constitutional history. First and foremost, of course, will figure the Charter itself, sometimes serving as an embodiment of the principle of limited monarchy and the evolution of the rule of law, again as a valued part of the private law, a "mere statute." But of none the less interest are its exponents and supporters: feudal barons of the type of Thomas of Lancaster; distinguished prelates like Stratford and Arundel; the ebullient yet practical citizens of London with a keen eye to business; local participants in village and county life; Tudor paternalists; and, last but not least, the distinguished succession of the gentlemen of the Inns of Court from the early pleaders of the Year Books to Sir Edward Coke, that "good commonwealth's man."

To set the stage for our first period—the later Middle Ages—the status of the Charters (Magna Carta and the Forest Charter) at the end of the reign of Edward I may be briefly summarized. It seems clear that Edward did not secure, or even seek, the annulment of the Charters.[1] Clement V's bull dated December 29, 1305, released the king from his obligation to observe the *additions* to the Charters made in 1297 and succeeding years as contrary to his coronation oath, but it contained a saving of the rights of the people existing before the concessions of November 1297.[2]

Edward made only a limited use of his release. He revoked the deforestations granted at the Lincoln parliament, and this was probably his main object.[3] The bull specifically mentions forest concessions. Most of the contemporary chroniclers, absorbed in their accounts of the war with the Scots, are silent on the whole matter. The one writer who does deal with it probably reflects contemporary opinion. He describes a ceremony at St. Paul's, June 5, 1306, in which the king was absolved from his oath,

[1] The contrary view has been expressed by M. Bémont, *Chartes,* p. xlviii: ". . . Edouard, en paix enfin avec la France et l'Ecosse, eut demande et obtenu du pape Clement V l'absolution de tous ses serments et l'annulation des chartes (1305, 29 dec. Textes, no. xvii). Le meilleur roi du xiiie siecle avait donc fait comme le pire . . ."

[2] The language of the bull is vague. It annuls "quasdam concessiones varias et iniquas, forestas, aliaque jura ad coronam et honorem tui culminis spectantia ab antiquo," but makes the reservation: "Per hoc autem non intendimus jus, siquod quibuscunque regnicolis dicti regni in premissis ante concessiones hujusmodi per te factas forsitan competebat, auferre." Bull *Regalis devotionis,* text in Bémont, *Chartes,* no. xvii, pp. 110–12.

[3] Stubbs, *Constitutional History,* II, 160–61; Tout, *Political History of England,* p. 229; Petit-Dutaillis, *Studies,* II, 226. Stubbs points out that the pope's act was referred to in only one contemporary official document, the Ordinance of the Forest, May 27, 1306 (*S. R.* I, 149).

and relates it to the forest only—the promised perambulations.[4] Certainly in after years it was not Clement's bull but the confirmations of 1297 and 1300 that were remembered and used.

The *Confirmatio Cartarum* reveals and emphasizes the contemporary conception of the Great Charter as common law, fundamental law, "to be observed in all points." Procedure for enforcement is prescribed:

> Our justices, sheriffs, mayors, and other officials who under us and by us have to administer the law of the land, shall allow the said charters in pleas before them and judgments in all their points; that is to say the Great Charter of Liberties as common law, and the Charter of the Forest according to the Assize of the Forest, for the relief of our people.[5]

The *Articuli super cartas,* recognizing that there are some provisions of the Charters for which there is no adequate remedy at common law, provides characteristically for the commissioning of local justices, "three substantial Men, Knights or other lawful, wise, and well-disposed Persons," chosen by the "commonalty" of each shire, to "hear and determine without any other Writ, but only their Commission, such Plaints as shall be made upon any Point contained in the foresaid Charters." [6] The desired publicity is to be secured through reading in cathedral churches twice a year and in full county court four times a year, and the greater excommunication is to be denounced twice a year.

Edward I's *inspeximus* of Henry III's Charter remained the standard for succeeding ages. It is the text most commonly included in the manuscript and printed volumes of the statutes.[7] In view of the fact that modern historians have devoted so much attention to John's Charter,[8] it must be emphasized here that it was the text of 1225—9 Henry III, as the lawyers commonly cited it—and this text exclusively that was known and in force. There are a few rare references to John's Charter in the thirteenth century.[9] Perhaps the statements of Wendover and Matthew Paris that the two texts, John's and Henry's, were alike in all points misled contemporaries as well as later generations.

Though it survived as so much parchment and ink, the now famous

---

[4] *Annales Londonienses*, I, 146 (R. S.). There is plenty of contemporary evidence that it was the forest concessions which Edward was so reluctant to yield.

[5] *Select Charters*, p. 492.

[6] *S. R.* I, 136. (When quoting from the sources I have used existing English translations where available, as for the *Statutes of the Realm* and the Selden Society edition of the Year Books. Where none exist, as for the *Rotuli Parliamentorum* and the Black Letter Year Books, I have supplied my own translation or paraphrase of the longer passages in the text, adding the original in notes where the passage is obscure, or the original French or Latin wording is particularly significant or attractive.)

[7] See below, Appendix B and Chap. VI.

[8] With the notable exception of McKechnie, whose commentary on the chapters of John's Charter indicates changes in the successive reissues of 1216, 1217, and 1225.

[9] For these see Thompson, *First Century of Magna Carta*, p. 65 (note A).

text of 1215 dropped completely out of sight until revived, first as a mere matter of antiquarian interest by Tudor historians such as Holinshed, then in more scholarly fashion by John Selden. As we shall see, it was virtually restored to the statute book by Coke and Selden in the parliamentary debates of 1628 and more definitely by the counsel for John Hampden in the *ship-money case*. He who reads on in the following pages, then, must resign himself to the text of 1225 and the stereotyped thirty-seven chapters thereof, even though it means abandoning so famous a designation as "chapter 39." [10]

[10] For the reader's convenience the text of 1225 is given in Appendix A, together with a summary comparison of the texts of 1215 and 1225 and a note on the Forest Charter.

PART I. THE LATER MIDDLE AGES

❀ CHAPTER I ❀

Parliamentary Confirmations and Supplementary Statutes

Parliamentary Confirmations of the Great Charter

"Magna Charta being confirmed thirty times, for so often have the kings of England given their royal assents thereunto."

". . . and the said two charters have been confirmed, established, and commanded to be put in execution by thirty-two several acts of parliament in all." (SIR EDWARD COKE)

THANKS to Sir Edward Coke everyone is familiar with the many parliamentary confirmations of Magna Carta and the Forest Charter.[1] Again and again in his reports, speeches, and treatises the great lawyer took occasion to emphasize these confirmations as evidence of the permanence of the Great Charter and its role as fundamental law. Modern historians have accepted Coke's count. In interpreting the contemporary purpose or value of such confirmations, they have been inclined to assume that provisions of the Charter early became obsolete and that medieval parliaments were seeking merely the moral victory of reminding the king that he was under the law.

Both these points need correction. First, a study of the sources reveals that there were more parliamentary confirmations than even Sir Edward's zeal collected. At no point in his commentary does Coke list entire his "thirty-two acts of parliament," though he cites for special features 52 Henry III, 25 and 28 Edward I, and 42 Edward III. A list has been supplied by the editor of the 1797 edition of the *Second Institute,*[2] and the

[1] This account of the confirmations summarizes material presented in an article, "Parliamentary Confirmations of the Great Charter," in the *American Historical Review,* 38: 659–72. For complete references to sources and secondary accounts the reader is referred to that article. Some additional illustrative and interpretive material has been added here.

[2] On the first page of this edition there appears a parenthetical note listing statutes of confirmation by regnal years as follows: for the reign of Henry III, one; Edward I, two; Edward III, fifteen; Richard II, eight; Henry IV, six; and Henry V, one. Following the lead of Bémont or McKechnie (both of whom cite the 1797 edition) historians ever since have been content to accept this list and have attributed it to Coke himself. Comparison with earlier editions of the *Second Institute,* wherein no such list appears, makes it clear that this note was not Coke's but the editor's.

same series is included in the *Statutes of the Realm*. It is a safe assumption that Sir Edward, the editor of the *Second Institute*, and the record commissioners followed the same method and hence reached a similar result: that of listing as "statutes of confirmation" those to be found in the early printed editions of the statutes—the *Antiqua Statuta* and *Secunda Pars Veterum Statutorum*.[3]

The main point to be made here is this: Based as it is on the old printed statutes, the traditional list does not give a complete count of confirmations of the Great Charter. The parliament rolls tell another story. Here are recorded seventeen confirmations for Edward III, twelve for Richard II, six for Henry IV, and two for Henry V—a total of thirty-seven. These, usually appearing on the roll as the first item of the *communes petitiones*, all receive some form of royal assent. Since the statutes contain confirmations for years in which none appears in the parliament rolls, and vice versa, the total number of recorded confirmations reaches forty-four as against the twenty-nine of the traditional list (that is, excluding those for Henry III and Edward I).[4]

The printed statutes are based on the statute roll rather than the parliament roll, but the former is not a complete or definitive record of the "approved bills" of a given parliament.[5] Some rolls have been lost; others are scanty or imperfect, such as those for the early part of Edward III's reign and part of the reign of Henry VI. Hence, even for years in which no confirmation is recorded on either roll, such negative evidence is not necessarily conclusive. Recent research has brought to light supplementary rolls for the parliaments of 1327 and 1334, and from among the Ancient Petitions the commons' request for a confirmation (with the royal assent) for the Candlemas parliament of 1339. This last adds one more to our

---

[3] For the basis of selection adopted by the record commissioners, see *S. R.* I, xxxi–xxxiii. As to Coke, the commissioners say: "On a Comparison, made for the Purpose of ascertaining the Fact, there is reason to conclude that the Copy used by Lord Coke in his Second Institute was that of 1587 (Totell's edition)." *Ibid*. I, xxii.

[4] The recorded confirmations are as follows:

NUMBER OF CONFIRMATIONS

REIGN	IN PARLIAMENT ROLLS	IN STATUTES	COMMON TO BOTH	TOTAL
Edward III	17	15	9	23
Richard II	12	8	7	13
Henry IV	6	6	6	6
Henry V	2	1	1	2
Total	37	30	22	44

[5] For light on the character and relations of these two types of record, see Gray, *Influence of the Commons on Early Legislation*. The petitions discussed in this chapter, it is interesting to note, usually appear as part of what Gray characterizes as a "comprehensive commons petition" (Chap. VIII) and contain phrases which he designates as the earmark of a commons petition—*Prayen the commons*, etc. (Chap. IV).

series, since it is not duplicated in either the *Rotuli Parliamentorum* or the statutes.[6] (The cartulary of Winchester cathedral records the petition and answer—missing from the parliament roll—for the 1340 confirmation.)[7] As to chroniclers, we are not fortunate enough to have a fourteenth-century Matthew Paris. The annals of the day devote more space to the French wars than to domestic politics, but they record some of the notable confirmations, such as those of 1340 and 1341.[8]

The absence from the traditional list of any confirmations for the reign of Edward II does not mean that there were none. Hemingburgh records one from the Easter parliament of 1309.[9] Although the formal roll yields only a few private petitions, the editors have supplied from another source the petition presented to the king by "the community of his realm." A most affecting plaint it is as to how "his poor people" have not been ruled, as they ought to have been, according to points of the Great Charter.[10]

The New Ordinances of 1311 contained as emphatic a confirmation of Magna Carta as can be found: "That the Great Charter be kept in all its points in such manner, that if there be in the said Charter any point obscure or doubtful, it shall be declared by the said Ordainours, and others whom they will, for that purpose, call to them, when they shall see occasion and season during their power."

According to article xxxi, other good statutes were to be maintained "so

[6] Richardson and Sayles, *Rotuli Parliamentorum* (C. S.) contains the request for a confirmation, 1 Ed. III (p. 117); a "whole" version of the petitions and answers so imperfect for this year in *Rot. Parl.* (pp. 99–179); and for 8 Ed. III the petitions and answers for which *Rot. Parl.* gives only Bowyer's transcript (p. 232). For the Candlemas parliament, 13 Ed. III, Ancient Petition 13584 is identified by the editors as the commons' request, and 13587 the customary affirmative "il plest a nostre seigneur le roi qe les dites chartres . . ." (pp. 268, 270–71). The petition includes with the Charters "lestatuz et ordeinaunces fetez sur les purveours et pernours pur les osteaux nostre seignour le roi et la roine et our enfaunz."

[7] *Chartulary of Winchester Cathedral*, p. 131.

[8] The confirmation of 1309 is noted by Hemingburgh, II, 275. For 1340, *ibid.* II, 354–55; *Eulogium Historiarum*, III, 204; Lanercost, p. 333; and the *Anonimalle Chronicle of St. Mary's Abbey*, York, p. 16 (the last two probably based on the same source). For 1341, Murimuth, p. 119, and Galfridi le Baker de Swynebroke, p. 73 (based on Murimuth down to 1341). For 1388, Henrici Knighton, pp. 299–300, and Ranulf Higden, IX, 190, app., who incorporate into their accounts the statutes of the Cambridge parliament of that year.

[9] "Anno Domini m.cccix. in quindena Paschae tenuit rex parliamentum suum Londoniis, et concesserunt sibi magnates xxv. denarium pro confirmatione Magnae Chartae et Chartae de Foresta . . ." Hemingburgh, II, 275.

[10] *Rot. Parl.* I, 443–45, app. It is prefaced with the statement that the petition was presented at the Easter parliament at London and answered *seriatim* at the Staunford parliament later in the year. The grievances rehearsed are a foretaste of those to be more effectively handled by the New Ordinances: abuses of escheators, purveyors, and constables of castles, the *new customs*, the jurisdiction of the Court of the Steward and Marshal, defeats and delays of suits at common law by protections, too liberal an issue of pardons to persons indicted for felonies.

"Les bones gentz du Roialme qi sont cy venuz au Parlement, prient a nostre Seigneur le Roy, q'il voille, si lui plest, aver regard de son povre poeple, qe molt se sente greve, de ceo q'il ne sont pas menez, sicome il deussent estre, nommeement des pointz de la Grant Chartre, e prie de ce, si lui plest, remedie." There are eleven specific grievances.

that they be not contrary to the Great Charter nor the Charter of the Forest, nor against the Ordinances by us made"; while article xxxviii again confirmed the Charters with a different proviso for interpretation.[11] The revocation of the Ordinances in 1322, of course, nullified their force as law (the same was true of the famous 15 Edward III, which appears in the traditional list) but did not affect the status of the Charters: "the Statutes and Establishments duly made by our Lord the King and his Ancestors, before the said Ordinances, abiding in their Force."[12] This parliament, moreover, provided for certain enactments to replace the Ordinances, the first of which reads: *Enprimes, Qe Seinte Eglise eit totes ses dreitures & franchises, sicome est contenue en la Grante Chartre, & autres Estatutz, de ceo fait avaunt ces houres.*[13]

Every attempt, from 1311 to 1322, to enforce the Ordinances involved a tacit, and sometimes an explicit, demand for the Charters. Supplementary articles issued some time between October 1311 and January 1312 asked that a certain measure be carried out according to Magna Carta and the Ordinances. The spring parliament of 1315 demanded a confirmation of the Ordinances and Magna Carta, and a perambulation of the forests. The Londoners, claiming their liberties as assured by Magna Carta, appealed to the Ordinances which had confirmed the latter. The York parliament of 1318 was to treat of points relative to Magna Carta and the Ordinances, and the Charter was read before the group assigned to this work.

First, It is accorded, That the Great Charter, and the Charter of the Forest, and all other Statutes, made as well in the time of the King's Progenitors, as in the King's time that now is be kept and maintained in all Points.   (4 EDWARD III, CA. I)[14]

IN THIS, the typical "parliamentary" confirmation of the Charter as it appears repeatedly in the statutes engrossed by the king's judges, the human

[11] S. R. I, 158, 165, 167. The rejection of the New Ordinances as evidence in *Bate's case* may have influenced contemporary and later writers against including them. See *State Trials,* II, 398, 497. Said Yelverton: "Great wars have been raised against the credit of this law in the parliament house . . . First, that it is no law; for it was enforced upon the king by some of the nobility that were too strong for him . . . The third objection is, that if it were a law, it is repealed."

[12] S. R. I, 189. According to one chronicle, "the parliament at York was opened, where the prosecution against the de Spencers was stopped, and they were restored to their lands, and the father was made earl of Winchester, and the king granted him the lands of sir John Gifford. And at that parliament were repealed the ordinances of the said earl of Lancaster which he and other nobles of his faction had passed; and if any profitable ordinance were found among them it was to be written and called a statute (*e sil y fust trove nul ordinaunce profitable, serroit escrit e averoit noun de statut . . .*)" *Chroniques de Sempringham* in *Livre de Reis de Brittanie,* pp. 344–45.

[13] *Rot. Parl.* I, 456, no. 35.

[14] S. R. I, 261. Cf. *ibid.* I, 345, 383; II, 32.

interest element has disappeared. One must turn to the parliament rolls for a more lively picture. As recorded there, the requests for a confirmation pass through infinite variations, revealing a far from perfunctory interest in the famous document and from time to time offering practical suggestions for its enforcement and interpretation. It is instructive to correlate with the request for a confirmation in a given parliament other petitions or enactments which relate to some specific provision of the Charter, as well as contemporary citations quite outside of parliament. The writer has found in fourteenth- and fifteenth-century sources appeals to at least twenty-two different chapters, some many times repeated. But these are to be the theme of later chapters. Here may be noted certain interesting variations in the confirmations as they are recorded in the rolls.

In the commons petitions the request for a confirmation of Magna Carta sometimes included, sometimes followed a plea for observance of the "liberties of the Church." [15] It became increasingly the practice to include with Magna Carta measures covered vaguely by the phrase "other good statutes," or to specify particular acts. This recurring phrase suggests that the Charters were being commonly called "statutes," but any conscious theorizing on their origin and status comes only in the next century from the lawyers—Littleton and others. Of these the Forest Charter (inseparably connected in popular opinion with its famous compeer ever since the issue of 1217) appears in every instance but one.[16] Observance of statutes on purveyance was urged in petitions of 25 and 38 Edward III, and 4, 6, 7, 8, and 10 Richard II; statutes of laborers in 4 and 8 Richard II.[17] In 1386 discontent with the administration brought a demand for the Charters and other good statutes, especially those relating to sheriffs, under-sheriffs, escheators, coroners, clerks of sheriffs, and purveyors. Occasionally other interests—rights and customs not embodied in statutes—received attention. The liberties of London and other towns were stressed in 1340, 1341, and 1376, and recurred constantly in a new formula adopted in Henry IV's reign. In the parliament of 1378–79 the commons asked observance of the common law as it had been used in the time of the king's progenitors, while in the troubled early years of Henry IV's reign their plea was for peace and justice to poor and rich alike.[18]

15 Cf. *Rot. Parl.* II, 7, 139 and III, 15, for instance.   16 25 Ed. III (*ibid.* II, 227).

17 *Ibid.* II, 238, 285; III, 93, 137, 173, 200, 221. Particularly elaborate in its enumeration of other statutes was the petition of 4 Rich. II: ". . . qe la Grande Chartre, la Chartre de la Foreste, & les Estatutz queux sont ordeignez pur la Pees, & les Estatutz des Laborers & Artificers, & des Purveours, & l'Estatut des fauxes Acusours, & les autres Estatutz & bones Loies, faitz si bien en temps nre Seigneur le Roi q'or est, come en temps de ses nobles Progenitours, soient bien tenuz & gardez en touz pointz, & duement executz."

18 *Rot. Parl.* III, 80. "Et qe touz voz liges & subgitz purront fraunchement & pesiblement, & en seure & sauf protection du Roy, aler & venir a voz Courtes, pur pursuir les Loies, ou les defendre, sanz destourbance ou impediment de nully. Et qe pleine Justice & Droit soient

Why thus repeatedly confirm a document long established as part of the common law? McKechnie comments on the fact that "Parliament in 1369 thus sought to deprive future Parliaments of the power to effect any alterations upon the terms of Magna Carta. Yet, if Parliament in that year had the power to add anything, by a new legislative enactment, to the ancient binding force of the Great Charter, it follows that succeeding Parliaments, in possession of equal powers, might readily undo by a second statute what the earlier statute had sought to effect." [19]

But that was not the medieval conception. To add something "by a new legislative enactment to the binding force of the Great Charter" was what fourteenth-century parliaments sought repeatedly to do. What Maitland aptly calls "this theoretical sanctity and this practical insecurity" of the Charters was part of the perennial medieval problem of law enforcement. Formal recognition by the king and his officials, as well as publicity among the various estates of the realm, was desirable; measures must be known to be enforced. Professor McIlwain has suggested that the whole of the fundamental common law was confirmed at the beginning of each parliament.[20] The idea was growing that the whole realm was present in parliament. The commons now ask reading of the Charters, not in county court or cathedral church, but before the whole parliament; interpretation, not by a baronial committee, but in parliament or by the council reporting to parliament; enforcement, not by local commissioners, but by the peers in parliament.[21]

In their petition of 1381 the commons themselves recognize the practice established by their ancestors and assume that it should bear fruit in law enforcement. They pray that since by the Great Charter it was ordained and affirmed commonly in all other parliaments (*communement en tous*

faitz si bien as poveres come as riches en voz Courtz." *Ibid.* III, 468. Cf. similar petitions, *ibid.*, pp. 433, 591.

[19] McKechnie, p. 159.

[20] "An examination of parliamentary rolls of the fourteenth and fifteenth centuries will show that the first business of a Parliament is the re-enactment or affirmance of the whole body of the fundamental law, including statutes of the King's predecessors." "Magna Carta and the Common Law" in *Magna Carta Commemoration Essays*, pp. 141–42. See also the same author's *High Court of Parliament*, Chap. II, "The Fundamental Law."

[21] Edward II's reign forms a transition period for these practices as it did for parliament itself. The New Ordinances provided first (ca. vi) for interpretation of obscure points by the ordainers and those whom they chose to consult; and then (ca. xxxviii) "that the Points which are doubtful in the said Charters of Franchises be explained, in the next Parliament after this, by the advice of the Baronage, and of the Justices, and of other Sage Persons of the Law." The method prescribed by cas. xl–xli for enforcing the Ordinances indirectly related to the Charters too. Officials (chancellor, treasurer, chief justices of the two benches, chancellor of the Exchequer, treasurer of the wardrobe, steward of the king's household, all justices, sheriffs, escheators, constables, holders of inquest for all purposes, and all other royal bailiffs and officials) were to take an oath to keep the Ordinances. In each parliament a committee composed of one bishop, two earls, and two barons was to be assigned to hear and determine complaints against any official false to his oath, penalties to be imposed at the discretion of the committee. *S. R.* I, 167.

autres Parlementz) that law be not denied or sold to anyone, that therefore fees be no longer taken by the chancellor for writs.[22]

In the fourteenth as in the thirteenth century, the Charters continued to be bought with a price. The feudal "gracious aid" had now become the parliamentary tax on movables, and bargaining for redress of grievances took the form of the parliamentary grant on conditions. In 1309 the magnates had granted a twenty-fifth for observance of the Charters.[23] The New Ordinances and the Charters which they confirmed were bought with a twentieth by the parliament of 1315. When collectors of the tax met with resistance on the grounds that the promise had not been fulfilled, the king was obliged to assure the sheriffs of the honesty of his intentions.[24]

In Edward III's first parliament appeared a petition asking interpretation of the Great Charter, while the confirmation of 1334 was followed by a proviso that "such statutes as be obscure by good advice shall be made plain." The unusual grant of the ninth sheaf, fleece, and lamb in 1340 was made in return for important concessions, not the least of which was a confirmation of the Charters. This is one of the few confirmations recorded by several chroniclers, all of whom note the bargain element.[25] The spring parliament of 1341 reminded the king of this grant and reproached him with his failure to fulfill its conditions, especially in regard to the Charters.

The elaborate arrangements made by this parliament for the confirmation, enforcement, and interpretation of the Charters, embodied in the famous but short-lived statute of 15 Edward III, are discussed below. With Edward's annulment of the statute, no such "king-yoking" schemes were adopted until the minority of Richard II, but from time to time the commons offered more modest suggestions to secure enforcement of the Great Charter and "other good statutes." In 25 Edward III they ask that *punissement de corps soit ordeigne a ses qe fount la encountre*; in 1354 that Magna Carta and the Forest Charter be read; in 1363 that officials be charged

---

[22] *Rot. Parl.* III, 116, no. 88; McIlwain, *High Court of Parliament*, p. 117.

[23] Hemingburgh (II, 275) stresses this element of bargain: "concesserunt sibi Magnates xxv denarium pro confirmatione Magnae Chartae et Chartae de Foresta."

[24] *Cal. Close Rolls,* 1313–18, p. 224 (April 20, 1315): Order to the sheriffs to make proclamation to the effect "that it was the king's intention from the time of the grant of the twentieth granted to him to resist the Scotch invasion, that the requests of the commons concerning the ordinances lately made and approved by the king and for the keeping of Magna Carta and the Charter of the Forests and for making perambulation of the forest shall be observed in all things, and the king has caused persons to be appointed to make the perambulations."

[25] Hemingburgh, II, 354–55: "Pro hac autem concessione remisit dominus rex et condonavit omnia catalla felonum et fugitorum . . . Confirmavit etiam Magnam Cartam, et Cartam de Foresta, et aliqua alia." *Eulogium Historiarum,* III, 204: "Pro hac autem concessione . . . et confirmavit Magnam Cartam de libertatibus Angliae et Cartam de Foresta." *Anonimalle Chronicle,* p. 16: "Sur queles grauntes et concessiouns le dit roi Dengleterre et de Fraunce une novelle chartre graunta et la graunte chartre ratifia et . . ."

with examining and showing to the council statutes and ordinances not duly executed.[26] Petitions of 29 and 38 Edward III sought remedy through writs granted by the chancellor.[27]

Special efforts to secure publicity and enforcement were put forth in Richard II's troubled minority. In his first parliament the commons asked that the Great Charter be read "point by point" before prelates, lords, all the baronage, and commons. Any points found obscure were to be declared between this parliament and the next by members of the continual council, in consultation with justices, serjeants, and any others they chose to summon. The resultant interpretation was to be shown to lords and commons at the next parliament, and *adonqes estre encresceez & affermez pur Estatut s'il semble a eux q'il soit a faire*. Both parliament and statute rolls state that the Charter was read in parliament.

The wording of this petition (1 Richard II) is particularly effective. The king is reminded of his coronation oath: *eiant regarde coment le Roi est chargee a son Coronement de tenir & garder la dite Chartre en touz ses pointz*. In quite the tone of American writers who extol the "fathers of the Constitution" the petitioners revert to the genesis of the Charter: *eiant regarde a la grante nobley & la sage descression q'estoit en la Roialme quant la dite Grande Chartre estoit ordene & establiz*. The Charter was read by the chancellor before some of the prelates and lords at Northampton in 1380, while waiting for others to arrive.[28] From this time on the petitions became more perfunctory and contained fewer variations.

Much has been made of one in this succession of confirmations, that of 42 Edward III: "That the Great Charter and the Charter of the Forest be holden and kept in all Points; and if any Statute be made to the contrary that shall be holden for none." Coke believed that this act restored the Great Charter to its full effect and pristine vigor. He cited it repeatedly in his writings and speeches. His conception of the document was pithily embodied in the oft-quoted "Magna Charta is such a Fellow, that he will have no Sovereign," and this conception was to be a great asset in the struggle against the Stuarts.

Bacon, like Coke, believed that the Charter was fundamental and unalterable, though Selden believed that it could be changed by parliament.[29] Among modern writers, McIlwain, with his thesis of the predominantly

---

[26] *Rot. Parl.* II, 227, no. 11; 259, no. 28; 276, no. 10.

[27] *Rot. Parl.* II, 265. For a similar petition, 38 Ed. III, see *ibid.* II, 285, no. 10.

[28] ". . . le primer jour de ce present Parlement, aucuns des Prelatz & Seigneurs de Roialme qi furent lors venuz a la Ville de Norhampton, avec les grantz Officers du dit nostre Seigneur le Roi, s'assemblerent en une Chambre ordenez pur le Conseil nostre Seigneur le Roy deinz la Priorie de Seint Andreu, & illoeques, en audience de toutz, l'Arcevesque de Canterbirs, adonques Chanceller d'Engleterre, fist faire lire la Grante Chartre de Libertatibus Anglie." *Rot. Parl.* III, 88.

[29] See below, pp. 241–42.

judicial character of medieval parliaments and the accompanying conception of fundamental law, accepts this view of the Charter,[30] while Mc-Kechnie, as indicated above, points out its conflict with the theory of parliamentary sovereignty. Professor Plucknett shows that in practice even fourteenth-century lawyers did not treat the Charter as unalterable fundamental law. While he finds in the act of 42 Edward III words "which at first sight suggest that this document was meant to be regarded thenceforward as fundamental . . . investigation makes it difficult to believe that this was the true meaning of the confirmation. Although Magna Carta was thus confirmed in general terms, considerable portions of it had long been repealed by previous enactments. Were these repeals still valid after 1368? The lawyers showed no doubts whatever and regarded the repeals as still operative." [31] But consistency was not a virtue of fourteenth-century parliaments and courts. There were "considerable portions" of the Charter not yet repealed. Its fame as a distinct entity was too great for anything but a confirmation *in toto*.

As a matter of fact, the petition of 42 Edward III goes farther than the statute. Not content simply to assume that statutes contrary to the Charters "be holden for none," it asks that such statutes be examined and *par la sage discretion & avisement des Seigneurs de Parlement repellez.*[32] There is no lack of evidence in these and succeeding years that ordinary statutes, at least, could be repealed by parliament. After 1368 no petition for a confirmation asked repeal of contrary statutes, but for a few years 42 Edward III is echoed in commons petitions such as those of 1376, 1377, and 1379: *qe la Graunde Chartre, & cele de Forest avaunt ditz, ove touz lour articles, estoisent en lour plenere force, nientcontreesteant auscun Estatut, Ordinance, ou Chartre depuis faitz ou grauntez a l'encountre.*

The commons, as well as popes and kings, could make use of *non obstante* clauses. In 1376 they had complained that in spite of confirmations, the Charters had been infringed by persons actuated by personal gain rather than the public welfare and *par sinistrers interpretations d'ascuns gentz de Loi,* while in 1 Henry IV they asked repeal of a statute of the king's grandfather as *expressement fait encontre la tenure e effect de la Grande Chartre.*[33]

In the later Middle Ages parliamentary confirmations of the Great Charter gradually became more perfunctory and intermittent and finally ceased altogether. A transition period—Richard II to Henry VI—is reflected in

[30] McIlwain, *High Court of Parliament,* pp. 51–66.
[31] Plucknett, *Statutes and Their Interpretation,* p. 27.
[32] *Rot. Parl.* II, 295. Compare the form of confirmation below which refers to "statutes not repealed."
[33] *Ibid.* II, 331, 364; III, 61. These instances are cited by McIlwain, "Magna Carta and Common Law," in *Magna Carta Commemoration Essays,* pp. 175–76.

the very form of the confirmations. In Richard II's reign for the first time appear requests for confirmations of statutes in general, with no mention of the Charters: *Primerement, qe toutes les bones Estatutz & Ordenances avant ces heures faitz, nient repellez, soient fermement tenuz & gardez, & duement executz en toutz lour pointz.*[34]

But it was the Shrewsbury parliament—that foretaste of absolutism—that initiated a new formula, couched in the same words as, perhaps suggested by, the speeches with which Richard's chancellors were opening the king's parliaments: "First, That Holy Church, and the Lords Spiritual and Temporal, and all Cities and Boroughs and other Commonalties of the Realm, have and enjoy their Liberties and Franchises from henceforth, as they have reasonably had and enjoyed in Time of his noble Progenitors Kings of England and in his Time."[35]

Here we seem to find abandoned that old spirit of *communitas* or *universitas* which had served to win and maintain the Great Charter, and we revert to the several discrete liberties and franchises of the various estates and communities of the realm.

The first parliament of Henry IV reverted to the earlier type of confirmation of the Charters. Then for several years the old and new forms are combined:

First, That Holy Church have all her Liberties and Franchises; and that the Lords Spiritual and Temporal, and all the Cities, Boroughs, and Towns franchised, have and enjoy all their Liberties and Franchises, which they have had of the Grant of the Progenitors of our said Lord the King, Kings of England, and of the Confirmation of the same our Lord the King; and that the Great Charter, and the Charter of the Forest, and all the good Ordinances and Statutes made in the Time of our said Lord the King, and in the Time of his Progenitors, not repealed, be firmly holden and kept.[36]

This form was used by two distinguished chancellors, Archbishop Arundel in opening the parliament of 1407 and Thomas Beaufort in 1411.[37]

---

[34] *Rot. Parl.* III, 290, no. 26 (15 Rich. II). The request for a confirmation for 8 Rich. II is more explicit, specifying statutes on sheriffs, escheators, purveyors, etc., but the more perfunctory form quoted in the text becomes customary: *S. R.* II, 38, 78; *Rot. Parl.* III, 210, 290, 318. 3 Rich. II (*Rot. Parl.* III, 80) includes the Charters, but the corresponding entry in *S. R.* II, 13, does not.

[35] *S. R.* II, 94. For the chancellor's speeches, for instance, that by William of Wykeham, 13 Rich. II, promising for the king: "Et voet qe si bien Seinte Eglise, come les Seigneurs Espiritels & Temporels & les Communes, eient & enjoient lour Libertees, Franchises & Privileges, si avant come ils les ont resonablement usez & enjoiez en temps de ses nobles progenitours Rois d'Engleterre." *Rot. Parl.* III, 257; also 277, 284, 309.

[36] 2, 4, 7, 9, 13 Hen. IV; 2, 4 Hen. V (*S. R.* II, 120, 132, 150, 166, 196; *Rot. Parl.* III, 468, 494, 591, 613, 659; IV, 19).

[37] Beaufort's: "Et outre ce, mesme le Chanceller declarra overtement en Parlement, q'y feust la voluntée du Roy, qe Seinte Esglise ait & enjoie toutz ses Libertee [*sic*] & Fraunchises, & qe la graunde Chartre, & Chartre de la Foreste, & toutz autres Estatutz & Ordenances faites devaunt ces heures, & nient repellez, soient tenuz & gardez, & mys en due execution." *Rot. Parl.* III, 647. Arundel's, at greater length, *ibid.*, p. 608. For the early part of Edward

Thenceforth the chancellors' speeches, as recorded by the clerk, promise merely "the liberties" as in Richard's reign—this regularly in all parliaments through 1417 and occasionally through 1435.[38] From this time on, the speech is either not recorded at all or receives the barest mention. For a time the commons petitions for confirmation follow the chancellor's lead with never a reference to the Great Charter. After 1423 the commons petitions cease to be headed by requests for a confirmation of any sort.[39]

Nevertheless, the confirmations were enshrined in parliament and statute roll, permanently recorded in such form as to convince later generations that here was something unique, not just one of the many "good laws and statutes not repealed," but *primus inter pares,* a law of laws, fundamental and enduring.

Supplementary Statutes

THE vitality of several provisions of the Charter is evidenced by their re-enactment or amplification in later statutes. As to thirteenth-century legislation, the Charter is specifically named and one or more of its provisions reaffirmed or elaborated in the Provisions of Oxford and Westminster, the Dictum of Kenilworth, and the Statute of Marlborough; in three great statutes of Edward I's reign, Westminster I and II and Gloucester; and in the *Articuli super cartas.*[40]

By the fourteenth century, tenures and the feudal incidents were fairly well regulated. There were writs and actions aplenty for almost any contingency. The few exceptions—matters yet needing legislative action—relate to the feudal aids, wardship, and escheat.[41] The series of statutes on waste during wardship was supplemented in 1340 by a provision against waste committed by escheators before turning over property to the heir.[42] As to escheats, chapter 31 of the Charter reaffirmed a distinction between

III's reign the rolls give only brief notice of the chancellor's speech (*les causes del Somons de cest Parlement*). Following the first attempt at quotation (1354) more and more space is devoted to the speech. Hence we are not in a position to know whether the chancellor customarily promised the Charters in those days.

[38] *Rot. Parl.* III, 454, 485, 522, 545, 567, 622; IV, 3, 15, 34, 62, 70, 94, 106; for the period after 1417, *ibid.* IV, 169, 261, 295, 316, 367, 388, 481.

[39] *Ibid.* IV, 49, 113, 120, 125, 146, 154, 253.

[40] See McKechnie's commentary on John's Charter, cas. 4, 5, 6, 9, 17, 18, 28, 30, 36, and 37; and Thompson, *First Century of Magna Carta,* pp. 55–57. In a few other instances where Magna Carta is not named, the wording closely parallels that of the Charter. As McKechnie points out, certain provisions of John's Charter, omitted from all revisions, were partly re-enacted later.

[41] As to feudal aids, 25 Ed. III, stat. 5, ca. 11, prescribes that there be only "reasonable aids to the crown," "after the form of the statute thereof made." But the statute here is West. I, ca. 36. The revised Great Charter contained no provision on aids. S. R. I, 322.

[42] 14 Ed. III, stat. I, ca. 13 (*S. R.* I, 285–86). It begins with a paraphrase of Magna Carta, ca. 3: "Item, whereas in the Great Charter it is contained, that after the Death of the Ancestors, which hold of the King in chief, and whose Heirs be within Age, that the King shall keep the Lands without Waste and Destruction, and restore them wholly to the Heirs

holdings originally granted by the crown and hence held *ut de corona* and holdings granted by a mesne lord whose barony subsequently escheated and hence held *ut de escaeta* (*ut de honore, ut de baronia*). The original text of 1215 had safeguarded this second class by providing against increase of reliefs and services, while the reissues added that the king would not claim escheat or custody over the tenants of such a barony. In practice there were other distinctions covered by the clause *Nos eodem modo eam tenebimus quo Baro eam tenuit.* It was profitable for the crown and the Exchequer to "forget" or ignore these distinctions, vital to the tenant to maintain them. The king's right to restrain alienation by tenants-in-chief was not questioned, but in 1325 complaint was made in parliament that the rule was being extended. The petitioners, purchasers of tenements held of honors forfeited in the recent rising against the king, alleged that whereas before the forfeiture they could purchase lands and take feoffments without having leave of the lords, now, escheators and other ministers "when lands within the honours are purchased, seize the lands as if they were held of the king in chief of the crown, which is contrary to the form of Magna Carta . . ." The complaint, which received a rather grudging recognition at this time, was dealt with in a statute at the beginning of the next reign.[43]

"All medieval laws," says Professor Tout, "were rather enunciations of an ideal than measures which practical statesmen aimed at carrying out in detail." [44] The general application of statutes such as Mortmain, Provisors, and certain commercial measures was weakened by the royal prerogative in making exceptions by *non obstantes,* the liberal dispensing power which medieval law and theory allowed its king. However, in respect to the laws to be discussed here, the problem was rather that of local law enforcement. Local officials, and sometimes local lords, were more to blame than the king and agencies of central government. In the following pages, even at the risk of wearying the reader, numerous supplementary details are introduced, especially from the close and patent rolls, for two reasons: (1) the examination of manuscript rolls reveals that a number of the original entries made by the clerks contain references to the Great Charter (always cited, by the way, as *magna carta de libertatibus anglie*)

when they come to their full Age; and against God and Right, and the said Establishment, the Escheators . . ." 36 Ed. III, ca. 13, imposes on escheators guilty of waste a penalty of treble damages to the heir, but this does not cite the Charter. *S. R.* I, 374-75.

[43] To this it was replied that "the king should have the same estate as to taking fines for the purchase of lands and tenements held of honours in the king's hands as the lords had, according to the purport of *Magna Carta,* saving to the king his rights and prerogative in other things." *Cal. Close Rolls,* 1318-23, p. 535 (C 54/143 m.15d); also *Rot. Parl.* I, 430. The statute does not cite the Charter. 1 Ed. III, stat. 2, cas. 12 and 13 (*S. R.* I, 256). See Pollock and Maitland, I, 338, for this episode, and p. 281 on escheated honors in general.

[44] *Political History of England,* p. 152.

which are omitted in the concise paraphrase of the modern calendar; (2) the provisions in question relate to everyday bread-and-butter matters—ships and fish, carts and cattle, weights and measures.

Grievances arising from purveyance continued in some form to vex the people until its abolition in 1660. For the period under discussion here it is enough to notice the heavy prises levied to supply Edward I's wars; the disorderly royal household of Edward II with its greedy and undisciplined servants, and purveyance for the Scottish war; Edward III's minority, with the maladministration of Isabella and Mortimer, then the burdens imposed by the long struggle with France. Magna Carta did little to limit purveyance, so little, in fact, that the lawyers of the sixteenth and early seventeenth centuries conceived chapters 19 and 21 as the sanction rather than the curtailment of this prerogative.[45]

The first real regulation of purveyance for the royal household appears in the *Articuli super cartas,* 1300. By chapter 2 purveyance was confined to the king's takers for the king's house; purveyors must pay or agree on payment, have a warrant, take no more than needful, take nothing as wages, answer in the king's wardrobe for the things taken; purveyance without warrant was constituted a felony; and purveyance at fairs, towns, and ports for the king's great wardrobe (which handled war supplies) was to be by warrant under the great seal.[46] No wonder that in succeeding years it was this, cited as 28 Edward I, chapter 2, that was confirmed by parliament rather than the limited clauses of Magna Carta. Nevertheless, for a generation or more after 1300 the Charter stood first in popular opinion as a remedy for the evils of purveyance. The *Articuli* either were considered, as their title implies, an expansion of and commentary on the Charter or were confused with the latter.

Instances of this popular attitude are found in the Easter parliament of

---

[45] In theory purveyance was "a right of pre-emption; the provisions seized were to be paid for at the market rate . . . In the absence of a neutral arbitrator to fix the value of the goods, the unfortunate seller was thankful to accept any pittance offered by royal officials . . . Payment was often indefinitely delayed or made not in coin but in exchequer tallies, 'a vexatious anticipation of taxation,' since these could only be used in payment of Crown dues." McKechnie, p. 330.

For complaints made to the commissions of investigation, 1340–41, see Hughes, *Study of Social and Constitutional Tendencies,* pp. 13–35, 95–96, 204.

Magna Carta ca. 19 permitted constables of castles to take supplies from persons outside the town where the castle was situated only on immediate payment and with the consent of the owner. For goods taken from the castle town, forty days' delay was allowed. Ca. 21 prohibited sheriffs from commandeering horses and carts except at fixed rates. Demesne carts of any "parson" or knight or lady were exempt. The last clause restricted the king and his officials to wood obtained from the royal demesne. West. I added restrictions slight except for the clergy. For the draft presented by the barons, 1297, Edward I substituted the vaguer terms "for no business from henceforth we shall take such manner of Aids Tasks nor Prises, but by the common assent of the Realm."

[46] S. R. I, 137–38.

1309, which granted a twenty-fifth on condition of redress of grievances,[47] and in the petition of the barons in 1310 resulting in appointment of the Lords Ordainers. This reads:

> And the land is altogether poor and devoid of all manner of treasure, so that you have not wherewith you may be able to defend your land, or to maintain your household, except by the extortions which your ministers commit upon the goods of Holy Church and of your poor people, without paying anything therefor, contrary to the tenor of the Great Charter, the which they pray may be maintained in its force.[48]

Efforts to enforce the New Ordinances, 1311–22, were concerned particularly with purveyance. Orders to sheriffs and constables enjoin observation of chapter 10 and direct victualling of castles "according to the tenor of Magna Carta." [49] One article of the *Great Eyre of Kent* (6 and 7 Edward II) had to do with unlawful prises.[50] On the repeal of the Ordinances, 1322, terms of the *Articuli super cartas* were confirmed, regulations on purveyance to be published every market day.[51]

In 1330 the treatise *Speculum*, ascribed to Archbishop Meopham, vigorously denounced abuses. Ten years later another archbishop, Stratford, was protesting the invasion of ecclesiastical privilege by Edward's war purveyance. He, too, had recourse to excommunication and in the multiple grievances of 1339–41 made much of Magna Carta.[52] In 1330, the same year that Meopham was writing his treatise, began the long series of stat-

---

[47] Cf. above, p. 11, note 10, for the preamble. Items 1 and 7 relate to purveyance.

[48] *Liber Custumarum*, pt. ii, 573–74 (French text, pt. i, 198). Ca. 10 of the New Ordinances affirms in much the language of the *Confirmatio Cartarum* the prohibition of prises "other than those anciently due and accustomed," and broadens into a principle of more general application ca. 19 of Magna Carta, restricting constables of castles. Violation of this prohibition is made a felony. *S. R.* I, 159.

[49] Orders to the sheriffs dated November 22, 1317, *Cal. Close Rolls, 1313–18*, p. 584 (C 54/135 m.15d). Order to cause proclamation to be made forbidding any minister of the king or other person taking corn, wine, meat, or other sorts of victuals, or horses, beasts, cloth, or other goods of clerks or laymen or merchants, native or alien, by land or by sea, for the use of the king or of anyone else, against the will of the owners thereof, unless the true value be forthwith paid for goods for sale or unless the seller give respite of payment of his good will, excepting the ancient prises of the king in places where the king's castles are situate according to Magna Carta and the other prises due to the king, except in the liberty of the church. Letters close, February 13, 1322, directing the victualling of eight castles. *Cal. Close Rolls, 1318–23*, p. 418 (C 54/139 m.19). For the struggle for enforcement, see Davies, *Baronial Opposition to Edward II*, p. 319.

[50] *Great Eyre of Kent*, 6 and 7 Ed. II, Vol. I (Y. B. Series, Vol. V) item 118. "Of prises taken by constables of castles upon the goods of such folk as be not of the town where the castle is; and of like prises made upon the goods of such folk as be of the town where the castle is, and not paid for within forty days; always excepting the ancient and accustomed prises; and through whose orders and through whose agency and when such prises were made. This is forbidden in chapter vii of the same Charter and in chapter ix of the Statute of Westminster."

[51] *Cal. Close Rolls, 1318–23*, p. 532 (C 54/139 m.15d).

[52] Stratford's letters, written from Antwerp to the bishops of Bath and Wells and London, dealing with this evil, are quoted by Hughes, *Social and Constitutional Tendencies*, pp. 111–12.

utes—thirty-six in all—intended more adequately to restrict purveyance.[53] Not one of them cites the Great Charter, nor do the parliamentary petitions upon which some of them were based. More to the point was it to cite Westminster I and the *Articuli super cartas* or to attempt new and more effective rules. The very fact that late fourteenth-century petitions asked confirmation of the Charters and also of statutes on purveyance indicates that Magna Carta alone was not thought to handle purveyance adequately. However, as we shall see, the practice of arranging chapters of statutes under alphabetical titles, used first in the manuscript and then in printed volumes, led to at least a physical paper-and-ink reunion of Magna Carta chapters 19 and 21 with these later statutes.

All kydells for the future shall be removed altogether from Thames and Medway, and throughout all England, except upon the sea shore.

(MAGNA CARTA CA. 23)

FOURTEENTH-CENTURY statutes supplementary to this chapter, 23, of Magna Carta, like those on purveyance, do not cite the Charter.[54] In the first half of the century, however, chapter 23 was the only recourse of complainants and was frequently cited both in petitions and in government directions to officials. The annoyance to merchants from obstructions in rivers, commonly called *kydells* or fishweirs, is obvious when it appears that persons went so far as to dam up the river on each side "so as to leave a narrow outlet only for the passage of the water across which a net was extended to intercept the fish." [55] Restriction of such devices in the Thames and Medway was one of the liberties early acquired and jealously guarded by the Londoners, and by Magna Carta extended to other rivers throughout England.[56] This regulation was repeated in subsequent confirmations of London's own charters as well as those of the Great Charter.[57] In the

---

[53] For instance, 4 Ed. III, ca. 3, restricts purveyance to royal purveyors and orders the latter to use correct measures; ca. 4 confirms 28 Ed. I, ca. 2; 5 Ed. III, ca. 2, confirms 4 Ed. III and 28 Ed. I and adds that prices are to be set by constables and four discreet men of the towns, tallies made and sealed, etc. 18 Ed. III is a general confirmation of all previous legislation; 36 Ed. III includes most previous enactments and provides "that the heinous name of purveyor be changed and named buyer . . ." See *S. R.* I and II, index, *purveyance*.

[54] There are four such acts, beginning with 25 Ed. III, stat. 3, ca. 4 (*S. R.* I, 315-16), which is confirmed with additional clauses on penalties and enforcement by acts of 45 Ed. III, ca. 2; 21 Rich. II, ca. 10; and 1 Hen. IV, ca. 12 (*S. R.* I, 393; II, 109-10, 115-16).

[55] Norton, *City of London*, pp. 305-6. Cf. McKechnie, p. 343: "This word [kydell] seems to have been used by the framers of Magna Carta in a wide general sense, embracing all fixed contrivances or 'engines' intended to catch fish, and likely by their bulk to interfere with the free passage of boats."

[56] London had received chartered rights granting "conservancy of the Thames" before Magna Carta. For the charters of Richard I and John, see *Liber Albus*, pp. 498-500. The confirmation of this liberty by the Great Charter is noted in chronological sequence by this compiler, p. 500.

[57] For instance, 1 Ed. III, a general confirmation of the liberties of London beginning, "In primis, cum in Magna Charta de Libertatibus Angliae, inter alia contineatur, quod civitas

Liber Albus, where these grants according London conservancy of the Thames are recorded, even legend is drawn into account. The series is prefaced with the story of the founding of London by Brut in imitation of Great Troy, telling how he was attracted by the advantages of the river Thames—hence the origin of the city's control over its waters.

Enforcement was no easy task against the opposition of the feudal magnates whose lands lay along the riverbanks and the likelihood of royal connivance in order to secure license fees. In 1316, for instance, men of Oxfordshire and Berkshire were complaining of weirs so high that the land on either side was flooded, and of obstacles called *lokes* on the weirs which hindered ships going to Oxford.[58] There was repeated need to evoke the authority of the Great Charter and to appoint special commissions for its enforcement.

One example may serve for illustration. On May 8, 1327, three men were commissioned to inquire by jury in four counties "with power to remove the said kidels, etc., and to punish offenders by fine and otherwise." This order resulted from a petition to king and council in parliament by citizens of London and others

who come to the city with their merchandise over the Thames, complaining that divers men of the counties of Middlesex, Surrey, Berks, and Oxford have kidels along the banks of the river between London and Oxford, have made weirs in the same river, and fixed pales and piles along its course, and tied the cords of their nets athwart the stream, to the obstruction of ships and boats, contrary to divers charters of the citizens, and more especially Magna Carta . . .[59]

This seems to have been a long-time arrangement, for several years later, 1334, a certain John de Bybury was appointed in the place of one of the four to work with the others

to remove all nets and kidels used in river Thames and other rivers in the counties of Oxford and Berks for taking fish contrary to Magna Carta wherein it is contained that all kidels should be wholly put down along the Thames and Medway, and throughout England save on the sea coast, to burn these when removed and to punish by amercements and otherwise those who use such instruments.

Londoniarum habeat omnes libertates suas antiquas et liberas consuetudines suas . . ." includes one specific item: "Et quod dicti cives ammoveant et capiant omnes kidellos in aquis Thamisiae et Medeveiae, et habeant punitiones ad ipsum Dominum regem inde pertinentes." *Liber Albus,* p. 505.

[58] *Cal. Pat. Rolls,* 1313–17, p. 501 (roll 145 m.16d, 9 Ed. II, pt. 2). Cf. *ibid.* 1338–40, p. 149 (roll 193 m.2d, 12 Ed. III, pt. 2).

[59] Thus the *Cal. Pat. Rolls,* 1327–30, p. 150. In the original manuscript (roll 167 m.24d) ca. 23 of the Charter is quoted verbatim. A similar commission directed to four others for Oxford and Berks only, August 9, 1327, *ibid.* m.5d. (This entry as calendared omits the Magna Carta citation entirely!)

As the supplementary statutes (25 Edward III to 1 Henry IV) do not cite Magna Carta, neither do the commissions to enforce them.[60]

It was not only the clauses of Magna Carta enunciating abstract constitutional principles which were subject to reinterpretation or misinterpretation but provisions like chapter 23 dealing with such concrete commodities as fish and ships. In popular opinion this chapter was gradually credited with a double purpose—the protection of fish and fishing rights as well as the removal of obstructions to navigation. McKechnie suggests a possible source of confusion in an episode of 1283.[61] Two years later the Statute of Westminster II, chapter 47, instituted the first legislation intended to protect fish. Confusion was natural, for the very devices that obstructed navigation destroyed the fish.

The mayor of London acted as

"chief conservator, and his jurisdiction extended from Staines to Yantlet Creek, near the mouth of the river. . . . The Thames fish was at this period a valuable source of London's food supply, and the city watched its preservation with a jealous eye. Those kidels which were not of the standard size would catch the young fish and so endanger the industry, and when any were seized they were publicly burnt and the owner fined £10. In 1381 the size of the mesh was ordered to be 1½ inch east of London bridge and 2 inches west of London bridge, in both cases the measurement to be reckoned transversely between the knots." [62]

The popular attitude is well illustrated by the wording of a commission issued in 1302:

that magnates and others having lands near the river in the counties of Middlesex, Surrey, Buckingham, Berks, and Oxford have constructed weirs, mills, and divers enclosures without license, and have made the weirs and enclosures narrower and higher than they used to be, so that vessels laden with victuals, and the fish living in the river cannot go through as they were wont: and that fishermen catch fish with too narrow nets, contrary to Magna Carta; and they are to abate the same.[63]

The intensity of rival interests is well illustrated by an episode as late as Henry IV's reign, recounted by Pendrill:

[60] Cal. Pat. Rolls, 1330–34, p. 542; 1350–54, pp. 93, 204, 276, 542, compared with close rolls 233 m.12d, 235, m.10d, 236 m.24d, 241 m.6d respectively; ibid. 1354–58, pp. 127, 547, with rolls 243 m.7d, 251 m.25d; ibid. 1364–67, p. 285, and roll 273 m.36d (De palis et kidellis amovend); ibid. 1367–70, pp. 201, 266, and rolls 278 m.12d, 279 m.17; ibid. 1374–77, p. 159, and roll 292 m.4d (De inquirendo gurgitibus et kidellis); ibid. 1413–16, p. 347; 1416–22, p. 78.

[61] This involved a misunderstanding of ca. 16, which related to hawking, not fishing, but does read fish into the Charter and perhaps eventually confused cas. 16 and 23. McKechnie, pp. 303–4.

[62] Pendrill, London Life, pp. 265–67.

[63] Cal. Pat. Rolls, 1301–1307, pp. 88–89 (roll 122 m.14d—"contra tenorem magne carte nostre de libertatibus Angliae in destruccionem piscium").

A sub-conservator of the Thames seized sixteen nets belonging to fishermen of Erith, Barking, and Woolwich, intending to take them to London for examination. Immediately the bells of the church on the shores of the river were rung to call the people to arms, who, to the number of 2,000, armed with bows, arrows, swords, bucklers, and clubs, and using doors and windows in place of shields, as we are told, put out in boats and pursued him to Barking, shooting at him as he fled. Unable to proceed farther, the sub-conservator landed and deposited his booty with the constables of Barking; but the mob, following in his wake, landed and rescued their nets, with which they returned in triumph. The ringleaders were afterwards arrested and brought before the King's Council at Westminster, but when they humbly apologised, the Mayor, who had appeared as prosecutor, not only agreed to forgive them, but magnanimously allowed them to continue using the same nets until the following Easter, by which time they were to have new ones made in accordance with the standard of the city.

A statute of 4 Henry IV, chapter 11, confirmed this series, together with the acts prohibiting obstructions in rivers, combining in one statement the two objectives of protection to fish and maintenance of free navigation.[64] None of these acts cites Magna Carta, nor do the commissions issued for their enforcement, but the Londoners, in a petition of 2 Henry V, do attribute to the Charter both objectives.[65] Officials do not seem to have shared this confusion. Throughout the reign of Henry VI commissions continued to be issued explicitly for the enforcement of one or the other—statutes on fish or on navigation.[66]

Only in the reign of Edward IV did a commons petition and the resulting statute complete the fusion or confusion of objectives. In much the words of the Londoners of Henry V's time:

Prayen the Commens in this present Parliament assembled; that where by the laudable Statute of Magna Carta, amonges other, it is ordeyned, that all Kidels by Thamys, Medewey and by all this Reame, shuld be put dowen, but by the Coostes of the See, which Statute was made for grete wele of all this

---

[64] 13 Rich. II, ca. 19, 17 Rich. II, ca. 9 (*S. R.* II, 67–68, 89–90); 4 Hen. IV, ca. 11 (*S. R.* II, 136) which reads: "Item, Because that by Wears, Stakes and Kidels, being in the Water of Thames, and (of) other great Rivers through the Realm, the common Passage of Ships and Boats is disturbed, and much People perished, and also the young Fry of Fish destroyed, and against Reason wasted and given to Swine to eat, contrary to the Pleasure of God, and to the great Damage of the King and his People . . ."

[65] ". . . qe come pur eschuir la distruction de brode & fry· & de pesson, & la disturbance des communes passages des niefs & bateulx parmy toutz les communes Rivers du Roialme, par la graund chartre ordeigne fuist, qe toutz les Kidelx parmy Thamise & Medeway, & tout le Roialme d'Engleterre forsque par le costier du Mier, serroient tout oultrement oustez & abatiez." A petition of the mayor, aldermen, and commons of London in parliament. They are promised the enforcement of existing statutes and the placing of the mayor or *gardein* of London on the commission for the river Lay. *Rot. Parl.* IV, 36, no. 15.

[66] For instance, commissions on obstructions to navigation: *Cal. Pat. Rolls,* 1422–29, pp. 123, 402 (roll 410 m.17d, 420 m.15d); *ibid.* 1429–36, pp. 527 (roll 438 m.13d); and others. Protection to fish, *ibid.* 1422–29, p. 494 (roll 423 m.25d).

land, in avoidyng the streytenes of all Ryvers, so that Shippes and Bootes shuld have theryn their free and large passage, and also in savyng of all frye of Fysch brought fourth in the same; uppon which Magna Carta, a grete sentence Appostelik of excommengement, by grete numbre of Bishoppes ayenst the brekers therof was pronounced . . . and in affirmaunce of the said Statute of Magna Carta, dyvers Statutes sithen have be made and ordeyned . . .[67]

Commissions for enforcement issued in 1476, 1478, and 1483 all recite the act.[68]

Let there be one measure of wine throughout our whole realm; and one measure of ale; and one measure of corn, to wit, "the London quarter"; and one width of cloth (whether dyed, or russet or "halberget"), to wit, two ells within the selvedges; of weights also let it be as of measures.

(MAGNA CARTA CA. 25)

THIS chapter, although not the first attempt at regulation in this field, remained the standard law on uniform weights and measures until the reign of Edward III. Here the barons "took a step in their own interests as buyers, and against the interest of the trade guilds as sellers." But these "sellers" proved incorrigible. Their evasions furnished a problem reign after reign; indeed, century after century. The consumer repeatedly complained of the deceits practiced, particularly of the use of one set of measures to buy and another, smaller, to sell. The Londoners, although proud that their weights and measures were the authorized standard, far from setting a good example, were reputed the worst offenders.[69] Henry III had attempted enforcement on his progresses. Edward I's *Assiza de Ponderibus et Mensuris* was a complete category of authorized weights and measures.[70]

There was considerable agitation on the matter in the reign of Edward II. A petition of 1314 asked that the same weights and measures be kept and used in Cornwall as elsewhere in the realm, "according to what is contained in the Great Charter."[71] Three years later eight commissions were appointed to correct false measuring of grain throughout thirty-six counties. Letters close to the sheriffs, warning of the coming of these commissioners, recite that frequent are the complaints of great men (*magna-*

---

[67] *Rot. Parl.* VI, 158–59. The statute, 12 Ed. IV, ca. 7 (*S. R.* II, 439–42).

[68] *Cal. Pat. Rolls*, 1476–85, pp. 23, 144, 344. Here the calendarer does include some such phrase as "pursuant to Magna Carta," but the manuscript roll repeats practically verbatim, though in Latin, the language of the petition and statute.

[69] McKechnie, p. 359. For a good sketch of the various enactments on weights and measures from Edgar on, see Leadam's introduction to *Select Cases in Star Chamber*, 1477–1509, pp. cxlvii–cli (S. S.).

[70] Leadam describes how Henry III personally superintended destruction of false weights and measures in 1228. For Edward's *Assize*, see *S. R.* I, 204–5.

[71] *Rot. Parl.* I, 308.

tum et procerum) in parliaments of the use of other than standard measures: "namely greater with which they buy, and smaller with which they sell, in great deception of the people of our said realm." The pertinent clause of the Great Charter is quoted, and the king recalls that he is sworn to observe all the rights and liberties therein.[72]

In 1320, in response to similar complaints, the treasurer and barons of the Exchequer were instructed to assay and prove the standard of the London quarter of corn and furnish measures made by that standard to the principal town of every county in the realm, "as it is contained in Magna Carta that there shall be one measure of corn, to wit the quarter of London, throughout the realm." [73] In the course of this assay at the Guildhall, the assayer asked the citizens whether they did not have other measures and whether a measure of ale (*lagena cervisiae*) was not larger than one of wine (*lagena vini*). The citizens corrected him on the authority of the Great Charter.[74]

Beginning with Edward III's reign this problem of weights and measures, like those of purveyance and obstructions to navigation, led to a long series of supplementary acts. Between 1340 and 1497 there are seven such statutes, besides letters patent, 1351, ordering for Ireland "the same assize of measures and weights as the king uses in England, as contained in the great charter of the liberties of England." All these acts confirm chapter 25 of Magna Carta, which they quote in their preambles.[75] Amplification is in the form of more explicit definition of weights and measures, penalties, and methods of enforcement.

It was something of a formality, perhaps, for the engrossers of a statute to incorporate previous enactments along the same line, yet quite in keeping with medieval emphasis on old law and custom. At least three of these statutes are the result of petitions which suggest the importance in popular

---

[72] "Cum inter cetera, in magna carta de libertatibus Anglie, contenta, contineatur, quod per totum regnum nostrum una sit mensura bladi, scilicet quarterium London . . . nos, qui jura & libertates in dicta carta contentas, prout vinculo juramenti astricti sumus, volumus in omnibus observari . . . February 20, 1317." Rymer, *Foedera*, Vol. II, pt. i, p. 316; *Cal. Close Rolls*, 1313–18, p. 455. The letters patent of March 1 constituting the commissions also cite and partially quote the Charter. *Parl. Writs*, Vol. II, pt. ii, pp. 111–12; *Cal. Pat. Rolls*, 1313–17, pp. 688–89.

[73] *Cal. Close Rolls*, 1318–23, p. 280. In pursuance of the plan, London officials were requested to show the clerk of the king's market the measures called "the standards of London." This request, like the letters to the sheriffs three years before, rehearses complaints in parliament, quotes the Charter, and notes the king's oath to observe the latter.

[74] ". . . quod una mensura vini et cervisiae erit concordans per totam Angliam sicut continetur in Magna Charta de Libertatibus Angliae; et sicut usi sunt semper et maxime a tempore Regis Ricardi, ab anno regni ipsius viii." *Liber Custumarum*, pt. i, p. 383.

[75] For instance, 14 Ed. III: "Whereas it is contained in the Great Charter, that one Measure and one Weight be throughout England . . ." The statutes are: 14 Ed. III, stat. 1, ca. 12; 25 Ed. III, stat. 5, ca. 10; 34 Ed. III, ca. 6; 13 Rich. II, stat. 1, ca. 9; 8 Hen. VI, ca. 5; 7 Hen. VII, ca. 3; 12 Hen. VII, ca. 5 (*S. R. I*, 285, 321–22, 365–66; and II, 63–64, 241–42, 551–52, 637–38). The letters patent to Ireland: *Cal. Pat. Rolls*, 1350–54, p. 123 (roll 234 m.14).

opinion of Magna Carta as a remedy for false measures. For instance, in 1351 in the casual French of the parliament roll: *Come ordeine soit par la Grande Chartre "Qe une Mesure soit usee parmy tut le Roialme des totes choses vendables"; quel Estatut n'est pas tenus; Prie la Commune ...*

In the petition of 1429 later statutes are given more attention, but even so comes the characteristic beginning, now in English: "Please to oure soverayn Lord ye Kyng to considere, how it was ordeinid bi ye grete Chartir of fredomys of ye Reme, bi a Statut maad ye xxvi zer of the reigne of Kyng E. III, and confermid bi a Statut made ye xiii yere of Kyng R. II yat on weizte and on mesure be bi al ye Reme ..." [76]

A petition of 1402 tries to extend the meaning of chapter 25 by the ingenious argument that since the Great Charter provides for one weight throughout the realm there ought also to be but one uniform fee for weighing: weighers in some cities and boroughs are charging outrageously for their services, three or four times the rate in the city of London. [77]

As to means of enforcement, the act of 1340 prescribed two or more "good and sufficient persons" per county. Letters patent for the appointment of these and for similar commissioners in the 1350's, like the statutes, commonly begin by quoting chapter 25. [78]

As was often the case with expedients for law enforcement in this century, the remedy proved worse than the disease. Some commissioners were overzealous in amercing offenders and in a few instances even absconded with their collections. [79] Again, justices commissioned to enforce the statute of 25 Edward III accepted a large number of indictments for offenses committed before the act was made. As it was not intended to be retroactive, these indictments were canceled by the government by writ of *supersedeas*. [80]

[76] *Rot. Parl.* II, 240; III, 270; IV, 349, no. 5. There are several other acts dealing with a special aspect of the problem, which naturally do not cite the Charter. 11 Hen. VII, for instance, is not concerned with affirming the principle, but with a device for its insurance. Standard weights and measures are to be taken home to every city, borough, and town by their members of parliament. *S. R.* II, 570–71.

[77] *Rot. Parl.* III, 496–97. The petition was referred to the council and does not appear to have resulted in any legislation to this effect.

[78] Here again it is not safe to rely on the calendars; the following commissions, as calendared, omit citation of Magna Carta, though the manuscript roll includes it: *Cal. Pat. Rolls,* 1340–43, p. 446; 1343–45, p. 72; 1348–50, p. 533; 1350–54, p. 510. (*Ibid.* 1354–58, pp. 236, 396, are exceptions.)

Commissions as recorded in the rolls for various years from 1341 to 1356, issued to groups of counties (as "Norfolk and Suffolk"; "Lincoln, Somerset, Dorset and Lancaster"; eight groups for sixteen counties, etc.) all cite the Charter. Officials and clerks naturally followed a set form. *Patent Rolls* 205 m.8; 206 m.32d, 40d; 208 m.8d, 15d; 209 m.37d; 211 m.35d; 230 m.5d; 240 m.21d; 241 m.10d; 243 m.16d; 245 m.12d; 248 m.13d.

[79] In 1344 complaints of exactions had led to the withdrawal of powers. *Rot. Parl.* II, 155, 156; *S. R.* I, 301. For a surveyor of weights and measures in county Lincoln about to abscond with the amercements, see *Cal. Pat. Rolls,* 1340–43, p. 553. For a commissioner who had gone off with his collections, *ibid.* 1343–45, p. 7.

[80] *Assize Roll* (Roll of the Peace) Yorkshire I J 1/1134 m.3d. The writ of *supersedeas* cites Magna Carta. I am indebted to Miss Bertha Putnam for this reference.

More acceptable to the country gentry and lesser folk throughout the kingdom was the plan adopted in 1361 of entrusting enforcement to justices of the peace. From this time on the statutes on weights and measures were included with the many other matters entrusted to these justices by their commissions. But these commissions did not, could not, undertake to recite the many statutes for which the justices were responsible and hence do not in themselves cite or quote the Great Charter. The conscientious justice, or his clerk, must perforce have consulted the abridgments compiled for his use, first in manuscript and then in print.[81]

It was left for the shrewd Henry VII, with his understanding of human nature, to find a really effective solution of the problem. Forty-three cities and boroughs were specified in which the authorized standards were to be kept; upon the town officials was put the responsibility of examining weights and measures twice a year and destroying faulty ones; moreover, and here lay the key to the success of the measure, to these local officials went fees for sealing. These two acts of Henry VII's thus close the series. They have their interest among the few citations of the Great Charter in the early Tudor period, though they do come to sound like a mere formality:

Prayen the Commens in this present parliament assembled, that where aswell by the Chartre of Magna Carta as by oder divers ordenances and Statutes made in diverse parliamentes in the tyme of your noble progenitours and predecessours, It hath be ordeyned that oon mesure and one Weight shuld be throughoute all this Realme of England . . .[82]

IMPORTANT as a defense against abuses in the local administration of justice was chapter 35, with its regulation of the time and manner of holding the county court, sheriff's tourn, and view of frankpledge. This chapter also served as a "legal barrier to the introduction of the system in places where it had not existed in the reign of Henry II."[83] Its rules were ex-

---

[81] See below, Chap. VI.

[82] Thus the petition of 1491. That of 1497 reads, "Whereas afore this tyme the Kynge our Sovereign Lord intending the commen wele of his people, and to avoide the great disceite of Weightis and Mesures longe tyme used within this his Realme contrarie to the Statute of Magna Carta and othre estatutes therof made by divers of his noble progenitours . . ." S. R. II, 551, 637–38.

[83] The county court was to meet not more than once a month; no sheriff or bailiff was to make his tourn through the hundreds more than twice a year or in other than the accustomed place; view of frankpledge was limited to once a year and the sheriff was not to "seek occasions," but to be content with what sheriffs were accustomed to have from their view in the time of Henry II; local customs dating from the time of Henry II or later were to be respected. Introduced as ca. 42 in the 1217 issue, this chapter really accomplished in a different way what had been intended by ca. 25 of John's Charter.

The itinerant justices did not enforce the rules in certain counties which had not had the sheriff's tourn or view of frankpledge in Henry II's reign. In at least eight

tended to leet jurisdiction. The sheriffs' abuses touched the common man in his purse and in his liberty. It was their practice to summon local courts with undue frequency, and at unusual times and places, and to amerce suitors who failed to attend. No wonder the close rolls abound in grants to individuals of the much coveted exemptions from suit of court, as well as from being impaneled in assizes, juries, or recognitions, and serving as coroners, verderers, and foresters.

This chapter of Magna Carta was confirmed by the Provisions of Westminster and the Statute of Marlborough. Articles of the Great Eyre of Kent (1313–14) assigned to the itinerant justices inquiry into violation of the rule for semi-annual tourns, as well as unlawful prises and amercements: "Of sheriffs who hold their turn more frequently than twice in the year contrary to the Great Charter of liberty [*magna carta libertatis*] and when they so did." [84]

According to Fitzherbert, if the sheriff distrain a man to do suit more than twice in the year, he may have an "action on the statute"—a writ upon Magna Carta—addressed to the sheriff.[85] A statute of 31 Edward III, chapter 15, reaffirmed the rule for a tourn "but two Times in the Year, in a Place due and accustomed" and prescribed as penalty "if they hold them in other Manner, that then they shall lose their Turn for the Time." [86] The preamble recites how persons have been summoned to tourns in Lent "when men ought to attend to devotion, and other Works of Charity, for Remedy of their Souls," and in harvest when "every Man almost is occupied about the cutting and entring of his corn." It is gratifying to find this act actually taking effect a few months later in letters close to Peter Nuttle, sheriff of York, for irregularities *ex clamosa insinuatione populi nostri*. Not only was the said Peter to desist from these evil practices, but the Great Charter and other statutes were to be proclaimed and enforced in full county court, cities, boroughs, market towns, seaports, and "other places where it shall seem expedient." Several of the sheriff's deputies were indicted before justices of oyer and terminer and removed from office, as was he himself eventually.[87]

Whether cited as a living force, or as a mere formality of enactment,

counties (and possibly a ninth, Cheshire) frankpledge suretyship was not a county institution in the twelfth or succeeding centuries. Morris, *The Frankpledge System*, Chap. II.

[84] No. 83, articles of the *Great Eyre of Kent*, I, 37 (Y. B. V, S. S.).

[85] See below, p. 48.

[86] *S. R.* I, 352.

[87] The sheriff was accused of holding his tourn as often as he pleased, and outside accustomed places; of taking indictments secretly without indenture and then imprisoning and fining the accused; and of failing to make tallies for receipt of debts, etc., contrary to Magna Carta and other statutes.

In spite of the recent statute, the Great Charter is cited and part of ca. 35 quoted. Rymer, *Foedera*, Vol. III, pt. i, p. 410. *Cal. Close Rolls*, 1354–60, pp. 534–35.

these supplementary statutes served to perpetuate the Charter along various practical lines, quite apart from constitutional principles and of interest to large numbers of the common people. In the manuscript and printed volumes of statutes, as we shall see, the chapters appear under one or more of the various titles so dear to the lawyers.

❖ CHAPTER II ❖

Magna Carta in the Plea Rolls
and Year Books

"He (Serjeant Maynard) had such a relish of the old year-books that he carried one in his coach to divert him in travel, and said he chose it before any comedy." (ROGER NORTH, MOTTO OF SELDEN SOCIETY YEAR BOOKS)

The Year Books—the Law Reports of the Middle Ages—"are the exclusive property of the legal profession. Written by lawyers for lawyers, they are by far the most important source of, and authority for, the medieval common law." (HOLDSWORTH)

THE best evidence of the lasting practical value of some chapters of the Great Charter, through the reigns of the first three Edwards at least, is that of the plea rolls and Year Books. Here are actions "founded on the statute" in which the original writ actually quotes a provision of the Charter or is traditionally believed to be based on it. Attorneys and pleaders cite it on behalf of litigants, sometimes accurately and justifiably in support of a major issue, again erroneously or as a frivolous exception, only to be corrected by their opponents or overruled by the judges.

Modern historians have put undue emphasis on the Charter as a statement of *public law,* a "liberty document" designed as a check on royal power and officialdom. It is to correct this overemphasis that the present writer has, in the following pages, made so much of the evidence from the plea rolls and Year Books. For it is instructive to note that in all these actions "founded on the statute" and in several of the instances in which litigants or their pleaders cite the Charter, it is being used as *private* law between parties in *common* pleas in which the king and his officials were not concerned.[1] In other words, viewed in this aspect, the Charter is a "mere statute." This fact must have been partly due to the operation of

---

[1] This dual aspect of the Charter is recognized in near contemporary (thirteenth-century) enactments such as Marlborough, ca. 5: "The Great Charter shall be observed in all his articles, *as well in such as pertain to the King as to Other*; and that shall be inquired afore the Justices in Eyre when they come into those parts." (Italics added by the author.)

the clause of chapter 37 (chapter 60 of John's Charter) which extends the benefits conceded by the king to his tenants also to the tenants of mesne lords, whether cleric or lay.[2] The action based on chapter 14 designed for tenants who have been "immoderately amerced" in court baron is a good illustration. Judges and lawyers of the fourteenth and fifteenth centuries certainly looked on Magna Carta as a statute much like other statutes and treated it as such.

What this treatment was likely to be is worth pausing to consider in its broader aspects. Recent studies based on the plea rolls and Year Books have thrown light on the attitude of the legal profession toward the laws: their conception of so-called statutes and of common law, the relation of one to the other, and the extent to which the king's judges might interpret and even modify the law. Sayles, drawing his evidence from the *coram rege* rolls, finds that discussion occasionally did arise over conflicts of statute law and the royal prerogative, but that such occasions were few and the conflict not serious.[3]

For the authority of the king, presumed to be acting with the advice of his ministers, lies at the back of both statute and prerogative: a judge can plainly declare that he had "a later warrant from the king and that is as high as a statute." It did not seem strange to contemporaries, therefore, that the king was not bound by statutes and could alter and suspend them, dispense with them and even annul them. . . . When he abrogated a statute, it was not evidence of bad faith; the public good might demand it, for . . . no one could be always sure that a statute would work beneficially.[4]

Plucknett, basing his studies on the Year Books, treats of the "methods and the principles of interpreting legislation which were evolved by the common law courts during the Edwardian reigns" (20 Edward I to 20 Edward III). He finds the judges in the earlier part of this period "wielding the wide discretionary powers of the king." They "make exceptions out of the statute," refuse to apply statutes, extend the words of a statute, and use discretion in the application of statutes comparable to an equitable jurisdiction, and all with "a singular absence of any feeling that constitutional problems of great difficulty were involved." These practices Plucknett attributes partly to the poor way in which the statutes were drawn, partly to the "fusion of powers"—the close relation of parliament

---

[2] "Moreover, all these aforesaid customs and liberties, the observance of which we have granted in our kingdom as far as pertains to us towards our men, shall be observed by all of our kingdom, as well clergy as laymen, as far as pertains to them towards their men."

[3] In his introduction to *Select Cases in the Court of King's Bench*, III, xxxvii–xlii, "Statutes and the Royal Prerogative" (S. S.). This in the reigns of Edward I and Edward II and the early part of Edward III's; Sayles finds a decided change in the attitude of parliament and the judges by the middle of the fourteenth century (1356).

[4] *Ibid.*, p. xxxviii.

Title page of Berthelet's edition of the statutes, 1531

or council and courts, and of law and equity.[5] As the period advances, the judges show a decided preference for strict interpretation. S. B. Chrimes deals with "statutory law and judicial discretion" as revealed by the fifteenth-century Year Books. Something of his findings will be indicated below.

Of the two types of record, a more exhaustive use has been made here of the Year Books than of the plea rolls, because the former contain the

---

[5] *Statutes and Their Interpretation, passim.*

pleadings.[6] It is true that in the *coram rege* rolls some pleadings are summarized, especially if the case has been brought before King's Bench because of royal interests, difficulty, or review of error. This is more apt to be true in the early part of our period when King's Bench was doing more of this supervisory work and the rolls record a greater variety of cases. As the century wears on, the entries become more stereotyped. The *de banco* rolls are apt to yield material where an action is founded on the Charter, and a chapter of the latter is quoted in the writ, but not when the citation is merely an exception by one of the litigants. As to the Year Books, the reporters occasionally quote a writ or note that an action is founded on the Charter, but the value of the books lies in their record of the pleadings, which is their primary interest.

Maitland, in an effective passage, describes the oral pleading—"tentative and experimental pleading," he calls it—of Edward II's day:

We are tempted to say that argument precedes pleading or that pleadings are evolved in the course of argument. . . . Counsel for the defendant, let us say, experimentally offers a plea. Some little discussion ensues. He discovers that the opinion of the Court is against him, or in other words, that if he definitely pleads that plea he will be defeated. So he will not abide [*demorer*] there; he will not let himself be "avowed" by his client; he tries some other line of defense. Then of all this tentative and experimental pleading the record takes no cognizance. . . . When it comes to the pinch, he will not demur; but his "inchoate demurrer" . . . has served its purpose; he has been able to make an experiment and to ascertain that a demurrer would be unsuccessful or at any rate dangerous. . . .

We are at present disposed to think, that very often, perhaps normally, nothing in the nature of "a pleading" went down on to the roll until the whole process of oral pleading was at an end.[7]

Of course the king, as a great property holder, was frequently a litigant. He could sue in any court he chose. The phrase "so-and-so who sued for the king (*qui sequitur pro rege*)" recurs frequently in the *coram rege* rolls. In suits where the king was plaintiff or claimant, a provision of the Charter might be cited on behalf of the defendant. Individuals might not sue the king directly by purchase of a writ but could "sue by petition," as the phrase went. Occasionally such a petition was referred to King's Bench and may be quoted in the rolls, but more petitions of this type have been found in the parliament rolls, and occasionally the close rolls, which thus supplement the court records described above.

[6] For a summary of and comment on the sources used here, see Appendix C.

[7] Y. B. III, pp. lxvi–lxviii (S. S.). This contrast between the reports and the official record is well brought out in the Year Books as edited for the Selden Society; the editors, whenever possible to identify a case, quote the corresponding "note from the record," usually the *de banco* roll.

In the early years of the fourteenth century the clerk was still enrolling considerable numbers of private petitions on the parliament roll.[8] It is here, rather than in the plea rolls, that are to be found petitions to king and council in which a provision of the Charter is cited in defense of rights as against encroachment by the king himself or his officials on his behalf. The petitioners are important people, usually tenants-in-chief of the crown; the issues relate to the various feudal obligations defined in the Charter. On the close rolls are enrolled some orders in answer to such petitions; in some instances the petition is quoted verbatim, in others only suggested or implied. In the following pages are described first, a few typical examples of this, the better known use of the Charter, that is, as a defense against the crown; then, in more detail, the less familiar uses in routine actions (common pleas) as private law.

But first one more question needs to be answered. In what form was the text of the Charter known to or available for judges, pleaders, and litigants?

The four originals of John's Charter have long received ample publicity. Historians have described them. Many a tourist from the United States and parts of the British Commonwealth have shared with groups of English school children a sight of the originals in the British Museum. The perfect Lincoln Cathedral copy, after a year's showing at the World's Fair in New York and a temporary residence in the Library of Congress, was installed with the Declaration of Independence in some secure repository for the duration of World War II. In originals of the definitive text of 1225 little interest has been shown in modern times. McKechnie does note the copies preserved at Durham Cathedral and at Lacock Abbey in Wiltshire. A facsimile of the former appears in the *Statutes of the Realm* and was used by the record commissioners for their printed text. They also call attention to the "Magna Carta of 9 Henry III under Seal, from which Blackstone printed a Copy in his Edition of the Charters,— still preserved by the Family of the Talbots, of Lacock Abbey, in that County"; to the *inspeximus* of 25 and of 28 Edward I on the statute roll, reciting and confirming the Charters; and to several original charters of *inspeximus* of these dates.[9]

More impressive as suggesting easy access to the text of the Charter in the later Middle Ages are the numerous manuscript volumes of statutes "not of record"—the *Antiqua Statuta* as they came to be called—preserved

---

[8] The regular enrollment of private petitions comes to an end about the year 1332 (according to Richardson and Sayles, *Rotuli Parliamentorum*, p. xvii), but the editors of the printed *Rotuli Parliamentorum* supplement what is found on the clerk's roll from the original petitions preserved in the Public Record Office.

[9] McKechnie, pp. 155, 165–70; J. C. Fox, "The Originals of the Great Charter of 1215," *English Historical Review*, 39:321–36; S. R. I, 22–23.

in libraries in England and even on the Continent. Miss Putnam thinks that some of these were intended for justices of the peace. That judges and lawyers in the central courts may also have used them seems probable. On the evidence of the early Year Books (20 Edward I to 20 Edward III) Professor Plucknett concludes that the judges were not well informed of the contents of statutes, and the pleaders even less so; that reference by the court to an official copy of a statute was unusual, and that the court did not possess a copy of its own for ready reference.[10] The volume of statutes multiply as time goes on; perhaps their use did too. Certainly judges and pleaders *cite* statutes frequently in the later Year Books.

The writer examined some score and more of these manuscript volumes "not of record" in the British Museum. They range in size from tiny volumes in a minute hand to thick quartos, from the occasional hasty and disordered to the more usual neat and even elegant. The script is not the court hand of the chronicles, but the law hand of the plea rolls. The *Antiqua Statuta* usually contain the so-called statutes from Magna Carta (9 Henry III) through those of Edward I and sometimes Edward II, in contrast to the *Nova Statuta* which begin with 1 Edward III and continue to the time of compilation, Richard II, Henry IV, or Henry VI, as the case may be. Some volumes contain both *antiqua* and *nova statuta*. One anticipates the printed abridgments of Rastell and Pulton. Some contain statutes only, others add a Register of Writs, and still others treatises such as *Britton*, the *Parva Hengham,* and others. Small wonder that the scribe of one of these comprehensive types sighed with relief as he wrote his last "here endeth" (*Explicunt capitula*) and added a fervent *Deo gratias*.

Where such a copyist begins his Magna Carta with an illuminated initial and/or other decorations, his motive was probably merely to adorn the first page, not to single out this document for special honor. Still, the mere chance standing in first place in the statute books, both manuscript and later print, must have lent a certain prestige and publicity.

[10] *Proceedings before the Justices of the Peace* (Bertha H. Putnam, editor), I, xxxi–xxxii. "It would be most interesting if one could say with certainty what copy of the statutes the court used—whether the statute roll, close roll, patent roll, or one of the semi-official registers now preserved in the Exchequer, or whether they had a copy for their own use—but as to this there is no evidence. It would seem that the court had not always a text at hand, judging as well from what has just been said as when a party brought into court a copy of the statutes 14 Edw. III st. 4, c. 2 sealed with the great seal, or where *Bereford* said to a party 'Show us the statute' and when he had seen it, told them that they were not in the case provided for in it. This impression is confirmed by the cases now about to be considered, the evidence all pointing to the same conclusion, namely, that reference by the court to an official copy of a statute was decidedly unusual, and that the court did not possess a copy of its own for ready reference." When the court did take the important step of "looking at the statute" this was "usually an occasion of great interest to the compilers of the Year Books." "Ignorance of the Statutes among Contemporary Lawyers . . ." in Plucknett, *Statutes and Their Interpretation*, pp. 104–5.

With a few exceptions Magna Carta, followed by the Forest Charter, stands as first of the *antiqua statuta*. The text is most commonly the Latin with *inspeximus* of 25 Edward I, although occasionally labeled simply as 9 *Henry III* or the *Charter of Henry III*. There are a few French texts. Numbering of the various provisions is not a modern invention. Though the well-known numbering of John's text may have had to wait for Blackstone, the current text of Henry III was so treated from early times. Even the author of the *Mirror of Justices* (c. 1285–90) was evidently using a numbered copy, since he speaks of the "law of this realm founded upon the forty articles of the Great Charter of Liberties (*fondee sur xl poinz de la grande chartre des fraunchises*)." In the volumes examined the Charter is divided into chapters indicated in a few instances by red or blue initial letters, but usually by numbers and sometimes by rubrics repeated in the table of contents. The numbering varies from copy to copy (35, 36, 37, 38) and in no instance corresponds exactly to the thirty-seven chapters of the later printed volumes of statutes.[11]

Provisions of Magna Carta Invoked for the Benefit of Crown Tenants

THESE provisions are embodied in petitions or in directions to officials as recorded in the parliament, close, and patent rolls. Some of the entries are of considerable length but are handled here as briefly as is consistent with clarity because of the commonplace character of most of them. They are concerned mainly with feudal law and custom governing the relationship of the king and his tenants-in-chief. Appeals to the increasingly famous and oft-cited chapter 29 (John 39) are reserved for a separate chapter. The petitioners include such notables as an abbot, two bishops, and three earls!

In 1306, a certain Aline, widow of John de Brerton, claims that her husband had held land of the honor of Knaresburgh, now in the king's hand, for a certain annual fee farm and not by military service. Hence she asks for the guardianship of her eldest son, still under age, *secundum formam et tenorem Magne Carte.*[12]

The rolls of the parliament of 8 Edward II are interesting in their grouping of petitions under various captions. One group headed *Adhuc de Responsionibus coram Rege et Magno Consilio* contains four petitions

[11] For references to the manuscript volumes examined, and a description of certain outstanding types, see Appendix B. For the printed volumes, see Chap. VI below.

[12] *Rot. Parl.* I, 197, no. 43. Based on ca. 27, in which the king promises not to exact wardship from lands held by fee farm, socage, or burgage; or possibly on ca. 31, where the king is made to promise in regard to lands held of honors which have escheated: "Nos eodem modo eam tenebimus quo baro eam tenuit." The case was referred to one of the justices, some instructed person to be present "ad dicendum pro Rege si quid dicere sciverit . . ."

which cite the Charter, while another headed *Responsiones Petitionum Anglie per Auditores earundum* contains a fifth. Isabel, wife of Hugh Bardolf, petitions for the restoration of a free tenement from which she has been ousted without a "reasonable judgment" against the form of the Great Charter and the Ordinances. William de Brewouse protests the exaction of *queen's gold* in addition to the relief which he has duly paid, *solonc la fourme & l'ordinance de la Grant Chartre le Roi Henry des franchises d'Engleterre* (chapter 2). The men of Cornwall, among other complaints, ask that the king's ministers and others in Cornwall use the same measures and weights as are used elsewhere in the realm, *selónc ceo q'il est contenu en la Grant Chartre* (chapter 25).[13]

The fifth of these petitions, that of Theobald, son and minor heir of Lord William Russell, relates to an aspect of wardship which calls to mind the comment on this provision of the Charter in the *Mirror of Justices*: "And note that every guardian is charged with three duties: to sufficiently maintain the child; to maintain its rights and inheritance without waste; thirdly to answer for the satisfaction of its trespasses." The first—"to sufficiently maintain the child"—is not specified in the Charter. As McKechnie says, "It was unnecessary to repeat the recognized rule that the minor must receive, out of the revenues, maintenance and education suited to his station." [14] Yet that is just what young Theobald is asking—proper support for himself from the issues of the land, which he complains he has not been getting from either the king or the grantees of the wardship. His petition, while representing correctly the spirit and implications of the Charter, "quotes" from it a clause it does not actually contain! [15]

There is little evidence of grievances connected with the method of amercing barons, but since they were amerced at a relatively high rate, instances occur of persons protesting being reckoned as barons in order to escape with a smaller payment. The Abbot of Croyland made good

[13] *Queen's gold* (*aurum Reginae*) is defined by McKechnie, p. 198, as originally exacted of all who paid reliefs, calculated at nine per cent of the relief, and paid "to the private purse of the Queen Consort by an official representing her at the Exchequer." This practice, protested by the barons in 1258, was discontinued except in connection with some special composition, as a fine in disputed succession. Hence, perhaps, Low's and Pulling's definition: ". . . a claim made by the Queen of England to the king on the renewal of leases or crown-lands on the granting of charters—matters of grace supposed to be obtained by the powerful intercession of the queen."

Rot. Parl. I, 299, 305, 308, nos. 42, 68, 81. The fourth, directed against the Earl of Cornwall rather than the king, complains of the putting *in defenso* of the banks of Ouse and Yor contrary to the Great Charter (ca. 16). For a similar petition, see pp. 410–11, no. 140.

[14] McKechnie, p. 208. The comment in the *Mirror of Justices* is on pages 176–77.

[15] *Rot. Parl.* I, 318, no. 128: "Et cum in Magna Carta de Libertatibus Anglie contineatur, quod custodes . . ." This as per ca. 5, but the petition continues: "Et quod hered' habeant sustentationem competentem de exitibus predictis."

such a claim against the Exchequer in 1322, as did a certain Thomas de Furnivall in 1326. In both instances Exchequer officials were directed to permit these individuals to be amerced according to the Great Charter.[16] Petitions of Hugh Despenser, the younger, and of Walter, Bishop of Exeter, make effective use of the last clause of chapter 29 promising no delay of justice.[17] Another (Robert Thorpe) makes interesting use of two chapters of the Charter. This petitioner is heir to a manor held of the king in fee farm, but formerly held of an honor which had escheated. On his father's death Robert "came and in ignorance did homage to the king by error" and had his seisin. And now he is being distrained by the sheriff of Suffolk for relief. He says that he sought remedy in Chancery and was adjourned thence into parliament, where he now prays remedy, according to law, *e solom les poyntz de la Graunde Chartre, ou est motee issint entre Eschietes, Nos eodem modo eam tenebimus quo Baro eam tenuit, &c.* But it apparently occurs to him that it may be difficult to undo his mistake since the king is actually "seised of the homage." Hence he calls attention to

another point in the conclusion of the said Great Charter where it is put thus. Moreover we have granted to them, for us and our heirs, that neither we nor our heirs shall demand anything by which the liberties contained in this Charter may be infringed or weakened, and if anything be sought after by anyone contrary to this, it shall be worth nothing, and held for naught.[18]

Several other petitions scattered through the reign of Edward III and the early years of Richard II indicate continued awareness and use of some provisions of Magna Carta. In the first parliament of Edward III a petition of the Bishop of Durham cites the Charter in connection with a manor and advowson alleged to be wrongfully detained in the king's hands.[19] Another abuse connected with wardship—the king's reluctance

[16] McKechnie, who discusses these cases (pp. 297–98), says that the abbot was not successful in his claim, but the record indicates that he was: for "it appears by the record and process before the keeper and barons that the abbot did not hold as a baron and ought not to be amerced as one, whereupon it was considered by them that the abbot should be discharged of the amercements, and should be amerced according to the form of Magna Carta." *Cal. Close Rolls,* 1318–23, pp. 442–43. The same in the roll 205 m.12, where the case is reviewed in 1341, quoting the order of 15 Ed. II. For Thomas de Furnivall's case, see also Madox, *History and Antiquities of the Exchequer,* I, 535–38.

[17] See below, pp. 75, 97.

[18] *Rot. Parl.* I, 419–20, no. 12 ". . . d'un autre poynt en la parclose de la dite Graunde Chartre ou est mote issint, Concessimus eciam eisdem, pro Nobis & heredibus nostris, quod nec Nos . . ."

[19] It is the procedure to which he takes exception, but the text (imperfect) does not make clear just what chapter of the Charter he had in mind—perhaps both the "fixed place" of chapter 11 and the "law of the land" of chapter 29 ("ne chose enroule ne record par fyn ne par iugement due nul part, et a la commune lei de la terre et la grante chartre et a la secunde estatut de westmoustier"). Richardson and Sayles, *Rotuli Parliamentorum,* p. 114.

to release a profitable estate when the heir came of age—was the grievance of David, Earl of Athol, in his petition (1334) for livery of the castle, manor, and honor of Chilham with appurtenances in Kent. He had petitioned in the parliament of 4 Edward III; had had a day "now in parliament, and now in chancery"; and asks livery of his heritage before the end of the present parliament: "as our lord the king is obliged to render to heirs within age and in wardship, their heritages fully when they come to their majority (*a lour plein age*). And the Great Charter made by his progenitors, and confirmed by himself, wills it." [20]

In 1380 "amends" for waste during wardship was assigned as a special favor to John de Mowbray, still a minor and ward of the crown. Where it should be proved that waste had been committed by the grantee of the wardship, he was to have all that appertains to the king by reason of the said waste, *secundum legem regni nostri Anglie et per formam magne carte de libertatibus Anglie.*[21]

A clause of chapter 8, providing that the king will not seize lands for debts if the chattels are sufficient to satisfy the debt, is invoked by two petitioners in right of their wives, heiresses of a certain John de Moeles, deceased, debtor to the crown.[22] As late as 1373 two pledges for debtors, having discharged a debt of two thousand pounds, claimed and had assigned to them part of the lands of the debtors in line with the first clause of chapter 8, praying the king "that he would order the lands of the said Thomas and Bartholomew to be delivered to them to hold according to the form of Magna Carta in which it is contained that, if a debtor default or will not pay his debt when he can, the pledges shall answer for the debt and have his lands and rent until they be satisfied of their debt." [23]

Magna Carta and the Register of Writs

"*. . . and that our justices, sheriffs, mayors, and other officials who under us and by us have to administer the law of the land, shall allow the said*

[20] *Rot. Parl.* II, 87, no. 60. "Et la graunt Chartre par ses progenitours fete, & par ly meismes conferme, le voet." Letters close (1346) on behalf of John de Wareme, Earl of Surrey, result from complaints against an escheator, but here it is not ca. 31 but ca. 29 that is involved: the escheator had taken the manor into the king's hand "without warning or calling the earl, contrary to the form of Magna Carta . . ."

[21] The letters patent on the young earl's behalf recite verbatim the clauses of ca. 4 on waste during wardship. *Cal. Pat. Rolls*, 1377–81, p. 488.

[22] *Rot. Parl.* II, 397, no. 110. The chattels had been seized by the sheriffs of three counties to satisfy the debt; then orders had gone forth to the sheriffs to turn the chattels over to the executors and to levy the debt from the lands. The petitioners secured recall of this order, "come cele est conceive encontre la tenour de la Grandre Chartere," and in the answer: "Pur ceo qe il n'est mye reson qe les terres de les dettours le Roy soyent charges come les dettours eient biens & chateux dont la dette purra estre leve . . ."

[23] The petition is quoted in letters patent to the sheriffs of London to turn over the lands in question. *Cal. Pat. Rolls*, 1370–74, pp. 281–83 (C 66/288 m.12).

charters in pleas before them and judgments in all their points, that is to say, the Great Charter of Liberties as common law, and the Charter of the Forest according to the Assize of the Forest, for the relief of our people."

(CONFIRMATIO CARTARUM)

"Nevertheless the King nor none of those that made this ordinance intend, that by virtue hereof any of the foresaid Knights shall hold any Plea by the power which shall be given them, in such case where there hath been Remedy provided in times past, after the course of the Common Law, by writ; nor also that any prejudice should be done to the Common Law, nor to the Charters aforesaid in any Point."   (ARTICULI SUPER CARTAS)[24]

SOME actions were founded on common law, some were created by statute. In the fourteenth century it was the opinion of the courts that "a new statutory remedy did not involve the abolition of the previous Common Law on the matter." [25] Some statutes set up a form of words to be used in a new writ; others did not.[26] In no instance does Magna Carta prescribe the form of a writ. Inasmuch as so many chapters of the Charter only reaffirmed common law, these distinctions are of less significance than for later statutes. Actions to enforce some of the principles laid down in the Charter already existed at common law, and the appropriate writs appear in Glanvill. Yet later legal tradition conceived of two of these as "founded on Magna Carta." [27]

Some statutory writs rehearsed the authorizing statute in their preambles and others did not. The printed Register contains four original writs which quote a provision of the Charter. Of several other writs which do not so quote, it is nevertheless noted in the Register that they are "founded on Magna Carta." In the case of still others, some connection with the Charter is indicated in the *regula* following the writ. A comparison of the lists of writs included in manuscripts of the Register compiled at successive periods indicates that some of the writs traditionally alleged to be "founded on the Charter" were comparatively late creations. The old *Natura Brevium* naturally notes these relationships and adds others in its explanatory comments on individual writs or groups of writs. Fitzherbert's *Natura Brevium,* "fuller and more readable" than the older commentary, does even more of this.[28]

---

24 These two quotations are enforcement clauses of the respective documents.
25 Plucknett, *Statutes and Their Interpretation,* p. 131.
26 For instance, West. II, ca. 35, contains the wording of a writ of "ravishment of ward."
27 "Ne iniuste vexes" and "de plegiis acquietandis."
28 "In the reign of Edward III, a selection of writs was published with a commentary under the title 'Natura Brevium.' After the publication of Fitzherbert's Natura Brevium it was called the 'Old Natura Brevium.' " Holdsworth, II, 522. It was printed by Pynson, 1524, and by Tottell, 1584. Fitzherbert's was printed in 1534, and reprinted 1537. For a list of the writs and some examples, see Appendix D.

DE MODERATA MISERICORDIA AND MAGNA CARTA CHAPTER 14

"Very likely there was no clause in Magna Carta more grateful to the mass of the people than that about amercements."[29] Amercement in proportion to the offence (*secundum modum delicti*); exemption of the means of livelihood of the offender; affeerment by local juries, or in the case of earls and barons, by their peers—such checks on the arbitrary practices of officials were indeed worth preserving. Westminster I, chapter 6, had repeated these rules more explicitly for the towns and lower classes and had granted affeerment by peers to freeman, merchant, and villein—a provision which came to be attributed to the Charter itself:

And that no city, borough nor town, nor any man be amerced, without reasonable cause, and according to the quantity of his trespass; that is to say, every freeman saving his freehold, (contenance), a merchant saving his merchandise, a villein saving his waynage, and that by his or their peers.[30]

In the thirteenth and fourteenth centuries, enforcement of these rules devolved upon the itinerant justices and was included in the articles of the eyre. An example in point is article 117 of the *Great Eyre of Kent* (1313–14), which reads: "Of such as have been amerced without reasonable cause and beyond the quantity of their trespass, and not by their peers, by whom alone they should be amerced. See the sixth chapter of the same statute [Westminster I], and the thirteenth [*sic*] of the Great Charter of Liberty."[31] Here the intent was no doubt to check up on local royal officials, particularly the sheriffs, as was the case in the eyre at the Tower of London, 1321, when it was the turn of the amercers to be amerced.[32] Similarly in an assize roll for Devon (25–27 Edward III) a sheriff was charged with having assessed a certain immoderate amercement (*immoderata misericordia*) *absque taxatoribus aut paribus suis ad hoc electis et iuratis, contra formam magne carte de libertatibus Anglie et eodem modo facit de omnibus amerciamentis in comitatu predicto hundredo de Shefthere et turno vicecomitis.*[33] An early fourteenth-century petition from the tenants of the manor of Bocking in Essex to their lord, the prior of Christchurch, Canterbury, assumes extension of this provision of the Charter to court leet and its tenants, both free and customary, quite properly in view of the fact that leet juris-

---

[29] Maitland, *Pleas of the Crown for the County of Gloucester*, p. xxxiv.

[30] *S. R.* I, 28.

[31] *Great Eyre of Kent*, I, 42 (S. S.). The practice is recognized by Bracton and by Fleta (*De Capitulis Corone & Itineris*). Cf. *Novi articuli corone* (Edward I) Harl. MSS 395, fol. 106: "Item de hiis qui amerciati sint sine rationabile occasione ultra quantitatem delicti et non per pares suos et per quem amerciati fuerint."

[32] The sheriffs of London were charged with amercing men in their courts at their will without affeerment of their peers. This, declared the justices, "the Lord King in no wise permits, according to the Great Charter of England, but it is beyond royal power to concede and against all justice." *Liber Custumarum*, I, 410–11.

[33] *Assize Roll, Devon*, 195 m.7. I am indebted to Miss Bertha Putnam for this instance.

diction was in theory a regalian right in private hands. The petition is worth quoting as one of the few from a group of this kind. Since their lord, the prior, is an ecclesiastic, they most appropriately remind him of the responsibility of "Holy Church" toward the Charter:

Furthermore, Sire, that whereas the aforesaid tenants who were liable to be amerced in court, ought when so amerced, to be affeered by their peers according to the extent of their trespass then came the said John le Doo (the steward) and refused to accept such affeerment, but has of his own conceit, increased their burdens twofold or even threefold and by such means has vexed the tenants and brought them to destruction, against all reason and the Great Charter that Holy Church ought to uphold. And for this they pray remedy.[34]

The protection afforded by chapter 14 was also extended to the tenants of mesne lords in court baron. In the Register, the old *Natura Brevium,* and Fitzherbert, the writ *de moderata misericordia,* "founded on Magna Carta," is explicitly designed for tenants in court baron. Says Fitzherbert:

The Writ of Moderata Misericordia lieth in Case where a Man is amerced in a Court Baron, or other Court which is not a Court of Record, outragiously for Trespass or other Offence; then he may sue this Writ directed unto the Lord of the Court or unto his Bailiffs, commanding them, that they moderately amerce the Party according unto the Quantity of the Trespass, Ec. And this Writ is founded upon the Statute of *Magna Charta,* cap. 14, *Quod nullus liber Homo amercietur nisi secundum quantitatem Delicti,* Ec. . . .

But what shall be said moderate Amercement, and what not, appeareth by the Words of the said Statute, which saith, *Secundum quantitatem Delicti:* By which it seemeth, that if it exceed the Value of the Trespass, it is not a moderate Amercement; and that shall be intended for the Value of the Trespass, which is done unto the Lord, and not to him who shall have the Amercement . . . But it seemeth this Amercement ought to be affeered by Persons certain, when they are amerced for any Trespass. And if the Amercement which is set be affeered by his Peers, then this Writ of *Moderata Misericordi doth not lie*; for then it is according to the Statute of *Magna Chart'* . . . And by the Statute of Magna Charta every amercement in a Court Baron ought to be affeered by Two Tenants of the Manor upon Oath. And if the Steward or Bailiff will assess any Amercement without Affeerment, then he who is amerced shall have such a Writ. . . .[35]

[34] For the full text of the petition, with discussion of the probable date and description of the manor, see Nichols, "An Early Fourteenth Century Petition from the Tenants of Bocking to their Manorial Lord," *Economic History Review,* 2:300–7. An extent of 1309 gives the names of eighty-six males, besides a vicar, a chaplain, and two clerks. Nichols says that it is hard to ascertain the exact status of the tenants. There were some free holdings and some customary or villein tenures. He adds that holders of the latter may not have been unfree personally. I am indebted to Professor Herbert Heaton for calling to my attention this interesting episode.

[35] Fitzherbert, *Natura Brevium.* He also notes the clause on amercement of clerks and gives a form of writ to the sheriff. As indicated in the bibliography, I have used

From the Year Book for 10 Edward II comes a perfect example of such an action, one of the few instances which the reporter specifically calls an action "founded on the Great Charter." One Richard le Gras had sued a writ of right against several persons before the bailiff in the court of the Bishop of Winchester. He essoined himself by casting one essoin against all of the parties instead of against each separately. He was amerced at one mark and distrained by two horses to pay the same. It was claimed for the bailiff that the amercement was affeered by Richard's peers, and issue was joined on this point.

According to the record (the *de banco* roll), the amercement

was awarded in the aforesaid court of Wargrave by the suitors of the same court . . . And this mercy Robert of Wargrave and William of Wargrave, free tenants of the same court and peers of the said Richard, sworn to affeer the said amercement, as should be according to the tenour of the said Great Charter, then assessed the said Richard at ten shillings . . .

According to the first version in the Year Book:

A writ of *moderata misericordia* founded on the Great Charter was brought against the Bailiff of the Bishop of Winchester, which said that the Bailiff had amerced him for a small trespass etc. contrary to the form of the Great Charter etc. And wrongfully for this reason . . . thereupon he sued a prohibition, and forbade him by the King etc., and delivered the prohibition on a certain day in a certain place etc. and he (distrained him) until he had paid the mark, wrongfully and to his damage etc.

Denham said for the bailiff that whereas he supposed that he delivered the prohibition to him, he delivered none, ready etc.

Burton. This is no answer, because our action is given to us by the Great Charter, wherefore you ought to answer.

The second version is interesting in its assumption that the Charter specifically relates to a lord's court.[36] What seems to be a similar action brought by an abbot against the bailiff of a royal honor is briefly recorded in the *de banco* roll for 18 Edward II.[37]

DE RATIONABILI PARTE BONORUM AND MAGNA CARTA CHAPTER 18

This writ, old enough to be found in Glanvill in the forms of the

both the early French and later English translations of Fitzherbert and the Register. Page references are not indicated. Material used in the following pages can be more easily found under the respective titles (*de moderata misericordia*, etc.).

[36] "(Richard le Gras) complained that whereas it was ordained by the Great Charter of the King, that no man should be amerced in his lord's court for small trespass and that naught should be taken from him save a reasonable amercement only . . ." Y. B. 10 Ed. II, pp. 3–5 (S. S.).

[37] H. 18 Ed. II, roll 255 m.154, to the effect that the bailiff had not followed instructions: ". . . prefato Ballivo preceperat dominus Rex quod iuxta tenorem Magne Carte de libertatibus Anglie moderatam ab eodem Abbate caperet Misericordiam, secundum

Register, does not quote the Charter, but parties and pleaders connected the two. Fitzherbert notices this discrepancy between theory and practice:

This writ lieth where the Wife after the Death of her Husband cannot have the third Part of her Husband's Goods after the Debts are paid, and Funeral Expences performed: For then she may have this Writ against the Executors of her Husband: And it seemeth by the Statute of Magna Charta c. 18. that this was the Common Law of the Realm; and so it appeareth by *Glanvil*, that it is the Common Law, that after the Debts paid, the Goods shall be divided into three Parts: One Part for the Wife, another Part for Sons and Daughters, and the third unto the Executors.

Then he adds, "but yet the Writs in the Register rehearse the Customs of the Counties, and are of this Form," and gives sample writs, one for the wife and one for a son or daughter, neither of which quotes chapter 18.[38] The author of the annotations (*regula*) of the Register notes that "in certain writs that writ is founded on Magna Carta" but seems to doubt their validity.[39] Very likely both commentators were familiar with the reports of the very cases to be described here.

In two of these the writ quotes chapter 18. The first is an action brought by a widow against her husband's executor (1314).[40] The second, an action of *detinue* brought by an infant, is reported in the Year Book as follows:

A. brought a writ against William, executor of the testament of Angarice, executrix of G. of B., and the purport of the writ was as follows:

Seeing that it is provided by the Great Charter of the liberties of England that children, after the death of their father, are to have their reasonable share of the goods and chattels which he had on the day of his death, and that one G., our father . . .[41]

In two other cases of the same reign, according to the pleadings, the writ follows the forms in the Register, alleging merely "the custom of the country," but counsel support the custom by citing the Charter.[42]

modum delicte illius, idem ballivus . . . ab eodem Abbate graviorem redemptionem per varias districtiones extorquere non cessat . . ."

[38] Fitzherbert, *Natura Brevium*. Glanvill does not give the writ but describes the customary practice, sec. xii, p. 5.

[39] On the grounds that what existed before the statute could not be established by the statute? "In quibusdam brevibus breve istud fundatur super Magnam cartam, sed non valet pur ceo que forpris de statute nest pas statuit."

[40] From the *Register of Walter de Stapleton*, Bishop of Exeter, p. 429, the writ of *venire facias* to the Bishop: ". . . ad respondendum . . . de Placito quare, cum in Magna Carta de Libertatibus contineatur quod uxores, post mortem Virorum suorum habeant racionabiles partes suas de bonis et catallis que fuerunt Virorum suorum predictorum, etc."

[41] Y. B. 6 and 7 Ed. II, pp. 30–31 (S. S.). Similarly in the *de banco* roll: "de placito quare cum in magna carta de libertatibus Anglie contineatur quod pueri post mortem patrum suorum habeant racionabilem partem suam . . ."

[42] Y. B. 1 Ed. II, pp. 39–40 (S. S.). In the second, P. 17 Ed. II, no. 16 (*detinue*), when the custom was questioned, it was replied, "The custom is such, and is proved by the Great Charter, which wills 'salvis uxori et pueris suis rationabilis partibus suis.'"

Fitzherbert describes a group of writs for being quit of toll (*breve de essendi quietum de teloneo*): one for citizens and burgesses, one for merchant strangers, others for spiritual and religious persons, and for tenants of ancient demesne. Of the last he says:

Tenants of Ancient Demesne by the Custom of the Realm ought to be quit of Toll, etc. in every Market, Fair, Town or City throughout the Realm; and upon that every one of them may sue to have Letters Patent under the King's Seal, to all the King's Officers, and to Mayors, Bailiffs etc. and the form of the Patent is, Whereas according to the Custom, etc.

None of these forms cites the Charter, but letters patent of the very nature he describes, dated as late as February 12, 1476, do so:

Mandate to all sheriffs, mayors, bailiffs, constables and other ministers of the king to permit the men and tenants of the manor of Kynton alias Quintone and Waleborne, which is of the ancient demesne of the crown, as appears by a certificate sent into Chancery by the king's treasurer and chamberlains, to be quit of prest and of toll, passage, pontage and picage throughout the whole of England according to the tenour of Magna Carta and the custom of the Realm.[48]

This from the calendar might leave us in doubt as to the provision of the Charter intended, but the roll makes clear that it is chapter 9. The guarantee of their liberties to cities and boroughs is extended to tenants on ancient demesne.

As we have seen above, the holding of the sheriff's tourn (further regulated by 31 Edward III, chapter 15) continued in popular estimation to be linked with Magna Carta chapter 35. The Register came to contain quite a group of writs for actions against unwarranted demands for suit of court—*pro exoneratione sectae ad Curiam Com' vel Baron'*. According to Fitzherbert: "And if the Sheriff will distrain a Man to do Suit to the Hundred or Wapentake more than twice in the Year, to do Things appertaining to that Leet, then he shall have a Writ upon the Statute of Magna Charta directed to the Sheriff, which shall be thus . . ." This group is illustrative of the infinite specialization in forms, as it contains variants fitted to the needs of wards, coparceners, "men and women of religion," parsons, women, tenants in ancient demesne, as well as persons summoned to a leet or tourn out of their hundred.

M. 30 Ed. III (c. no. 50), in an action of detinue of chattels by a widow against executors of her husband, to the allegation that a writ was abated before Sir William Herle, it was replied, "The reason the writ of which you speak was abated was because it made mention that it was given by the Great Charter, whereas it was not."

[48] *Cal. Pat. Rolls*, 1467–77, p. 565. In the roll 537 m.8, this entry, like writs for "actions on the statute," begins with and quotes ca. 9: "Sciatis quod cum in magna carta de libertatibus Anglie inter cetera contineatur quod Civitas Londoniarum habeat . . ."

A WRIT OF PROHIBITION DIRECTED AGAINST UNLAWFUL
USE OF THE WRIT PRAECIPE

The writ which is called praecipe shall not for the future be issued to anyone, regarding any tenement whereby a freeman may lose his court.

(MAGNA CARTA CA. 24)

RATHER obscure in its place in the Register, but most interesting as an example of an action founded on the Great Charter, is a writ òf prohibition whereby a lord could claim his court.[44] According to chapter 24, writs of *praecipe* could still be issued to tenants-in-chief of the king but not to tenants of mesne lords. The letter of the law was observed: the Chancery ceased to issue this form of writ to subtenants. The real intent of the provision was evaded in practice.

Almost too sweeping is McKechnie's conclusion that by Edward I's reign "legal machinery was brought to perfection so that thereafter no action relating to freehold was ever again tried in the courts baron of the magnates." More in harmony with the evidence of the sources is the statement of Pollock and Maitland that throughout the thirteenth and even in the fourteenth century a good many actions were begun in feudal courts by writ of right although they were seldom disposed of in these courts. They quote Hengham, who "tells us that in his day the lords rarely asserted this jurisdiction over freehold land, for they could get little or no profit out of it." [45] The evidence of the Year Books indicates that occasionally in the reigns of the three Edwards, lords did claim their courts, sometimes successfully, and based their claim clearly on the Great Charter.

The old *Natura Brevium* has the most interesting description of the prescribed procedure.[46] It is to the effect that since by the Great Charter chapter 24, "which begins *Breve quod vocatur precipe in capite* it is provided that this writ never be granted to anyone whereby any freeman may lose his court," anyone who wants to use this writ must make oath on his faith (*ferra suerte par sa foy*) that the tenement which is in demand is

[44] Fitzherbert includes it in a group "On Prohibition and Inhibition." In the old *Natura Brevium* it is recited and discussed in connection with the writ *praecipe*. For a description of the devices used to evade ca. 24, see McKechnie, pp. 353–54.

[45] Pollock and Maitland, I, 587–88: ". . . to get them removed first into the county courts, and then into the king's court was easy, and if the tenant (the passive party in the litigation) chose to reject the duel and put himself upon the grand assize, the competence of the lord's court was at an end."

[46] Old *Natura Brevium*, pp. xiii–xiiii, "Briefe de Droit precipe in capite." Cf. Fitzherbert, pp. 93–94: "And one Writ in the Register is, where a man sueth a *Praecipe in Capite* against another in the Common Pleas, of Lands or Tenements which are not holden of the King, but of another Lord; then the Lord of whom the lands are so holden may sue this Writ directed to the Justices of the Common Pleas, commanding them, that if it do appear unto them that the Lands are not holden of the King, &c. but immediately of another, that they do not meddle with the Conusance of that Plea, but that they bid the Party sue for his Writ of Right Patent, *If it shall seem expedient to him.*"

held of the king in chief as of his crown (*come de son corone*) and of no other. But if any man purchase the *praecipe in capite* by false suggestion made in the king's court in order to deprive the lord of his court, the latter shall have a writ directed to the justices to inquire whether the tenements be held of the said lord, and if it be so found, then the demandant if he wishes may bring his writ of right patent in the court of the lord.

Recognition of the right of a lord to such an action is found in a case of 6 Edward II. A demandant brings his writ of right before the justices in the Great Eyre of Kent. Says Passeley, on behalf of the lord:

This is a *precipe in capite,* and we tell you that the tenements are not holden of the Crown, but of the manor of Eltham, which is the King's peculiar and is in the hand of the Queen; and you have the bailiff here who claims the right of his court, for the tenements ought to be demanded in that court by a writ of right overt.

The judges, Staunton and Spigurnel, recognize the claim, citing a previous case as precedent:

In a precipe in capite, after gage of battle and when the champions were in their places to wage battle on behalf of the Abbot of Launceston and another, the chief lord came with a writ from the King, in accordance with the Great Charter, informing the Justices that the tenements were holden of the bearer as chief lord, who ought to hold his court. So here, in accordance with the Great Charter, this challenge cannot hold . . .[47]

In a rather obscure case of about the same time (8 Edward II), the Abbot of Edmundsbury, in seeking abatement of a writ of right, secured from the king some such prohibition based on Magna Carta. Interesting here is the assertion that Domesday Book and "the charter of liberty" were "inspected." [48]

Early in Edward III's reign two lords relied on the same provision in successfully claiming their courts, not against the crown but against the Bishop of Durham. However, they proceeded by petition before king and council in parliament, not by this writ of prohibition.[49]

---

[47] Y. B. 6 Ed. II, pp. 86–87 (S. S.).

[48] Y. B. 8 Ed. II, pp. 172–73 (S. S.). "And the King sent his writ to his Justices which recited that the Abbot of Edmundsbury had shown that John of Dagworth had impleaded him in our Court by the *precipe in capite* and claimed from him the manor etc. to hold of us in chief, and further we have inspected Domesday, in which it was found that the Abbot holds the manor etc. of us in chief, and we have also inspected the charter of liberty which provides that a precipe in capite which would put any free man in danger of losing his Court is not to be granted to anyone, and we bid you, etc."

[49] The king's letters close (dated November 15, 1331) to the Bishop on behalf of the petitioners, *Cal. Close Rolls*, 1330–33, p. 372. The two lords protested "that they like other free men of the realm, ought to have their court concerning lands of the manor that are to be pleaded by writ of right, according to the law and custom of the realm and the tenor of Magna Carta . . ."

Less successful, apparently, was a second method of recourse open to a lord (also noted in the old *Natura Brevium*) which was simply to appear before the justices before whom the writ *praecipe* was pending without having purchased any writ of prohibition. In two instances recorded in the Year Books for Edward I's reign, a mere verbal claim based on the Charter, made by a bailiff on his lord's behalf, was overruled or ignored by the justices. "The lord should have purchased his writ, as is proper in such case, for by reason of your plea, we will not stay the suit." [50] Similarly (3 Edward III) when a lord himself appeared before the justices to claim his court, he was told by Herle, "The issue is joined, buy a writ to have a remedy for this if you wish."

These episodes seem to indicate that the justices sanctioned the use of such writs (prohibition). Yet presently we come upon indications of reluctance to grant them. A clerk of the Chancery comes into the bench "to see what the justices would do, for those of the chancery did not want to grant any writ for this W. Plais to the justice of the bench." [51] Again (6 Edward III) when two lords clearly claim their court by writ based on Magna Carta, counsel for the demandant maintains that the Charter merely forbids Chancery to issue the *praecipe* in certain circumstances, but once the writ is issued, does not prohibit the justices from holding the plea! Herle, J. denies this: "The law wills that the writ be not granted, whereby a free man lose his court, whether the law is effectual or not, if it be effectual, we must have regard for it even though the writ be here, for otherwise the law would have no effect . . ." Yet presently, "Herle had the inquest summoned and sworn." [52]

As late as 17 Edward III, Thomas de Bello Campo, Earl of Warwick, used a third method described in the old *Natura Brevium,* applicable when an action based on a false suggestion that land was held in chief of the king had resulted in judgment for and recovery by the demandants:

And the Earl of Warwick, who said that he was lord of the same land, sued an *Audita Querela* directed to the Justices on the ground that the *Praecipe in capite* was brought to deprive him of his court. And at his suit, by force of this writ, an inquest of office was taken in the Bench to inquire who committed the deceit, etc.[53]

[50] Y. B. 20–21 Ed. I, pp. 72–74, and 30–31 Ed. I, pp. 232–34 (R. S.).

[51] Y. B. T. 3 Ed. III, no. 7, *droit.* Ralph Dacre brought his writ of right against Roger de Maunby, and process continued until the issue of the grand assize was joined. Then W. Plais came and said that the tenements were held of him, and that the writ was purchased on false suggestion, and against the form of the Charter, and begged the court not to hold this plea.

[52] Y. B. P. 6 Ed. III, no. 16, *droit.*

[53] Y. B. 17 and 18 Ed. III, p. 282 (R. S.). The editor supplies from the *de banco* roll the "audita querela" which recites how the parties had obtained the writ "fraudulenter contra formam Magnae Chartae de libertatibus Angliae, in qua continetur quod breve quod vocatur

Provisions of the Charter Cited by Pleaders

IN THE following instances from the Year Books of the first three Edwards, it will appear that the citing of provisions of Magna Carta usually comes from the pleaders and attorneys; that while there is an occasional misconception or frivolous exception, the claim is usually a bona fide one, the chapter in question is correctly quoted and relates to the main issues in the case. All this contrasts with instances from some of the fifteenth-century Year Books and especially the sixteenth-century reports in which the citing of chapters of the Charter comes more often from the judges than the pleaders and is often incidental to the issue in the case, a matter of mere academic interest, by way of illustration, analogy, or precedent.[54]

MAGNA CARTA CHAPTER 4, WASTE DURING WARDSHIP

Of all the feudal incidents, wardship had been the most difficult to regulate. Chapter 4 of the Charter gives the king damages for waste in the estates of any of his tenants-in-chief where the waste is committed by the sheriff or other official administering the wardship for the king ("we of him will take amends"). For the other type of wardship—one granted by the king to some private party—the penalty prescribed was different: "he (the grantee or lessee) shall lose that wardship." To this the statute of Gloucester, chapter 5, added, "And where it is contained in the Great Charter, that he which did waste during the custody shall lose the wardship, it is agreed that he shall recompense the heir his damages for the waste, if so be that the wardship lost do not amount to the value of the damages before the age of the heir of the same wardship." [55]

Pleaders tried to defeat such actions by confusing the two types of wardship or ignoring the second. In an unsuccessful attempt to defeat an action of waste against one of the executors of a lessee, says Denom for the defendant:

These tenements are holden in chief of our lord the King by services which give wardship etc.; and we do not think that of tenements which are holden of the King and of which wardship belongs to the King anyone but the King ought to have amends for waste, for the Great Charter says "we from him will take amends."

Staunton, J. That refers to a case where the wardship is in the King's hand; and here [the plaintiff] is of full age and desires to aver that you have made waste to his disinheritance. Therefore plead over.[56]

Praecipe in capite non fiat alicui de aliquo libero tenemento unde liber homo perdat curiam suam."

[54] See below, pp. 60–67 and Chap. VII.

[55] S. R. I, 48.

[56] Y. B. 3 Ed. II, pp. 89–90 (S. S.). The editor apparently makes the same mistake the pleader (Denom) does here for in a note prefixed to the case he says "The heir of one of the tenants in chief of the King can bring an action for waste against the grantee of the ward-

This case constitutes an excellent example of the difference between the Year Books and plea rolls described above. The record from the *de banco* roll contains nothing of these pleadings but merely the issue finally joined on the fact of waste committed. A similar exception erroneously based on the Charter was raised by counsel for the defendant in an action of waste against a lessee (7 Edward III) with the same outcome: the heir is declared of age and entitled to his action, and issue joined on the fact of waste made.[57]

MAGNA CARTA CHAPTER 7, DOWER

It has been suggested above that the Charter, as a definition of feudal law and obligation, might serve the lord as well as the tenant. An effective illustration of this point is afforded by the use of chapter 7[58] in two instances, one on behalf of the king himself (1292), and the other for a mesne lord, the Bishop of Coventry and Lichfield (1313).[59] Here, instead of the usual complaint of a widow that she has not received *enough* dower land, her rightful third, *too much* has been assigned or claimed and the lord counters with only a third. The first, from the *coram rege* rolls,[60] is the rather complicated case of one Hawise, widow of Griffith ap Wenonwen, who petitioned the king for the manor of Ashford with which her husband had dowered her and from which she had been ejected in time of war. The argument on the king's behalf seems to have been that as this manor was all the land her husband held in England, she should have received only a third of it and that no part of this English manor could be used as dower for the lands he held in Wales.

ship, notwithstanding Mag. Cart. c. 4." Plucknett, p. 74, uses this case as an example of "the extension of the words of the statute," but the statute of Gloucester, ca. 5, had made the extension.

[57] Y. B. H. 7 Ed. III, no. 3, *waste*. In another attempt to defeat an action of waste against the lessee of a wardship by a similar exception, counsel for the plaintiff says, "You cannot aid yourself except by the Great Charter and the Charter wills, *Et si nos comiserimus vel dederimus etc. nos ab eo capiemus emendas*—There the Charter supposes that he will take amendes from him to whom he leased it . . ." What follows seems to mean that the wardship is no longer in the hands of the original lessee. Y. B. P. and T. 14 Ed. II, no. 12, *waste*.

[58] The last clause of ca. 7 of the 1217 and 1225 (not 1215) texts: "Assignetur autem ei pro dote sua tercia pars tocius terre mariti sui que sua fuit in vita sua, nisi de minori dotata fuerit ad hostium ecclesie." *Dos* or dower was one-third of the husband's lands, often set apart at the church door at marriage.

[59] Compare with these the interesting defensive exposition of this chapter made by Earl Warenne, 1299 (*King's Bench Rolls*, III, 88–95). The earl sued by petition to the king, complaining that while the king was in Flanders, and he himself in Scotland, the king's escheator had assigned dower to the widow of one of the earl's tenants, "much more than she ought to have." "And it seems to the said earl that the wrong done in this assignment cannot be redressed either for him or for others in such a case until they have been given seisin again, for though the Great Charter requires that dower should be assigned to ladies within forty days after the death of their husbands, that is to be understood as referring to such as of right ought to assign dower, for otherwise it would follow that the king or some other man can assign dower to the prejudice of other tenants from the best possessions of an inheritance (whereas she ought to be assigned to have her third both of good and of bad) . . ."

[60] *King's Bench Rolls*, II, 57–58 (S. S.).

And Hugh of Lowther, who sues for the king, says that no action is available to the aforesaid Hawise for demanding the aforesaid manor in dower. For he says that she has plainly acknowledged that the aforesaid Griffith her husband, on the day when he married her and ever afterwards had no other lands or tenements within the realm of England than the aforesaid manor, and the assigned dowry cannot exceed a reasonable dowry, which is a third part of all the lands. He prays judgement whether she is able or ought to have the aforesaid manor as her dower by the aforesaid endowment, and especially since it is contained in the Great Charter of the lord king that a woman ought not after her husband's death to be dowered save of the third part of the lands which belonged to her husband or of less,[61] and thus no one can fix his wife's dower to exceed a third part of his tenements without violence to law and the aforesaid lord king's charter etc.

Then we have the astonishing spectacle of the king's attorney insisting that the king will abide by the common law, while it is the counsel for the lady who claims that the king is above the law; for Hugh of Lowther goes on to say that Griffith's deed is void since it is "entirely contrary to common law, neither ought the royal grant, made upon this, to hold or be valid, especially as the lord king had no wish by that grant to change the common law of his realm." Hawise counters with the affirmation that "the lord king Henry, father of the present lord king, confirmed that endowment for himself and his heirs, and since the king himself is above all law and gave her the aforesaid manor in dower, she prays judgment if she ought to be repelled from her action etc."

In the case of *Beaumont v. the Bishop of Coventry and Lichfield* the plaintiff claimed a half of each of three manors, alleging that the manors were held by socage in counties (Norfolk and Suffolk) where it was customary for the wife to receive half as dower. The bishop's counsel countered with the argument, "The Great Charter wills (*la Graunte chartre veut*) that a wife is to be dowered with the third part of the tenements which were in the seisin of her husband etc. and therefore your claim is contrary to common law." [62]

MAGNA CARTA CHAPTER 10, EXACTION OF EXCESSIVE SERVICES

Although the following is a *replegiari* and not the action of *ne iniuste vexes* traditionally believed to be founded on the Charter, the same chapter 10 is used here as a defense against excessive services. In answer to a dis-

---

[61] The Charter does not actually say this, but only "if she had been dowered less at the church door."

[62] And again, "The Great Charter speaketh generally, and so is to be understood as well of socage tenure as of tenure by knight's service . . ." Y. B. 6 and 7 Ed. II, pp. 53–56 (S. S.). This case furnishes another good example of the difference between the Year Books and the plea rolls. Each of the three versions reported in the Year Books gives the pleadings citing the Charter. The *de banco* roll merely states that the bishop by his attorney denied the claim as contrary to "the law and custom hitherto had in the King's Realm," and as "contrary to the

traint the plaintiff produced a deed proving that former services had been commuted for the render of seven pounds of pepper a year. "The abbot tried to get behind the deed by alleging that he and his predecessors had been seised continuously of the original services." [63]

Claver, for the plaintiff: The Charter of Liberty of England wills (*la chartre de fraunchise D'engleterre veot*) that no man should be distrained to do more services for his free tenement than are due from the words: *quam inde debetur* etc. *Debetur* aids us, and by these words we shall be received on this plea to discharge ourselves by this deed. Judgment.

Bereford, C. J. held that the deed did discharge the original services.

MAGNA CARTA CHAPTER 34, APPEAL

Professor Sayles has pointed out that in spite of Magna Carta chapter 34, which limited a woman's appeal for death to that of her husband, there are recorded in the plea rolls appeals "for the death of a son, a brother, a nephew or a mother, and such are brought not only before the king's bench but also before the common bench and into the county courts. Even for robbery women came forward to voice their appeals. But whenever the Great Charter was invoked in bar, the appellor was non-suited. As a rule however, the woman lost her action through failing to continue the prosecution." [64] In a rather odd case of 11 Edward II chapter 34 was invoked in vain, the judge ruling that "appeal is given to the son of the aunt of him that is dead." When the appellee tried to avoid battle on the grounds that "by the law of the land he [the appellor] cannot be of better condition with regard to this appeal than his mother would be if she were living," Scrope, J. ruled, "At common law appeal is given to a woman as much as to a man and by statute a woman's appeal is only restricted. The son, therefore, remains at common law, so let the appeal stand in the matter." [65]

MAGNA CARTA CHAPTER 28

Nullus ballivus ponat decetero aliquem ad legem manifestam vel ad

common law." The outcome is not indicated. Bereford, C. J. tells the claimant, "If you want to allege a custom contrary to common right, you must establish it by some title, such as its observance since, a time, etc; and peradventure the Court will receive you."

[63] For the editor's analysis of the case, Y. B. 10 Ed. II, p. xvi (S. S.); for the quotation from the report, *ibid.,* p. 17.

[64] "The bringing of such appeals was clearly contrary to law; why then was such a practice tolerated not only by the courts but by the accused themselves? The simplest explanation appears to be that the injured had little hope of seeing the evil doers indicted and were willing to lose their suit and submit to imprisonment and subsequent fine in the knowledge that once their grievance had been brought to the notice of the royal courts the king would usually proceed further on his own account." *King's Bench Rolls,* III, lxxii–lxxiv (S. S.). For cases of Edward I's reign where the rule was applied in bar, *ibid.* II, 25, III, 148; and Thompson, *First Century of Magna Carta,* p. 48.

[65] Y. B. 11 Ed. II, pp. 263–64 (S. S.).

juramentum simplici loquela sua, sine testibus fidelibus ad hoc inductis.

No bailiff for the future shall upon his own unsupported complaint, put any one to his manifest law nor to an oath without credible witnesses brought for this purpose.

THE words *manifestam* and *ad juramentum* do not appear in the text of John's Charter but were inserted in the 1217 issue. It was the *ad juramentum* which made it possible for the Puritan lawyers in Elizabeth's reign to use the provision as a defence against the oath ex officio. The clause was originally directed mainly against unfair treatment of accused men in criminal prosecutions.[66] Both McKechnie and Plucknett have commented on the general obscurity into which this chapter had fallen within a century of the granting of the Charter, and both cite by way of illustration a little Latin note of the early fourteenth century containing three alternative suggestions. The third and preferred of these is substantially the meaning assumed by the defendant quoted below. In the words of McKechnie:

A third opinion is stated and eulogized as a better one, namely, that the Charter prohibited bailiffs from showing undue favour to *plaintiffs* in civil pleas. The defendant on a writ of debt (or the like) should not, in this interpretation of Magna Carta, be compelled to go to proof at all (that is, to make his "law") unless the plaintiff had brought "suit" against him (that is, had raised a presumption that the claim was good, by production of preliminary witnesses or by some recognized equivalent).[67]

This was the sense in which the chapter was used by a defendant in an action of debt (1313–14). The plaintiff had used the formal words producing suit although he had none.[68] The defendant contended that consequently he should not be put to his wager of law: ". . . you have tendered suit, and suit you have not got; and so we ask for judgment after what fashion we shall go away. For the Great Charter says that *nullus ponatur*

---

[66] "No one ought to be put to his '*lex*,' in the sense of 'ordeal,' on mere grounds of vague suspicion or on the unsupported statement of a royal bailiff. After 1166, at least, the voice of an accusing jury of neighbours was a necessary preliminary, under normal circumstances, before any one could be put to the ordeal in England. Magna Carta confirmed this salutary rule: no bailiff should put any one to the ordeal except after formal indictment, due evidence of which was presented at the diet of proof." McKechnie, p. 373. Cf. *Assize of Clarendon*, ca. 4.

[67] McKechnie, p. 371, and note 1: "These appear as an appendix to the Year Book of 32–3 Edward I, p. 516; but the handwriting is supposed to be of the reign of Edward II."

[68] *Anon. v. Anon., Great Eyre of Kent*, II, 34–35 (S. S.). Perhaps the plaintiff already considered suit unnecessary. In 1343 it was decided that "the 'suit' must be in existence, but need not be produced in court; and that if they did appear they could not be examined." McKechnie, p. 371, note 2. Plucknett, commenting on this case, says that the defendant misquoted the Charter, which rightly applied to those who sue in court baron as it only specifically mentions "bailiffs." Yet Plucknett notes that Fleta "tacitly assumes that the provision applies equally to all courts." Both McKechnie, p. 370, and Pollock and Maitland, II, 604, assume that "bailiff" is used here in its widest sense of any royal official.

ad legem manifestam etc.; and here you can give no evidence but by the testimony of suit, and no suit have you got . . ." We wish that Chief Justice Bereford had given his interpretation of this chapter, but all the report gives us is his explanation of how the case should have been pleaded: "A good pleader would not have tendered suit in this case, but would have counted in this wise: *And if he will deny it, see here his deed in proof thereof . . .*"

MAGNA CARTA CHAPTER 11

Common pleas shall not follow our court, but shall be held in some fixed place.

Moreover, no common pleas shall be from henceforth holden in the Exchequer, contrary to the form of the Great Charter.

(ARTICULI SUPER CARTAS, CHAPTER 4)

CHAPTER 11 was one of the best known and oft-cited provisions of the Charter. In the reigns of Elizabeth and James I it was commonly believed to be the origin of the Court of Common Pleas. As a feature of the opening of the new law courts in the Strand in 1882, Queen Victoria was handed a golden key, the key to the " 'certain place' in which, according to the ancient law, justice should be administered." [69] In the thirteenth, fourteenth, and even fifteenth centuries, this chapter was invoked from time to time by the parties to some suit to avoid litigation in King's Bench, Exchequer, or Chancery. By 1300 (as chapter 4 of the *Articuli super cartas* indicates) the clause was assumed to forbid the trial of common pleas in the Exchequer, and in the fourteenth century was popularly held to mean that King's Bench could not hold pleas of land.

In the cases to be described here it will be observed that such exceptions raised by litigants were sometimes allowed, but the justices, especially those of King's Bench, always felt free to overrule them and to uphold their own jurisdiction.[70] Two cases in *Bracton's Note Book* reveal their attitude in early days (1236–37): one litigant was told that even though common pleas be prohibited from following the king, "it does not follow on this account that uncommon pleas may not follow the king and ask judgment"; and to another's protest it was answered that this common plea was not a private plea but specially touched the person of the king (*specialiter tangit personam Dom. Regis*).[71] In 1290 the judges interpreted

---

[69] Burdick, *The Bench and Bar of Other Lands*, p. 48.

[70] Plucknett cites their attitude in one such instance as an example of "exceptions out of the statute" (*Statutes and Their Interpretation*, p. 62), yet the removal of "difficult" cases *coram rege*, while not specified in Magna Carta ca. 11, was really only what had been intended by Henry II in establishing the bench at Westminster in 1178, if we accept the account of a contemporary chronicler, Benedict of Peterborough: ". . . si aliqua quaestio inter eos veniret, quae per eos ad finem duci non posset, auditui regio praesentaretur, et sicut ei et sapientoribus regni placeret terminaretur." *Select Charters*, p. 155.

[71] *Bracton's Note Book*, III, cases 1213; 1220.

the Charter to mean merely that common pleas ought not to begin *coram rege*. The exception and the ruling, both so explicitly put here, are worth quoting:

And whereas it asserted with regard to this, that it is contained in the Great Charter that common pleas may not follow the king himself but are to be held in some definite place, this is to be understood that common pleas ought not to be begun before the king himself, but if common pleas, which have begun before any justices whatever, have been transferred by the king's command before the lord king himself on account of any difficulty and exigency [*propter aliquam difficultatem et necessitatem*], whether before judgment has been given or after, in point of fact all things, without which the aforesaid pleas cannot be determined, ought to be attracted hither to them.[72]

Yet a case might be sent back to the bench as more expedient to be handled there, as was eventually done in this very instance and another (1294); or after error in process had been corrected by the King's Bench (1298).[73]

In the reign of Edward III the popular interpretation was voiced by counsel in the case of *Nutil v. Kyllum* (1340): "A plea of land shall not be pleaded in the King's Bench; for that would be against the Great Charter, which says that 'common pleas shall not follow our Court' . . ." But two years later in a plea of land in Common Bench a writ of entry was abated because of error:

And now in the King's Bench because the demandant cannot have a writ in any other form, the judgment was reversed; and the demandant continued his suit there in the same Court, notwithstanding the words of Magna Carta to wit, *communia placita non sequantur curiam nostram*, because the plea is there by default of another.[74]

The judges also made exceptions to the rules laid down by the Charter (chapter 12) for holding the possessory assizes. McIlwain relates how in 18 Edward II it was decided "that an assize of *novel disseisin* to regain a lordship in the Marches of Wales was rightly held in the English county of Gloucester, though this was a violation of a negative command of Magna Carta itself, 'and the reason is notable, for the Lord *Marcher*, though he had *jura Regalia*, yet could he not do Justice in his own case,' 'and therefore' says Coke, 'this case of necessity is by construction excepted out of the Statute.' "[75]

---

[72] *King's Bench Rolls*, II, 11–12.

[73] *Ibid*. III, 19–21, 69–73. For other instances from the *coram rege* rolls of Edward I's reign in which litigants cite the Charter in excepting to the jurisdiction of the court, with what success the record does not indicate, *ibid*. I, 133, and III, 112–14.

[74] Y. B. 14 and 15 Ed. III, p. 144; and 16 Ed. III, pt. ii, p. 444 (R. S.).

[75] McIlwain, *High Court of Parliament*, pp. 285–86, quoting Coke's *Second Institute*; Fitzherbert's *Abridgement*, assize no. 382. This case is also used by Plucknett, *Statutes and Their Interpretation*, p. 62, as an illustration of an "exception out of the statute."

As a matter of fact, this chapter of the Charter as revised in 1217 (and retained in the 1225 issue) in itself provided for exceptions. Litigants were apt to cite the first clause only—"Inquests of novel disseisin and of mort d'ancestor shall not be taken elsewhere than in their own county courts"— whereas the justices relied on the clauses permitting unfinished assizes to be concluded elsewhere in their circuits and difficult cases to be referred to the bench at Westminster. Good examples of exceptions by litigants are recorded in the Black Letter Year Books for 17 and 24 Edward III.[76] In the first case, Hingham, forced to answer, told "how he entered by purchase and not by disseisin, etc. and prayed the assize, moreover the Great Charter provides that assizes be taken in their counties." [77] In the second, *novel disseisin* before King's Bench at York, the exception was raised but disallowed, on the same principle the justices had laid down in 1290, that it was enough that the plea had been *begun* in its county.[78]

One more case as reported for 19 Edward III is of interest for the spirited defense of their jurisdiction and their reputation by the justices of King's Bench. The case, again a *novel disseisin,* was an involved one, begun before the justices in Suffolk. The justices of King's Bench admitted that the original writ was extinguished by the removal of King's Bench out of the county, but maintained their authority to award the assize "at large," and granted a *nisi prius.* When the defendant "sued by petition to the king," "the bill of Petition enclosed in a letter under the Privy Seal, was sent to Sir William Scot, who said that this suit was a slander against the Court in so surmising dishonesty in its Justices. Therefore Robert was ordered into custody and was put on mainprise to answer to the King." It was in connection with this same case, we are told, that Sharshulle, then chief baron of the Exchequer, came into King's Bench and said, "The plea is not to the jurisdiction, because it is an established fact that in certain cases all kinds of pleas are pleadable in this Court—a writ of Right as well as other writs." Counsel for the plaintiff, Pole, goes so far as to say, "The Justices of this Court do not hold Assises only in the manner limited by Statute, but as they previously did in this Court before the making of the Statute." [79]

---

[76] For thirteenth-century instances of such exceptions see Thompson, *First Century of Magna Carta,* pp. 45–46.

[77] Y. B. H. 17 Ed. III, no. 18, *petit breve de droit*: ". . . auxi come la grante chartre voleit qe les assises serront prisez en countees."

[78] Y. B. H. 24 Ed. III, no. 7.

[79] Y. B. 19 Ed. III, pp. 104–6, 138–44 (R. S.). The Charter is not so mentioned, but the phrase "because by statute" undoubtedly refers to the familiar and much cited ca. 12.

Scot said further: "This award of the Assise was made in accordance with the opinion of all the Justices of all the Courts, who told us that such award had often been made in like manner between other parties, and I have often seen it made myself. And others, our fellow-justices, said that we should prejudice this Court if we did not act in that manner; and therefore we hold the award of the Assise to be good."

The rule laid down by the Charter (chapter 13) that assizes of *darrein presentment* be taken before the bench was sustained in the only instance of its use which I have found. Jurisdiction claimed by the bailiff of an Abbey (who produced a royal charter granting cognizance of all manner of pleas within a certain hundred) was rejected: "The now impedient has brought an assize of last presentation against the now bailiff and that Magna Carta says that such assizes are to be taken before the justices of the Bench." [80]

Magna Carta in the Later Year Books

A RECENT study by Professor Chrimes has made use of the fifteenth-century Year Books to throw light on the so-called Lancastrian constitution: "to investigate the spirit behind the forms," and "to deal with constitutional theory as distinct from constitutional practice." [81] He has little occasion so much as to mention Magna Carta, which, as we have seen, served as private rather than public law. However, some of his generalizations afford a helpful background for the cases to be described below. .

In the first half of the fourteenth century the common lawyers had been jealous for the common law—it was not to be modified by statute more than necessary. By the fifteenth century the supremacy of statute law over common law was unquestioned. A statute "in the affirmative" would not abolish remedies pre-existing at common law (this would still be available as an alternative) but the contrary was true of a statute in the negative. Statutes were classified as introductory of new law or declaratory of old, affirmative or negative, general or particular. If declaratory of old law, a statute might be interpreted equitably. If introductory of new law, negative or particular, it should be interpreted *stricti iuris*.

Chrimes finds that considerable judicial discretion was still being exercised in the fifteenth century. Sometimes it is held within bounds by restrictive rules such as reference to the original intention of the legislature (so much insisted on later by Sir Edward Coke) [82] or the assertion that certain statutes must be interpreted strictly or "without equity." Broad interpretation "by the equity of the statute" includes various types of ex-

[80] "Assise de ultima presentatione semper capiantur coram justiciariis de banco et ibi terminentur."

"Subsequent legislation vacillated between two policies, actuated at times by a desire to restrain the discretionary powers of the justices and at others by experience of the hardships inflicted upon litigants by inflexible rules." See McKechnie, pp. 283–84, for an account of these measures, including two statutes of Richard II's reign.

Y. B. 2 and 3 Ed. II, p. 202, no. 21, app. (S. S.). The editor calls this "a carelessly made copy of the record of a *quare impedit* brought by William de Lucy against Edward Burnel." The argument, he says, "would be that the Abbot's court, being unable to entertain the assize, could not do justice in the counter-action."

[81] Chrimes, *English Constitutional Ideas*, in four chapters: "The Estate of the King"; "The Nature of Parliament"; "Statutory Law and Judicial Discretion"; "The Theory of the State." Generalizations which follow here are based on chap. 3.

[82] "Et en chescun statut on covient de construire l'entent de eux que fesoient le statut."

tension such as to include a plea not named because the "mischief" was the same as in the one named; to include an offense analogous to, but not identical with one made felony by statute; where a statute prescribed a writ only, to add process; and so on.[83]

Of course it is impossible to apply these rules to Magna Carta *in toto*. Parts of it were declaratory of the common law [84] (and the lawyers commonly pointed to Glanvill to prove this), parts were new; chapter 34 was to become a favorite example of a "statute in the negative"; while other clauses were broadened at the discretion of the judges "by the equity of the statute."

For the purpose of this study a comparison of the fifteenth-century Year Books with those of the earlier period reveals both likenesses and contrasts. Not as many different provisions of Magna Carta figure as in the earlier period. More detailed legislation had altered or superseded the Charter in some points. Pleaders still draw on it to make "frivolous exceptions." As Chrimes puts it, "the arts of advocacy were often more ingenious than ingenuous then as they are now." A few of the old standbys still serve to support a claim or defend against an abuse, notably chapters 9, 11, 12, 14, and 35. Now and then citing of "the statute" by pleaders or judges may be quite incidental, introduced by way of illustration, analogy, or precedent, a mere "academic reference." To be sure, the cases to be described here are few in number in proportion to the bulk of the reports, but they suffice to show that the Charter was neither obsolete nor forgotten.

A "frivolous exception" which had been used by earlier pleaders was repeated in 12 Henry IV.[85] Counsel for the defendant tried in vain to defeat an action for waste by citing Magna Carta chapter 4 to the effect that the king is to have amends. This pleader was evidently hard put to it, for this was the third of a series of futile exceptions all ruled out by the judges.

Common Pleas and King's Bench continued to uphold their own juris-

---

[83] For illustrations of all these, Chrimes, *English Constitutional Ideas*, pp. 294–98. "This interpretation 'by the equity' of the statute, was due, in part at least, Sir Peter Maxwell suggests, to the lax and over-concise construction of early statutes; furthermore, 'the ancient practice of having the statutes drawn by judges from the petitions of the commons and the answers of the king may also account for the latitude of their interpretation. The judges would be disposed to construe the language with freedom, knowing like Hengham, C. J. and Lord Nottingham, what they meant when framing them."

[84] "A statute . . . admittedly in affirmance of common law obviously differed from the common law only in being written and enacted. No question of the one's overriding the other could arise . . . they were necessarily identical in substance." Chrimes, *English Constitutional Ideas*, p. 284.

[85] M. 12 Hen. IV, no. 6, *waste*. Hankford, J. rejected his claim that a ward come of age does not have action against a guardian; both judges upheld the procedure of the sheriff in taking a view in one vill, though waste was committed in two; and as to the Charter, he was reminded that it applied to land held of the king, for which he had committed the wardship to another.

dictions and to interpret at their discretion chapters 11 and 12 of Magna Carta. In a certification of assize adjourned before Common Pleas at Westminster the judges themselves were in disagreement as to whether the adjournment was proper in this case.[86] When Thirning inquired "How comes this certification here before us?" Hankford replied that it was by adjournment according to Magna Carta chapter 13 (*sic* for 12)— that is, on account of a difficulty involved. As to the meaning of this clause, he explains, "my colleague and I are not in agreement, and though the statute does not speak of adjournment on certification in an assize of novel disseisin, still I understand that it is adjournable here as the assize is."

Again in a *novel disseisin,* counsel for the plaintiffs argued that the adjournment to Westminster was unlawful on three counts, the third, that removal from the locale in Surrey to Westminster violated the *in itinere suo* of Magna Carta chapter 12. At Westminster, Hull ruled the adjournment lawful (*assez bon*) even though he discovered no "difficulty" in the matter found by the verdict. When counsel reiterated his *in itinere suo,* Hankford, J. rejoined, "By the equity of the statute, which says *in itinere suo,* it is customary to adjourn to Westminster before the justices, and this is law, or otherwise we would make many errors." [87]

When a party was summoned before King's Bench by *scire facias,* counsel demanded judgment of the writ, "for this *scire facias* is a common plea which ought to have been pleaded in Common Bench, where the fine is levied, and the statute of Magna Carta wills that common pleas shall not follow our court [*communia placita non sequantur Curiam nostram*]." But Hankford, J. retorted, "Would you restrict our jurisdiction? . . . This belongs to us, so answer." [88]

This same chapter 11 was quoted in an "action on the statute" (that is, *Articuli super cartas,* chapter 3), a plea to the jurisdiction of the Court of the Steward and Marshal.[89] As late as 14 Henry VII the reporter records a pronouncement by Fineux, chief justice of King's Bench, on the removal of cases to his court, in spite of, or at least not contrary to chapter 11.[90]

---

[86] M. 12 Hen. IV, no. 18, *certificat d'assise.* Certification was "a process by which an obscure or incomplete verdict given before justices of assize was sometimes brought before the central court by summoning the jurors to Westminster to certify the justices as to the oath they have made." The "difficulty" was the question whether certification could be made since two of the original jurors had died. The justices adjourned the case to Westminster, where Gascoigne of King's Bench ruled out the objection; the case was then adjourned to Common Pleas, where the discussion quoted above took place.

[87] P. 12 Hen. IV, no. 5, *assize.*

[88] H. 5 Hen. V, no. 4, *scire facias.* "Voiles vous restreigner nostre Jurisdiction? Vous ne deves point, car ceux del Common Bank ont atteint devant eux, uncore ceo appertient a nous, per que respoignes tc."

[89] M. 10 Hen. VI, no. 43, *Action sur le Statut.*

[90] The ruling is to the effect that if a plea be begun in some other court where pleadable and then is removed to King's Bench for any reason before its determination, King's Bench

Chapter 14 had not lost its popularity or value. In an action for debt brought against a tithing man, amerced because he had refused to "do his office" (make presentments) in court leet and had left the court, the question was raised as to the authority of the steward "then judge of the same leet." It was argued on his behalf that as the leet is a king's court for the time being—a court of record—the steward has power to amerce at his discretion one who will not do his office. To the contrary one of the barons held that the plaintiff would be barred:

"for the Statute of Magna Charta wills that no one be amerced but according to the quantity of the offence, and such has not been done in this case, for the amercement ought to have been affeered by the suitors and this was not done. Wherefore the action can not be upheld, otherwise the statute would be void." [91]

Another of the justices spoke to the same effect, adding, "And as to what is said that he is a judge of record, I concede that, but that does not prove that he may amerce a man according to his discretion."

For 6 Henry VII is recorded an instance, unusual in that the judges, if correctly reported, confuse the terms of a chapter of Magna Carta and those of a supplementary act. Such confusion may well have arisen from the summary forms of the printed abridgments. The question whether an indictment before a sheriff was void if taken in a tourn held at other than the prescribed times led to a review of successive regulations, the practice at common law, Magna Carta chapter 35, and 31 Edward III. Fairfax and Fineux, ruling that the presentment was good, assumed that the Great Charter set the number of tourns at two, but that it remained for 31 Edward III to specify the seasons. [92]

It is no surprise to find the city of London as late as 7 Henry VI relying on Magna Carta chapter 9 to defend a custom. The sheriffs had refused to act on a writ *de nativo habendo,* alleging that, by the ancient custom of immunity after the "year and day," no action for recovery lies, with the astonishing assertion that the defendant had dwelt within the city for forty years! Against the city it was argued that the sheriffs ought to be amerced

will have jurisdiction and will determine it there by the same form and process it would have had in the other court. H. 14 Hen. VII, no. 3. "Nota, que Fineux Chief Justice disoit si un ple . . ." In another such note (one of a series) we find rights of distraint allowable to a lord whose tenant alienated too much land, defined as before and after Magna Carta ca. 31. M. 10 Hen. VII, no. 26. Where the citing of statutes comes at the end of a report with a *vide* such as Coke used so much, one may suspect the reporter or even the editor. For instance, H. 7 Hen. IV, no. 14: "Vide statutum Magne charte ca. 3, 4, 5, & 6. Merton ca. 6."

[91] M. 10 Hen. VI, no. 22, an action of debt for 100*s.* brought against the defendant amerced in that sum by the plaintiff for one J. C. the steward.

[92] P. 6 Hen. VII, no. 4, *enditement, leet, tourne de vicomte.* Keble argued that since by the statute of 31 Ed. III (stat. 1, ca. 15) the sheriff who offended "loses his tourn," the presentment could not be good. King, for the king, held that the "loss" intended by the statute meant only the fines and amercements due the sheriff; what is presented for the king, to whom alone appertains the punishment of a felon, is not voided.

and a *sicut alias* awarded since their defense was unsound. They had ex-
cused themselves on two grounds, one that the city of London is ancient
demesne, the other by force of a custom. Yet when *Domesday Book* was
brought by *certiorari* from the Exchequer, the treasurer and barons certified that the city was not ancient demesne, and *Domesday Book* was upheld as *general et universal que n'est traversable*. Further, a custom against
common right prejudicial to the whole realm (unlike one affecting Londoners only) could not be admitted. But the sheriffs were undaunted.
They begin their *return* with the time-honored eulogy of London as "the
most ancient City in the realm, the chamber of the king, which is his
most ancient demesne (*antiquissimum dominicum Regis*)," equate the
Charter with an act of parliament, and rely on the fact that their city is
older than Domesday.

It would be strange indeed to defeat now a custom used from time immemorial; since they have claimed this custom as one of the liberties of the
City, and all the liberties were ratified and confirmed by Parliament, namely
by the Great Charter of Magna Charta [*sic*] that should be as strong as the
franchise of Westminster or St. Martin. Furthermore the City of London is
older than Domesday Book. At the time of the making of it the City covered
at the widest estimate only the half of its present area [*ne comprend tant come
fait a or, par plus estimation qe le moity*]. It might well be that the soil onto
which it has since expanded was ancient demesne.[93]

The relation of custom and statute raised in a case of 8 Henry VII involved these same chapters of the Charter, chapter 35 directly and chapter
9 by way of analogy. The question was, "Given that Magna Carta [chap-
ter 35] provides that view of frankpledge be held only once a year,
whether it could be held twice by prescription?" Brian held that it could
not:

"I think not, for one can not use prescription against a statute unless it [the
prescription] be saved by another statute, as those of London can give land in
mortmain without licence, and that is by the statute of Magna Carta ca. 9
which is confirmed, and through which their liberties and customs are
granted."[94]

A good example of indirect use of the Charter appears in 10 Henry VII,
when counsel for the plaintiff used the analogy of the obligations of a
guardian during wardship as defined in chapter 5 to support an action
against the bailiff of a park.[95] It was argued for the defendant that a bailiff

[93] Y. B. P. 7 Hen. VI, no. 27, *de nativo habendo*. When the case was continued M. 8
Hen. VI, it was not Magna Carta but the confirmation of their liberties by Richard II and
by parliament which they emphasized.
[94] Y. B. T. 8 Hen. VII, no. 1.
[95] Y. B. 10 Hen. VII, no. 12, an action of account brought by Sir William Say against
John S., bailiff of his park of W. "A park was any piece of ground enclosed with a paling,

is not accountable for deer since they are wild beasts (*sont feres bestes*) and he could be held responsible only for something in which his lord had actual property. But Keble, for Sir William, the plaintiff, defended the action on the grounds that a person may be held to account for anything in his care, as for instance an officer of the court for the king's records in his keeping. It is not the enclosure alone but all within it that constitutes a park. "I may give some one permission to take yearly a deer, a hare or a connie, or grant to my parker the shoulders and humbles of each deer killed, even though I have no more property in the deer than in the fish in the river!" (Whether because we are getting into more modern times or are dealing with matters close to the soil, the pleader's law French fails him here and he falls back on English for such humble terms as *parker, shoulders,* and *humbles.*)[96] Furthermore, he argues, it appears by the statute of Magna Carta that a guardian must keep up houses, parks, fish ponds, and so on, and if a guardian destroys beasts he is chargeable in an action of waste, and "I do not doubt that if a guardian in socage made similar waste he would be chargeable for it on account." All the judges agreed that action of waste does lie in such a case.

It is interesting to find the Charter figuring either directly or as an analogy in the discussion of nice points of law by all the judges in Exchequer Chamber at a time when both Littleton and Fortescue were on the bench. In an appeal for the "death of an ancestor" it was the opinion of the judges that the appeal did not lie, for the question was whether the right of appeal could be conveyed through a woman who herself could never have had appeal.[97] It was Portyngton, king's serjeant, who cited "the statute." The opinion evidently impressed the reporter, who concludes with a *quod nota bene.*

And the justices were in the Exchequer Chamber and Fortescu [C. J. K. B.] Chief Justice, said to Neuton [C. J. C. P.] I wish to hear your opinion of this matter, for I and my fellow judges are agreed.

Portyngton. It seems to me that the appeal does not lie, for he cannot have this appeal unless he claims to be heir by the same removes, and he cannot [claim to be heir] except through a woman who can never have action, for the statute provides that no one shall be taken or imprisoned on the appeal of a woman except for the death of her husband; therefore the woman shall not have appeal. And this is an action ancestral which is by descent, and it cannot

or hedge, whether with the object of protecting wild beasts or otherwise, and the right to effect this was quite independent of royal grant. Neither parks nor warrens were protected by the forest law, but by that part of the common law which related to theft and trespass." McKechnie, pp. 422–23.

[96] ". . . grant a mon parker les shoulders et les humbles et uncor jeo n'ay properte en le Deer." The same arguments are repeated in Trinity term. "Quod omnes Justiciarii concesserunt quoad hoc: auxi accion dAccompt gist de park."

[97] E. 20 Hen. VI. *Select Cases in the Exchequer Chamber,* pp. 95–97 (S. S.).

descend unless it [the right of appeal, be] given to his ancestor and this was never done; therefore etc.

. . .

And the opinion of all the justices except Neuton was that the appeal did not lie. And then on another day Fortescue by assent of all the justices of both Benches in the King's Bench said to the defendants: "Go in peace." (Which note well).

A few years later the same clause was serving the lawyers as an example of a statute in the negative, in this instance as an analogy to Marlborough, chapter 3.[98] In an action for trespass *vi et armis* against a lord (cattle taken for arrears of rent) the writ was "abated by office of the court."

He will not have judgment of recovery because the statute is in the negative, —a lord may not suffer the penalty etc. . . . just as in case an appeal is brought by a woman of the death of her father etc., however much the defendant has affirmed the writ etc. still the court will abate it because the statute is in the negative, that "no one be taken etc. on account of the appeal of a woman concerning the death of anyone but her husband."

In an important case relative to wardship, the judges in Exchequer Chamber differed as to the interpretation of Magna Carta chapter 3. The case was that of one "who held of the King in chief, died, leaving issue a daughter fifteen years of age, and the question was whether the King should have the wardship and marriage. . . . It was the opinion of the majority of the judges that she should not be in ward."[99]

The discussion turned mainly on the interpretation of the statutes of Merton and Westminster I ("whether the age of the male and female was all one") but one of the counsel, Chokke, went back to Magna Carta to support his view. Prypot, C. J. made a different interpretation. Six of the justices agreed with Prypot, while two, Fortescue and Nedeham, supported Chokke's interpretation.

We shall have occasion in another connection to describe Littleton's interpretation of *judicium parium*.[100] Another notable pronouncement which influenced his successors of bench and bar was his explanation of when and how Magna Carta became a statute. A statute, he said, "was limited to a certain time at which it had been made and to a reign and a place in which it had been enacted. For *Magna Carta* was not a statute at the beginning, but only after it had been confirmed by the statute of Marlborough (c. 5); and *Quia Emptores* and divers other statutes had a definite time limit in respect of the specified date of their enactment."[101]

[98] Y. B. 10 Ed. IV, 49 Hen. VI, pp. 64–66, no. 17, *trespass* (S. S.).

[99] Editors' summary. *Select Cases in the Exchequer Chamber*, pp. 138–43 (S. S.).

[100] See below, pp. 85–86.

[101] As paraphrased by Chrimes, *English Constitutional Ideas*, pp. 43–44. (For the original, his app. no. 61 ". . . en chescun statute est limit un certein temps quant ceo fuit fait

Professor Richardson has called attention to the attempt of another fifteenth-century commentator to explain why Magna Carta, despite its form, should be regarded as a statute:

He cites the opening words of Chapter I. *concessimus et hac presenti carta confirmavimus,* and says that "it was used that what statute that the king and his council made, it was ever set in the king's confirming, so that the king, being chief of his council, spake in his own name and his council's . . . But nowadays, for that the king is intrinsic within his council and may not do without them, therefore it is written underneath [that is, after the preamble of a statute] in this form, *Ordinatum est.*" [102]

It is rather disappointing to turn to the treatises of the two famous lawyers. Fortescue does not document his conversation with the young prince, nor is it likely that he would have cited Magna Carta had he done so. Littleton does have occasion to use chapters 2 and 6 in his *Tenures,* but only incidentally. [103] Other later statutes such as Merton, Marlborough, and Westminster I and II had elaborated more effectively on feudal law.

All told, the instances described in this chapter are not numerous in proportion to the great bulk of the two centuries of Year Books from which they are drawn. Still they are enough to show how some chapters of the Charter continued in current use, and how these and others persisted as part of the statutory lore of the legal profession. They became enshrined in "our books" to the edification of lawyers in the days of Lambarde and Coke.

et en temps de quel Roy et en quel lieu, *quia magna carta* ne fuit statute a commencement tanque ce fuit confirm par Marlebridge cap. 5, et la est le temps limit en certain quant ce fuit fait . . .") This statement was made by Littleton in agreement with Choke, J. to the effect that the so-called *Statuta Prerogativa Regis* was not a true statute, but an affirmance of the common law. M. 15 Ed. IV, no. 17.

[102] Richardson, "The Commons and Medieval Politics," Transactions of the Royal Historical Society, 4th series, xxviii, 1946, in a passage beginning: "The baronage had not only made good in practice their claim to control an evil king; they had climbed into power and sat perpetually and without question beside the king. This truth is recognized by a commentator on Magna Carta writing in the middle of the fifteenth century."

[103] Under these titles: *Graund sergeantie; Homage, fealtie,* and *escuage.* "And if the tenaunt which holdeth by escuage die, his heire being of full age, if hee helde by a knyghtes fee, the heire shall pay but an C. s. for his reliefe, as it is ordeined by the statute of Magna charta cap. 2, but he that holdeth of the kinge by graunde sergeantie . . ." In interpreting Merton, ca. 6, he says: "Also it hath bene a question how these words should be understand, *Si parentes conquerantur* &c. And it seemeth unto some that considering the statute of Magna charta cap. 6 that willeth that *heredes maritentur absque disparagatione* &c. upon which this sayde statute of Merton upon this point is grounded as it seemeth . . ."

❄ CHAPTER III ❄

Magna Carta and Liberty of the Subject

No freeman shall be taken and imprisoned or disseised of any free tene-
ment or of his liberties or free customs, or outlawed, or exiled, or in any
other way destroyed, nor will we go upon him nor send upon him, except
by the lawful judgment of his peers or by the law of the land.[1]

To no one will we sell, to no one will we refuse or delay, right or
justice. (MAGNA CARTA CA. 29)

As the Goldfiner will not out of the dust, threds, or shreds of Gold, let
pass the least crum, in respect of the excellency of the metal: so ought not
the learned Reader to let pass any syllable of this Law, in respect of the
excellency of the matter. (SIR EDWARD COKE)

MODERN commentators have successfully divested chapter 29 of the clouds
of glory with which it has come trailing down the centuries. The blame
for the elaborate glosses which made of this chapter the "palladium of English liberties" has been laid with some justice at the door of the seventeenth-
century protagonists of the common law such as Coke and Selden. Arguments of counsel in the *five knights case* and debates on the Petition of
Right effectively linked chapter 29 with the writ of habeas corpus. By 1628
Coke had completed his *Second Institute.* These interpretations of the
Great Charter, forged as a weapon of the Puritan-parliamentary party
in its struggle against the Stuarts, were accepted by later historians and
believed to apply to 1215 as well as to 1628. It was left for the recent "scien-
tific" historian to carry the document back to its irreducible minimum, the
meager aristocratic concept of 1215. In their zeal for this task, commentators
have devoted less attention to any detailed study of the long and fascinating process of growth and gloss and the successive circumstances which
produced it.

Much of the material to be presented here is not new. Pike and Vernon-
Harcourt have outlined the history of trial by peers. Stubbs, Maitland,
Holdsworth, McKechnie, and, most recently, Miss Clarke have called atten-

---

[1] The words "of any free tenement or of his liberties or free customs" were not part of the
original ca. 39 of John's Charter, but were inserted in the reissues, 1217 and 1225. They added
greatly to the possibilities of interpretation.

68

tion to some of the fourteenth-century interpretations of the *per legem terrae*.[2] Yet none of these writers tells the whole story, nor has anyone honored chapter 29, for all its fame, with a historical sketch of its own—something it amply deserves.

The two main views of the original meaning of the phrase *per legem terrae* have been admirably stated by Professor Holdsworth.[3] The present writer accepts his conclusion that the *lex* as here used is not the test—battle, ordeal, or compurgation—but that *lex terrae* means simply "the law of the land." Holdsworth finds that "the weight of contemporary exposition is in favor of this view," and thinks that "it makes better sense": "It would seem to be clear that there might be circumstances in which a man might lawfully be 'taken or imprisoned or disseised or exiled' otherwise than by a judicium parium"—for instance, disseisin as the result of a verdict in an assize of *novel disseisin*; or outlawry following appeal or indictment and proper proceedings in county court. And, it may be added, there might be a judgment by peers which was conducted unlawfully in some particulars. Still, it must be admitted that it was fourteenth-century usage and interpretation that fully equated the phrase with *due process of law*—the common law—and thus enabled parliament and the common lawyers to use it with such effect in the seventeenth century. It is that evolution that is to be dealt with here.

Taking the fourteenth century as a whole, the sources examined reveal more references to chapter 29 than to any other one provision of the Charter. Moreover it becomes apparent that this famous provision had its reputation pretty well established in these years and that there was less of novelty in later interpretations than is commonly supposed. In this period the *per judicium parium* was still appealed to as a guarantee "that execution should be preceded by a judgment." It was believed to confer trial as well as judgment by peers, and trial in which lawful procedure must be observed. In this period the *liber homo* lost whatever aristocratic connotation it had ever had and was construed as equivalent to "any freeman" or even "anyone, whoever he may be." The phrase *per legem terrae* was interchanged with the magic formula *due process of law*; it was made to cover the indicting jury and procedure by original writ; it was believed to limit the jurisdiction of the council, other prerogative courts, and commissions armed with special powers; and it was supposed to insure trial in common-law courts by common-law procedure.

---

[2] Pike, *A Constitutional History of the House of Lords*; Vernon-Harcourt, *His Grace the Steward and Trial by Peers*; Stubbs, *Constitutional History*, 11, 633–34; Maitland, *Constitutional History of England*, p. 217; Holdsworth, *History of English Law*, I, 487–89; McKechnie, *Magna Carta*, pp. 380–81; M. V. Clarke, "The Origin of Impeachment," in *Oxford Essays presented to H. E. Salter*.

[3] *History of English Law*, I, 60–63.

Before turning to the more significant episodes in which chapter 29 was being exploited by "peers of the realm" and by the commons in parliament, a few miscellaneous uses deserve attention. These indicate that even at the beginning of the century interpretations were free and varied.

The author of the *Mirror of Justices* (c. 1290) presents an early instance of the possibilities of juggling with this chapter and yet is not far from contemporary points of view. He makes these clauses cover the indicting jury and the right to an action of *novel disseisin*. He paraphrases with "the right course and right rules of law," uses "lawful judgment" apart from the "of peers," and concludes that *cest mot si non par loial jugement* has reference to all the clauses of this chapter.[4]

Legal historians find the first instance of the identification of judgment by peers with trial by jury in a case of 1302 (as reported in Year Book 30–31 Edward I) and assume that it is based on Magna Carta. A knight accused of a felony objected to his trial jury both because they had presented him and because they were not his peers. The court recognized his second objection as valid and a jury of knights was substituted. Neither in this case nor in that of the bishop (Year Book 12 and 13 Edward III) who as "peer of the realm" demanded knights on an inquest is the Charter actually cited.[5] The right to a jury of one's peers may have come by analogy with the early principle that one's judges (those owing suit of court in local popular or manorial courts) should be one's peers. It does not figure in the possible challenges to jurymen listed by Fortescue except to the extent of excluding persons of villein tenure. As far as the records reveal, it seems to have remained for Lambarde in the sixteenth century first to make the connection with Magna Carta chapter 29. Selden does it in his commentary on Fortescue (chapter 26) but Fortescue himself does not. Perhaps these very Year Book cases were ultimately responsible. Once enunciate the principle that a jury must be peers and it would be natural for later generations to assume, conversely, that peers must mean a jury. But, as we shall see, in the fourteenth century it is not the identification of the *judicium parium* of Magna Carta with jury trial that confronts us again and again in the records, but rather the insistence that the *per legem terrae* of Magna Carta guarantees jury indictment.

More significant are the following cases in which individuals complain of disseisin of freehold without judgment by the law of the land, as contrary to Magna Carta. One, though claiming free status, is declared a villein; another is widow of a mesne lord's tenant; the other two are tenants of the

---

[4] *Mirror of Justices*, pp. 179–80 (S. S.).

[5] Y. B. 30–31 Ed. I, p. 531 (R. S.). Cf. Pollock and Maitland, I, 622–23, note; Holdsworth, I, 324; and Plucknett, *Statutes and Their Interpretation*, pp. 150–51. These writers all assume that the claim is based on Magna Carta. In the second case (Y. B. 12 and 13 Ed. III, pp. 290–91) the judges are quoted as saying "this challenge is usual, when a Peer of the Realm is a party . . ."

crown. None is concerned with judgment by peers but each with some of the various ordinary forms of common-law procedure (though what is claimed is not always technically "lawful").

The first is a *novel disseisin* (1292).[6] On review at Westminster the verdict had been reversed and the tenement in question restored to the prior of Butley on the grounds, among other errors, that Martin, as the prior's villein, had not been entitled to the assize. Now in King's Bench, Martin, by his attorney, insists that he is of free status and says that he recovered the tenements

by the recognition of the assize in a general verdict on dissesin according to common law, and the auditors without a writ of the king addressed to them thereon and without any notice properly made to that Martin,[7] have judged him to lose the aforesaid tenement against common law and against the tenor of the Great Charter of the lord king.

This is vague enough, since no clause of the Charter is quoted, but the complaint of disseisin of freehold without proper forms according to common law seems to point to chapter 29 (rather than chapter 12 on the assizes).

In 1299 the Earl of Warenne complains that while he was in Scotland on the king's business, the widow of one of his tenants was dowered in Chancery as if her husband had held of the crown, and "with much more than she ought to have." He asks seisin of the lands in question and £200 damages. The widow, Alice, protests that what the Earl is asking would amount to disseising her of her dowry lands without lawful judgment:

And inasmuch as it is contained in the Great Charter of the liberties of England that no one shall be disseised of his free tenement without lawful judgment and she has been seised in this way by the lord king's delivery as it were by lawful judgment, she prays that she may not be removed or disseised against the form of the aforesaid Charter.[8]

Among the petitions submitted in the parliament of 8 Edward II is the complaint of Isabel, wife of Hugh Bardolf, that she has been disseised of a certain free tenement by inquest based on a "false suggestion," and writ under the privy seal to the escheator to seize the land into the king's hands "against the form of the Great Charter of liberties, which contains that neither the king nor any of his ministers will oust any man of his free tenement without reasonable judgment . . ." [9]

6 *King's Bench Rolls*, II, 86–97 (S. S.).

7 Though the prior claims that Martin was warned by a writ of *scire facias* and "vouches the writ in the bundle."

8 *King's Bench Rolls*, III, 88–95 (S. S.).

9 ". . . and likewise against the form of the Ordinances which the King has accepted, which provide that common right be not defeated nor delayed by letter of privy seal." The council ruled that by proof of her charters Isabel was entitled to recover her lands. *Rot. Parl.* I, 298, no. 37.

In the York parliament of 1318 Margaret, one-time widow of Peter Gaveston, and her second husband, Hugh d'Audley, presented an ingenious petition asking restoration of the earldom of Cornwall and other of Gaveston's confiscated estates:

as her right, to hold in manner aforesaid, having regard to the Great Charter, which wills that her inheritance and marriage shall be rendered to a widow immediately after her husband's death, that no one's right shall be delayed, and that no one shall be ousted of his freehold without the award and judgment of the law of the land (*saunz agard et jugement de ley de la terre*) and to the second statute of Westminster . . .[10]

From this point the subject falls both logically and chronologically into two parts: (1) the circumstances of the reign of Edward II and the early years of Edward III led to emphasis on the *judicium parium* with the phrase *per legem terrae* assumed to assure trial with lawful procedure; (2) from time to time throughout the long reign of Edward III, and occasionally in the reign of Richard II, the content of the *per legem terrae* was expanded, quite apart from any connection with judgment by peers.

Per iudicium parium

BY THE early fourteenth century neither the theory nor the practice of trial by peers had been reduced to precision. No clear-cut group of hereditary peers had yet been formed, and the crime of treason was still ill-defined. Bracton had "justified the principle on the ground that no man can be judge in his own case. If therefore the king is taking legal proceedings against his vassal, he cannot judge, nor can his judges, because they represent him. But in order that serious misdeeds may not go unpunished, 'curia et pares judicabunt.'" Hence the principle "should be applied only to those greater wrongs which involve forfeiture and capital punishment. This suggestion tentatively put forth by Bracton is stated as settled law by Fleta and Britton." [11] Pike indicates that the "troubled reign of Edward II afforded many instances of conspiracy against the King, and of execution for treason," but concludes that "in the midst of arms laws are silent." [12] Yet it is sometimes in a lawless or despotic age that appeals to law may be most frequent. The constant harping on the coronation oath in this reign, as well as the use of chapter 29, are cases in point.

The reign of Edward II was marked by factional struggles:[13] the Lords Ordainers over against the king and his household; Thomas of Lancaster,

---

[10] ". . . which will that lands given in tail shall remain to whom they are given and their heirs according to the will of the donors." *Cal. Close Rolls,* 1318–23, p. 143. But this petition was emphatically denied, and the confiscation of Gaveston's estates upheld.

[11] Holdsworth, I, 386–87.

[12] Pike, *House of Lords,* pp. 174–75.

[13] Tout, *The Place of the Reign of Edward II in English History.*

now leader of a united baronial opposition, again with his personal adherents, a party by himself; 1318–22, the "middle party," combining the more moderate of the barons with the better element of the court; 1322–26, the ascendancy of the Despensers; and finally the revival of an opposition sufficient to overthrow the favorites and dethrone the king. Thus whatever was done—reform of the household and exile of a royal favorite like Gaveston, or the execution of a baronial leader like Lancaster—was the work of the particular clique in power. Their action was challenged by the opposing faction on the grounds that it was not approved by the "whole community of the realm." Three practices resulted: the claim advanced by the barons (as in earlier reigns) that they were the rightful counselors of the king; the more recent assertion that a "full parliament" was the only proper place to concert policies; and the claim to *lawful trial* and *judgment by peers*—the whole body of the magnates—as against mere judgment by a clique or official coterie.

It was in the reign of Edward II that the whole body of the magnates began loosely to be called peers. Pike indicated the year 1322 and the charge against the Despensers as "the earliest known use of the expression 'Peer of the Realm,' or Pier de la Terre." [14] Pollard points to an earlier instance, *par agard des pieres,* in the treaty of Leake between Edward II and Earl Thomas, August 1318.[15] If the text of two earlier documents be given correctly by the chroniclers, the Lancastrian opposition used the phrase *par commun assent des pieres* as early as 1312, and *paribus terrae* in 1317.[16] In some instances the peers are referred to in their capacity of counselors, not judges, or, as Tout puts it of a later period, "the magnates who were habitually summoned to parliament."

The next few years saw the various partisan executions, followed by reversal of judgment when the opposing faction recovered power. As the "lands of traitors were forfeited for treason and could be granted to others, there were excellent grounds for passing judgment, but none for fair and impartial trial. . . . Each party said that the misdeeds of the other were 'notorious,' and notoriety sufficed in place of any trial in due form." [17] Again the victims or their heirs protested acts done without the consent of the "peers of the realm," but their appeal now was to the peers as judges—to the *judicium parium* of Magna Carta.[18]

[14] Pike, *House of Lords*, pp. 157–58. Actually the date is July 1321; *S. R.* I, 181–84. The phrase occurs several times in this document.

[15] Pollard, *Evolution of Parliament*, p. 93, citing *Rot. Parl.* I, 453–54.

[16] Lancaster's letter of July 1317, justifying his failure to answer the king's summons, reminds Edward that the business for which the king has summoned him should be treated *in parliamento paribus terrae praesentibus*; December 1312, in the answer of the three earls to the proposed pacification, *Annales Londonienses*, p. 227, cas. iii, iiii.

[17] Pike, *House of Lords*, p. 178. This procedure is suggestive of the later bill of attainder.

[18] In an age when the business of parliament was still largely judicial, and the same group of magnates served there at once in counseling and in judicial capacities, either use of the

One of the first to suffer arbitrary arrest and execution was the royal favorite, Peter Gaveston. He had been banished by the Ordainers under sentence of being treated as a public enemy if found within the realm after a day named. On his return he was captured and beheaded on Blacklow Hill, June 1312. Thus in a sense he had a sort of judgment by *some* peers —the Lords Ordainers—but no trial. The judgment was never reversed. Few voices were raised on behalf of the hated Gascon. One chronicler writing late in the century, however, states that Gaveston was beheaded, *paribus terrae nec praesentibus nec vocatis*.[19]

Much more striking is the evidence in connection with the Despensers. Even before the sentence of exile had been imposed on them, the Charter had been invoked on behalf of the younger Hugh. In a letter to two of the barons, the king justified his refusal to dismiss his favorite on the grounds that Hugh had been made chamberlain by counsel of the magnates in full parliament at York.[20] Furthermore

we cannot and ought not to commit the aforesaid Hugh or any other to custody without cause since that would be contrary to the tenor of the great charter of the liberties of England and the common law of our realm, and also contrary to the ordinances to the observance of which you are bound by oath, and contrary to our oath by which we are bound to exhibit justice to all and singular . . .

These sentiments of righteous constitutionality sound odd enough from an Edward II. Perhaps Hugh himself was responsible for them in this and the following documents. In Gaveston's day he had been in the ranks of the opposition. He was accused of making the distinction between king and crown and insisting on the barons' right to coerce a lawless or tyrannical sovereign. Hugh's influence at court, together with his aggressiveness in rounding out great estates for himself in Wales and the Marches, finally led to civil war.

In the summer of 1321, in a parliament dominated by the western and northern lords and their armed followers, sentence of forfeiture and exile was pronounced against the two Despensers by their lay peers in the presence of the king, a reluctant party to the judgment. The accused were not present and there was no actual trial, merely a finding by these peers that their alleged misdeeds were notoriously true. This judgment was reversed

term "peers" must have influenced the other. The appeals to Magna Carta described below probably contributed to the increasing use of the term to be found in the parliament rolls of Edward III's reign. In the charges against the Despensers (1321) and against Mortimer (1330), the word is used several times, now of the counselors whose functions the favorites have usurped, again in connection with trial by peers. *S. R.* I, 181–84; *Rot. Parl.* II, 52–53.

[19] Bridlington, p. 44. This chronicle was completed about 1377.

[20] *Parl. Writs*, Vol. II, pt. ii, pp. 231–32; letter dated April 23, 1321, directed to Humphrey de Bohun, Earl of Hereford and Essex, and to Roger Mortimer of Wigmore.

the next year in response to nearly identical petitions of father and son.[21] Errors alleged include charges that the magnates were both prosecutors and judges in their own cause, that they came to parliament in "undue manner" with horses and arms, that the award was made without consent of the prelates who are peers in parliament, that the victims were not called into court nor to answer, and that the award was made contrary to the Great Charter of the liberties of England, "wherein it is contained that no one shall be forejudged or destroyed in any manner except by lawful judgment of his peers or by the law of the land."

The Repeal of the Process against the Despencers, a long document in French, rehearses these errors, and makes clear that it was the "not being called into court nor to answer" that was conceived to be contrary to the "law of the land" of the Charter.[22] Toward the close of this document, the king reverts to his obligation by his coronation oath to "do right to all our subjects and to redress wrongs done them"; *et que en la dite graunt chartre est countenutz, Qe nous ne nieroms ne delaieroms a nuli droit ne justice* . . . This is one of the rare instances found in which both parts of chapter 29 (John 39 and 40) occur in the same passage.[23]

By 1322 it was the turn of the Lancastrian opposition to suffer. Earl Thomas, the Mortimers of Chirk and Wigmore, and Bartholomew de Badlesmere received much the same treatment at the hands of the victorious king and restored favorites. Lancaster, after his defeat at Boroughbridge, was brought before the king and several nobles at Pontefract. His misdeeds were recorded, judgment was pronounced on behalf of the king, and execution followed. He was not allowed to say a word in his defense. Certain persons were commissioned to visit each of the others and to pass judgment according to a schedule attached to the commission. This document contained the formula that the crimes of the accused were notorious and that the king records the fact.[24] None of the commissioners was a peer. Badlesmere was executed. The sentence of the Mortimers was commuted to perpetual imprisonment. The nephew escaped in August 1324, while the uncle died in prison two years later.

[21] *Cal. Close Rolls,* 1318–23, pp. 542–43 (the petition of "Hugh, the son"). The exiles were recalled by the king early in December 1321, the judgment annulled informally in January 1322, and formally by the York parliament which marked the complete royalist triumph in May.

[22] Given in full, Vernon-Harcourt, *His Grace the Steward,* pp. 324–26; *Cal. Close Rolls,* 1318–23, pp. 544–46: ". . . que les ditz Hugh et Hugh n'estoient appeletz en court ne a respouns sicome est susdit. . . ."

[23] Three other documents issued on behalf of the Despensers adopt the same righteous tone, based on the coronation oath, the Charter, and the Ordinances, but in each case quoting only the *quod nulli negabimus aut differemus rectum aut justitiam*: a safe-conduct, dated December 8, 1321 (Rymer, *Foedera,* Vol. II, pt. i, p. 463); letters close to ten bishops, January 4, 1322 (*Parl. Writs,* Vol. II, pt. ii, p. 173); the statute revoking the pardon granted the pursuers of the Despensers (*S. R.* I, 187).

[24] Vernon-Harcourt, *His Grace the Steward,* pp. 299–300; for the commissions and recorded judgments, *Parl. Writs,* Vol. II, pt. ii, app., pp. 216–17 and 264–65 respectively.

This procedure against Lancaster and his adherents and that against Mortimer later, in 1330, are discussed by Professor Plucknett as examples of "conviction by record" and "conviction by notoriety" respectively. He assumes that, though protested later, at the time they were used these were recognized methods of procedure.[25] But this is not the impression one gets from the reversal of the "judgments" early in Edward III's reign. In his first parliament Earl Thomas' brother Henry, Roger Mortimer, the nephew, and Badlesmere's son Giles, in the presence of king and lords, emphasized the illegality of such proceedings "in time of peace when the king was not riding with banners displayed, and when the Chancery of the king and the justices of either bench were sitting." Each petitioner quoted chapter 29 and alleged its violation in that the victim had, without lawful judgment of his peers, been condemned to death contrary to the law of the land—that is, without being arraigned or allowed to answer.[26] Besides these individual protests, we have petitions of the "commonalty of the realm," asking annulment of the record and process of false judgments, restitution of property, and special compensating privileges for widows and heirs. These requests, following one for maintenance of the estate of "holy church" and the Great Charter (some points of which are to be interpreted), conclude with this declaration for the future: *Et qe desormais soit nul mys a la mort par record le roy saunz respons iugez.*[27]

Similar episodes were to recur under the arbitrary regime of Isabella and Mortimer. One of the few nobles who had remained loyal to the king in 1326, Edmund Fitzalan, Earl of Arundel, was executed under Mortimer's direction and his estates were confiscated, and this action was confirmed in the first parliament of Edward III. After the fall of Mortimer, Edmund's son Richard was restored to his rank and most of his possessions, not on grounds of injustice done but because the king "had great hope of good in

[25] Though "as a battle cry for fourteenth century parliamentarians" he says, it was effective to insist on appeal, indictment, or original writ, "the common law itself admitted without question several other procedures," bills and *querelae,* informations, and also conviction by record and notoriety. These, he thinks, are the true forerunners of impeachment. He rejects the theory that "the Commons were the grand inquest of the nation, and the whole proceeding was merely the common law trial of indictment transferred to the larger scene of parliament." Plucknett, "The Origin of Impeachment," Transactions of the Royal Historical Society, 4th series, xxiv, 47–71 (1942).

[26] These documents are given by Vernon-Harcourt, *His Grace the Steward,* pp. 327–34. Henry of Lancaster's quotes entire ca. 29, paraphrased in the third person, i.e., "nec dominus rex super ipsum ibit nec super eum mittet . . ." The petition of the nephew of Andra Harcla, Earl of Carlisle, uses the odd expression, "ne fuit attaint par enquest de ses piers."

The charges brought against the younger Despenser in 1326 blame him for this fate of Earl Thomas and others: "in his own hall within his castle, by the royal authority which you had usurped over our Lord the King, you caused him to be condemned upon a false charge, against law, and reason and the Great Charter, and also *saunz respounz* you caused him to be martyred and murdered by a painful and piteous death. *Litterae Cantuarienses,* III, 407 (app.). This does not appear on the parliament roll.

[27] Imperfect in *Rot. Parl.* II, 7, nos. 3 and 4. For the better text followed here, Richardson and Sayles, *Rotuli Parliamentorum* (C. S.), p. 117.

the young man." Yet an attractive variant is furnished by the first clause of Richard's petition: *qe come la Grant Chartre voet, que nul Counte, Baroun, ne nul autre due Roialme, soit jugge mes par proces de ses Peres . . .* In this phrase—*par proces de ses Peres*—is tersely embodied the double principle of judgment and lawful trial.[28] The petitions of John Maltravers do not name the Charter, yet his precise defining of *forms* of procedure, his citing of the declaration of 1 Edward III, and his warning of dangerous precedent are too effective to pass over. In the same parliament that condemned Mortimer, Maltravers was adjudged a traitor but he escaped to France. His cause was prosecuted in parliaments and council for years by his wife and friends *cum magna instantia*. The petition of 1339 protests that the judgment of 4 Edward III

was and is erroneous in many respects, for in your first parliament it was ordained that no man be judged without response; and in that the said judgment was made in the absence of the greater number of the peers of the realm, and without their knowledge or their will, and without calling the said John to answer; and in that our lord the king and the said peers of the realm had no knowledge (*purpense*) or information by appeal or indictment of the thing which was surmised in his absence . . .

Maltravers professes to be ready to answer to all, *solom la loi de la terre,* concerning whatever may be charged against him *en fourme de loi*. The 1347 petition, in the same vein, includes the warning that these errors might be most perilous and damaging to all the great ones (*grantz*) of England in time to come.[29]

In this period the phrase *nec super eum ibimus* was still taken quite literally. We are far from the "pass upon him" of the later Englished versions. It was necessary to remind Edward II and Edward III, as it was John, that they must not proceed with armed forces against their subjects. Edward II had marched into Gloucester (March 1321) to support Hugh in his territorial ambitions in South Wales. Hence it was charged against the Despensers that they

falsely and wickedly counselled our Lord the King to go with Horse and Arms towards the parts of Gloucester, and made him traverse the country with Horsemen, and make incursions with his armed men in those parts upon his

[28] *Rot. Parl.* II, 55–56, no. 13.
[29] He was finally restored to his former estate and a charter granted him to that effect. This ignores the alleged errors and bases restitution on the king's gratitude for Maltravers' services against his enemies. *Rot. Parl.* II, 53, no. 3; 173, no. 65; 243. For his 1339 petition. Richardson and Sayles, *Rotuli Parliamentorum* (C. S.), pp. 285–86. At about the same time (1346) the Charter was evoked on behalf of John de Warenne, Earl of Surrey, in regard to a manor falsely seized by the escheator on the claim that it was held in chief of the king. It is the seizure "without warning or calling the earl" that is alleged to be contrary to Magna Carta. *Cal. Close Rolls*, 20 Ed. III, pt. 1 (C 54/179 m.7): "ipso Comite super hoc non praemunito nec non vocato captum est in manum nostram in ipsium comitis grave dampnum et contra formam magne carte . . ."

good People, contrary to the Form of the Great Charter, and the Award of the Peers of the Land; and so by their false and evil Counsels they would have moved a War in the Land, to the Destruction of Holy Church and of the People, for their own proper Quarrel.[30]

A similar incident resulted from the fact that by 1328 Mortimer had usurped the powers of the council of regency and was advising young Edward III to "forcibly and speedily assail certain Lords and others of the land." Civil war was averted through the mediation of Archbishop Meopham. A communication, probably from Meopham's pen, was sent to the king on December 29, reminding him that at the recent parliament at Salisbury proclamation was made by common assent that "all matters respecting the subjects of the realm should remain in suspense until the coming parliament at Westminster." The letter, in words worthy of a Stephen Langton, then continues:

let your councillors who are about you be mindful of the points to which you pledged your oath at your coronation, among which are comprised, that you would observe the laws and customs granted to your people of England by your predecessors, and that you would maintain peace and concord with all your might for God, Holy Church, the Clergy, and the people both great and small; and it is commonly known that in the Great Charter it is contained, that you shall not go nor send nor ride against any of your realm,[31] and this was afterwards ratified by several Popes, and established as a law of the land, and confirmed by you yourself, and you are bound by your said oath to maintain it.

The king is urged to desist from the reported design of assailing certain Lords by force, "and if there be anyone of your realm, peer or other who may have committed an offence, or done anything against your Lordship that he ought not to have done, then let him come to your said parliament at Westminster and make amends, and let him be duly punished according to the laws of your land."

After the overthrow of Mortimer there was little further occasion for the

---

[30] S. R. I, 183. In 1326 a similar charge was brought against the younger Hugh, this time with reference to the defeat of Earl Thomas and his adherents: ". . . you Hugh, came to our Lord the King and caused him to assail by force of arms peers and others his faithful and liege people, in order to ruin and despoil them, *encountre la Grante Chartre et les Ordinaunces* . . ." *Litterae Cantuarienses*, III, 407. The charge was repeated in the first parliament of Edward III, *Rot. Parl.* II, 7.

[31] I have substituted my translation for this clause—"qe vous ne irrez, ne voyerez, ne chivacherez sur nul de vostre terre," which is inaccurately rendered "that you shall not make attack, nor *sue*, nor assail any subject of your realm," another example of how difficult it was for nineteenth-century scholars to escape the influence of later interpretations of the Charter. *Litterae Cantuarienses*, III, 414–17 (French with English translation) headed Supplicatio Praelatorum . . . facta Domino Regi . . . The Summary in English, *Calendar of Plea and Memoranda Rolls of the City of London*, 1323–64, p. 84, is an inaccurate rendering of the French text; it uses the phrase "due process of law" where the text reads "solum les leis et les coustumes de vostre terre."

repetition of such incidents. Edward III, with his love of chivalry and the tourney, his round table, and his profitable ventures in France, pleased the nobles and on the whole struck a happy medium between the extremes of baronial and administrative dictation.[32] The exigencies of the French wars, however, did produce a crisis, 1340–41, in which trial by peers and the Great Charter again became issues.[33] The leadership of Archbishop Stratford in this episode raises the question of whether the prelates claimed trial by peers. The spiritual lords were being called peers of the realm at this time and calling themselves such.[34] The stand taken by certain individual bishops in Edward II's reign, as well as Stratford's policy in 1341, indicates that in cases of treason or felony they preferred to hold to clerical privilege.[35] As Holdsworth remarks, we ought to say with Selden that the bishops were peers but did not want trial by peers. Stratford, as will appear, did ask trial by peers in parliament for such prelates as were royal officials charged with misconduct in office. Yet both Bishop Langton and Stratford made some interesting use of Magna Carta chapter 29.

Walter Langton, Bishop of Coventry and Lichfield (or Chester, as the see was sometimes called) and distinguished minister of Edward I, was accused by Edward II of various misdemeanors as treasurer, arrested, and sent to the Tower in the summer of 1307.[36] A special commission of judges (none a peer) was appointed to try him. The trial was postponed until after the coronation, but before the end of March judgments were being levied

[32] See Tout's effective characterization, *Chapters,* Vol. III, ca. ix, sec. ii.

[33] Miss Clarke suggests that "the strong accord between king and magnates might have neutralized the movement back to Magna Carta and the common law, if it had not been for the crisis of 1340–1 and the vigorous action of Archbishop Stratford . . ." "The Origin of Impeachment," in *Oxford Essays presented to H. E. Salter,* p. 168.

[34] For instance, one of the errors alleged by the Despensers was that the award against them had been made "sauntz l'assent des prelatz qui sount piers du roialme en parlement." Again (3 Ed. III) John, Bishop of Winchester, refused to answer in King's Bench the charge that he had withdrawn from parliament without the king's license; "and the said bishop came in his own person and defended etc. And said that he is one of the peers of the realm and prelate of holy church (unius de paribus regni et prelatus sacre ecclesie)" and maintained that such an offense ought to be corrected and amended in parliament and not elsewhere. *Coram rege* roll 276, m.9d. A jury was rejected as insufficient, "et nomement quant Levesqe qe pere de la terre est partie." Y. B. 12 and 13 Ed. III, pp. 290–91 (R. S.).

In 25 Ed. III a petition of the clergy reads, "Item, come Ercevesqes & Evesqes tiegnent lour Temporaltes du Roi en chief, & par tant sont Pieres de la terre come sont autres Countes & Barons." *Rot. Parl.* II, 245, no. 66. In 1397 when Thomas of Arundel was accused of high treason by the commons, "le Roy nostre seignur disoit, qe par cause que les ditz Accusementz & Empeschementz touchent si haute person & Pere de son Roialme, il volloit ent estre advisez." *Ibid.* III, 351.

[35] The right to exemption from lay jurisdiction for an offense for which a man could be brought into peril of life or member was believed established beyond question by ca. 15 of the *Articuli cleri* (9 Ed. II). Exception in cases of high treason seems to have been assumed even before the passing of this act, but was definitely established only by the Statute of Treasons, 1352.

[36] In the formal charges he was not specifically charged with either treason or felony, but of having "presumptuously usurped power, under colour of his office, and effected sales, alienations, and waste of the King's lands, to the disherison of the Crown, and in derogation of the King's royal estate . . ." Pike, *House of Lords,* p. 181.

on the lands belonging to the bishop's see. His lands, together with silver, gold, and jewels hoarded in the New Temple, were seized by the king and Gaveston. Gaolers, appointees of the latter, carried the bishop from castle to castle and finally shut him up in the king's prison at York. In July 1311 he was moved to the archbishop's prison, thus partially satisfying the claims of clerical privilege.

The following January he was set free. His release was due partly to the intervention of the pope, but others had protested on his behalf: "Sire, the Prelates, Earls, and Barons pray you that you will do right unto the Bishop of Chester as to his lands, and in especial as to his other goods, according to the Great Charter, and according to the Ordinances." [37] This may point at chapter 1, which to the prelates was all sufficient as a defense of clerical privilege. On the reconciliation of king and barons in 1318 Langton put before the new council a claim for £20,000, the alleged amount of his losses. In this petition we have his own statement of his case:

That the said King had the said bishop without being arraigned, or called in judgment, against the form of the law of the land, and against the points of the great Charter, suddenly taken and imprisoned, and held in prison a year and a quarter . . . in the meantime all his lands were seized and retained in the hand of our lord the king, as well of his bishopric as of his lay fee, and all his moveable goods . . . [38]

The bishop does not here raise the question of trial by peers, or even of clerical privilege (except in the allusion to seizure of his "spiritualities"). It is the unlawful procedure—the being seized and imprisoned without being arraigned or called in judgment—that is against the law of the land and the Charter.

Much has been written on the crisis of 1340–41.[39] It makes a dramatic story: Edward's reluctant conclusion of the truce of Esplechin (September 25, 1340) on the failure of expected money and supplies from England; his secret escape from Ghent, where his allies fairly held him a hostage; his wrathful descent on the Tower of London late on the night of November 30; the summoning by torchlight of scapegoat ministers; the consequent

[37] One of certain articles supplementary to the New Ordinances, drawn up between October 1311 and January 1312; French text and translation, *Liber Custumarum*, pt. ii, p. 686. Also *Annales Londonienses*, pp. 198–200.

[38] French text, *Cole's Documents*, pp. 4–5 (the translation is mine). No action resulted from the petition; the bishop received nothing. Both Pike and Vernon-Harcourt discuss Langton's case, but neither seems to know this petition of 1318. Pike concludes that though the ecclesiastical power may have saved Langton as a bishop, "he was, as the King's officer, regarded as being amenable to the jurisdiction of the King's Justices."

[39] Pike and Vernon-Harcourt in connection with trial by peers; Tout (*Chapters*, III, sec. iii) from the administrative point of view, as a result of the attempt at administrative efficiency initiated by the Walton Ordinances; others for its interest for parliamentary history. See also such essays as Lapsley, "Archbishop Stratford and the Parliamentary Crisis of 1341," *English Historical Review*, 30:6–18; Hughes, *Study of Social and Constitutional Tendencies*; Clarke, "The Origin of Impeachment," in *Oxford Essays presented to H. E. Salter*, pp. 168–72.

dismissals and arrests; the long quarrel with the archbishop, John de Stratford—a veritable war of words; the partial victory for the constitutional cause in the spring parliament of 1341. The chancellor and the treasurer, both bishops, were dismissed from office but escaped imprisonment. Others not so fortunate were five clerks (four from Chancery and one from Exchequer); three leading merchants; and such lay ministers as the warden of the Tower, the keeper of the Channel Isles, the chief justice of King's Bench and four justices of the Common Bench. Only one of the greater nobles, Thomas Wake, a member of the council of regency, was arrested, and he was soon released.

On January 13, 1341, three justices were commissioned to arraign these officials, both clerks and laymen, singly at the king's suit. This meant in a few instances that commissioners were to sit in judgment on peers. Already in December the king had appointed sixteen commissions (each for one or a group of shires) to hear and determine oppressions and extortions by the king's ministers.[40] A general eyre was to sit at the Tower of London.

Meanwhile Stratford, object of Edward's greatest wrath, had eluded him. Taking refuge in his own church of Canterbury, December 2, 1340, the archbishop remained there until his appearance at parliament the following April. Like Langton, he was accused of misdemeanors in office, in particular that he had assumed responsibility for the war with France, then negligently failed to send the necessary money and supplies. Later, as a result of the propaganda used in his spirited defense, he was charged with having "traitoriously" stirred up the people against their king. For himself Stratford asked trial by peers to the extent of investigation in parliament of his official conduct. He maintained the traditional attitude of the clergy in regard to more serious charges. His case has greater significance than Langton's, for the archbishop did not stop with his own defense. By means of sermons, letters to king and council, letters to his diocesan clergy, and sentence of excommunication, he became spokesman for clerk and layman, peer and commoner, in a real constitutional struggle.

His influence must have been great. To the weight of high office and zeal for his order he added a sense of the dramatic. For instance, he waited until St. Thomas' Day (December 29) for the first public demonstration. If we may accept one account,[41] after celebrating mass and preaching a sermon in praise of the martyr (on the text *in diebus suis non timuit principem*) he confessed to the people his undue absorption in temporal affairs and proclaimed his intent henceforth, like Becket, to champion the rights of the church. This he followed up with a protest against the arrest

---

[40] All the escheators and most of the sheriffs were dismissed, and writs were issued for the election of new coroners.

[41] Gross, quoting Tait, says that this chronicle is wrongly ascribed to Birchington, in Wharton, *Anglia Sacra*, pp. 21–22.

of certain Chancery clerks, justices, and knights contrary to Magna Carta, the defamation of the archbishop, and attacks on other liberties of the church. Then sentence of excommunication was pronounced against persons guilty of such offenses.

The question of arbitrary arrest and imprisonment, though not the only issue, alone can be discussed here. It will appear that, under Stratford's leadership, the following use was made of Magna Carta: (1) in respect to clerks below the rank of bishop, appeal to the "liberties of the church," or to the Charter for its guarantee of these liberties in chapter 1; (2) for Stratford himself and his fellow bishops, as well as for lay peers, an attempt to extend the *judicium parium* to misdemeanors, especially misconduct in office; (3) for layman or clerk of whatever rank, appeal to the *per legem terrae* of chapter 29 as an assurance of lawful procedure.

Stratford's letter to the king, January 1, 1341, shows the fruits of the publicity accorded chapter 29 in the previous reign.[42] The archbishop gives the king an ominous reminder of his father's misdeeds and fate:

... for by the evil counsel which our lord your father, whom God assoil had, he made seize, against the law of the land and the great charter, the peers and other people, and put some to a shameful death, and of others he made seize their goods and what they possessed, and some he put to ransom; and what happened to him for that cause, you, Sire, do know . . . And now, by evil counsel, abetted by certain people of this land which are not so wise as were needful, and by counsel of others which seek rather their own profit than your honour or the safety of the land, you begin to seize divers clerks, peers, and other folk of the land and to make suit nothing fitting against the law of the land the which to keep and maintain you are bound by the oath taken at your coronation, and contrary to the great charter, against which all who come counter are excommunicate by all the prelates of England, and the sentence confirmed by the pope's bull, which we have by us.[43]

The letter of January 28 to king and council defends the excommunication Stratford had authorized by rehearsing misdeeds of king and officials and demanding redress.[44] The archbishop fully exploited the possibilities of the greater excommunication, even incorporating chapters of the Charter into the text of the sentence. As pronounced under his direction, the first article is directed against those who deprive the church of her right, violate the liberties and free customs of the church of Canterbury, or disturb the peace of the realm; the third deals with unlawful purveyance of clerical

[42] Stratford had finished his clerical training before 1311, held minor offices in church and state, and was made bishop of Winchester, 1323, in opposition to Edward's candidate.

[43] Avesbury, pp. 327–28; Rymer, *Foedera*, Vol. II, pt. ii, p. 1143; Hemingburgh, II, 363–65.

[44] Listing by name the clerks detained, he protests this violation of the "liberties of the church," then more broadly demands the release of those—"personae, laici, hominesque liberi, contra Magnam Cartam, leges ac terrae consuetudines capti." Hemingburgh, II, 370. His letter of March 14 contains a similar passage. Wilkins, II, 666.

goods; and the fourth with the arrest and detention of clerks. The second article, reciting in full chapter 29, paraphrased to read in the third person, and chapter 9 on the liberties of London, is directed against all who infringe these or any other provisions of the Great Charter or the Forest Charter.[45] Stratford ordered the promulgation of this imposing sentence in all the dioceses of his province. The Bishop of Exeter, noting that some offenders (the king's commissioners, perhaps) remained obdurate, had the sentence repeated in his diocese again during Lent and Easter, with bells ringing and candles lighted.

The parliament which met April 23, 1341, marked a temporary victory for Stratford and the constitutional cause. A partial reconciliation was patched up between king and archbishop, although the latter was not allowed to defend himself publicly as he desired. In spite of Edward's unfavorable response to some of the petitions, the statute of 15 Edward III was forced through. This enactment has been more famous for its repeal than for its passage.[46] Taken as a whole, however, it is largely concerned with the observance of the Charters. Chapter 2, based on the report of the committee of twelve, reiterates the right to trial by peers and extends it to misdemeanors, especially alleged misconduct in office:

Whereas before this time the Peers of the Land have been arrested and imprisoned, and their Temporalties, Lands and Tenements, Goods and Cattels, asseised in the King's hands, and some put to death without judgment of their Peers: It is accorded and assented That no Peer of the Land, Officer nor other, because of his Office, nor of things touching his Office, nor by other cause shall be brought in judgment to lose his Temporalties, Lands, Tenements, Goods, and Cattels, nor to be arrested, nor imprisoned, outlawed, exiled, nor forejudged, nor put to answer, nor to be judged, but by award of the said Peers in the Parliament.[47]

This principle was intended to include the spiritual lords. Bishops had been members of the committee. In the report of the latter the question is raised and answered in the affirmative whether "if any of the Peers be or have been Chancellor, Treasurer, or other officer whatsoever, this privilege should operate as well with regard to their office as in any other manner." The reference to peers who "be or have been chancellor, treasurer," was clearly suggested by the treatment accorded the two bishops so recently removed from these offices.

[45] Hemingburgh, II, 377–78. For the bishop's letter, repeating the articles of excommunication in French, see Wilkins, II, 669–70.

[46] The annulment by the king after the close of the session and repeal by the parliament of 1343 have been used to illustrate ideas as to the relative authority of king and parliament in legislation. Administrative historians have played up its provisions for the appointment and control of the king's ministers in parliament.

[47] S. R. I, 295–96; based on Rot. Parl. II, 132, no. 51 (the petition). For the repeal, ibid. II, 139, no. 23.

The act of repeal (17 Edward III) contained the proviso, "because some articles are comprised in the same statute which are reasonable, and in accordance with law and reason," that "of such articles and others agreed on in this Parliament there be made a statute anew, by the advice of the justices and other learned men, and kept for ever." No such act was made. Magna Carta remained the only "statutory" basis for trial by peers.[48] Some advantage was gained for the lay peers by the definition of treason in 1352, and for the spiritual lords by the confirmation of benefit of clergy in the statute *Pro Clero* of the same year. Pike thinks it fortunate that the claim to trial by peers for misdemeanors was lost. Somewhat the same end was effected by impeachment later, but initiative came from a different source.

To the seeker after immediately practical results, the various appeals to chapter 29 described above may seem but the battle cry of a losing cause. They added little to the technical development of trial by peers. Despenser's citing of the Charter in 1321 did not save Lancaster from a worse fate next year. Nor can it be maintained that when judgments were reversed, the Charter was the main factor. Even the famous 15 Edward III was a dead letter. But in the long, slow progression toward the "rule of law," as in many another hard-won cause, propaganda and iteration count for much. Who can gainsay that even the hapless Edward II contributed something when he saved his favorite with the excuse, "the king cannot and ought not to commit Hugh or any other person to custody without cause, since this would be contrary to Magna Carta and the common law of the realm." The right of subjects—peer and commoner, clerk and layman alike—to be tried by "process of law" was taken up by the commons and continued to be agitated by the series of petitions and statutes to be described in the next section.

Richard II's reign suggests a parallel with that of Edward II: the factional struggles, the few years of successful despotism, ending in deposition. Yet there is no such agitation, either individual or collective, for the *judicium parium* of Magna Carta in the later reign. One explanation may be the irregular practice of criminal appeals in parliament. Each party in turn "appealed of treason" the leaders of the opposing faction whether they were peers or not.[49] But the very type of episode which was sure to

---

[48] Cf. Pike, *House of Lords*, p. 197: "The Statute of 15 Edward III was ever afterwards treated by the lawyers as non-existent, and Magna Charta, as confirmed by Henry III, was always considered the statutory basis of the right of Peers to be tried by Peers."

Statute of Treasons, 25 Ed. III, stat. 5, ca. 2 (*S. R.* I, 319–20);*Ordinacio pro Clero,* ca. 4, 25 Ed. III, stat. 6, ca. 4 (*ibid.* I, 324–25). "That all manner of Clerks, as well secular as religious, which shall be from henceforth convict before the secular Justices aforesaid, for any Treasons or Felonies touching other Persons than the King himself or his Royal Majesty, shall from henceforth freely have and enjoy the Privilege of Holy Church, and shall be without any Impeachment or Delay delivered to the Ordinaries demanding them."

[49] Holdsworth, I, 388: "The Act of 1399 eliminated this cause of confusion and helped to establish the principles, firstly that such appeals were not to be tried by the House, and secondly that the only persons who were entitled to be so tried were peers."

evoke an appeal to chapter 29 earlier in the century fails to do so now. With an occasional exception, such as that of Thomas, Earl of Salisbury, who petitions in quite the earlier manner,[50] this holds good for the three Lancastrian reigns. Examples in point are the cases of Thomas Despenser (1398), Mowbray (1405), Henry, Lord Scrope (1415), and Lord Saye (1450), who claimed trial by peers but, as far as the records show, with no reference to Magna Carta.[51]

Here may be illustrated again the growing effacement of the Charter described in earlier chapters. But by this time the definition of treason, the end of criminal appeals in parliament, and especially the clearer delimitation of the peerage itself with the evolution of a select group of hereditary peers, all must have had their effect. The right to the *judicium parium* hardly needed the backing of Magna Carta. It was enough to say, as did Lord Scrope: *ipse est Dominus & unius Parium Regni Anglie, & petit quod ipse per Pares suos Regnie Anglie, prout moris est, trietur & judicatur.* Yet the "statutory" basis, Magna Carta, was not entirely forgotten. When in 1441, as a result of the famous case of Eleanor, Duchess of Gloucester, trial by peers was extended to peeresses, that statute was based on Magna Carta chapter 29, quoted accurately in full. Of course, if the act was drafted by "sages of the law," this was natural enough.

Later in the century the Year Books (10 Edward IV) record the well-known ruling:

Note by Littleton J. who says that in appeal sued against a lord and peer of the realm trial shall not be by his peers, but shall be as in the case of a common person, etc., and thus it was adjudged before *Fortescue* in an appeal sued against lord Grey of Codnore, father of the present lord Grey, etc. But on indictment of felony or treason, which is at the suit of the king, trial shall be by peers, because the statute of Magna Carta rules (*qar lestatut de magna carta voet*) that by the words "nor shall we go upon him nor shall we send upon him" shall be understood the suit of the king (*nec super eum ibimus nec super eum mittemus est entendu le suite le roy,* etc); and he says that when a lord is indicted, etc., this shall be referred to the parliament; and there the seneschal of England shall require him to make reply, and if he shall say he

---

[50] (1414) He asks reversal of the judgment against his father, John Montacute, a favorite of Richard. Involved in the conspiracy of the earls of Huntington, Kent, and Rutland, he was seized and beheaded by a mob at Circenster, and afterward in the parliament of 2 Henry IV (along with the other conspirators) judged a traitor notwithstanding, as the record has it, "q'ils feurent mortz sur le dit leve de Guerre saunz processe de Ley." *Rot. Parl.* III, 459, no. 30. The son's petition alleges several errors, among them "de ceo qe l'avaunt dit Johan Mountagu, jadis Count de Sarum, fuist mys a la mort saunz nulle accusement, & saunz estre mesne en juggement ou en respounce, encountre droit, ley, & custume de la Terre, & la fourme de la Graunde Chartre des Fraunchises d'Engleterre, en laquell est contenuz, Qe null Frank homme ne soit exile, ne forjugge, n'en autre manere destruit, sinon par loial juggement de ses Pieres, ou par Ley de la Terre." *Ibid.* IV, 18.

[51] The Duke of Suffolk waived his right to trial by peers and put himself on the king's mercy. For these episodes, and also the case of the Duchess of Gloucester, see Appendix E.

is not guilty this shall be tried by his peers, etc., and then the spiritual lords who cannot consent to the death of a man shall appoint a proctor in parliament etc.; and then the seneschal must examine first the most puisne lord there is as to whether the accused be guilty, and then in turn all the lords who are there.[52]

Here clearly the literal "going and sending" of earlier days has become judicial procedure, "the suit of the king," and no doubt inspired the "pass upon him" of the early English translations of Magna Carta which antedate Coke by nearly a century. Any dictum from Littleton, the distinguished judge of Common Pleas and author of the famous *Tenures*, must have carried great weight. This one is enshrined in Tottel's editions of the Year Books and in the much used *Grand Abridgement* of Fitzherbert.

Per legem terrae

"For mine own part, I shall be very glad to see that old, decrepit Law *Magna Charta* which hath been kept so long, and lien bed-rid, as it were, I shall be glad to see it walk abroad again with new vigour and lustre, *attended and followed with the other six statutes*; questionless it will be a great heartening to all the people." Thus Sir Benjamin Rudyerd spoke in the course of the famous 1628 debates on "liberty of the subject." The so-called *six statutes* were fourteenth-century interpretations of Magna Carta chapter 29, ranging in point of time from 5 to 42 Edward III. They were used by counsel for the five knights; formally grouped with the Great Charter in one argument by the commons in conference with the lords, April 7, 1628; cited as the *six statutes* in succeeding debates; and partly incorporated as precedents in the Petition of Right.[53]

Legal historians [54] have shown that the writ of habeas corpus, as a safeguard to liberty of the subject, did not derive from Magna Carta or from any medieval device such as the writs *de odio et atia* and *de homine replegiando,* but rather from various writs of habeas corpus in use as procedural writs.[55] Nevertheless, Holdsworth believes that it was the happy (if his-

[52] Y. B. 10 Ed. IV and 49 Hen. VI, p. 63 (S. S.), with a second shorter version. Cf. Fitzherbert, *Grand Abridgement*, title "Corone," no. 34. This ruling is noted by Pike, *House of Lords*, pp. 217–18; and by McKechnie, p. 382, based on Pike: "Pleas following upon accusations by the injured party were held in 1471 not to fall within the words of Magna Carta."

[53] See below, Chap. XI.

[54] Holdsworth, IX, 104–25; Jenks, in *Select Essays in Anglo-American Legal History*, II, 531–48.

[55] Such as *habeas corpus ad respondendum, habeas corpus ad subjiciendum.* These developed into "something more than a procedural writ due to the desire of the courts of common law to extend their jurisdiction at the expense of rival courts." In the medieval period these rivals were local and franchise courts; in the late fifteenth and sixteenth centuries, the central prerogative courts of Chancery, Council and Star Chamber, and Admiralty. "It was in the second period that the power of this weapon was seen on a larger stage, and that the course of the struggle with some of these rival courts showed that it could be used in a new way to protect the liberty of the subject."

torically unjustified) connection of the writ of habeas corpus with the Great Charter, effected in the seventeenth century, which made possible its later benevolent role:

Whether or not the famous clause of Magna Carta, which enacted that "no free man shall be taken or imprisoned or disseised or exiled or in any way destroyed except by the lawful judgment of his peers or by the law of the land," was intended to safeguard the principle that no man should be imprisoned without due process of law, it soon came to be interpreted as safeguarding it. Because it was interpreted in this way, it has exercised a vast influence both upon the manner in which the judges have developed the writs which could be used to safeguard this liberty, and upon the manner in which the Legislature has assisted that development. Without the inspiration of a general principle with all the prestige of Magna Carta behind it, this development could never have taken place; and equally without the translation of that general principle into practice, by the invention of specific writs to deal with cases of its infringement, it could never have taken practical shape.[56]

The writ of habeas corpus thus needed the support of the Great Charter. It may be suggested that the latter, to be effective for this purpose, needed the support of the *six statutes*. Had the Charter "walked abroad again" unattended by the "other six statutes," could it have been used as effectively as it was? "For these words 'per legem terrae,'" said Noy, "what 'Lex terrae' should be, I will not take upon me to expound, otherwise than I find them to be expounded by acts of parliament; and this is, that they are understood to be the process of the law, sometimes by writ, sometimes by attachment of the person." Similarly Littleton, "Out of this Statute I observe, that what in *Magna Charta,* and the Preamble of this Statute [25 Edward III, chapter 4] is termed by *the Law of the Land* is, in the Body of this Act, expounded to be *by Process made by writ Original at the Common Law,* which is a plain interpretation of the words *Law of the Land* in the Grand Charter." [57]

The various interpretations of chapter 29 among which the *six statutes* are to be found, occur usually as commons petitions (or statutes based on such petitions) protesting the jurisdiction and procedure of the council, or the summary procedure of special commissions, and in Richard II's reign, of the Court of the Constable and Marshal. A few individual petitions also take exception to the Exchequer as a non-common-law court. The petitioners are not concerned with the *judicium parium* either in the technical sense or in the sense of trial by equals or trial by jury; in fact the phrase is usually omitted in the partial quoting (or misquoting) of chapter 29. It is rather the magically elastic *per legem terrae* which is invoked to secure

[56] Holdsworth, IX, 104.
[57] See below, Chap. XI.

trial in common-law courts, and by routine common-law procedures such as original writ or indictment.

Both parliament and the lawyers distrusted the jurisdiction of the council. It was "identified with the crown and the prerogative." It not only exercised a competence outside the common law but tended to encroach on the field of the latter. It was feared for its power and disliked for the very efficiency of its procedure.[58] Furthermore, "the council took up criminal cases on 'information' or 'suggestion' by whomsoever it was offered. This was a mode of accusation that was creeping in as the earlier method of criminal appeal declined. It differed from the appeal in that it was unaccompanied by any challenge to battle; it might be offered either publicly or secretly, and without traditional safeguards. . . . the danger of the system lay in its being applied on the slightest suspicion and even falsely and maliciously." [59] This practice was especially resented. As a result the jury of *presentment* was becoming valued as a jury of *indictment*—a safeguard against false accusation. It is in this period (the 1360's) that Miss Putnam finds the juries in quarter sessions, in addition to their presentments, certifying individual complaints or bills with the now familiar "This is a true bill (*Hec est billa vera*)." [60]

As to special commissions, parliament and the administration differed over personnel and powers. It was hard to strike a happy medium between the weakness and inefficiency of local keepers or justices of the peace preferred by the commons and the strong-arm methods of commissions staffed with administrative officials and "great men" favored by king and council. Every student of the parliament rolls is familiar with the alternation of complaints of lawlessness and miscarriage of justice with protests against the methods devised to deal with these very evils. The remedy was worse than the disease. Miss Putnam has worked out in detail the ups and downs of this conflict throughout the fourteenth century. The mediocre talents and services of local men, justices of the peace, were preferred to commissions granted to "distinguished lawyers, or to magnates and lawyers." The use of specially strong commissions was naturally revived in times of special disturbances such as the peasants' revolt and Jack Cade's rebellion.[61]

---

[58] "The parties to the action could be examined; the writs of subpoena or *quibusdam de certis causis* by which defendants were summoned to appear gave them no warning of the nature of the plaintiff's cause of complaint, and it sometimes executed its orders by the summary method of despatching a serjeant at arms." Holdsworth, I, 486.

[59] Leadam, in *Select Cases before the King's Council*, pp. xxxvi–xxxvii (S. S.).

[60] *Proceedings before Justices of the Peace in the Fourteenth and Fifteenth Centuries*, pp. c–cii: "The crucial point," Miss Putnam says, "is to discover just when jurors began to make indictments as well as presentments. . . . The earliest clear examples that I have noted of this procedure (by no means necessarily the earliest in fact) are in Suffolk for 1361–2."

[61] *Ibid.*, pp. xxxvi–lvi: "The Competitors of the Justices of the Peace." Pertinent to this study and to be described in the next few pages are: the Ordinance of Northampton, 1338, which provided that notorious suspects be summarily attached (issued by a great council fear-

Attempts to restrict the holding of common pleas in the Exchequer had been made in 1284, 1300, and 1311. It was the second of these, the *Articuli super cartas,* chapter 4 (based on Magna Carta chapter 11, not 29), that was to be remembered and used in later years.[62] Yet certain individual petitioners in the 1330's do direct the magic "law of the land" clause against the Exchequer. They protest the action of a chamberlain in impleading them in that court for trespass (as his privilege of place entitled him to do), thus "cunningly contriving to maliciously aggrieve them and to deprive them of the common law." The first group (a prior, a chaplain, two monks, and one other) while not ignoring the "fixed place" for common pleas, base their case mainly on the right of free men to the common law: it is contained in the Great Charter "that no free man shall be taken, imprisoned, disseised, etc. except by the judgment of his peers or by the law of the land," and they show the king "that they were free men and ought to be treated according to the common law of the land." [63]

Other jurisdictions encroaching on the field of the common law may be noted briefly. A series of statutes, of which again the *Articuli super cartas* (chapter 3) was the most fundamental, defined and restricted the jurisdiction of the Steward and Marshal for the king's household "within the verge," especially as to common pleas, but I have found no protests against this court based directly on Magna Carta.[64] More opposition was aroused by the Court of the Constable and Marshal. A military court nominally under the control of the constable and marshal was in existence at least as early as the reign of Edward I. By the reign of Richard II this court had "developed apace." As the duel of law declined, the treason duel of chivalry made its appearance. French influence, the pleasure of the king and of such nobles as delighted in the splendid rites at royal expense, and, later in the reign, the increasing extension of the prerogative were responsible. The restrictive statute of 13 Richard II best defines what the proper jurisdiction

ing an outburst of lawlessness on the king's departure for France; not to be confused with the statute of Northampton, 2 Ed. III, ca. 3); the commissions of 1340–41; and the statute of Gloucester (2 Rich. II, stat. 1, ca. 6), authorizing commissions armed with powers of summary arrest.

    [62] 12 Ed. I, Statute of Rothlan; *Articuli super cartas,* ca. 4; New Ordinances, ca. 25 (*S. R.* I, 70, 138, 163). The *Articuli* reads: "Moreover no Common Pleas shall be from henceforth holden in the Exchequer contrary to the Form of the Great Charter." Although the Exchequer had long had its "fixed place," it had spent long periods at York during Edward I's Scottish campaigns, and besides, the "fixed place" prescribed in the Charter for common pleas had come to be identified with the Bench. For a petition citing the *Articuli* to this effect, see *Rot. Parl.* III, 563, no. 6 (1404).

    [63] The second group, a knight, his son, and six others, protested in much the same vein, quoting ca. 29, and claiming that they were all free men "who ought to be treated according to the common law." *Cal. Close Rolls,* 1333, pp. 359–60, 727.

    [64] In their petition of 1376 the commons ask that the steward and marshal "ne tiegne ne se melle de nul autre Plee mes tiel come est ordeigne en l'Estatut appelle Articuli super Cartas. Et qe touz ceux qe voillent autrement suir eient lour suites a la Commune Ley." *Rot. Parl.* II, 336, no. 91.

of the court was thought to be, yet as the same statute complains, the court has encroached and "daily doth incroach Contracts, Covenants, Trespasses, Debts, and Detinues, and many other Actions pleadable at the Common Law, in great Prejudice of the King and of his Courts, and to the great Grievance and Oppression of the People." [65] But according to Vernon-Harcourt the business of the court increased: "it took cognisance of actions for debt *causa fidei lesione pretense,* and also continued to deal with appeals of treason and felony on practically the same simple and comprehensive pretext. . . . From and after (if not before) the reign of Richard the Second the proceedings seem to have been exclusively in accordance with the civil law. Trial was by witnesses, or failing sufficient evidence, by battle."

From the Westminster parliament of 1331 comes the first of the group later to be dubbed the *six statutes*:

It is enacted, that no man from henceforth be attached by any Accusation, nor forjudged of life or limb, nor his lands, tenements, goods, nor chattels seised into the king's hands against the form of the Great Charter, and the law of the land.

It has no corresponding petition in the incomplete record of the parliament roll for this session. It may have been prompted by the arbitrary regime of Isabella and Mortimer.[66]

Had it not been repealed, the statute of 15 Edward III might well have served as the second in this series. The circumstances which produced it have been described above. Against the commissioners authorized to hear and determine oppressions and extortions by the king's ministers it was alleged that they had imposed exorbitant fines without regard to the degree of the offense; that sheriffs were charged to return all free men, whether resident or nonresident, to serve on juries and to seize the lands of those who failed to appear; that persons were convicted by their indictors, whom they were not allowed to challenge. Judge Willoughby, arraigned at the bar at Westminster, objected "that he ought not to be tried without indictment or suit of party, and that the 'plusours billes' which were produced were not affirmed by pledges in the usual manner." [67] In fact, the commission to try Willoughby and the other great officials bases charges of their misconduct in office on the "common report and clamour of the people and divers

---

[65] Vernon-Harcourt, pp. 362–66. According to 13 Richard II, "to the Constable it pertaineth to have cognizance of Contracts touching Deeds of Arms and of War out of the Realm, and also of things that touch War within the Realm, which cannot be determined nor discussed by the Common Law, with other Uses to the same matters pertaining . . ." *S. R.* II, 61.

[66] 5 Ed. III, ca. 9 (*S. R.* I, 267). For the formal charges against Mortimer and individual complaints of injustices inflicted by him or his adherents, see *Rot. Parl.* II, 52–53.

[67] *Rot. Parl.* II, 128, no. 14; Y. B. 14–15 Ed. III, pp. xx–xxi, 258–63 (R. S.); Murimuth, p. 118; *Cal. Pat. Rolls,* 1340–43, pp. 110–11; Hughes, *Study of Social and Constitutional Tendencies,* p. 183.

petitions shown before him [the king] and the council against some of them." Professor Plucknett concludes that here notoriety served as a substitute for indictment, and was technically correct.[68]

Such was not the view of the April parliament, which protested these abuses, secured repeal of the Ordinance of Northampton, and in 15 Edward III, chapter 3, sought security for the future.[69] Though short-lived, it must have crystallized and expressed popular opinion. The commons were not entirely silent in the next few years. The parliament rolls record two petitions, one for 1347 and one for 1351, which protest some aspect of the council's procedure, but neither cites the Charter.[70]

The second of the *six statutes* (25 Edward III, statute 5, chapter 4) emanated from the same parliament which enacted the famous Statute of Treasons. This act follows almost verbatim one of the commons petitions; it is a clear-cut protest against the practice of accusation by "suggestion" to king and council, and is the most explicit exposition thus far of the "law of the land":

Whereas it is contained in the Great Charter of the Liberties of England, that none shall be imprisoned nor put out of his freehold, nor of his liberties or free customs, unless it be by the law of the land; it is accorded, assented and stablished, that from henceforth none shall be taken by petition or suggestion made to our lord the king, or to his council, *unless it be by indictment of good and lawful people of the same neighbourhood where such deeds be done, in due manner, or by process made by writ original at the common law*; nor that none be out of his liberties nor of his freeholds, *unless he be duly brought in to answer, and forjudged of the same by the course of the law*; and

---

[68] He concludes that his "submission to the King's grace must be taken as, technically at least, an admission of the correctness of the procedure, although it need not imply an admission of the charges against him." Plucknett sees here a change in the role of notoriety—"the crown alleged that the notoriety of the prisoner's misdeeds was sufficient to put him upon his trial without an indictment. Notoriety therefore enters upon a new role, that of serving instead of an indictment as the basis for a common law trial; no longer does it work an instant conviction."

[69] "Because that the points of the Great Charter be blemished in divers manners, and less well holden than they ought to be, to the great peril and slander of the king, and damage of his people, especially inasmuch as clerks, peers of the land, and other free men, be arrested and imprisoned, and out of their goods and cattels, *which were not appealed nor indicted, nor suit of the party against them affirmed*; It is accorded and assented, that from henceforth such things shall not be done. And if any minister of the king, or other person, of what condition he be, *do thus, or come against any point of the Great Charter, or other statutes, or the laws of the land,* he shall answer in the parliament as well at the king's suit, as at the suit of the party, where no remedy nor punishment was ordained before this time, as far forth where it was done by commission or commandment of the king, as of his own authority, notwithstanding the ordinance made before this time at Northampton, [which] . . . is repealed . . ." *S. R.* I, 296 (italics mine). Where *S. R.* reads "if any minister *do or come against* any point," I substitute "do thus" for the French "*E si nul les face,* ou viegne contre nul point."

[70] *Rot. Parl.* II, 168, no. 28; 228, no. 16. The first protests summoning persons before the council "par suggestion ou certification d'ascunes acusours volentriment." The second questions the council's jurisdiction in cases involving freehold, but not "de chose qe touche vie ou membre, contemptz ou excesse." See pp. 165–72, nos. 6, 34, 54, 60, for more "negative evidence"— commons petitions which might appropriately cite the Charter but do not.

if anything be done against the same, it shall be redressed and holden for none.[71]

A similar enactment (1354), much briefer in compass, constitutes the third of the *six statutes*.[72] In this instance Magna Carta is not cited, but the provision follows close upon a confirmation of the Charter (chapter 1). In these acts of 1352 and 1354 the *liber homo* of the Charter has become in one case simply "none (*nul*)," in the other "no man of whatever estate or condition he may be (*nul homme, de quel estate ou condicion qil soit*)." [73] The second uses the phrases "in due manner or by process made by writ." The third is the first instance I have found where *due process of law* occurs in connection with chapter 29.[74] Three years later the Charter is being invoked to secure "due processes" for "divers men of Ireland, great and small":

Whereas certain of our justices of Ireland have arrested, taken and imprisoned divers men of Ireland Great and Small, by Writs, Precepts, Bills, and otherwise, at their Will, and without Indictments, Presentments, or due Processes (*seu debitis processibus*), and have detained them in dark Prisons and bound in fetters, until through Duresses, Imprisonments, and Pains inflicted, they paid Fines and Ransoms to the Justices and their private Counsellors and Brocagers according to their Pleasure, to their own personal Profit and not ours, against the form of the Great Charter and other our Statutes thereupon made, and against the Law and Custom of the said Land; . . . We will and stedfastly command, that men being our Subjects, without Indictments, of Presentments, or other due Processes, against the form of the Charter and statutes aforesaid and the Law and Custom abovementioned, by our Justices of Ireland for the time being, or their Lieutenants, or by their Precepts, or Commands, or by Bills, shall by no means be taken nor imprisoned. . . .[75]

---

[71] *S. R.* I, 321 (italics mine). For the petition, see *Rot. Parl.* II, 239, no. 19. The record includes a confirmation of the Charters and petitions which cite other chapters of Magna Carta; see pp. 238–41, nos. 14, 26, 40.

[72] "That no Man of what Estate or Condition that he be, shall be put out of Land or Tenement, nor taken, nor imprisoned, nor disinherited, nor put to death, without being brought in answer by due process of the law." 28 Ed. III, ca. 3 (*S. R.* I, 345). This act may have resulted from complaints recorded (*Rot. Parl.* II, 258, no. 22): that persons are put in *exigend* in counties where they are not resident, as well at the suit of the king as of a party; thus they are outlawed without their knowledge and in case of felony their chattels are forfeited and themselves put in danger of life and limb.

[73] For interesting comments on how the attitude of the common law militated against any aristocratic connotation in this phrase, had such been originally intended, see Vinogradoff, in *Magna Carta Commemoration Essays*, pp. 81–82; and Pollard, *Evolution of Parliament*, p. 72.

[74] ". . . saunz estre mesne en respons par due proces de lei." The phrase *process of law* appears in documents emanating from the Lancastrian opposition some years earlier. The first comes from enemies of the Despensers in the pardon drawn up for themselves, 1321: "and for the obtaining by force that which could not be obtained by process of law." *S. R.* I, 185–86. The other is one of a group of petitions presented in the parliament of 1325, protesting arrests, imprisonments, seizure of lands of knights and ladies (chivalers, dames) and others: "pleise a vostre haute Seignurie qe desore tieux attachmentz ne se facent par simple acusement *sans proces de lay*, & qe de ceux issi pris & emprisonez voillez comander deliverance solonc la leye de vostre terre." *Rot. Parl.* I, 430 (app.).

[75] 31 Ed. III, stat. 4, ca. 16 (*S. R.* I, 362).

"Against the form of the Great Charter and *other statutes thereupon made*"
—here is evidence that the latter are beginning to serve as precedents. This
phrase recurs in 1362 and 1363.

In their selection of a fourth interpretation of chapter 29, counsel for the
five knights made a bad blunder. Their 36 Edward III, number 9, is a general confirmation of the Charters and has nothing to do with arbitrary
arrest, as Attorney General Heath ably demonstrated.[76] The common lawyers were on surer ground in citing another petition of the same parliament.[77] To be sure, this did not appear on the statute roll, but, as Digby
said, it is "the answer to the petition which makes it an act of parliament."
Certainly it must have had an especial appeal in 1627 and 1628 for it protests arrest by special command. Their fifth statute, 1363 (again based
almost verbatim on a commons petition), not only complains of false suggestions to the king himself, contrary to the process of the law of Magna
Carta, but provides that henceforth such accuser find sureties before the
council, and "if his suggestion be found evil," incur the same penalties the
accused would have suffered.[78]

It is interesting to find that the last of the *six statutes,* 42 Edward III,
chapter 3, was cited in cases of the nineteenth and twentieth century. "This
is treated by the Supreme Court of New Zealand as a statutory prohibition
of commissions of inquiry as to offenses committed; and is also relied on
by the counsel for the University of Oxford." [79] Actually here the commons
were not complaining of commissions but of false accusers who made their
accusations rather for vengeance or their own profit than for that of the
king or his people, and that persons thus accused were brought before the
council by writ or other command of the king under heavy penalty (*sur*

[76] *Rot. Parl.* II, 269. "Primerement, Qe la Grande Chartre, & la Chartre de la Foreste, &
les autres Estatutz faitz en son temps & de ses Progenitours, pur profit de lui & de la Commune,
soient bien & ferment gardez, & mis en due execution, saunz destourbance mettre, *ou arrest
faire a l'encontre par especial mandement,* ou en autre manere." Its wording, its place at the
head of the commons petitions, and the royal answer mark it unmistakably as the usual request for a confirmation. No doubt the words italicized attracted the overeager "counsel for
the defense."

[77] *Ibid.* II, 270, which reads in part: "Item, Come il soit contenuz en la Grande Chartre &
autres Estatutz, *qe nul homme soit pris n'emprisonez par especial mandement,* saunz enditement ou autre due processe a faire par la Lei: Et sovent foitz ad este, & uncore est, qe plusours
gentz sont empeschez, pris, & emprisonez, saunz enditement ou autre proces fait par la Lei sur
eux . . . Qe plese a nostre dit Seignur commander a delivrer ceux qe sont issint pris par tiele
especial mandement, countre la fourme des Chartres & Estatutz avant dits."

[78] *Ibid.* II, 280, no. 37 (the petition); *S. R.* I, 382 (the statute). The procedure prescribed
for offenders was amended by 38 Ed. III, stat. 1, ca. 9 (*ibid.* I, 384).

[79] W. Harrison Moore, "Executive Commissions of Inquiry," *Columbia Law Review,*
13:500–23. In 1850 it was cited by the "four very distinguished lawyers" who advised the
University of Oxford as to the illegality of the Oxford University Commissions. In *Cock v. Attorney-General for New Zealand* (c. 1908): "The limitations and their extent were demonstrated by legislation, by *42 Edward III, c. 3,* and the Act for the Abolition of the Star Chamber,
16 Car. I, c. 10, as well as the resolution of the judges in the case of Commissions of Inquiry
temp. James I." As Moore points out, 42 Ed. III, ca. 4, would have been more to the point.

grief peine), apparently the writ of subpoena. Following a summary statement of the grievance, the statute proceeds in the identical words of the last part of the petition:

It is assented and accorded, for the good governance of the commons, that no man be put to answer without presentment before justices, or matter of record, or by due process and writ original, according to the old law of the land: and if any thing from henceforth be done to the contrary it shall be void in the law, and holden for error.

Neither petition nor statute cites Magna Carta, but both follow almost immediately after a confirmation of the Charters, and are followed (chapter 4) by a regulation as to irresponsible and abusive commissions of inquiry.[80] In the parliament roll the king's answer reads: *pur ce qe ceste Article est Article de la Grand Chartre, le Roi voet qe ceo soit fait come la Petition demande.* What more did the seventeenth-century interpreters of "law of the land" in Magna Carta need than this?

This, the last of the *six statutes*, is also the last in the series of petitions giving specific content to the *per legem terrae* of chapter 29 which find a place in the statute roll. There are, however, a few petitions of allied character in the reign of Richard II. These protest respectively "false suggestions," overpowerful commissions, expanding jurisdiction of the Court of the Constable and Marshal, and some form of extralegal procedure. In the Gloucester parliament of 1378 the commons complain of a particular kind of false suggestion: persons intimate that certain lands are in the king's hands and then buy patents to have the same, thus ousting people from their freeholds to their great damage and disinheritance, *sanz respons, & encontre la fourme de Grande Chartre.*[81]

Yet it was this same parliament which attempted to cope with the more than usual disorders in the country, especially in Wales and the western shires,[82] by confirming the statute of Northampton and providing for special commissions of "sufficient and valiant persons, lords or other," with power over offenders "to arrest them incontinent without tarrying for indictments or other process of the law," and to have them detained in gaol until the coming of the justices "without being delivered in the meantime by mainprise, bail, or in other manner." This law was repealed in the very next parliament. The commons had protested it as "very horrible and dan-

---

[80] *S. R.* I, 388. The petition (*Rot. Parl.* II, 295, no. 12) includes details (omitted from the statute) for safeguarding the interests of the king if the "suggestion" be to his profit.

[81] *Rot. Parl.* III, 46, no. 66. To their request that no such patents be issued henceforth the response is *Le Roi le voet.*

[82] The chancellor's opening speech and the commons petitions describe the riotous proceedings of confederacies of armed men (*ibid.* III, 33, nos. 8 and 9; and 42, no. 44); the statute refers to "assemblies, routs, or ridings of offendours, baratours, and other such rioters in affray of the people." *S. R.* II, 9–10. Repealed by 2 Rich. II, ca. 2. *S. R.* II, 12; based on *Rot. Parl.* III, 65.

gerous for the good and lawful people of the realm," likely to result in misinformations and false accusations against persons by their enemies, or through the ill will of the commissioners themselves, "the which ordinance is openly against the Great Charter, and divers statutes made in the time of the progenitors of our lord the king, that no free man can be taken nor imprisoned without due process of law." At the same time another petition protests that persons are being appealed by bill before the constable and marshal for treasons and felonies done *within* the realm, imprisoned against the law of the realm "and against the form of the Great Charter, which wills that no man be imprisoned nor in any manner distrained except by the lawful judgment of his peers and the law of the land." [83]

Again at the end of the reign, one of the charges incident to Richard's deposition reveals the abuses to which the Court of the Constable and Marshal was being put. After a recital of chapter 29 it accuses the king of having willfully committed perjury in violating this, one of the statutes of his realm: by his own command persons have been maliciously prosecuted for scandalous words against the person of the king, seized and imprisoned, and led before this military court, where they were allowed to make no answer except not guilty, and must defend themselves with their bodies against adversaries young and strong, although the accused were old, weak, maimed, or infirm. [84]

After 1379, throughout the remaining twenty years of Richard's reign, chapter 29 falls into comparative oblivion. There are two exceptions, both interesting for their free "gloss on the text." Oddly enough the first comes from the Lords Appellant, in accusing Nicholas Brembre, "false knight of London," of having traitorously encroached on royal power in taking some twenty-two prisoners from Newgate, and having all but one beheaded at the "foul oak" in Kent, without warrant or process of law. The charge begins with a free rendering of chapter 29 appropriate to the occasion: *Item la ou par la Graunt Chartre, & autres bones Leis & Usages de Roialme*

[83] *Rot. Parl.* III, 65, no. 47. The matter was postponed, as one requiring great deliberation, and because the heirs claiming the offices of constable and marshal were under age. As to one case, an appeal of treason allegedly done in Cornwall, it was promised that the king would appoint special commissioners. Petitions of 1384 and 1389 and the statutes to which they led (8 and 13 Richard II) are based simply on the common law, with no reference to Magna Carta. *S. R.* II, 37, 61; based on *Rot. Parl.* III, 202, no. 31; 265, no. 26.

The statute of 1399, effective in abolishing appeals in parliament, "contrary no doubt to what its framers intended," only "gave a fresh impetus to the court of chivalry. Frequently during Henry the Fourth's reign, the commons presented petitions on the subject." These cite the statutes of Richard II and the common law, but not Magna Carta. In two the Admiralty is a cause of protest also. *Rot. Parl.* III, 473, no. 79; 498, no. 47; 530, no. 39; 625, no. 24.

[84] *Rot. Parl.* III, 420, no. 44. If the petition and statute of Henry IV be the result of this charge, neither follows its form in quoting the Charter. *Rot. Parl.* III, 442; *S. R.* III, 116. The statute provides that criminal appeals for matters done out of the realm are to be determined in this court, but appeals for matters done within the realm are to be "tried and determined by the good Laws of the Realm."

d'Engletere, 'nulle homme ne serra pris, enprisone, ne mys a mort saunz dewe processe de Lai' . . .[85]

There are a few other petitions of parliaments of Richard II and of Henry IV, V, and VI, protesting some aspect of the jurisdiction of the council, its use of letters of privy seal and the prerogative writs of *quibusdam certis de causis* and subpoena, but they no longer cite chapter 29. The practice in question is merely said to encroach on the common law; no resulting enactment appears on the statute roll, and the answers recorded in the parliament roll are evasive or qualified with reservations.[86]

One more voice is raised in 1415, the voice of the "good people of Sandwich," who plead for the common law against the jurisdiction of the constable of Dover Castle in a dispute arising in connection with the trade with Flemish merchants. Their quaint petition, extremest example of a free rendering of the Charter, shows how far, in this age no less than in later centuries, one could depart from the letter yet hold to the spirit of the old law: *Plese a Vous, honurables Sires, considerer la matier suis dite, & auxi l'estatut del graunt chartre, qe fait mencion qe null Homme serroit jugge sinoun par la commune ley, et auxi en autres estatutz d'aucien temps ordeignez, nully ne serroit moleste ne greve saunz due Processe de ley* . . .[87]

As was usually the way with medieval legislation, no one enactment produced definitive results. There was the inevitable reaffirmation and amplification, the pleas for more effective enforcement. Holdsworth concludes that these statutes did have one important result: "They prevented the Council from dealing with questions of freehold which were properly determinable by the common law courts by the machinery of the real actions; and they prevented it from dealing with questions of treason or felony, a

---

[85] *Rot. Parl.* III, 231, 319, 470. The second, a petition of 17 Richard II, repeated 2 Henry IV, against arbitrary arrest and imprisonment, does not specify the exact grievance, but also paraphrases: "depuis q'il est contenuz en la Grant Chartre, 'Qe nul serra arestu, n'emprisone, saunz responce, ou due proces de la ley': & a ceo sont jurrez le Roy, les Seigneurs, & Prelatz, & conferme en chescun Parlement . . ."

[86] 9 Henry V does remind the king of "divers statutes" made in the time of his noble progenitors to the effect that none of his "lieges" be brought "en respounce sinon par Brief Original & due Proces selonc la Leie de la Terre." *Rot. Parl.* IV, 156, no. 25. For the others see *ibid.* III, 267, no. 33; 323, no. 52; 471, no. 69; IV, 84, no. 46; V, 407 (articles for the council, no. iii). The first, for instance, protests summoning of persons by suit of the party or on suggestion by *quibusdam certis de causis* or other such writs, before chancellor or council, "de respondre d'ascune manere dont recoverer est done par la commune ley." The answer is evasive: "Le Roy voet sauver sa Regalie, come ses progenitours ont faitz devant luy," though in another instance it is assumed the council may act if one of the parties is poor and his adversary great and rich.

In 3 Henry V the protest is against writs of subpoena and *certis des causis,* and also procedure "solonc la fourme de ley cyvyle & ley de Seinte Esglise, en subvercion de vostre commune ley." This petition attributes the invention of such writs to John Waltham, Bishop of Salisbury, "de sa subtiltee." He was keeper of the Chancery rolls, 1381–86, keeper of the privy seal, 1386, and finally treasurer, 1391–95. *D. N. B.*

[87] Presented through the commons: "Item les ditz, Communes baileront, en ycell Parlement, une Petition, pur les gentz de Ville de Sondwyck." *Rot. Parl.* IV, 67, no. 9.

conviction for which involved the death penalty and escheat or forfeiture of freehold." [88] On the other hand they did not effect any essential alteration in the procedure of the council. Nevertheless, chapter 29 had certainly been made to mean more things to more people, to connote the later "liberty of the subject." The next steps, as we shall see, were to come rather incidentally through the compilers and printers of the statutes.

Delay and Sale of Justice

"No words of that famous document," remarks Stubbs of Magna Carta, "were better known or more frequently brought forward than the fortieth clause, 'nulli vendemus, nulli negabimus, aut differemus rectum aut justiciam.'" Yet it is something of an anticlimax to turn to this passage (the last clause of chapter 29 in most copies of the definitive text), for the sources indicate that it had a somewhat less notable career than the preceding clauses. It offered fewer possibilities than the *judicium parium* or the *per legem terrae*. Eventually it came to serve as an effective rhetorical flourish in arguments in courts or parliament. It was a great favorite of Sir Edward Coke, who used it as a maxim on the title page of his *Eighth Report* (printed in 1611) and in many a speech. Even in his time, however, it occasionally had a more specific application, as in the charges of "sale of justice" brought against Sir John Bennett. Fourteenth-century citations of the clause occur in connection with (1) a few miscellaneous protests against denial or delay of justice, and (2) repeated complaints in the commons petitions of sale of writs at exorbitant rates.

The kind of delay so characteristic of medieval justice is well illustrated by the petition of Walter, Bishop of Exeter (18 Edward II). His was a long dispute between himself and the crown, originating in Edward I's reign, over the advowson of the church of St. Burian in Cornwall, which he claimed was a parish church with cure of souls in his diocese, but which by "false suggestion" of a royal appointee had been treated as a free chapel of the king. The bishop complains that his plea has been pending before the justices for eight years, and a note appended to the petition states that he has presented it in every parliament the past seven years. Evidently parliament was not always the effective aid in expediting justice that litigants hoped for, especially when royal interests were involved. He asks that his petition be sent to the justices with a command to do right "without further delay, least souls be imperilled, by the grace of our lord the king, who ought to will and does will that right be not delayed nor denied to any against the Great Charter." [89]

[88] Holdsworth, I, 488.
[89] ". . . sanz etre plus delaye, pur peril d'almes, de la grace nostre Seigneur le Roi, qe deit voler et veust qe droit ne soit delaye ne denie a nulli encontre la Grant Chartre. Responsio: Coram Rege, quia tangit ipsum." *Rot. Parl.* I, 421, no. 18.

On the roll of the Lincoln parliament (9 Edward II) is recorded the famous case of the Gloucester inheritance arising on the death of Gilbert de Clare, Earl of Gloucester, without male heirs. His three sisters, with their husbands, claimed as coheiresses. The petition of the importunate Hugh Despenser the younger demands the portion of his wife Alianor, professes himself ready to do homage and all service due, and asks prompt livery: "And as it is contained in the Great Charter that our lord the king will not delay or sell right, nor take away right from any (*ne droit delaier, ne vier, ne purloigner droit a nully*), the which Charter he himself has confirmed." But settlement was deferred, pending investigation of rumors that a posthumous heir might be born to the countess. The two officials assigned to answer Hugh for the king retorted that the Great Charter of liberties ought to operate as much in the interests of the countess as of Hugh and Alianor and others.[90] It has been seen above that letters and documents issued by the king in behalf of the Despensers in 1321–22 quoted this clause, and that the Londoners used it in their petition of 1377 protesting delay occasioned by royal protections allowed before the king's justices in pleas of debt, account, or trespass, where the plaintiff was a freeman of the city.

As to sale of justice, the original intent of the Charter had been to check certain abuses of John's reign, not to stop the legitimate sale of writs, or the customary fees for expediting justice or securing some special procedure.[91] But "elaborate glosses overlaid the king's promise that he would sell justice to none, for a line between the price of justice and those mere court fees, which are demanded even in our own day, is not easily drawn." Kings never ceased to exact large sums for writs of grace, and evaded, or even explicitly repudiated, popular interpretation of the clause. The author of the *Mirror of Justices* was probably voicing the popular view when he said:

The article whereby the king grants to his people that he will not sell, nor deny, nor delay justice, is disregarded by the chancellor who sells remedial writs and calls them writs of grace, and by the chancellor of the exchequer who refuses to give acquittances under green wax for payments made to the king, and by all who delay judgment or other right.[92]

The commons petitioned repeatedly in parliaments of Edward III and Richard against the practice in Chancery of charging a fine in addition to

[90] "Adicientes, quod tantum operatur Magna Carta de Libertatibus Anglie pro Impregnatura prefate Comitisse in hoc casu, quantum pro predictus Hugone & Alianora, ac alius Jus vendicantibus in hac parte." *Rot. Parl.* I, 353–54.

[91] For practices along these lines in the reign of Henry III, see Pollock and Maitland, I, 174.

[92] *Mirror of Justices*, p. 180. Cf. p. 179: "As to the clause forbidding the king and his chancellor to take anything for granting the writ *de odio et atia*, this ought to be extended to all remedial writs . . ."

the customary set fee for writs. They asked that writs be issued without fine on payment of the fee for the seal, or as one petition puts it, *resonablement pur l'escrivre & pur le Seal*. In six out of ten such petitions in parliament rolls the *nulli vendemus* clause is quoted or paraphrased, in Latin or French, as justification for the request.[93] The second, 1352, is most eloquent, reminding the king that writs are a prime element (*primere partie*) of his law, "which law is the sovereign right of his realm and of his crown," and cleverly reminding him that all told more would accrue to him in fees, issues, and amercements if writs were granted freely without fine.

Succeeding petitions, those which quote the Charter and those which do not, are brief. None results in a statute. In spite of representations of the commons to the contrary, officials usually assume that fines are being taken for writs of grace only, and so rightfully. Answers to the petitions seldom go beyond directions to the chancellor to follow previous practice, to be "reasonable," or "gracious." In one instance it is frankly admitted that the king has no intention of curtailing so valuable a source of revenue. Again, even more emphatically, the practice is defended on grounds of profit and prescription: "Our lord the king has no intention of relinquishing such a great commodity which has been used continually in the said chancery, as well before as after the making of the said Charter in the time of all his noble progenitors, who have since been kings of England."[94]

[93] 1334: "Item prie la dite commune pur ceo qe la chauncellerie est une place la ou homme covient avoir recoverer et comencement par brief a pursuere son droit, qil puisse avoir les ditz briefs santz rien doner ostre la fee du seal, desicome la grande chartre voet 'Nulli vendemus, nulli negabimus aut differemus rectum et iusticiam,' qar multz des gentz ont este delaiez de lour droit et ascunes desheritez pur ce qe les clerks de la chauncellerie les ont viez briefs qi autrefoitz soloient estre grantez santz rien doner, et auxint le roi ad eu de ce grant pert.

"Responsio: Les briefs qi sont de cours soeint de cours, et des briefs qi sont de grace le roi comandra son chaunceller qil soit gracious." Richardson and Sayles, *Rotuli Parliamentorum*, p. 234. (The editors substitute *niez* for *viez*, but I think *viez* is correct; i.e., *sold*. It is the same word that Despenser uses in his petition in paraphrasing ca. 29, *ne droit delaier ne vier*.) For the others, see *Rot. Parl.* II, 241, no. 40; 261, no. 39; 313, no. 38; 370, no. 58; III, 166, no. 88. In 1354, for instance, the clause is in French: "Qe a nully serra vendu, nye, ou esloigne droit ou Justice." Others which do not cite the Charter: II, 170, no. 45; 229, no. 29; 287, no. 23; 305, no. 19.

[94] 1352: "qe le chanceller . . . soit si gracious come il poet estre bonement, en eise du poeple"; and in answer, "Homme ne poet toller le profit le Roi qe soleit estre donez pur Briefs de grace en auncien temps." 1381: "Nostre Seignur le Roi n'entende mye de soi demetre de si grant comodite, q'ad este usez continuelment en dite Chancellerie, si bien avaunt come apres la confection del dite Chartre en temps de touz ses nobles progenitours, qi depuis aient este Rois d'Engleterre."

❖ CHAPTER IV ❖

Magna Carta and Special Interests: The City of London

Now to treat of the great and notable Franchises, Liberties, and Customes of the City of London, would require a whole Volume of itself. . . . These notable, rare, and special liberties we have attempted to remember: but whether herein we have done that good to the City that we intended, we know not, for we have omitted many more of no small number and great rarity and consequence too long to be remembered.

(SIR EDWARD COKE)

Two miles from London lay Westminster, clustering round its Abbey, and its Hall which Rufus had built and which Richard II was adorning with rafters of Irish oak. Westminster had become the recognized center of royal administration, law and Parliament, although it had no commerce and no municipal privileges of its own, and was only a village at great London's gate. There was no royal foothold inside the English capital corresponding to the Louvre in Paris. When the King came up to town, he lived sometimes at Westminster on one side of London, sometimes in the Tower on the other. But the City that lay between was not his ground, and Richard II was no more able than Charles I to dictate to its militia, its magistrates and its mob. The medieval balance and harmony of powers from which modern English liberty has sprung, is clearly illustrated in the relation of the Plantagenet Kings to their capital.[1]

London had played no small part in the winning of Magna Carta. The city had opened its gates to the insurgent barons. Its mayor was one of the committee of twenty-five assigned to enforce the Charter. The reward which London and other towns received for their support was merely the general confirmation of their "ancient liberties and free customs, as well by land as by water," [2] for they possessed charters of their own, defining in detail the "liberties" granted by successive rulers. Still the sanction of

[1] Trevelyan, *English Social History*, pp. 31–32.

[2] Ca. 13 of John's Charter. As ca. 9 of the 1225 issue (which will be cited hereafter) this provision reads: "Civitas Londonie habeat omnes antiquas libertates et liberas consuetudines suas. Preterea volumus et concedimus quod alie civitates, et burgi, et ville, et barones de qinque portubus, et omnes portus, habeant omnes libertates et liberas consuetudines suas."

the Great Charter was not without value as a very notable confirmation of these private charters and of customary rights for which no written grant could be produced. As we have seen, parliamentary confirmations recognized the interests of London in the Charter, and the citizens valued their conservancy of the Thames and Medway, and restrictions on purveyance. On the other hand chapter 25, providing for uniform weights and measures, benefitted the consumer—here merchants and craftsmen were the chief offenders. The freedom of trade promised by chapter 30 was so liberally interpreted by Edward II and Edward III as to nullify London's local trade monopoly. The very terms of chapter 9 contained contradictions, for one town's "liberties" might interfere with those of another. In 1298 for instance, the mayor and aldermen of London had declared that merchants of Sandwich could not trade with aliens in London and that only freemen of the city could sell wine there. Archbishop Winchelsea backed the Cinque Ports, claiming that this action of the London officials was contrary to Magna Carta.[3]

Copies of the Charter were preserved among the city's archives at the Guildhall, as is evidenced by a table of contents of the *Liber Custumarum* as it appeared in the time of Henry IV or V.[4] Three of the long series of London's charters granted after 1215 (the ninth charter of Henry III, the first of Edward III, and the first of Henry IV) recall the confirmation of the city's liberties by Magna Carta.[5]

In the fourteenth century no less than in the thirteenth, London continued to play an important role in national affairs. To cite only the more striking episodes, its citizens helped turn the tide for Isabella and Mortimer against Edward II, had their part in the crisis of 1340–41 led by Archbishop Stratford, displayed active hostility to John of Gaunt in the 1370's and 1380's, opened their gates to the revolting peasants, and in 1399 received Henry IV with enthusiasm.

The city, with the nearby Westminster, was gradually becoming the capital of the nation and was well aware of its prestige and importance. A petition of the commons (1354) describes London as the abode, as nowhere else in the realm, of "our Lord the King, and of all the great ones,

---

[3] For his letter to the mayor of London, *Cal. Letter Books*, C, 31–32.

[4] A *Tabula Contentorum* including among many items the following: *Magna Charta, Charta de Foresta, Confirmatio ejusdem, De Perambulatione Foreste, Confirmatio Chartarum Regiarum in Flandria factarum, Novi Articuli super Chartis, Charta de Ronemede, Statutum de Foresta. Liber Custumarum*, pt. ii, pp. 488–89. Cf. the list, pp. 491–98, 513–14, noted by the editor as "portions of the *Liber Custumarum* which have been omitted in the present volume, as having been previously printed in Government Publications."

[5] *Liber Albus*, pp. 137–39, 144, and 167 respectively. The last item of the ninth charter of Henry III reads, "Item, de Magna Charta liberis hominibus regni Angliae concessa." The first item of the first charter of Edward III reads "Quod cives Londoniarum habeant libertates suas, secundum formam Magnae Chartae, etc. et quod impedimenta seu usurpationes eis in hac parte facta revocentur et adnullentur." The first charter of Henry IV is identical with the above.

a great part of his commons, merchant strangers and others." [6] Later in the century a passage in the *Letter Books* refers to London as the safest place within the realm, whither the most people resort for business, "and more particularly, seeing that it is the capital city and the watchtower of the whole realm, and that from the government thereof other cities and places do take example."

Thanks to Chaucer and his many exponents, there is no lack of physical description of London, at least as it was in the latter half of the century, with details ranging from the first use of "sea" coal to the red tile roofs replacing thatch, and the hundred churches, "the chief architectural glory" of the city. Though the walls of the houses were still of mud and timber, "the number of fine stone mansions built by great lords or wealthy citizens was on the increase, like John of Gaunt's Savoy on the way between London and Westminster." [7]

Most effective for its picture of the character and situation of the city— the "lay of the land"—is the description of Chaucer's London by a reader of the Middle Temple. He reminds us that we must

> Forget six counties overhung with smoke,
> Forget the snorting steam and piston stroke,
> And dream of London small and white and clean,
> The clear Thames bordered by its gardens green
> While nigh the thronged wharf Geoffrey Chaucer's pen
> Moves over bills of lading.

London was then only what we now call the City and some distance away was Westminster. Outside Ludgate the open Fleet Stream flowed under a bridge to join the Thames. Then along the Riverside came the Dominican House of the Black Friars and the Carmelite House of the White Friars with their extensive buildings and gardens, and next to them was the Temple. On the North of these ran the street of Fleet, merging into the road leading by way of the Strand or bank of the River to Westminster. The way to reach the Tabard Inn from the Temple would have been either by road through the City under the shadow of Old St. Paul's and over old London Bridge or by ferryboat from the Temple Stairs to the Southwark side and thence onwards. [8]

From 1355 on London sent her four members to parliament, paying considerably more than the customary wages and providing lavishly for their expenses when parliament was at a distance (*in aliquo loco regni remoto a civitate*) or when some extra outlay was needed *pro proficuo et honore*

[6] ". . . en la Citee de Loundres soit la demoere nostre Seigneiur le Roi, & des touz les Grantz, & grante partie de ses Communes, & Marchantz estraunges & autres, plus qe nulle part aillours en le Roialme d'Engleterre . . ." *Rot. Parl.* II, 258.

[7] Trevelyan, *English Social History*, p. 31.

[8] John Mahan Gover, A Reading delivered before the Honourable Society of the Middle Temple, 1935.

civitatis.[9] From the early days of parliaments, London's representatives were men of consequence. They had perhaps served not only as mayor or alderman but as king's butler or escheator, were owners of considerable property in or near the city, and financiers of note, such as Sir John Philpot. and Richard Whittington.[10]

According to custom, royal jurisdiction in the city was confined to the following: sessions of gaol delivery at Newgate, constituted each year by a fresh writ from the king with the mayor as one of the judges; the king's justices sitting at St. Martin-le-Grand (outside the walls) with jurisdiction over matters in the city affecting the king or his heirs, writs of error, and proceedings against the mayor and aldermen in their corporate capacity; the periodic iter at the Tower, with its burdensome inquests, trial of felonies, and so on. But there was always danger of the extension of this royal jurisdiction at the expense of London's own courts, of the use of special commissioners armed with unusual powers, or of the extreme measure of being "taken into the king's hands." The proximity of the court and of the courts lent prestige and was good for trade but had its disadvantages. Common Pleas had long been settled at Westminster, and King's Bench was tending to settle there. The king's purveyors "could walk the city at their pleasure, bearing their white wand of office, and mark with the broad arrow whatever goods were required for the King's use." [11]

Most vital to the craftsmen and merchants of the city were the various economic "liberties" both within its own walls and throughout the land. Within the jurisdiction of the city, merchant strangers could deal by wholesale with citizens only, not in any way by retail and not with other aliens. Foreign merchants must lodge with a freeman and remain no more than

---

[9] With the exception of the parliament of 1371 "four names are found on every return made between 1355 and 1500." McKisack, *Parliamentary Representation of the English Boroughs*, p. 40. The normal rate of pay was never adopted in London. For details of the "extraordinary liberality" with which the city treated its representatives, *ibid.*, pp. 82–84. In the fifteenth century expenses were limited and regulated; there was to be a certain allowance for cloth and fur and generous wages, but an allowance for extra expenses only when parliament was meeting at a distance.

[10] "Richard de la Pole, who represented London in the parliament of September 1332, combined the offices of alderman of Bishopsgate and kings butler. John de Grantham who sat in the parliaments of February 1328, November 1330, and February 1338, owned property in eight London parishes and in the town of St. Omer."

The great financier, Sir John Philpot, acted as paymaster to Edward III. "Among Philpot's acts of munificence were the equipping of a squadron of 1000 armed men in 1377, and the defrayal, during his mayoralty, of the cost of one of the two stone towers built below London Bridge. In the summer of 1379, he provided ships for Buckingham's expedition to Brittany, and a few years later undertook the transport arrangements for Despenser's 'crusade.' On his death in the summer of 1384 he bequeathed lands to the city for the relief of three poor people for ever." For these and other examples, *ibid.*, pp. 101–2.

[11] Pendrill, *London Life*, pp. 237–38, 268. The Court of Husting at the Guildhall, presided over by the mayor and aldermen, heard pleas of land and tenements, suits for rents or services, disputes over wills. The Sheriffs' Court heard personal actions such as pleas of debt or trespass, seizure of goods, or claims of account between merchants.

forty days in the city. Londoners trading throughout England were quit of stallage, had their own courts at fairs, and were exempt from various tolls (such as the so-called *brudtol, yeres giue,* and *scotale*). Should any town try to impose such tolls on London citizens, the latter could use *withernam* or distraint on such goods of men of the offending town as were to be found in London.[12]

Magna Carta Chapter 9 as a Blanket Guarantee for Various Economic and Political Liberties

IN THE reign of Edward II, the main economic issue between king and citizens was an inherited one, the *carta mercatoria,* secured by Edward I in 1303. The Gascons, in return for paying increased customs, were to be exempt from unjust prises of their goods, could sell in gross to natives or aliens, and could lodge where they pleased. London merchants promptly contested the *carta* on the grounds that it was contrary to Magna Carta and their city charters. Later they complained that increased customs meant higher prices.[13] Little wonder, then, that the citizens welcomed the work of the Ordainers. Article 11 of the New Ordinances, after describing the *new customs,* provided:

We do ordain, that all manner of Customs and Imposts levied since the Coronation of King Edward, Son of King Henry, be directly put out, and altogether extinguished for ever, notwithstanding the Charter which the said King Edward made to the Merchants Aliens, because the same was made contrary to the Great Charter and the Franchise of the City of London, and without the assent of the Baronage . . .

Repeated attempts, 1311–22, to enforce the Ordinances thus favored London's interests. Even so, in 1319 Edward, wanting much Gascon wine in view of the war with the Scots, granted the Gascons temporary right to sell in gross to native or alien, and in December 1320 confirmed the privilege without time limit. With the repeal of the Ordinances in 1322, the *new customs* were restored. The same year the king suspended London's mayoralty which was not fully restored until December 1326. It was this matter of the *new customs,* together with various political grievances, which brought the citizens so warmly to espouse the cause of the queen and led to the riotous disturbances in the city, culminating in the murder of Bishop Stapleton, treasurer and chancellor of the Exchequer.

On the vexed question of exemption from tallage, the Londoners apparently tried from time to time to claim a "liberty" which no king had actually recognized. A tallage was fixed in amount by the king's justices

---

[12] *Ibid.,* pp. 260–61, for specific examples.
[13] For the details of the dispute in this reign and the next see Sargeant, "The Wine Trade with Gascony" in Unwin's *Finance and Trade,* pp. 257–311.

and "assessed by them on individual citizens who were subject to direct distraint by agents of the Crown." London preferred the aid which was voluntary, the amount named by the citizens, assessed, collected, and paid over by them. The Articles of the Barons had not asked abolition of tallage, but merely that neither tallage nor aid be levied without the consent of those so burdened. McKechnie believes that the dropping of the word tallage from chapter 12 of the Great Charter, far from indicating that the Londoners were subject to aids only, gave the king a free hand to tallage at will. Royal practice after 1215 seems to bear out this view.[14]

As late as 1304 tallage was levied apparently without opposition, but in 1312 London resisted a similar demand by reverting to its old tactics of denying liability. It is significant that in so doing the citizens did not, and apparently could not, allege any specific grant or precedent as they did for other liberties, but had to fall back on general confirmations including that of Magna Carta chapter 9. Mayor, alderman, and sheriffs, called before the king's council and informed of the impending tallage, asked leave to consult the commonalty:

After consultation, the Mayor, Aldermen, &c. came and said that although the King could tallage his demesne cities and boroughs at will, they of the City of London, as they understood, were not subject to tallage, inasmuch as they enjoyed by charter all franchises, &c. which their ancestors enjoyed in the time of King Henry I., and since that day they had been quit of all tallages. Moreover, the great charter of liberties of England allowed the citizens all their ancient franchises and free customs, and inasmuch as they were of old so free as not to have been customarily tallaged in manner aforesaid, they ask that they may not be now so tallaged, if it please the king.[15]

While they did not receive recognition of the claim, they were respited until the next parliament by a grant of one thousand pounds. But the parliament which was to have settled the question of their liability, meeting at York, September 1314, was too far away and too busy with Scottish affairs. The king sent another set of tallagers, and again the Londoners bought themselves off, this time for six hundred marks. With that the matter was apparently dropped, leaving a practical if not a theoretical victory with London. An end to tallage was due, not to Magna Carta or to any fancied liberties of London, but rather to the development of the special aid into the parliamentary grant, the tax on movables. Tallage practically ceased in

[14] See McKechnie's whole discussion, pp. 234–39. Although ca. 12 was omitted from all reissues of the Charter, Henry III and his son usually asked consent in levying the special "gracious aid" from the country at large. Pressure was sometimes brought upon London in setting the amount of the "voluntary" gift desired. These kings both tallaged their demesne towns. In 1255 Henry III demanded three thousand marks' tallage of the Londoners. The latter flatly denied liability to tallage and offered an aid. Entries in Exchequer and Chancery rolls proved the contrary, and the citizens had to submit.

[15] *Cal. Letter Books*, D, 305–7; *Parl. Writs*, Vol. II, pt. ii, p. 84 (app.).

1332 when Edward III accepted a tenth and fifteenth granted by the September parliament of that year, as a substitute, and recalled the letters for the collection of tallage which he had issued the previous June. Already by his first charter to London, the king had granted the citizens the privilege of being taxed according to county, not borough, ratings, and had given the long-coveted recognition of exemption from other forms of imposition.[16]

Most jealously guarded among "liberties" connected with self-government was the privilege that exempted the citizens from pleading outside the walls except in pleas affecting outside tenures.[17] Pendrill cites the instance of a citizen (1299) who incurred the heavy penalty of loss of the freedom of the city for impleading a fellow citizen in the Court of the Steward and Marshal, a dangerous "precedent." Here again the proximity of the court at Westminster was a disadvantage. With increasing sojourns of the king there, steward and marshal were common offenders. They attached citizens to appear before them in pleas of trespass committed within the city. On a visit of royal officials to the Guildhall (1312)[18] this and other grievances were rehearsed by the recorder as *contra magnam cartam et contra libertatem nostram per cartas progenitorum regum Anglie confirmatas.* The citizens were told to come to Westminster next day. Meanwhile a riot occurred in the city and when the mayor presented himself, it was blame, not redress, that was forthcoming.

To the parliament of 1315 a similar complaint was presented on behalf of two London citizens. They were released on bail, pending consideration of their case *coram rege.* Meanwhile a writ to the offending officials confirmed the city's privilege as granted by their charter, confirmed by Magna Carta, and this in turn by the New Ordinances.[19] A copy of this writ was treasured by the citizens along with their charters. They used it to good effect on behalf of a certain William the Fleming, armorer of London, attached in a plea of trespass within the verge.[20] But there was no finality about such proceedings. Eternal vigilance was required. At the York parlia-

---

[16] *Liber Albus,* pp. 146–47: "quod cives Londoniarum, in auxiliis, concessionibus, et contributionibus, taxentur et contribuant cum communitate regni, sicut homines comitatuum et non sicut homines civitatum et burgorum; et quod de omnibus aliis tallagiis sint quieti." This meant not only a lower rate (fifteenth instead of tenth) but also more exemptions. In the counties persons with less than ten shillings paid nothing, while in the boroughs only those with less than six shillings were exempt.

[17] First granted in Henry I's charter to London: "Item quod cives Londoniarum non placitabunt extra muros civitatis de ullo placito." Henry II's adds "excepto de tenuris exterioribus"; and Richard I's, exceptis monetariis et ministris Regis." *Liber Albus,* pp. 128, 130, 131. Similarly in the charters of John, Henry III, Edward I, Edward III, and Richard II, pp. 132, 135, 139, 148, 154.

[18] September 20, to ask security for the citizens' loyalty to the king. *Annales Londonienses,* I, 216.

[19] *Liber Albus,* pp. 478–79.

[20] The claim was allowed and the plaintiff directed to prosecute her case: "coram Baillivis dictae civitatis, et infra muros ejusdem, juxta tenorem dictorum chartae et brevis." *Rot. Parl.* I, 300–2.

ment (12 Edward II) the citizens are again complaining of attachments and amercements by the steward and marshal. Proof had to be produced all over again. As London's representatives did not have the "evidence" with them the matter was postponed.[21]

Certain matters, such as escheats and appeals of death, could be dealt with only by the justices itinerant at their periodic iters in the Tower, not by the royal courts at Westminster. Why the citizens should have insisted on this as a privilege is not apparent at first thought. An iter at the Tower was as burdensome and costly as those throughout the shires, and the Londoners could not flee to the woods as the people of Cornwall were said once to have done. The justices amerced for errors great or small since their last visit, and it was necessary for the citizens to go through the laborious process of proving their liberties one by one.[22] But delay had its advantages. Iters were infrequent (at intervals of seven years or longer), and the citizens were acting in a somewhat collective capacity, representing the corporation.[23] In 1312, for instance, in a case involving property in London claimed by the king as an escheat on outlawry for felony, the mayor and "commonalty" produced their *inspeximus* (Edward I's):

They further say that it was granted to the same citizens by the Great Charter of the Liberties of England, that they should have all their ancient liberties and customs, unimpaired, and that the custom of the City is that such pleas of escheats of tenements within the liberty of the City be pleaded before the Justices Itinerant at the Tower, and not elsewhere.[24]

The parties were finally released *sine die*, not on the basis of London's "liberty," but because a jury testified that the alleged outlawry had not taken place.

Persons appealed of a death in the city were allowed to find sureties for appearance at the next iter. This custom was defended at about the same time as the above (6 Edward II). When a certain widow appealed two citizens for the death of her husband, the attempt of royal officials to bring the case *coram rege* was resisted, first by one of the appellees and eventually

---

[21] For consideration by some of the council. Shortly we find the citizens petitioning again, quoting the king's recent *supersedeas* to Exchequer officials as to the amercements, and complaining that no action had been taken.

Cole's Documents, p. 31. The original petitions in French, Ancient Petitions File 59, no. 2927; the second complaining of no redress, Ancient Petitions File 120, no. 5973. The first begins with the characteristic appeal to Magna Carta: "A nostre Seigneur le Roi et a son counseil monstrent le meire e le Communalte de la Cite de Loundres qe come en la grante chartre soit contenu qe la dite Cite eit totes ses aunciens custumes fraunchises et fraunches custumes. Et en les chartres des Rois Dengleterre faites as Citeins de la dite Citee par nostre seigneur le Roi Edward qe mort est confermez soit contenu qe nul des ditz Citeins pleide hors des mures de la dite Citee de nul plee horspris pletz de tenure foreins forsqe moneoures et ministres le Roi. Et en les ordinaunces soit contenu qe la grant chartre soit garde en toutz ses pointz."

[22] Pendrill, *London Life*, pp. 226, 252.

[23] For the advantage of delay, see the episode described below, note 26.

[24] *Cal. Letter Books*, D, pp. 289–90; and more fully, *coram rege* roll 208, m.11d.

by the city officials. Mayor and aldermen persistently denied receipt of the king's writ and even the command to appear to certify their custom. Finally on the third summons they did appear and made a comprehensive certification of their liberties in regard to crown pleas.[25]

No array of charters, however imposing, saved London from the extreme penalty of being occasionally "taken into the king's hands." This meant suspension of the rights of self-government as exercised by mayor and aldermen, and the substitution of a royal agent as governor. The most notable instance in the thirteenth century had been that suffered under Edward I, 1285 to 1298. During the greater part of Edward II's reign, the Londoners, in spite of Lancastrian sympathies, politicly kept the king's favor. On February 23, 1321, however, the city was taken into the king's hands. In May the citizens were again permitted to elect a mayor but with limitations on the restored mayoralty. Full restoration of their liberties came only November 6, 1326, through Isabella and Mortimer.[26]

As compared with the reigns which preceded and followed it, that of Edward III was one of moderation and accommodation. Just as the government itself was never "put into commission" nor the king faced with actual revolt, so London was never "taken into the king's hands." The reign began auspiciously with new chartered rights: the city would not be taken into the king's hands because of personal misdemeanors by its officials, nor need formal proof of all liberties be proffered at the iters.[27]

In 1328 the exemption of London juries from attaint was successfully maintained by a characteristic appeal to the Great Charter, and this in spite of a recent statute. It was argued that the liberties and free customs of the city used from ancient time are not altered or infringed by a statute unless express mention be made therein.[28]

[25] They "deny having received the writ, and as to certifying the King on the franchise and custom aforesaid, they cite the Charter granted to the City anno 27 Edward I., and the Great Charter of liberties of England which confirmed to the City all its ancient liberties and customs. Thereupon the King sent a 'bill' under the Great Seal to Roger le Brabazon and his fellow-justices to the effect that the citizens should be allowed to enjoy all their ancient privileges." The widow was left to prosecute her suit at the next iter. *Cal. Letter Books,* E, 34–36.

[26] *Cal. Letter Books,* E, vii, ix–x, xviii, xix–xx, 155. The alleged cause of the seizure was that justices at the Tower had discovered that John de Gisors, while mayor in 1314, had, under bribe, bestowed the freedom of the city on one appealed of felony, antedating the admission so that he might avail himself of the citizen's privilege of being replevied until the next iter!

[27] "Item, quod libertas civitatis Londoniarum non capiatur in manum Domini Regis pro aliqua personali transgressione, vel judicio personali alicujus ministri ejusdem civitatis; nec quod Custos in eadem ea occasione deputetur." *Liber Albus,* p. 147.

"Better still, Edward IV granted a charter by which, if any of their liberties were called in question in any court of the King, it should be sufficient proof of such liberty if the Mayor and aldermen, by the mouth of their Recorder, pronounced it to be good and true." Pendrill, *London Life,* p. 252.

[28] The statute (1 Ed. III, ca. 6) provided for "an attaint as well upon the Principal, as upon the Damages, in Trespass." *S. R.* I, 253.

The city occasionally suffered the king's indignation if not his wrath. When Edward, angered because of inadequate war supplies, returned unexpectedly from the continent (November 30, 1340) to arrest scapegoat ministers and to appoint commissioners to check up on tax collectors and other delinquents, London was not excepted. The brothers William and Richard Pole, financiers, and the merchant John Pulteney were arrested and imprisoned. A special commission was to sit at the Guildhall "to inquire into the misdoings of the King's ministers and others during the King's absence abroad." But when, a few days later, the appointed justices ordered London's sheriffs to summon twenty-four men from each ward to appear before them at the Guildhall, the commission was challenged through the recorder. Eventually, at the king's orders, there was substituted an iter at the Tower. There the justices sat March 5 to 17, were twice adjourned owing to the meeting of the April parliament. By letters patent of June 3, the citizens were released from the iter and, though promised only the usual seven-year respite, were never subjected to another. London's challenge of the commission does not cite Magna Carta,[29] but the city's liberties had been linked with the Charter directly in Archbishop Stratford's sentence of excommunication (which quotes chapter 9) and indirectly in the short-lived statute of 15 Edward III.

A modified but no less resented method of disciplining London officialdom appeared in a statute of 28 Edward III, chapter 10. Failure of city officials to correct misgovernment was to entail at the first default one thousand marks to the king; at the second default, two thousand marks; and only at the third was the city to be taken into the king's hands. What particularly aroused the citizens was the authorization of inquests by "People of foreign counties, that is to say, of Kent, Essex, Sussex, Hertford, Buckingham, and Berks, as well at the King's Suit as others that will complain." A petition of protest was immediately presented to the king but apparently without results, as it was repeated more emphatically in 1357:

Also show the said good folk that whereas it is recorded in the Great Charter that the said City should have its franchises and customs, it had lately been

The king's attorney insisted that every liberty must be proved in the affirmative by showing actual use, and not by nonuser, but Stace (he who had applied for the jury) could not show that any attaint had ever been taken in the city. *Cal. Letter Books*, E, xxviii.

[29] *Cal. Letter Books*, F, 59–61, compared with manuscript of the same. The iter was challenged by the recorder, "on the ground that the Commission was contrary to the City's franchise, which allowed no Justices to sit within the liberty of the City except at the Tower when an *Iter* was being held, and at Neugate for gaol delivery, and at St. Martin le Grand for correcting errors and taking inquisitions. And the Mayor, Aldermen and Commonalty asked that the said franchise might be allowed them, as allowed beyond the memory of man." See also *Cal. Pat. Rolls*, 1340–43, p. 224. According to Tout, *Chapters*, III, 130–31, release of the iter meant that William Pole and others remained in prison without trial and were released only in 1342.

decreed that matters done in London should be tried by men of foreign counties, to the derogation of the said franchises, whereby the good folk of the
said City refuse to become Mayor, Aldermen or other officer within the same,
and the more substantial of them refuse to live or traffic therein, and others
refuse to come to the City.[30]

No redress was secured. This ordinance was still an object of protest as
late as 1 Henry IV.

Conflicting Interests: London and Alien Merchants

*All merchants unless publicly prohibited beforehand shall have safe and
secure exit from England and entry to England, with the right to tarry
there and to move about as well by land as by water, for buying and selling
by the ancient and right customs, quit from all evil tolls, except (in time of
war) such merchants as are of the land at war with us. And if such are
found in our land at the beginning of the war, they shall be detained,
without injury to their bodies or goods, until information be received by us,
or by our chief justiciar, how the merchants of our land found in the land
at war with us are treated; and if our men are safe there, the others shall be
safe in our land.*   (MAGNA CARTA CA. 30)

CHAPTER 30 (John 41), in its original intent, contained little comfort for
English merchants. In John's day, truly, if not in James I's, as the crown
lawyers then sought to maintain, the control of commerce was vested in the
king. Foreign merchants were dependent on royal favor for the privilege
of trading and even for personal safety. "No alien could enter England or
leave it, nor take up his abode in any town, nor move from place to place,
nor buy and sell, without paying heavy tolls to the king. . . . John had
increased the frequency and amount of such exactions, to the detriment
alike of foreign traders and their customers." [31]

Magna Carta benefited foreign traders and their English customers, the
wealthy consumer class of rich nobles and ecclesiastics, by conferring on
alien merchants three privileges: (1) safe conduct (protection of their persons and goods); (2) liberty to buy and sell in time of peace; (3) a confirmation of the ancient stereotyped rates of customs. These rules applied
to aliens—foreign traders from friendly states—and not to native traders.
In fact, aliens such as the Gascons, Italians, Flemish, and Hanse merchants
continued to monopolize the carrying trade between England and the

---

[30] The statute reads: "Because that the Errors, Defaults, and Misprisions which be notoriously used in the City of London, for Default of good Governance of the Mayor, of the
Sheriffs, and the Aldermen, cannot be enquired nor found by People of the same City; it is
ordained and established . . ." S. R. I, 346–47. The measure was to extend to other cities
and boroughs too. *Cal. Letter Books*, G, 86. For the first petition we must rely on the original
manuscript Letter Book, G, f19b (*Cal. Letter Books*, G, 53, omits the reference to Magna Carta).
[31] McKechnie, p. 399.

continent for 150 years after 1215. Home traders were not consenting parties and indeed this provision, as used by successive monarchs, conflicted with the various local charters confirmed to London and other towns by chapter 9, especially their retail monopoly and the principle that "foreigners must be kept at the wharf-head!" In the reissues of the Charter, the king's discretionary power was emphasized by insertion of the clause "unless publicly prohibited beforehand" (*Omnes mercatores nisi publice antea prohibiti fuerint*).[32]

That alien merchants were aware of chapter 30 and its value to them is apparent from an episode of 1320, odd as it seems to hear an appeal to the Charter from men bearing the names of Bonus Philippi, Dinus Forcetti, and Manenttus Francisci! A fixed obligatory staple at St. Omer had been established in 1313. The Bardi and other aliens less privileged than the Gascons preferred free export from England subject only to paying the customs. Before a full council at Westminster, including king, ministers, justices of both benches, barons of the Exchequer, and others, April 13, 1320, the Bardi

asserted that they ought not to be restricted to the said staple, saying that they never consented that the aforesaid charter (establishing the staple at St. Omer) should be obtained from the king, and that they ought not to be restricted by it to go with their wool or wool-fells to that staple . . . and that it is contained in Magna Carta that all merchants may come into the realm, stay therein and return thence safely and securely with their goods upon paying the due and accustomed customs.

But arguments of native merchants, including the diplomatic suggestion that by means of this staple "the king can constrain the men of the aforesaid lands by whom his Scotch enemies are cherished," carried the day with king and council.[33]

Every student of this period is familiar with the policy of Edward III. Besides the well-established *antiqua custuma* and the *new customs,* increases known as "subsidies" and eventually as "tunnage and poundage" were occasionally imposed by the crown and reluctantly sanctioned by parliaments. Though usually accompanied with a proviso against constituting a precedent for the future, by 1371 such increased rates were accepted as justifiable. In the reign of James I the crown lawyers used these increases as evidence of the king's right to impose. The parliamentary lawyers emphasized the restrictive clauses, as well as drawing inferences from the mere fact that parliament was consulted at all.

[32] *Ibid.,* p. 404: "This was a material alteration, the effect of which was to restore to the King full discretionary authority over foreign trade, since he had only to issue a general proclamation, and then to accept fines for granting exemption from its operation."

[33] *Cal. Close Rolls,* 1318–23, pp. 234–35; *Parl. Writs,* Vol. II, pt. ii, pp. 217–18.

Magna Carta chapter 30 and two fourteenth-century statutes based on it were variously interpreted by the two sides. In the 1610 debates Hakewill maintained correctly that these statutes, in confirming and expanding the clause of Magna Carta, specifically included denizens as well as aliens. But neither Hakewill nor his opponents understood their real import or the character of the fourteenth-century conflict of interest between native and alien merchants. The first, while *verbo in verbis* confirming free trade to all "merchants strangers and privy," could have advantaged but few of the latter. The second was a short-lived relief to London and other cities from the damaging effects of the Statute of York which especially favored the Gascon wine merchants.[34] It was this last as re-enacted in 1351 and enforced until 1376 that so aggravated the citizens of London and led them to appeal repeatedly to their own local charters supported by Magna Carta chapter 9, for it placed strangers and denizens on an equality in all branches of trade, retail as well as wholesale, brushing aside local franchises with an insidious *non obstante* clause. When the measure was re-enacted in 1351 it was explicitly applied to London.

In spite of the seeming futility of their appeals, the citizens never lost faith in the Great Charter. Chapter 9 was cited again in the letters patent[35] which gave them some fourteen years respite (1337–51) and repeatedly in petitions—eight of them between 1351 and 1376. Naturally the city officials followed somewhat the same formula in each instance, but with variations and amplifications.[36] The petition of 1368 (probably prompted by writs to

[34] 2 Ed. III, ca. 9 (*S. R.* I, 259): "Item, It is enacted, That the Staples beyond the Sea and on this Side, ordained by Kings in Times past, and the Pains thereupon provided, shall cease; and that all Merchants Strangers and privy may go and come with their Merchandises into England, after the Tenor of the Great Charter; and that Writs thereupon shall be sent to all Sheriffs of England, and to Mayors and Bailiffs of good Towns, where need shall require."

14 Ed. III, stat. 2, ca. 2 (*S. R.* I, 290): "Item, where it is contained in the Great Charter, That all Merchants shall have safe and sure conduct to go out of our Realm of England, and to come and abide, and . . . so always, that Franchises and free Customs reasonably granted by us and our Ancestors to the City of London, and other Cities, Boroughs, and good Towns of our Realm of England, be to them saved."

According to Sargeant ("The Wine Trade in Gascony" in Unwin's *Finance and Trade*), the Statute of York was the result of the withdrawal of the Gascon traders from the country owing to violence against them in Bristol and London, 1334, and to the king's desire for increased customs.

S. R. I, 270–71. It granted to "all Merchants, Strangers and Denizens" the right to sell to "what Persons it shall please them, as well to Foreigners as Denizens," save only the king's enemies, "Corn, Wines, Aver de pois, Flesh, Fish and all other Livings and Victuals . . . Woolls, Clothes, Wares, Merchandises, and all other Things vendible," in cities, boroughs, vills, ports, etc., within liberties or without. "Notwithstanding Charters of Franchise granted to them to the contrary, nor Usage, nor custom, nor Judgement given upon their Charters, Usages or Customs that they can alledge."

[35] Letters patent, March 26, 1337 (*Cal. Pat. Rolls*, 1334–38, p. 460).

[36] 1351, 1352, 1355–56, 1365, 1368, 1372. As summarized in the calendars, four of these do not cite Magna Carta, but comparison with the manuscript Letter Books indicates that the Charter was cited in every instance. *Cal. Letter Books*, F, 229, 242–43; G, 14–15, 52, 185, 206; and the corresponding manuscript Letter Books.

Those of 1368 and 1372 were presented in parliament, *Rot. Parl.* II, 296, no. 16; 314, no. 46. The first included other cities and boroughs.

the sheriffs enjoining strict observance of the statute) spoke for other cities and towns as well as London. That of 1372 argued that the trade of native merchants was *a grant eyde & maytenance de la dite Citee, sustenance & encresce de Navie de la dite terre.* This elicited the temporary concession that only freemen of London might sell victuals at retail, and this until the next parliament, *sur condition q'il soit bien reule & governee en les meen temps a commune profit: Et est l'entention du Roi, qe nul prejudice soit fait as Aliens q'ont Franchises par chartres des Rois.*

In the last decades of the century, economic issues were complicated by a division of interests within London itself. Victuallers within the city and "of the freedom," subject to many civic burdens, felt that outsiders who escaped these should be restricted. Non-victuallers such as the goldsmiths, drapers, and saddlers favored a cheap and continuous supply of food brought by outside grocers, butchers, and fishmongers, and accused their opponents of aiming to raise prices to their own profit.[37] The rising tide of discontent in the last years of Edward III was felt throughout the country. Petitions in the parliaments of 1373 and 1376 were couched in broad terms to cover the interests of all cities and boroughs. The first asks confirmation of local liberties notwithstanding statutes to the contrary, and quotes chapter 9. The second is combined with a request for confirmation of the Charters, and accompanied with another dealing specifically with the grievance as to aliens. They were charged with acting as brokers and retailers. "They had also become householders, and as such were accused of harbouring spies, while they were also responsible, it was believed, for the impairing of the navy." [38]

Some satisfaction was obtained by Richard II's first charter to London, only to be offset next year by a modified confirmation of 9 and 25 Edward III. At last in 1383 by Richard's second charter, London secured a confirmation of its liberties, plus a *non obstante* clause, this time in its own favor, explicitly exempting the city from the provisions of the hated Statute of York. The government's policy was not consistent in this reign or the next.[39] Nevertheless this charter seems to have rather supplanted Magna Carta in the citizens' esteem as the chief bulwark of their liberties. Because it was granted in parliament it came to be reputed and called a statute (7 Richard II). Norton says of it:

[37] For the details of this protracted conflict see Pendrill, *London Life,* chap. v.

[38] *Rot. Parl.* II, 318, no. 16; 331, no. 52. That of 1373, from "ses poveres liges Communes des Citees & des Burghs deinz le Roialme d'Engleterre," quotes: "desicome en la Graunt Chartre soit contenuz, Qe la Citee de Loundres eit toutz ses Fraunchises, & ces auncienz Custumes; Et qe toutz autres Citeez & Burghs, & Villes, & Barons des Cynk Portz, eient toutz lour Fraunchises & fraunks Custumes deblemez." The response is grudging: "monstront en especial queles Franchises lour sont tolues, & reson serra fait." Sargeant, "The Wine Trade in Gascony," in Unwin's *Finance and Trade,* p. 310.

[39] See *S. R.* II, 53–54, 153–54; *Rot. Parl.* III, 613; *Cal. Letter Books,* I, 69; Sargeant, pp. 310–11.

Restoration of the ancient Thoroughfare from Westminster to London

114

This charter is continually spoken of in the older law authorities, and often referred to in records, as the grand charter of confirmation of all the City liberties, franchises, and customs. It is a transcript, *verbatim*, of the last charter, confirming by *inspeximus* that and all the preceding charters recited or referred to in it. The grant was made in parliament, as the last was; and from the date we may conjecture that it was intended as a ratification of the former charter by the king, on attaining an age of greater discretion and in deference to the services of the citizens and their celebrated mayor Walworth on the occasion of Tyler's rebellion.[40]

London suffered from the financial exactions of Richard II. One chronicler estimates the merchants' losses by "selyng of blank chartres." [41] In 1392 the king's displeasure was incurred by the refusal of a £1000 loan. Accounts vary. According to one, the merchants went so far as to beat a man who offered to lend the sum to the king. Richard deposed and imprisoned mayor and sheriffs, appointing a warden and royal sheriffs in their place. A commission composed of the dukes of York and Gloucester was to inquire into alleged misgovernment in the city. The citizens finally succeeded in ransoming their liberties for ten thousand pounds. Stow, in his *Annals,* describes how the principal citizens met the king and queen at Wandesworth "where in most lowly wise they submitted themselves unto his grace," and requested him "to ride through his Chamber of London." The streets of the city "were hanged with cloth of golde, silver, and silke, the conduite in Chepe ran with red and white wine." Their majesties were presented with many costly gifts, "also golde in coyne, precious stones and jewels, so rich, excellent, and beautifull, that the value and price might not wel be esteemed, and so the Citizens recovered their ancient customs and liberties." [42]

This was a profitable transaction for the king, but one which contributed to bring the Londoners out in full force to welcome Henry of Lancaster a few years later. How they must have relished the contrast now presented by their erstwhile oppressor. "Lancaster forced him to enter the capital riding on a little hackney and robed in a plain black gown; he was greeted with hoots and insults, while the victor was welcomed with royal honours." [43] In Henry's first parliament they sought protection for the future

---

[40] The clause reads, "Quod cives Londoniarum habeant omnes libertates et liberas consuetudines suas illaesas, non obstante statuto edito apud Eboracum anno Regis Edwardi Tertii nono."

For the charter, see *Liber Albus,* I, 155–62, and Norton, *The City of London,* pp. 367–71. In the Year Book case described above, pp. 195–96, London uses both Magna Carta and 7 Rich. II. For later practice, see below, pp. 270–72.

[41] *Chronicle of London* (Nicholas, editor), p. 83. See also *Gregory's Chronicle,* pp. 98–101, (C. S.).

[42] Quoted by the editor, Thomas Wright, in notes on *Richard de Maidston's Poem,* pp. 58–59 (C. S.).

[43] Oman, *Political History of England,* p. 150.

in an elaborate petition which reminds the king that the statute of 28 Edward III, chapter 10,[44] conflicted with the city's charters, and especially with Edward III's promise that no forfeiture of liberties would be incurred for individual misconduct of a citizen. The petition concludes: *considerantz auxi, qe le dit Estatut est expressement fait encontre la tenure & effect de la Grande Chartre.*[45] Although the statute was only slightly modified at this time, London was not again taken into the king's hands until the famous *quo warranto* case of 1683. According to Norton, Richard II was the last to seize the city for individual offences of the magistrates or others. Charles II's forfeiture was grounded on corporate acts of the whole body of citizens.

Conflicting Interests: London and Other English Towns

OTHER cities and boroughs made no such use of Magna Carta as did London. One may venture an explanation as follows. Many were young as urban communities. Their own charters, the most comprehensive and valuable of them, were granted later than London's, later indeed than Magna Carta. They were not involved in the same degree in the dramatic events of 1215. There were, to be sure, some older communities—Norwich, Northampton, and Nottingham, Hereford, and Great Yarmouth[46]—which, like London, had a series of charters going back to the reign of John or before, and confirmed by *inspeximi* of later kings, sometimes with grants

[44] Cf. above, p. 109. They evidently thought that Richard's action was in line with this act.

[45] *Rot. Parl.* III, 442–43. Ancient Petition 1068. In line with the royal reply, 1 Hen. IV, ca. 15, rehearses the statute and repeals the specific penalties imposed on mayor, sheriffs, and so on, for neglecting to redress errors and misprisions, and leaves penalties discretionary. *S. R.* II, 117–18. Norton, *The City of London*, p. 118.

[46] These negative conclusions are based on the following sources: in manuscript, scores of the Ancient Petitions preserved in the Public Record Office (which in view of their negative interest, it has been thought hardly worth while to list here by number); in print, the parliament rolls, and the borough records of Hereford, Leicester, Northampton, and Nottingham (listed in bibliography); *inspeximi* of borough charters in the charter rolls. Some collections, such as the *Coventry Leet Book,* are not apt for the purpose in mind.

The *Records of the Borough of Northampton,* Vol. I, for instance, contains charters from Richard I on, with later *inspeximi.* Hereford's *Book of Customs* dates from the reign of Henry II. The city was "sold to itself" by Richard I, and received additional liberties or confirmations from John, Henry III, Edward I, II, and III (*inspeximi* of 1 and 5 Ed. III), Richard II, Henry IV, Edward IV, and even the Tudors and Stuarts. Only as late as the reign of Richard II was the city's "chief bailiff" permitted to take the title of mayor.

Charter Roll C 53/114 m.29 contains Edward III's *inspeximus* of Great Yarmouth's charters (Edward III confirming 7 Ed. II which in turn confirms Edward I's *inspeximus* of charter of Henry III and John).

Two of Henry III's *inspeximi,* quoted in Edward II's, do cite Magna Carta: For Scardeburgh, following a series of items each relating to a separate "liberty"—"and that the burgesses and any coming to the said borough shall not be vexed or troubled by anyone contrary to the liberties contained in the great charter made to the magnates and other free men of England."

For Gloucester, granting return of writs and that the bailiffs shall answer by their own hand at the Exchequer—"and that if the burgesses shall be amerced for any fault before the king or any of his justices, they shall be amerced according to the form of the great charter of the liberties of England; and that the burgesses through all the king's land and power shall have all their liberties and free customs . . . as fully as the king's citizens of London . . ." *Cal. Charter Rolls,* pp. 190, 201.

of additional liberties. Yet it is noticeable that *inspeximi* of these towns do not cite Magna Carta as do those of the Londoners. It is London, not Yarmouth, that cites Magna Carta in the famous interurban quarrel to be described below. Even the Cinque Ports are more inclined to rely on their comprehensive charter of Edward I than on chapter 9.

The very fact that chapter 9 favored London may have been a deterrent, for London's liberties and interests crossed and outweighed those of lesser communities. Many such throughout the kingdom possessed some of the same privileges as London, but

it was of no use for the King to give out new charters to provincial towns or to increase their existing rights, for the citizens of London would simply decline to admit them. In 1319 they refused to admit the charter of Colchester, merely permitting the merchants of that town to trade in London free of one toll only—murage. In the same way Edward II had granted a charter to Cambridge exempting their merchants from liability to pay not only murage, but other tolls in London known as pavage and pickage. In 1331, when these privileges were claimed, the Mayor and aldermen, after examining the charter in question, remitted murage only.[47]

Typical of intercity conflicts and rivalries was the protracted quarrel in the early years of Edward III's reign between Great Yarmouth on the one hand, and London, Norwich, Little Yarmouth, and Gorleston on the other. The men of Great Yarmouth, in King's Bench, accused certain individuals of these communities of infringing the charter granted them by Edward I and confirmed by Edward II. On behalf of the defendants it was claimed that this recent concession to Great Yarmouth contravened older chartered rights of theirs. The lusty fisher folk of Great Yarmouth had by force and violence denied their neighbors of Little Yarmouth and Gorleston their accustomed right of way through the port. They had prevented the Londoners from access to and use of their "houses" in Little Yarmouth and Gorleston where they and their ancestors, time out of mind, had been wont to dress and prepare fish, sell and buy, and had monopolized the fishing trade by violence and brokerage. But it is not Great Yarmouth, it is London who asks that the rival's charter be revoked since its operation weakens their own ancient liberties "against the tenor of Magna Carta etc. and the great damage and manifest prejudice of the same citizens." Again, following Yarmouth's detailed denial of the charges, the Londoners ask judgment, concluding with the emphatic "maxime cum in magna carta de libertatibus Anglie contingatur quod civitas London' habeat libertates et liberas consuetudines antiquas illesas etc." True, Little Yarmouth and Gorleston cite the Charter in their petition, inspired perhaps by the exam-

[47] Pendrill, *London Life*, p. 261.

ple of their greater fellow-sufferer, or the influence of their lord John, Earl of Brittany.[48]

Entries in the patent rolls constitute a telling commentary on the conflict of urban liberties and the complexity of interurban relations.[49] In April of 1334 a commission was appointed as a result of complaints in parliament of even greater outrages by the men of Great Yarmouth.[50] Again early in Richard's reign these vigorous and turbulent fisher folk were exercising chartered rights (including a recent grant of 31 Edward III) to the detriment of others.[51]

"*Preterea volumus et concedimus quod omnes alie civitates, et burgi, et ville, et barones de quinque portubus, et omnes portus, habeant omnes libertates et liberas consuetudines suas."* As was befitting "their wealth, their situation and their fleet," the Cinque Ports received specific mention in the reissues of Magna Carta. But it was the very comprehensive charter of Edward I which constituted the basis for their "liberties" in the later Middle Ages and even in the Tudor and Stuart periods. It was this which was confirmed reign after reign, culminating in the *inspeximus* of Queen Elizabeth: "all the former are but preambles of other Kings and Queens of

---

[48] The evidence seems to begin with Michaelmas term 1 Ed. III. The case was postponed from term to term, and finally referred to the council. *Coram rege* roll 270, m.38; 271, m.101 and 104; 274; 275, m.94. File 164, Ancient Petition 8172, undated, seems to fit this time and episode. It is a good example of the easy casual French versions of the Charter, in its complaint that Great Yarmouth's charter operates not only to London's "destruction," but to the king's "disinheritance," and "encountre la graunt chartre qe veut voloms e grauntoms qe touz nos cites bourgs et villes eient lour fraunchises e lour usages."

[49] *Cal. Pat. Rolls*, 1330–34, p. 124 (1331). Ratification by a committee of the council of an attempted solution of the dispute as follows: "That the port of Yarmouth is the only port there and belongs to the town of Great Yarmouth for ever. That ships entering the port or river of Yarmouth with cargoes whereon customs ought to be levied by the king's customers are to come to Great Yarmouth there to pay such customs but ships belonging to Little Yarmouth and Gorleston may then discharge their cargoes at those towns and shall not be compelled to pay any dues to the burgesses of Great Yarmouth against their will, except in the case of such of their ships as may be unloaded at Great Yarmouth. That ships entering the port or river laden with herrings or other fish or cargoes whereon no customs are due to the king shall be discharged at Great Yarmouth only, unless such ships belong to Little Yarmouth or Gorleston, in which case they may discharge their cargoes where they will without let by the burgesses of Great Yarmouth, provided that ships of others be not claimed as belonging to Little Yarmouth or Gorleston on pain of forfeiture of such with their cargoes to the king. And that neither party be now molested by reason of any cause depending in any of the king's courts touching the aforesaid disputes, saving always any right of the citizens of London, of Norwich, the barons of the Cinque Ports or others. Any infringement of the foregoing ordinances by either party is to be punishable by fine of 100 l." And cf. *ibid.*, p. 317, for a further definition by letters patent of July 10, 1332.

[50] The Londoners petition in the same vein as before. File 59, Ancient Petition 2901. (Cf. File 133, Ancient Petition 5607.)
For individual petitions also citing Magna Carta, see File 59, Ancient Petitions 2902–2907. These were in line with the government's instructions that individual Londoners sue individual Yarmouthers before commissioners for the trespasses complained of.

[51] As evidenced "on complaint by the commons of Norfolk and Suffolk that notwithstanding that in the parliament of Northampton the statute was passed (and in that of Gloucester confirmed) that grants by charters or letters patent contrary to statutes of general utility should be of none effect, yet the burgesses of Great Yarmouth pleading their charter, confirmed and renewed by the king . . ." *Cal. Pat. Rolls*, 1377–81, p. 633.

this land," as the contemporary copyist quaintly puts it. There were valuable additional grants, for instance those conferred by Edward IV, and even Charles II. The *inspeximus* of Edward IV, oddly enough, is the only one which notes the confirmation of the liberties of the Cinque Ports by Magna Carta, a clause based on the "humble petition of the said barons, and honest men of the Cinque Ports aforesaid." [52] As we shall see, when the infringements of certain liberties of the Cinque Ports were aired in parliament, it was not the representatives of the ports, but Sir Edward Coke, who linked them to Magna Carta chapter 9.

Yet occasionally the Great Charter was cited on behalf of one or other of the five ports.[53] As we have seen, the men of Sandwich in a parliamentary petition of 1415 used their own paraphrase and application of chapter 29. In 1446 Hastings secured the revocation of letters patent which had granted Thomas Stoughton "the king's purveyor of sea-fish" the office of baillage of Hastings. One John Tamworth made known to the king that

"the said town is one of the Cinque Ports, whereof the barons and men have enjoyed time out of mind divers liberties by reason of the shipping which they ought and are wont to prepare yearly for the king, . . ."; that the custom of the town was to elect its bailiff by the commonalty assembled at the "Hundred-place" on Sunday three weeks after Easter, and that the said John was thus duly elected.

In support of this and other chartered rights and liberties he quotes chapter 9 in full.[54]

Outside London and the Cinque Ports, appeals to chapter 9 are rare. There are a few, such as those of Little Yarmouth and Gorleston taking their cue from London, collective petitions of all cities and boroughs such

[52] For a contemporary manuscript copy of Queen Elizabeth's *inspeximus,* see Harl. MSS 306, no. 8, fol. 46. Charles II's *inspeximus* of Elizabeth's, and so on back to Edward I's, is in print with the title *The Great and Ancient Charter of the Cinque Ports and its Members, From the First Granted by King Ed. the 1st To the Last Charter Granted by King Charles the 2d. Printed from an Ancient Copy dated 1668. By C. Mate at the Shakespeare Office no. 9 Market Place, Dover.* Here, p. 21, the *inspeximus* of Edward IV, citing the Charter reads: "And we being certified by the humble Petition of the said Barons, and honest men of the Cinque-Ports aforesaid, and their Members, that notwithstanding, it is contained in the Magna Charta of the Liberties of England, (amongst other things) that the Barons of the Cinque-Ports may have all their Liberties and Free-Customs, yet they by reason of the ambiguity, obscurity, and doubtful meaning of certain Words, and general Terms contained in the Charters, Letters and Confirmations aforesaid, have been, and are at this time hindered from the enjoying of certain of their Liberties and Free-Customs, as also the Priviledges and Acquittances which they were wont freely, peaceably and quietly to enjoy in the Ports aforesaid . . ." For the original, 5 Ed. IV, in Latin (Charter Rolls C 53/194 m.32).

[53] Two such instances, naturally, appear late in Edward I's reign: Archbishop Winchelsea's backing of the men of Sandwich v. the Londoners (see above, p. 101) and ca. 7 of the *Articuli super cartas* forbidding the constable of Dover Castle to distrain the men of Dover to plead elsewhere or in other manner than provided by their charters—"according to the form of the charters which they have from kings concerning their ancient liberties confirmed by the great charter."

[54] *Cal. Pat. Rolls,* 1441–46, p. 427, which reads simply "in support whereof he cites Magna Carta," but the roll 462, m.33, quotes the chapter in full.

as that of 1376, and tenants on ancient demesne using the chapter to substantiate their peculiar "liberties" dating back to Domesday Book. Very likely there are others, which I have not spotted, like that of little Bloxham, in 1440, as appears in the calendar of patent rolls, an order to the

sheriffs and others to permit the men of the town of Bloxham to have all their ancient liberties and free customs, as they ought to have and as they and their ancestors have been reasonably used to have from time immemorial, in accordance with the Great Charter wherein it is contained amongst other things, that the city of London shall have all its liberties and customs, and all other cities boroughs and towns, and the barons of the Cinque Ports and all ports to have all their liberties and free customs.[55]

Obviously Magna Carta was no magic "open sesame" to civic liberties. If the king's interest and the king's income were too deeply involved, even London had perforce to yield. Still, on occasion, the Charter added substantial backing to successful claims. Certainly the citizens' perennial faith in it must have contributed to its fame and name. In the constitutional crises of Tudor and early Stuart periods, as we shall see, London played a no less vital, but rather different role.

[55] *Cal. Pat. Rolls,* 1436–41, p. 468. Such letters patent often reflect the language of a petition. For tenants on ancient demesne, see above, p. 48.

❋ CHAPTER V ❋

Magna Carta and Special Interests: The English Church

That the English Church shall be free, and shall have all her rights entire and her liberties inviolate. (MAGNA CARTA CA. I)

The Great Charter that Holy Church ought to uphold.

(PETITION FROM TENANTS OF BOCKING IN ESSEX)

No COMPLETE separate account of Magna Carta in its relations to the English church need be given here. The clergy were the literal, physical, and spiritual guardians of the Charter: they kept copies of it in their cathedral archives and contributed to its enforcement by their anathemas. Earlier chapters have shown the clergy as interested in confirmations of the Charter and as playing important roles in constitutional crises as did Archbishop Winchelsea in 1311 and Stratford in 1341. Provisions on purveyance and amercements were of value to individual "clerks," great and small, while bishops and abbots who held by barony also had an interest in some of the feudal clauses. Three topics, however, merit further treatment: (1) the extent to which the clergy still saw in chapter 1 the guarantee to the *Ecclesia Anglicana* of any and all specific "liberties"; (2) whether excommunication continued to be used as a means of enforcement; (3) exposition of the Charter in ecclesiastical constitutions and treatises.[1]

Liberties of the Church

IF THE English church were to seek in the Great Charter a defense against king and pope, it was upon the single clause quoted above that it must base its claims. Vague as it was, throughout the thirteenth century faith in its efficacy persisted. From time to time this, that, or the other particular power, privilege, or immunity was claimed as one of the *jura* or *libertates*

---

[1] This chapter is based on the evidence of parliament and statute rolls, chronicles, and especially Wilkins' *Concilia* (Vols. I-III), which contains many documents from the registers of Canterbury and York, and also selected bishops' registers in print. (See the Bibliography.) No attempt has been made to examine all the extant printed registers or any of the manuscript registers.

confirmed by the Charter. Again comprehensive lists of grievances—
gravamina—were drawn up in protest on the same grounds.[2]

As time went on, this very elasticity became an advantage to the crown
rather than to the church. Such general terms could not avail against the
policies of an Edward I who would be likely to expect from the clergy
the same definiteness, the actual parchment evidence of chartered rights,
which he demanded of the barons in his *quo warranto* proceedings. Nor
could they avail against the attitude of king and council in response to
certain articles of the clergy in the Lincoln parliament of 1316: "such
Things as be thought necessary for the King and the Commonwealth
ought not to be said to be prejudicial to the Liberty of the Church." [3]
In the fourteenth century the English clergy were subject to new financial
burdens. Annates became a regular source of papal revenue; crusading
tenths continued to be levied, the king sometimes sharing in these. Foreign
ecclesiastics were permanently established in England as papal collectors.
Appointment to bishoprics by direct papal nomination was not uncommon. Professor Tout has described the policy of "mutual accommodation"
between Edward II and the Gascon Pope Clement V, and his successor.
King and pope divided the spoils. In Clement's time the crown received
the most, in John XXII's the pope.[4]

Henry III had gloried in his role of vassal of the pope. Fourteenth-
century kings were not quite such obedient sons of "Holy Mother
Church." The lord and vassal relationship was formally repudiated in
1366 with parliamentary sanction. Some years before this, king and parliament had cooperated in placing on the statute roll the acts of *provisors*
and *praemunire,* though *provisions* continued to be tolerated by royal
connivance. The residence of the popes at Avignon further complicated relationships. Wycliff's advocacy of disendowment found supporters.
Through his influence heresy for the first time appeared in England.
With the activities of the Lollards and the extension of theories of dis-

[2] The *gravamina* drawn up in convocation at Merton, 1257, consist of some fifty items.
In six instances it is alleged that practices complained of are against the "liberty of the
Church." The document concludes, "Although our lord the king swore at his coronation to
preserve the rights and liberties granted to churches, and although he has confirmed them
in the beginning of the great charter, these are nevertheless, constantly attacked, disturbed,
and mutilated by his officers . . ."

[3] *Articuli cleri*, ca. 8; S. R. I, 172. "The King and his Ancestors since Time out of
Mind have used, That Clerks which are employed in his Service, during such Time as they
are in Service, shall not be compelled to keep Residence at their Benefices; and such
Things . . ."

[4] Tout, *Place of the Reign of Edward II in English History,* Chap. VI. Edward II secured
favors and dispensations which enabled him to reward his faithful clerk John Sandall with
numerous livings. About 1314 he held two dignities, eight prebendal stalls, ten rectories, and
received a salary of five hundred pounds as chancellor. He was Bishop of Winchester,
1316–18. John XXII secured for his clerk Rigaud, born at Assier (north of Cahors), advance-
ments in England culminating in the bishopric first of Lincoln, and then of Winchester. John
Sandall and Rigaud of Assier, *Winchester Registers* (1316–23), prefaces.

endowment to lay holdings, church and state, nobles and clergy rather drew together again, on the defensive. Still the voice of the *Ecclesia Anglicana* was not entirely silenced. As we shall see, one of the articles of charges on the deposition of Richard II alleged violation of a liberty of the church confirmed by Magna Carta, and at least three notable fifteenth-century archbishops—Arundel, Chicheley, and Stafford—made some use of the document.

Archbishop Winchelsea had been active in securing the *Confirmatio Cartarum*, 1297, and was appointed one of the Lords Ordainers. We may assume that he was responsible for the confirmation of the liberties of the church by chapter 1 of the Ordinances. His register gives evidence of considerable agitation by his clergy in provincial council shortly before, in 1309. Their *gravamina* include an emphatic reminder of clerical liberties as confirmed by the Great Charter of Henry III supported by the great excommunication.[5] In 1307 Ralph Baldock, Bishop of London, had used chapter 1 to secure from the king immunity of the local clergy from arrest by city officials.[6]

Nevertheless it was more effective to secure recognition of specific liberties or limitation of specific abuses from king in council or king in parliament, and thenceforth to cite them rather than the Charter. Such had been Westminster I, chapter 1, forbidding compulsory prises of clerical goods. This was formally recited and confirmed in 10 Edward II.[7] Such were the *Articuli cleri* approved in the Lincoln parliament of 1316, of which it was said that they had been presented in vain in many previous parliaments.[8] Such was the statute of 1340, though this act, perhaps due to Archbishop Stratford, begins with the characteristic "old fashioned" preamble:

> Edward, by the Grace of God, &c Greeting. Know Ye, that whereas in the first article of the Great Charter it is contained that the Church of England be free and have all her Rights entirely and Franchises not blemished and

[5] *Gravamina cleri in concilio provinciali Cantuar. proposita.* Wilkins, II, 314–15. This is followed by *gravamina antiqua in hoc concilio repetita*, with an item on purveyance which reads: "Item ministri domini regis capiunt equos, et carectas praelatorum, et aliorum virorum ecclesiasticorum ad faciend. cariagia contra libertatem ecclesiae, et seriem magnae chartae."

[6] Register of Ralph Baldock, pp. 154–56. "Royal writ forbidding the arrest of adulterous clergy in London," dated March 16, 1307, and followed by one in similar vein, January 2, 1313. Both begin "cum in magna carta de libertatibus ecclesie contineatur quod . . ."

[7] *De Statuto pro Clero inviolabiliter observand.* S. R. I, 175–76. Wilkins, II, 459, the same from the Register of Walter Reynolds. The same later in the century in William of Wykham's Register, Vol. II, pt. iii, p. 523.

[8] These regulate prohibitions to court christian, "distresses on the clergy," benefit of clergy ("the privilege of the church shall not be denied to a clerk becoming an approver"), sanctuary and abjuration, burdensome corodies and pensions, "the king's tenant excommunicate not privileged," examination of a parson as to fitness "belongeth to a spiritual judge"; and one on "free election to dignities of the Church" answered with a vague, "They shall be made free according to the form of Statutes and Ordinances." S. R. I, 171–74.

also in all the whole Establishments made, as well in times of our Progenitors as in our own time, the same article is often ratified and confirmed: Nevertheless in our Parliament holden at Westminster the Wednesday next after the Sunday of Middle Lent it is shewed unto us by the Reverend Father in God, John Archbishop of Canterbury, Primate of (all) England, and the other Prelates and Clergy of our Realm, how some Oppressions and Grievances be done in divers Manners by some of our Servants, to people of Holy Church, against (the Franchise of) the Great Charter and the Establishments aforesaid, which Oppressions they shew in Petition, praying upon the same Remedy: Wherefore We, their Petition seen and regarded and thereupon deliberation had with the Peers of our Realm, and other of our Council and of the Realm summoned to our said Parliament, and having regard to the Great Charter and to other Statutes aforesaid, and at the request of the said Prelates and Clergy, which have much aided us, and daily do, by the assent and accord of the said Peers, and of all other summoned and being in our said Parliament, have granted and do grant for us and our Heirs and Successors to the said Prelates and Clergy, the things underwritten, perpetually to endure . . .[9]

This statute (framed by a committee of judges, prelates, barons, knights, and burgesses) was one of the four important statutes secured from the king in the spring parliament of 1340 in return for liberal war grants.

The so-called *Ordinacio pro Clero* of 25 Edward III, like the *Articuli* of 1316, consists of a series of specific regulations. It begins simply "First, That all the Privileges and Franchises granted heretofore to the Clergy be confirmed and holden in all Points."[10] To be sure, the usual request for a confirmation of the Charters had been proffered at the beginning of the session. The petition which led to the first statute of *praemunire* cites the Great Charter in connection with free elections and rights of advowson, though the wording is obscure.[11] Again among the commons petitions in the parliament of 1373 is one which complains of papal reservations and provisions by which treasure is drawn out of the realm to the impoverishment of the realm and enrichment of the king's enemies, and pro-

[9] 14 Ed. III, stat. 4 (*S. R.* I, 292): *De diversis libertatibus ecclesiasticis per dominum Regem concessis.* Ca. 1 deals with purveyance with an additional clause that the clergy be not "charged with hostages, horses or dogs"; ca. 2, the king shall not present to churches in another's right but within three years after voidance; cas. 3–5 regulate seizure of temporalities, waste during escheat, etc. This *nova carta* is noticed by the chroniclers, as *Chronicon de Melsa*, III, 44; Lanercost, p. 333. 14 Ed. III, stat. 1, ca. 1, is a confirmation of the Charters, and ca. 13 provides "Escheators shall not commit waste in lands of the king's wards contrary to Magna Carta."

[10] Ca. 2 modifies 14 Ed. III, stat. 4, ca. 2, as prejudicial to the crown. Then follow concessions relating to benefit of clergy, presentments to benefices, seizure of temporalities, etc. *S. R.* I, 324–26.

[11] Did the petitioners have in mind ca. 1, or the more specific ca. 33 which relates to vacancies, yet supports rights of patrons? "Et aussint contre ceux qi par nul especial Privilege occupient ou font debate en ascunes Dignites, Priories, ou Possessions, as queux attient franche Election, ou pertient le Presentement au Roi, ou a nul de sa ligeance, solonc l'article ent purveu en la Grande Chartre, come ad este de tut temps en Roialme d'Engleterre." *Rot. Parl.* II, 252.

longation of the war: "And also, in disturbance of free elections to the said elective benefices against the Great Charter, and the intent of your progenitors and of the others, nobles of the said realm, founders of the churches." [12]

Excommunication

THE practice of excommunicating violators of the Charters, or rather of pronouncing a general sentence of excommunication to be incurred *ipso facto* by all who should infringe them thereafter, had been used throughout the thirteenth century.[13] Particularly impressive and long remembered was the great sentence pronounced in 1253 by Archbishop Boniface and his bishops in the presence of Henry III, confirmed in 1254 by Pope Innocent IV and in 1256 by Alexander VI. This sentence was included in early printed volumes of the statutes, the *Antiqua Statuta* beginning with Magna Carta.[14] The impressive ceremony, performed as it was with candles burning and bells ringing (*candelis accensis et campanis pulsatis*), the sentence which "aweth the heart, and whosoever heareth it, both his ears shall tingle," both afforded publicity and added to the reputation of the Charters. The practice was in line with the custom of the clergy in excommunicating not only violators of the liberties of the church, but also disturbers of the peace. Maitland has reminded us that there are special reasons for reenacting old law which might not occur to the mind of a modern layman. Whereas a secular legislator is content if he can punish those who break his edicts, the church desires to legislate not only for the *forum externum* but for the *forum internum* also. She does not merely want to punish those who break her laws; she wishes to be able to say that they have sinned in breaking them. . . . Now in the *forum internum* we can hardly assert that ignorance of a rule is never an excuse for breaking it. Hence a more than usually strong desire on the part of ecclesiastical legislators to deprive their subjects of the plea of ignorance.[15]

In the course of the fourteenth century, respect for the church and its anathemas was diminishing. The clergy themselves, however, kept faith in the power of excommunication, yet they weakened it through overuse. It was used as warning or intimidation, penalty or mere process.[16] In

---

[12] *Rot. Parl.* II, 320.

[13] Thompson, *First Century of Magna Carta*, pp. 97–102. Formal sentences against Charter-breakers were pronounced in connection with the reissues of 1416, 1217, 1225, and the confirmations of 1237, 1253, 1255, 1276, 1297, and 1300.

[14] See below, Chap. VI.

[15] Maitland, *Roman Canon Law in the Church of England*, pp. 35, 36.

[16] The bishops' registers abound in examples. For instance, from Adam of Orleton's, pp. 314–15 (1325), "The Bishop of Salisbury threatens excommunication against any who should despoil the Church of Wootten Rivers of its tithes or any part of them," and similarly against any "who should despoil the Church of Patney of anything belonging to it." These both refer to the sentence "a sanctis patribus latis," as do some of the following.

pronouncing the great excommunication, it was customary to use the text of a sentence pronounced by a distinguished prelate or used upon some notable occasion, such as that of 1222 by Stephen Langton at Oxford, that of 1253 by Boniface, and that of 1268 by the legate Ottobone. Such a sentence would be reverently referred to as promulgated "by the holy fathers of the church," *a sanctis patribus ecclesiae*. Texts though similar were not identical. The early Oxford sentence, for instance, contained no clause on the Charters. A given archbishop or bishop might select one or the other of these famous forms and use it either *in toto,* or just those clauses which fitted the needs of the time. Just as king and parliament had to meet periods of special lawlessness, the church was confronted with crises in encroachment upon its "liberties." One prelate might be more aggressive or zealous than another, and so on.

The *Confirmatio Cartarum* of 1297 had prescribed

that all Archbishops and Bishops shall pronounce the Sentence of great Excommunication against all those that by (Word), Deed, or Counsel do contrary to the foresaid Charters, or that in any point break or undo them. And that the said Curses be twice a year denounced and published by the Prelates aforesaid.[17]

When we raise the question as to just how long and how regularly this rule was obeyed, the evidence of the sources is not clear-cut. On the one hand we find repeated references in the present tense—"the great sentence which *is pronounced.*" On the other hand, we find from time to time that convocation, or a particular archbishop or bishop, finds it necessary to repeat an old constitution or issue a new one reviving or enjoining the sentence in whole or in part. We may perhaps conclude that the rule was presupposed in theory but sometimes lapsed in practice.

Something of this same variability then confronts us when we turn to the policy of the church toward actual or potential Charter-breakers. For instance, the sentence pronounced by Archbishop Winchelsea in Christ Church, Canterbury (1310), against violators of the liberties of the church throughout his province does not mention the Charters or Charter-breakers specifically, though their inclusion may have been implied.[18]

In the Register of Durham, I, 52–54, 161–65, we find a general sentence "contra rapientes bona ecclesiastica," and "contra ingredientes parcos."

From Hereford comes a mandate (1346) "to promulgate the bishop's sentence against unknown persons who occupy the church with armed force," and, more elaborate, a mandate (1353) to a dean to pronounce sentence in all churches of his deanery "against disturbers of the peace in church and state, conspirators, perjurors, mainteners of false pleas, and hinderers of a free making of wills whether by wives or dependents, where a right to make them is customary." John de Trillek's Register, pp. 99, 179.

For various sentences pronounced by the Archbishop of Canterbury see Wilkins, III, 49–50, 86, 133.

[17] S. R. I, 123. Cf. Archbishop Winchelsea's decree to the clergy, Wilkins, II, 240–42.

[18] Wilkins, II, 401–3. He confirms statutes and ordinances of Otto, Ottobone, and Stephen, and refers to the sentence of the great excommunication *per sacros canones infligitur*

On the other hand, the model sentence prescribed by the Archbishop of York the next year not only includes such an item but implies its common use throughout England:

Item excommunicantur omnes illi, qui scienter veniunt, vel faciunt contra magnam chartam, vel aliquem articulum in ea contentum; et sunt articuli 35, aut contra chartam de foresta, vel aliquem ejus articulum, et habet articulos 15, de quibus plene habetur in dicto tractatu, qui "Pupilla" dicitur. Et haec sententia lata est per omnes episcopos Angliae, et per sedem apostolicam perpluries confirmata.[19]

This same impression of continuous usage is conveyed by incidental statements in documents of Edward II's reign such as the Despensers' protest against their exile by award of parliament: "excommunicated four times a year are those who presume to attempt anything against the aforesaid charter." [20] Constitutions of Bishop Richard de Kellawe of Durham order publication of the general sentence in all the cities and churches of the diocese three times a year, as if it was a rather routine matter.[21]

From time to time in the thirteenth century Henry III had been supported by papal bulls exempting him and his officials from the force of the sentence. In 1328 Archbishop Meopham, admonishing the young Edward III to observe the Charter, recognizes the exception of "the king, the queen, and their children," [22] but a few years later in his *Speculum,* denouncing abuses of purveyance, he implies that even the king may incur the curse. We have already seen what dramatic use Archbishop Stratford made of the great excommunication in the crisis of 1340–41, incorporating into the sentence whole clauses of Magna Carta, the which were most contravened at the time. In subsequent letters to king and council Stratford, like Meopham, did not hesitate to charge violations "contrary to the great charter, against which all who come counter are excommunicate by all the prelates of England, and the sentence confirmed by the pope's bull which we have by us: *the which things are done at the great peril of your soul and the minishing of your honour.*" [23] Some years later, in 1364, it is the Oxford sentence which the Bishop of Ely revives throughout his diocese.[24]

"pronounced by us and our suffragans" in cathedral churches on the four principal holy days (*festis principalibus*) of the year. The one specific item relates to purveyance.

[19] Constitutions and a sentence of excommunication in twenty-nine items, *ibid*. II, 409–15.

[20] *Chronicles of Edward I & II*, pp. 70–71 (Bridlington). Similarly in other documents connected with the Despensers: a letter of the king to the Bishop of Exeter (Wilkins, II, 509–10) and the revocation of the pardon to their pursuers (*S. R.* I, 187).

[21] Though the text is not quoted, the sentence is treated as a routine matter. Register of Durham, III, 578 (app.).

[22] *Calendar Plea & Memoranda Rolls of the City of London,* 1323–64, p. 84, a letter dated December 23, 1328.

[23] Avesbury, p. 328.

[24] He complains that many churches do not have the text promulgated at the Oxford council. and prescribes its use yearly. Wilkins, III, 59–61. In 1351 constitutions of the

The register of Bishop Brantyngham of Exeter, under the date of 1373, enumerates offenses for which the sentence of excommunication is incurred *ipso facto*. The bishop deplores that through ignorance of holy scripture, the canons, and the traditions of the fathers, some of his parish clergy employ excommunication unlawfully and indiscreetly. The twenty-six articles of this monition are to be "read in all colleges and Parish churches of the Archdeaconry of Totnes on Sunday and solemn days at least four times in the year, and are to be fixed up within a month in a place within each church where they can be clearly seen." But here it is the *magna charta de Foresta* (*sic*) not the Great Charter which is cited, and more particularly, chapter 7 of the same, regulating abuses of *scotale* and other exactions by the foresters.[25] Occasionally, as in 1368 and 1376, the commons in their parliamentary petitions for confirmation of the Charters, resort to warning against the danger of incurring the sentence.[26]

Treatises

THE lawyers were not the only "treatisours." Ecclesiastics contributed not only through "constitutions" but by essays on special themes. Perhaps the most scathing denunciation of purveyance is to be found in the *Speculum*, penned probably by Archbishop Meopham about 1330. This treatise, addressed to the young king, Edward III, attempts to bring home to him a sense of responsibility for the evils perpetrated by his agents. Although the archbishop is especially concerned with purveyance of the goods of ecclesiastics, he does not confine himself to this aspect. The evils of the system as it affected the poorer classes are vividly portrayed: seizures against the will of the owner or without payment; underpayment—for example, three pence for a bushel of oats worth five; farmers left without enough grain for seed corn; taking from the poor widow the very hens which constitute her livelihood, and from the debtor the ox with which he had expected to save his land from confiscation; men, carts, and horses forced to go ten leagues from home and labor for many days; easy duplication and imposture—the village which has suffered from one set of purveyors only to find these followed a day or two later by others from the household of the queen or the king's sister.

Archbishop of Dublin provided for pronouncing the sentence three times a year, the text to be that of his previous constitutions or those of his predecessors, the sentence to be pronounced in the native tongue on occasions when many people are present, with candles burning and bells ringing. The matters itemized relate to various purely ecclesiastical matters. *Ibid*. III, 20. See also II, 749.

[25] *Articuli pro quibus incurritur sententia excommunicat. ipso facto*. Bishop Rede's Register, editor's note, p. 181, in connection with Rede's sentence of 1404. Wilkins, III, 95–96.

[26] 1368. ". . . pur le profit de la dite Commune, & pur la graunde sentence eschure q'est contenu en les Chartres & Estatuz sur ditz."

1376. ". . . a l'honour de Dieu & de vostre Roial Majeste & pur Salvation de tout la Roialme, & pur eschuire les grosses sentences qe chaient sur touz ceux qi fount au contraire." *Rot. Parl*. II, 295, 331.

The author is a resourceful preceptor and every possible form of admonition is at his command: quotations from Augustine; scriptural denunciation of Old Testament princes; a reminder to Edward that he is not emperor but king of England, a fief of the papacy. Even were he emperor, granted that the emperor is not under the laws, it beseems him nevertheless to live according to the laws.[27] Only a brief part of the treatise is concerned with restrictions on purveyance, but that part is significant. The young king is reminded that he has taken an oath to observe "the rights and laudable customs and especially the ecclesiastical liberties of the realm"; that all who go against articles of the Great Charter are *ipso facto* excommunicate, a sentence several times confirmed by the apostolic see. The king's agents by their evil practices have certainly incurred this sentence. They force the "servants of the Lord (*servos Christi*)" to labor day and night in the king's service, yet fail to pay the prescribed rates: for a cart with two horses ten pence per day and for a cart with three horses fourteen pence per day, *ut patet in Magna Carta, et quia non solvunt ut statuitur in Magna Carta sunt excommunicati.*

Pound, in his *Spirit of the Common Law,* reminds us that John Wycliff was a legal as well as religious reformer:

It is not an accident that the first reformer in English legal thought was also the first reformer in English religious thought. John Wycliff is known for his resistance to authority in the church and his translation of the Scriptures to bring them home to the common man. But in his tract *De Officio Regis* he attacked authority in law and asserted the sufficiency of English case law—for such it had fairly become—against the venerable legislation of Justinian and the sacred decretals of the Popes. . . . "The Pope," says Boniface viii in the fourteenth century, "holds all laws in his breast." Wycliff said boldly that men might well be saved "though many laws of the Pope had never been spoken," that Roman law was "heathen men's law" and that there was no more reason and justice in the civil law of Rome than in the law of England. He appealed from authority to the local custom of England, from the rules imposed externally by Roman law and the Pope, to the rules which Englishmen made for themselves by their every-day conduct. . . . In law and in religion he appealed to the individual against authority.[28]

As Maitland has pointed out, Wycliff actually proposed "the introduction of English law as a substitute for Roman law into the schools of

----

[27] ". . . quod licet imperator non subjuciatur legibus, decet tamen sibi seipsum vivere secundum leges." *Speculum* has been attributed to Simon Islip. *De Speculo Regis Edwardi III seu tractatu de mala regni administratione conscripsit Simon Islip.* Joseph Moisant, editor, Paris, 1891. For probability of Meopham's authorship, see Tait, in *English Historical Review,* 16:110–15. Meopham was Archbishop of Canterbury 1327–33; Islip was archbishop 1349–66. The treatise is quite in keeping with the policy of Meopham, as revealed by the letter of advice to Edward III described above. Stratford mentions Meopham's excommunication of violators of rules on purveyance.

[28] Pound, *Spirit of the Common Law,* pp. 39, 40.

Oxford and Cambridge." [29] Pound refers to "the sufficiency of English case law—for such it had fairly become," but actually it is the "king's statutes" in general and Magna Carta in particular which Wycliff names:

It were more profit both to body and soule that oure curatis lerneden and taughten many of the kyngis statutis, than lawe of the emperour. For oure peple is bounden to the kyngis statutis and not to the emperours lawe, but in as moche as it is enclosid in Goddis hestis. Then moche tresour and moche tyme of many hundrid clerkis in unyversite and other placis is foule wastid aboute bookis of the emperours lawe and studie about hem. . . . It semeth that curatis schulden rather lerne and teche the kyngis statutis, and namely the Grete Chartre, than the emperours lawe or myche part of the popis. For men in oure rewme ben bounden to obeche to the kyng and his rightful lawes and not so to the emperours; and they myghten wonder wel be savyd, though many lawes of the pope had never be spoken, in this world ne the tother.[30]

From the pen of a contemporary of Wycliff, John de Burgh, comes a little treatise, *Pupilla Occuli,* on the seven sacraments and the ten commandments. The author was chancellor of the University of Cambridge and vicar of Collinham. In this treatise he treats of offenses for which excommunication is incurred by force of the constitutions of legates and of provincial statutes, and more particularly in chapter 23: *De sententia lata super magnam chartam et super chartam de foresta.* Not only does he recite the sentence pronounced by Archbishop Boniface in 1253—the sentence "several times, so it is said, confirmed by the apostolic see"—but he includes the text of the Charters almost verbatim, with the warning: *Hos articulos ignorare non debent quibus incumbit confessiones audire infra provinciam Cantuariensem.*[31]

Fifteenth-Century Practices: Repetition or Variation

IN THE first half of the fifteenth century, clerical interest in Magna Carta seemed to revive rather than decrease. The church continued to be served by a rather able succession of primates. In 1399 Henry and Arundel, the exiled prince and the deposed prelate, returnd to England together, the one to attain the throne, the other to recover his archbishopric.[32] Both

---

[29] Maitland, *English Law and the Renaissance,* p. 63, n. 20.

[30] As quoted by Maitland from *Select English Works* (Arnold, editor), III, 326.

[31] Although he says the articles are inserted briefly ("Articuli vero in dictis chartis contenti hic breviter inserunt"), actually most of them are quoted verbatim. Although they are not numbered, he says there are thirty-three articles in Magna Carta.

Cf. Bémont, *Chartes,* p. xlix, n. 1, where this treatise is described. The author, Bémont says, more than once admits his indebtedness to an earlier document, *Oculus sacerdotis:* "l'auteur de ce dernier parait etre Guillaume 'de Pagula' (de Pagham), carme, qui fut eveque de Meath de 1327 a 1349." It may be noted that in the constitutions of 1311 cited above, the Archbishop of York refers to a treatise *qui Pupilla dicitur.*

[32] Arundel had been accused of complicity in the conspiracy of the three earls, Richard's Uncle Gloucester, Warwick, and his own brother, Arundel. The archbishop was translated to St. Andrews, a see which being then schismatic, he could not occupy.

had suffered from the tyranny of Richard II as had other individuals and "estates" throughout the realm. The accession of the first Lancastrian seemed to offer clergy and laity alike a promise of better times to come. Arundel was an active agent both in the deposing of Richard and the enthroning and coronation of Henry. It may well have been due to the archbishop that one of the formal charges against Richard accuses him of issuing by letters under his signet prohibitions to court christian, and that in "causes mere ecclesiastical or spiritual," in which prohibitions had already been justly (*ex justitia*) denied by the chancellor, "wickedly violating the ecclesiastical liberties approved in Magna Carta, to the preservation of which the king is sworn by oath. He is thus guilty of perjury and has incurred the sentence of excommunication launched by the holy fathers." [33]

In the new reign, just as the Great Charter resumed its old role in parliamentary requests for royal confirmations of liberties, so it reappeared in clerical petitions and *gravamina*. Arundel, one of the witnesses before whom Richard read his abdication, opened proceedings at Henry's first parliament on St. Faith's Day, October 6, 1399, and a few days later conducted the coronation. The convocation which met at St. Paul's in October was assured by the Earl of Northampton that the king was making no requests for money grants, indeed, would tax the clergy only in case of war and special needs and promised vigorous support in the suppression of heresy. This convocation framed an elaborate series of articles, sixty-three in number, directed some to the archbishop from his clergy, some to the pope, and some to the king. The last group seeks in quite the old form a sweeping confirmation of "all the privileges, liberties and rights of the church, especially those contained in Magna Carta and the statute of *circumspecte agatis*." [34]

Arundel is best known, perhaps, for his vigorous suppressing of Lollardy: as the sponsor of the statute *de heretico comburendo,* the prosecutor of John Oldcastle and of Lollard influences in the University of Oxford, and as the enemy of disendowment. It was in the unlearned parliament at Coventry, 1404, that the bold commons (*omnino illiterati*) proposed to devote church property to the use of the king for one year. As the chron-

[33] ". . . libertates ecclesiasticas in Magna Charta approbatas, ad quas conservandas juratus extiterat, nequiter infringendo; perjuriam et sententiam excommunicationis contra hujusmodi violatores a sanctis partibus latam damnabiliter incurrendo." *Rot. Parl.* III, 421.

[34] "Inprimis, supplicant humiliter et devote praelati et clerus praedicti, quatenus omnia privilegia, libertates, et jura, et specialiter in Magna Charta, et in statuto 'Circumspecte agatis' contenta . . ." The list of liberties most desired as usual relates to prohibitions, benefit of clergy, purveyance, appropriation of ecclesiastical revenues from temporalities in the king's hands, and with special reference to the *Articuli cleri* of Edward II. Wilkins, III, 243. On the other hand, the petition which convocation presented in parliament in 1402 cites not Magna Carta but the *Ordinatio pro clero* of 25 Ed. III, since it is benefit of clergy with which the petition was most concerned. *Ibid.* III, 270–72.

icler indignantly puts it, they labored only to one end: to "rob the patrimony of Christ, and take away the temporalities formerly granted by holy men and kings."

Arundel roundly censured them for their folly and greed and was supported by the Archbishop of York, but it was the shrewd Bishop of Rochester who effectually silenced the advocates of disendowment. This bishop, says the chronicler, was dubbed the "Mercury" of my Lord of Canterbury, though the latter was not lacking in eloquence, for what the archbishop conceived in his mind, that the said bishop spoke out freely. He produced a book containing Magna Carta and read it to them. When he further showed that they were excommunicate, as indeed were all who subverted the liberty of the church, many of them next day confessed their sin and begged absolution! [35]

Arundel was not so successful the next year in his effort to save Richard Scrope from the king's wrath; in fact he was hardly afforded an opportunity to invoke Magna Carta. The Archbishop of York was allowed neither benefit of clergy nor the privilege of a peer, but with Mowbray was arraigned and condemned precipitately before a special commission of about six peers and three or four *puisne* judges and executed at once, all this while his fellow primate and would-be defender slept! Arundel had been deluded by the king into expecting a delay in the proceedings.[36]

A mandate from Bishop Rede of Chichester to his archdeacon in this same year, enjoining publication of the general sentence four times a year, sounds as if it were directed against the Lollards.[37] In 1413 the Canterbury clergy petitioned for better enforcement of canons and provincial constitutions, including Archbishop Peckham's command for publication of articles of the general sentence four times a year.[38]

In 1414 Arundel was succeeded by Henry Chicheley, a milder man than his predecessor, who nevertheless "kept down Lollardism with a firm hand." His biographer pictures him as "a lawyer of no mean repute," who was served by the famous canonist William Lyndwood as his vicar-

---

[35] "Roffensis vero qui Mercurius dicabatur Domini Cantuariensis eo quod ea quae mente conceperat Archiepiscopus, ipse protulit voce libera, quanquam Domino Cantuariensi non deesset facundia, offerri fecit librum in quo continebatur Magna Charta, legitque coram eis; ostenditque excommunicatos, et omnes qui subvertere nitebantur Ecclesiae libertatem. Quo tonitrus repercussi, proparaverunt in crastino plurimi, fatentes peccatum, et petentes absolutionem . . ." *Annales Henrici,* pp. 393–94.

This chronicler (anon.) gives a graphic account. He describes elections to the parliament under a new form of writ "sub breve novi tenoris, ne, videlicet, eligerentur milites, sive cives, qui gustassent aliquid de jure regni, sed omnino illiterati."

[36] Oman, *Political History of England,* pp. 196–98.

[37] Bishop Rede's Register, pp. 83–84: "The separate conversation of the wicked is rending faith and unity from the members of Christ, while people neither fear God nor the effects of ecclesiastical censure . . ."

[38] They refer to certain constitutions of Otto and Ottobone, the Oxford council, Boniface, Peckham, and Stratford. *De publicandis articulis generalis sententiae quater in anno. constitut. Peckham iisdem temporibus.* Wilkins, III, 351–52.

general and who pursued a successful national church policy while Henry V lived. After 1422 it was more difficult to withstand papal encroachments such as those of the aggressive Martin V, who urged repeal of the statutes of *provisors* and *praemunire*.

It was the proposal for disendowment (renewed in 1410 and now in 1414) which figures in the opening lines of Shakespeare's Henry V. Says the archbishop to the bishop of Ely:

> My lord, I'll tell you; that self bill is urged,
> Which in the eleventh year of the last king's reign
> Was like, and had indeed against us pass'd,
> But that the scambling and unquiet time
> Did put it out of farther question.

Chicheley did not resort to threats and fulminations. Though he supported Henry's war policy and invasion of France, he did not, as Shakespeare following the chroniclers implies, deliberately instigate it as a diversion, that is, "in the hope of foiling the attacks made by the Lollard party on the church." [39]

However, in 1429 Chicheley reverted to the sentence of excommunication directed against Charter-breakers, and quoted chapter 25 of Magna Carta, with the very practical purpose of stamping out the use of a false weight—the so-called auncel weight—which "ill-doers" were using throughout Canterbury province "to the defrauding of the people and endangering of their own souls." [40] A few years later, in 1434, at an adjourned meeting of convocation at Oxford, whither it had resorted to escape the plague, it was complained that the practice of promulgating the sentence had fallen into desuetude through oblivion or neglect. A committee of the clergy presented an abbreviated form of the general sentence in English (*in lingua materna, sub breviori modo*). After corrections and emendations this was adopted for publication in all the churches of the province three times a year on specified Sundays when the most people were present. It is disappointing to find that, perhaps due to this very brevity, none of the ten articles cites the Great Charter. [41]

[39] "Hall in his account of the parliament held at Leicester on April 30 1414 makes Archbishop Chichele warmly advocate war with France, in the hope of foiling the attacks made by the Lollard party on the church. (Hall, Chron. 35.) This passage, which forms the basis of the speech given to the archbishop by Shakespeare (H. V. Act 1 sc. 2) must not be accepted as accurate." Chicheley was not sitting in this parliament as archbishop, and his name does not appear in *Rot. Parl.* IV, 15. "He probably did belong to the war party, and he and the clergy exerted themselves to find means for carrying it on, but didn't just instigate the king to embark on it to serve their own purpose." *D.N.B.*

[40] He refers particularly to the form of sentence in the constitutions of Archbishop J. Peckham. Wilkins, III, 516–17.

[41] It is not quite clear from the form of the entry in the Register whether the clerk quotes verbatim or abbreviates further, as he says "quorum articulorum tenor inferius describitur." Wilkins, III, 523–24. The articles relate to liberties of the church in general and to ecclesiastical jurisdiction, "the peace and tranquility of the realm," false witness,

In the 1430's and 1440's the English church seems to have been vexed over interpretation of the great statute of *praemunire* (16 Richard II) and the use being made of the writs of *praemunire facias*. Pope Martin V had urged repeal of the statutes of *provisors* and *praemunire,* but now the danger came from nearer home, from the common lawyers. Archbishop Chicheley in 1439, then John de Stafford in 1444 and 1447, raised the issue in convocation. The statute was being interpreted as applying not only to the papal curia, but to court christian and even to the temporal courts of English nobles, and the writ was directed against persons suing in such courts, thus having much the effect of a writ of prohibition. In a way this was the kind of use of the statute for which Sir Edward Coke was ridiculed when he tried to apply the phrase "in the court of another" to Chancery. Perhaps Sir Edward was inspired by these fifteenth-century "precedents" of his intellectual ancestors in the Inns of Court.

The practice was protested in convocation as too stringent and indeed leading to the final destruction of all spiritual jurisdiction as well as the franchise courts "granted by the progenitors of our lord the king"; as against faith and conscience, and to the great detriment (*emblemishement*) "of the estate and liberties of holy church, granted by the Great Charter of England and by our lord the king, and several of his progenitors in divers parliaments heretofore." The petitioners ask that the statute be strictly interpreted to apply exclusively to those who sue in the papal court or elsewhere "outside the realm of England." Writs of prohibition such as were in use before the statute would serve for any contingency within the realm. The matter was postponed until the next parliament, writs of *praemunire facias* to be restricted in the meantime.[42] As far as the records indicate, convocations of 1444 and 1447 were content with reiterating the specific grievance, without reference to the Charter, or in fact any prefatory statements, though that of 1447 has the novelty of being in the English tongue.[43]

The charter confirming liberties of the church which Edward IV granted at the beginning of his reign and which Richard III was asked to confirm, does not cite Magna Carta, yet it was not in complete abeyance

slander, failure to take excommunicated persons, infringement of sanctuary, purveyance, witchcraft, Lollardy, falsifiers of papal letters, wills, withholders of tithes, false weights and measures, felons, conspirators, maintenors of false quarrels. Here again Chicheley reverts to Peckham and the council of Reading. *Ibid.* III, 523–24.

[42] Wilkins, III, 533–34; Cf. Chicheley's biographer in the *D.N.B.*: In November 1439 in a speech before a synod held in London the archbishop declared "that many wrongs were inflicted on ecclesiastical judges by the interpretation put by the common lawyers on the statute of *praemunire.* A petition was presented to parliament asking that the operation of the statute be limited to those who invoked the interference of foreign courts."

[43] Wilkins, III, 540–41, 555–56 (from Stafford's Register). In 1444 they ask revision of the statute, "praesertim propter terminum alibi."

even in these rather absolutist reigns. The sentence against Charter-breakers was cited as current practice in a petition and the resulting statute of 1472, and in letters patent of 1476 for the enforcement of Magna Carta chapter 23:[44] "uppon which Magna Carta, a grete sentence Appostelik of excommengement by grete nombre of Bishoppes agenst the brekers therof was pronounced, and the same sentence, iiii tymes in the yere openly is declared, according to the lawe of the Church."

More distinguished than Archbishop Chicheley himself was his vicar-general, William Lyndwood, civilian and canonist, envoy for the government on a number of diplomatic missions in the 1420's and 1430's, and from 1433 keeper of the privy seal.[45] His *Provinciale* or *Provincial Constitutions* is a "digest in five books of the synodal constitutions of the province of Canterbury from the time of Stephen Langton to that of Henry Chichele," fourteen archbishops in all. It is "accompanied by an explanatory gloss in unusually good Latin." There were many editions, including an English translation published by Redman as early as 1434.[46]

As this work became the principal authority for English canon law, it must have continued to exert some influence, among civilians at least, even after the Reformation. Under the rubric *De Sententia Excommunicationis* Lynwood includes the notable sentences pronounced by Stephen Langton, Boniface, and Peckham with the note: *Magnam Chartam, Cujus Capitula sunt xxxvii ut in eadem plenius apparet & recitantur in Pupilla oculi parte quinta F.22.*[47] Thus, in an academic way at least, the Charter was established in constitutions and canonical treatises as it was in the literature of the common law.

The pre-Reformation *Ecclesia Anglicana* evidently continued promulgation of the sentence in some form into the years of the Reformation parliament, for it was thought necessary in 1534 to forbid its use.[48] It is interesting to find a reader in one of the Inns of Court in the reign of Charles II discussing the question of the effectiveness and survival of

[44] Wilkins, III, 614, 616; *Rot. Parl.* VI, 158-59; S. R. II, 439; *Cal. Pat. Rolls*, 1476-85, p. 23.

[45] Appointed in 1414 as Chicheley's official of the court of Canterbury, he later (1426) became Dean of the Arches and Bishop of Hereford. *D.N.B.*

[46] The Latin edition has a very long title, which reads in part: *Provinciale, (seu constitutiones Anglie) continens Constitutiones Provinciales quatuordecim Archiepiscopum Cantuariensium, viz. . . . cum Summariis . . . revisum atque impressum Auctore Guilielmo Lynwood, J.U.D. . . .* First printed at Oxford, c. 1470-80; then with Caxton's cipher and Wynkeyn de Word's colophon; reprinted 1499, 1508, 1517, and 1529.

[47] Peckham's, based on Langton's and Ottobone's, reads: "Item excommunicati sunt ab omnibus Archiepiscopis & Episcopis Angliae omnes illi qui venunt aut faciunt contra Magnam Chartam Domini Regis, quae Sententia per Sedem Apostolicam pluries est confirmata & approbata."

[48] Strype, *Memorials*, I, 253: "In the year 1534, when orders came for the regulating of preaching, and bidding of the beads, the *general sentence*, as it was called, was also forbidden to be used any more."

these sentences. He says that the "perticular Denunciacions and Custome of Excommunicacion twice every yeare remain'd in the Offices of the Church as I have heard till the Reformacion and in most of the Provinciall Counsells ever since there is one Canon or Constitution for it." He concludes that the sentences must have been effective since "these Charters have bin lesse obnoxious to Invasions and we have them at this day without any other blemish then what Tyme hath given them." [49] Arnold saw fit to include a paraphrase of it, including an article against the Charter-breakers, among the many miscellaneous items in his *Customs of London* (printed in 1502 and again in 1520 or 1521).[50] The version of the sentence in the *Festival,* a handbook for priests, as printed by Wynken de Worde in 1532, reads: "And al those that be agaynst the great charter of the Kynge, that is confermed of the court of Rome." [51] Christopher St. Germain complained:

Thoughe there be dyvers good and reasonable artycles ordeined bi the church to be redde openlye to the people at certayn dayes by the churche therto assygned, which commenly is called the general sentence: yet many curates and theyr paryshe prestes sometyme rede onely parte of the artycles, and omytte parte therof, eyther for shortnes of tyme, or else to take suche artycles as serve mooste to theyr purpose.[52]

Whether pronounced by the better type like Chaucer's poor parson, or mumbled by some ignorant "mass-priest," it must have become more or less a formality, a far cry from the impressive curse upon Charter-breakers of the thirteenth century.

[49] The lecturer was lending the support of his talents to the recently re-established Anglican church by reading on Magna Carta ca. 1.

[50] A summary in English (perhaps Arnold's own paraphrase of some old Latin text) of the curse as provided in the "councel of Oxenford," in thirty articles. Arnold's *Chronicle,* or *Customs of London,* pp. 174–78. Article xxix: "Also they ben acursed of all ye Archbisshops and Bishops of Englande alle they which comen or done ageynste the grete charters which conteynen xxxvi. chapiters or artycles which sentence and many mo been confermed by the apostolicall seete, that is to saye of the lybartyes and of forest and theis thingis ben done and made of the consent and wyl of oure lorde the Kynge."

[51] Strype, *Memorials,* Vol. I, pt. ii, no. xlvi, p. 189.

[52] *A Treatise concerning the Division betwene the spiritualtie and the temporaltie,* Leaf 12v–13.

PART II. THE TUDOR PERIOD

❧ CHAPTER VI ❧

Magna Carta and the Printers and Chroniclers

Emonges all writers that have put in ure
Their penne and style, thynges to endite,
None have behynd theim left so greate treasure,
Ne to their posteritee have dooen suche delite
As thei whiche have taken peines to write
Chronycles and actes of eche nacion,
And have of the same made true relacion.

(GRAFTON)

M. Bémont's historical sketch of the Charter concludes that from the reign of Henry VI to the Stuarts it was no longer an issue. "Parliament approved docilely the political and religious coups d'états of the fifteenth and sixteenth centuries, and the Great Charter rested in the shade." [1] Historians have been content to accept this conclusion. Professor Cross, for instance, after enumerating certain great principles "embedded in the momentous document," concludes "nevertheless machinery had later to be devised to make these principles operative, and there were long stretches when they were practically forgotten." In a note he adds, "Shakespeare in his great drama *King John* does not mention Magna Carta at all." [2] Examination of various pertinent records of the Tudor period substantiates this conclusion for the late fifteenth and first three quarters of the sixteenth century, so far as the use of the Charter as a constitutional or "liberty" document is concerned, but even in this period it was not so completely in the shade as hitherto supposed.

We have seen in earlier chapters the extension of its use at least into the reigns of Edward IV and Henry VII: the rather routine quoting of a provision in an occasional petition or statute; the citing of others for their practical or theoretical value in cases reported in the Year Books;

---

[1] "A partir de Henri vi et jusqu'aux Stuarts, il n'en est plus question. . . . Le Parlement approuva docilement les coups d'etats politiques et religieux du xve et du xvie siecle, et la Grande Charte resta dans l'ombre." Bémont, *Chartes,* I.

[2] Cross, *Shorter History of England and Greater Britain,* p. 94 and n.

and the document *in toto* still "protected" and perpetuated in a mechanical sort of way by the church through the great excommunication.

In the throes of the Reformation the Charter was not entirely eclipsed. Defenders of the old order, the church universal, invoked it, in vain of course, against king and parliament. But when these forces had worked their will, just what was rightly to be considered the true *Ecclesia Anglicana?* Only relatively late in the century was chapter 1 appropriated by proponents of the state church. When the Puritans, in alliance with the common lawyers, entered the lists against the bishops and the Court of High Commission, it was chapter 29, not chapter 1, which was to serve their turn.[3] A few episodes of the 1530's, together with some negative evidence of the succeeding decades may be briefly sketched before turning to the more significant aspects of sixteenth-century Charter history.

Rather well-known are the protests of two persons in high place who cited chapter 1 of the Charter against the legislation of the Reformation parliament and the questionable legality of proceedings of the crown. Archbishop Warham, charged with a *praemunire*, declared that "the liberties of the Church are guaranteed by Magna Charta, and several kings who violated them, as Henry II. [*sic*], Edward III., Richard II., and Henry IV., came to an ill end." [4] Warham also lodged a formal protest on February 24, 1532.[5] Arraigned in King's Bench, Sir Thomas More, according to Roper's account, declared the indictment against him was

grounded upon an act of parliament directly repugnant to the laws of God and his holy church, the supreme government of which, or any part thereof, may no temporal prince presume by any law to take upon him, as rightfully belonging to the See of Rome . . . And for proof thereof, like as amongst divers other reasons and authorities, he declared that this realm being but a member and small part of the church, might not make a particular law disagreeable with the general law of Christ's universal Catholic church, no more than the City of London, being but one poor member in respect of the whole realm, might make a law against an act of parliament to bind the whole realm. So further showed he that it was both contrary to the laws and statutes of this our land yet unrepealed, as they might evidently perceive in Magna Charta, *quod Ecclesia Anglicana libera sit, et habeat omnia jura integra, et libertates suas illaesas,* and also contrary to the sacred oath which the king's highness himself, and every other Christian prince always with great solemnity, received at their coronations.[6]

---

[3] For these two phases, see below, Chap. VIII.

[4] *Letters & Papers, Henry VIII*, V, 542. "The draft of a speech apparently intended to be delivered in the House of Lords. Warham died August 23, 1532, and this speech appears to have been composed very shortly before his death." (Editor's note.)

[5] "Protestatis archiepiscopi Cant. de non consentiendo ad statutum promulgatum in praejudicium ecclesiasticae potestatis." Wilkins, III, 746.

[6] Roper, *More*, 86–87. Roper says that he was not present at the trial, but had this by the "credible report" of Sir Anthony Saintleger, and partly of Richard Haywood, and John Webb, and others.

Participants in the Pilgrimage of Grace "cited Magna Carta with its ecclesia libera sit as their warrant for rebellion." From one of them, Robert Aske, captain of the Yorkshire group, comes testimony, oddly indirect, of a practice reported current until the Reformation: that of the lords at the beginning of each parliament in confirming the liberties of the church as granted by Magna Carta. In answer to interrogatories on his relations with Lord Darcy:

To that the said Aske sayth they had comunicacion togedere toching the said acts of parliament and saith by his faith he kane not well remember nowe any notorious comunicacion betwix the lord Darcy and him in the denyall of the auctorite of the supreme hed but he rememberyth this that the same lord Darcy declared to him he had in the parliament chamber declared befor the lords his holl mynd toching any mater ther to be argued toching ther faith but that the custome of that house emongst the lords befor that tyme had been that such maters should alwaies toching spirituall affaires [?] be referred into the convocacion house and not in the parliament hous and that befor this last parliament it was customed amongst the lords the first matter they alwais communed of after the masse of the holy ghost was to affirm and allow the first Chapter of Magna Carta toching the Rights and liberties of the Church and it was not now so.[7]

The *Lords Journals* contain no evidence of such a practice.[8]

In the following years neither extreme—papist or puritan—cited the Charter in defense of his conception of "liberty of the church" (chapter 1) or "liberty of the subject" (chapter 29). Although it would be rash for this or any other researcher in this field to assume that no such instance has eluded his vigilance, the negative character of the most promising sources consulted seems convincing.[9] In the pages of Foxe are indicated the characteristic lines of protest and defense of those subjected to religious persecution: the pre-Reformation martyrs,[10] the old style "heretics"; then those late in Henry VIII's reign too advanced toward protestantism to

---

[7] *Exchr. T. R. Misc. Books*, vol. 119, 233/117. The *Calendar of State Papers* entry reads "commoned," but the manuscript seems to be "communed," which makes better sense.

[8] The journal for the first parliament of Henry VIII records the three readings and unanimous approval of a bill "pro Libertatibus Ecclesie Anglicanae," *L. J.* I, 4, 5; but there is no corresponding act in the statutes. Cf. Reid, *The King's Council in the North*, pp. 131–32: "They [the pilgrims] were equally desirous that the old customs of the House of Lords, always used before the last Parliament, should be revived: namely, that matters touching the Faith should be referred to Convocation and not discussed in Parliament; that the first act of the House should be the affirmation of Magna Carta; and that bills touching the King's prerogative, or between party and party, should be scanned by the learned counsel in case they should perceive anything in it prejudicial to the prerogative or to the Commonwealth."

[9] It has not been thought worth while to consult the many controversial works obviously concerned mainly with religious doctrine.

[10] Most of Foxe's data on this group consists of the articles produced against them, statements of doctrine and their answers. There are a few protests on procedure as "contrary to all due order of law," but usually on the grounds that the heresy laws and accustomed rules of procedure in ecclesiastical courts have not been properly observed. For example, Foxe, *Actes & Monuments*, V, 35–36.

conform to the six articles; in Edward's reign Catholic divines such as Bishops Bonner and Gardiner (though, of course, these last receive very different treatment at Foxe's hands); and finally the more numerous "Marian martyrs." Many of Foxe's sources on the latter relate to doctrine: their stanch testimony to their beliefs in response to the articles administered to them, and speeches and letters rejoicing in their martyrdom and encouraging coreligionists to be equally steadfast.

The doctrine of passive resistance so clearly enunciated by the Puritans in Elizabeth's reign does not find conscious expression here. Yet a few of the martyrs do complain of proceedings contrary to law, both the ecclesiastical law and the common law: they are imprisoned without cause, held in prison some time before cause is shown or trial permitted, and the oath required of them is unlawful. One John Philpot approaches the later conception of "liberty of the subject" in his demand for "the benefit of a subject," and by his contention that his deprivation of his archdeaconry is against the common law.[11]

The distinguished Catholic divines, Bonner and Gardiner, bishops over a number of years and trained canonists, naturally would not condemn the ecclesiastical courts and procedure which they themselves had used against Protestant "heretics," or seek support in the common law. It is surprising that at some point in their elaborate defenses they did not, like More and Warham, at least appeal to the *Ecclesia libera sit* of Magna Carta. But perhaps the document was too royalist in its origin, too insular in its character, and it eventually was to be appropriated by the new Erastian *Ecclesia Anglicana*. English Catholics, as their writings and speeches reveal, took refuge rather in the church universal, its theology and canons. Gardiner does recall how the charges against Wolsey included the "staying of the common law" contrary to Magna Carta.[12] Both bishops

[11] On his first examination he said: "I desire your masterships that I may have the benefit of a subject, and be delivered out of my long wrongful imprisonment where I have ben this twelfth month and this half, without any calling to answer before now, and my living taken from me without all law." Foxe, *Actes & Monuments*, V, 607. As to his deprivation: "Master doctor, you know that the common law is otherwise; and besides this, the statutes of this realm be otherwise . . ." On his second examination Philpot claimed that statements with which he was charged had been spoken in convocation, which as a part of parliament should allow free speech! *Ibid.*, p. 629.

Robert Glover charges "my masters have imprisoned me, having nothing to burden me withal." Again, "so remained I a prisoner in Coventry by the space of ten or eleven days, being never called to my answer of the masters, contrary to the laws of the realm, they having neither statute, law, proclamation, letter, warrant, nor commandment for my apprehension." *Ibid.* VII, 389–90.

John Roger says: ". . . it had been time enough to take away men's livings, and thereto to have imprisoned them after that they had offended the laws . . . But their purpose is to keep men in prison, so long until they may catch them in their laws; and so kill them." *Ibid.* VI, 599. Also VI, 589; VII, 161, 299, 308, 310; VIII, 105, 236, 409; and others.

[12] In a letter to the Lord Protector, dated at the Fleet, October 14, 1547. Foxe, *Actes & Monuments*, VI, 42–46. "And one article against my lord cardinal was, that he had granted

point out flaws in the personnel and procedure of the commissions appointed to deal with them.[13]

Only after long and fruitless protests along these lines do they seek help in the "laws of England," and "the liberty of an Englishman." Thus Gardiner: "and if I might have the liberty of an Englishman, I would plainly declare I had neither offended law, statute, act, proclamation, nor his own letter neither." And again, even more emphatically:

The bishop of Winchester maketh most instant suit, to have the benefit of the laws of the realm, like an Englishman, and not to be cast in prison without bail or mainprize, without accusation or indictment, without calling to any presence to be charged with anything; [how like the "being called to answer" of the *six statutes*!] and so to remain these eighteen weeks, and could have no relief to know what is meant with him.[14]

Meanwhile still other forces of the age were quietly, almost mechanically, and little noticed at first, playing a part in Charter history. In Trevelyan's delightful vein:

if Chaucer's spirit could have peeped over the shoulders of Edward IV at the machine which Master Caxton had brought from Flanders, as it stamped off in quick succession copies of the *Canterbury Tales* to look almost like real manuscripts, the flattered poet would have smiled at so pleasant a toy. He would hardly have foreseen in it a battering ram to bring abbeys and castles crashing to the ground, a tool that would ere long refashion the religion and commonwealth of England.[15]

Chaucer's spirit, like the modern literary historian, with thoughts intent on *Canterbury Tales,* the *Morte d'Arthur,* and translations of *Cicero* and

injunctions to stay the common laws. And upon that occasion Magna Charta was spoken of, and it was made a great matter, the stay of the common law." Quoted by McIlwain, *Constitutionalism, Ancient and Modern,* pp. 103–4.

[13] Bonner repeatedly refers to "the law," "law and reason," "equity," "his Majesty's ecclesiastical law." He questions the authority of the commission and especially the addition to it of Sir Thomas Smith, and accuses Smith of tampering with the articles against him. In the fourth session, showing why he ought not to be "declared for cast and convicted," he protests the "nullity and invalidity, injustice and iniquity, of your pretensed and unlawful process made by you against me . . ." He accuses the commissioners of having "confounded all kind of legal process; sometimes proceeding 'ad denunciandum'; sometimes 'ex officio mero'; sometimes 'ex officio mixto'; contrary to the king's ecclesiastical laws and contrary also to this commission directed in this behalf . . ." He questions the lawfulness of his "strait imprisonment," which prevented his prosecuting his appeal to the king. Gardiner points to his forced absence from the upper house, quotes the Act of Uniformity, raises exceptions to the witnesses, who as peers were not on oath, though "the law ecclesiastical requireth the oath corporal . . ."

Foxe devotes some sixty pages to Bonner (V, 741–800) and more than two hundred to Gardiner (VI, 24–267).

[14] Foxe, *Actes & Monuments,* VI, 74, 111. In similar vein, Bonner, V, 788–89, 793. In his third appeal he complains "that he had found heretofore, at the hands of the archbishop of Canterbury and the rest of the colleagues in this matter, much extremity and cruelty, injuries, losses, and griefs, contrary to God's law, and the laws and statutes of this realm, and against justice, charity, and good order."

[15] Trevelyan, *English Social History,* p. 58.

Aesop's Fables, would probably have overlooked the fact that one law book also slipped from Caxton's press—the first of the great series soon to follow.

Gentlemen and citizens alike were reading, besides "endless romances in prose and 'rhyme doggrel' about Troy, King Arthur and a hundred other traditional tales," chronicles of England and France in verse and in prose, recounting the deeds of their sovereign's "illustrious predecessors." The rise of the cult of "antiquities"—not classical lore but Britain's own past—led in the search for manuscripts to the finding and publishing of more ample historical sources, chronicles hitherto lost or dispersed. There was a revival of ancient tongues (Celtic and Anglo-Saxon) and a keen interest in history and archaeology.

The illustrious succession of "literate lawyers" perennially praised and perpetuated the common law in compilations and treatises. Trained in Latin and classical mythology, something less of mathematics and philosophy in the universities, and in legal lore and social graces in the Inns of Court, they were also well practised as city recorder, king's serjeant, justice of the peace, and judge, had served one or more sessions in the House of Commons and sometimes in the privy council. "Master Silence, J. P. is at the cost of keeping his son, Will, at Oxford, for some years before he goes on to the Inns of Court; and after that double training in the humanities and in law, the young man will be fit to succeed his father as a Gloucestershire landowner and Justice of the Peace." [16]

It remained, however, for the late years of Elizabeth's reign and the indomitable combination of Puritan and lawyer in such men as Robert Beale, James Maurice, and Nicholas Fuller to recreate the Great Charter in its role of "liberty document." In this they anticipated Coke by several years, while he, in fact, still the Tudor statesman and dutiful official, as speaker of the commons pocketed, at his queen's direction, the bill to confirm Magna Carta and "liberty of the subject."

The Printers and Magna Carta

The former booke intituled Magna Charta [contained some things not very necessary to be had] in one so portable a volume, and the same confusedly and not orderly digested, and in many places . . . verye faltye. This conteyneth the most necessarie of those olde statutes, and divers later and newe statutes most convenient to bee had, perfect and ready, not onely by al students of the lawe for their private studies, readings, mootes, boltes, cases and other exercyses, but also by the practisers of the same for their daylie affaires . . .

(ANTIQUA STATUTA, TOTTELL'S EDITION)

[16] *Ibid.,* p. 182.

AT THE very time when the Great Charter is assumed to have fallen into obscurity, the printing press was giving it a sort of mechanical physical publicity in the successive editions of statutes that rapidly appeared. The printing press was established in Westminster in 1477, Oxford 1478, St. Albans 1479, and London 1480. From Caxton's press at the sign of the "red pale" in the Almonry at Westminster there appears to have come only one law book, the *Statutes 1–4 Henry VII.* Caxton, "the individualistic Englishman following out his own 'hobbies' with business capacity and trained zeal," was also the man of letters, translator as well as editor and publisher, serving royal and noble patrons who wanted romances or religious works such as *Morte d'Arthur,* the *Golden Legend,* and the *Sarum Ordinale.*

For the first forty years after the introduction of printing into England, most of the persons connected with the book trade were foreigners. Only in the second forty years do Englishmen replace foreigners in numbers and status. In 1480 John Lettou, a skilled printer, set up his press in London. When two years later he formed a partnership with William de Machlinia (of Mechlin, Brabant), the lawyers came into their own. Machlinia's strong point was legal printing: "during his continuance in the business (1482–86) he seems to have printed all the law books issued in England." For Lettou's "neat type" he substituted "a small cramped black letter abounding in abbreviations, designed after the law hand of the period." By 1483 their press had produced Littleton's *Tenures,* an abridgment of the statutes, and the Year Books of 33, 35, and 36 Henry VI.[17]

More notable was Machlinia's successor, Richard Pynson of Normandy.[18] Pynson had probably been educated at the University of Paris and had learned printing from Richard le Talleur, a noted printer of Rouen. For the printing of law books, his knowledge of Norman French must have been an asset. If he did start in Machlinia's shop he moved shortly to St. Clement's parish outside Temple Bar, and in 1500 to Fleet Street within Temple Bar at the sign of the George, where he remained until his death (c. 1530). Other printers settled nearby, and Fleet Street became the "printers' row" of the sixteenth century, as it is the "newspaper row" of the present day. When Pynson first arrived in London he was without material, so he commissioned Le Talleur at Rouen to print for him the two law books most in demand, Littleton's *Tenures* and Statham's *Abridgement.* Duff characterizes Pynson as "an enterprizing

---

[17] Duff, *A Century of the English Book Trade.* The type used by Lettou and other printers had none of the abbreviations necessary for printing law books.

[18] Duff thinks that he succeeded Machlinia promptly (between 1488–90), otherwise "England would have been left without a printer who could set up law French"; Pynson did not actually work with him or inherit his type, but occupied his vacated shop in Holborn and used waste materials (his earliest bindings are lined with waste leaves of Machlinia's printing).

and careful printer" whose work became even more scholarly as time went on. Notable was his edition of the beautiful *Morton Missal* and of the plays of Terrence, with one exception the first classic printed in England. Distinguished and learned men like Cardinal Morton were his patrons. In 1508 he became official "king's printer," in which post he published Henry VIII's works against Luther, and the current *session laws.* Beale calls him the first to print law books in considerable numbers.[19] Among these were editions of the *Antiqua Statuta* or *Boke of Magna Carta* and the *Grand Abridgement* to be described below.

About 1525 the shrewd and practical Robert Redman began to print in St. Clement's parish outside Temple Bar. His unscrupulous adoption of Pynson's sign (the George) and imitation of Pynson's publications led to bitter controversy. On Pynson's death, Redman bought out his business, used his type and devices, and even assumed, unsuccessfully, to be his successor as king's printer. He is of interest here only as the printer of the *Great Book of Statutes* and Ferrers' translation of the statutes, 1534. Pynson's true successor as king's printer was Thomas Berthelet, who served in this post from 1530 to 1547. In the capacity of bookbinder he gratified his royal patron's taste for the magnificent by producing gilttooled bindings in the Venetian manner, and is believed to have brought Italian workmen to England for this purpose. The output of his press in law books was as impressive in number and variety as Pynson's, including new editions of works printed by his predecessor.[20]

A different kind of printer appears in the persons of John and William Rastell—father and son, both trained lawyers and Lincoln's Inn men—who were editors as well as printers. John, who married Sir Thomas More's sister Elizabeth, has received more attention, perhaps because of his literary proclivities,[21] but William's editing was the more scholarly. John had for a time an excellent law practice, and he represented Dunheved, Cornwall, in the Reformation parliament. As to his press, "he appears," says Duff, "not to have attended closely to his business, but to have passed much of his time at his house in the country, leaving his workmen to attend to the printing." Yet John himself refers to the pros-

[19] All told he printed over three hundred different books. Of his output, 1490–1500, more than one fourth were law books. Besides the works mentioned above, these included the *Old Tenures, Natura Brevium, Carta Feodi, Court Baron, Novae Narrationes, Diversity of Courts, Justices of the Peace, Hundred Court,* and a number of Year Books. For a complete list, see Beale, *A Bibliography of Early English Law Books.*

[20] Beale, *Bibliography*, pp. 176–78, 191–92.

[21] Most notable of the law books issuing from his press were the *Liber Assisarum*, Fitzherbert's *Grand Abridgement*, and the abridgment of the statutes to be described below. "The majority of the books he issued were legal," says Duff, "but besides these are some of great interest, such as 'The Mery Gestys of the Widow Edith,' 1525; 'The Hundred Mery Talys,' 1526; 'Necromantia,' n.d.; and others." He himself compiled a popular chronicle, *The Pastyme of People,* and wrote a moral play, *A New Interlude and a Mery of the Nature of the iiii Elements,* 1519. E. Gordon Duff, in *D.N.B.*

perous years when he "printed every year two or three hundred ream of paper, which was more yearly profit to me than the gains that I got by the law . . ." [22].

William Rastell followed his father's craft of printer from 1530 to 1534.[23] While still so engaged he was admitted student at Lincoln's Inn, 1532, was called to the bar in 1539, chosen autumn reader in 1547, and treasurer in 1555. He, too, practiced law with considerable success. A Catholic, he remained at Louvain throughout Edward's reign. On Mary's accession, he was made serjeant-at-law and served as judge of Queen's Bench, 1558–63. During this period comes his really valuable contribution as editor rather than mere printer: the complete edition of More's English works, and several important law books, including the *Collection of all the Statutes,* to be described below.

To George Ferrers (1500–79) goes the distinction of making the first English translation of Magna Carta and other statutes (unabridged).[24] Ferrers is one of those interesting and notable persons in the reigns of Henry VIII and Elizabeth—that age so prolific in notables—who have been rather lost sight of amid the galaxy of brilliant contemporaries. "Poet and politician," Sir Sidney Lee calls him. To students of English literature he is the poet, writer of masques, and inventor of the *Mirror for Magistrates.*[25] To constitutional historians he is the politician, the member of the commons who figures as the principal in *Ferrers' case,* 1542, vindicating the parliamentary privilege of freedom from arrest. He was also a lawyer, a member of Lincoln's Inn, and "his oratory gained him a high reputation at the bar."

To anyone familiar with the manuscript volumes of statutes described above, the early printed volumes present little novelty. They simply reproduce in print the same varieties that had already proved their usefulness to bench and bar, and justices of the peace. In point of time there ap-

---

[22] This is a letter to Thomas Cromwell, 1536, in which he speaks of the loss of business and friends, and poverty: "for wher before I gate by the law in pleading in Westminster Hall forty marks a year, that was twenty nobles a term at least, and printed every year two or three hundred ream of paper, which was more yearly profit to me than the gains I got by the law, I assure you I get not now forty shillings a year by the law, nor I printed not a hundred ream of paper in this two year." *D.N.B.*

[23] In these years he printed at a house in St. Brides' churchyard, Fleet Street, whence issued some thirty books, including plays, interludes, and his uncle's controversial works—*The Works of Sir Thomas More, knight, sometyme Lorde Chancellour of England; written by him in the Englysh Tonge.* J. M. Rigg, in *D.N.B.*

[24] That is, the first translation in the printed statutes. There may have been others in manuscript, but this is Ferrers' own, not a copy. Whether the popularity of Rastell's *Abridgement* in English suggested the project, or the practical and aggressive Redman pressed for it, Ferrers' biographer attributes the publication definitely to Ferrers himself: in 1534, "he published an English translation of the Magna Charta and of other important statutes." Redman reissued the book without date in 1541, and Thomas Petyt produced a new edition in 1542.

[25] His "chief claim to literary distinction lies in the fact that he shared with Baldwin the honour of having invented the series of historical poems entitled 'Mirror for Magistrates.' " S. L. Lee, in *D.N.B.*

peared from the press first, the currently enacted statutes (session laws);
then the *Nova Statuta* and *Antiqua Statuta*; special collections such as
the *Great Book of Statutes*; and abridgments arranged under alphabetical titles.[26] It is intended to select for description here, of course, only
those which contain the Great Charter or related documents.

The small edition of the *Antiqua Statuta* was first printed by Pynson in
1508, and afterwards frequently reprinted. The little volume issued in
1514, for instance, is a 16mo (13½ x 7½ centimeters), of 150 numbered
leaves, and contains some sixty-three so-called *statutes, ordinationes, articuli*, and a supplement with names of the kings of England, and *aliqua
parva documenta valde necessaria* (counties, lists of writs, and geograph-
ical data). For Magna Carta and nine other statutes there are lists of
numbered *capitula*[27] with leaf references. The text of the Charter is Edward I's *inspeximus* (28 Edward I) in thirty-seven numbered chapters.
With rare exceptions such variations in numbering as occurred in the
manuscript volumes cease and this same thirty-seven is repeated from
Ferrers to McKechnie.

Variants from other presses, such as Berthelet's (1531), include an interesting additional feature, perhaps suggested by the abridgments—an
alphabetical table of matters. The method of reference, simply to numbered leaves, is vague, yet it seems possible to spot intended references to
some twenty-six chapters of Magna Carta.[28]

The title *Antiqua Statuta*, used by the record commissioners, M. Bémont, and others, was not that commonly used by these early printers and
editors. True, the colophon of Pynson's little volume of 1508 concludes
Parvum codex qui Antiqua Statuta vocatur explicit. But the title commonly used in the many successive editions was, in Latin, *Magna Carta
cum aliis antiquis statutis*; and, in translation, *The Boke of Magna Carta
with divers other statutes*. Publishers of later sixteenth-century collections
cited it simply as *The Boke of Magna Carta*.[29] The full titles appealed to

---

[26] Beale's classification is as follows: 1. Collections: (a) Nova Statuta, (b) Magna Carta
(antiqua statuta), (c) Secunda Pars, (d) Great Book of Statutes, (e) Statutes from 1225,
(f) Statutes at Large, (g) Collected Statutes; 2. Abridgments: (a) the Great Abridgment,
(b) Rastell's Statutes, (c) Pulton's Penal Statutes, (d) Abridgments of Session Laws; 3. Session
Laws.

[27] Examples of the *capitula* for Magna Carta: "Quod communia placita tenentur in loco
certo," "De amerciamentis assidend' secundum quantitatem delicti," "De precipe in capite,"
"Quod una mesura sit per totum regnum," "Quod Ballivus non ponat aliquem ad legem,"
"Quod nullus liber homo capiatur nisi per legale iudicium," "De conductione marcatorum."

[28] Cas. 2, 3, 4, 6, 7, 8, 10, 11 (?), 12, 13, 14, 16, 18, 19, 20, 22, 23, 25, 26, 28, 30, 31,
35, 36, 37. Examples of the titles: amerciementes, assise, Baillies, comitatus, Dette, Distresse,
Liber homo, Terre felonum. Berthelet's *Statutes from 1225* (1543) also has such a table of titles
though the references are incomplete and inaccurate. The title page of Berthelet's volume is
reproduced above, p. 35.

[29] ". . . the former booke intituled Magna Charta," preface to Tottell's 1576 edition. "Se in
the newe printed booke commonlye called Magna Carta, late printed by Rychard Tottel, An.
domini 1556 . . ." Rastell's *Statutes*, 1574 edition, leaf 374v.

the reader in quite the style of the modern publisher's "jacket": "Magna Carta in f.[olio] hereunto is added more Statuts than ever was imprynted in any one boke before this tyme with an Alminacke and a Calendar to know the mootes Necessarye for all yong studiers of the law."

The first English edition of the statutes is not that of the full texts, but the *Great Abridgement* (to 11 Henry VIII), translated and printed by John Rastell, 1527. In his preface Rastell attributes the printing of the current statutes (session laws) in English to Henry VII, and justifies his Englishing of the old statutes on the same grounds:

> But yet besyde this now of late days the moste noble prynce our late soveryn lorde kynge henry the vii. worthy to be called the seconde Salomon (whiche excellyd in polytyk wysedome all other pryncis that reygned in this realm before his tyme) concyderynge and well persevynge that our vulgare englissh tong was marvelously amendyd and augmentyd by reason that dyverse famous clerkys and lernyd men had translate and made many noble workys into our englisshe tong wherby there was moch more plenty and haboundance of englysshe usyd than there was in tymys past and by reason therof our vulgare tong so amplified and sufficient of itself to expound any lawys or ordinauncis which was nedeful to be made for the ordre of this realm, and also the same wyse prince consyderyng that the unyversall people of this realm had greate pleasure and gave themself greatly to the redynge of the vulgar englysshe tonge, ordeynyed and caused that all the statutys and ordinaunces which were made for the commeyn welth of this realm in his dayes shulde be indytyd and wryttyn in the vulgare englyssh tonge and to be publysshyd declaryd and imprinted so that than unyversally the people of the realm myght sone have the knowleg of the sayd statuts and ordynauncys which they were bound to observe and so by reason of that knowlege to avoid the daunger and penaltes of the same statutys and also the better to lyfe in tranquylyte and peace.

Henry VIII continued the practice, and so concludes Rastell:

> All which goodly purposys and intentys in my mynde often tymys revolvyde hath causyd me to take this lytell payne to translate out of frenche into englysshe the abbrevyacyon of the statutys made before the fyrst yere [of the reign of Henry VII].

This first *Great Abridgement* is actually a small, thick volume, 16mo (13 x 9½ centimeters), of 264 leaves. Its manuscript prototype is to be found in Harleian MSS 1317, described above. Some twenty-four chapters of Magna Carta are distributed under one or more titles each, twenty-six in all.[30] Short chapters are given in full; for the longer provisions a brief

[30] These are 2, 3, 4, 5, 6, 7, 8, 11, 12, 13, 14, 19, 21, 22, 24, 25, 27, 28, 29, 30, 31, 34, 35, 36. Titles are: Accusacion, Amerciemente, Appeles, Assise, Common Plees, Novel disseisin, Darrein presentment, Dette, Dower, Eschete, Merchantes & Merchandises, Mortmaine, Mordauncestre, Piers of the realme, Prerogatyf of the King, Purveiours, Quarentine, Reliefe, Right, Turne, View of fraunkpledge, Wager of lawe, Wardes, Waste, Weights and measures.

paraphrase may epitomize some main point, ignoring qualifying clauses.[31] Worth quoting for its notable influence on the current understanding is this for chapter 29 under the caption *Accusacion*: "no man shall be takyn or imprisonyd or any wyse destroyed nor we shall not go nor sit upon hym but by lawfull iugement of his peerys or by the law of the land."

It remained for George Ferrers to translate the full text of the Charters and other statutes antedating 1 Edward III from the current editions of the *Antiqua Statuta*.[32] Ferrers, if we may assume the *To the reder* to be his, recognizes the difficulty of the task but justifies it on the grounds of its practical value:

specyally when many of the termes as well French as latyn be so ferre out of ure by reason of theyr antyquyte, that scarsely those that be best studyed in the lawes can understande them, much les then shal suche as come rawly to the redynge therof perceyve what they meane. And yet in the same yf they be well sought, is conteyned a great part of the pryncyples and olde groundys of the lawes. For by serchyng the great extremities of the comon lawes before the makynge of statutes and the remedyes provyded by them, a good student shal soone attayne to a perfyte iudgement. And bycause the moste parte of them retayne theyr force, and bynde the kyng's subiectes unto this day, me thought it necessary to set them forth in such sorte as men myghte beste have knowledge of them and knowledge can they have none except they rede them and what dothe it avayle to rede, yf they understande not, and how shulde they understande the meanyng which understande not the text. For this cause I saye was thys boke translated into the Englyshe, which thoughe percase it shal not satysfye the lerned, yet shall it be a good helpe for the unlerned.

Cay, in the preface to his 1758 edition of the statutes, attributes the translation of the statutes Henry III–19 Henry VII (Berthelet 1543) to Ferrers also, and comments thus on it:

It is not a good one, and the Mistakes in it are very numerous and considerable: It has often been desired that a new Translation should be made, but as this has been used for some Ages, not only by the Public in general, but even the Parliament, and many Statutes are recited in subsequent Acts in the Words of this Translation, *it seems to be too much authenticated for any Editor to presume to reject it.*[33]

---

[31] "Recognicions of assise shall not be taken but in theyr countes, magna carta c. xii.

"Comyn plees shal be holdin in a place certein, magna cart. c. xi.

"They thyrde parte shal be assignyd to the woman for her dowry of all the land that was to her husband in his lyfe except that she were redowed of lesse at the churche dore, m. carta capitulo septimo."

[32] *The Boke of Magna Carta, with divers other statutes . . . translated into Englyshe by George Ferrers*, Redman, 1534. This contains the greater part, but not all, of the matters included in earlier volumes, but does not arrange them in chronological order. Successive editions with some amendments and additions were printed: 1. by Redman's widow Elizabeth, 1540, *The great Charter called in latyn Magna Carta with divers olde statutes . . . newly correctyd*; 2. by Thomas Petyt, with the same title and preface, 1542.

[33] Italics mine. *S. R.* I, xxii. xxiv.

Just so must these early translations of Magna Carta have had their influence and become "too much authenticated" for any lawyer or parliament man, even the great Sir Edward Coke, to presume to reject them.

Ferrers' translation of the Charter is awkward and wordy in parts. In a few instances incorrect sequence of words and phrases (chapters 26 and 31) or faulty punctuation (chapters 35 and 37) obscures the meaning. Naturally the same clauses are omitted that are missing from his Latin models. Yet on the whole he does rather well. Clauses and phrases may be in inverted order and nearly every word of a given chapter different from that of the modern version, yet the general meaning be the same. The translator does not seem to have worried about the niceties of *et* and *vel* and wades bravely through the difficult archaic words over which modern scholars have labored so hard: the *vivaria* of chapter 5 (Mc-Kechnie's "fishponds") is translated "warrens" (and Coke does the same); in chapter 14 *wainagium* is simply "waynage," but *contenement* is equated with "freholde"; in chapters 15 and 19 *villa* is wrongly translated "town"; in chapter 23 *kidelli* are "werys"; and the archaic textiles of chapter 25 become "one bredth' of dyed clothe, russettes and haberiectes," as compared with McKechnie's "one width of cloth (whether dyed, or russet, or 'halberget' "). Even McKechnie had to give up on this last word and simply guesses that it may have meant some kind of heavy cloth worn under a hauberk. Some renderings are those which would come naturally to the pen of a common lawyer of the sixteenth century: in chapter 10 "freholde" (McKechnie's "free tenement"); in chapter 30 "saufe and sure conduyte" (McKechnie's "safe and sure exit from England and entry to England"); in chapter 24 "the wryt that is called precipe in capite." [34] Quite in the spirit of the year when the translation was published, the *Ecclesia Anglicana* is rendered "church of England." More significant than any of these is Ferrers' rendering of chapter 29, the clause *nec super eum ibimus, nec super eum mittemus.* He uses not the literal "nor will we go upon him nor send upon him" of the feudal age of John and Henry III, not the modified "nor we shall not go nor sit upon hym" of Rastell's abridgment, but the complete equation with legal process which has been credited to Coke—"nor we shall not passe upon hym, nor condempne hym."

The alphabetical index of matters improves upon that of the Latin and French editions of 1529 and 1531. The terms chosen are more scholarly or, better, more lawyer-like: "aiornement," "ne iniuste vexes," "precipe in capite," "Peers of the realm," "wager of law" (for chapter 28 where others have "baillies").

---

[34] Other errors: ca. 7 omits the clause *dum vivere voluit sine marito*; ca. 18, to *attache & arrest* instead of to *catalogue* (*imbreviare*); ca. 21, *lord* instead of *lady*; ca. 35, *perquisivit* is translated *purchase.*

The *Great Boke of Statutes* (1 Edward III to 25 Henry VIII) in English, also published by Redman, does not, of course, contain the text of the Charters. Its elaborate table of statutes reign by reign and parliament by parliament does list successive confirmations of the Charters and other statutes and indicates the relationship of certain fourteenth-century statutes to Magna Carta.[35]

After the middle of the century, interest centers on better editing of the original Latin and French texts and on better translations.[36] Tottell's press succeeds Pynson's and Berthelet's in printing of new editions of the *Antiqua Statuta,* now again in the original tongues but emended by comparison with the official rolls.[37] In a preface "to the Gentlemen studious of the lawes of Englande," Tottell claims that his publications are more accurate, better printed, and cheaper than those of his predecessors, and that he has procured "learned help" where he could. In Tottell's 1576 edition, a small thick volume of 247 leaves, a more selective method has been used, and corrections explicitly indicated. The preface describes the shortcomings of "the former booke intituled Magna Charta," and the virtues of the new edition (as quoted at the head of this section) and explains that words between "two plain strikes" show what is corrected or added, "the corrections whereof are to be warranted by divers auncient copies . . ."[38] It was apparently the 1587 edition of Tottell's statutes that was used by Sir Edward Coke in his *Second Institute.*[39]

William Rastell combined in his publications the best features of earlier works and improved on them. He seems to have found his father's *Abridgement* all too sketchy and inaccurate and, unlike Ferrers, was skep-

---

[35] *The great boke of statutes conteynyng all the statutes made in the parliamentes from the begynnyng of the fyrst yere of the reigne of kyng Edwarde the thyrd tyll the begynnyng of the xxv yere of the moste gracyous reigne of our Soveraigne lorde kyng Henry the VIII.* In eight instances the table specifically mentions a confirmation of the Charters. In twenty other instances some such phrase is used as "a confirmation of all statutes not repealed," "All statutes not repealed confirmed," "All liberties and good statutes confirmed." For instance:
"Here begynneth the second parliament holden at Northampton in the seconde yere of kyng Edward the Thyrd.
"A confirmacyon of the great chartre & the chartre of the forest, ca. 1."
. . .
"The xxiii parliament holden at Westminster the xlii yere of kyng Edward the thyrd.
"The great chartre and the chartre of the forest confirmed, ca. 1."
[36] This is about the time (1569) of the fine and scholarly edition of Bracton, whose editor (the mysterious "T. N.") collated eight manuscripts.
[37] As indicated by his title: *Magna Charta, cum statutis quae Antiqua vocantur, iam recens excusa, & summa fide emendata, iuxta vetusta exemplaria ad Parliamenti rotulos examinata;* also published by Myddlyton with statutes to 34 Henry VIII.
[38] Thus clauses omitted from the text of the early editions are supplied and a number of minor corrections in a single word or phrase indicated. Take for instance his treatment of ca. 7: "Nulla vidua distringatur ad se maritandum // dummodo voluerit vivere sine marito // Ita tamen . . ."
The table of chapters of Magna Carta, based, as the preface states, on Rastell's compilation, is of interest because like that it includes ca. 29 as the first item under *Accusation.*
[39] See below, Chap. XII.

tical of translations. His statutes, like the abridgments, are distributed under alphabetical titles but on a more selective basis. As he explains in the preface to his first edition ("William Rastell seriant at law to the gentill readers," 1557): "all the printed statutes expired or repelled, or concernyng private parsons or some private places" have been omitted. The rest of the printed statutes are included, "worde for worde as they be in the great statutes," only leaving out "certeyn superfluous wordes, as also the most part of the preambles," except those "without whiche the body of the statutes cannot be well perceived." As a further help to the reader, he explains, "the wordes in the small letter within the parentises ( ) be not the wordes of the statute, but my wordes planted in there, for the better understanding of the statute." Moreover, he continues: "I have put every statute in the tonge that it was first written in. For those that were first written in latin or in frenche, dare I not presume to translate into Englishe, for feare of misse interpretacion. For many wordes and termes be there in divers statutes both in latyn and in frenche, which be very hard to translate aptly into English."

After Rastell's death, however, Barker and other printers produced the same collection in English translation. Rastell's original preface continued to be used, simply omitting the passage on retaining the original tongues! Many of Rastell's titles are identical with those of the *Great Abridgement,* but there are additions and substitutions, more apt and lawyer-like.[40] His arrangement permits the inclusion of all the chapters of Magna Carta, quoted in full, and with only one interpolation "planted in there" by the editor.[41] Under the title *Accusacion* appears not only chapter 29, but in chronological order five [42] of the *six statutes,* with 17 Richard II, chapter 6, and 15 Henry VI, chapter 4, that all who run might read.

A variation from collections such as Rastell's appeared in 1560 with the first edition of Pulton's *An Abstract of all the penal Statutes which be generall, in force and use, wherein is contained the effect of all those Statutes which do threaten to the offenders thereof, the losse of life, member, lands, goods, or other forfeiture whatsoever.*[43] A practical and successful book, it was reprinted in 1577, 1594, and 1596. Ferdinando Pulton had more university training and connection than many of the active

[40] For instance, some of his titles correspond to those of the Natura Brevium for "actions founded on Magna Carta": *moderata misericordia, precipe in capite, rationabile parte bonorum.* Ca. 22 is given appropriately under *forfeiture* instead of *escheat.* Interesting captions are *franchises & liberties* (under which Magna Carta, cas. 1, 9, and the last clause of 37 are included), *confirmacion,* and *excommengement.*

[41] Ca. 37—*Omnes autem consuetudines & libertates (s. in magna carta) quas concessimus in regno* . . .

[42] Excluding the inappropriate 36 Edward III, no. 9, introduced by the lawyers in 1628.

[43] This title continues: "Whereunto is also added in their apt Titles, the effect of all other generall Statutes, wherein is there any thing material and necessarie for each Subiect to know. Moreover the Authoritie and duetie of all Iustices, Sherifes, Coroners, Escheators, Maiors . . ."

members of the legal profession. He was a commoner of Brasenose College, Oxford, and a fellow of Christ's College, Cambridge. Though a member of Lincoln's Inn, he was never called to the bar because he was a Roman Catholic. It may fairly be said that he devoted his life to the editing of the statutes. The *Penal Statutes* contains an epistle "To the Right worshipful Sir William Cordell, Knight, Master of the Roules." It has the usual eulogy of England's laws so characteristic of this age but, as we might expect from a scholar of Pulton's type, with rather more reference to Roman law and God's law (the law of nature and reason). For instance, after describing the drawing up of the *Twelve Tables* of the Romans and the ten commandments and other law of the Children of Israel, he continues:

With which good examples, and such like . . . the vertuous Princes and Governours of this Realme being mooved, have not onely provided for the due observation of the Lawes of GOD within these their Kingdomes and Provinces, picked foorth the purest iuice and pithiest marrow of the Lawes of the Romans and other regions, and from time to time by the advise of their nobles, and consent of their commons, decreed, altered, and refourmed the same according to the inclination of their subiects . . .

but have published and made them known, that each person might know that whereby he was to live

alwaies intending that these Lawes, which the finger of God hath written in the heart of man, or nature infused into him upon his first creation, or reason, the onely cognisaunce of mankinde, instilled into his breast, or which the auncient Maximes and Customes of the Realme, the verie ground of all our Common Lawes, have instructed him, be not to any English man, having the clear use of *Synderisis,* wholly unknown.

In explaining the English practice of publicizing the laws, Pulton uses as one of several examples how "King Edward I ordeined by Parliament that the statute of *Magna Charta,* and *Charta Foresta,* should be openly read in the Churches."[44] The task he has set himself is necessitated by the condition of the statutes "growen to be so many, some much differing, and some mere contrary and repugnant to others." But their chronological range has already been definitely set by his predecessors, from the time of Henry III "in the ninth yere of whose raigne Magna Charta the first statute that we have in print was made." Under eighteen alphabetical titles are included twenty-one chapters of the Charter.[45]

[44] ". . . and further they have foreseene, that some special statutes, which be most dangerous and into the perill whereof the ignorant people are likest to slide, should be openly read in the foresaid Courts, that the hearers thereof should not onely understand themselves, but also instruct their neighbours at home, of those most Penall Lawes, and of the great daungers thereof."

[45] From *Accusation,* ca. 29, to *Weares,* 15, 16, 23. Of the sixteen omitted, a few were obsolete, and others not "penal."

Pulton uses the title *Accusation,* as do the others, but with the marginal caption "No man shall be condemned without lawfull triall." His translation of chapter 29, slightly different from Rastell's, is followed by interesting cross references to or summaries of one or other of the *six statutes.*[46]

The novelty of Pulton's editions lies partly in this selective treatment but even more in bringing the Charter up to date by combining a provision with one or more later enactments[47] and by rephrasing. A statute which is thus made to deal in easy colloquial fashion with the "Queen's wards," "any other mans villein except the Queenes," "none which holdeth of the Queene in capite," "if any Earle, Baron, or other of the Queenes tenants, which holdeth of her Grace in Capite by knights service doe die," "if anie man do make a Suggestion to the Queenes Maiestie," is indeed far from seeming obsolete, archaic, or obscure!

The Chroniclers and Magna Carta

THE reading of history was a popular pastime in Tudor England.[48] To scholar and amateur alike its value was believed to lie in examples to be imitated or shunned. Chronicles were most in favor with bourgeois readers, especially chronicles of London which gratified civic pride, although the standard chronicles of England, such as those of Hall and Holinshed, enjoyed wide circulation. Richard Grafton, grocer-printer, and John Stow, merchant-tailor, catered particularly to bourgeois tastes. While some accounts dealt narrowly with London and its interests or with recent and contemporary events,[49] another group attempted to cover the whole known history of England and to glorify the ruling monarch by an account of his "illustrious ancestors," reign by reign. It was in such as these last—briefly in the pages of Caxton and Fabyan, and in more detail in the great chronicle of Holinshed three generations later—that the

---

[46] His translation and summary are as follows: "No freeman shal be taken or imprisoned, or disseised of his freehold, liberties or free custome nor shall be outlawed, banished, or by any meanes brought to destruction: neither shall any passe, or sit in iudgement upon him, but by the lawfull iudgement of his equales, or by the law of the Realme." (Note the "neither shall *any* passe," instead of *we*; and "equales" instead of *peers*.) Then, "neither shall iustice or right be sold, denied, or deferred to any man. Magna Charta 9 Hen. 3 29. 5 Ed. 3 9. And if any man be taken or put to answere without a presentment before Iustices, or some matter of record, or by due proces, or by writ originall, the same is void and erronious. 25 Ed. 3. 4. 28 Ed. 3. 3 42 Ed. 3. 2. See Suggestion." Under another title, *Wager of Lawe,* is a suggestive translation of the obscure ca. 28 of the Charter: "No Bailife shall put any man to his open law, nor to his oth, upon his own bare report, without faithfull witnesses brought in for the same. Mag. Chart. 9 Hen. 3. 28."

[47] For instance, Magna Carta ca. 14 and West. I, ca. 6, on amercements; ca. 36 with Mortmain; ca. 31 with statutes of 1 Ed. 3, ca. 13, and 1 Ed. 6, ca. 4 (prerogative); grouping cas. 15, 16, and 23; and combining the substance of three of the *six statutes.*

[48] Wright, "The Elizabethan Middle Class Taste for History," *Journal of Modern History,* 3:175–97.

[49] *The Grey Friars of London Chronicle* and Richard Arnold's *Customs of London* ("a popular hodgepodge of information about London"); *Hall's Chronicle* (1399–1547), the best contemporary history of the reign of Henry VIII.

story of John's reign, the original granting of the Charter of Liberties, and its reissue by Henry III were set forth.

In the words of *Caxton's Chronicle* and its replica, the *St. Alban's Chronicle*:[50]

"Ther began a gret debate bitwene king John and the lordis of englond" for reason that he would not keep the laws of Saint Edward, "for he wold hold no law bot did all thing that he likid." He had disinherited men without consent of lords and peers of the land, and would disinherit the "good Erle Randulf of Chestre" for reproaching him "of his wykkednesse" . . . The archbishops and other great lords "assembled them before the fest of sent Johan baptist in a Medow besides the toune of Stanes yt is called Romnemede. And the kyng made them ther a chertour of fraunches [*sic*] such as they wold aven and in soch maner they were accordid and that accordement last not full longe, for the kyng him selfe soone after did ayens the pointis of the same chartre that he had made wherefor the moste parte of the land of lordis assembled them and began to were upon him ayen."

What follows is superior to some later chronicles in that it recounts two of the reissues (although confusing what was done in 1217 with 1225), and makes clear the connection between John's charter and Henry III's "wich yit bene holdein."

How Lowys turned ayen into Fraunce and of the confirmacion of kyng Johanes chartre

. . . And afterward the kyng and the Erchebishop and erles and Barouns assembled them at London at Michelmasse that next come thosewyng and held ther a great parlament and ther wer tho renewed all the fraunches yt king John had graunted at Romnemede and king Henri tho confirmed by his chartre the wich yit bene holdein thrugh out all englond.

. . .

Of the quinzeme of goodis that wer grantid, for the new chartre and of the purveance of Oxford.

And it befell that the lordis of englond wold haven somme addicions mo in the chartre of fraunches that thei had off the kyng and spekyn thus bitwen them anon the kyng graunted them all ther axyng and made to them ii chartres that on is called the gret chartre of fraunchises and that other is called the

[50] *The Chronicles of England*, called *Caxton's Chronicle* (though merely an imprint of the popular chronicle of *Brut* (first edition folio Westminster, 1480; second edition folio Westminster, 1482. There are extant thirteen copies of the first edition; eight of the second. Hardy, in his introduction to Waurin, I, lxi–lxiii (R. S.), describes the *Brut* as existing in several "anonymous prose versions in Anglo-Norman, apparently of English origin—reducible, as it would seem, to two distinct classes, or types"; one written shortly after the period at which it terminates, 1333; the second written about the middle of the fourteenth century, from which *Caxton's Chronicle* was translated.

Chronicles of England, St. Albans, 1483. "The St. Albans reprint is called the *Fructus Temporum*, and contains precisely the same text as Caxton's, with the addition of slight notices of Popes and Emperors." *Dibden's Library Companion*, p. 170.

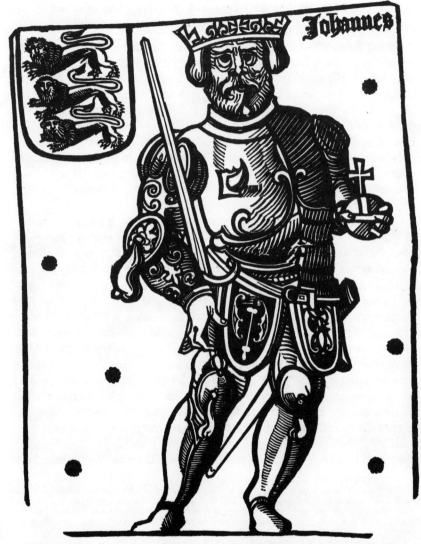

King John—a woodcut from John Rastell's *The Pastyme of People*

chartre of forest and for the graunt of thes ii charters prelatis Erles and barons and all ye commyns of englond yaf to the king a m marke of silv[er].

Robert Fabyan was one of the early citizen chroniclers. He was a member of the Drapers Company, alderman of the ward of Farringdon Without, and sheriff in 1493. He knew French and was the best skilled in Latin of any layman of his age. He endeavored, says a modern editor of his work, "to reconcile the discordant testimonies of historians: adding the fruits of personal observation in the latter and more interesting portion of his Chronicle." [51] Some of his authorities he must have known only in manuscript; a few such as Caxton's were in print. It is Caxton which Fabyan quotes on the causes of dissension between John and the barons. His account of the granting of the Charter, however, is brief [52] and he makes no mention of any reissue by Henry III.

John Rastell reprinted *Fabyan's Chronicle,* and was himself the author of *The Pastyme of People or The Cronycles of Dyvers realmys and most specially of the Realme of England* (1529). As the title page professes, these accounts are "brevely compyled" [53] from earlier chronicles, Caxton, Machlinia, St. Albans, Fabyan, and the Polychronicon. Like the compiler's volume of statutes, it is a careless piece of work; in fact, says its modern editor (T. F. Dibden), "it is hard to conceive a book more rudely printed." Yet to contemporary readers typographical defects must have been partly offset by the striking full-page woodcuts of the kings of England, though they appear a bit ludicrous to the modern eye. The passage on the causes of the "great discencyon" between John and his "lordes" is an abbreviated statement of Caxton's. In what follows, Rastell, not mere chronicler but printer and lawyer as well, refers to the charter as *Magna Carta* and adds a few words on its contents.[54]

In 1534 appeared the *English History* of the learned Polydore Vergil,[55] the friend of Bishop Fox of Winchester, More, Erasmus, and others. Nat-

[51] Henry Ellis' edition, p. xiii.

[52] "Soon after, to stablysshe ye peace atwene the kynge and his lordys, an assemble was made on Berhamdowne; where the kynge and the lordys mett with great strengthe upon eyther syde, where a charter or wrytynge was devysed & made, and there sealyd by the kyng, so that the barony was with it contentyd, and departyd in peasyble wyse, everych man into his countrey." *Fabyan's Chronicle* or *The New Chronicles of England and France,* pp. 320–21.

[53] "Brevely compyled and emprynted 1529 in Chepesyde, at the sygne of the mearemayd, next to pollys gate."

[54] "About the viii. yere of this kynges reyne, the charter called Magna Carta was confyrmed, and dyvers artycles addyd therto, howe the kynge shoulde have the warde and maryage of the lordes heyres, beynge within age, and the fyrst statute of Mortmayne then made." Additions had been made to ca. 3 on wards in the 1217 issue, but nothing new on marriage of heirs. Ca. 36 is, in a sense, the first enactment on mortmain.

[55] A native of Urbino, educated at the University of Bologna, Polydore became chamberlain to Pope Alexander VI and was sent to England in 1501 as subcollector of Peter's pence. He had been recommended to Henry VII while the latter was still in exile. In England he received a succession of benefices and was naturalized. About 1508 Henry had commissioned him to write the *English History* which appeared, 1534, in twenty-six books dedicated to Henry VIII

urally this scholarly Latin account by a foreign author (and one of whom the native writers were inclined to be jealous) was not as widely read as the popular English chronicles. Holinshed cites passages from it as do some of the later "antiquaries," but actually it was too good for some of them. Ellis calls it "the first of our histories in which the writer ventured to compare the facts and weigh the statements of his predecessors; and the first in which summaries of personal character are introduced in the terse and energetic form adopted in the Roman classics. In the choice of expression, and in the purity of Latin style, Polydore Vergil exceeded all his contemporaries."

This critical faculty and skill at characterization appear in the account of John's reign, but the story of the granting of the "liberties" is couched in Polydore's fine Renaissance Latin, not in the terms natural to the pen of an English chronicler or lawyer. The encamped *principes* present the king with a schedule of petitions, demanding *leges ac vetera instituta*, and after Louis' withdrawal, Henry confirms the *leges antiquas*. Polydore does not specifically relate the issue of 1225 to John's Charter. He had very likely seen one of the little volumes of statutes like Pynson's that were just coming from the press, as he speaks of the laws then granted as "collected in a little book which is called Magna Carta." [56] Other episodes of Charter history recorded by Polydore (in which he always uses the term *Magna Carta*) are: the restoring of ancient laws (*leges antiquas*), 1258; their confirmation "at Marlborough," 1257; the enacting of the statute of *Mortmain* in amplification of Magna Carta chapter 36; the confirmation at Lincoln, 1301; and a confirmation which he describes as taking place in a "council" at Westminster on which occasion the princes were made dukes, and various liberal measures were enacted in honor of the king's fiftieth birthday. [57]

For more comprehensive accounts we have to await the chroniclers of Elizabeth's reign who had ampler sources at their command. The appointment of John Leland by Henry VIII as "King's Antiquary" marked the

(*Polydori Vergilii Urbinatus Anglicae historiae libri vigintisex*, folio, Basle; other editions, 1546, 1555, and after). He had already produced his *Proverbium Libellus*, 1498 (which anticipated Erasmus' *Adagia*) and the *de Inventoribus Rerum*, 1499. His *History* was criticized by Leland, Savile, and others. Ellis defends Polydore against the charge of burning manuscripts or shipping them off to Rome. The English, he says, did not like his discarding *Brute* and discrediting Geoffrey of Monmouth, and, in fact, were jealous that the task was committed to him. "The truth is that Polydore Vergil's attainments went far beyond the common learning of his age." Ellis, *Three Books of Polydore Vergil's English History*, pp. xxiv–xxv (C. S.).

[56] *Polydori Vergilii*, book xv. "Multa privilegia ordini sacerdotali atque reliquo populo . . . multaque leges latae, quas reges qui secuti sunt, ita approbarunt, ut inde bona pars iuris collecta sit, quemadmodum in eo extat libello, qui inscribitur, Magna charta, & altera vulgo de foresta id est de ferarum saltibus."

[57] Like the contemporary chronicles which he used, Polydore's account of the fourteenth century plays up the French and Scottish wars, the papacy, Edward's "Round Table," and so on, rather than domestic and political affairs.

beginning of the cult of "antiquities" in Tudor England. The contemporary meaning of this term was not classical lore but Britain's own past. Leland's antiquarian tour or "itinerary" occupied the years 1534–43. His *New Year's Gift* (1545) heaps at his patron's feet, as it were, the fruits of his labors—what materials he has amassed and how he intends to embody them in lasting form. The various motives, the lines along which antiquarianism was to develop are all anticipated. Leland, the humanist, will write in elegant literary style (whereas "men of eloquence hath not enterprised to set them forth in a floryshynge style in some tymes past") thus avoiding the reproach of foreign nations, not only the Germans but the Italians themselves "that counte as the Grekes ded full arrogantly, all other nacyons to be barbarouse and unlettered, savinge their owne, shall have a direct occayson openly of force to say That Britannia prima fuit parens . . ." The fame of his Maecenas will be fittingly extolled: "The fourth book of the *De Viris Illustris* begynneth with the name of your Maieste, whose glorie in learnynge is to the worlde so clerely knowne . . ." The reformation in the church will be bulwarked for "profyte hath rysen by the aforsayd iourneye, in bryngynge full many thynges to lyght, as concernynge the usurped autoryte of the Byshopp of Rome and hys complyces, to the manyfest and vyolent derogacyon of kyngely dygnyte . . ." Britain will be glorified by description of "the actes of your most noble predecessours, and the fortunes of thys your realme, so incredyblye great . . ." "I trust," he concludes, "that thys your realme shall so wele be knowne, ones peynted with hys natyve colours, that the renowne thereof shal geve place to the glory of no other regyon." [58]

With Archbishop Matthew Parker, the chief motive was controversial: to justify the state church, its organization and doctrine, by reverting to an ancient native church antedating and independent of Roman Catholic authority. In strict logic this carried him back to the Celtic, not the Anglo-Saxon church, yet in respect to customs and doctrine the latter afforded some support. [59] In 1568 his activities received the sanction of the privy council in a commission:

That the Lord Archbishop of Canterbury should have a special care and oversight in the conservation of such ancient records and monuments as were written of the state and affairs of the realm of England and Ireland; which were heretofore preserved and recorded, by special appointment of her Majesty's

[58] John Leland, *New Year's Gift.*
[59] Parker justified the translation of the Bible into English by his finding Saxon translations of portions of the Scriptures. His treatise defending marriage of the clergy makes use of Saxon precedents. He sets forth a Saxon sermon which speaks "plainly and evidently contrary to the novel doctrine of transubstantiation." It is surprising upon what slight crumbs of comfort these scholars sometimes relied. Salisbury writes to Parker of meeting the phrase *clerico uxorato* in an old register or record, although he adds that *clericus* did not always mean "priest" in those days.

ancestors in divers abbeys, to be treasurehouses to keep and leave in memory such occurrences as fell in their times . . . So as, when need should require, resort might be made for the testimony that might be found in them; and also by conference of them, the antiquity of the state of those countries might be restored to the knowledge of the world . . .[60]

He and the scholars who collaborated with him displayed tremendous zeal in the pursuit of manuscripts and endless labor in mastering ancient tongues and scripts. Much was accomplished. The exportation of manuscripts abroad was arrested and many recovered by agents on the continent. As to the manuscripts collected, says Strype, "All the antique pieces that he got, for the better and surer preservation of them, he bound up together in volumes, and covered with vellum." Some of the most notable were published, among them *Gildas, Asser, Aelfric*, the *Saxon Gospels, Flores Histoirarum, Walsingham,* and *Matthew Paris*. The last named was to be important not only for its narrative story, but for what it sets forth as the text of John's Charter. It was this, not one of the originals, that scholars such as Selden and Coke used.[61]

Although history was not divorced from useful ends or its study from ulterior motives, to such men as Lambarde and Camden, Britain's "antiquuities" became a veritable cult in itself, and there is a caressing touch in their very use of the term. Although history in the universities meant the classical historians (and this was true even in 1623 when Camden's chair of history was endowed) England's history came to be considered a study most fit for gentlemen as well as for citizens. Thomas Wotton, "To his Countriemen, the Gentlemen of the Countie of Kent," presenting to them, as it were, Lambarde's *Perambulation of Kent* (1576), writes:

And yet this much I may breefly say . . . that (the sacred word of Almightie God alwaies excepted) there is nothing either for our instruction more profitable, or to our minds more delectable, or within the compasse of common understanding more easie or facile, than the studie of histories; nor that studie for none estate more meet, then for the estate of Gentlemen: nor for the Gentlemen of England, no Historie so meete, as the Historie of England. For the

---

[60] Quoted, Strype, *Parker*, I, 523.

[61] According to Strype (I, 220, 552, 554) Parker had written to Matthias Flacius Illyricus (c. 1561) that "Matthew Paris's Chronicon could not be found among us here in England." Eventually copies of the chronicle or of portions of it were secured from Stow, Cecyl, Edward Aglionby, Henry, Earl of Arundel, and Sir Henry Sidney—the latter's copy "writ by Matthew Paris's own hand." Strype praises the archbishop's painstaking work in piecing together and collating the various manuscripts at his disposal.

Luard, the modern editor of the *Chronica Majora*, II, xxii–xxviii (R. S.), accuses his predecessor of altering the text, "almost at random," omitting or introducing matter from other sources, although as he went on with the work "he altered less." Very likely Parker did well enough for a pioneer. His edition was published in 1571. There were reprints in 1616, 1640, and 1684. For a description and comments on Paris' and Wendover's texts of Magna Carta, see Appendix F.

dexteritie that men have either in providing for themselves, or in comforting their friends (two very good things) or in serving their King and Countrie (of all outward things, the best thing) doth rest cheefly upon their owne and other folkes experience. Which I may assuredly accompt . . . to be the very mother and maistres of wisdome. Now that, that a number of folks doth generally, is much more then that, that any one of us can do specially, and so by folks experience, are we taught largely. And that, that other folkes for their King, their countrie, themselfes, their friends, like good men do vertuously, ought to provoke us with good devotion inwardly to love them; and with good words openly much to commend them, and in their vertuous actions rightly to folowe them. And that, that other folkes against their King, their countrie, their friends (and so against themselves) like foolish men do ignorantly, or like leude men do wickedly, ought to move us first (as our neighbours) Christianly to bewaile them, and then . . . dutifully and wisely to beware by them. . . . Thus you see what experience doth, and thus you see where other folkes experience is to be had; which, for the good estate of England (resting chiefly upon the good iudgement and service of the Gentlemen of England) is, as I thinke, most properly set from the Historie of England.

Stow, "the most accurate and businesslike of English annalists of the sixteenth century," [62] was a tailor by profession, a member of the Merchant Taylors Company. From 1560 on he was more and more concerned, as he puts it, "with the search of our famous antiquities." He knew Lambarde, Camden, and Fleetwood, furnished manuscripts (including *Matthew Paris*) to Parker, edited some under the latter's direction, and was a member of the Society of Antiquaries. His great work was to the glorification of his native city, the comprehensive *Survey of London* (1598, 1603). But as early as 1565 he had prepared one of those abridgments popular with his fellow citizens, the *Summarie of Englyshe Chronicles*.[63] On John's reign and the granting of the Charter, this account follows Fabyan almost verbatim. For the years of Henry III's minority it deals with affairs of London rather than constitutional issues. In 1580 Stow published a more substantial work of some thirteen hundred pages, *The Chronicles of England from Brute unto this present yeare of Christ, 1580*, better known by the title of the second edition (1584), *The Annales of England*.[64]

Little is known of Holinshed's early career or education. Early in Elizabeth's reign he came to London and was employed as a translator in the

[62] Sidney Lee, in *D.N.B.*, who also quotes a contemporary of Stow's: "He always protested never to have written anything either for malice, fear or favour, not to seek his own particular gain or vainglory, and that his only pains and care was to write truth."

[63] With a dedicatory preface to Roger Martin, then lord mayor, the aldermen and commoners of London. Nine successive editions with additions bringing the information up to date appeared 1567–1604.

[64] ". . . faithfully collected out of the most authenticall Authors, Records and other Monuments of Antiquitie." Eight editions had been issued by 1631.

printing office of Reginald Wolfe, who planned to produce a universal history and cosmography. Holinshed worked for several years under Wolfe's direction and had free access to Leland's manuscripts, which Wolfe had inherited. He also drew largely on Stow.[65] After Wolfe's death in 1573 other publishers took up the work but, finding the original project too vast, decided to confine the work to the British Isles. Thus appeared in 1577 *Holinshed's Chronicles of England, Scotland, and Ireland.*[66]

At last in Stow's *Annales* and Holinshed's *Chronicles* the crisis between John and the barons, the granting of the Charter, the events of the minority of Henry III, and the reissue of 1225 are set forth with the rich detail of Matthew Paris. Holinshed is preferred for quotation here as the more detailed work and also the better known name to modern readers because of its association with Shakespeare. The errors are those of the medieval predecessor, Matthew Paris—the attributing to John of the issue of a separate Forest Charter in 1215, and the assumption that the reissue was identical with the original grant. On the other hand, there is made clear the connection of Henry III's charter with John's, as also its permanence— "so that a great part of the law now in use dependeth of the same."

Finally, when the king measuring his owne strength with the Barons, perceyved that he was not able to resist them, he consented to subscribe and seale suche articles concerning the libertyes demaunded, in forme for the most part as is conteyned in the two Charters *Magna Carta* and *Carta de Foresta,* beginning *Johannes Dei gratia,* &c. And he did not onely graunt unto them their petitions touching the foresayde liberties, but also to win him further credite, was contented that they should choose foorth certaine grave and honourable personages, which should have authoritie and power to see those things performed which he then graunted unto them.

. . .

1225. King Henrie holding his Christmas at Westminster, called his high court of Parliamente there the same time, and demaunded a reliefe of mony, towardes the mayntenaunce of his warres in France, and had granted to him the fifteenth peny in value of all mooveable goodes, to be founde within the Realme, as well belonging to the spiritualty as temporalty, but under condition, that he should confirme unto his subiectes their often demaunded liberties. The king upon desire to have the monie, was contented to condiscende unto theyr requestes, and so the two Charters were made, and by the king confirmed, the one entituled *Magna Charta,* & the other *Charta de Forresta.* Thus at this Parliament were made and confirmed these good lawes and laudable ordi-

[65] Sidney Lee calls him a "conscientious compiler," the only part of whose work with independent value is that on Elizabeth's reign, and adds that "the valuable part of Holinshed is Stow's work."

[66] This first edition was compiled by Holinshed, William Harrison, and Richard Stonyhurst. Perhaps it was because Holinshed was chiefly responsible for the *Chronicles of England* that the work bears his name. After Holinshed's death, a new edition was brought out by John Hooker, assisted by Francis Thynne, Abraham Fleming, and John Stow.

nances, which have bin from time to time by the Kyngs and Princes of this realme confyrmed, so that a greate parte of the law now in use dependeth of the same. The same charters also were directed and sent foorthe into everie Countie within the Realme to be proclaimed.

Later passages note in proper chronological place the confirmation of the Charters by the *parva carta* of 1237, the confirmation of 1253, complaints of nonobservance in 1255 and 1258, and the confirmation of 1268 (Marlborough), 1297, 1300, and 1341.[67]

Now if we attempt to account for the omission of Magna Carta from Shakespeare's *King John* we must consider not only the content of the chronicles but the point of view and historical attitude of the age. To find these details thus set forth in the chronicles is not to say that Tudor readers necessarily paid much attention to the political episodes or their constitutional significance. King John must have afforded an "example to be shunned," but the supposed murder of Arthur was more dramatic than the granting of the Charter. It was the former which was utilized by Elizabethan playwrights. Shakespeare was catering to the already existing enthusiasm for historical drama. Reigns already embodied in plays of genius like Marlowe's *Edward II* he let alone, preferring to deal with reigns not hitherto used, or to rewrite inferior plays. The material for *Richard II, Henry IV, Richard III*, and *Henry VIII*, he drew from Holinshed.[68] *King John* was based on the older, anonymous, chronicle-history drama, *The Troublesome Raigne of John King of England*, which, like Shakespeare's play, omits the events connected with the granting of Magna Carta.[69] Although John is not portrayed in too favorable a light, Shakespeare does put into his mouth speeches that would have sounded pleasantly in the ear of a Henry VIII or Queen Elizabeth, notably the defiance of Pandulph, a perfect exposition of the divine right of kings:

> What earthly name to interrogatories
> Can task the free breath of a sacred king?

[67] *Holinshed's Chronicles of England, Scotland, and Ireland*, 1577 edition, II, 649, 736–37, 751, 779, 828–30, 835, 914.

[68] The theme of *Richard II*, the "serious matter" of *Henry IV*, the plot of *Henry V* (together with the play called *The Famous Victories of Henry the Fifth*), derive from Holinshed. It is freely used in all three parts of *Henry VI*. For *Richard III* "the outline in the chronicler seems to have been Shakespeare's prime authority." Although some use may have been made of Hall and Foxe, *Henry VIII* is based mainly on Holinshed, in fact, "more of Holinshed's actual wording has been retained in this play than in any of the other dramas. Characterization, episode and dialogue owe directly to the chronicler." Josephine and Allardyce Nicoll, *Holinshed's Chronicle as Used in Shakespeare's Plays*, pp. 20, 52, 90, 138, 177.

[69] "There is no doubt that Shakespeare based his play of King John on the older anonymous chronicle-history drama, entitled *The Troublesome Raigne of John King of England*, which, first published in 1591, was reprinted in 1611 as by W. Sh. and in 1622 as by W. Shakespeare. His use of Holinshed was therefore at second hand, although for the King's outburst when he learns of the supposed murder of Arthur it would seem that he had in mind the corresponding passage in the chronicler. This, however, appears to be the only (and it is doubtful) evidence to show Shakespeare's acquaintanceship with the original narrative." *Ibid.*, p. 1.

> Thou canst not, cardinal, devise a name
> So slight, unworthy and ridiculous,
> To charge me to an answer, as the pope.
> Tell him this tale; and from the mouth of England
> Add thus much more, that no Italian priest
> Shall tithe or toll in our dominions;
> But as we, under heaven are supreme head,
> So under him that great supremacy,
> Where we do reign, we will alone uphold,
> Without the assistance of a mortal hand:
> So tell the pope, all reverence set apart
> To him and his usurp'd authority.[70]

John was not always presented as the tyrant king. After the Reformation parliament had done its work, propagandists pictured him as the innocent victim of an overweening papal power. This theme appears as early as 1535 in Coverdale's "epistle dedicatory" to his translation of the Scriptures directed to Henry VIII. "Whose heart would not pity it, yea, even with lamentation, to remember but only the intolerable wrongs don by the antichrist of Rome unto your graces most noble predecessor, king John . . ." [71] In editing *Harding's Chronicle,* Grafton thinks it unfit "to alter and chaunge that olde men have wryte." He is content to excuse the author for his "Popyshe errour" by the blindness of the times, and to rejoice in the change effected in his own age.

> In other thinges the tymes were suche
> That, though this werke have some spice of blindnesse,
> Yet is the authour not to be blamed much,
> for Popyshe errour, that season, doubtlesse
> Did all the worlde overgo and oppresse.
> Therefore such thinges we must in good part take,
> And pardon that faulte for the tymes sake.
>
> Yet have we thought best, the autour to set out
> Even in suche fourme as hymselfe dyd endite;.
> It wer an unquod thyng yf we should go about
> To alter and chaunge that olde men have wryte.
> Secondly, to us it may bee greate delyte,
> The blindnesse of those tymes to consider,
> From whiche hathe pleased God to us to delyver.
>
> Fynally, the darkenesse of those dayes to see,
> To the honoure of our kyng dooeth redound,
> To whom, by Goddes helpe geven it hath bee,

---

[70] Shakespeare, *King John,* Act III, Scene 1.
[71] Quoted Strype, *Annals,* Vol. II, pt. ii, p. 492 (app.).

All popyshe trumperye for to confounde;
Which thyng al trew English hertes hath bounde
Incessauntly to praye for kyng Henrye ye eyghte,
Whose godly wisdome hath made all streyghte. [72]

The editor of the later edition of Fabyan exercised no such scholarly restraint. Passages unfavorable to John are omitted or qualifying statements added in the margin.[73] John's speech as quoted in Fabyan's text— "Here I resigne up the croune of the realme—into the popis handys, Innocent the thyrde, & put me hole in his mercy and ordynaunce"— evokes the comment, "What chrysten hert, but must wepe and lament to here a crysten prynce to be thus abused."

Stow's *Annales,* on the other hand, set forth the worst tales about John with no apologies. Holinshed, after discussing the causes of the discord between John and the barons as variously detailed in Fabyan, Caxton, and Hector Boetius, concludes: "These seeme to be coniectures of such writers as were evill affected towards the kings cause." [74] The 1586 edition contains some anti-papal passages not in the original.[75]

We shall find some evidence that lawyers and scholars in the reigns of Elizabeth and James I knew and used these chronicles. Early in the reign of Charles I such protagonists of the crown and the prerogative as Laud and Bagg tried to discredit the Charter by demonstrating its unsavory origin in the events of 1215. However, the charm of the chronicles must not lead us to overrate their influence. To the Tudor lawyers Magna Carta was the "statute of 9 Henry III." To these men we must now turn.

[72] *Harding's Chronicle,* edited and published with continuation by Richard Grafton, 1543. Grafton's "To the Reader" in thirty-one stanzas. Pope is changed to *Romyshe byshoppe,* p. 271, 3rd stanza, 1st line; 272, 1st stanza, 6th line.

[73] For example of omissions, the words italicized: in connection with the interdict "but all this myght not move the kyng *from his erroure,*" "also chyldren were crystened thoroughe all the lande, & men houselyd & anelyd, excepte suche persones as were exceptyd by name in the bull, *or knowen for maynteyners of the kynges ill entent.*"

For examples of marginal additions: "It is affermyd of some autours, that the Frenshe kynge made this warre upon kynge John, by excytynge of the pope, for his contumacy agayne ye church," *"it is said, 'the byshop of Rome was the sturrar up of these warres.' "* Following the passage describing John's submission to the pope— *"the great misery that this prynce was in, beyng so oppressed wyth the tyrannye of the B. of Rome, that monstrous and wicket beast."*

Such editing, of course, is not confined to John's reign. Throughout the work *Pope* is uniformly changed to "Bishop of Rome." Thomas à Becket is no longer a "glorious martyr" and a "blessed saint," but a "traitorous bishop." Miracles are omitted, especially when taken from the *Legend of the Saints* or attributed to the popes, as are passages tending to encourage houses of religion, penance, pilgrimage, preservation of relics; offences done the Church of Rome, shrines, etc.

[74] *Chronicles,* p. 319 (late edition).

[75] Pandulph's speech to John is entitled "The saucie speech of Proud Pandulph the popes lewd legat, to king John, in the presumptuous popes behalf." In connection with release of the interdict, the reader is reminded, "Ye have heard before how pope Innocent (or rather Nocent) who was the root of much mischiefe and trouble, which qualities are nothing consonant to his name . . ." (p. 316).

❖ CHAPTER VII ❖

The Lawyers and Magna Carta

We find it necessarie in all commonwealthes, for subiects to live under the direction of Lawes, constitutions or customs, publickly knowen and received, and not to depende only upon the commandement and pleasure of the governor, be the same never so iust or sincere in life and con-versation. For that the Law once enacted and established, extendeth his execution towards al men alike without favour or affection. Whereas if the word of a Prince were a lawe, the same being a mortall man must needes bee possessed with those passions, and inclinations of favour or disfavour yt other men be: and sometimes decline from the constant and unremoveable levell of indifferencie, to respect the person more than the cause. Wherefore it was wel agreed by the wisest Philisophers and great-est politicks, that a dumme lawes direction is to be preferred before the sole disposition of any living Prince, both for the cause afore touched, and for other reasons which I will here omit.

(THE LAUDABLE CUSTOMS OF LONDON)

NOTHING gives one such a surprising sense of peace and calm, stability and continuity, as to retreat from the hurly-burly of the usual textbooks and narrative histories of the Tudor period, with their wars and rumors of wars, threats of disputed successions, Edwardian agitators and Marian martyrs, into the reports and treatises. Something of the continuity in law and institutions which persists throughout this period Holdsworth attributes to the policies of that "consummate statesman," Henry VIII, who planned and induced the nation to accept "the policy of making a Reformation in religion by way of evolution and not by way of revo-lution"; who "created a modern state upon the basis of medieval institu-tions and the common law, and not upon the basis of new institutions and Roman law." [1] But the actual adaptation of medieval law and insti-tutions to modern needs was the work of that "school of literate Eliza-bethan lawyers" to which such men as Plowden and Lambarde, Bacon and Coke, belonged. The gentlemen trained up in the Inns of Court, ultimately to become king's serjeants or judges, like the common law

---

[1] Holdsworth, IV, 32.

167

itself, pursue their way serenely from reign to reign. In the pages of Dyer and Plowden nice points of law are argued at length by bench and bar. In Michaelmas term (2 and 3 Philip and Mary) there were created seven new serjeants who argued their case called the *Serjeants' case* in Easter and Trinity terms while the judges argued the same case in the following Michaelmas term.[2] There argued for the defendant four of the new serjeants, and for the plaintiff three, one of whom was William Rastell, while the bench included such distinguished judges as William Staunford and Robert Brooke, C. J. Again judges and serjeants are concerned over the correct title or "style" for their new Catholic queen, Mary Tudor. In his reports Plowden interpolates an epitaph for two serjeants and verses in praise of Judge Brown or indulges in a long disquisition on the meaning of equity. Dyer notes a ruling on the liability of the owner of a dog who kills sheep and records how members of a jury were fined forty pence each because they ate and drank before giving their verdict, notwithstanding their defence that on their way to court, after having agreed on their verdict, "they saw Rede Chief Justice going on the way to see an affray, and they following him, and in going, they saw a cup and drank out of it."[3]

"Ben Jonson, in 'Every man out of his Humour' (1616), apostrophises the Inns of Court as 'the noblest nurseries of humanity and liberty in the Kingdom.' It is true to say that the Inns of Court in medieval and in Tudor days were always training up and sending out, as the Temple Bidding Prayer has it, 'a due supply of persons, well qualified to serve God both in Church and State.'"[4] James I, himself no mean scholar, recognized their value to the commonwealth. In letters patent conveying the Temple to grantees representing the Inner and Middle Temple, he speaks of those two Inns as places to which

"many young men, eminent for rank of family and their endowment of mind and body, have daily resorted from all parts of this Realm, and from which many men in our own times, as well as in the times of our progenitors, have by reason of their very great merits been advanced to discharge the public and arduous functions as well of the state of justice, in which they have exhibited great examples of prudence and integrity, to the no small honour of the said Profession, and adornment of the Realm, and good of the whole Commonwealth."[5]

[2] An action of trespass in Common Bench. See below, p. 171.

[3] Dyer, fols. 98, 25; Plowden, fols. 180, 356, 376. As to Mary Tudor, the question was whether writs issued for her first parliament were lawful since the title *supremum caput ecclesiae anglicanae* was omitted. In addition to the verses, Plowden refers to Anthony Browne as "un des Justices del common bank, que fuit Judge de profound ingeny et graunde eloquence."

[4] Sir Lynden Livingston Macassey, K.B.E., K.C., LL.D., Autumn Reader to the Honourable Society of the Middle Temple ("after dinner," November 13, 1930), "The Middle Temple's Contribution to the National Life," p. 19.

[5] Quoted *ibid.*, pp. 18–19.

A modern Reader of the Middle Temple has listed from its membership through the ages, "representatives of almost every department of intellectual activity," as well as "statesmen and politicians, soldiers, sailors, courtiers, ambassadors, and even of merchants and agriculturalists," including such Elizabethans as Raleigh, Drake, Frobisher, and Hawkins! [6] The "judicious Hooker," author of the *Ecclesiastical Polity,* served as *master* (chaplain) 1589–91. Among Middle Temple lawyers were many whose names figure in the following pages: Dyer and Plowden, William Fleetwood, Richard Martin, Sir Henry Calthorp, Francis Ashley, James Whitelocke, Edwin Sandys, John Brampston, and others. "More Americans have entered Middle Temple than any other of the Inns of Court." On the other hand, Gray's Inn may claim the Bacons, Nicholas and Francis; Lincoln's Inn, Fortescue and Lambarde; the Inner Temple, Littleton, St. Germain, Selden, and Coke, as well, of course, as many others.

In the following pages these and other eminent members of the Inns of Court will appear as contributors to the use and interpretation of the Great Charter: in an academic way by the writing of learned treatises and handbooks, and by readings before their respective societies; in a more active capacity by arguments and judgments in the courts and debates in parliament, now in mere routine matters, again in great constitutional crises.

The Early Reporters, Plowden and Dyer

HOLDSWORTH calls Edmund Plowden (1518–85) "perhaps the most learned lawyer in a century of lawyers, who, it is said, might have been Lord Chancellor of England but for his adherence to the Roman Church." [7] He was a Cambridge man and a Middle Temple lawyer in days when the Inns of Court inclined to be conservative in religion. Naturally his active political career falls in the reign of Mary Tudor when he sat in her first three parliaments, was a member of the council of Wales and the Marches (1553), and one of the justices of gaol delivery at Shrewsbury at which were decided important crown cases from several Welsh counties (1554). A writ (October 27, 1558) directed him to take the degree of serjeant-at-law in Easter term following, but with the death of Mary the writ abated, and Elizabeth did not renew it. Although Elizabeth's privy council regarded him with some suspicion, they did not proceed against him. Acknowledged by contemporaries as "the greatest and most honest" lawyer of his age, he continued to follow a distinguished pro-

---

[6] "Raleigh was the brightest of a galaxy of gentlemen-adventurers who were members of the Inn. Francis Drake was admitted before 1590; Martin Frobisher in 1592; and John Hawkins in 1593. Think of finding yourself next to a mess composed of this historic Four." Gover's Reading, p. 6.

[7] Holdsworth, V, 372.

fessional career.[8] A modern member of the Honourable Society of the Middle Temple thus pays tribute to him:

Edmund Plowden's bust in marble has for many years stood beneath our Minstrel Gallery and his coat of arms is in the great South Window. Camden said of him that he was "in knowledge of Law *facile princeps* and in integrity of life second to none." . . . It was he who was mainly responsible for the building of our glorious Hall in place of the older and smaller one which stood in Pump Court. Plowden died in 1585 and was buried in the Temple Church. The dignified monument containing his recumbent effigy in coloured alabaster has recently been placed in the North Aisle of the Church after being hidden from sight in the Triforium for nearly a century.[9]

Although at some disadvantage to myself and to the reader, perhaps, I have used the first editions of the reports in the original law French rather than the modern English Reprints. My object was to discover just what was being said and thought about the Charter at the time these reports were written. Where Magna Carta is concerned, the modern editor and translator is apt unconsciously to incorporate conceptions of a later day. Short passages are quoted in the original French, longer ones in my translation or paraphrase.

Plowden's is "the pioneer of the modern style of law report," in which the interest tends "to shift from the argument leading to the formulation of the issue to the decision upon that issue; and to make it clear that, as a general rule, reportable cases were those which turned, not on an issue of fact, but upon an issue of law." [10] In his prologue, directed to the students of the common laws of England and especially to his companions of the Middle Temple, he says, "there is no Record entered but such upon which there is a Demurrer in law, or a special verdict conteigning a matter of law." [11] In five cases reported by Plowden, as in the later Year Books, a clause of Magna Carta, cited like any other statute, or a case from the Year Books which turns on a provision of the Charter is used as a precedent or analogy by counsel or judges, more often the latter. In one instance the reporter himself supplies such a "precedent."

In two cases the court found for the defendant because of error in the plaintiff's writ, even though the defendant failed to take advantage of the same.[12] In the second, among precedents for such a ruling, are in-

---

[8] He was double Lent Reader for his Inn (1560–61) and treasurer of the same, 1561. In Michaelmas term 1562 he was one of the counsel of the Court of the Duchy of Lancaster. He successfully defended Bonner against Bishop Horne and supported Gabriel Goodman in defeating a bill in the Commons for abolition of sanctuary for debt. *D.N.B.*

[9] Gover's Reading, pp. 4–5.   [10] Holdsworth, V, 371–72.

[11] The reports cover the years 1549–80, and include cases in King's Bench, Common Pleas, and Exchequer. Made originally for his own use, they were edited and published by the author from his manuscripts in law French, lest incorrect versions be published.

[12] These are both cases of debt, 4 and 6–7 Ed. VI. In the first, it is ruled "if it appears to the court that the plaintiff doesn't have title, he will not have judgment however much the

cluded a trespass case of 10 Edward IV, and the familiar chapter 34 of the Charter: "And thus if the defendant would admit good an appeal brought by a woman for the death of her father, still the court must abate it, as is there held: Because the statute is, No one shall be arrested or imprisoned upon the appeal of a woman for the death of any other than her husband."

In the case referred to above in which the new serjeants tried their mettle, six points were moved and debated by bench and bar on the demurrers raised by the parties. Alone of interest here is the question whether in a statute the words "by the king" or "in the name of the king" include his heirs or successors.[13] Three chapters of the Charter were cited in the arguments, which may be paraphrased as follows:

when a thing is said to be *by the king* or *in the name of the king,* that in many instances it will include his heirs or successors. As the statute *de Religiosis,* which prohibits mortmain, provides that if the immediate lords do not enter within the time limit, *Nos statim terras & tenementa capiemus in manum nostram* . . . And likewise the statute of Magna Carta 17 says *Nullus Vic' &c. vel alii Ballivi nostri teneant placita Coronae nostrae.* Thus the statute *de Praerogativa Regis,* that in some points is a statute, and in others not, says *Dominus Rex habebit &c.* And also the statute that says *Communia placita non sequantur Curiam nostram &c.* And such other statutes of which there is an infinite number which speak of the king only, have been expounded to extend to the heirs and successors to give them the benefit, or to bind them. And the reason is because the king is body politic, and when the act says the king, or he speaks (*Nos*) it is always spoken in his person as king, and in his dignity royal, and therefore includes all those who have that function.

Brooke, C. J. argued that the plaintiff was not within the words, but was within the "equity of the statute":

For we see where an act is made to remedy any mischief, that to aid things in like degree one action has been taken for another, one thing for another, one place for another, one person for another . . . As the statute of Magna Carta c. 12 gives power to the justices of assize to adjourn the assizes before them in their iter or for difficulty into the common bench, Thus it was adjudged in 12 Henry 4 that by the equity of the statute they could adjourn the assizes before themselves at Westminster which is out of their circuit.

In a case of debt[14] brought by writ in the Court of Exchequer and tried at *nisi prius* with verdict for the plaintiff, when the latter appeared in the Exchequer to demand judgment, it was denied him. Four points

---

defendant admits his title." In the second, the plaintiff is in error in failing to recite the statute which is the ground of his suit, even though the defendants in their demurrer have confessed to such an act of parliament as the plaintiff declares. Plowden, fols. 66v, 85.

[13] *Hill v. Graunge, trespass,* 2 and 3 Philip and Mary. Plowden, fols. 176v, 178.

[14] *Stradling v. Morgan, debt,* 2 Eliz. *Ibid.,* fols. 207–8.

were argued, the fourth being whether the court had jurisdiction to deal with such a common plea. Counsel for the defendant and two of the barons argued that it did not, as the plaintiff had not shown that he was privileged. Luke "said also that by the statute *Articuli super cartas* ca. 4 it is ordained that no common plea be henceforth held in the Exchequer against the form of the great charter. And he recited also the statute of Rutland . . ." Saunders, C. B. upheld the broader view of the jurisdiction of his court. He said that the Exchequer from great antiquity had been a court to hold common pleas and cited as evidence the passage with which Glanvill introduces his treatise.[15] This is a good example of how lawyers and scholars of this age might be misled by the wording of medieval treatises and histories, for Glanvill's *curia regis ad scaccarium* was not the specialized Court of Exchequer over which Chief Baron Saunders presided. The so-called statute of Rutland, he maintained, was merely an ordinance made by the king for the order of the Exchequer, without the authority of parliament. Furthermore, "as to the other statute referring to Magna Charta [the *Articuli*]," he pointed out correctly, though contrary to popular tradition, "that in Magna Charta there was no such restraint on the authority and jurisdiction of the court."

A case of 3 and 4 Elizabeth illustrates very well how Magna Carta had been reduced to a "mere statute" and some of its clauses relegated to the realm of private law. In a plea of *eiectione firmae* in which both parties demurred in law, the main discussion turned on whether the king was bound by the statute *de donis*.[16] Incidentally there were interesting arguments in which serjeants for the defense expounded the theory of the two capacities of the king, the body natural and the body politic, maintaining that the two remain distinct (that King Henry VII had held the grant in question in his capacity of body natural and hence is bound by the statute) and also set forth a rather strong statement of limited monarchy. The king has many prerogatives, but the common law has admeasured his prerogatives.[17] Serjeants for the plaintiff maintained that the body natural and body politic are merged; hence if the body politic could alienate the land, so could the body natural. Judge Weston, to the same effect, made a strong statement for the prerogative, though Browne and Dyer were more moderate.

Both sides discussed the extent to which the king is bound by statutes

---

[15] ". . . et illas solum leges continet & consuetudines secundum quas placitatur in curia Regis ad Scaccarium &c." There was never any restraint by statute, he says (*nemy de rigore iuris*). It was rather "by reason of the multitude of the affairs of the king than by default of power" that the court in later times ceased to hold all kinds of common pleas.

[16] *Eiectione firmae*, 3 and 4 Eliz. Plowden, fols. 234–44.

[17] "Et coment que le roy ad moults prerogatives par le common ley touchant sa person, ses biens, ses dets et duties, et autres choses personal, uncore le common ley ad tielment admesure ses prerogatives que il ne tolleront ne preiudiceront le inheritance de ascun."

and admitted that there are some which do not bind the king by general words if he be not specifically named.[18] Such is Magna Carta chapter 11. As put by counsel for the plaintiff, "the statute of Magna Carta chapter 12 [*sic* for 11] which says, *Communia placita non sequantur curiam nostram* does not bind the king; but he can sue in king's bench for debt, or other common pleas, in which he is plaintiff." This is to assume that pleas affecting the king's property rights are *common* not *crown* pleas, and thus to exempt the king from the operation of the clause, as he may sue in any court he pleases. As the bench had now been so long established at Westminster, the original intent of chapter 11 was lost sight of.

Judge Weston, arguing to the same effect, afforded a still more striking example of reading the king out of the Charter when he cited Magna Carta chapter 10 as a statute which does not bind the king. Surely this was a chapter emphatically directed against King John: "No one shall be distrained for performance of greater service for a knight's fee, or for any other free tenement, than is due therefrom." But because it had become a tradition enshrined in the Register of Writs that the action of *ne iniuste vexes* was "founded on Magna Carta" chapter 10, and one cannot proceed against the king by writ but only by petition, the king is not fully bound by the statute since he is not named in it!

A briefly recorded action of debt[19] is interesting for the comments it evokes from the reporter himself (*Sur cest recorde diverse choses sont destre note*). Among these Plowden calls attention to the fact that an act of Henry VIII has modified a provision of Magna Carta:

But the king up to the statute in 33 Henry VIII, could not for debt touch the land, or the heir of any debtor, if the goods of the debtor were sufficient to satisfy the debt, and this was by the statute of Magna Charta *cap. 8* where the words of the act are: Neither we nor our bailiffs shall seize any land or rent for any debt, so long as the existing (*praesencia*) chattels of the debtor are sufficient to repay the debt, and the same debtor is ready to make satisfaction &c. But other persons were unrestrained (*laisse a large*).

Plowden's great contemporary, Sir James Dyer (1512–82), was an Ox-

---

[18] Such statutes as deal with usury, usurpation, and others that concern real estate (*realtie*) or inheritance or the public welfare of the realm do bind him, and such is *De Donis*. Like Weston in the passage described below, counsel for the defense also quotes ca. 10 "on which the *ne iniuste vexes* is founded for avoiding encroachment." If the king encroaches more rent or service, the party, by petition and not otherwise, will have remedy against the king by this statute, because the king is not named.

[19] *John Davie v. Fermer Pepys, debt*, 15 Eliz. Plowden, fols. 438v–41v: Davie is suing F. Pepys, son of Thomas Pepys, on an obligation of eighty pounds. It is adjudged that J. D. is to recover the debt from a rectory and six acres which F. P. says is all that he has, and an inquest is held to determine the value of the land. It is evidently this which brings to the reporter's mind the chapter of Magna Carta restraining the king from levying on land for debt. The statute in question, 33 Hen. VIII, ca. 39 (*S. R. III, 886–87*), does not explicitly repeal the Charter or make any reference to it.

ford man and a Middle Temple lawyer. He, too, sat in parliament as member for Cambridgeshire in 1547, and again in 1553 in which session he was chosen speaker. He also served as recorder of Cambridge and counsel to the university. He was made king's serjeant and knighted in the fall of 1552; made a judge in Common Pleas in 1556; transferred to Queen's Bench a year later; and returned to Common Pleas by Elizabeth, to become chief justice in January 1559. Dyer's reports, like Plowden's, though more concise, mark the transition from the Year Books to the modern system.[20] As the reports cover the period 1513–82, it is obvious that some must have been copied from various sources. However, the cases of interest here all fall within Sir James' active career as king's serjeant and judge.

In two cases, as reported by Dyer, clauses of Magna Carta are cited in the traditional way as analogy or precedent. In the first it is again chapter 34, that favorite of the lawyers as an example of a statute in the negative, the theory being that when a statute was so worded the judges could not make a broad construction or allow exceptions.[21] In the second, chapter 12 (and 11 indirectly through the *Articuli super cartas*) is used among examples of correct procedure in review of error.[22] In a third case, arguments to the effect that injustice would be done if infants did not have to answer to the law were prefaced by an eloquent eulogy of the common law's rendering justice to all, irrespective of person. Here was introduced the episode recorded in the Year Books (Henry IV):

It seems first that each subject of this realm for injuries done to him in goods lands or person [has the right to] seek redress from the king and against any subject whether he be bond or free, whether it be woman or child, whether he be religious or outlawed, or excommunicated, or any other without any exception, and against him who is able to render the thing claimed. And the king being personally in the Chancery, said *nulli vendemus, nulli negabimus aut differemus Iusticiam vel remedium* as Magna carta says [*come magna charta dit*].[23]

In two other instances the Charter appears in a more important and less incidental role. A complicated case led to a discussion of the right of a wife in property given by her ancestors, in the course of which chapter 7

20 Compiled originally for his own use, they were first published by his nephews, R. Farewell and J. Dyer, 1585. Lord Ellesmere in Star Chamber said of them: "In Diar are reports as he heard them, and also opinions and doubtes, and thus are strange things printed which detract greatly from the authority of Diar's book." Holdsworth, V, 364–65.

21 *Debt*, 2 and 3 Philip and Mary, Dyer, fol. 119v. Here the reference is simply to "the statute": ". . . mesme la ley d'un appeale port par feme de morte patris sui coment que le defendant admit l'appeale, le court ne doient suffer le plaintiff daver iudgment, eo que le statut est en le negative."

22 That is, the relationship of one court to another. *Error*, 10 Eliz. Dyer, fol. 250v.

23 *Anderson and others v. Ward, error,* 1 and 2 Philip and Mary. Dyer, fol. 104.

was cited as authority on inheritance and marriage.[24] In the other, a dispute over a grant of office, the action of the justices was upheld in refusing, as prothonotary in the bench one who was not sufficient and maintaining one who was. There was cited as precedent the instance of a sheriff who for misconduct in office was removed by King's Bench (8 Henry VIII) without summons or trial. The said John Savage, knight and sheriff of Worcestershire, was indicted on three counts: two were escapes of felons *felonice & voluntarie,* "and also he was indicted for holding his turn in an unaccustomed place and against the form of the statute of Magna Carta," [25] an indication that chapter 35 was still in use.

Early Treatises

IN ADDITION to the reports, Tudor lawyers contributed several notable treatises: Christopher St. Germain's unique *Doctor and Student* and the resulting controversial tracts; handbooks for justices of the peace compiled successively by Fitzherbert, Crompton (an enlarged and revised edition of Fitzherbert), and Lambarde; Staunford's *Pleas of the Crown* and *Praerogativa Regis*; descriptions of the courts, such as *Diversity of Courts,* Crompton's *Jurisdiction of Courts,* and most notable, Lambarde's *Archeion.* As will appear, except for St. Germain's, those treatises which belong to the latter half of Elizabeth's reign are most interesting both for their more reasoned discussion of principles of the common law and their increasing awareness af Magna Carta.

Christopher St. Germain (c. 1460–1540) was a barrister of the Inner Temple, well-versed both in English common law and in the literature of the canon law. He "did for the canonist principles which he took from Gerson," says Holdsworth, "what Bracton did for the civil law principles which he took from Azo. Both writers adapted foreign principles to an English environment." [26] Thus St. Germain, by the mouth of the doctor of the dialogue,[27] was able to point out to the student of the common law

[24] Item in the last clause of the statute of Gloucester on alienation in the wife's lifetime of the heritage or marriage of his wife; if he alienates property purchased by his wife with warrant he is outside the statute for heritage and marriage will not be intended purchase. For this see Magna Charta ca. 7 *de maritagio et hereditate femine. Ibid.,* fol. 148.

[25] *Sir. J. Savage v. the sheriff of Worcester, indictment,* 4 and 5 Philip and Mary. Dyer, fol. 151v. "Et auxi fuit pur tener de son turne, in loco non consueto, contra formam Statuti de Magna Charta."

[26] Holdsworth, V, 266–69; IV, 275–81. He points out that St. Germain adopts the medieval point of view (still that of the current scholastic philosophy of the late fifteenth and sixteenth centuries as expounded in the works of the great jurist, John Gerson), which "regarded the world as ruled primarily by the law of God and by the law of nature or reason, and only secondarily by the human law of the particular state. . . . Thus the rules of equity were really special applications of the overriding law of God, or of reason or nature to the treatment by merely human law of particular cases."

[27] St. Germain, *The Dialogue of the Doctor and the Student.* The first *Dialogue* was published in Latin in 1523, reissued in 1528, revised and published in English by the author, 1531. The second *Dialogue* was published in English in 1530. There were many subsequent

those parts of it which "needed the help of equity if it was to fulfil the main object of law—the furtherance of justice and the promotion of virtue." St. Germain, like the reporters, knows and treats Magna Carta as a statute, a "mere statute," but as such, superior to customs and maxims. As the doctor is largely concerned with equity, it is not in his exposition, but in the introductory chapters in which the student explains the "six grounds of the laws of England," [28] that three provisions of the Charter are used by way of illustration. Although it is not yet here treated as a "liberty document," interestingly enough, besides chapter 3, the passages cited are the two clauses of chapter 29 (John 39 and 40).

After listening to the student's definition of the general customs of the realm, says the doctor, "I pray thee show me some of these general customs." Whereupon the student gives a number of examples, among them one custom which is confirmed by Magna Carta and another which is more precisely defined thereby:

Also by the olde custome of the realme no man shalbe taken imprisoned disseased nor otherwise destroyed, but he be put to aunswer by the lawe of the land: and this custome is confirmed by the statute of Magna Carta the xxvi chapter [*sic* for xxix].

The second is that of the lord's right of relief from an heir of full age:

which at the common law was not certayn, but by the statute of Magna carta it is put in certayn, that is to say for every hole knights fee to pay C. s. And for a hole Barony to pay C. markes for relief. And for a hole Erledom to pay a C. li. and so after the rate.

The student concludes that customs may be changed by statute for they "cannot be proved to have the strength of a law only by reason . . . And a statute made against such general customes ought to be observed because they be not merely the law of reason."

Customs are rather generally known, says the student, but "divers principles that be called in the law Maximes," these "be knowen onely in the kynges courts or among them that take great study in the law." For example:

Also there was sometyme a Maxime and a lawe in England that no manne should have a writte of right but by speciall suite to the king, and for a fyne to be made in the chancery for it. But these maximes be changed by the

editions. I have used those of 1531, 1554, 1613. The passages quoted in the text are from the 1531 edition, chapters vii, viii.

[28] The doctor describes the law eternal as known only to God, but made known to his "creatures reasonable" in three ways: by the law of nature or reason, God's law, man's law. Then he asks the student to show on what the laws of England are grounded, and he names six grounds: the law of reason, the law of God, the general customs of the realm ("and these be the customs that properly be called the common law"), maxims, particular customs, and statutes. The student then discusses each in turn (in separate chapters).

statute of Magna carta, the xvi [*sic* for xxix] Chapter, where it is said thus, Nulli negabimus, nulli vendemus rectum vel iusticiam. And by the wordes nulli negabimus, a man shall have a writte of ryght of course in the Chauncerie without suing to the Kyng for it. And by the woordes, nulli vendemus, he shal have it without fyne; And so many times the old Maximes of the lawe be chaunged by statutes.

In one more instance only does the student call to mind the Charter, and that in discussing "where ignorance of the lawe excuseth in the lawes of Englande and where not": "For ther is no statute made in this realm but by the assent of the lordes spirituall and temporal and of all the commons . . . And every statute there made is of as strong effect in the law, as if all the commons were there present in their own person . . ." He concludes that ignorance excuses in only a few cases, one such exception being "he that offendeth agaynst Magna carta is not excommenged but he have knowlage that it is prohibit that he doth." [29]

St. Germain's popularization of the canonist conception of equity apparently aroused the jealousy of certain of the common lawyers educated narrowly in their own system. Shortly after the publication of the English version of *Doctor and Student* an anonymous serjeant-at-law produced a tract in defense of the common law.[30] He refuses to recognize that it has any defects at all. "The lawe of the realme is a sufficient rule to order you and your conscience what ye shall do in everie thinge, and what ye shall not do." Conscience is a dangerous and variable substitute; the chancellor, usually a "spiritual man," does not know the common law well enough to appreciate and understand it. The serjeant inveighs particularly against the writ of subpoena and the practice of "uses." Procedure by subpoena (in Chancery) is really contrary to, and sets aside the common law, although the king and the judges and serjeants are bound by oath to observe and administer the laws of the realm. Uses "began of an untrue and crafte invention to put the king and his subjects from that which they ought to have of right by the good true common law of the realme." Yet in all this the serjeant says not a word of chapter 29 which was to be invoked so pointedly against Chancery and this very writ in later years.

It remained for his adversary, St. Germain, in his rejoinder, the "Little Treatise concerning Writs of Subpoena," to suggest incidentally one such argument the serjeant might have used. St. Germain justifies the writ on the grounds that it has been used long, often, and publicly, hence pre-

[29] "For they be only excommenged by the sentence called (Sentencia lata super cartas) that doth it wilfully or that doth it by ygnoraunce, and correct not themself within xv dayes after they have warnyng."

[30] "A Replication of a Serjaunte at the Lawes of England," *Hargrave's Law Tracts*, pp. 323–31.

sumably by the authorization of king and council, and even by the advice of the judges.[31] He discusses the chancellor's responsibility if he "grante a subpoena upon a bill that appeareth evidentlye to belonge to the common law and not to the chauncerie":

And some men say, that if the chanceller grante a subpoena upon a bill that appeareth evidentlye to belonge to the common law and not to the chauncerie, and though he there taketh surtie accordinge to the said statute of Hen. 6. yet in that case he is bounde nevertheless to yielde damages to the defendant, though the bill be proved true because he had done against the lawe. And some men will say, that in that case an action lieth upon the statute of Magna Charta against the plaintiff. Howbeit I will not determinately speake therein, but will likewise remit it to other that will furder treate thereof for the plainer declaration of that matter.

Treatises designed to inform justices of the peace of their duties naturally rehearsed the various statutes which the justices were to enforce. However, the statutes which so heaped tasks upon the justices that they incurred the name of "statute creature" were those of the later Middle Ages and the Tudor period. Only a very few provisions of Magna Carta were involved, and even these were largely supplemented or superseded by later enactments.

Fitzherbert's first tract on the justices of the peace was published anonymously as early as 1510.[32] In 1538 he published under his own name a larger tract on the same subject. It begins with an exposition of the justices' commission and then sets out the articles of their charge to the jury. Grouped separately are those articles which depend on specific statutes, and in the summary of the latter are included just two provisions of Magna Carta, the meetings of the sheriff's court and the office of coroner.[33] In 1583 William Crompton issued an enlarged edition of Fitz-

[31] In chapter 1, "Whether a subpoena ought to lye in any case." Here he notes two statutes, 17 Rich. II and 15 Hen. VI, restricting the use of the writ in some cases, and thus by implication, assuming its use in others. In succeeding chapters he discusses specific uses of the writ and also some cases in which it may not be used. And for the following, *Hargrave's Law Tracts*, p. 350.

[32] See Holdsworth, IV, 115–16 and note, for a description of this tract, assignment of authorship to Fitzherbert, and the statement that "from it many other similar tracts were copied." For Fitzherbert's *Natura Brevium* and *Grand Abridgement*, see above, Chap. II.

[33] In the 1541 edition these read: "The Office of Shyreff. Shyreffes shall holde their courtes from moneth to moneth. And where greater tyme is wonte to be, greater shalbe." Magna Carta ca. 33 (*sic* for 35). Rules for holding the sheriff's tourn are based on 31 Ed. III, ca. 14 (*sic*), rather than this same chapter of the Charter, although the times prescribed are the same.

"The Office of Coroner. For to declare playnelye the offyce of a Coroner, it appereth by the statute of M. Carta in the xv [*sic* for 17] Cha. that no Coroner ought to holde any plees of the Corone. But Breton declareth the offyce of a Coroner in forme folowynge. Fyrst that in everye countye Coroner[s] shalbe the principall conservatours of the peace to beare recorde of all plees of the croune, as of abiuracyons, utlagaries, and such lyke."

The series on weights and measures begins with 25 Ed. III, and that on purveyance contains nothing earlier than that reign.

herbert, in law French. The same clauses of the Charter are quoted in respect to sheriff and coroner. Under the caption *Fynes, Amerciaments, & Forfaitures* now appears: "When a man shall be amerced, this shall be according to his offence, saving his contenement. Magna carta ca. 14." [34] These treatises were superseded by the greatly superior *Eirenarcha* of William Lambarde which first appeared in 1581. Before the contributions of this genius of legal antiquarians are described, however, the works of William Staunford merit attention.

Sir William Staunford (1509-58), another learned lawyer and contemporary of Dyer and Plowden, was judge of Common Pleas, 1554-58. He is said to have edited the earliest printed edition of Glanvill. He makes much use of Glanvill and of Bracton, then not yet printed. His treatise on the pleas of the crown, which Holdsworth characterizes as· "founded almost entirely upon Bracton and the Year Books," was posthumously published in 1560. It is divided into three books: I, various offenses; II, jurisdiction, appeals, indictments, and defenses; III, methods of trial and consequences of conviction. Besides some routine allusions to Magna Carta[35] there are passages of greater interest in which the Charter is conceived as an especially authoritative statement of the law midway between Glanvill and Bracton. This point of view is even more clearly emphasized in the second treatise to be described below.

On occasion he finds discrepancies in his authorities, and in one instance marvels that Britton should seem to authorize something prohibited by Magna Carta. After repeating Britton's description of the process of outlawry, he comments:

And whereas Britton has said before that the appellee of the deed will be outlawed if he doesn't come, tc. that seems astonishing [*merveilous*] to me that the sheriff or coroner could award process of outlawry in such a case, for the statute of Magna Carta cap. 17 is Quod nullus Vicecomes, Constabularius, Escheator, Coronator, vel alii Ballivi nostri, teneant placita Corone nostre. On which statute divers have held opinions that on appeal begun before the sheriff and coroner, although they can award process against the appellees up to the outlawry still the outlawry they cannot award, nor if he appears, put him to answer, but only assign him to prison by reason of this statute of Magna Carta. Ideo Quaere, for Britton and the Book of Assizes before mentioned are to the contrary, the which were written a long time after the making of the said statute.[36]

[34] For a description of this treatise see Holdsworth, IV, 116, note 9.

[35] Staunford, *Pleas of the Crown*, Book II, fols. 55v, 84. Under the caption "De que mort Feme avera appeal," he begins with the well-known rule of Magna Carta ca. 34. In two instances he quotes statutes which embody a clause of the Charter: West. II, ca. 29, quoting Magna Carta ca. 26; 31 Ed. III, ca. 14, on the order of indictments to be taken in turns or leets, quoting Magna Carta ca. 35.

[36] *Ibid.*, fols. 64-64v.

In his discussion of "year, day and waste" Staunford arrives at an interpretation of chapter 22 different from that of modern commentators, namely, that the absence of reference to waste meant that it was remitted in favor of the lords to whom the property would escheat.[37] Like Littleton, he sees trial by peers as founded on Magna Carta. Following a nicely detailed description of the correct procedure, based as he says on two Year Book cases (1 Henry IV and 13 Henry VIII), he concludes:

And this manner of trial is given so it seems [*come semble*] by the statute called Magna Carta chapter 29: which is to this effect [*in cest manner*] Nullus liber homo . . . [quoted in full in large print] In this statute there is that word *homo* which includes as well male, as female, and moreover it was not intended of male only, as appears by the statute made in the year 20 *Henry 6 ca. 9*, the latter of which is thus.[38]

Staunford's other treatise, as its title indicates, was "an exposition of the kinges prerogative collected out of the great abridgement of Justice Fitzherbert and other older writers of the lawes of Englande." The author hoped that his work might inspire some of the judges or other learned men to deal similarly with other titles in Fitzherbert.[39] Staunford adopted for his plan of treatment the chapters of the so-called *Praerogativa Regis*, adding certain procedural privileges which had been developed since its compilation—the legal process which could be used by or against the crown.[40] The *Praerogativa* has been assigned to some time between the years 1255 and 1290. Holdsworth calls it a tract which may have been "merely private work, or have emanated from some official on the instructions of the king." But from Edward III's reign to Coke's time it was accepted as a statute. Because in manuscript volumes of the statutes it was inserted between the *Vetera Statuta* and the *Nova Statuta*, it was assumed to date from Edward II's reign.[41] Its sixteen chapters constitute

---

[37] Cf. below, p. 182, for the same subject dealt with in his second treatise.

[38] Staunford, *Pleas of the Crown*, chap. 1, "Triall per les pieres."

[39] Published 1568, but the dedication to Nicholas Bacon is dated November 6, 1548. "I would wish that amongest such plenty of lerned men as bee at this day some thing were devysed to help the students of their long jorney . . . whiche thing might wel come to pass after my poore mynd, if such titles as bee in the great abrijment of Justice *Fitzherbert* were by the Judges or some other learned men labored and studied, that is to say, every title by itself by special divisions digested, ordered, and disposed in such sort as that all the judicial acts and cases in the same might be brought and appere under certain principles, rules and grounds of the said lawes."

[40] Staunford realized that this treatment did not exhaust the subject; "Dyvers other Prerogatives there bee, whiche the king hath by order of the common lawe, that bee not within this statute comprised, a greate parte whereof under the title of Prerogative Maister Fitzherbert hath most diligently noted in his greate Abridgment, and so well placed there, that I doo, of purpose omit to release them here." *Praerogativa*, fol. 50v. Holdsworth comments, "as Staunford recognized, it did not tell lawyers or politicians anything of the new position in the state which the king and his prerogative were taking." III, 460.

[41] *English Historical Review*, 5:753. Holdsworth, I, 473, note 8. In S. R. I, 226-28, it appears among statutes of uncertain date. Staunford uses internal evidence to support his dating. Littleton, he says, doubted of the time of the making of the statute, but he himself is

a statement of the feudal rights of the crown, "the powers of other feudal lords magnified"; or again, "exceptions in favour of the crown to those general rules that are established for the rest of community." For that was the meaning of *prerogatives,* used in the plural, not singular, in the thirteenth and fourteenth centuries. Later, indeed by Staunford's time, these were becoming merely the "ordinary private rights of the crown as contrasted with the sovereign position it held or claimed to hold in public law." [42] Magna Carta, too, had been primarily a statement of feudal law, but with emphasis on the limitation, rather than the privilege, of the crown. For this reason, perhaps, the *Praerogativa* makes no reference to the Charter, but Staunford was quick to see parallels between the two documents.

He points out correctly that passages of the *Praerogativa,* chapter 4, merely restate clauses of Magna Carta chapter 7, which in turn but confirmed the common law as stated in Glanvill. For example, after summarizing all that Glanvill says on the position of heiresses and widows (tenants of mesne lords), he concludes:

so it aperes plainly here by *Glanvill* that this hole statute of prerogativa should be but a confirmation of the common law. And that the law was so as Glanvill toke yt, it may partly apere by the statute of *Magna carta* cap. 7. For the words are not onlie *quod vidua securitatem faciet quod se non maritabit sine assensu nostro si de nobis tenuerit,* but are also *vel sine assensu domini sui si de alio tenuerit.* And Bracton agrees also with Glanvill.[43]

In two instances Staunford completes his discussion of certain prerogatives by additions from the Charter. To the definition of royal rights of *primer seisin* (*Praerogativa,* chapter 3) as they apply to knight's service tenure he adds the limitation: "But otherwyse yt ys where the tenure is but a tenure by Socage in capite, for there the kynge shall have noe primer seisin in landes holden of other, namely if theye be holden of other by knyghtes service, as it appearethe plainlye by the statute of Magna charta ca. 27 and in the newe Natura brevium fo. 288." [44] Again, after distinguishing between *tenure in capite,* that is to say *ab antiquo de Corona,* and tenure "which is but newlye come," he adds, "and the statute of Magna Carta ca. 3 [*sic* for 31] did helpe this matter by expresse woordes,

sure from the words "tempore Regis H[enrici] partris Regis E[dwardi]." If written in Edward I's day, the words would be "patris nostri." *Praerogativa,* fol. 6.
[42] Holdsworth's phrases, III, 460–61.
[43] *Praerogativa,* fol. 20. Passages preceding this relate to the widow's required promise not to marry without the king's or other lord's license, and her protection against a forced marriage. Magna Carta is cited in both connections.
[44] *Praerogativa,* fol. 13v. Ca. 27 relates to *prerogative wardship,* not to *primer seisin.* What the Charter says is that when the tenure is *socage in capite* the king shall have no *wardship* in the lands holden of another by knight's service. Staunford's interpretation seems to be an instance of "extension of the words of a statute": where wardship is specified, *primer seisin* by analogy is included.

if such an honour came to the crowne by waye of discent or any other
waye." [45]

In commenting on other provisions he is biased by his penchant for
equating all with the early common law. His interpretations here afford
an excellent example of the effect of looking back through the centuries
to the Charter as the statute of 9 Henry III, with no knowledge or understanding of it as a corrective of earlier practices or of John's abuses of
the law. The intent of Magna Carta chapter 32 was probably to check the
greater freedom of alienation prevailing before its enactment. But, says
Staunford, quoting the chapter, this statute "is but a confirmation of the
common law, as it doth appere by that which is written in Glanvill." [46]

Again, as in his *Pleas of the Crown,* he holds that the king's right to
waste in lands forfeited for felony was abolished by Magna Carta chapter
22 and restored by *Praerogativa Regis,* chapter 16. "Thus up to this day,
it appears plainly that the king is entitled to all three namely year, day,
and waste." Incidentally he hits on the more correct interpretation, but
abandons it because it does not fit with Glanvill. [47]

William Lambarde

IF CAMDEN was the foremost scholar of his day for his broad knowledge of
Britain's "antiquities" in general, William Lambarde was prince of legal
antiquarians. He combined a successful law career with that of antiquary
and historian. Born in London in 1536, William was the son of John
Lambarde, draper, alderman, and sheriff. On the death of his father in
1554 he inherited the manor of Westcombe in Greenwich, Kent, and
readily identified himself with the interests and loyalties of that county.
He was called to the bar of Lincoln's Inn in 1567; was made a bencher
of his Inn in 1579; and in August of the same year became justice of the
peace for Kent. In later years he was appointed successively master in

[45] "And that statute doth set forth certeine honours by name whiche bee not of the
auncientnes of the Croune, that is to say the honour of Wallingforde, Nottingham, Bolingbroke
[*sic*] and Lancaster."

[46] *Praerogativa,* fols. 28–28v. After commenting on the justice of such a rule he discusses
evidence in Bracton of a tendency toward more liberal rule for alienation and concludes, "It
seemeth by *Bracton* that it was verie doubtful notwithstanding the statut of Magna carta
whither the king's tenant might alien his whole tenancy or not. And therefore was that statute
of *Quia emptores terrarum* made . . ."

[47] "By this [Magna Carta ca. 22] it should seme this statute doth remitte the wast because
it speaketh nothing of it or els per aventure you will saye that this word *Nisi* argues and
proves that the kinge before the statut of Magna carta might have holden it as long as he
would, but to the contrarie of that exposition is Glanvile, as appereth before." *Ibid.,* fol. 48v.
Then Staunford quotes Bracton to the effect that the king "before the making of the sayd
Statute of Magna Carta" had nothing but the waste, then accepted the year and day instead
of waste. This is the interpretation which Coke uses (*Second Institute,* p. 36) and which
McKechnie (p. 338) attributes to Coke himself, but wrongly, I think, as Coke probably got it
from Staunford or direct from the same passage in Bracton.

Chancery (1592), keeper of the rolls and the House of the Rolls in Chancery Lane (1597), and keeper of the records in the Tower (1601). At this time he was personally noticed by the queen, to whom he presented an account of the Tower records which he called his *Pandecta Rotulorum*.[48]

Lambarde's interest in antiquities seems to have been inspired while he was a student at Lincoln's Inn by his studies in history and Anglo-Saxon with Laurence Nowell.[49] It was at the latter's suggestion that he made his collection and paraphrase of the Anglo-Saxon laws, the *Archaionomia*, 1568, which, as his subtitle puts it, *a tenebris in lucum vocati . . . G. Lambardo interprete*. These "restored the forgotten Anglo-Saxon laws to the students of the common law. Because they had a direct bearing upon constitutional and legal antiquities, they could be pressed into the service of those who fought the battle of the constitution in the following century . . ."[50] Succeeding scholars, lawyers, and parliament men must have known Anglo-Saxon institutions as they were presented in the words of Lambarde's translation. Matthew Parker and Lambarde were drawn together by their common interests. The archbishop recommended him to Lord Burghley as "an honest and well-learned observer of times and histories." Says Strype:

> William Lambard and our Archbishop conferred much their notes of antiquity together; and did mutually impart to each other their collections, and particularly the antiquities of Kent, Lambard left in the Archbishop's hands. . . . As to his skill in the Saxon language and laws, thus he spake, *Et in ejusmodi rebus perscrutandis sagaci certe ingenio, et peracri . . .* To this Antiquarian the Archbishop communicated an ancient copy of Matthew Paris, before an edition of it, who took the pains to transcribe this learned Abbot's history, which transcript yet remains in the Cotton library . . .[51]

Lambarde is best known as the author of the first county history, his *Perambulation of Kent: containing the Description, Hystorie, and Customes of that Shyre*,[52] the model for others to follow such as Richard

---

[48] Nichols, *Biblioteca*, I, 525–26, app. vii.

[49] Laurence Nowell (or Nowel, d. 1576), brother of Alexander Nowell, dean of St. Paul's, was not a lawyer. Educated at Oxford and Cambridge, he was for a time master of a grammar school, tutor to Richard de Vere, Earl of Oxford, and in 1560 dean of Lichfield. "He was a diligent antiquary, and learned in Anglo-Saxon, being among the first to revive the study of the language in England (Camden, *Britannia*, col. 6) and having as his pupil William Lambarde, the editor of the laws of the Anglo-Saxons, with whom he used to study when staying at one period in the chamber of his brother Robert Nowell (d. 1569) attorney-general of the Court of Wards, in Gray's Inn." His *Vocabularium Saxonicum* passed successively to Lambarde, Somner, and Selden. William Hunt, in *D.N.B.*

[50] Holdsworth, IV, 117.

[51] Strype, *Matthew Parker*, p. 517.

[52] The first draft was published by Wotton, 1576. He had collected materials for an account of all England, but abandoned this larger design on hearing of Camden's undertaking. His materials were published in 1730.

Carew's on Cornwall. The story goes that Cecil prepared by a study of the *Perambulation* to regale Elizabeth with the antiquities of Kent on her progress into that county.

Lambarde's legal treatises were equally distinguished. His *Eirenarcha* for justices of the peace, based on his profound knowledge of the law as well as on actual experience as justice, was superior in content and organization to Fitzherbert and Crompton.[53] In his preface he says that he has set himself to compare the older treatises on the justices of the peace, "to conferre their writings with the Booke cases and Statutes that have arisen of latter times, and out of them to collect some one body of discourse, that may serve for the present age, wherein wee now live, and somewhat further the good endevour of such gentlemen as be not trained uppe in continued studie of the lawes." In his dedicatory letter to Lord Bromley he relates how he had collected material for his own use and then was persuaded to have it published for the use of others: "Then againe, I tooke the booke into my handes, and ripping (stitch by stitch) my former doing, I enlarged the worke, graunting unto it more breath and roôme of speech: I planted *Precedents* here and there in it; I gave it some light of Order and Method; and added withall some delight of history and Recorde . . ."

The comprehensiveness of his scholarship is revealed by his further account in the same letter of the authorities he has used: Marrowe's Reading (18 Henry VII); Fitzherbert's and another anonymous treatise; the "olde and newe bookes of the Common Lawes" (which included Glanvill and Bracton, both now in print); and the "volumes of the Actes and Statutes." In the course of his treatise, besides making numerous citations from these authorities, he corrects errors in Fitzherbert's historical treatment, points out anachronisms and errors in the commission of his own day, and includes interesting etymologies for many terms, Latin, French, Greek.

In the *Eirenarcha*, as in Crompton's edition of Fitzherbert, the statement on amercements appears,[54] but now in connection with Lambarde's

---

[53] *Eirenarcha* was published in 1581. It was followed in 1583 by a companion tract on the duties of constables and other officials dependent upon the justices—*The Duties of Constables, Borsholders, Tythingmen, and such other lowe Ministers of the Peace.* These two were the most practical, useful, and popular of Lambarde's works. They "exactly supplied a want long felt by that numerous and important class who were called on either to act as justices of the peace, or to advise them as to their powers and duties." Blackstone could still recommend the *Eirenarcha* to students in his day. Its popularity is attested by the numerous editions— seven between 1583 and 1610. There were six reprints of the companion tract, 1584–1610. Holdsworth, IV, 118 and note 2. My citations are from the first edition. In the 1610 edition the arrangement in books and chapters is entirely different.

[54] On the other hand, the series of statutes on purveyance goes back to 28 Ed. I, ca. 2 (*Articuli super cartas*). As to weights and measures, 9 Hen. III, ca. 25, is listed in the table though not quoted. The table is headed as "conteining (verie neare) all the imprinted Statutes, both generall and particular, wherewith Iustices of the Peace have in any sorte to deale."

interesting discussion of fines and amercements, the etymology of the words, the difference between them, and the tendency to blur this distinction in everyday speech and the language of the later statutes:

Hereof also the *Fine* tooke firste his name, of the Latine *Finis,* because it maketh an end with the Prince, for the imprisonment for the offence committed against his Law. And in that respect chiefly doth it differre from an *Amercement*: For when the offender hath not so deeply trespassed, that thereby he deserveth any bodily punishment at all (as if he be nonsuit in an action, or do commit any such like fault) he is said to fall into the Kinges *Mercie,* because he is therein mercifullye to be dealt with: and by the *Great Charter* (ca. 14) that Amercement and summe of money which he is to paye for the same, ought to be asseased and affeered by the good and lawfull men of the neighburhoode, which also *Glanvil* lib. 9 ca. 11 affirmeth to have bene the Law of the lande long before that time, saying . . .[55]

But it is in Lambarde's "planting a precedent" and adding those "delights of history and record" that the most interesting references to Magna Carta occur. Chapter 30, along with other statutes, serves to illustrate the difference between "such an Alien as is of the Enmitie of the Queene, and him that is of hir Amitie."[56] More striking is his account of the experiment tried in the second year of Richard II, which he inserts in connection with his discussion of the powers of two justices (out of sessions) in "punishing riots, routs, and unlawful assemblies."

This auctoritie of assembling the power of the countie, and of arresting and imprisoning Riotters, til due execution of law were done upon them, was once before this time (namely 2 R. 2. c. 6) committed to some, and was by and by after resumed in the same yeare of the same king's raign, as a thing too greevous to be suffered, that any man shoulde be imprisoned without an Indictement (or *Sine legali iudicio parium suorum,* as *Magna Carta* speaketh) first had agaynst him.[57]

Here Lambarde clearly equates the jury—in this instance the indicting jury—with the *iudicium parium* of chapter 29, whereas, as shown above,[58]

[55] *Eirenarcha,* Book II, chap. xvi. "Of the Processe of the Fine of the Queene, and of the assessing thereof: and of Estreating for the Queene."

[56] He is discussing suretie of the peace and "good abearing," and expresses some doubt touching aliens because the commission seems to authorize the justices "no further than to provide for the Queene's people, of which number no Alien seemeth to bee." Yet "some think there ought to be a difference between such an Alien as is of the *Enmitie* of the Queene, and him that is of hir Amitie: for the Statuts (Magna Carta ca. 30, 9 Edward 3 ca. 1; 14 E. 3 sta. 2 ca. 2 and sundry other) do al use that difference in *Marchant strangers,* and do provide, that such of them as be not *Enimies* of the *Realme,* may both safely come into the Realme, and tarie heer, and go thence at their pleasures." Book I, chap. xvi, 88–89.

[57] Book I, chap. xxii, 233–34. In later editions (1592 and 1619, pp. 305 and 314–15) this passage concludes "(. . . as Magna Charta speaketh) until that the experience of greater evils had prepared and made the stomake of the comon wealth able and fit to digest it."

[58] See above, Chap. III.

in this incident and other like instances in the fourteenth century, the commons always found guarantee of jury indictment in the other phrase —*per legem terrae.* In a subsequent passage (*Of Hearing or Triall by Traverse*) Lambarde not only makes the identification of the *judicium parium* with the *trial* jury, but extols jury trial as the ancient heritage of the freeborn man. Although he may have been merely voicing the current opinion of his day, this passage seems to mark Lambarde as the original author of this famous "error." Anticipating Coke by many years both in this point and in the conception of the Great Charter as a liberty document, it deserves to be quoted in full:

The most solemne, and antient Triall of the fact, against an offendor that will not confesse it, is that which we see performed by the verdite of twelve good and lawfull men of the Countrie; and it also doth best contente and quiet the guiltie man, for that it passeth by his owne Countriemen Neighbours, and *Peeres,* according to the antiente libertie of the Lande, whereunto everie Free borne man thinketh himselfe inheritable. And thereupon it is named (*Mag. Chart.* cap. 29) *Legale iudicium parium suorum,* the lawfull iudgement of a mans owne *Peeres,* or *Equalles*: because as the Nobilitie, so also the Communaltie are to be tryed, in treason, felonie, or misprision of treason, not the one by the other, but eache by men of their owne estate and calling: I meane by the word *Nobilitie,* as our own Law speaketh (which calleth none *Noble* under the degree of a *Baron*) and not as men of forraine Countries doe use to speake, with whom every man of *Gentile* birth is accounted *Noble*: for wee daily see, that both *Gentlemen* and *Knights* do serve in the *Parliament,* as members of the Communaltie. Howbeit, in cases of forcible *Entrie, Riot, Rout, unlawfull assemblie,* or suche like, they of the *Nobilitie* shal be tried by twelve men, as wel as other inferiour subiects . . .[59]

In the gradually dawning conception of the Great Charter as a "liberty document," Lambarde's *Archeion* is also of extraordinary interest. But this historical commentary on the central courts of justice, though composed in 1591,[60] was not published until 1635. There is little evidence of its influence. Wood, commenting on Fleetwood's works, says that he saw in manuscript "Observations upon the Eyre of Pickering and on Lambarde's Archeion." [61] Whether the latter was read by other contemporaries, or whether the author himself shared its content in conversation with friends and colleagues may only be conjectured.

Lambarde's description of the granting of Magna Carta in a full parliament of the three estates (king, lords, and commons) need not surprise

[59] Book II, chap. xiii, 436–37.
[60] The *Epistle Dedicatorie* to Sir Robert Cecil, dated at Lincoln's Inn, October 22, 1591, says, "Whereof, some I penned sundrie yeeres sithence, others not long agoe, and the rest so lately, that your Honour may, if it please you, take the first view and reading of them . . ."
[61] Wood's *Athenae,* I, 598.

us, for he carries parliament back to remote times.[62] More specifically, here he is relying on *Matthew Paris* and on the wording of later confirmations of the Charter—"authenticke Records of the Parliaments themselves." But it is still the living statute 9 Henry III of which he writes; in spite of his acquaintance with the chronicle, he makes no mention of John's original grant or the circumstances which produced it. Yet he is aware that the document is something precious for which Englishmen have striven:

I read moreover in the same *Matthew Paris,* That King *Henry* the 3. did, *Anno Dom.* 1225. call together *Omnes Clericos, & Laicos totius Regnie,* which Assemblie the same writer in some places expresseth by the words *Universitas Regni.* But what need I to hang long upon the *credit* of *Historians,* seeing that from this time douneward the Authenticke Records of the *Parliaments* themselves doe offer me present helpe. The great Charter of England, which passed from this King about this time, and for which the Englishmen had no lesse striven than the *Trojans* for their *Helena;* beareth no shew of an *Act* of *Parliament:* and yet I will prove, by the depositions of two sundrie *Parliaments,* that it was made by the common consent of all the Realme, in the time of K. Henry 3. for so saith the *Statute* called *Confirmatio Chartae, Anno* 25. *Edward* I in flat termes; and the *Statute* made at *Westminster, Anno* 15 *Edward* 3. ca. 1 saith That it was made by the *King, Peeres,* and *Commons* of this Land.

After citing other statutes he concludes:

if you shall finde any acts of Parliament, seeming to passe under the *Name* and *Authoritie* of the King onely, as there be some that have that shew indeed; yet you must not by and by judge, that it was established without the assent of the other Estates . . . And though Magna Charta, and sundrie other old Statutes, doe run in the Name of the Prince onely, yet the other two Estates are supplied in all good understanding.[63]

After his definition of the various courts ("Ecclesiasticall Courts, what they be," "The Division of Meere Lay Courts at this day") he proceeds, as he says, to go back to history from William the Conqueror on "and descend from him downward, untill I have set them all on foot." As to the Court of Common Pleas, Lambarde finds its origin in a deliberate creation of Henry III by Magna Carta chapter 11.[64] This view was com-

---

[62] He is misled, as many of his contemporaries must have been, by his translation and understanding of Anglo-Saxon words and terms in his *Archaionomia,* valuable as this work was on the whole. In the *Archeion,* pp. 238–46, for instance, drawing on Tacitus, Bede, the laws of Ine, Alfred, and others, he interprets *witana* (wise men) as including the commons.

[63] *Archeion,* pp. 264–70.

[64] The lay courts are discussed under these subdivisions: civil matters between king and subject; civil matters between subject and subject; courts of conscience for civil causes; criminal causes. Of the origin of the court of Common Pleas he says:

"In this plight that High Court of the King continued untill that *Henry* the third, in the

mon to most scholars and lawyers of the time. Coke repudiated it, to be
sure, but on the other hand gave the court too ancient an origin.

Lambarde, good Elizabethan lawyer and statesman that he is, sees no
irreconcilable conflict or rivalry among the various courts he describes, or
between council and courts. The latter, "derived from the Crowne their
originall," are all "roses from the garland of the Prince, leaving nevertheless the *Garland* itself *undespoyled* of that her *Soveraign vertue*, in the
administration of Iustice." Yet he recognizes historic conflicts as well as
criticisms in his own day. It is in the section entitled "The Kings Councell" in which he discusses the king's "supreme Court of Prerogative,"
that he treats of the "conflicte betweene the law absolute and ordinarie."

> But here have I mightie Adversaries to encounter withall; the which main-
> taining with their whole Forces the ordinarie Iurisdiction, will in no wise yeeld
> to any such absolute and unbridled *Authoritie*, as I may seeme to advance.
>
> And therefore first of all, that *Great Charter* of the *Liberties* of *England*,
> (which I may call the first Letters of *Manumission* of the people of this
> *Realme*, out of the *Norman* servitude) doth by the *Mouth* of the King
> (amongst many other Freedomes) specifie this one: *Nullus liber homo capiatur,
> vel imprisonetur, aut disseisietur de libero tenemento suo, vel libertatibus, vel
> liberis consuetudinibus suis, aut utlagetur, ut exuletur aut aliquo modo destrua-
> tur, nec super eum ibimus, nec super eum mittemus, nisi per legale iudicium
> parium suorum, vel per Legem terrae.*
>
> By pretence of which *Grant*, the common *Subject* thought himselfe free
> from that irregular *Power* which the former Kings and their Councell of Estate
> had exercised upon him; and phantasied, that he ought not thenceforth to be
> drawne to answer in any *Case*, except it were by way of Indictment, or by
> tryall of good and lawfull men (being his Peeres) onely after the course of
> the Common Law."

Then Lambarde hastens to correct this misconception of the "common
subject," yet this same misconception was to be revived with ardor a few
years hence:

nineth yeare of his reigne . . . finding by experience, that it was either chargeable or dilatorie,
or both, for his subjects to have no other remedie for tryall of their rights, but either before
himselfe, in that *Supreme Court*, (which removed with him wheresoever he went) or before
those *Iustices in Eyre* (which came not yearely into the Countrie) granted unto his subjects
that *great Charter* of the Liberties of *England*, in the 11. Chapter whereof, he ordained thus:
Communia Placita non sequantur Curiam nostram, sed teneantur in aliquo certo loco. Whereupon followed two things: The first, that a new *Court* was erected for the determination of
such *Pleas* as did not concerne the *Croune* and *Dignitie* of the *Prince*, but were meerely *Civill*,
and did belong to the subjects betweene themselves: The second, that this Court was established in a place certaine, and that was at *Westminster*; to the end, that the people might have
a standing seat of Iustice, whereunto they might resort, for the tryall of their oune Causes,
and not be driven to follow the *King* and his *Court*, but onely where the matter respected him.
And after this, all the Writs that are recited in *Henry Bracton's* Booke, (which was written in
the latter end of the reigne of this King *Henry* (the third) have this commandement to the
partie: *Quod sit coram Iusticiariis meis apud Westminster*, and not *Coram me vel Iusticiariis
meis*, as the former form in Glanvile was. And thus began that *Court*, which, because it hath
power over *Common Pleas*, wee now call the *Common Pleas*." *Archeion*, pp. 34–36.

Whereas indeed, these words of the Statute ought to be understood of the restitution then made of the ordinarie *Iurisdiction* in common *Controversies*, and not for restraint of the absolute *Authoritie*; serving onely in a few rare and singular Cases. And therefore see what followed; some *Cases* dayly creeping out of Suits, for which no *Law* had been provided; and some misdemeanors also happening from time to time, in the distribution of those *Lawes* that were already established.[65]

Then in a fascinating passage which has not had the publicity it deserves,[66] Lambarde traces from Magna Carta to 15 Henry VI (and into the sixteenth century as a prelude to his description of the Star Chamber) the swing to and fro between the seeming need for the special jurisdiction of the council and attempts to limit that jurisdiction by the rules of the common law, or, as he puts it in a later passage, "the tossing of this Ball to and fro, betweene the Councell and Commons." After commenting on the return to prerogative justice for some time in the reign of Edward I,[67] he sketches the fourteenth-century struggle of parliament to limit the jurisdiction of the council, or at least to modify its procedure:

Neverthelesse, (such is the weaknesse and imperfection of man) the time was not long, but the *Subject*, which so desirously fled to the King and his Councell for succour, did as hastily retire, and run backe to the ordinarie *Seat* and *Iudge* againe. . . . But this is certaine, that within five yeeres next after the beginning of the Reigne of King *Edward* the third, it was commanded by *Parliament*, that the forme of the *Great Charter*, in this point, should be wholly and inviolably observed.

Thus does Lambarde introduce and rehearse five of the parliamentary measures later to be known as the *six statutes*, together with 17 Richard II, chapter 6, and 15 Henry VI, chapter 4. All these, as he tells us, were provided by parliament "for the more assured suppression of all attempts that might breake forth to the contrary." [68] Although no doubt Lambarde had access to the official rolls, it seems hardly a coincidence that these acts are identical with the series quoted in Rastell's *Statutes* under the title *accusacion*.

[65] *Archeion*, pp. 108–10.
[66] Holdsworth is an exception.
[67] "It came to passe, that many finding none other helpes for their griefes were enforced to sue to the Kings *Person* itselfe, for remedie: And hee againe knowing himselfe to be the *Chiefe Iustice* and *Lieutenant* of God within his owne Realme, thought himselfe bounde to deliver *Iudgment* and *Iustice*, whensoever it should be required at his hands. . . . The which thing was so farre from offending the *Subject* for a long time together, that in the Parliament 28 *Edw.* I *cap.* 5 the *Commons* assented to an Act, by which it was provided, That the Chancellor and the Iustices of the Kings *Bench* should follow the King wheresoever hee went; to the end, that he might alwaies have at hand men learned, and able to advise him in such *Cases* as he admitted to his hearing."
[68] *Archeion*, pp. 110–21. Of course he does not include 38 Ed. III, no. 9, which, as has been shown above, was not in the statute roll and did not mean what counsel for the five knights claimed it did.

But with the spirit of compromise and moderation characteristic of Elizabeth's reign, Lambarde does not find this "repugnancie" insoluble:

The which howsoever in appearance it may seeme great and irreconciliable, yet if recourse may be had to that *golden Mediocritie*, which both *Religion, Reason* and *Law* doe maintaine in this point, the Controversie will soon be decided, and that without any derogating from the *Authoritie* of the *King* and his *Councell*; or prejudicating that lawfull *Freedome* of the Subject, which is claimed for him.

It is inseparably annexed to the office of king to be judge. If the subject were once utterly barred of this access to the person of the king "in case of such his distresse,"

he would cry out upon the ordinarie *Law,* for the *Authoritie* whereof he so eagerly striveth; and would not sticke to lay to the Kings charge, that hee bare the *Sword* in vaine; that he kept not the promise of the *Great Charter*; *Nulli negabimus aut differemus Iustitiam*; and that hee violated the solemn *oath* and *vow* of his Coronation, *faciam fieri justitiam.*[69]

Readings in the Inns of Court

"EATING for an education" is the way one writer sums up the life of a law student, "for the 'eating of dinner' is the method adopted by the four Inns of Court for ensuring that a student is actually present in his college . . ."[70] His real education consisted not only of attendance on the nearby courts at Westminster during term times, but also the practice moots (mock trials) held in the great hall after dinner, and in the series of learned lectures given by an appointed Reader, an obligation imposed on the benchers of each society.

As revived in modern times, a reading, as the distinguished Middle Temple Lent Reader, John Mahan Gover, puts it (1935), "involves more honour than obligation." On the contrary, in Elizabethan and Stuart times the position of Reader of the Inn was "a seriously burdensome one."[71] Gover illustrates from the account which Sir James Whitelocke gives in his *Liber Famelicus* of "his experiences as Reader in the year 1619 and

[69] He proposes as a *"meane"* fair to king, courts, and client, that "the ordinarie *Iurisdiction* of the *Common Court* be not hindred by this infinite authoritie, but onely where either (as I said) they have no. Warrant to receive the *Plea*, or where the tenure of their due proceedings is disturbed; or where the matter is such, as deserveth to be heard from the *highest Stage*, or the partie such, as is unable to run the wearisome race of *solemne Law & Processe*; or where some other rare, extraordinary, & weighty *consideration* shall promote the same."

[70] Blackham, *The Story of the Temple*, p. 163.

[71] John Mahan Gover, a reading delivered before the Honourable Society of the Middle Temple, Lent Reader, 1935. "It will be remembered that the practice of Readings by the Readers of the Middle Temple was discontinued from 25 June 1680, until it was revived by Mr. Justice McCardie, when, during his term as Lent Reader in 1927, he gave a Reading on 'The Law, the Advocate, and the Judge.' " Macassey, "The Middle Temple's Contribution to the National Life."

sets out an account of his perquisites in that office and also his expenditure including the provision of '80 fat bucks' for dinners in the Hall. The account shows a lamentable adverse balance of £239 which, translated into its modern equivalent in value, leaves me with a profound sense of satisfaction that the Readership has been shorn of most of its ancient responsibilities."

The character of such a reading and the circumstances attendant on its delivery will be set forth in detail in connection with Francis Ashley's reading in Middle Temple Hall, 1616. The Reader usually selected a statute, introduced his subject with an introduction in English (and this was occasionally of enough general interest to be printed separately), then followed, in law French, with a most exhaustive exposition, phrase by phrase and word by word. This treatment was well described by a member of the Middle Temple, Edward Bagshawe:

for Reading of Law in the Inns of Court and Chancery (in both of which I have been Reader) are, as they speak in Schools, rather *Problemata* than *Dogmata*, Mootes and Questions of Law (though of the Prerogative itself, the highest of things) for the Ventilation of Truth, and extricating the obscurities of Law, for the benefit of Students in those Societies, then Resolutions and Judgments of Law in Westminster Hall . . . it was the manner of Readers to lay the points of their Case so close, that what seemed strange to the hearers, when the Readers came to argue, he made those things so clear, that usually the Reader came off well.[72]

Among the statutes upon which were based readings in the Inns of Court in the fifteenth and sixteenth centuries, recent legislation of note naturally received the most attention.[73] Yet medieval statutes were not entirely neglected. It is natural to find Littleton, author of the *Tenures,* reading on Westminster II, chapter 1 (*de donis conditionabilis*), and Fitzherbert, compiler of the *Grand Abridgement* of the Year Books, on the statute of Marlborough. Coke cites a reading by Sir Robert Brook (2 Philip and Mary) on Magna Carta chapter 28. A reading by Brook on chapter 17 of the Charter was printed in 1641. But here the chapter in question, like the texts of some sermons, is just a point of departure, in this instance for a dissertation on the pleas of the crown.[74] No lawyer

[72] As to arrangement, continues Bagshawe, "I expounded my whole Statute, being an ancient Law, according as all ancient Readers were wont to do. I made ten divisions, according to the manner of Readings," upon every division put ten cases, and for each case a number of points. In the defense which he published in 1660 of his Reading of 1639, criticized by Laud in that he "read against the bishops." See below, pp. 368–69.

[73] Such were Sir Thomas Audley's readings on 4 Henry VII, ca. 17 (aids); Robert Brook's on 28 Hen. VIII, ca. 2 (limitation of actions); Sir James Dyer's on 34 and 35 Hen. VIII (explanation of the Statute of Wills); and Sir Thomas Williams' on 35 Hen. VIII, ca. 6 (trial by jury).

[74] The cover of the tract reads "The Reading of Mr. Robert Brook, seriant of the Law, and Recorder of London upon the Stat. of Magna Carta, chap. 16 [*sic*] Printed London 1641."

would have thought of reading on Magna Carta *in toto* any more than Littleton would have undertaken the whole of Westminster II.

In the Harleian Manuscripts are notes of a reading on Magna Carta, some twenty-three "lectures," anonymous, undated, and seemingly incomplete.[75] There is no title, but in the Reader's introductory statements to his audience he refers to "the Statute of Magna Carta which I meane by your patience and favours to read upon." As usual the introduction is in English, the actual exposition of the text of the "statute" in law French. Although undated, internal evidence marks it unmistakably as of Elizabeth's reign.[76] The style immediately suggests that of Sir Thomas Williams in his reading on 35 Henry VIII, chapter 6, said to have been delivered as the Lent reading at the Inner Temple (1557–58).[77] Williams was a member of parliament in 1555, 1557–58, and 1562.[78] In this last session he was elected speaker, but the parliament was prorogued more than once, and Williams died July 1, 1566, before it met again. He was also Lent Reader for his Inn in 1560 and possibly in 1561, but the Inner Temple records do not record the subject of his readings.

In the course of twenty-five rather large quarto leaves written on both sides, the Reader treats of the preamble and chapters 1 and 2 of the

In the manuscript collections of the sixteenth and early seventeenth centuries are what appear to be students' notes of readings on various chapters of Magna Carta, but they are too fragmentary to be worth comment here. For instance:

MS Rawl. C. 85, fol. 2. "Lectura sur [le statut?] de Magna Carta, ca. 19" (among notes on cases of Elizabeth's reign and Coke's reading on the statute *De Finibus*).

Harl. MSS 1210, no. 13. A Lent reading, 8 Henry VIII on ca. 17; and 1336, no. 4, "Like Readings upon Magna Carta, beginning at cap. VIII and short explanations of certain passages in some other statutes."

[75] Harl. MSS 4990 154–79 (146–71), some twenty-five rather large quarto leaves written on both sides.

[76] For instance, his discussion of the law of the land as relating to the church is clearly post-Reformation law: "par la course del comon loy le roy est le supreme governer del spiritualtie et auxi del temporaltie en cest terr' et nemy le Pape. Car come appert par le common ley et auxi par diverse ancient estatuts ceo authoritie que le pape avoit gayne en cest terr' fuit par usurpacion." Leaf 163. Leaf 176, he refers to the time "avant le primer an del roigne nostre seignor le roygne q'ore est."

[77] Published in 1680 as "The Excellency and Praeheminence of the Law of England above all other Lawes in the World, asserted in a Lent Reading upon the Statute of 35 Henry VIII cap. 6 concerning Tryals by Jury of Twelve Men" (and incorrectly stated to have been delivered in Lent of 1556–57). The striking peculiarity of style in these two readings consists in the repetition at the beginning of each lecture throughout the series (with slight variations): "In my last lecture I set forth to you . . . Now, with your patience I will show you . . . (En mon daren lecture . . . Et ore Jeo montra a vous par vostre patience sur eux parols . . .)"

From Inner Temple Records we learn only: "*At Parliament 4 & 5 Philip and Mary 1557,* Reader for Lent Vacation next, Master Williams. *At Parliament 2 Elizabeth 1560,* Reader for Lent Vacation next, Master Williams. *At Parliament 18 May 3 Elizabeth 1561,* Order that Master Williams shall pay 40 li. in Trinity Term for the clear discharge of his reading, but should he come himself or send his letter undertaking to read at Lent next and read accordingly that then he be discharged of his fine."

"Whether he paid his fine or gave his Lent reading we have no record." (Data kindly supplied by the librarian of the Inner Temple Library.)

[78] D'Ewes' *Parliaments of Elizabeth* quotes his speeches of January 15 and 28 and April 10, 1562.

Charter only, but his exposition, as was characteristic of such readings, is most exhaustive and is interspersed with illustrative hypothetical cases in which "J. S." plays the role of the modern "John Doe." Occasionally he cites Glanvill and Bracton, and in some instances gives a fairly sound historical interpretation; for example: his explanation of the grievance of the barons in regard to relief, his definition of *ecclesia anglicana* both as to persons and areas, and the principal grievances of the clergy at the time of the making of the "statute." [79] Again characteristically, however, most of the dissertation is designed to inform the student audience on the law of their own day. Marvelous was the ingenuity with which this and other Readers contrived to complicate a seemingly narrow and simple passage. To mention only a few of the many topics treated: a discussion of grants past and present and what would constitute a good grant *en ces iours* (in connection with *Inprimis concessimus Deo*); what privileges the church has by the words *libera sit,* and the respective technical meanings of *omnia jura sua* and *libertates suas*; benefit of clergy including its limitation by 4 Henry VII, chapter 13; the ranks of the nobility, how an earl and a baron may be created, and the relief of each grade including the later creations of duke and marquis; all sorts of complicated relationships and types of tenures; and the meaning of *liber homo* (in the clause *Concessimus etiam omnibus liberis hominibus regni nostri*).

The Reader applies the same forms of interpretation to the Charter as were accorded other statutes. Words should not be taken according to the letter but according to the intent of the parties. It is not to be concluded from the wording of chapter 2 that only those holding *in capite* pay relief, for "by the equity of this statute" he who holds an honor (*par le reason del honor*) pays relief; neither is it to be concluded that only those holding by military service pay relief, for "by the equity of this statute" he who holds in socage pays relief. Some provisions of the Charter are not liberties but restraint of liberties, such as that no one shall alienate in mortmain; that a woman shall have an appeal for the death of none other

---

[79] "Qui fuit le myschief concernant Relief avaunt le fesaunce de cest estatute?" Earls and barons, he says, had to pay relief at the will of the king; John had promised to make reliefs certain, but had not done so. The words "antiquum relevium" suggest that relief had been certain earlier but this was not true as evidence from Glanvill (whom the Reader calls Chief Justice of the Common Bench in Henry's reign).

"Et qui serra dit ecclesia Anglicana & queux Esglises sont include en eux parols et que nemy." In the Scriptures this term means the congregation of the good and faithful, both lay and spiritual. It may mean material churches, the profits and revenues of the church, or ecclesiastical persons. Again it means the ecclesiastical persons who are in the church, and thus it is intended by this statute. This grant to God and the church is understood of such persons and in none of the other respects before rehearsed.

As to areas, he excludes the Irish churches (as Ireland was not a party to the quarrel between the king and his subjects) and those of Normandy and *auters lieues,* but includes Welsh churches, as Wales was then, he says, *parcell de angliter* and Henry III made his son prince of Wales!

than her husband; and that the king may not retain a felon's land held of another more than a year and a day. The wording of the Charter is not to be taken too literally, for specific words will not restrain general words. One cannot argue that nothing but liberties was granted, nor from the word *heredibus* that corporations like London and other towns (the Cinque Ports) and ecclesiastics who do not have heirs are not included.

The introduction contains the usual eulogy of the common law but is unique in its account of the issuing of the Great Charter by King John, not the usual 9 Henry III of the lawyers:

> The Comonwelthe of everie Contrie consisteth and dependethe upon three things—upon the kinge, the lawe and the people: upon the kinge as the Chief governor, upon the lawe by the which the kinge doth governe, and upon the people which under the kinge by the Lawe are rewled and governed; which. Comonwealthe being a bodye politique may verie fyttlie be compared unto the naturall bodye of a man, namely the kinge unto the heade, the Lawe unto the hart, and the people unto all the rest of the parts of the bodie.

This figure of speech is then further developed, showing the disorderly conditions that will ensue in a country without law, and continues:

> But to come nearer unto the matter and to showe unto you the particular causes of the makeinge of this statute. [There were laws in the realm made by early kings for some time before this statute—and here he names Lucius, Canute, Edward the Confessor, William the Conqueror, "and others."]
>
> . . . in the tyme of King John, in whose tyme this Statute of Magna Carta was made, there were almost none of the said auncient Lawes of this Realme put in use, whereby the nobles and subiects of this Realme did fynd themselves much grieved and did thynke that the kinge had thereby not onlie incrotched upon the libertyes of the Church, But also had otherwise done many wrongs and Iniuryes unto diverse of his subiects, contrarie to the said auncient Lawes of this Realme, by reason whereof great warres and discentyon did growe in this realme betwixt the foresaid kinge and his subiects . . .

He says that these are called the "barons warres" in "our Cronicles." He goes on with the story very well, how the king, driven to distress, asked what was required of him, whereon the "nobilitie and others the subiects of this Realme" asked three things: to restore to the clergy the dignities and privileges he had taken from them, to restore to the people their ancient laws and customs, and especially those of St. Edward the Confessor (who was the last king before the Conquest), and to redress the injuries done and recompense for the wrongs to his subjects.

Whereupon the kinge did make unto his subiects a Charter at a place which is called Roundemeade in the Countye of Oxford; calleinge [it] at that tyme the Charter of Roundmeade, in which of [*sic*] the auncient Lawes of this Realme were mencioned and diverse of them augmented and inlarged, as by the same Charter maye appeare. And after that the said Charter in the lii yeare of kinge Henrye the third was made a Statute and a generall lawe to contynue for ever as may appeare by the statute of Marlebridge cap. quinto made in the tyme of the said kinge; the like maye appeare in the tyme of Edward ye first, and Edward the thirde, and in the tyme of other kings that have lived sythence that tyme. Furthermore this Charter was thought so necessarie for the comonwelth of this Realme that in the tyme of kinge Edward the first a general Curse was pronounced by all the byshopps of England against suche as should break the great Charter.

Perhaps this Reader was caught up in the enthusiasms of Parker and his group as well as the contemporary chroniclers. Certainly he is a better historian than some of his successors in the next reign.

The City of London Again

IN THE writing of law treatises London was not overlooked, as witness *A Briefe Discourse, declaring and approving the necessarie and inviolable maintenance of the laudable customs of London,*[80] published in 1584. It is intentionally anonymous, for in his "apostrophie to the reader" the author says "I keep myselfe unnamed, and unknown." It is the type of thing the city's recorder might have done, unless we suspect someone interested in the particular custom discussed. The author's eulogy of the city outdoes those of his medieval predecessors. Just as Rome was the *epitome totius orbis* so is London the *epitome totius Anglie* and *totius occidentis emporium.* There is the characteristic compliment to the queen—the city is notable not only for the assembly of all the estates, but "chieflie because of the favorable and often soiorne of our most roiall and gracious soveraigne." The citizens "trayned by harde education in great use of service and affairs" and also "by their travaile and traffique beyond the seas," and "continuall negotiation with other Nations," "procure unto themselves great iudgement and sufficiency to manage a politicke regiment in their city . . ." Their government is headed, not by cruel viceroys as in Naples and Milan, proud podesta "as be most cities in Italie, or insolent Lieutenantes or presidentes, as are sundry Cities in France . . ." but "by a man of trade or a meere marchant."

Getting more particularly to his subject, the writer characterizes customs as "the principal ioyntes and verie sinowes of all good corporations and fellowships."[81]

---

[80] *Namely, of that one whereby a reasonable partition of the goods of husbands among their wives and children is provided. At London, printed by Henrie Midleton for Rafe Newberie, 1584.* A tiny volume 16mo of forty-eight pages. Beale (T. 260) does not assign any author.

[81] A custom which justly deserves the name "is of no lesse reverent regarde and authoritie than a written lawe, passed and allowed in Parliament . . ." ". . . the Custome taketh his force by degrees of time, and consent of a certaine people, or the better part thereof, but a lawe

And to come neerer to the matter, this famous and renowned citie of London hath many laudable and aunccient Customes: which though they derogate and differ much from the rules of the common Lawe, yet have they beene not onely approved by inviolate experience of sundrie ages, but also have beene of olde ratified and confirmed by sundry actes of Parliament, and charters of Princes, and namely by the statute of *Magna Charta,* by these wordes following, *Quod civitas London habeat omnes libertates suas antiquas & consuetudines quas habere consuevit,* which is, That the citie of London have all their aunccient liberties & customes which they have used to have. The words folowing for other cities etc. be, *Quod habeant omnes libertates & liberas consuetudines* which signifieth, that they shall still retaine their liberties and free customes, that is to say, their freedomes and immunities, as to be discharged of tolles, pontage, and such like: Whereas the Citie of London hath provision made by that estatute, for all usages and customes what soever. Verily as ye citie of London beareth oddes, and prerogative over other cities in England, being the Metropolis or mother Citie thereof, so are the inhabitantes of it no lesse necessarie than profitable members of the common wealth, in transporting our commodities into other lands, and enriching us with the benefits and fruits of other countries.

The writer's horizon is not confined to his native city but takes in the whole commonwealth. His illustrations are broad in scope, ranging from scriptural passages, Aristotle on cities, customs of ancient Rome, to Bartolus and Year Book cases. Like so many treatises in this age, the *Discourse* includes the defense of a regime that is not mere "princely government" but involves the rule of law. However much writers with other points of view, contemporary or modern, elect to play up Tudor absolutism, the common lawyers were all sure that England had such a regime as this author describes. It is typical enough to have been chosen as the introduction to this chapter.

springeth up in an instant, and receiveth life from him that is of soveraigne authoritie to command."

❧ CHAPTER VIII ❧

The Puritans and Magna Carta

*That wonderful and to us more or less mysterious change in England
from a series of feudal ranks to an organic nation, which was complete
in the reign of Elizabeth, made the feudal regime incomprehensible.*

(MC ILWAIN, HIGH COURT OF PARLIAMENT)

As a result of the interests and activities described in the last two chapters,
there was available by the latter part of Elizabeth's reign much of the
"ammunition" to be used in the constitutional struggle of the next reigns.
There were in print the works of Glanvill, Bracton, Britton, Fleta, and
Fortescue; the Register of Writs and Fitzherbert's *Natura Brevium*; the
Year Books and the more recent reports of Dyer and Plowden; and
treatises on the justices of the peace and the courts, such as Staunford's and
Lambarde's, as well as on more specialized subjects such as the church
and the city of London. These all contributed in themselves to the impression of the "toughness" and the fundamental character of the common
law, and in several instances were also prefaced with a laudatory "To the
Reader," setting forth an idealized picture of Tudor government and the
rule of law.

More particularly, as to Magna Carta, there were in the various editions
of the statutes complete texts of the Charter in Latin and English;
epitomes and paraphrases of its chapters under the alphabetical titles so
dear to the lawyers, and followed by later enactments in the same field.
The *nova statuta* contained a record of the successive parliamentary confirmations and the text of the great excommunication directed against
Charter-breakers. The Year Books and nominate reports contained cases
in which a clause of the Charter figured, either as an actual issue or as
an effective "academic reference." The publication of the famous old
chronicles like Matthew Paris and the newer popular "histories" of Grafton, Stowe, and Holinshed afforded some knowledge of the vivid drama
of Charter history, although, as has been pointed out, the lawyers were
not apt to think back of "9 Henry III."

In the various episodes of the coming constitutional conflict, of course,
Magna Carta was usually only one of several "precedents." Yet any read-

ing of the sources about to be described here reveals how much this knowledge of Charter history—the repeated royal and parliamentary confirmations, the statutory interpretations, the curse upon Charter-breakers—did to contribute to the conception not only of Magna Carta as the "law of laws," but of fundamental law as a whole.

However, we do not have to wait for the advent of the Stuarts. Although no exact chronological line can be drawn, in the last years of Elizabeth's reign (1578–1603) the Charter begins to have something more than mere academic reputation and to be put to practical use. The interests and talents of some of the common lawyers unite with those of the Puritans to effect an irresistible combination.

Practical Applications of Various Chapters of the Charter

As REVEALED by D'Ewes' *Parliaments of Elizabeth,* members of the Commons make an occasional illustrative reference to some clause of the Charter. Naturally these come from the lawyer M.P.'s. William Fleetwood, distinguished recorder of London, makes the point that "the words of an Act of Parliament are not ever to be followed; for that sometimes the construction is more contrary to what is written, as in the Statute of Magna Charta; *nisi prius homagium fecerit.*"[1] In the 1593 session Mr. Henry Finch of Gray's Inn, later distinguished for his treatise on the common law, offered arguments pro and con in the debate on Fitzherbert's case:

On the other side, Utlagus ne Villein cannot be a Champion, which is as a Judge to decide: then *a fortiori,* he can be no Judge in this House. Outlawry is as an Attainder, therefore the party so stained is no competent Judge. The Great Charter is, all Tryals ought to be *per legales homines & parium suorum.* The outlawed man is not of the number of *Parium,* so not to be a Judge.[2]

More significant are a few contemporary cases in which some provision is cited actually to support a claim.[3] In a *replevin* (30 Elizabeth) Magna Carta chapter 14, and Westminster I, chapter 6, were used, unsuccessfully,

[1] D'Ewes, *Parliaments of Elizabeth,* p. 174, the debate on the bill against usury, 1571. Fleetwood argued against usury as something *malum in se,* "for that of some other transgressions, her Majesty may dispence afore with; but for Usury, or to grant that Usury may be used, she possibly cannot."

[2] Whether Thomas Fitzherbert, arrested (two hours after election as burgess) in an outlawry after judgment for debt at the queen's suit, was a member of the house, and if so, ought to have privilege. *Ibid.,* p. 480, for the speech, p. 518, for account of the case. It was in this same session that Finch supported Morice's bill on the oath ex officio, citing historical precedent.

[3] To be sure, some of these cases are reported by Sir Edward Coke, who customarily amplified and embellished his reports from his own vast knowledge of the law, but an attempt has been made to distinguish between instances in which the citation is obviously Coke's, and those in which the wording of the report seems to indicate that the citation was actually a part of the arguments of bench or bar.

by the plaintiff to maintain that his fine, if legally imposed by the steward, ought to have been affeered.[4] It was ruled that this was a fine and not an amercement and hence not within the meaning of chapter 14. In 36 Elizabeth, in a case of sufficient interest to be argued by all the judges in Exchequer chamber, chapter 36 was cited in connection with *uses* and the "mischiefs" that existed before the statute of 27 Henry VIII.[5] Other contemporary cases involving chapter 29 are described below.

Before describing the controversy between the civilians and the common lawyers, and the famous case of monopolies, both of which involved constitutional issues carrying over into the next reign, something may be said here of various other practical, though less dramatic, uses of the "statute."

Elizabethan officials were making a routine and uncontroversial kind of use of the Charter for the benefit of the crown. Here the "researcher" apparently simply used the material at hand in such printed statutes as Rastell's where the required data was already conveniently arranged under alphabetical titles. Among the Burghley papers, for instance, is "A brief Abstract of all the statute Lawes concerninge purveyance" (1588), which begins with Magna Carta.[6] In the State Papers is "A shorte discours touching the marriage of the Queenes widows without Licence" with the object of so defining "her highnes trew Prerogatyve" as to prevent evasions, and thus greatly increase her Majesty's yearly revenue, and lastly that "her Matie may have the comendinge of any her servauntes to any her widowes in marriage which wilbe verie honorable to her highnes and profitable to them." Here "the proofes of the premisses" are the common law (as set forth in Bracton and Britton); statutes, including Magna Carta chapter 7 "beinge in effecte but the comon Lawe"; *prerogativa regis* as expounded by Staunford; and precedents "provinge the practice in former ages." This compiler notes further, "Many other precedents are in the Tower of London to the like effecte, which for that there is noe Kalendar unto them require the more Labor to be found out."

[4] At a court leet, the plaintiff, being elected constable of the manor of Kingston and charged by the steward to take the oath of office, "utterly refused and departed in contempt of that court," whereupon the steward fined him one hundred shillings and the bailiff seized his beasts as distress.

The wording seems to indicate that the objection quoting Magna Carta ca. 14 and Westminster I was actually made by or on behalf of the plaintiff. The report concludes, however, with a distinctly Cokesque *Nota*, elaborating on the two "statutes" and the distinction between fines and amercements. Coke, *Reports*, VIII, 38–42, *replegiare*.

[5] *Ibid*. I, 120–40 (called the *case of perpetuities*). The passage in question cites the statute *de Religiosis*, 7 Ed. I "in enlargement of the statute of Magna Carta cap. 36 which provided . . ."

[6] Lansd. MSS 56, no. 21, endorsed "Purveyors—all ye statute laws concerning them"; including statutes from Magna Carta to Ed. 3. A margin is lined off at the left where the successive statutes are listed and a brief summary statement in English written opposite—

"Magna Charta   No mans wod shalbe taken but by the will of them whose the wod is.
ca. 22   None shall take corne hides or goods of any man without the will and
9 Hen. 3   assent of him whose the goods be."

The same kind of thing appears early in James' reign as officials sought to define and describe to the king the perquisites of his newly acquired kingdom and to fill his ever-depleted treasury. In Sir Julius Caesar's papers there is a memorandum "concerning the spedy payment of the kings Maiesties Reliefes" (January 1607) which sets down rules to correct abuses such as delay or evasion of payment. Here (as always down through the centuries, since there was no further regulation) the accustomed rates of relief are quoted as per Magna Carta chapter 2.[7] There is also a table of "Statutes concerninge the kinges Exchequer 9 April 1607," with pertinent acts from Magna Carta (chapters 8, 11, 18) to 1 Jacobi.[8]

Other treatises are in a more controversial vein. The striking character of the rivalries between prerogative and common law has tended to overshadow the lesser conflicts among the common-law courts themselves. Chapter 11 of Magna Carta was the lawyers' favorite for proof of the origin of the Court of Common Pleas (by creation of the king, "9 Hen. 3") and for its jurisdiction. This was the view held by Lambarde, Stowe, Camden, and Cowell,[9] and is the one set forth in an anonymous little treatise included in Bacon's collected Works, but which editors of the Spedding edition are positive was not Bacon's.[10] Coke repudiated this origin but on the other hand carried the court too far back. In his Eighth Report he quotes from the Year Books how in 10 Edward 4 "all the Iudges of England did affirme that the Chancery, Kings Bench, Common place and Eschequer, be all the kings Courts, and have bene time out of memory of man; so as no man knoweth which of them is the most auncient."

Others as well as Staunford were misled by Glanvill's statement that the

[7] This is followed by a table (*Rata pro Releviis, Magna Charta none Henrici tercii,* ca. 2) itemizing reliefs all the way from the one hundred pounds of an earldom down to twelve pence from a fraction of a knight's fee. Lansd. MSS 166, fols. 200-2 (208-9). Cf. *ibid.,* fol. 213 (219v) for similar data in even more detail, endorsed "A sute touching the improvement of the kinges reliefs, 18 May, 1611."

[8] Lansd. MSS 168, no. 46, a table of acts in two columns, with no indication of contents.

[9] For Lambarde, see above, Chap. VII, and for Cowell and Coke, below, Chap. IX. Camden in the *Britannia,* II, 8 (Gough edition), and Stowe, *Survey of London,* p. 522 (1633 edition), both introduce their comments in connection with the "fixed place," that is, their descriptions of Westminster Hall "In this Hall," says Stowe, Henry III "ordained three judgment seates, to wit . . ."

[10] This is a brief but effective description of the common-law courts, central and local, their jurisdiction and procedure, the main features of the criminal law and a little on the law of land and of chattels. Except for mention of the Court of the Marshalsea there is not so much as a hint of the existence of other courts and systems of law in England, hardly a Baconesque quality!

After naming the various types of pleas for which the court was erected at Westminster "which were wont to be either in king's bench, or else before the justices in eyre," he concludes, "but the statute of Mag(na) Chart(a) cap. 11, is negative against it, namely, Communia placita non sequantur curiam nostram, sed teneantur in aliquo loco certo; which *locus certus* must be the common pleas; yet the judges of circuits have now five commissions by which they sit."

pleas he describes were held "in the Exchequer" (*curia regis in scaccarium*). Hence the natural conclusion that the Exchequer was "the originall courte of the whole Realme," [11] and "originally the king's only court." [12]

Two little late-Elizabethan treatises, both anonymous, attempt to defend the Common Pleas against encroachment by King's Bench, particularly the use by the latter of a device known as writ of *latitat*. In the first treatise, "Reasons concernynge common pleas should not be sued in the kynges bench," the writer pictures the Exchequer as originally the king's only court; then King's Bench, Chancery, and Common Pleas were created by the king—none other than Edgar! The Charter is not quoted but applied as an emphatic marginal commentary. [13]

As described by a modern writer the procedure by writ of *latitat* is as follows:

". . . if a defendant could be brought, even on a trumped-up charge, into the Marshalsea prison, which was the one used by the King's Bench, any civil action could proceed against him before the King's Bench. This desired imprisonment was achieved by what was called a bill of Middlesex, an order to the sheriff of Middlesex to arrest the defendant on a criminal or semicriminal charge, such as trespass, and lodge him in the Marshalsea. If the defendant did not reside in Middlesex, this bill was supplemented by a writ called *latitat* addressed to the proper sheriff informing him that the suspect was lurking (Latin, *latitat*, he lurks) and running about in his country and ordering him to apprehend the accused and put him in the power of the court. Once that was done the civil action was begun and the more serious charge was forgotten. [14]

Before describing and denouncing this procedure, the larger treatise [15]

[11] Data copied from the records for Sir Julius Caesar, Lansd. MSS 170, fols. 46–50 (47–51), "A Treatise of the exchequer beinge the Originall Courte of the whole Realme." It states that "the Comon Place was utterly put out of the kinges Eschequer by Statute, except betwene parties whereof one of them at least, was in the same court privileged."

[12] Lansd. MSS 106, no. 13, now to be described.

[13]The wholle Course of Comon Lawe and Magna Carta prove it.	"The king in Chauncerie directed his subiectes to the Courte of Common plees for their Common Causes which Court only servd for the Comon Causes."
The Auncient Recordes of that Courte & magna Carta prove it.	"The kinges benche being appoynted only for pleas of the Crowne, doe also tak examinacion of errors in the other Courte, because it was a superior Courte, but proceeded not in accions either reall or personall between partee and partie."
. . .	. . .
The statute is playne and the records there doe prove it for long time.	"The statute of magna carta was made against that Courte concevying those Inormities and it semeth that verie fewe such Accions were used there of long time together till of late yeares."

[14] Knappen, *Legal and Constitutional History*, p. 285.

[15] "Certaine notes or Remembrances, sette downe towards a Reformacion desired to bee had of the unlawfull holding of Common Pleas in the Kinges Benche, and especiallie con-

introduces a rather sound historical description of the *curia regis* of post-Conquest days, the current view of the origin of Common Pleas as created by Magna Carta chapter 11, the later erection of King's Bench, and the regulation of subsequent "confusion of jurisdiction" by the *Articuli super cartas*. After expatiating at length upon the evils of the writ of *latitat*,[16] the writer concludes that it is "contrarie and repugnante to the Auncient Lawes and Statutes" as proved "by the first and most auncient lawe afore recited called Magna Charta," and others. The practice has been "impugned by writs from Chancery," not only the usual prohibition and *supersedeas,* but "an auncient presidente in this forme," that is, a prohibition which quotes Magna Carta chapter 11.

Common Pleas was also issuing prohibitions to the Court of Requests. In one such case, and perhaps others, the prohibition was based on Magna Carta. For an account of this conflict we are also indebted to Sir Julius Caesar.[17] He explains that finding "a great contention on foote betwene the Judges of the Comen Pleas and the Mrs. (masters) of Requests then being, touching yᵉ iurisdiction of her Majesties court at Whitehall," he undertook to "breed hereafter a continewall peace, between yᵉ Judges of the Common Lawe and her Majesties Counsell." Data collected with this aim includes "Prohibitions &c granted out of her Majesties Court of Comon Pleas to stay the Parties proceeding in her Majesties Courte of Whitehall since the 32th yeare of her Majesties most happy Reigne. The like whereof is not remembered to have beene done in former tyme." Here is recorded (1594) a complaint against one William Parsons, defendant, guilty of "divers contempts" against "the dignitie of this Court," who "in further manifestation of his contemptuous disposicion preferres an Information into his Majesties Court of Comon Pleas against the

cerning a Certaine kinde of Proces called a Latitate, latelie yssuinge forthe of that Courte Contrarie to the dewe and Auncient Course of the Common lawes of the Realme, without Originall writt as followethe." Lansd. MSS 64, no. 85, dated 1590.

[16] The fact that upon "one onelie latitat" for a "supposed transgression" a man might have to answer to five, six, or more declarations put in by the first, or any other plaintiff; the Court of Common Pleas is defrauded of actions of *debt, detinue, eiectione firmae,* and others which rightfully belong to it; "every utter barrister or other are bringers of such suits by covin," whereas serjeants at law are properly the only counselors at Common Pleas; men of sufficient freehold are "arrested by the body for verie vexacion, where by the Common lawes of this Realme they oughte at the uttermost to bee but returned in yssues"; there is "hindrance and decay of profit to her majesty" (six pence paid for sealing a *latitat* may replace the fees for several original writs).

[17] My account here is based not on the original manuscripts, but on Leadam, *Select Cases in the Court of Requests* (S. S.), introduction and sources (using Lansd. MSS 125 marked "Sr. J Caesar on the Court of Requests"). According to Leadam, "The assaults by the Judges of the Common Law Courts upon the authority and jurisdiction of the Court of Requests appear to have begun in 1590, if we may trust a contemporary defence of the Court contained in the volume of collections from which extracts have already been taken . . . ." The Court of Requests, he says, "was constantly in collision with the courts of Common Law, as is apparent from the common form of plea that 'this suit is determinable at the common law.' . . . Its injunctions 'to stay the rules at common lawe' were numerous." P. xxii.

Plaintife upon the statute of Magna Charta and divers other statutes in that case made."

It is further set forth that "All Courtes in England have their beginning by one of theise three wayes. 1. By graunte from the King. 2. By Parliament.[18] 3. By use and custome." But the king is the "fountaine of all English Justice in all causes" whence all judges "derive their ordinary or extraordinary authority." Hence it follows: "That ye King of England never did nor doth graunt any jurisdiction to any Court in his Dominions, but so, as hee still retaineth in himselfe & his Counsell attendant uppon his person, a supereminent authority and Jurisdiction over them all . . ." (Britton).

It would appear to be something of a draw in point of time as to which was first to make effective practical application of chapter 29 and one or other of the attendant *six statutes*, the Puritan lawyers, Beale, Morice, and Fuller on behalf of their clients, or Bacon (if it be Bacon) in "A Brief Discourse upon the Commission of Bridewell," but the latter seems to have antedated slightly the more important activities of the former.

The editors of the Spedding edition of Bacon's works attribute the "Brief Discourse" to him,[19] and furnish a setting as follows: "An order of Common Council, now at Guildhall, dated Augst. 4th 1579, professed to give the Governor of the Hospital very arbitrary powers over the rogues and vagabonds of London," but later ordinances of a "much less stringent character" were adopted. "Nothing seems more probable than that the question had been in the meantime discussed, whether it was quite safe to rely on the charter, and to ground on it such strong measures as were at first contemplated."

The main contention of the "Brief Discourse" is summed up in the words: "Now if we do compare the said Charter of Bridewell with the great Charter of England both in matter, sense, and meaning, you shall find them merely repugnant." This, the crowning point of the argument, is preceded by a little discourse on the law, "the most highest inheritance the King hath; for by the law both the King and all his subjects are ruled

---

[18] The first example of creation by parliament is the traditional "the Court of common pleas by the statute of Magna Charta, 9 H. 3 cap. 11. communia placita non sequantur Curiam meam . . ."

[19] They say that it was first printed in a report on Bridewell Hospital from Harl. MSS 1323. Another copy, anonymous, is in Cambridge University Library. "It appears, however, to be a legal opinion, to which a name must from the first have been attached, and I see no intrinsic reason for doubting its being Bacon's of a time when he was a young man. . . . If the paper be really Bacon's, it appears to me to be very interesting, as it ascertains in the most authentic way the constitutional opinions with which he entered life." The date may be fixed "without much hesitation as of some time before Oct. 11th, 1587."

McIlwain, quoting from the *Brief Discourse*, accepts this judgment as to Bacon's authorship. *High Court of Parliament*, pp. 64–65.

and directed . . . That a King's grant either repugnant to law, custom, or statute is not good nor pleadable in the law, see what precedents thereof have been left by our wise forefathers." To be sure, the author admits, it is possible to cite commissions which seem to change or infringe law, yet in every such instance on inspection it appears that "this is by authority of Parliament." Indeed even the powers of the high commissioners are authorized altogether by parliament! His evidence includes not only Magna Carta but the many confirmations from Marlborough to Henry VI, and notably that of 42 Edward III.

If the unofficial and informal manuscript version may be trusted, a case of about this same time (*Skinner and Catcher's case*, 31 Elizabeth) also concerned with Bridewell and the underworld of London, elicited a eulogy of the Charter with a comment on its origin from no less a person than the Lord Treasurer himself, and that in Star Chamber.[20]

My Lord Treasorer in the Starre chamber in Michaellmas tearme 30 et 31 Eliz. sayd that this fredome no Countre butt oures (noe not in Fraunce) can challenge by the Lawes of their Realme, and that the procuring of this Statute of Mag[na] Chart[a] cost manye a noble mans lyfe, and was the Cause of the Barons warr, and therefore beinge so hardlye gott wee ought not easely to suffer yt to be lost. Allso it was then agreed by all the Courte and the Queenes learned counsell, That if the Queene graunte a Commission and expresse lycence to punishe any offence in this or that sorte, yet yf the same kynde of punishment bee nott suche as by lawe ought to bee inflicted for that faulte, the partye punished hathe good remedye against them. And to punishe one suspected to bee an harlot by whippinge, as the case was there . . . my Lord Treasurer said that such were often whipped at Westminster, but that it was after they were convicted by an enquest. Also it was then and there agreed per touts, that Imprisonment is noe punishment by the Course of the lawe but onelie a meanes to have the partyes forthcomminge till the tryall be had of that which is layd to their Charge or els till they paye the kinges fyne, and all this was in Skinner and Kechers case Shriefes of London for whyppinge Mistres Nevill and Mistres Newman.

In this reign it is not surprising to find Star Chamber in the role of champion of the oppressed. Lambarde in his *Archeion* has nothing but praise for it. There is in Harleian Manuscripts (Elizabeth) the text of a

---

[20] Cott. MSS Cleopatra F I 68–73 (69–74) and Harl. MSS 358, 201–13. This is not a report of the case, but is introduced in connection with arguments against procedure in High Commission. It follows a reference to Rastell, title *Accusation*, and quotation of ca. 29 as Englished there. I have not succeeded in finding the case in any of the printed reports. Star Chamber records contain the interrogatories and depositions of the two sheriffs, the Master of Bridewell, and others.

Harl. MSS 2143 (Star Chamber Reports, Eliz. and Jac.), beginning "Damages, a misdemeanor in Skinner and Catcher in causing Mrs. Nevell to be whipped uniustly," contains a brief statement of the charges brought by "Mr. Attorney" and the damages and fines imposed on the offending officials.

proposed bill to the effect that if justice or right be denied or delayed to anyone lawfully demanding the same, the offender pay one thousand marks, half to the queen and half to the injured party. No person or persons are to be imprisoned or "put to answere, but onely by due course of the lawes Statutes and ancient laudable customes of the Realme and no otherwise." The preamble of the bill bases these principles clearly on the Great Charter:

To the honor and glory of almightie god the furtherence of Justice and inheritance of the ancient lawes and liberties, allowed granted and confirmed by our Sovereigne Lady the Queenes Majesties most noble progenitors by the great Charter comonly called magna Carta, and by diverse Actes of parliament to the Subiectes and people of this Realme of England, Be it enacted by the Queens most excellent Majestie . . .[21]

Church and State: "Prerogative" Acting through High Commission

And my Lord Chancellor in his oration did amongst other things give a special admonition unto this House [Commons] not to deal with matters touching her Majesty's person or estate or touching religion.

(D'EWES, PARLIAMENTS OF ELIZABETH, 1580)

"Her Majesty's person or estate or touching religion," or again, as put by the speaker in 1593, "the said matters of state or reformation in causes ecclesiastical"—these were the fields which, in successive parliaments throughout her reign, Elizabeth sought to reserve to the crown. In the speeches of Puritan zealots like Strickland and Peter Wentworth the issues were "God's cause" and the privilege of parliament—freedom of speech in its broadest aspect. The adroitness of the queen and her councillors made it appear that the Commons were the aggressors, encroaching on the prerogative. We do have statements such as Yelverton's (1571) in which he "shewed it was fit for princes to have their prerogatives, but yet the same to be straightened within reasonable limits." But it was the growing power and activities of High Commission in the 1580's that led the common lawyers in the courts and the press as well as in parliament to anticipate Coke in turning the tables—in picturing the prerogative as the aggressor against the common law.

The fundamental issue here was not new. In its broadest aspects it has been admirably stated by Professor Pollard for Henry VIII's reign and after:

A much neglected but very important constitutional question is whether

---

[21] The bill recites the acts of 3 Henry VII and 21 Henry VIII, prescribes some enlargement, but also careful definition of jurisdiction, and safeguards for defendants. Harl. MSS 6847, fols. 133–40.

the King quâ Supreme Head of the Church was limited by the same statute and common law restrictions as he was quâ temporal sovereign. Gardiner raised the question in a most interesting letter to Protector Somerset in 1547 (Foxe, VI. 42). It had been provided, as Lord Chancellor Audley told Gardiner, that no spiritual law and no exercise of the royal supremacy should abate the common law or Acts of Parliament; but within the ecclesiastical sphere there were no limits on the King's authority. The Popes had not been fettered, — *habent omnia jura in suo scrinio*; and their jurisdiction in England had been transferred whole and entire to the King. Henry was in fact an absolute monarch in the Church, a constitutional monarch in the State; he could reform the Church by injunction when he could not reform the State by proclamation. There was naturally a tendency to confuse the two capacities not merely in the King's mind but in his opponents; and some of the objections to the Stuarts' dispensing practice, which was exercised chiefly in the ecclesiastical sphere, seem due to this confusion. Parliament in fact, as soon as the Tudors were gone, began to apply common law and statute law limitations to the Crown's ecclesiastical prerogative.[22]

Rival theories came to include the whole question of ecclesiastical jurisdiction, its origin and consequent powers. The common lawyers contended that the Act of Supremacy conferred on the crown only a limited ecclesiastical jurisdiction, those powers delegated to it by statute. Their opponents saw that act as "restoring" to the crown any and all jurisdiction formerly exercised by the pope, "the ancient jurisdiction ecclesiastical and spiritual." This was their stand in *Cawdry's case* (1591) at which time even the judges of King's Bench concurred in attributing to the ecclesiastical courts a coordinate and independent status. James I, in turn, and the civilians upon whom he relied took the same view of all the non-common-law courts. He as sovereign was head of both groups: the law that was administered in Chancery, Admiralty, and High Commission was "law of the land" no less than that in King's Bench, Exchequer, and Common Pleas. Thus to the common lawyers the High Commission was created and hence limited by the act of 1 Elizabeth. Letters patent could not rightfully confer upon it powers not specified in this act nor commonly exercised by the ecclesiastical courts before 1559. To the civilians, High Commission was created by royal prerogative and invested with authority according to the broadest interpretation of successive letters patent. The latter view was historically the more correct.[23] As a sort of "ecclesiastical

[22] Pollard, *Henry VIII*, 329–30.

[23] As Usher has demonstrated, the commissions created successively by Henry VIII and his three children (including at least Elizabeth's early ones) were temporary but conferred wide powers and untrammeled procedure. The commissions were: those employed first by Henry VIII and Cromwell in trying heresy cases; the Edwardian commissions; that of Mary who "gave the Commission the shape it retained until 1583"; the early Elizabethan commissions which followed the model of Mary's letters patent. Usher, *Reconstruction*, I, 101–2.

privy council" the commissioners were intended to uphold the church settlement of the moment and with it the occupant of the throne.

Little is known of the methods employed by the commissioners in early days. "Contemporaries (and indeed most Church historians) were interested in doctrinal discussions, and recked little of procedure and jurisdiction, so that the accounts of the inquiries and trials we can identify contain little of any service to us." The discretion of the commissioners "was infinite and their decision final." Only by a gradual evolution did the commissioners become the Court of High Commission on a permanent footing with regular duties, including a concurrent jurisdiction with the other ecclesiastical courts.[24] It developed a more precise personnel (mainly bishops and civilians) and a staff of clerks and officials under the jurisdiction of the Archbishop of Canterbury (Whitgift) and the Bishop of London (first Aylmer, and then Bancroft). "Proctors and advocates were regularly licensed to practice before its bar." It followed forms and precedents like those of the regular ecclesiastical courts but retained some special prerogative powers. Although it filled the need for some adequate coercive agency in the Anglican church, the very features which made it so effective came to be resented and feared not only by nonconformists but by the common lawyers; not only as a bar to liberty of conscience but to liberty of the subject.

As the controversy developed, the court came to be challenged on a number of counts: its jurisdiction; the extension of its authority over all England; its process, not only summons by citation but the use of pursuivants to arrest by attachment and bring by force, and excommunication for contumacy (the equivalent of outlawry at common law); its penalties, not restricted as the bishops' were to ecclesiastical censures and excommunication but extending to fine and imprisonment "at discretion" and deprivation of benefices (which, as the lawyers maintained, were to the minister as was his freehold to the layman). It could compel the clergy to specific performance of any of its orders. Excommunication was no longer effective as either process or penalty when "laymen cheerfully remained excommunicated for years as was not uncommon in Elizabeth's reign!"[25] But it was its method of trial, especially the proceeding *ex officio mero* and the use of the oath ex officio, that was most disliked and feared,[26] and first to be opposed. Eventually the deprivation of Cawdry,

<hr />

[24] Usher, *Rise and Fall*, pp. 43–44 and Chap. III.

[25] Usher, *Reconstruction*, I, 104–7; *Rise and Fall*, pp. 45, 99.

[26] For the Puritans "to take the oath and then not tell the truth was to commit perjury and was manifestly out of the question; but, as the Commission's procedure, like all civil-law procedure, required for the proof of the guilt of the accused no further evidence than the admissions in his own sworn testimony, it was evident that the Puritan who took the oath and told the simple truth would instantly provide legally perfect proof of his nonconformity." *Ibid.*, p. 126.

the imprisonment of Cartwright and others increasingly focused attention on those powers.

The oath ex officio,[27] though employed earlier, was first specifically authorized by the letters of 1583, the sixth commission. The form used in the late sixteenth century was: "You shall swear to answer all such Interrogatories as shall be offered unto you and declare your whole knowledge therein, so God you help." The defendant was called upon to " 'answer the Articles or Interrogatories truely (being matters of his owne facte and knowledge so farre foorth as by lawe he is bound), before everie particular thereof be made knowen unto him.' " [28] The common lawyers recognized the legality of the oath in certain classes of cases and on certain conditions. The issue then turned on the character of the preliminaries. As stated by Wigmore:

There must be some sort of presentment to put any person to answer. But must that come from accusing witnesses or private prosecutors or the like (corresponding to our notion of a "qui tam" or a grand jury)? Or might it be begun by an official complaint (somewhat like our information "ex relatione" by the attorney-general)? Or might the judge "ex officio mero" summon the accused and put him to answer, in hopes of extracting a confession which would suffice? And in the last method, must the charge at least be brought first to the judges' notice "per famam," or "per clamosam insinuationem," "common report," or "violent suspicion"? [29]

The last, action by the judge *ex officio mero* (which gave the oath its name), was favored by the commissioners as most effective in searching out nonconformity. But the temptation was great for the judge to overlook the condition *per famam* or *per clamosam insinuationem* and to indulge in a "merely unlawful process of poking about in the speculation of finding something chargeable." To the common lawyers, however, even "common report" and "violent suspicion" hardly constituted a true *presentment* worthy of the name. They viewed such practices with the same dislike and used against them the same arguments and "statutes" as had their intellectual ancestors of the fourteenth century against *informations* to the council. Eventually they came to contend that the oath was illegal in any form. Although sanctioned by letters patent it was not

---

[27] "This was a witness's oath which ecclesiastical authorities by virtue of their office—hence the name—might administer to accused persons, who were thereupon questioned about their supposed misdemeanors. In current ecclesiastical theory this was a device intended to encourage something like auricular confession. In practice it was indistinguishable from the Roman law procedure of forcing a man to incriminate himself—a procedure from which it had, indeed, been originally borrowed. It had long been in use in ecclesiastical courts, though not frequently employed." Knappen, *Tudor Puritanism*, p. 272.

For the origin and history of the oath, see Maguire, "Attack of the Common Lawyers on the Oath Ex Officio," in *Essays in honor of C. H. McIlwain*.

[28] Usher, *Rise and Fall*, p. 112.

[29] Wigmore, *Evidence*, IV, 800.

expressly authorized by the statute of 1 Elizabeth. It might be demonstrated to be against the law of God and the canon law; certainly it was against the common law, the *per legem terrae* of Magna Carta.

The conflict between the common lawyers and the civilians is now an oft-told and well-told tale, but for the most part the tellers thereof have not been Magna Carta conscious.[30] It was in this struggle that the Charter definitely emerged as a "liberty document." The issues were forced by such stanch Puritan nonconformists as Cawdry and Cartwright. The weapons were forged by the Puritan lawyers Robert Beale, Sir James Morice, and Nicholas Fuller from principles of the common law formulated in the fourteenth century (especially the interpretation then put upon Magna Carta chapter 29) and put into usable form in the printed statutes and treatises of the sixteenth.

Although these Puritan lawyers were not immediately successful, they had "briefed a case" for Coke and others in the next reign. In what follows it will be apparent that Magna Carta was not yet the main "precedent"; emphasis was upon rival interpretations of the statute of 1 Elizabeth and other pertinent acts of her father, and upon the claim of the common lawyers to be the sole interpreters of *all* statutes, versus that of the civilians for interpretation in the ecclesiastical sphere. But if 1 Elizabeth was to be made to accord with the "law of the land" as before 1559, that law as to "liberty of the subject" was best upheld by Magna Carta and the *six statutes*.

The vicissitudes of Puritanism in Elizabeth's reign have been ably analyzed by Professor Knappen:[31] the vestiarian controversy in which opposition to government coercion was weak and unorganized; 1568–73, "years of revival" characterized by greater activity in parliament, since the government was absorbed in the problem of Mary Stuart and Catholic plots; a period of polemical writings, the famous *First Admonition to the Parliament* (1572) and others; 1575–83, the "prophesyings" countenanced by Grindal; and finally the more fundamental attack on the episcopal system with the aim of substituting a presbyterian "discipline." During these years some criticism of ecclesiastical courts and discipline and of the arrest and imprisonment of nonconformists was voiced in tracts, private petitions, and parliamentary petitions and bills. Perhaps the doctrine of

[30] Either that, or else its use seems to these writers too commonplace to notice. For instance, R. G. Usher, in *The Reconstruction of the English Church*, treats of the episodes and persons and uses some of the sources described below, but never so much as mentions Magna Carta in the two volumes. In his *Rise and Fall of the High Commission*, he does indirectly, in that he quotes or paraphrases Coke's writs of prohibition.

An exception is Mrs. Mary Hume Maguire's "The History of the Ex-Officio Oath in England" (Radcliffe College dissertation, 1923) which treats extensively of Morice, Beale, and Cosin, and their treatises.

[31] Knappen, *Tudor Puritanism*, chaps. x–xii.

passive resistance avowed by certain groups and individuals [32] made more aggressive protests less likely. Characteristically some of the imprisoned ministers were more concerned for their parishioners than for themselves, such as one who complained to the Bishop of London that his imprisonment would do harm "to a great many of poore simple souls . . . about the Minories" who were not getting enough sermons.[33] Furthermore, the lawyers had not yet come to the rescue. Sources here, then, like those for the Marian martyrs, have only a negative interest. Although we have nothing as copious as Foxe's *Actes and Monuments* for this period, its place is fairly well-supplied by the great Register, intended to be "the Puritan's Book of Martyrs." [34]

With the exception of Grindal who had encouraged conventicles, harmony usually prevailed between the queen and her bishops. Walton says of Whitgift:

His merits to the Queen, and her favours to him, were such that she called him her little black husband, and called his servants her servants: and she saw so visible and blessed a sincerity shine in all his cares and endeavours for the Church's and for her good, that she was supposed to trust him with the very secrets of her soul, and to make him her confessor.

---

[32] For instance, Robert Crowley, the poet-controversialist, in *A Briefe Discourse against the Outwarde Apparell and Ministering of the Popishe Church* (1566) says, "Our goods, our bodies, and our lives we do with all humble submission yield into the hands of God's officers upon earth: but our consciences we keep unspotted in the sight of Him that shall judge all men." About 1582 Robert Browne stated that the queen "may put to death all that deserve it by law, either of the church or commonwealth, and none may resist her or the magistrates under her by force of wicked speeches, when they execute the lawes." These and others in similar vein quoted by Knappen, *Tudor Puritanism*, pp. 198–99, 213, 307, 314.

[33] Seconde Parte of a Register, doc. 75, pp. 128–29.

[34] Knappen, *Tudor Puritanism*, p. 301. Most of the copies of the first part were seized as they came into England from Middelburg in 1593; the other half was not printed until recent times.

The First Admonition to the Parliament contains passages indicating growing animosity toward the ecclesiastical courts: the loose issuing of licenses by the Court of Faculties; abuse of excommunication; "great sinnes eyther not at al punished . . . or else sleightly passed over. . . . Againe such as are no sinnes . . . grevously punished." As for the commissaries court, "that is but a pettie little stinking ditche that floweth oute of that former great puddle robbing Christes church of lawful pastors, of watchfull Seniors and Elders, and carefull Deacons." *Puritan Manifestoes*, pp. 12, 17, 33.

Individual petitions in the *Seconde Parte of a Register*:

Doc. 51: John Field and Thomas Wilcox, imprisoned as the authors of the *Admonition*, protest that they had been imprisoned three months without cause: "We wrote a boke in the parliament tyme (which should be a free tyme of speakinge or wrytinge) justly cravinge a redress and reformation of many abuses, and for that we are imprisoned and so uncourtiouslie treated."

Doc. 99: "Articles sent to the Bishops & Cleargye in the convocation house . . . From the Marshalsye by John Nasshe the Lordes pirsoner" has general charges against the bishops of imprisoning and persecuting true Christians.

For other individual petitions, see docs. 66, 111, 113, and others.

As to action in parliament, the "six bills" introduced in 1566, and enacted in altered form, 1571, were measures so moderate, as Knappen points out, as to be supported by the Anglican clergy, even the bishops. In 1572 a bill to legalize Puritan nonconformity was dropped at the queen's command.

Nevertheless, there was one grievance which led even Whitgift, while still Bishop of Worcester, to appropriate Magna Carta chapter 1 in the interest of the Anglican church. This was the practice of the queen and her courtiers of granting patents for finding out concealed lands. Strype has vividly described the abuses in regard to what he calls these "pretended concealed lands to be forfeited to the Queen," the which "deprived Churchmen, Bishops, and others, of great part of their revenues, and left the state of the Clergy, by means of those greedy cormorants (who commonly got these forfeitures to themselves) in a very mean state." [35]

After warning the queen of the danger of sacrilege (since "princes are deputed nursing fathers of the Church, and owe it a protection") and of the curse upon those who alienate its immunities and lands, Whitgift continues:

And to make you that are trusted with their preservation the better to understand the danger of it, I beseech you forget not, that to prevent these curses, the Church's land and power have been also endeavoured to be preserved (as far as human reason, and the law of this nation, have been able to preserve them) by an immediate and most sacred obligation on the consciences of the princes of this realm. For they that consult Magna Charta shall find, that as all your predecessors were at their coronation, so you also were sworn before all the nobility and bishops then present, and in the presence of God, and in his stead to him that anointed you, "to maintain the church-lands, and the rights belonging to it"; and this you yourself have testified openly to God at the holy altar, by laying your hands on the Bible then lying upon it. And not only Magna Charta, but many modern statutes have denounced a curse upon those that break Magna Charta; a curse like the leprosy that was entailed on the Jews; for as that, so these curses have and will cleave to the very stones of those buildings that have been consecrated to God; and the father's sin of sacrilege hath and will prove to be entailed on his son and family. And now, madam, what account can be given for the breach of this oath at the last great day, either by your majesty, or by me, if it be wilfully, or but negligently violated, I know not.

Further, the bishop "begs posterity to take notice of what is already become visible in many families: that churchland added to an ancient and

---

[35] Strype, *Whitgift*, I, 172–73. Cf. Strype's *Annals,* Vol. II, pt. i, p. 309. "When monasteries were dissolved, and the lands thereof, and afterwards colleges, chantries, and fraternities were all given to the crown, some demeans here and there pertaining thereunto were still privily retained and possessed by certain private persons, or corporations or churches. This caused the queen . . . to grant commissions to some persons to search after these concealments, and to retrieve them to the crown." Contrary to all right and the queen's intent the commissioners challenged "lands of long times possessed by church-wardens, and such like, upon the charitable gifts of predecessors, to the common benefit of the parishes; yea, and certain stocks of money, plate, cattle, and the like. They made pretence to the bells, lead, and such other like things, belonging to churches and chapels, used for common prayer. Further they attempted to make titles to lands, possessions, plate, and goods belonging to hospitals, and such like places, used for maintenance of poor people . . ."

just inheritance, hath proved like a moth fretting a garment, and secretly consumed both . . ." and continues in even bolder vein:

And though I shall forbear to speak reproachfully of your father; yet I beg you to take notice, that a part of the Church's rights, added to the vast treasure left him by his father, hath been conceived to bring an unavoidable consumption upon both, notwithstanding all his diligence to preserve them. And consider that after the violation of those laws, to which he had sworn in Magna Charta, God did so far deny him his restraining grace, that as king Saul after he was forsaken of God, fell from one sin to another; so, he, till at last he fell into greater sins than I am willing to mention.[36]

It was Archbishop Whitgift's institution of a stricter regime that led to the alliance between the Puritans and the common lawyers. In 1583 he issued a set of orders, and the next year twenty-four articles to be administered to nonconformist suspects by the oath ex officio, a procedure which even Lord Burghley protested "as written in a Romish stile, smelling of the Romish inquisition." [37] At first, help from the lawyers came not so much in the taking issue on broad principles as in raising legal technicalities.[38] But protests against the oath, and against imprisonment and deprivation as violations of the "law of the land" become increasingly vigorous in both private and parliamentary petitions.[39] As yet these do not cite the Great Charter. There were few tangible results. Mary Stuart and the threat from Spain overshadowed lesser causes. After their failure to secure results through the parliaments of 1585 [40] and 1586,

[36] Strype, *Whitgift*, I, 174–75, paraphrases the bishop's remonstrance in the third person. I quote above the direct form given in Walton's *Life of Hooker*, pp. 32–35. Among those that abused this trust of the queen's, says Walton, was the Earl of Leicester. Earl and bishop fell "to an open opposition" before the queen, then the bishop, finding her alone, addressed her as quoted!

[37] The orders provided that no one might exercise any ecclesiastical function unless he subscribed to the three articles devised by Parker in 1571: to acknowledge the royal supremacy; to attest of the Prayer Book that it "containeth nothing in it contrary to the Word of God"; and to accept the thirty-nine articles as agreeing with scripture. Knappen, *Tudor Puritanism*, pp. 266–67. For the twenty-four articles, Burghley's letter, and Whitgift's reply, Strype, *Whitgift*, III, app. nos. iv, ix, and x respectively.

[38] It was pointed out, for instance, that even the Act of Uniformity itself was not strictly followed by the bishops. Robert Beale took this line of attack in his first tilts with Whitgift. Knappen, *Tudor Puritanism*, chap. xiii, "The Alliance with the Lawyers," especially p. 271.

[39] For private petitions, see the *Seconde Parte of a Register*. Particularly full is "A Declaration of the unjuste proceedings of the L. B. of London againste Edmond Allen and Thomas Carew, contrarie to the lawes of this realme" (doc. 189, 1585–86). This includes a statement by Carew himself: "I was defended by lawyers and nothing was proved against me." For others, pp. 202–8, 221, 227, 242, 254.

Puritan activities in the sessions of 1584–85, 1586–87, 1588–89, are described by Knappen, *Tudor Puritanism*, pp. 277–79, 290–92, 297.

Typical documents are the sixteen articles framed by the Commons, 1585, and submitted to the lords, Strype, *Whitgift*, III, app. no. xiii and the archbishop's answer, I, 358–59; and the comprehensive "A General Supplication to the Parliament, Anno 1586, November," so-called in the Register, doc. 204.

[40] One of the sixteen articles submitted by the Commons in 1585 urges as to the oath: "Furder, that it may please the reverend Fathers aforesayd, to forbeare theire examinations

the policy of "tarrying for the magistrate," the Puritans turned with increasing vigor to the development of the *conference* or *classis* movement, based on the Book of Discipline, and designed to establish the Presbyterian system of church government. "They realized the danger of misinterpretation and acted secretly . . . But they made a studious effort to keep within the letter of the law. Legal counsel was frequently taken and carefully followed." [41] Cartwright took a prominent part in this movement.

Before turning to Morice and Fuller, "counsel for the defense," a brief statement of the two famous cases, Cawdry's and Cartwright's, may be in order. In 1586 Robert Cawdry, parson of South Luffenham, Rutland, was cited before High Commission and forced under protest to answer on oath articles on his use of the Prayer Book. He was convicted of nonconformity, deprived of his benefice, and suspended.[42] In 1591 Cawdry sued the new incumbent of his benefice for trespass, thus bringing the case into the common-law courts (Queen's Bench). James Morice, as Cawdry's counsel, argued to prove the illegality of the deprivation.[43] If he also dealt with the oath along the lines of his later treatise, there is no evidence of it in the famous (and only) report we have, that by Sir Edward Coke.[44] Under the title *De Jure Regis Ecclesiastico,* the report is primarily concerned with the judgment. It constitutes an eloquent vindication of High Commission even by the common-law judges, further elaborated by Coke himself, along the lines indicated above: The High Commission is a prerogative not a statutory court, the oath ex officio is lawful as authorized by letters patent; the ecclesiastical courts are coequal with the common-law courts and thus may have their own procedure.

About the same time that this final sentence of deprivation was being executed upon Cawdry, Cartwright and others of the *classis* movement were imprisoned.[45] Their refusal to take the oath blocked proceedings in

ex officio mero, of godly and learned preachers, not detected unto them for open offense of lyfe, or for publike maynteyning of apparent error in doctrine; and only to deal with them for such matters as shall be detected in them." (Ca. 11.)

[41] Knappen, *Tudor Puritanism,* p. 288 and chap. xiv.

[42] The sentence of deprivation, May 30, 1587; that of degrading and deposition from the ministry, May 14, 1590.

[43] On the grounds that by the statute of 1 Eliz.: Cawdry might be deprived only for the second offense; he was not deprived either "by the verdict of 12 men, or by confession or by the notorious evidence of the fact," but by default "in respect he appeared not"; sentence was given by Alymer "with the consent" of others, whereas three or more commissioners ought to have "joined" in it; it did not show that the commissioners were natural-born subjects of the queen. His opponents claimed that (1) by his own confession he said the Book of Common Prayer "was a vile Booke and fye uppon it," and that he had failed to follow it; (2) that he was warned and exhorted, yet failed to conform. Lansd. MSS 68, no. 47, fol. 108. Also no. 45, fol. 104, endorsed "the opynion of certein counsellors at Lawe touching Mr. Cawdrys deprivation," signed "Ja. Morice, Nich. Fuller, Geo. Croke," and no. 46, fol. 106, endorsed "attorney of the Courte of Wardes touching Mr. Cawdry's Deprivation," signed "Ja. Morrice."

[44] Coke, *Reports,* V.

[45] Cartwright was sent to the fleet probably in late October 1590.

the Court of High Commission and focused attention on the legality of
the oath. As Thomas Cartwright was "the Patriarche" of the Puritans
and "their chiefest counsaylor," his case was of particular importance.
His influence throughout Warwickshire was summed up by an early
biographer as follows:

> His carriage and deportment was such, that there was not a Nobleman or
> Gentleman of equality in all the country that looked Heavenward, or was
> of any account for religion and learning, but they sought to enjoy his com-
> pany, and found much pleasure and content therein, for his conversation was
> such, that scarce a word came from his mouth that was not of some good use
> and concernment.[46]

Cartwright appeared first before the high commissioners, but as he
blocked the trial by refusing to take the oath,[47] they handed him over to
Star Chamber as better able to deal with him. The evidence here is more
ample than in Cawdry's case. Most of the documents connected with his
appearances in High Commission have been transcribed by his biographer, Pearson, and by Strype.[48] In his report to Lord Burghley, Cartwright justifies his refusal of the "generall and indefinite" oath, as "I
esteemed it contrarie both to the lawes of god and of the Land, to require
such an oath, especiallie of a minister." Then he strikes the keynote of
his whole line of defense, denial that the actions of himself and his group
were in any way illegal.[49] The letter of the imprisoned Puritan ministers
to the queen "in vindication of their innocency" follows the same course.[50]
    Cartwright's experience before the commissioners in May[51] was dis-

---

[46] Pearson, *Thomas Cartwright*, p. 305, quoting Samuel Clarke. Although he had spent
the years 1577–85 in the Low Countries, he had kept in touch with the Puritans in England.
In 1585 he had been permitted to return home, and in 1586, through the influence of his
patron the Earl of Leicester, he was installed as master of Warwick Hospital. In addition to
Leicester he could count among his friends and patrons the Earl of Warwick; Knollys; Lady
Russell; John Puckering, serjeant at law and recorder of Warwick (later to become lord
keeper); and Lord Burghley himself. *Ibid.*, chaps. iv, v. vi.

[47] Thus the court might fine or imprison for contumacy, but could not convict. "In later
years in order that such an impasse might not hinder the activities of the High Commission
it was legally affirmed that refusal to take the oath was a sign of guilt and the recusant was
declared *pro confesso*." Cf. Usher, *Reconstruction*, I, 62–64. Maguire, "Attack of the Common Lawyers on the Oath Ex Officio," in *Essays in honor of C. H. McIlwain*.

[48] From Lord Burghley's papers, Lansd. MSS. These include his report from the fleet to
Lord Burghley of the proceeding against him, "the sum of that which passed at both their
sittinges"; a supplication from Cartwright and others "suggesting that th'othe which was
tendered was not according to law"; and the account of a meeting of six of the commissioners
(Saturday, May 1 or 8, 1591) with Cartwright alone, with the intent of breaking down his
resistance to the oath.

[49] Pearson, *Thomas Cartwright*, app. xxiii.

[50] "Whereof, for that the oath is the next and immediate cause of our trouble, we have made
our answer first to that; and then after also to the crimes that are suggested and secretly informed against us." Strype, *Annals*, IV, app. lx. (Their attack on the oath is based on 25 Hen.
VIII, ca. 14, and 35 Hen. VIII, session 3, ca. 15, rather than on general principles of the
common law.)

[51] "Th'effect of th'answer of Mr. Cartwright before certen her maiesties high Commissioners in causes Ecclesiasticall, namely the B. of London (Aylmer), the Atturney generall,

couraging. In spite of learned counsel such as Morice and Fuller, the weight of evidence and authority was still too great on the other side. After a long speech by the bishops, concluding with a command to take the oath,

Then Mr. Cartwright beginning to speak, Mr. Attourney (Sir John Popham) took the speech from him, and made also a long speech th'effect whereof was to show how dangerous a thing yt was that men should upon the conceits of their own heads, and yet under colour of conscience, refuse the things that have bene receyved for lawes of long time, and that this othe that was tendred was according to the lawes of the land which he commended above the lawes of all other lands, yet so that because they (were) the lawes of men, they carried alwayes some stayn of imperfection. Also that he was now to deal with Mr. Cartwright in two poynts, one was the peace of the land which was broken by him and others . . . Th'other was the justice of the land, which he and others had offended against, in refusing th'othe now tendred, which (as he said) was used in other Courts of the land. Nether was there anie in his conscience, learned in the lawes that did judge yt unlawfull . . .

After further argument and Cartwright's continued refusal to take the oath

Whereof when they demaunded the reason, his answer was, that he had layd the chief strength of his refusall upon the law of god: secondly upon the lawes of the land, which in some mens judgment professing the skill of the lawes, did not warrant such proceeding. But seeing that he heard Mr. Atturney affirm as he did, and that he had no eyes to look into the depth and mysteries of the law: that he would most principally relie and stand (at this praesent) upon the law of god.

According to Strype, Nicholas Fuller was Cartwright's counsel in his appearance before Star Chamber.[52] Unfortunately we do not have any such report of Fuller's arguments here as we do those on behalf of his clients Allen (the case of monopolies, 1602) and Ladd and Mansell (1607).[53] Pearson calls Cartwright's answers to the forty-three interrogatories administered to him "singularly meagre" and "deliberately noncomittal,"

Mrs. D. Lewin, D. Bancroft, D. Stanhop and another whom I know not, which two last were silent. The place was the B. chamber secretlie kept, least anie that favoured the cause (as seemeth) should come in. The time upon Saturday last in th'afternoon, without (as I have heard) anie warning aforehand, which is usually given to prisoners." Pearson, *Thomas Cartwright*, app. xxv.

[52] Strype (under date May 13, 1591) says, "When Fuller, their counsel began to answer Mr. Attorney the Lord Chancellor interrupted, according to a letter written by Sir Fr. Knollys next day; and moved the archbishop to appoint one D. D. and one D. C. to join with the judges for their information against Cartwright."

[53] *Star Chamber Proceedings*, 33 Eliz., A 56, no. 1. In addition to these official bundles of interrogatories and depositions of the witnesses, there is a letter from Cartwright to Burghley with an abstract of the accusations and the prisoners' replies in parallel columns. For the letter, see Pearson, *Thomas Cartwright*, app. xxviii; for the abstract, Strype, *Whitgift*, III, no. 14, 242–60. This contains twenty-one items (not forty-three); no. 18 relates to the oath.

disappointing alike to his examiners and to the historical student. Pearson finds in them enough to throw some light on the Presbyterian movement, but the lords of the Star Chamber did not succeed in proving "seditious conduct *de facto*." Even so, Cartwright and the others were kept in prison for a time as they stanchly refused to accept the subscription drawn up by Popham. Cartwright was finally released at some time before May 21, 1592, a practical victory but hardly a theoretical vindication.

When the case of the preacher Cartwright and his followers, for refusing to take Whitgift's oath and make answer, was brought for a final settlement, all the chief judges and law officers gave it as their opinion that the refusal was unlawful. Up to this time then it would seem that the stricter ecclesiastical rule was conceded by the highest authorities to be unimpeachable by common-law Courts.[54]

To be sure, there is little evidence of the use of Magna Carta in our story thus far. It is to the treatises and their authors—the common lawyers, Beale and Morice, and the civilian, Doctor Cosin—that we must turn.

The "Treatisours"—Beale, Morice, and Cosin

ROBERT BEALE, diplomatist and antiquary, was clerk of the privy council, sat in five parliaments, and served on a number of commissions and diplomatic missions.[55] Most extraordinary of these, congenial to one of his Puritan leanings, was his mission in 1578 to the Protestant princes of Germany "to obtain a toleration for such of the reformed churches as did not agree with the ubiquitaries. He made a journey during winter of 1400 miles, visited nine princes personally, and sent the queen's letters to three others." He was a member of the Society of Antiquaries, acquired great knowledge of languages, and was an ardent collector of books and manuscripts "which last he purchased at almost any cost, so that in early life he formed one of the best historical libraries in Europe." Little is known of his education. He seems to have studied at Cambridge. In a letter to the archbishop he says of himself:

Touchinge my studies, I have by the space of xxvi yeres and upwards bene a Student of the Civill Lawes, and long sith could have taken a degree, if I had thought, (as some doe) that the substaunce of learninge consisteth more in forme and title, then matter: and albeit, for lacke of use, my skill be impayred; yet would I be lothe that the greatest Doctor that is about your Lord-

---

[54] Wigmore, *Evidence*, IV, 804–5. These "judges and law officers" were the two chief justices, the chief baron, Serjeant Puckering, Attorney General Popham, and the solicitor general.

[55] The *D.N.B.* and Cooper's *Athenae Cantabrigenses*, II, 311–12. The first says little of his education. The latter, though including him in its pages, can only say "It seems probable that he had a part of his education in this university, but we have not succeeded in ascertaining in what college or house."

ship could so teache me what lawe is, but that, with a little studie, I could discerne, whether he saye trulie or no. In divinitie, I think I have redde as much as anye Chapleyne your Lordship hath.[56]

Perhaps he was also self-taught in the common law. After reading his assured and vigorous pronouncements on the latter, it is hard to believe that he did not have some training in one of the Inns of Court. For instance, note his surprise that his civilian opponents dare impugn the Register:

Wherefore I never harde the originall wryts were other wise taken then as rules and foundacions of the knowledge of the common law of the Lande: wherto men oughte to geve faithe and not to denye them, for uppon these foundacions all the whole Lawe dependethe, as Fitzherberte saithe in his preface before his Natura brevium and as Britton saythe . . . and as Bracton saythe Brevia communia inter omnes pro iure generaliter observari debent . . .

He is equally scornful of their "wrangling Accursian glosses" on the language of the law.[57]

Beale had his first tilt with Whitgift on the appearance of the *orders* of 1583. Then the twenty-four articles and the increased use of the oath focused his attention on the latter.[58] Probably about 1588 he drew up his *Certain Brief Notes*. The longer treatise (c. 1590), *A Collection Shewinge what Jurisdiction the Clergie Hathe Heretofore Lawfully Used,* was

---

[56] Strype, *Whitgift,* III, app. no. v.

[57] "Wherto I aunswere that the common Lawe of this realme is not wrytten in any such Ceceronian or Justinian Latin, wherat Gramarians may so cavill at there pleasures: But it was wrytte in such termes and phrases as seemed beest unto ye law makers to expresse theire meaninge. And if anie doubt do arise theruppon, it is to be resolved by other words and place of the same Lawe and Lawe makers and not by such wrangling Accursian glosses which rather overthrowe then explaine ye true texte and meaninge of the same."

[58] The *D.N.B.* lists amongst his writings, "*A Book against Oaths ministered in the Courts of Ecclesiastical Commission from her Majesty, and other Courts Ecclesiastical,* printed abroad and brought to England in a Scotch ship about 1583." "*A Book respecting Ceremonies, the Habits, the Book of Common Prayer, and the power of Ecclesiastical Courts,* 1584." See Strype, *Whitgift,* I, 401–2, for a schedule of charges (fourteen points) drawn up by the archbishop against Beale's writings, including:

"1. Before the last Parliament he writ a book against oaths that be ministered in the courts of ecclesiastical commission from her Majesty, and in other courts ecclesiastical."

"2. Hereof he gave out copies; and thereby many flew abroad in sundry men's hands."

"3. A little before that Parliament, the said book was published by print in foreign parts, and the copies printed were brought hither in a Scottish ship."

. . .

"5. He hath since penned another great book in defence of his said former book against oaths, and in impugnation of sundry parts of ecclesiastical jurisdiction, practised in courts of her Majesty's commission, and in inferior ordinary courts ecclesiastical."

. . .

"9. But especially against the driving of any offender by that commission, to put in their answers to the matters objected upon their oaths; albeit the offences touch neither life nor limbs."

. . .

"13. He condemneth (without exception of any cause) racking of grievous offenders, as being cruel, barbarous, contrary to law, and unto the liberty of English subjects."

apparently an expansion of the *Brief Notes.*[59] As a result of his activities in 1593 he was temporarily sequestered from court and parliament but eventually restored to favor, for he served on several commissions, 1597, 1599, 1600, and 1601, in which year he died.

Sir James Morice, attorney of the Court of Wards, was for many years recorder of Colchester, and represented it in the parliaments of 1586, 1588–89, and 1593. He was counsel for Cawdry, "his first great chance to champion the Puritans."[60] It was probably soon after he had lost this case (about 1591 or 1592) that he drew up his *Briefe Treatise of Oathes exacted by Ordinaries and Ecclesiastical Judges,* though it was not published until 1598.[61] Morice also served as counsel to Cartwright and was particularly active in the parliament of 1593.

Doctor Richard Cosin was dean of the Court of Arches and "one of the most influential of the high commissioners." His able and elaborate statement of the position of the civilians includes a summary of the whole scope of ecclesiastical jurisdiction; a description of the various forms of procedure in ecclesiastical courts (the *inquisitio* was only one of three); and a dissertation on oaths with a long, learned discussion on the nature of an oath. In his second edition, 1593, he is answering both Beale, whom he calls "the Note-Gatherer," and Morice, whom he calls "the Treatisour."

The main arguments on both sides have been indicated above. Doctor Cosin, like the judges in *Cawdry's case,* insisted on the equality of lay and ecclesiastical jurisdiction under the crown. High Commission, drawing its authority from the prerogative, might well have its own forms of procedure. The oath was further justified by expediency if heresy were to be effectively ferreted out. Its abuse need not be feared, because of

---

[59] The original of the *Brief Notes* has not been found. All we have is Cosin's resumé of the "Note-gatherer's" arguments, and Strype's abstract of a "pamphlet" which he assigns to Beale, *Whitgift,* II, book iv. The most important part of the longer treatise is transcribed in Mrs. Maguire's thesis, pp. 261–75, from Calthorpe MSS 44, fols. 99–202. This, she says, can be assigned to 1590 "with reasonable certainty."

[60] Mrs. Maguire's thesis, p. 96. "Soon after he defended the archdeacon of Essex who had refused to conform absolutely, and advised Whitgift to be more circumspect in his dealings, as in his opinion, whoever proceeded by civil or canon law, in a manner repugnant to the Word of God, laws of the realm, or liberty of the Subject, was liable to the penalties of praemunire." (Based on a letter of Vincent Skinner to Burghley, March 14, 1591.)

[61] *Briefe treatise of Oathes exacted by Ordinaries and Ecclesiastical Judges, to answere generallie to all such Articles or Interrogatories as it pleaseth them to propound. And of their forced and constrained Oathes ex officio, Wherein it is proved that the same are unlawful.* Morice sent the treatise to Burghley who sent it to Whitgift who showed it to Dr. Cosin who wrote his *Apology* confuting it. Morice then wrote a *Defence* which "more fully showed the injustice of administering the oath." He "retained his Defence in private," but the archbishop insisted on seeing it. Morice complained that Cosin might publish all he wrote, while he himself was prohibited. Strype, *Whitgift,* II, 28–30. According to Mrs. Maguire, the best manuscript is Lambeth 234, which contains Morice's defense in answer to Cosin, and the original treatise, which he elaborated to refute Cosin's arguments. Others are Harl. MSS 5247, fols. 1–60, and Cott. MSS Cleopatra F I, fols. 50–69. I used only this last and the printed edition of 1598 which follows it.

the probity of the ecclesiastical judges, who were much to be preferred to the ordinary "accuser."

To what extent Beale and Morice were indebted to each other does not appear. Certainly they must have been thrown together both by their official positions, membership in the Commons, and even more by their sympathies for their Puritan clients. To the "Note-Gatherer" and the "Treatisour," High Commission was a statutory creation: the statute did not authorize the oath; the ruler's sanction could not make it legal. If the canon law had ever permitted it, such "foreign made laws" ceased to have any force in the land after 25 Henry VIII. But as they saw it, the oath was contrary to the law of God (the Scriptures) and the canon law, and above all to the "law of the land," both customary and statutory. As to penalties, the ecclesiastical courts had customarily used "ecclesiastical censures," and could fine and imprison only as specifically sanctioned by parliament. The same must be true of High Commission. It was as old "law of the land," of course, that the Great Charter and its interpreting and reinforcing statutes came into play. Here the cumulative effect of the early printed statutes, treatises, and chronicles becomes apparent. Both writers make emphatic statements of limited monarchy and the rule of law. Magna Carta is something fundamental and absolutely unalterable that royal letters patent are powerless to touch. As Beale puts it, it is "the law of laws." "Magna Carta against which I truste neither anie Common or Ecclesiastical Lawyer will make any exception at all."

The allegation, says Morice, that the ruler in commissions gives power, by express words to the commissioners ecclesiastical, to examine by oath persons accused or presented is no sufficient or lawful justification

inasmuch as we have proved, and further shall proove such examinations and inquiries upon oath, to be injurious both to the Prince and people of this Realme, and to impugne our gouvernement and forme of Iustice. In which cases the Kings graunt or commission is of no force in lawe. For as *Bracton* well hath written, *Potestas Principis juris est non injuriae, & cum ipse sit author juris, non debet inde injuriarum nasce occasio unde jura nascuntur.* That the King by his Commission or graunt, or otherwise then by Parliament, may not change or alter the lawes of this Realme, nor the order, maner or fourme of administration of Iustice, is rightlie also noted unto us by that grave and learned Iudge Maister *Fortescue,* saying *Non potest Rex Angliae ad libitum suum leges mutare. Regni sui Principatu, namque nedum Regali sed & politico ipse suo populo dominatur.* And by that booke also of Anno 11 H. 4 where it is agreed that neither the King by his graunt, nor the Pope by his Bulles (for all his triple Croune) can change or alter the lawes of the lande, whereunto concurre divers others bookes of the report of the lawe.[62]

[62] Morice, *Briefe treatise of Oathes.* This passage continues with precedents from the Year Books, including the commission of 42 Ed. III, voided as unlawful, and that memorable saying of Justice Scrope, "If the King (sayeth hee) commaund anything impossible that

Morice is evidently well-read not only in the law books but in those chronicles with an anti-Catholic bias, perhaps the late edition of Grafton or the second of Holinshed. He holds up as a warning "the contention and strife of Anselme Archbishop of Canterburye with kinge Rufus, the manifold practices of Thomas Becket against kinge Henrie the seconde, the tragicall liefe and pitifull end of king John occasioned by the malicious meanes of the Archbishop Stephen Langton." He knows something of Charter history: the confirmations, and the curse against violators which he quotes.[63] Although the practices denounced in this passage are charged to "the unbridled Cleargie men in the Papistical time," they suggest the treatment so recently accorded Cawdry and Cartwright.

It is in declaiming against the "general citations" of the ecclesiastical judges, their "arrests, distresses, impeachments, excommunication, imprisonments thereuppon ensuyinge," that Morice uses a paraphrase of Magna Carta chapter 29, and the most pertinent two of the *six statutes*:

But to returne againe to our prohibition and attachment it is evidente thereby that all the sommons and citations which those Ecclesiastical Judges send forthe under their generall terms *propter salutem animae* or *ex officio mero*, and all their arrests distresses impeachments excommunications imprisonments thereuppon ensuyinge are altogether injurious bothe to the Prince and people. And of this opinion seemethe to bee that learned Judge Mr. Fitzherberte who in his booke de Natura brevium saithe uppon these writtes in this manner. By this appearethe yt those generall citations which Bishoppes make to cite men to appeare beefore them *pro salute anime* without expressinnge any cause especiall, are against the lawe. And true it is for by the statute of *Magna Charta* (contayninge manie excellente lawes of the liberties and free customes of this kingdome) it is ordained that no free man bee apprehended imprisoned distrayned or impeached but by the lawe of the land. And by the statute made anno 5 E. 3. ca. 9 It is enacted that no man shalbe attached uppon anie accusation contrarie to the fourme of the greate Charter & the law of the Realme. Moreover it is accorded by parliament ann. 43 E. 3. ca. 9 for the good gouvernement of the Cominaltie that no man bee put to answere without presentment beefore Justices, or matter of record, or by due processe, or by writte Originall after the aunciente lawe of this land. And how then shall that kind of proceedinge *Ex officio* by forced oathes and the urging of this generall oathe and straighte imprisoninge of such as refuse to sweare bee justifiable?

Beale also rules out by "historical evidence" any claim of his opponents for a jurisdiction *jure divino*. Although he admits that there was some "usurpation" by the pope and clergy after the Norman Conquest, after

which the lawe will in the case must be done: if he commaunde any thing contrarie to lawe, his Iustices ought not to do it."

[63] Evidently using the text as printed in the early volumes of statutes, attributed to Boniface, but erroneously dated 12 Hen. III.

the Becket affair, and under John and Henry III, he plays up the episodes in which kings and common-law judges held their own. Like Morice he knows something of the Charter's stormy origin and long history, its fundamental character as established by parliamentary confirmations, coronation oaths, and the curse against Charter-breakers.

And therfore it were a great pittie that a Lawe that was debated by the espace of a hundred yeres with the losse of the lives of mo Englishe subiects then be at this daie lyvinge in the Lande; so solumnlye made, and so often confirmed in sondrie parliaments and corroborated by the othe of all the kinges and Queens and subiects, should be now overthrowen and made voyde by reviving of that tiranicall custome which the Clergie seeketh to bringe in agayne.

Beale makes more exact and discriminating use of specific chapters of the Charter than does Morice. Thus he attempts to offset his opponents' use of chapter 1 by a counter interpretation: "Whereas they stand much upon the wordes of Magna Charta quod Ecclesia Anglicana libera sit, & habeat omnia iura sua integra et libertates suas illaesas first it behooveth them to shewe what liberties they then had." [64] Chapter 29 (which he quotes more accurately than Morice) he does use rather broadly against both the alleged excessive penalties employed by the commissioners and the practices of pursuivants.[65]

Beale is unique in using chapter 14 (rather than 29) as a defense against the deposing and depriving of ministers. They ought not to lose their benefices (which he calls their "freeholdes") for offences "meere temporall, for speaches or makinge of bookes," for the Great Charter provides that clerks are not to be amerced according to their ecclesiastical benefice. His use of chapter 28 is certainly nearer in spirit to the original intent of

[64] The Charter, he explains, granted them *their* liberties, not the liberties of the Roman Curia, liberties held in England as granted by the king not by the Roman pontiff. "And so it appeareth that the Clergie should enoiye the Liberties of the Churche accordinge to the Lawes and customes of the realme, yeilding themselves to the Lawes of the realme . . ."

[65] As to punishments, "*Bracton* wryteth that a consideracion is to be had of the cause, of the person, of the place, of the tyme, of the qualitie, of the quantitie, and of the event, which if they were duelie considered as they ought to be I doubt not but mens offences wold be lesse agravated then they are, and that the Juries shold not be commaunded to fynd the fact onely without the qualitie for that the qualitie was alredie determined by others. What is become of the great Charter of England which saith that no freeman shall be taken or imprisoned or disseised of his freehold or liberties or free customes, or be outlawed or exiled or otherwise be distrayned but by lawfull iudgment and by the lawes of the land." And what has become of the rules governing process (literally, "of the auncient writts of the land") "when every pursuivant by a warrant under the hande of the Commissioners shall enter into mens houses, break upp their chests and chambers, extortionouslie exact excessive fees both against the Canons and the Commission Ecclesiasticall, cary away what they list, and afterward pick matter to arrest and committ them, whereof there is no other proofe, but that the partie must be compelled by oth to answer unto the same. I wold to God her Majestie were trulie enformed of these indignities offered unto her poore and loyall subiects and then I doubt not they wold be reformed accordingly."

that rather obscure provision than the far-fetched interpretation of Doctor Cosin.[66] After defending the writ of prohibition, as given in the Register and Fitzherbert, against a variant which his opponents found in Rastell, he says:

But to shewe that the said wrytte in the Register and Fitzherberte is a lawe and ought to be esteemed as a Lawe, this may be truelie said, that it conteynethe nothing els then that which is conteyned in the lawe of Lawes, that is the greate Charter of Englande touching the othe now unlawfully used by the Clergie and sought to be mainteyned with the overthrowe of the authoritie or the Lawe, and discredite of the authenticall bookes and reverent Judges of our Lawe.

Magna charta in the 28 or 29 chapter hath these wordes: Nullus Ballivus de cetero ponat aliquem ad legem manifestam nec ad iuramentum simplici loquela sua, sine testibus fidelibus ad hoc inductis—which in the English Statutes is translated thus: No Bayliffe from henceforth shall putt anie man to his open Lawe, nor to othe, uppon his owne bare sayinge, without faithful witnesses brought in for the same.

After supporting his interpretation of chapter 28 [67] with three of the *six statutes,* quoted almost exactly as they appear in Rastell's *Statutes,* Beale concludes: "Whereby I doe inferre that by the Statute of Magna Charta and the olde Lawes of this realme, this othe for a man to accuse himself was and is utterlie inhibited."

Cosin's learned description of procedure in ecclesiastical courts does admit of certain rules and limitations. He says, for instance, if the ordinary proceeds *ex officio mero,* the charge must be grounded (1) upon some presentment of a fame or crime by church wardens; (2) proved by other witnesses; or (3) *clamosa insinuatio.* Yet the rule that a fame ought to appear or be proved before a judge may proceed when there is no

[66] He is on sounder ground than the civilians in his historical interpretation of the word *bailiff* as used in this chapter: "But some will perhappes descant uppon the words Nullus ballivus as though other officers and especiallie those of the Clergie were not bounde therunto. To the first I answer, that when the Lawe of Magna Charta was made, the Bayliffe was the kings Judge and officer, and afterwards were brought in conservators of the peace, Justices of Oyer and Terminer, Justices of bothe Benches, Justices Itinerant, as appeareth in Bracton and by the Statute of Articuli super chartas and Westm. the 2. In the time of kinge Edw(ard) the first and sondrie other Statutes of kinge Edwarde the 3. After which time the worde Bayliffe grew out of use, to be taken for officers of Justice but was most commonlie reteyned for officers of Liberties and Manors." Beale even cites Linwood's interpretation of the word, the "custome book of Normandy" and Bracton, and says that *bayliffe* is still used in the old sense in Guernsey, Jersey, and Normandy!

[67] After an attempt to explain the practice in Norman times, in which he evidently confuses the oath ex officio and compurgation, he reverts to chapter 28: "But seeing by this Law of Magna Charta the Judge was inhibited to proceade to the puttinge of a man to his open lawe or othe: So I doubte not but the accuser or informer was bounde to the lyke: and therefore doe assure my self, that I maye lawfullye, according to the said Lawe of Magna Charta inferre that in an accusation uppon the bare informacion of anie man, Judge or accuser, without other lawful witnesses, none ought to be putt to his othe or proceaded against without better proofes." The three of the *six statutes* which he quotes are those of 5, 25, and 42 Edward III.

presentment "has divers exceptions in law." One such exception is when special inquiries are framed by the prince himself, and this may be by means of the ecclesiastical commission! [68] This and other passages show how little real defense there could be for "liberty of the subject" when rules of law could be thus excepted against. As to Magna Carta, Doctor Cosin makes incidental reference to the general excommunication, the oaths for its observance taken by kings at their coronations, and the confirmations by act of parliament. Under his handling, chapter 1 again comes into its own as a sweeping confirmation of the liberties of the church.[69] He is historically more correct than his opponents when he points out that this confirmation came at a time when "it was holden" (though untruly, he adds) "that the state Ecclesiastical . . . had not their Iurisdictions from the Prince, but from God alone, derived downe to them by means of the Pope." Furthermore, as this chapter stands first and apart from all the others, the latter must apply only to lay, not ecclesiastical matters, unless so specified—"a confirmation of their rights and liberties before any graunt was made to the rest of the Realme besides." [70] *Ergo,* chapter 29 could not rightly be taken to limit ecclesiastical courts and procedure as the common lawyers contended! In another passage, upholding the power of the queen to authorize by letters patent the use of process other than by citation (letters missive, attachment, and so on) and of punishment by fine and imprisonment, Cosin ingeniously reads chapter 29 quite out of the picture, concluding, "it is manifest, that the wordes have no relation to Iurisdiction ecclesiasticall." Yet again inconsistently, if he cared for the support of chapter 1, he contends that the Charter is not unalterable law—"and albeit if Magna Carta had bene to the contrary, yet an act of Parliament coming after, might change that law . . . It is assured that par in parem non habet imperium; and none authority can so binde it selfe by any law, but that (upon good occasion and by like power) it may be abrogated again."

As to chapter 28 (which he says he "supposes" the "Note-Gatherer" has in mind), like others before and after him Cosin admits "that these words are something too obscure and darke for mee to understand, what

---

[68] Cosin, *An Apologie for Sundrie Proceedings,* Pt. II, chap. vii (especially pp. 59-60). "The Civill and Canon lawes allowe sundry meanes to grounde a speciall Enquirie of Office against a crime, besides Accusation and Presentment." He cites four exceptions.

[69] "The Great Charter (to the observation and propugnation whereof, the King and the great Nobles and Officers were wont to be sworne) layeth this groundworke of all which followeth: We have granted to God, and by this our present Charter confirmed, for us and our heires for evermore, that the Church of England shalbe free, and shall have all her whole right and liberties inviolable. But that the Church had these rights and liberties then, (which are now claimed) the Actes of Courtes Ecclesiastical in those former times, and in all succeeding ages, (without prohibition or oppugnation), with the statutes and reports, (some whereof were made not long after) and so from time to time downeward (till these late challenges) do make it very manifest." *Ibid.,* chaps. ii, iii, and pp. 7-9, 175.

[70] For an example of Cosin's arguments and style, see Appendix G.

is positively meant by them, and so much the rather, because I know not
the usage afore that time, which (thereby) was meant to be remedied."
His attempted explanation, though wide of the mark, is like one of the
three suggested in the early fourteenth century and is partly borne out
by the translation he uses. As to chapter 26, this learned civilian goes even
further astray in his misreading of the common law when he equates
this *inquisitio* (the writ of inquisition of life and member which called
for a jury) with the *inquisitio ex officio*. This must have indeed impressed Beale as a "wrangling Accursian glosse" of the first magnitude!

Since pamphlets failed to bring results, Morice turned to action
through parliament. In February 1593 he presented two bills, one against
unlawful oaths, inquisition, and subscription, the other against unlawful
imprisonment and restraint of liberty. The speech that Morice made in
the Commons (February 27) and the text of the first bill are given in full
in his own account of the whole affair,[71] which concludes, "This my
Speeche ended, I delivered my twoe Bills unto the Speaker, who then
was Mr. Edwarde Cooke hir Majesties Sollicitour." Other speakers, pro
and con, followed Morice, among the latter Oliver St. John, one of three
gentlemen by this name who figure in Magna Carta history.[72] Coke skill-
fully shelved the bill by asking leave to consider it, but promised to keep

[71] "A Remembrance of certaine Matters concerninge the Clergye and their Jurisdiction,"
1593, transcribed by Mrs. Maguire (pp. 276–318) from Baker MSS, vol. 40 (Cambridge
University Library MSS, Mm. 1.51, fols. 105–34). As she points out, the *Commons Journal*
for this year is lost. D'Ewes, who used it, omits Morice's speech given there and supplies others.
[72] This member of the parliament of 1593 was Oliver St. John, Viscount Grandison and
Baron Tregoz (1559–1630), a Lincoln's Inn man, most of whose career after 1593 lay in
Ireland, where he ultimately became lord deputy.
"Then stood up Mr. Oliver St. John, as may be collected out of the aforesaid Original
Journal-Book of the House of Commons . . . and speaking to the Bill said: 'it is and hath
been the manner of this House to allow a mixture in speaking and after the Grave, Honourable and Wisest, then to hear the meanest also. For my self, I am but young, yet will I
shew unto you matter which is old. In Answer to them that spake last, the Antient Charter
of this Realm says, *Nullus liber homo*, &c. which is flatly violated by Bishops Jurisdiction.
You know what things Thomas Becket stood up against the King, which things are now
also crept in. And for more full Answer of one that spake before, his Antiquity and prescription cannot be allowed in this Government for any reason; for so were the official prestitute
to take and exact Fees, because out of mind they had done so. And set it down that it was
Answered in the Parliament House, That Thieves may prescribe to take Purses on *Shooters-
Hill*, because time out of mind they had done so . . . So I think the Bill very worthy and
fit to be read.' " D'Ewes' *Parliaments of Elizabeth*, p. 475b.
Others followed, pro and con. Sir Francis Knollys, well-wisher of the Puritans, supported
the bill on the grounds that it did not attack the ecclesiastical jurisdiction, but only sought
to reform abuses ("If the canon law went contrary to the laws of the realm, it was a usurpation
and encroachment and should be restrained"), and Robert Cecil advised referring the bill to
the queen. *Ibid.*, 474–79; Mrs. Maguire, "History of the Ex-Officio Oath," pp. 295–96.
According to Morice, Mr. Lewyn a civilian "discoursed at large of government and
justifienge the proceedings *Ex officio*," and affirmed that subscription was practised at Geneva.
"To whome for the matter of Inquisition Mr. *Fynche* of Greys Inne replyed affirming the
same to be contrary to the lawes of the Realme: shewinge withall that it was an Article
aggreed uppon betwene the Kinge and Thomas Beckett Archbishop of Canterbury that no
such Courts of Inquisition by oathe should be practised within this Realme."

it secretly. Meanwhile the queen commanded him to tell her what the bill contained and sent back by him her command "that no Bill touching the said matters of state or reform in Causes Ecclesiastical be exhibited." In Morice's words:

The Speaker also reckoninge the leafes of the Bill, said it was longe, consistinge of manie parts, and therefore it would be very hard for him on the suddaine to deliver the contents thereof to the House. Whereupon I desired, that the Bill concerninge Imprisonment might be read: which not obtayned, the Conclusion was, the Speaker promised the House to bringe those Bills again the next daie, and in the meane time safelie to kepe them from the view of any man. But as I have heard, he was in the meantime commaunded to come with the Billes to the Court, which accordinglie he did. What became of them after, he best knoweth. It is affirmed, that in respect of his promise, he was suffered to retorne them to the House. But most certaine it is, they were never read there, nor any Determinacion nor order of the House made concerninge them, only a Commaundment was delivered from her Majestie that there should be no dealing in matters of Estate, eyther Civill or Ecclesiasticall.[73]

What became of them after, he best knoweth! One can only speculate as to whether Sir Edward remembered and was influenced by their contents in later years! Morice was reprimanded by some of the privy councillors and temporarily suspended.[74]

Both the speech and the first bill which it introduces denounce ecclesiastical jurisdiction on three grounds, each of which is enlarged upon in vigorous terms: "an ungodlye and intollerable Inquisition," a "lawlesse Subscription," and a "bindinge absolution." [75] Naturally both speech and bill reflect the same views already set forth in the treatises. Interest lies not in novelty but in the wider audience for the speech in the Commons. It begins with the characteristic Puritan note which puts God's cause above the queen's, but also definitely plays up "liberty of the subject" and concludes with the usual idealized conception of the Tudor monarchy— "our Estate and Pollicie exquisitelie planted and established in great wisdom."

[73] Maguire, "History of the Ex-Officio Oath," p. 297.

[74] He was told that he should have presented the matter privately to the queen. He replied that he would be content if the queen effected the desired reforms, but maintained that it should be possible to bring up such matters in parliament. He was placed in the custody of Sir John Fortescue for eight weeks. A second time before the council, accused of uniting with Peter Wentworth in his bill on the succession, Morice admitted that Wentworth tried to discuss the matter with him, but claimed that he had refused to have anything to do with it.

[75] Entitled "An Act against unlawful Oathes, Inquisitions, and Subscriptions." The bill describes in much the language of the *six statutes* what judicial procedure should be according to the Great Charter and other "laws of the land"; what it actually is in the ecclesiastical courts, then forbids the three specified evils under pain of "praemunire as per 16 Richard II." The Charter is cited twice, in connection with deprivation of freehold, and with forced subscription. For passages from the speech (Mrs. Maguire's transcription), see Appendix G.

Although Morice's account reads, "This my Speeche ended, I delivered my twoe Billes unto the Speaker, who then was Mr. Edwarde Cooke his Majesties Sollicitour, the true copies whereof doe ensure," the text of the second bill is not included. Though I cannot identify it absolutely, there is a bill in the Harleian Manuscripts which may be Morice's.[76] It is a huge double folio sheet in large writing, labeled on the outside in a small note, "To confirme a branch of Magna Charta, comitting to prison without process or arrest punishable." According to its terms, any person imprisoned contrary to "the provisions and prohibitions of the said Great Charter and other Lawes in that behalfe made" is to receive treble damages (recoverable by *action on the case* in any court of record), and to be released on writ of habeas corpus, fine and damages to be imposed on any warden for detention after receipt of the same.

About the same time that the lord treasurer was being importuned by the imprisoned Cartwright and his fellows, petitions came from another group. These were the strict separatists, followers of Henry Barrowe and John Greenwood, and popularly nicknamed "Brownists." Their numbers and influence in London increased in the years 1586-92. By 1592 some seventy of them were in prison in London "not to speak of other Gaoles throughout the land." Although some were people of small means and little learning, petty tradesmen and the like, the leaders were men of more distinction. Francis Johnson had been a fellow at Christ's College, Cambridge, until expelled for his religious views. In 1592 he became pastor of Greenwood's church and was leader of the London group until 1597. John Penry was a young Welshman of good family and Oxford training who aspired to be the apostle for Wales.[77]

Strype quotes what appears to be an appeal to Lord Burghley from the prisoners themselves. It bears the names of fifty-nine persons in the Gatehouse, Fleet, Newgate, Bridewell, the Clink, the White-lion, the Woodstreet Counter, the Poultry Counter, and "dead in prison" ten.[78] This is followed by a second, "The Petition of the London Church to the privy

[76] See Appendix G. However, a discrepancy appears. One of the lords of the council is quoted as saying to Morice: "You do well in your Bill of Imprisonment to except the Queene, her Councell, and the Justices, but none of us can (if that were lawe) commytt any man to Prison, without express cause in wrightinge. But in fayth my Lords for my parte, I commytt as fewe as any man . . ." This bill has no explicit exception, but merely "by sufficient warrant and authority." Morice's bill wàs referred to in connection with the "Magna Carta bill" introduced in the Commons in 1621, and again in one of the conferences between the houses in 1628.

[77] Knappen, *Tudor Puritanism*; Burrage, *Early English Dissenters*; William Pierce, *John Penry*; Strype, *Annals*, Vols. III and IV. Barrowe and Greenwood had been imprisoned about 1588. These two and Penry were later executed; the remaining Barrowists were allowed to go into exile.

[78] Strype, *Annals*, Vol. IV, no. lxi, pp. 127-30. He calls it the humble petition "put up of many poor Christians, imprisoned by the bishops in sundry several prisons in and about London."

council" which Penry's biographer, Pierce, is convinced was his work.[79] In spite of professions of "loyalty" and "innocency," it contains a most sweeping rejection of the whole establishment. The clauses charging unlawful proceedings against the prisoners read like something of an echo of those of their more conservative brethren, perhaps composed without benefit of lawyer, as they appeal rather vaguely to the "public charter of this land." [80]

Whereas Warham and More had invoked chapter 1 of Magna Carta on behalf of the Catholic Church, and Whitgift and Cosin had used it in defence of the Anglican establishment, it remained for Francis Johnson and John Penry to invoke it for the separatists' conception of the "true church of Christ." Francis Johnson, in prison, writes to the lord treasurer (January 8, 1594) enclosing a paper "That F. J. for his writings is not under the danger of the statute of 35 Eliz. ca. 1 made to retain the queen's subjects in their due obedience, appeareth thus." This consists of ten arguments and a short conclusion asking his release, the seventh being: "His writings are in defence of the right and liberty of the Church of Christ; which the great charter of England granteth shall be free, and have her whole rights and liberty inviolable, &c." [81] Penry was apprehended in the spring of 1593 and tried for felony in violating the Act of Uniformity, convicted, and executed May 28, 1593. "In his defense, as in his last tract, he maintained that the Queen was bound to rule in accordance with the law, both divine and human. Ordinances contrary to either were of no validity." " 'Her Majesty (he declared) hath granted in establishing and confirming the Great Charter of England that the church of God under her should have all her rights and liberties inviolate for ever.' Asked by the judge whether a subject has the right to scan what oaths princes take and charge the rulers to keep covenant with the ruled, Penry replied in the affirmative, repeating that the prince must rule by

[79] Pierce, *John Penry*, p. 372. "The most influential person still free was Penry, and it was his advice and help they sought . . . Penry drew up a petition to the Privy Council in which the grievances of the Separatist Church were set forth." And (note 3)—"The petition is in Penry's characteristic style and its authorship cannot be mistaken."

[80] Strype, *Annals*, Vol. IV, no. lxii, pp. 131–36. They are "emboldened to express before your honours our most lamentable usage and distressed estate; whose entire faith unto God, loyalty to our sovereign, obedience to our governors, reverence to our superiors, innocency in all good conversation towards all men, cannot avail us for the safety of our lives, liberty, or goods, not even by her highness's royal laws, and the public charter of this land, from the violence and invasion of our adversaries, her majestys subjects, whose dealing with us your honours shall further understand, when we have briefly declared the true cause thereof unto you; which is this . . ." Again in conclusion: "In the mean time they prayed in the name of God, and our sovereign queen, for the present safety of their lives, the benefit and help of her majesty's laws, and of the public charter of the land; (to the observation and preservation whereof your honours have sworn;) namely, that we may be received unto bail, until we be by order of law convict of some crime, deserving bands . . ."

[81] Strype, *Annals*, Vol. IV, nos. xci and xcii, pp. 187–94. For further details on Francis and his brother, see Knappen, *Tudor Puritanism*, pp. 316–17.

law. 'Hence it is that the judges of this land are bound by law to administer justice and equity unto the poor subjects, notwithstanding that the prince's letters be directed to the contrary.' " [82]

Nicholas Fuller and "Liberty of the Subject" *versus* Monopolies

USHER, who has done much to rescue Nicholas Fuller from oblivion, does not carry his career back of 1604, except to note that he was already known to the commissioners as counselor for the Puritans.[83] But, as we have seen, among these was no less notable a client than Cartwright, and in 1602, Fuller was also one of the counsel for Allen in the famous case of monopolies (*Darcy v. Allen*). Whether Allen was a Puritan does not appear, but like the issue over ecclesiastical jurisdiction, this case involved the "prerogative" and "liberty of the subject." Furthermore, Fuller used some of the same arguments, indeed, the very phrases he was to employ in the better known "speech" or tract of 1607.

Darcy v. Allen involved liberty of the subject in the sense of liberty to engage in any trade or occupation and, in Fuller's arguments at least, liberty of recreation. Unlike the medieval privileges granted to boroughs and guilds, the monopolies of the Tudor period were manufacturing rather than commercial privileges and were not controlled by the crown.[84] "The patentee applied for the grant, and having got it was left free to act under the powers conferred by it." Abuses appeared when to persons who had introduced nothing new into the country were granted "all kinds of commercial privileges, oppressive powers to enforce these privileges, and dispensations from the existing law." In James' reign the powers of patentees to proceed against "interlopers" were to constitute an additional grievance, another infringement on common-law procedure and its safeguards, but the immediate issue in 1602 was rather the economic one of freedom of occupation.

Opposition to monopolies was voiced in parliament in 1597 and again in 1601 when a bill was introduced and extensively debated. A memorandum in the State Papers directed to "your Lordship" (Robert Cecil?)

[82] Examination before Fanshawe and Young, April 10, 1593, consisting of about fifteen items designed to incriminate him. The quotation is from Knappen, *Tudor Puritanism*, p. 312. (Cf. Pierce's account, p. 425.) Several petitions and depositions from other Barrowists in the early 1590's are quoted by Burrage, *Early English Dissenters*, but none of these cites Magna Carta.

[83] "Nicholas Fuller: a forgotten exponent of English liberty," *American Historical Review*, 12:743–60; *Reconstruction*, II, 134–54; and more briefly, *Rise and Fall*, Chap. VII. "He was a barrister of standing and a member of Gray's Inn. He was one of the lawyers with whom the Puritan leaders had long been in the habit of consulting; and he had already conducted cases for the ministers and their friends in the common law courts." *Reconstruction*, II, 136–37.

[84] "The essence of these grants of industrial monopoly licences was this: In return for the introduction of a manufacturing process, formerly unknown in this country, the introducer was granted a monopoly of using that process for a specified length of time. The aim was to introduce into this country 'those industries the products of which had hitherto figured most prominently on the lists of imports.' " Holdsworth, IV, 345.

perhaps submitted about this time, asks "To Leave to the Judgment of the Common Lawe disarmed of her Maties protection all such Monopolies, privileges and grants as are allreddy put in practise to the preiudice of every particular Subiect of this Lande; being of no better strength then her Maties prerogative and that contrarie to the greate Charter of England." [85] It was accounted a diplomatic triumph for the queen when she secured the abandonment of the bill on the promise "to leave the validity of the patent to the judgment of the common law." The opportunity for such a test case came when Darcy, patentee for the sole importation and sale of playing cards, sued Allen, a haberdasher of London, for infringing his patent. [86] The case was argued for the patentee, and hence indirectly for the crown, by Altham, Fleming, solicitor, and Coke, attorney general, and for Allen by Dyer, Croke, Dodderidge, and Fuller.[87]

The case was important enough to attract three reporters, Coke, Moore, and Noy. Sir Edward's account has the fullest summary (*Eleventh Report*) of the main arguments on both sides and the judgment in which Popham, C. J. and the whole court resolved in line with counsel for the defendant "that the said grant to the plaintiff of the sole making of cards within the Realm, was utterly void, and this for two reasons: (1) That this is a monopoly, and against the common law; (2) That it is against various acts of Parliament." [88] Moore's report is interesting for Dodderidge's arguments: his emphasis on the rule that the validity of patents be tested by law; his observations on the constitutional significance of the case (*Et Dodderidge dit que le case fuit tender concernant le prerogative de Prince et liberty del subject*); and his admission that some patents are justifiable, among these *que le Roy poit prohibiter commerce & traffique ove forraigners & ceo est prove per Magna charta cap. 30,* an anticipation

[85] *State Papers,* 12 276 fol. 97 (calendared among undated items, c. 1600). This is the last of three items: the first, that three of the privy council issue a general pardon under the great seal; second, to dispense with penal laws "such as shall appeare . . . to tende rather to the endangering of good men and the advantage of the worser sorte then to any publike good of the realm." These pardons to be ratified and these lawes abrogated by act of parliament when the same shall next be called. Then follow "Reasons that may induce her Matie to yeald unto the granting hereof," and "the good that will ensue hereof."

[86] Darcy brought an *action on the case* against Allen. The latter demurred, and the court upheld the demurrer, though it was admitted that a monopoly patent might be defensible on certain grounds. (Cf. Holdsworth, IV, 350–53.)

[87] Though Coke's *Eleventh Report* contains the statement, "And this case was argued at the bar by Doderidge, Fuller, Fleming, Solicitor, and Cooke, Attorney General, on the part of the Pl' and by Croke, G. Altham, and Tanfield on the part of the Def'," which puts Fuller and Dodderidge on the wrong side.

[88] (1) Que ceo est monopoly, et enconter le comon Ley. (2) Que ceo est enconter divers acts de Parliament.

Against the common law for four reasons: (1) All trades which keep people busy and support them and their families, and serve the queen when need be are profitable for the public weal, so the grant to have the sole making is against the common law, and the benefit and liberty of the subject. And "with this accords Fortescue in Laudibus Legum Angliae capitulo 26." Such a charter of monopoly against freedom of trade and traffic is against divers acts of parliament (*9 E. 3 cap. 1 & cap. 2. 25 E. 3 ca. 2*). "Vide Magna Charta ca. 18; 27 E. 3. ca. 11 &c." Coke, *Reports,* XI, 84–88.

of the use of this chapter of the Charter by the proponents of impositions later on.[89]

Noy gives what purports to be the arguments of Fuller quoted *in toto*. Although Noy is not one of the most reliable of the reporters, Holdsworth does not hesitate to accept this as Fuller's, and certainly it is quite characteristic, anticipating in many respects the better known "speech" of 1607. Noteworthy are the comments on the prerogative and liberty of the subject, the coronation oath, the quoting of Bracton, the passage beginning "The law knoweth no commandment but by writ," the Puritan touch ("we are now the house of God and the people of God" and the quoting of scriptural "law"), the emphasis on the law and the judges as arbiters, and finally the citing of the Great Charter as a defense of "liberty of the subject." To be sure, it seems a bit incongruous to find a Puritan defending the right to play cards, but the "reign of the saints" was still far off!

First it is not to be confessed, that the Queen may by letters patents without Parliament restrain all card-playing, which I will prove by reason, use, and by intent of statutes.

For this is true without any contradiction, that no man can continue alwaies in labour, alwaies in reading, or alwaies in meditation, but he must have reasonable recreation, and all persons cannot take recreation abroad, for some be sick, weak, or impotent, that need refreshing, some seasons are such, as that there is no recreation abroad, and in these times, and to these persons to make restraint is wrong.

For as Mr. Solicitor said, that the benefit of government was not that the subjects should live safely only, but tute vivere, pacifice vivere, honeste vivere, & jucunde vivere. And the law in ages past alloweth as much: for Cicero saith, that lex est vinculum civitatis, fundamentum libertatis, & sons aequitatis; and how can it be said that freemen should according to the Statute of Magna Charta, use libertatibus & liberis consuetudinibus suis, when Mr. Darcy hath a patent to restrain cards, another to restrain tennis play, another hawking and hunting, &c. Is not this to make freemen bondmen? And if the Queen cannot to maintain her war, take from her subject 12 d. but by Parliament, much lesse may she take moderate recreation from all subjects, which hath continued so long and is so universal in every country, city, town and household, but to punish the abuse is necessary: for common-weals are not made for Kings, but Kings for common-weals. (Magn. Car. c. 29. 25 E. 3 c. 8.) [90]

<hr />

[89] Moore, *Reports*, p. 672.

[90] Moore's report (p. 674) has ónly this on Fuller: "Fuller que argue e contra, insist sur le liberty des subjects en le use de lour trade quel il semble ne poit estre toll ne restraine per patent le Roy." Then brief arguments and names of cases cited. Coke does not indicate Fuller's arguments separately, but sums up the arguments which Fuller was answering: "As to the first question, it was argued on the part of the pl' that the said grant of the sole making of cards within the Realm was good for 3 reasons." Playing cards are an article of vanity, not of necessary use, a wasting of time, patrimonies, and substance; the queen has the prerogative to prescribe moderation in matters of recreation and pleasure; as she may suppress completely for abuse or deceit, surely she may regulate.

PART III. THE EARLY STUART PERIOD

❧ CHAPTER IX ❧

Scholarship and Controversy Intensify

You that have been
Ever at home, yet have all countries seen,
And, like a compass keeping one foot still
Upon your centre, do your circle fill
Of general knowledge; watched men, manners too,
Heard what times past have said, seen what ours do.

(BEN JONSON ON SELDEN)

ELIZABETH'S successor was well-received at first. It was not yet apparent how the personality and polity of James Stuart were to jar the nice balance of crown and parliament, prerogative and common law—the *dominium politicum et regale* of Fortescue, "that golden mediocritie" of Lambarde, or "our estate and pollicie exquisitlie planted and established in great wisdome," as Morice puts it. Trevelyan, with his usual felicity, has described how

The first of these four Stuarts, who have left their indelible negative impression upon England, ushered in the tragedy of King and people with a pageant of royal progress from Berwick to London, which then excited to ecstasies the loyalty and curiosity of a simple nation, and has since, in the reflex light of all that followed, became a theme for the irony of historians. For a month of spring weather James rode south. The land seemed bursting into bud to welcome him, growing greener each day as the ever increasing train of courtiers wound slowly down out of the north country into the midland valleys; through shouting market-places where the masque of welcome and the corporation with its address were lost in the press of men; by ancient steeples rocking with the clash of bells; along open roads hedged with countrymen who had come on pilgrimage across whole counties.[1]

One trait of the new ruler was to be significant. Himself no mean scholar and writer, James loved learned conversation and argument, whether at the dinner table [2] or in the more formal debates such as the

---

[1] *England under the Stuarts*, p. 74.
[2] "A well-known trait of James I was his fondness for learned conversation, especially at the dinner table. As a boy in Scotland he was accustomed to the reading and discussion of

Hampton Court conference and the later disputations between the civilians and the common lawyers over High Commission. All this helped to make possible the defining of positions on both sides, the veritable war of words, precedents, documents, which in the end was to be more lasting than the actual civil wars of the 1640's.

With Robert Cecil and others of the old queen's officials still in office, there was a certain continuity in "statecraft" and traditions for a time at least. "Antiquaries" as diverse as John Selden, Ferdinando Pulton, and Doctor Cowell added their contributions to the history and interpretation of the Great Charter. Its clauses came ever more readily to the minds and lips of lawyer members of the Commons. It was cited as the "ancientest" of laws regulating purveyance. The issue over impositions led to rival interpretations of chapter 30. The Puritan lawyers, undaunted by their earlier failures, continued to labor in parliament and courts, keeping faith in chapter 29 until their cause was raised from obscurity by a more powerful advocate of the common law, Sir Edward Coke. At the same time in the courts there were being made various practical applications of the magic formula, *per legem terrae,* but as yet safely remote from intrusion on the "prerogative" of council and crown.

In all this it is not easy to fix upon any satisfactory approach, either chronological or logical, or to be sure of cause and effect, action and interaction of one episode with another. Let us then, in this chapter and the next, rather arbitrarily, take as a unit the first twelve years of James' reign; our goal, Francis Ashley's reading in his Inn of Court in 1616, on Magna Carta chapter 29; and as our cue, his explanation of his choice of that "statute," "the finding how obvious this law was upon all occasions."

Handbooks, Reports, and Antiquarian Lore

INTEREST in editing of the statutes continued and was stimulated by the plans of James and Bacon for some fundamental revision or codification of the law. Ferdinando Pulton, now well along in years, was still active and produced two works of distinction in James' reign. He followed his *Penal Statutes* with the even more practical and successful *Kalendar or*

the Scriptures during his meals; and later in England he loved to gather round him at table his favorite divines and a few selected laymen whose learning and dispositions were such as he could appreciate. 'It was the custom of King James,' wrote Francis Osborne, '. . . to discourse during meals with the chaplain that said grace or other divines concerning some point of controversy in philosophy.' 'That King's table was a trial of wits,' wrote Hacket. 'The reading of some books before him was very frequent while he was at his repast. Otherwise he collected knowledge by variety of questions which he carved out to the capacity of those about him. . . . He was ever in chase after some disputable doubts which he would wind and turn about with the most stabbing objections that ever I heard. And was as pleasant and fellow-like in all those discourses as with his huntsmen in the field.' " D. H. Willson, "James I had his Literary Assistants," *Huntington Library Quarterly,* Vol. VIII, no. 1, p. 35.

Table of all the statutes from Magna Carta (9 Henry 3) to 3 Jacobi.[3] Most notable was his last work, the *Statutes at Large*. Holdsworth, following the record commissioners, characterizes this as an advance on all earlier editions of the statutes, although defective in certain respects.[4] Pulton himself described in a letter to Sir Robert Cotton his plan for his project and also secured Cotton's help in getting access to the records, promising to respect the opinion of "some of the learned Judges" as to the exclusion of certain statutes which might seem dangerous to publish.[5]

The sympathies of most modern writers of seventeenth-century constitutional history are so strongly with the common lawyers that the virtues and talents of their opponents are apt to be overlooked. Unquestionably there were many distinguished and sound scholars among the civilians. Their services were valued not only in the ecclesiastical courts but in Chancery and Admiralty, and the privy council might employ them in nice points of diplomacy and international law. They were elected to membership in the Commons where as specialists in certain fields they served on committees. The lists of committee members in the *Commons Journals* for James' reign not infrequently contain the item "all the civilians in the House."

After Cosin's death in 1597, Doctor John Cowell figures most prominently. At Cambridge he was regius professor of civil law, master of Trinity Hall, and vice-chancellor. He was a member of *Doctors' Com-*

---

[3] First published in 1616, this had gone through five editions by 1618: *A Kalendar, or Table, comprehending the effect of all the statutes that have been made and put in print, beginning with Magna Carta, enacted 9 H. 3, and proceeding one by one until the end of the session of Parliament 3 R. Jacobi: showing which are repealed, expired, altered, worn out of use, made for particular persons or places, and which are general in force or use. Whereunto is annexed an Abridgment of all the Statutes whereof the whole or any part is in general force or use.* It thus consists of two parts: (1) the statutes arranged chronologically; (2) their contents summarized under alphabetical headings.

[4] The promised text of the statutes in the original language was not included; the edition was the work of a private scholar, not official; the selection of the items to be included depended on Pulton's opinion as to which were in force and which repealed; some, but not all, were copied from and examined with the original records.

[5] " 'Mr. Pulton seeketh to print the statutes at large. He promiseth to set down which statutes or parts of statutes are repealed, and which, being at first but temporary, are since expired and void because not revived. This hath already done in his late abridgment. . . . Now, to make this new book at large saleable, he promiseth to print the statutes first in the language the same were first written; and such as were originally in French or Latin, he will translate and print likewise in English. When the statute has no title he will devise a title out of the body, and print it with the statute. He will set down which statutes are warranted by the record and which not. He will correct the printed book by the record. For which purpose he requireth free access at all times to the records in the Tower.' Bowyer and Elsyng, the keepers of the Tower Records, threw some difficulties in his way; but their opposition was over-ruled by the intervention of Cotton, and in 1611 the requisite access was granted by the Council. Pulton tells us that he had compared as many as possible of the old statutes 'as be chiefly in use' with the original records; and that the rest he had corrected by the help of such books as the Register of Writs, the old and new Natura Brevium, the books of Entries, the Books of Years, and the Terms of the law." Holdsworth, IV, 309–10. Pulton's letter to Cotton, dated March 8, 1612, is in Cotton MSS Julius C III, fol. 78 (310).

mons and vicar-general to Bancroft. He had drafted for the archbishop the complaints of the clergy against prohibitions and had an important part in the preparation of the canons of 1604. It was also at Bancroft's suggestion that he wrote and published (1605) his *Institutiones Juris Anglicani*, which followed the exact arrangement of Justinian's *Institutes*. Its object was "to promote the union of Scotland and England by pointing out the resemblance between the common law and the civil law; to give the student of the common law some knowledge of the general principles of law; and to show the students of the civil law that if they would study the common law, they would improve their knowledge of both laws and cease to be regarded as mere children in legal knowledge." [6]

Cowell's better known *Interpreter or Booke containing the signification of words* resulted from the *Institutiones*. In writing the latter Cowell was "obliged to consider the meaning of the principal technical terms of English law," and added a glossary. Then he set himself to supply "a law dictionary of the kind familiar to the civilians." [7] Usher suggests a rather different and more propagandist motive when he describes the *Interpreter* as "a little dictionary of political terms in which he sought to set before the English reading public such definitions of the various ordinary phrases then in use, as would in his opinion more nearly accord with precedent and history than did the views which were espoused both by the Puritans and the common lawyers." [8] First published in 1607, the dictionary was reissued in expurgated form in 1637 and had passed through seven editions by 1727. When the animus against it had died down, it became and long remained the standard dictionary of English law. In Holdsworth's estimate "the book is clearly expressed and many of the definitions are happy—Blackstone copied from it his definition of the Prerogative, with only a slight (though a very crucial) verbal alteration."

The *Interpreter* is best known through its condemnation by the Commons, which has made famous (or rather infamous) the definitions of *parliament, prerogative,* and *subsidy*.[9] Yet many of Doctor Cowell's definitions ought to have satisfied even the common lawyers. He drew on all their most noted "treatisours" directly or indirectly for his data: Glanvill, Bracton, Britton, Fleta, Fortescue, Fitzherbert, Staunford, Crompton,

[6] Holdsworth, V, 20–21. The full title: *Institutiones Juris Anglicani ad methodum et seriem institutionum Imperialium compositae et digestae.*

[7] Holdsworth, V, 22.

[8] Usher, *Reconstruction*, II, 211.

[9] According to Usher, the attorney general suggested at a conference of the two houses that the definitions given for these three words offered "the only legal pretext for proceeding against the author, inasmuch as they could punish only for contempt or breach of privilege. The Commons accepted his advice with ill grace, for apparently they had set their hearts upon censuring the views expressed in the book in regard to the common law which they felt had been attacked." *Reconstruction*, II, 248–49.

Lambarde, Kitchin, and Manwood. There is even a rather nice "defini-
tioñ" of Magna Carta, though for this, at least for any description of the
document *in toto*, its origin and character, the learned doctor had to draw
on the chroniclers Holinshed and Polydore Vergil rather than the lawyers.

Magna Charta, called in English the great charter, is a charter containing
a number of lawes ordained the ninth yeare of *Henry* the third, and confirmed by *Edward* the first. The reason why it was tearmed *Magna Charta*,
was either for that it conteined the summe of all the written lawes in England, or else that there was another Charter called the Charter of the Forest,
established with it, which in quantitie was the lesser of the two. I reade in
Holinshed, that King *John* to appease his Barons, yelded to lawes or articles
of government much like to this great Charter, but wee nowe have noe
auncienter writen lawe, then this, which was thought to be so beneficall to
the subiect, and a lawe of so great equitie in comparison of those, which were
formerly in use, that K. *Henry* the third was thought but hardly to yeld
unto it, and that to have the fifteenth peny of all the moveable goods both of
the spiritualtie and temporaltie throughout his realme. *Holinshed* in *Henry*
the third. And though this Charter consist not of above 37 chapters or lawes:
yet is it of such extent as all the lawe wee have, is thought in some sort to
depend of it. *Polydorus* and *Holinshed, ubi supra.*[10]

Most of us are used to consulting law dictionaries in which old Latin
and French terms are listed and "Englished." Such in fact was Rastell's
Termes of the Lawe.[11] For the readers he had in mind, Doctor Cowell
did the reverse, listing terms to be found in the current English versions
of the statutes and in the treatises, followed by a Latin or French
synonym, a brief definition or a longer exposition, and a citing of the
pertinent authorities. Besides *"Magna Carta"* there are some eighteen
words or phrases from fourteen of its chapters so treated, as well as two
from the Forest Charter. For instance,

Contenement (*contenementum*) seemeth to be the free hould land, which
lyeth to a mans tenement or dwelling house, that is in his owne occupation.
For in *magna charta ca.* 14. you have these words: A free man shall not be
amerced for a small fault, but after the quantity of the fault: and for a great
fault, after the maner thereof, saving to him his contenement or free hould.
And a merchant likewise shalbe amerced saving to him his merchandise: and
any other villaine then owers, shalbe amerced saving his wainage, if he take

<hr />

[10] This and the following quotations are from the 1607 edition by titles (the book is not
paged).

[11] Rastell's *The Exposicions of the termes of the lawes of England, with divers proper rules
and principles of the lawe, as well out of the bookes of Master Littleton as of other.* This is
quite different from Cowell's. The first edition, 1529, is entirely in French, both terms and
definitions, and as the subtitle (*out of the bookes of Master Littleton*) suggests, is largely
concerned with tenure, land laws, and so on. Later editions have parallel columns in French
and English "for the benefit of young students." Only the very late editions, 1598, for
instance, include a few old English terms such as *heriot, sok, infangethief.* Rastell does not
cite treatises, and only rarely a statute. There is no reference whatever to Magna Carta.

him to our mercy. And Bracton, li. 3. tracta. 2. ca. 1 hath these words: . . .
quod miles & liber homo amerciabitur . . .

Common plees (communia placita) is the kings Court now held in *Westminster* hall, but auncient time moveable, as appeareth by the Statute called
Magna charta, cap. 11. as also *anno* 2 *Ed.* 3. *cap.* 11. and *Pupilla oculi, parte*
5. *cap.* 22.

This is followed by a brief history of the origin of the central courts,
based on "M. Givin in the Preface to his readings." [12]

The term *Peeres (pares)* is not related to Magna Carta but has the
characteristic twofold definition used by others (Lambarde and Selden):
"plurally those that are empaneled in an Enquest," but "most notoriously
used for those that be of the Nobilitie of the Realme . . ." [13]

In view of its early unpopularity and prompt suppression, it is unlikely
that the *Interpreter* played much part in the publicizing of the Charter,
but the dictionary affords further evidence of how Cowell's "sources"—
the various treatises on the common law—were sprinkled through with
fragments of the Charter, as it were, like raisins in a cake!

It is interesting to compare with this the elaborate entry in Spelman's
Glossary, a veritable panygeric and historical treatise under the title
*Diatriba de Magna Charta: Ejus nomen, origo, deliquum respiratio, dis-
crimen multiplex, & confirmatio numerosa.*[14] The Glossary is more properly an encyclopedia, the *Interpreter* a dictionary. Still, the difference in
the treatment of Magna Carta reflects a generation of Charter history.

[12] More briefly he does well with the etymology of *escheate*, merely quotes the Charter on
open lawe, and gives up on the mysterious *haberiecte*: "*Escheate (Eschaeta)* commeth of the
French (*escheoir i.e. cadere, accidere, excidere*) . . . any lands or other profits that fall to a
Lord within his maner by way of forfeiture, or the death of his tenent, dying without heir
generall or especiall, or leaving his heire within age or unmarried, *Magna chart, ca.* 31. *Fitzh.
nat. br.* fol. 143. T &c. *Open Lawe (Lex manifesta, Lex apparens)* is making of Lawe which
by *Magna charta ca.* 28. Bayliffes may not put men unto upon theire owne bare assertions,
except they have witnesses to prove their imputation. *Haberiects (Hauberietus pannus)* Magn.
chart. ca. 25 & pupilla oculi parte 5 cap. 22 (no definition attempted)."

[13] "*Peeres (pares)* commeth of the French (*per,* i. *par*) it signifieth in our common lawe,
plurally those, that are empaneled in an Enquest, upon any man for the convicting and clear-
ing him of any offence for the which he is called in question. And the reason thereof is,
because the course and custome of our nation is, to trie every man in this case by his equals.
West. prim. cap. 6. *anno* 3 *Ed. prim.* So Kitchin useth it fol. 78 in these wordes: *Mais si le
amerciament soit affirre per pares . . .* But this word is most notoriously used for those
that be of the Nobilitie of the Realme, and Lords of the Parlament, and so is it used in *Stawnf.
pl. of the Crowne, lib.* 3. *cap. Triall per les peeres,* being the first."

[14] Henrico Spelmanno, *Glossarium Archaiologicum,* London 1664, edited by Dugdale,
with a preface to Edward Hyde. Vol. I (A–L) was published in 1626. Spelman continued
collecting materials for the second until 1638. He died in 1641.

The article on Magna Carta covers more than five folio pages in double columns (pp.
374–79). The first paragraph will serve to suggest the tone and style: "Magna Charta.
Augistissimum Anglicarum libertatum diploma, & sacra anchora: condita prout extat hodie
in libris juridicis, anno 9. Henrici 3. & confirmata denuo annis 25 & 28 Edouardi 1. Inter
Regni constitutiones (quae Statuta nuncupamus) prima est, majorumque nostrorum opibus
& fortunis saepius comparata; sudore autem & cruore plurimo aegre adeo conservata, ut
Erythream dixeris, & sanguineam.

"For the first time a first-rate scholar and historian, who was also a first-rate lawyer, applied his talents to the criticism and elucidation of the sources of English law." Thus does Holdsworth characterize the worth of John Selden, quoting Maitland's statement that "History involves comparison, and the English lawyer who knew nothing or cared nothing for any system but his own hardly came in sight of the idea of legal history." Continues Holdsworth:

None of the other eminent scholars and historians of that day possessed quite the same combination of qualities and range of interests that he possessed. . . . And these talents and this industry were applied in accordance with the most modern canons of historical scholarship. *None but the best evidence was sufficient. The documents were made to tell their own tale in their own way,* with as little intrusion as possible of the author's own point of view. . . . No doubt his experience as a lawyer and a member of Parliament helped him to avoid "the sterile part of antiquity." It gave him the power, not only *to discern in the remote past what were the ideas and institutions which influenced the age in which he lived, but also to give a convincing account of their original contents and form, and of the manner of their development.* He was able to do this effectively because, besides being a profound common lawyer, he had also a profound knowledge of other systems of law . . .[15]

It was only natural then that it should have been John Selden who was the first to really analyze the text of John's Charter as given in Matthew Paris, and to compare it with the standard 9 Henry III of the statutes. *England's Epinomis,* one of the historical tracts published as early as 1610 while the author was still a student of but two years standing in his Inn of Court, goes back of and also supplements Lambarde's collection of Anglo-Saxon Laws.[16] For the material of chapter 10, "King John and his Grand Charter," Selden uses Matthew Paris (Parker's transcript and the printed copy of the same), "divers old written copies of the common and usual Magna Charta," and "our printed volumes of old acts of parliament." His historical account of the granting of the Charter and its reissue by Henry III is characteristic: a bit stilted in style but clear cut and precise, marked by a masterly choice of words, with neither errors nor exaggeration:

After the transaction of that great controversy betwixt the king and Inno-

---

[15] Holdsworth, V, 411. Italics mine.

[16] *England's Epinomis,* London, 1610. An English version of his *Jani Facies Altera* (early British, Saxon, and Norse customs) with additions. In chap. vi, "Henry Beauclerc restored and invented common liberties," Selden includes the coronation charter, the Latin text from Matthew Paris, characterizing the copies aptly as "charters of state-amendment—sent into every county." Chap. viii—"Henry Fitz l'Empres, and his Clarendon constitutions restored to themselves, and purged from the faults where with they have been published"—also contains the *Assize of Clarendon* with critical interpolations. Chap. ix—"Richard Coeur de Lion," —contains the *capitula placitorum coronae,* and an assise of the Forest.

cent III. bishop of Rome, publick commandment was given for observation and maintenance of the laws of *Henry* his great grandfather. . . .

But notwithstanding those general forms of reformation, a more serious and recapitulated was desired by the whole baronage. A grand council is appointed at *Paul's* in *London,* and there, by *Stephen* archbishop of *Canterbury* is produced a copy of Henry Beauclerc's free charter, (which is before expressed) and the same delivered to the chief clerk there, to be openly read and pronounced. As soon as the barons heard it, was an uniform consent, that maintenance and assertion of those liberties should rest, as of more dear account, in their martial resolutions, than blood or life. Nay in short space after, mutual combination by solemn oath taken upon the altar was made among them, that their band of fealty dissolved (for so they deemed *John's* government had occasioned) their swords should compel him to enseal their demands. To that place, which now is called the *Temples* (then the *new-Temple*) where the king lay in warlike order, they go to execute their designs; he binding himself with an interlocutory sentence and giving caution of future satisfaction, takes day until *Easter* following but all was no less delusory than dilatory: nor any thing done with a face of composition, until the appointed meeting of the king and barons (whose part hourly encreased) in *Renimid,* alias *Runingmede,* near *Stanes in Middlesex* . . . where an instrument of publick liberties, through mediation of what is above all law, necessity, was, as you shall hear it speak, sealed and delivered to the baronage.

Then follows his comparison of the two texts, and in conclusion:

The concluding date of these granted franchises, and restored laws, John Stow saith, was Given by our hand in Runingmede, betwixt Stanes and Windsor, the xvi of June, the xvii of our reign: unto which all the whole realm was sworn. But the fluxile nature of this deceitful prince, aided by pope *Innocent* III. and his nuncio Pandulph, soon loosed that kind of royal faith and promise; as quick were the barons (they by oath had bound themselves to constrain him by arms, if their expectations in his future carriage were frustrate) and ready to, and did, revolt. Death of the king prevented their projects, which for this purpose in the ix year of the succeeding Henry FitzJohn (as the first page of our printed volumes of old acts of parliament give to every reader testimony) were with some ease attained, and by his posterity, as the main freedom of the English commonwealth, have been since more than thirty times, by the true authority of the state, in their high court confirmed.

Selden's comparison is quite perfect for the two texts he had before him: the 9 Henry III of the printed statutes and the hybrid "John's Charter" of Matthew Paris. He quotes entire John's preamble and the *Imprimis concessisse Deo* and *concessimus* clauses, and comments that

these premisses are in the grand charter of Henry III commonly published in our printed statutes, nor in any word of moment is there a difference found betwixt this of *John* and that of *Henry,* until the prohibition of disparagement in marriage of young wards; which thus commandeth . . .

This reveals his method, to present the document itself "as you shall hear it speak." [17] As Paris' hybrid includes the 1225 variations within chapters, Selden is correct when he says, for instance, that from the tenth "unto the xviiith chapter of Henry's charter from hence, are in both almost the same syllables"; and again for the last chapters—"what follows in either is the same as well in words as sense." What was new to his readers then (those familiar with the printed 9 Henry III) were the chapters of the 1215 text which he quotes *in toto,* 10, 11, 12, 14, 15, 27, and 42. His comments are few. Even chapters 12 and 14 elicit no remark, though later, when need required, it was Selden who first publicized them in the parliament of 1628.

In others of Selden's learned works published later in the reign, occasional passages interpreting clauses of Magna Carta may be briefly noted. In his treatise of the *Disposition or Administration of Interstates Goods* Selden finds in chapter 27 (John's text) the basis of clerical control in this field. It originated "by virtue of that *per virum ecclesiae,* which was, I think the textual ground of right of committing of administration by the clergy." [18] He attributes its inclusion in 1215 to the influence of the great prelates—"the care of souls being the chiefest part of their common pretences for increase of their power and greatness." Rather oddly he pictures them as being of the king's party: "And it is to be understood that the greatest prelates of the clergy of that time, as Canterbury, London, Winchester, Pandulphus the pope's nuncio, the master of the Temple, and divers other bishops were on the king's part when that of king John was granted."

The *Priviledge of the Baronage,* drawn up by order of the House of Lords, 1621, has a passage in connection with trial by peers which is interesting for Selden's matter-of-fact insistence that Magna Carta, like other statutes, is to be interpreted "as it is clearly taken in continual practice, and in the books, according to the known use of the legal proceedings,

[17] After indicating variations in chapters 6, 7, and 8, he equates Henry III's chapters 10–18 with John's 16–26, and 19–30 with 28–41; 31, 33, and 34 respectively with 43, 46, and 54; and the new ones, 32, 35, 36, 37, with the same which Paris includes. Of course Selden does not thus number the chapters of John's Charter (as I have done for convenience), which are not numbered in Paris' text. He usually treats additional clauses as part of the preceding chapter of 9 Henry III. For an analysis of the texts of the Charter as given in Wendover and Paris, see Appendix F.

[18] Chap. iii, "In whom after the time of king John." It is this chapter of Magna Carta, he thinks, that is intended in one of Cardinal Ottobon's legatines, and in a constitution of Archbishop Stratford. In chaps. i and ii he has discussed procedure in the Saxon and Norman period, and concludes that the clergy had nothing to do with it before Magna Carta. He minimizes omission of the chapter from Henry III's Charter (chap. iv). He interprets ca. 18 of 9 Henry III by comparison with Bracton and evidence from the close rolls.

and not by literal interpretation of words." [19] Similarly in chapter ix, "Amerciaments of a spiritual or temporal baron," he points out that practice has modified the rule of the Charter, the justices now "supplying the room of peers" there specified.[20]

In his edition of Fortescue, the chapter on jurors (xxvi), Selden supplies an elaborate note, significant for its translation and exposition of Magna Carta chapter 29. As to the clause *nec super eum ibimus nec super eum mittemus,* he says, "I would English it thus, *Neither will we enter on his possession nor commit him* (for in that place of the Charter of 17. of K[ing] John by which this was made, it is *nec eum in carcere mittemus,* perhaps it should be *carcerem,* as the language requires) . . ." It was Selden who was to use these words—"commit him to prison"—to strengthen the force of this clause in the interest of the five knights shortly. As to the other phrases, he equates *judicium parium* with "legal judgment of his peers or men of his condition, that is by jury." Quite unique for those days, he narrows the *per legem terrae* to wager of law, concluding, "And *Ley gager* and a Jury are the two trials, as I suppose, there thought on."

In these same years Sir Edward Coke was educating the reading public through his reports published in eleven parts, 1600–15. These appeared so rapidly and opportunely that, as a critic put it in one instance, "While the arguments were even warm in the Judges Mouths, the Case was likewise warm in the Press." [21] Though they were popular with bench and bar, the author evidently intended them for a wider audience; as he put it, the truths thus revealed would help to insure to every subject his patrimony—"the auntient & excellent Lawes of England are the birthright and the most auntient and best inheritance that the subiects of this realm have, for by them he inioyeth not only his inheritance and goods in peace and quietness, but his life and his most deare Countrey in safety . . ." [22]

The reports vary, depending upon the nature of the cases.[23] Holdsworth

---

[19] "Trial by Peers." He is discussing Magna Carta ca. 29 and 25 Edward III together here (Pt. II, chap. ix). For these passages, see Appendix H.

[20] In another connection (Pt. II, chap. i) he writes as follows: "All oaths are either promissory or assertatory; the first being that which binds to a future performance of trust; the second, that which is taken for discovery of a past or present truth. The first kind, they as occasion required, used, in taking the oath of all barons for maintenance of the great charter, and the like under king John and Henry III."

[21] The *Magdalen College Case, Observations on the Lord Coke's Reports,* attributed to Ellesmere, to the effect that "the report of the judgment is not warranted by the record, or by the authority alleged," and that cases were published while writs of error were pending.

[22] Coke, *Reports,* V, "To the Reader."

[23] "Sometimes for instance, in the cases which he reports on points of practice, he makes the case a mere text for a summary of the law on the subject. . . . Sometimes he collects a number of cases bearing upon a particular topic, e.g., on copyhold, usury, by-laws, executions, slander, and appeals and indictments; and then he gives a summary account of the decisions

reminds us that at the time when Coke wrote, "there was no agreement as to the form which a law report should take. Every law reporter had a distinct style of his own." Coke's "skill as a reporter and the benefits which his Reports had conferred on the law were publicly recognized by the court of Star Chamber in 1613 . . .." Even such able opponents as Bacon and Ellesmere "could not, though encouraged by the king, find any serious errors in his Reports, except in cases of a political or semi-political character." To be sure, in Bacon's apt phrase, there was in his reports too much of himself (*de proprio*). The author of the *Observations* voices the same criticism in harsher terms, accusing Coke of "scattering or sowing his own conceits almost in every case, by taking occasion (though not offered) to range and expatiate upon bye matters."

Sometimes Magna Carta figures only in these "conceits," incidental asides suggested by some aspect of the case, or in one of the characteristic interpolations beginning *Nota Lecteur.*[24] Again the report seems to indicate that the Charter was actually cited by bench or bar. Cases pertinent to these studies are described below in their appropriate place. Here something may be said of the mere prefaces of the reports, which contain much antiquarian lore. These prefaces, first a Latin version addressed *ad lectorem* (*docto lectori; Deo, patriae, tibi,* and so forth), are followed by an Englished "to the Reader." They range from three to twenty-three pages, and vary as much as do the reports.

Coke's eulogies of the common law and Tudor government are no more enthusiastic or aptly phrased than those of his predecessors quoted above.[25] The *Second Report* is novel in its gracious tribute to the old queen. If Whitgift, many years before, had reminded her that she was sworn to observe the Great Charter, her attorney general now credits her with having done so.

For of all Lawes (I speake of humaine) these are most equall and most certaine, and of greatest antiquitie, and least delaie, and most beneficiall and easie to be observed . . . If the beautie of other Countries be faded and wasted

in each case, and the reasons for them. When the case deals with an important principle of law, he often gives the pleadings at length, a summary of the arguments on both sides, and the decision, together with the reasons for it. . . . To his mind the ideal report was a summary account of the effect of all that was said on both sides, 'beginning with the objections and concluding with the judgment of the court.' " Holdsworth, V, 462–63, 477–78.

24 For examples of these "conceits," introducing cas. 10, 11, 14 and 26, see Appendix H.

25 The preface to the *Fourth Report* (on the "making, correcting, digesting, expounding, learning, and observing" of the laws) uses the figure already employed by Lambarde—the laws are the "Sweet and fruitful flowers of his Crowne." As to the form of government, says Coke, one must take into consideration the type of government—whether monarchicall, aristocraticall, or democraticall. In England: "Our kingdome is a *Monarchie Successive* by inherent Birthright, of all others the most absolute and perfect forme of governement, excluding Interregnum, and with it infinite inconveniences; The Maxime of the Common law being, That the King of England never dieth, which is true in respect of the ever during, and never dying politique capacitie."

wyth bloudie warres, thank God for the admirable peace wherein this Realme hath long flourished under the due administration of these Lawes: If thou readest of the tyranny of other Nations, wherein powerfull will and pleasure standes for Law and Reason, and where upon conceit of mislike, men are sodenly poysoned, or otherwise murthered, and never called to aunswere; Praise God for the Justice of thy gracious Soveraygne, who (to the worldes admiration), governeth her people by Gods goodnesse in peace and prosperity by these Lawes, and punisheth not the greatest offendor, no, though his offence be *crimen laese Maiestatis,* Treason against her sacred person, but by the iust and equall proceedings of Law.

If in other kingdomes, the Lawes seeme to governe: But the Judges had rather misconster Law, and do iniustice, then displease the kings humour, whereof the Poet speaketh; *Ad libitum Regis, sonuit sententia Legis*: Blesse God for *Queene Elizabeth,* whose continuall charge to her Justices agreeable with her auncient Lawes, is, that for no commaundement under the great or privie Seale, writtes or letters, common right be disturbed or delayed. And if any such commaundement (upon untrue surmises) should come, that the Justices of her Lawes should not therefore cease to doe right in any point: And thys agreeth with the auncient Law of England, declared by the great Charter, and spoken in the person of the King; *Nulli vendemus, nulli negabimus, aut differemus Iusticiam vel Rectum.*

The *Third Report* (1602) eulogizes the ancient records. These "for that they contain great and hidden treasure, are faithfully and safely kept (as they well deserve) in the kinges treasurie. And yet not so kept but that any subiect may for his necessarie use and benefit have accesse thereunto, which was the auncient lawe of England, and so declared by an acte of Parliament in 46 E. 3. in these wordes . . ." This, the subject's right to search records as based on 46 Edward III, was actually cited by the Commons in 1610 to justify their search of records in the Tower in connection with impositions. Very likely Roger Owen who suggested it was inspired by Coke's preface. It is in the *Sixth Report* (1607) that Coke expatiates on the "ancientness" of the law as described by Fortescue.[26] Perhaps this was the "key" to some of the historical errors scattered through his works.

The *Eighth Report* (1611) bears on its title page what came to be Coke's oft-quoted favorite: *Magna charta cap. 29: Nulli vendemus, nulli negabimus aut differemus iusticiam aut rectum.* Defending his theory of the "antiquitie and excellencie of our laws of England," he traces

---

[26] He is answering "some of another profession" who are not persuaded that the common laws are as ancient as he has alleged in an earlier report. He praises Fortescue for his "profound knowledge in the Law," and "being also an excellent Antiquarie." The passage in question (ca. 17 of the *De Laudibus*) relates how England was inhabited successively by Britons, Romans, Saxons, Danes, Normans, yet governed continuously by the same customs. If they had not been very good surely some of these kings would have changed them, "especially the Romanes, who did iudge all the rest of the world by their own Lawes."

from the confirmation of the good laws of King Edward by William the Conqueror the charters of Henry I, Stephen, Henry II, John, and Henry III, playing up the phrases indicating that each is a confirmation of old laws and liberties. His account of John's Charter and its identity with Henry III's, based on Matthew Paris, adds nothing to what we have already seen from other pens but it must have carried added weight from Coke's pen. Here appears his explanation of the name, which he was to inject into many a parliamentary speech later—"the great charter of the liberties of England, so called of the effect, because they make free," and also his reckoning of the confirmations—"by the wisdome and authoritie of 30 severall parliaments and above." Since the "ancientness" of the laws is under discussion, it is here naturally that Sir Edward presents his views on the origin of jury trial and of the Court of Common Pleas, denying that the former came in with William the Conqueror and carrying the latter far back of the traditional Magna Carta chapter 11.

". . . But yet before I take my leave of these Historians, I must incounter some of them in two maine points. First, that the trial by Iuries of 12 men (which is one of the invincible arguments of the antiquitie of the common laws, being only appropriated to them) was not instituted by the powerful wil of a Conqueror, as some of them peremptorily affirme they were. The 2. that the Court of common pleas was not erected after the statut of Magna Charta (which was made in the 9. yere of king H. 3.) contrary to that which others do hold . . ."

The arguments which follow are not entirely illogical, and suggest the problems which documentary evidence posed for these early scholars.[27]

All this ignores that prince of antiquaries, Sir Robert Cotton, descendant of Robert Bruce and hence cousin of King James I, and one of the founders of the Society of Antiquaries. His house in Old Palace Yard by Thames-side, Westminster, was the rendezvous of scholars, poets, lawyers, and parliament men—Lambarde, Camden, Ben Jonson, Selden, John Eliot, and many others. In the House of Commons he was indefatigable in serving on committees, especially when search

---

[27] For instance, he argues correctly that the Bench must have existed before 9 Henry III, for "in the same great Charter, and in the next Chapter saving one, the Court of common pleas is expressly named; *Assises of Darreine presentment shall alwaies bee. taken before the Iustices of the Bench*, and .no man doubteth but Iusticiarii de Banco are Iustices of the Common pleas." Furthermore, Martin de Pateshull was made a justice of the Bench in 1 Henry III.

Of course he is impressed with the testimony of the Year Books: "And in an. 10. Ed. 4. fo. 53 all the Iudges of England did affirme that the Chauncery, Kings Bench, Common place, and Eschequer, be all the kings Courts, and have bene time out of memory of man; so as no man knoweth which of them is the most auncient."

Thus far his evidence is not bad, but, misled by one of his sources, he confuses the words of the *later confirmation* of a charter of Henry I to an abbot with the terms of the *original* charter. Further, a case in Plowden shows fines levied before the Conquest—*ergo*, the implication seems to be that the court existed then too!

for precedents was involved. A diffident speaker, his collections served to furnish materials to his friends for their speeches rather than for his own. "In later days he was wont to say to his intimates 'I myself have the smallest share in myself.'"[28] On the whole in the reign of James I he was as often employed by king and council as by his parliamentary colleagues. It was in the early years of Charles I, following the studied slight visited on him at the coronation through Buckingham's influence, that he became closely identified with leaders of the opposition. Prynne accords him first place in his list of sponsors of the Petition of Right, "the learnedest lawyers and antiquaries England ever bred." On the whole, contributions from his library seem to have come rather from the chronicles than the law books—historical episodes of "evil" ministers such as figured in the speeches of his friend Eliot and others in the sessions of 1625 and 1626 or in his own *Henry III* [29]—not cases and precedents from "our books."

To be sure, many a reader will recall that the Cottonian Library contained two of the original parchment copies of John's Charter, now known as the British Museum copies. These came into Sir Robert's hands only after the Petition of Right had become law, one a gift of Mr. Humphrey Wyems, January 1629, the other sent by Sir Edward Dering, Warden of Dover Castle, in May 1630.[30] The establishment of these facts deprives us of the picturesque legend recorded by Disraeli (*Curiosities of Literature*) to the effect that Sir Robert discovered one of the originals by accident in a London tailor's shop! Possibly Cotton had the pleasure

[28] Edward Edwards, *Lives of the Founders of the British Museum*, p. 53.

[29] "A Short View of the Long Raign of King Henry the third" (also called "The Troublesome Life . . . of Henry III") first appeared in print February 13, 1627. It was published again in 1641 and twice in 1642, once separately and once with Hayward's Henry IV.

It contains one reference to Magna Carta, based on Màtthew Paris: *"Dies datur fuit in tres septimanas ut interim Rex excessuos corrigeret, & magnates voluntati ejus obtemperarent.*

"At which day upon new grant of the great Charter, admittance to his Councell of some persons elected by the Commons, and promise to rely upon his Natives, and not Strangers [*sic*]; for advise hereafter; they spare him such a pittance as must tie him to their Devotion, for a new supply."

[30] McKechnie, *Magna Carta*, pp. 194–96. Cotton's first copy is the *"British Museum Magna Carta, number two*—cited as 'Cotton, Augustus, II. 106.' The early history of this document is unknown, but it came into the possession of Mr. Humphrey Wyems, and by him was presented to Sir Robert Cotton on 1st January, 1628-9. Unlike the other Cottonian copy, this one is happily in an excellent state of preservation . . ."

Cotton's second copy is the *"British Museum Magna Carta, number one*—formally cited as 'Cotton, Charters XIII 31A.'" The recent history of this document, which is possibly the original copy delivered to the barons of the Cinque Portes, is well known. It was discovered in the seventeenth century, among the archives of Dover Castle, by the Warden, Sir Edward Dering, and by him presented to Sir Robert Cotton. (Dering's letter, dated May 10, 1630, is in B. M. Cotton, Julius C III, fol. 191.)

In 1628 Selden was still relying on Matthew's Paris' text of John's Charter and even in the *ship-money case* in 1637 St. John, quoting John's ca. 12, says "though it be not Printed, yet it is of Record and Inrolled in the Red Book of the Chequer, and cited in Matthew Paris Pag. 343."

of showing the first to his friends before the library was sealed in November 1629, but apparently no current use was made of it. Cotton died May 6, 1631; "he would tell me they had broken his heart that had locked up his library from him." It was restored to his son, Sir Thomas, a few years later.

James' First Parliament

IN SUCCESSIVE sessions of James' first parliament (1604–11) the Great Charter figured incidentally in connection with attempts to regulate purveyance and to effect the union with Scotland; more prominently in the debates on impositions, 1610, and the bill for confirmation of "a branche of Magna Carta" (chapter 29), persistently introduced by the Puritans session after session.

It was only natural that it should have been cited in the debates on purveyance, for any recourse to the printed statutes under this title would disclose the long series beginning with Magna Carta chapters 19 and 21. For instance, Sir Francis Bacon, reporting to the House (April 30, 1604) on the committee's delivery of a petition to the king, shows how he had artfully urged on James the example of his predecessors: "It was no Part of their Thoughts to abridge his Majesty's Prerogative: It was only their Desire to have the old Laws confirmed. . . . Since Magna Charta, in H. III's Time, a Part of every King's Glory to make a Law against Purveyors. In E. III's Time, Ten Laws . . .[31]

Bowyer's Diary gives us an account of the conference between Lords and Commons, February 14, 1606, on which occasion Mr. John Hare, clerk of the Court of Wards, "attacked purveyors in a rather violent manner which offended the Lords." It was probably the chapters on purveyance which suggested the Charter, though it is the *nulli negabimus* clause which he actually quotes:

The matter which now wee complain of is the oppression by theis purveiors: which is three-fold: viz. in Cartakinge; secondly in Purveing for victualles woods etc. and lastlie in takings for the stable; The thing which wee desier is only execucion of such good lawes as now stande in force in that behalfe. We are not ignorant that his Majestie is swoorne to Magna Charta, which saieth *Nulli negabimus, nulli vendemus Justiciam aut rectum*; and we know and are assured by his gracious message . . . yet wee finde that if anie man gaine saie theis ungodlie people the purveiors in their uniust commaundes, such person is straight waie sent for and punished by imprisonment and otherwise by the officers of the Greene Cloath contrary to Law, and Justice . . .[32]

[31] *C. J.* I, 193b. Similarly in debate, March 5, 1606, Magna Carta seems to be taken as a sort of landmark in the origin and history of the practice. Various speakers contribute information as to what purveyance was in early days. *Ibid.*, pp. 277b, 278a.

[32] Bowyer, p. 40, and editor's comment, p. 38, note 3.

In the debate on March 11 "whether to proceed by composition with the king" (substituting some other source of revenue) or by some bill "further limiting purveiors," one speaker asserted that the "certaine price" set by Magna Carta for carriage alone "is woorth the compounding for." [33]

The lengthy proceedings in connection with the proposed union with Scotland evoked a few apt citations of the Charter. Again we are indebted to Bowyer for the report from the committee for the conference touching naturalization. Here Sandys equates the Charter with the Englishman's heritage:

A second Point debated by the Committees was whether the word Naturalization, shall be used in the Conference, for that the Lawyers thought a new Word, and therefore not determinable in seaven yeares. 2. The word is too Generall. 3. That word maketh a Man Inheritable unto Magna Charta, and then not limitted, nor to be restrained; And therefore it was rather thought fitt we should use the word (Enable).[34]

Again "Mr. Sollicitor" (Bacon), in a long speech urging acceptance of what the commissioners for the union had proposed, used chapters of Magna Carta to convince his hearers that the royal prerogative could be restrained.[35]

More significant, in view of its growing importance, was the citing of chapter 29 in connection with another aspect of the union, the bill for abolishing hostile laws, and more particularly "the remaundinge offenders interchangeable." Following a long report by Bacon [36] on the proceedings of the committee on the bill, Sir Roger Owen spoke vigorously against remanding:

The questions among us at the committee weare twoo.

1. First whether as the Lawe now standeth a man having committed felonie or treason in Scotland and being returned and abiding in England may

---

[33] *Ibid.*, pp. 75–76. Cf. *C. J.* I, 283a, for the clerk's version of the speech. Also a rather obscure allusion, *ibid.*, p. 297b.

[34] Bowyer, p. 219. This continues, "It was hereunto answered, That in the Civill Lawe, the word is used, and it is more fitt to use the Generall Word, then to expresse it particularly. Then by One of the Kings Councell it was said, That the word should never be put into the Act; so it was agreed, That in the Conference, the word should be used with Protestation etc." More on this whole matter, Bowyer, pp. 218–28.

[35] "I am cleere of Opinion, That the Kings Prerogative may be bound by an Act of Parliament. . . ."

"The Kings Prerogative was, That if a Baron died holding of the King, the King might seise his Relief as he pleased, and this was taken from him by the Statute of Magna Charta cap. 2. The King might have cutt downe the Timber of any Person to build Shipps But by the Statute of Magna Charta C. 21 this is taken away. Many of these I could enumerate, but it hath beene said, What Course shall wee take? By disabling the Persons? If so, the King will dispence with it; I say no, the King cannot; For where a disability is laid on the Person by Act of Parliament, the King cannot dispence with all." *Ibid.*, p. 286. A somewhat similar conception seems to be implied in a rather obscure statement, *C. J.* I, 185a.

[36] Bowyer, pp. 300–4.

by such commissions as are already sent foorth be remanded and sent back into Scotland:

2. And secondlie what remedy: To the first I saie negatively, and first not by the Canon Lawe . . . Then not by the Civill Lawe . . . (the laws of Artois, Picardy, and Spain not parallel examples) Againe this cannot be by commen law for felony committed in Scotland is no offence here: *et econverso.*

Likewise for 12 other reasons:

1. It is against Magna carta: *Nullus etc. capiatur imprisonetur etc. aut utlagetur aut exuletur aut aliquo modo destruatur nec super eum ibimus, nec super eum mittemus nisi per legale iudicium parium suorum,* etc.[37]

The use of certain clauses of the Charter in resisting financial claims by the crown in this period are commonplaces: chapter 30 in *Bate's case* and in the debates on impositions in succeeding parliaments; chapters 12 and 14 of John's text some years later in the famous case of *ship-money.* Chapter 29 was used in connection with forced loans and monopolies, not as a defense against these practices but against arbitrary arrests in enforcing them. Pecuniary exactions by the Tudors had been "neither frequent nor severe." There were loans from richer subjects (all those of Elizabeth's reign were repaid); rearrangements of tariffs to promote English trade; and some requirements in ships and ship-money for defense against the great enemy, Spain. The Stuarts used all of these devices, but for less popular purposes and with a sweeping application which boded ill for the powers of parliament and liberty of the subject.

Bate's case is too famous to need much exposition here. It clearly revealed that "the principle that the crown cannot impose new customs duties without the consent of Parliament and the principle that the crown can make re-arrangements of the tariff to further the commercial interests of the subjects might easily conflict." [38] The government's policy in regard to the Levant Company was designed primarily to regulate the Venetian trade, and only secondarily to increase revenue.[39] But such could not be claimed for the new book of rates, 1608, in which revenue interests were obviously paramount, and which affected internal as well as foreign commodities, and which, as Holdsworth puts it, "fell within the *dicta* rather than the decision in the case." The Exchequer judges in *Bate's case* decided that the new imposition on currants which Bate had refused to pay was entirely legal. They argued for the king's absolute power, *salus*

---

[37] Six more of the twelve are listed, at which point Bowyer breaks off with "The other reasons I observed not." *Ibid.,* pp. 304–5.

[38] Holdsworth, VI, 43.

[39] When the Levant Company surrendered its charter and trade was again thrown open, the government, deprived of the four thousand pounds a year it had received from the company, reverted to impositions (such as had been formerly levied by the company itself against nonmembers).

populi, that aspect of the prerogative in the conduct of foreign affairs which included the power to admit, exclude, or discourage by impositions.[40] They also cited precedents from their own Exchequer records. The pleadings in *Bate's case* have not been handed down to us, and of the judgments, only those of Clarke and Fleming have been preserved. We have to rely on Clarke's judgment for an indication of the statutes and precedents "objected" by counsel for Bate.[41]

The original import of Magna Carta chapter 30, and of the fourteenth-century statutes which cite it, has been explained above, as well as the true character of the conflict occasioned by the royal concessions to aliens at the expense of native merchants.[42] The debates on impositions in the Commons in 1610 reveal how little these fourteenth-century economic issues were understood, but, as was so often the case, the historical evidence was not clear cut. On the one hand there were medieval statutes and precedents which seemed to indicate that while there had been old customs duties of pre-parliamentary origin, the king had gradually lost any powers he might originally have had to impose new duties or to increase old rates without consent of parliament. Counsel for Bate and the parliamentary lawyers in the 1610 debates naturally stressed the restraining clauses in the medieval statutes and precedents, and of course attributed to each a permanent binding effect on the crown. The crown lawyers stressed the pre-parliamentary customs such as the great custom on wool, woolfells and hides, emphasized not the restraining but the saving clauses in some medieval statutes, and ruled out others as not pertinent, or only temporary in effect.[43] Each side accused the other of specious arguments. Dodderidge answers what he calls "arguments of the lowest rank," that

[40] As per Clarke's arguments: he that can do more can do less—the ports all belong to the king, as is indicated by the writ *ne exeat regnum.* If he can prohibit persons, then goods; if goods absolutely, then goods on condition, that is, by paying imposts. State Trials, II, 382–94.

[41] "And now for Statutes. The statute of Magna Charta, cap. 30. which was objected, that thereby all merchants may have safe, &c. to buy and sell without ill tolnets; but there is a saving, viz. by the ancient and old customs. The statute of Articuli super chartas, cap. 2 hath a saving in the end of it, that the king or his counsel did not intend thereby to increase the antient prices [prises] due and accustomed. So are all the other statutes of purveyors. The statute of the 45 E. 3. cap 4 which hath been so much urged, that no new imposition shall be imposed upon woolfels, wooll, or leather, but only the custome and subsidie granted to the king; this extends only to the king himself, and shall not bind his successors; for it is a principal part of the crown of England, which the king cannot diminish. And the same king 24th of his raign granted divers exemptions to certain persons; and because it was in derogation of his state imperial, he himself recalled and annulled the same."

[42] See above, pp. 110–12.

[43] Fleming justifies the so-called *maltolte* "bought off," 25 Ed. I, on the grounds that if it had not been lawful, parliament would not have paid such a "big subsidy" to secure its relinquishment! Among "ancient precedents in this Court" Clarke cites the custom for a tun of wine and its increase from Edward I to Mary—"no act of Parliament gave this to the king." Fleming, C. B says: "To prove the power of the king by precedents of antiquitie in a case of this nature may be easily done, and if it were lawful in antient times it is lawful now, for the authoritie of the king is not diminished and the crown hath the same attributes that it then had."

is, "many witty Inferences." Hakewill accuses the crown lawyers of "arguments of inference and presumption."

Although chapter 30 and its fourteenth-century confirmations were inconclusive for the immediate issue, the debates of 1610 are noteworthy as the first in which a chapter of the Charter figures as a major "precedent," and the Charter's origin, history, and fundamental character are publicized. This was an occasion on which both the search for and the exposition of the precedents were undertaken very seriously and methodically, and were even justified by "a precedent for searching precedents," "a copie of an Act of parliament 46 Ed: 3" produced by Sir Roger Owen, "that a subiect may have free accesse to recordes uppon any occasion."

Upon motion made that Mr. Speaker by direction and warrant of the house should require the Keeper of the records in the Tower and the Exchequer to give accesse to such of the house as should be ymploied to serch touching ymposicions And that such of the Kings Councill as had vouched Recordes in their Arguments for his Maty in the Exchequer in the informacion preferred against Bates for denying to pay imposicions should deliver notes of such Recordes as they had vouched, that they might be seene. It was obiected that Recordes are the Kings evidence, and that wee had not power to comaund the sight of them Whereuppon by Sr. Roger Owen was produced a copie of an Act of parliament 46 Ed: 3. That the subiect may have free accesse to recordes uppon any occasion But bycause it was not under the hand of any officer Therefore the reading therof was forborne and Mr. Lieutenant of the Tower and with him 2 or 3 more of the house appointed to examine the Copie and to certify the house in the afternoone following. The Committees report that it was a true copie and that they had seene the Recorde., Maii . . .

Hereuppon Committees are appointed to search, some in the Tower some in the Exchequer.

Because there was but one Copie of the Recordes, a time was appointed for the reading of them, when every one that list to be present might take notes of them, and it was ordered whether they were in French or Latine they shold be read in English, and afterwards the substance of them opened by him that read them, and when he found himselfe wearie, he should appointe some other to supplye that office, the appointed place was the parliament house, and to sitt as a Comittee without the Speaker. and which was accordinglie done. And by that meanes every one of the meanest capacity and learninge understood the effect of the Recordes before the Matter came to be debated of, which was resolved to be at a Comittee . . .[44]

[44] About May 1. Cott. MSS Titus F IV, "Proceedings in Parliament 1609 and 1610." Fols. 112–29 relate to the fourth session. A later entry relative to the search concludes: "The records brought in were delivered to the Clerke and it was reported from those that were employed to search the custome bookes in the Exchequer that no Imposicions could appear to them, though they had made diligent search, to have bene laid, save onelie by Q. Marye upon French Comodityes, Clothes and Wyne, and for French Comodities, they were taken onlie the first year of Q. Elizabeth 22. Jun: 1610 . . ." Cf. *Commons Debates, 1610,* p. 45.

The Charter is mentioned briefly in a number of speeches on both sides [45] but receives its fullest exposition in the speeches of Whitelocke and Hakewill. For the opposition, Hakewill's speech is the most convincing and masterly.[46] It was the one chosen to be printed in 1641. He admits that he accepted the judgment of 1606 at the time, but his recent search of records has led him to "stagger in his opinion"; some of the records urged were "untruly vouched and many misapplied." He wisely grants his opponents' contention that custom did not originate through parliament but is due at common law.[47] Even so, the common law leaves no doubt that it is a "duty certain," not an absolute power in the king to demand more or less:

That the common law of England, as also all other wise lawes in the world, delight in certainty, and abandon uncertainty, as the mother of all debate and confusion, than which nothing is more odious in law: — and therefore the rule is, *quod certum est retinendum est, quod incertum est dimittendum*; nay further, *quod incertum est nihil est.*[48]

It is under his third head, "whether or no hee (the king) bee not bound to the contrary by acts of parliament," that Hakewill accords the Great Charter its first public eulogy and history in the Commons since Morice's in 1593.

The first statute is in Magna Charta cap. 30 . . .

The statute, of which this is a branch, is the most ancient statute-law we have, wonne and sealed with the blood of our ancestors; so reverenced in former times, that it hath been by parliament provided, (25 E. 1, cap. 1, 2, 3, 4) that transcripts thereof should be sent to all the cathedrall churches of England there to remaine; that it should be twice every yeere publikely read before the people; that likewise twice every yeere there should be excommunication solemnly denounced to the breakers thereof; that all statutes and all judgments given against it shall be held as void; that it should be received and allowed as the common-law, by all such as have the administration of justice;

[45] For the crown: Sir Robert Hitcham and Yelverton; on the popular side, William Jones and Thomas Hedley. Hoskyns and Tate both note that Magna Carta goes back to King John. *Commons Debates, 1610, passim,* pp. 64–97.

[46] He develops three propositions: first, "whether custom were due to the king by the common law"; second, admitting the first, "whether it were a summe certain, not to be increased at the king's pleasure or otherwise"; third, if by the common law the king might have increased custom by his own will, by his absolute power without assent in parliament, "whether or no hee bee not bound to the contrary by acts of parliament." State Trials, II, 407–31, 455–70.

[47] The word *consuetudo* as used in ca. 30 of Magna Carta, he admits, means *custom,* but it is not the *custuma* of law Latin, but *consuetudo* which "implies an approved continuance without a known beginning." Furthermore, "in all cases where the common-law putteth the king to sustaine charge for the protection of the subject, it always yeeldeth him out of the thing protected some gaine towards the maintenance of the charge." In defining words such as *consuetudo, tolnetum, maltote,* Hakewill makes good use of the comparative method—the obvious meaning of such words in other contexts.

[48] He develops this point by showing that limitation either exists from the first, or is created by a "legal course," that is, by parliament, judges, or jury.

and it hath been no lesse than 29 times solemnly confirmed in parliament. I will, therefore with so much the more care, endeavor to free this law from all the objections that have been made against it.

His answer to the first "objection"—that chapter 30 applies to merchant strangers only—affords a characteristic example of the common lawyer's practice of putting a broad and "beneficial" construction upon a statute, but also reveals how little Hakewill knew of the mutually "beneficial" relations of a fourteenth-century king like Edward III and the alien merchants:

First, it is improbable, that the makers of the law should be more carefull to provide for the indemnity of merchant-strangers than of English; except perhaps they might imagine, that English merchants were already sufficiently provided for by the common-law. If that were their reason, as there could be no other that I can imagine, it doth as much maintaine my opinion, as if they had been conteined within the statute. Again, the words are generall, "all merchants"; and, "qui omnes dixerit, nullos excipit."
Besides, the statute is a beneficiall law; in which case particular and speciall words doe alwayes admit a generall extent: and therefore, to restraine generall words, as the objectors would, is against all reason and rule of law. As for the latter words, 'tis true, they doe indeed extend only to merchant-strangers; but the sense of the first sentence is perfect without this: and as long as no absurdity nor contradiction doth follow by interpreting the first words to extend to all merchants in generall, and the latter onely to merchant-strangers, the most ample and beneficiall construction is ever the best, as in all other statutes of this nature.

Though Hakewill can thus present an argument based merely on construction of the text of the Charter, it is the fourteenth-century interpretation implied in the statutes of 2 and 14 Edward III which he finds most convincing: "But this Objection is, in my opinion, cleerly removed by two statutes made by Edward 3, in declaration of this very clause." Further evidence of the influence of the printed statutes is to be found in his inclusion of the so-called statute *de tallagio non concedendo*. Like most of his contemporaries, he does not question that it is a statute but does a nice bit of critical work in attempting to date it, comparing printed and manuscript copies, official records, and the testimony of chronicles.[49]

---

[49] "Touching the time of the making of which there is great variety of opinion; for it is not, for ought I could ever learne, found any where upon record. Justice Rastall accounts it to have been made 51 of H. 3, and with him agrees an old manuscript which I have seen. It may well bee; for in one of the statutes you shall finde a pardon to Humfrey earle of Boham earl of Hertford and Essex constable of England, and to Roger Bygott earle of Norfolke and Suffolk marshal of England, who both lived in that time. Thomas of Walsingham in his history of England saith it was made in the 25th yeere of Ed. 1. Hee reciteth the statute *de verbo in verbum* as it is in our printed bookes; otherwise I should have thought he had meant another statute against impositions made indeede 25 E. 1, and found upon the records of that

As to Magna Carta itself, he points out, though it is the first recorded statute, "the first parliament was not kept 9 H. 3. though it be the first in our books." His account of the antiquity of parliament is based on Lambarde ("Mr. Lambert," as contemporaries called him) and gives evidence of the great influence of Lambarde's Latin translation of the Anglo-Saxon laws, suggested above.

Whitelocke's speech, delivered in the Commons on July 2, supplements Hakewill's. It is, he says, upon the first and fourth of the four "reasons" on which he grounds his opinion that he will put most emphasis: (1) "It is against the naturall frame and constitution of the policie of this kingdome, which is *jus publicum regni,* and so subverteth the fundamentall law of the realme, and induceth a new forme of state and government," and (4) "It is against the practice and action of our commonwealth, *contra morem majorum.*" His arguments, then, are most interesting for their broad implications. He clearly raises the question·"where the sovereigne power is in this kingdome," but it is too early for a theory of parliamentary sovereignty. Hakewill finds the *jura majestatis,* that sovereign power which is *potestas suprema,* a power that can control all other powers, and cannot be controlled but by itself, in *the king in parliament.*[50]

The speeches of Dodderidge and Bacon are typical of the defense for the crown. They naturally follow the lines of the judgment in *Bate's case,* plus attempts to explain away the additional precedents now cited by their opponents. Dodderidge pays due reverence to the Great Charter but finds in the *nisi publice antea prohibiti fuerint* clause a saving of the prerogative.[51] He disposes of 14 Edward III, chapter 2, by assuming that in the words "customes subsidies and other *proffittes* thereof," *profits* means impositions.

Bacon, in carrying the origin of customs back of acts of parliament

yeere. In our printed statutes at large, it is placed last of all the statutes of E. 1. Though there be some disagreement about the time of the making of this statute, yet they all agree the occasion to be the laying of a great imposition upon wool . . ."

[50] He answers objections against the statutes, "rather than to enforce the sense and meaning which is very plain and open." Like Hakewill, he uses 2 Ed. III and 14 Ed. III to prove extension of the provision to denizens. He defends 25 Ed. I, ca. 7, 34 Ed. I, ca. 1, and even the New Ordinances of which last he says "great wars have been raised against the credit of this law in the parliament house." He insists that it was approved by king and parliament, and that the searchers for precedents cannot find any evidence of its repeal! State Trials, II, 478–520, erroneously attributed to Yelverton.

[51] ". . . you will tell me this is directly contrary to the Statute of *Magna Carta,* against that Lawe which was written in Blood, and is of no lesse reverence with us then the Romayne Tables was with them. I aunswere no for by the Great Charter such Restraints may be in tyme of Peace, for that Lawe almost in the enterance conteyneth this restrictive Clause in the Lycence of free trade *nisi publice prohibiti fuerint,* which appeareth to be intended of peaceable tymes, since after in the same Chapter it provideth other wise what shalbe don in tyme of war . . ."

("and if by the common law, then what other means can be imagined of the commencement of it but by the king's imposing?"), makes the sage observation that "acts of parliament were not much stirring before the Great Charter, which was 9 Hen. 3." [52] As proved true in more than one instance, interest and scholarship combined to make of king's counsel the better historians!

It might be supposed that members of the Commons in the short and stormy session of the "Addled Parliament" would have had plenty of occasion to cite the Great Charter, but the sources are too meager to be conclusive. Besides the *Commons Journals,* there are only two brief diaries.[53] To be sure, the clerk records a long speech by Winwood on April 12, asking grant of supplies and reciting concessions the king will make in return, in which the secretary suggests "that his Majesty's Grace offered us, may be termed another Magna Charta." [54] The legality of certain patents was being questioned—"the patent for glasses" and the patent for the French Company. The latter had evidently been opposed on the grounds that it interfered with the freedom of trade granted by Magna Carta, for Serjeant Montague defends it as valid in spite of the Charter, that is, as a justifiable exception to the law.[55] Two years later Serjeant Ashley in his reading before the students of the Middle Temple objected to the same patent on the grounds to be used against a number of the patentees in the next parliament (1621): the patent to the French Company "allowing them to make ordinances and imprison those who infringe them is void, and such imprisonment is against this statute (Magna Carta)." [56]

Impositions were debated and denounced, and the king's right to impose denied in no uncertain terms by Sandys and others. No doubt much the same precedents were alleged as in the 1610 debates. In fact, we are told that the arguments on impositions were rehearsed for the new members, of which there were three hundred in this parliament. But we have no reports of proceedings in committee of the whole and subcommittees

---

[52] State Trials, II, 395–400.

[53] One of these is included in *Commons Debates,* 1621, VII, 628–56, App. C. This, say the editors, aside from the *Commons Journals* and the six-page account of this parliament in H.M.C. Portland MSS (9:132–39) "is the only record available of debates in 1614."

[54] In the ensuing debate Mr. Serjeant Mountague follows this cue: "Moveth to consider of the King's Offers of Grace, which before *Magna Charta*; for that but to declare, this to reform, the Common Law." *C. J.* I, 461b–462a.

[55] *C. J.* I, 469b, April 20: "Reporteth the Matter for the *French* Company. . . . Mr. Serjeant Mountague: That when heareth *London* named, he summoned.—Speaketh not for the Patent.—That in Acts negative or penal, a *Non-obstant* will dispense, notwithstanding a special Provision against a *Non obstante* . . . That many Things done against the Laws of the Kingdom. holden good. The Law of *Magna Charta* general for the Liberty of Merchants in trading. That 4 *Jac.* a Law made for *Exeter,* for a Patent for meritorious Causes, which crossed both the Law of 3 *Jac.* and of *Magna Charta.*"

[56] See below, p. 290.

such as the diaries give us for the sessions of 1621, 1624, and 1626. Furthermore, after the dissolution, James had the notes and papers of the members who were to have spoken at the conference with the Lords burned, probably to avoid publication.[57]

Fuller's case: Sir Edward Coke and Prohibitions

JUST as *Bate's case* crystallized the issue on impositions, so did *Fuller's case* in the next year that of prohibitions and the powers of High Commission. In the years since Morice's bills (1593) there had been some further defining of position on both sides. About 1598, for instance, a statement was framed by the bishops for consideration by the lords and judges. It consists of ten items, each questioning as an abuse some particular practice of the common-law courts in issuing prohibitions. It concludes with an effective statement of the duality and equality of the two jurisdictions, assuming the sanction of the ecclesiastical by certain statutes "and Magna Carta." [58] "Particularly touching the commission ecclesiastical" they say:

Seeing ecclesiastical authority is now as highly and truly vested in the prince, as is her temporal, whether her temporal authority should any more restrain her ecclesiastical, than her ecclesiastical should her temporal.

And for avoiding of confusion, and encroachment of jurisdictions distinct, why the prince's supreme ecclesiastical authority may not be as jealous over the temporal, as the temporal is over the ecclesiastical: seeing the common oath of obedience tieth all indifferently to the assistance and defence of all preeminences, united to the Crown.

The Charter did not figure in the Hampton Court conference, at least according to such reports as we have of it, although at the third session there was some discussion of the High Commission. James himself defended its procedure by oath ex officio.[59] In the next few years both the

[57] "All those also lawyers and gentlemen, who were assigned to parts in the conference propounded, and refused by the Lords, concerning impositions, were commanded to bring their papers thereabouts, which upon Thursday they brought to the Council chamber door at Whitehall and there burnt them; and were all commanded to stay in the town and not to depart without licence." The conclusion of a passage in *Holles Diary* describing what befell various members of the Commons after the dissolution of parliament, and the cause or "aggravation" therefore.

[58] "Since all the ecclesiastical jurisdiction is now united to the Crown, and from thence derived, whether may not the old prohibitions still retained be accounted offensive and dangerous; *viz.* whereby a severance is made of all ecclesiastical jurisdiction from the Crown, as not being the right thereof, nor belonging to it: and whereby it is *aliud forum regio foro*: yea though it be under the Great Seal of England authorized by Parliament. If in these, or some of these, not to be impeached, be indeed liberties and franchises of the Church, to the observation whereof by statute all the great officers and judges of the land are to be sworn; whether, by virtue of these statutes and Magna Charta, they ought not still to be holden as inviolable as ever they were, or ought to have been." Strype, *Whitgift*, II, 397–400.

[59] Usher, *Reconstruction*, Vol. I, Book II, Chap. II; *Rise and Fall*, pp. 164–66. The *Millenary Petition*, of course, contained a clause against the oath, but the Charter is not cited there, or in Bancroft's *Articuli Cleri* of 1605. Wilkins, *Concilia*, IV.

Puritans and the common lawyers attempted to influence James to restrict the authority of High Commission. The judges were making increasing use of prohibitions. The Puritans were instructed by their leaders to make use of them. Yet the judges had not taken such a united stand against High Commission as Coke attributed to them.[60]

The new canons, a veritable code of ecclesiastical law, drawn up by Convocation in 1604, "bound down the whole clergy and laity of England to perpetual uniformity." [61] The canons, 141 in number, are in print in Latin and English.[62] They have been exhaustively analyzed by Usher. The innovation, he says, "so far as there was any, lay in the definite and uncompromising form in which they were couched, in their inclusion in the Canon law of the Church, and in the provision of explicit penalties for their infringement." [63]

According to Gardiner these canons were offensive not only to the Puritans but to all the Commons, who resented the claim of the clergy to legislate for the whole people of England, "and especially their attempt to create punishable offences, a right which they held to be inherent in parliament alone." [64] Naturally, however, it was the Puritans who were most affected and hence most zealous in voicing opposition. January 1606 a bill, one of a group "for the better establishing of true religion," was introduced in the Commons and supported by Fuller, Morice, and others. On March 15 they "much urged" the cause of the deprived ministers, and on March 17 Fuller rehearsed grievances against High Commission. On May 3 the bill was read a third time and sent up to the Lords where it was rejected through the influence of the bishops. The Commons then had recourse to a petition. Though this was graciously received by the king, parliament was soon afterwards prorogued. The bill was revived in the next session (1606–1607), and again in 1610, and its substance embodied in the great petition of that year.[65]

What seems to be the text of this bill appears in the Cotton manuscripts

[60] At least, according to the unreliable *Thirteenth Report*, pp. 19, 26.

[61] Gardiner, I, 195.

[62] In Cardwell's *Synodalia*, Vol. I.

[63] These new penalties "fell upon every one from the bishop and the archdeacon to the humblest curate and ran the whole gamut of ecclesiastical retribution from excommunication to the smallest penance. The bishop who ordained unfit men, the minister who failed to read the service as directed in the Prayer Book, who preached in a private house or held a conventicle, the laymen who attended the conventicle, the ecclesiastical judge who connived at it, or who performed any act out of court, all felt the weight of the new Canons." For this and his analysis in various categories, see Usher, *Reconstruction*, Vol. I, Book II, Chap. V.

[64] Gardiner, *History of England*, I, 195, 291–92. Several of the Puritan tracts issued before the 1606 session (listed by Usher, *Reconstruction*, II, 115–16) had hinted that the canons were illegal because not confirmed by parliament, and "the point had been included among those sent out by the leaders in the summer and fall of 1604." But Usher thinks that until at least 1640 the canons of 1604 were considered "by the common law judges, as well as by the ecclesiastics and statesmen, to be legally binding upon both clergy and laity." *Ibid.*, pp. 116–17.

[65] Cf. Usher, *Reconstruction*, II, 246–50.

dated 3 Jacobi and headed "An Act for the due observance of the Great Charter." [66] It begins by reminding the king of the original grant by Henry III and the repeated confirmations by "your hyghnes roiall progenitors, kinges and queenes of this your highnes realme of England and pleadable in judgment before the kings Justices . . . as the common law of the realme in such sorte that if any judgment should be given contrarie to the tenor of the said great Charter that the same should be undon and holden for naught." That Fuller and his friends were the authors is suggested by the fact that the "precedents" are those used shortly after in Fuller's "tract."

The preamble rehearses "where by the great charter of England it is . . . graunted enacted and established." What follows is actually a paraphrase of 15 Edward III quoting Magna Carta chapter 29; the text of the great sentence of excommunication; Magna Carta chapter 1; and the second of the *six statutes!* [67] The enacting clauses are profuse: the framers have just about exhausted the dictionary in their zeal to cover all contingencies and avoid all loopholes, but stated simply, they ask a confirmation of "the said great charter, lawes, statutes and liberties yet in force." They signal out by number twenty-three of the canons of 1604 to be voided as having proved "hurtful to the prerogative roiall, onerous to the people, contrarient to the said great charter, and other lawes, statutes, liberties and free customes of this realme." All persons that have suffered from these canons, especially those prosecuted and the various ones penalized for their nonobservance, are to be "acquitted and absolved" therefrom. Severe penalties are prescribed for any attempt to make or put into effect in the future canons repugnant to the Great Charter and other laws of the land. Twenty-three of the canons, listed by number, are proscribed as unlawful.[68]

[66] Cotton MSS Cleopatra F II, fol. 191. Usher calls this the *petition* to James after rejection of the bill by the lords, 1606. If so, it nevertheless contains text of the bill verbatim.

[67] 25 Ed. III, though given as *xxvith* here. The sentence of excommunication of Charterbreakers is evidently taken from the English version of the early printed statutes (cf. Berthelet's edition, 1543, of the statutes Hen. III to Hen. VIII: "the sentence of curse gyven by the byshoppes agaynst the breakers of the greate charter"). Then follows a reminder that 25 Hen. VIII provided that constitutions, ordinances, canons provincial or synodal, prejudicial to the king's prerogative royal, repugnant to the laws and statutes of the realm, and onerous to the subjects are to be abolished and made void; only those found to be consonant with the law of God and the laws of the realm to stand in their full strength.

[68] They are 17, 36, 37, 49, 53, 58, 62, 63, 67, 77, 80, 90, 97, 98, 101, 107, 115, 127, 130, 131, 135, 139, 140. There is not as much correspondence as one might expect between these and Usher's categories, for instance, his "new canons," "aimed without doubt against the Puritans," and canons containing new penalties. It is easy to appreciate the Puritans' animus against some of them: the wearing of surplices; that ministers "not allowed preachers may not expound"; "no public opposition (that is, doctrinal debate or confutation) between preachers"; "inhibitions not to be granted factious appellants unless they first subscribe"; ministers and church wardens not to be sued for presenting; a national synod is the church representative and such synods "conclude as well the absent as the present"; and especially 36 and 37, governing subscription.

Fuller's was a test case arranged by the Puritans. He was the barrister expressly chosen to "impeach" the Commission before the common-law judges and to ask the latter to declare its practices illegal. Fuller had already gained notoriety and the disfavor of the king by his activities in parliament. He had favored delaying the subsidies, presented bills on pluralities and nonresidence among the clergy, defended in the House and in the courts the Puritan ministers deprived in 1605, opposed impositions, and most offensive to the king, opposed the union with Scotland in speeches bristling with uncomplimentary epithets on James' fellow countrymen.[69] Spedding even goes so far as to say that he "seems to have been recognized as leader of the opposition, in so far as that office can be said to have been recognized in those days." [70] In March 1607 he had acted as counsel for some twenty persons from Yorkshire committed for contempt on failing to appear in London to answer charges before the High Commission.

Usher has dealt so exhaustively with *Fuller's case* [71] that it may serve here to remind the reader that there was really a series of "cases" which brought Fuller successively before King's Bench, High Commission, and King's Bench again, involving respectively writs of habeas corpus for his clients imprisoned by High Commission,[72] and a writ of prohibition and a writ of habeas corpus for himself. The hearing on the habeas corpus took place before King's Bench, May 6 and June 13. In his argument Fuller "proceeded to prove to his own satisfaction at least that his clients must be released because the High Commission had no legal authority to imprison them." It is this "speech," in the revised form in which it was later published by Fuller's wife and friends, that is of main interest here.[73] This printed tract, thinks Usher, may be accepted as containing the

---

[69] Usher, "Nicholas Fuller, A Forgotten Exponent of English Liberty," in *American Historical Review*, 12:743–60; *Rise and Fall*, p. 169.

[70] Spedding, *Life and Letters*, III, 307.

[71] Usher, *Rise and Fall*, pp. 173–79; *Reconstruction*, Vol. II, Book III, Chap. V. Fuller was imprisoned by High Commission for slander and contempt in his arguments before King's Bench. The judges finally issued a *consultation* which authorized High Commission to proceed against him on grounds of heresy, schism, and error. Thus they did not uphold this particular prohibition, but made reservations as to their powers to issue prohibitions. In November Fuller appeared before the King's Bench on a habeas corpus. Usher thinks that he had intended to test the question of the right of High Commission to imprison at all, but lost courage. At the hearing only technicalities were discussed. The judges, satisfied that the return agreed with the consultation, remanded Fuller to prison. He paid his fine about December 30, and after some trouble about the form of his submission was released January 8, 1608.

[72] Thomas Ladd, merchant of Yarmouth, tried in ecclesiastical court at Norwich for attending a conventicle, was summoned to Lambeth on a charge of perjury, whereupon he refused to take the oath unless first allowed to read the answers he had made at Norwich. Richard Mansel, nonconformist minister, arrested as one of the movers of a petition to the House of Commons, which the government thought offensive, also refused to take the oath unless he was allowed to see the libel.

[73] "An Exact Copie of the Record of Nicholas Fullers case of Grayes Inne Esq. Termino Trin. Anno 5 Jaco. Regs." Lansd. MSS 1172, contains not the entire speech, but the passages

main legal contentions, the substance of what he said on May 6 and June 13, though "much expanded and embellished, and with many significant omissions." The main arguments are naturally the same as those used by Beale and Morice, and probably Fuller himself, fifteen years before. They are to the effect that before 1559 the bishops had not had power to fine and imprison, and that the statute of 1 Elizabeth did not expressly sanction any such powers as the commissioners had been exercising. As in his arguments in *Darcy v. Allen,* Fuller presents an attractive picture of a government based on the rule of law, and "a sweet harmony" between laws and people:

That the lawes of England are the high inheritance of the Realme, by which both the King and his subjects are directed. And that such grants, Charters, and Commissions, as tend to charge the body, lands, or goods of the subjects, otherwise than according to the due course of the lawes of the Realme, are not lawfull, or of force, unless the same Charters and Commissions doe receive life and strength from some Act of Parliament. Which lawes, by long continuance of time and good endeavor of many wise men, are so fitted to this people, and this people to them, as it doth make a sweete harmony in the government; all things being as readily obeyed on the one parte which are agreeing to law, as they are willingly commanded on the other parte according to law: every officer by the rule of the law, knowing the duties of their places . . .

Yet now that harmony is so disturbed by recent practices (such as use of the oath ex officio) that it seemed to him "that he was in a new world and other Common wealth." There is the same Puritan touch—"we being now the people of God the Jewes being cut off"; the quoting of Bracton, though not the same passage as in 1602; [74] and the same trenchant "the law admeasureth the king's prerogative." No wonder the common-law judges dealt leniently with the barrister who "did demand, why the exposition and construction of all statutes is left to the Iudges of the law, but for this cause, for that they are, and always have been thought the most carefull, iudicious and jealous preservers of the lawes of England."

It seems hardly a coincidence that Fuller uses the same three chapters of Magna Carta that Beale used, and in much the same way, as well as 42 Edward III. Not content with these printed statutes, he quotes from

which were to be used against him—the disrespectful statements about High Commission which were omitted from the printed version. The printed copy: *The Arguments of Master Nicholas Fuller in the case of Thomas Lad, and Richard Maunsell, his Clients. Wherein it is plainely proved, that the Ecclesiastical Commissioners have no power, by vertue of their Commission, to imprison, to put to the Oath Ex Officio, or to fine any of his Maiesties Subiects.* Imprinted 1607 (a tract of thirty-two pages, in B.M. copy bound with other tracts).

[74] "And as Bracton saith, *nihil aliud potest rex in terris, cum sit Dei minister et vicarius, quam quod de iure potest: quia illa potestas solius Dei est; potestas autem inuriae diaboli est, et non Dei; et cuius horum opera fecit rex, eius minister est.*"

the parliament rolls in the Tower, the petitions of 15 Edward III and 2 Henry IV.[75] It is in connection with his contention that it was no part of the ancient ecclesiastical jurisdiction "to imprison subiects, to fine them, or to force them to accuse themselves upon their own enforced oathes there being no accuser known," that he cites chapter 29 and its "inforcements," these parliamentary petitions, and the statute of Edward III:

For the lawes of England did so much regard and preserve the liberty of the subjects, as that none should be imprisoned, *nisi per legale iudicium parium suorum aut legem terrae,* as it is sayd in *Magna Charta, cap.* 29 which Charter by divers other statutes after, is confirmed with such strong inforcements in some of them as to make voyd such statutes as should be contrary to Magna Charta.

Fuller uses chapter 28 as Beale had used it—as forbidding use of an oath such as that ex officio. Chapter 14, however, he employs, not as a defense against depriving ministers of their benefices, but in connection with the heavy fines imposed by the High Commission on those twenty poor Yorkshire clients of his.[76] In his conclusion he reverts to his favorite figure of speech, showing "which kind of proceedings how farre they doe differ from the common lawe of England, which is the inheritance of the subjects, and what Iarres & harsh tunes they make in the sweet harmony thereof . . ."

As Usher concludes, "some of the best known sentences attributed to Chief Justice Coke might be almost a quotation from this pamphlet." But in 1606–1607 Coke had not yet taken the emphatic stand he was to take later. He had rather been acting as mediator between High Commission and King's Bench and had even received James' thanks for his efforts.[77] Nevertheless, although the Puritans won no considerable victories in these

---

[75] The first is the petition that resulted in the famous but short-lived "statute" of 15.Ed. III described above, pp. 83–84. The petition of 2 Hen. IV is quoted in the original French of the roll, but for the benefit of the reader stands in translation at the beginning of the tract.

[76] "Only so much as came under his owne view, he said, that, the last day of *Easter terme,* he moved at the *Exchequer* barre for 20 persons, his *Clients,* dwelling in *Yorkshyre;* whereof some, as they told him, were very poore, who were fined by the *Ecclesiastical Commissioners* for not appearing at their dayes appoynted, many of them to 30 pounds a peece, one only at ten, and all the rest at twenty a peece, which was not *salvo contenemento,* according to the statute of Magna Charta cap. 14."

Beale used the last clause, *Nulla ecclesiastica persona amercietur secundum quantitatem beneficii sui ecclesiastici* . . . Fuller the first, *Liber homo non amercietur pro parvo delicto nisi secundum modum ipsius delicti, et pro magno delicto* . . . *salvo contenemento suo* . . .

[77] Usher, *Reconstruction,* II, 210 and note 2. The dramatic altercation between James and Coke which Gardiner brings in here seems to belong to a later period. Coke's views at this time are probably represented in the conclusions of the twelve judges following Fuller's hearing on the habeas corpus. Coke, *Reports,* XII, 41–44, "Nicholas Fuller's Case." This consists of a series of conclusions to the effect that a consultation cannot be issued out of term time; it is for the common-law judges to interpret statutes and decide points of disputed jurisdiction, and it is also in their province to punish for slander, though High Commission may proceed for heresy and schism.

years, High Commission was soon to find in the Chief Justice of Common Pleas a much more formidable opponent than Fuller.

The next few years saw the issue of increasing numbers of writs of prohibition and an occasional habeas corpus. It cannot be denied that some of these prohibitions were issued for persons guilty of flagrant offenses (in spite of the common lawyers' denial that they were "enormous") and that their cumulative effect constituted a dangerous attack upon the whole authority and jurisdiction of High Commission. In the 1580's and 1590's the Puritan lawyers had questioned, not so much the jurisdiction of High Commission as its procedure by oath ex officio and its use of the penalties of fine and imprisonment. Coke questioned these powers but also tried to narrow its jurisdiction (1) by evaluating the degree of the offense—it might try all "heresies, errors, schisms, abuses, offences, contempts, and enormities whatsoever" only when any such was "enormous"; (2) by excluding entirely from its jurisdiction cases not specified in the statute of 1 Elizabeth even though conferred by letters patent (such as tithes, legacies, matrimony, adultery, and the like).[78] Wigmore and Mrs. Maguire have summarized those cases in which prohibitions were connected with use of the oath ex officio. Gardiner and Usher have described several of the most flagrant cases, those which particularly aroused the bishops and civilians, and indeed, the king himself. Usher alone, and that in only one of his three accounts, reveals the interesting fact that the "suggestions" upon which Coke's prohibitions were grounded included and quoted Magna Carta chapter 29. The inspiration may well have come from Fuller's recent arguments. These prohibitions were issued (1) for persons imprisoned by High Commission for refusal to take the oath; (2) for persons imprisoned as penalty after conviction; (3) for persons arrested in some allegedly arbitrary fashion by pursuivants and summoned out of their diocese.[79]

---

[78] This amounted to claiming that the letters patent issued for the past sixty years were illegal and that the king did not possess residual authority. A new court could be formed only by act of parliament. Usher suggests that in the tracts of 1590 and 1591 and perhaps a few of the individual petitions, these views of Coke's were anticipated.

[79] Usher, *Rise and Fall,* pp. 204–9; examples (though not grouped in these categories) from Stowe MSS 424, fols. 158–64, "probably a copy made for the Archbishop's use." On examination I find this manuscript (fourteen large folio pages) contains notes on seventeen cases, each dated, with caption as to the offense ("A wicked & lewd practise to dissolve a legall contract, & for being abettors of adulterie." "Simony, gross ignorance, insufficiency in a minister and other offences."). In some there is also a summary of the handling of the case in ecclesiastical court, and the order of the lay court (Coke's) for suspending sentence, releasing from prison, and so on.·

The grounds of the prohibitions, varying from five to nine items, all include chapter 29, listed first in the first three cases, and second or third in the others: "The Judge takeinge notice of the articles sendeth his prohibition upon these Suggestions. 1. That by the Statute of Magna Charta nullus liber homo caperetur aut imprisonaretur [*sic*] tc. nisi per legale Judicium parium suorum aut per legem terrae." The clerk's recordings become progressively sketchier and more illegible, and he settles down to a mere "That by Mag. Charta nullus liber homo tc."

Some of the cases in point are summarized in the unreliable but some-times useful *Twelfth* and *Thirteenth Reports*.[80] Coke's own account of *Withers and Heliers' case* is interesting for his strong assertion that the prohibition was, and properly so, grounded on Magna Carta.[81]

And though it be therein truely said that the Construcion of the statute of 31 Eliz: do belong to the Judges of the Realme yet was not that the ground of the prohibicion But upon the informacion of the statute of MAGNA CARTA and the whole matter above said therein comprised the Prohibicion was graunted as it ought to be by Lawe.

Usher has worked out in detail, with critical analysis and dating of the pertinent manuscript and printed sources, the series of conferences spon-sored by James in the years 1608–1611. Only those arguments which in-volve rival interpretations of Magna Carta need be noted here. There was little novelty beyond what had already been presented by Doctor Cosin and the "Treatisours" in Elizabeth's reign.

Hobart, in the spring of 1609,[82] answering the charge that the high com-missioners "inflicte punishments not warranted by law," rules out Magna Carta chapter 29 on the grounds that it is abrogated by later statutes:

And now lately in Mr. Fuller's Case uppon solleme argument in the Kings benche, it was adiudged that his Imprisonment by the High Commission was Lawfull. And therefor to alledge now the Statute of Magna Charta cap. 29 Nullus liber homo capiatur vel imprisonetur nisi per legale Iudicium parium suorum, vel per Legem terrae against this Imprisonment by the Highe Comission, is out of Season, because this latter Law abrogats the former and the Statutes are infinite that have given Imprisonment in sondry Cases synce that Statute of Magna Charta.[83]

Coke's formal written answer to Hobart presented in the fall of 1609 or spring of 1610 consisted of a preface exalting the common law,[84] and

---

[80] *Porter and Rochester's case*, M. 6 Jac. Coke, *Reports*, XIII, 5–9, and for the prohibition, Cott. MSS Cleopatra F II, fol. 434 (429).

Allan Ball's case. Ibid. XII, 49–50. Ball, arrested, had apparently resisted the pursuivant. Arrest by pursuivant before any answer or default made "will be against the Statute of Magna charta, and all the ancient Statutes, which see *Rastall, Title Accusation* . . ."

[81] "A declaration of the true grounds of the prohibitions to the High Com. with answers to the obiections made to the contrary." Cott. MSS Cleopatra F I, fols. 168–69.

[82] The first conference, November 1609, has been reconstructed by Usher ("James I and Sir Edward Coke," *English Historical Review*, 38:664–75). He thinks that in the *Twelfth Report*, 63–64, Coke condensed the substance of several meetings. The precedents, Magna Carta and certain of the *six statutes* which Fuller had used, may have been used in the con-ference, but here they look like notes added for reference, each prefaced by a *Vide*.

[83] "The grounds of the Prohibitions to the High Commission and the answers unto them," signed Henry Hobarte. Cott. MSS Cleopatra F I, fols. 128–35 (127–34).

[84] "A Preface to the Answers of the Judges of the Court of Comon Pleas unto the obiections and arguments made (on behalf of the Lord Archbishop of Canterbury) against Prohibicions." Cott. MSS Cleopatra F I, fols. 116–26. This goes so far as to maintain that the civil law has all these superiors, not only royal authority, but common law, acts of parliament, and customs of England!

"five treatises knit into one"—that is, an answer to each of the "five heades" used by his opponents.

In answering the civilians' claim that there should issue "no prohibicion out of the Comon place but upon suites dependinge there by original [writ]," Coke uses Magna Carta chapter 11 to substantiate for the Bench a sweeping jurisdiction over all common pleas. Since it "hath the immediate proper and naturall Jurisdiccion," it may issue prohibitions, prohibit usurpation on its jurisdiction, and punish contempt.[85]

The civilians seem to have had the last word for the time being.[86] May 20, 1611, in another debate before the king, there were presented in refutation of Coke's latest propositions, "arguments drawn up by the Archbishop." These maintain that "the kinge hath power in his owne person to heare and determine all kinde of causes when it shall so please his Majestie"; and that "the kinge hath authoritie to certifie both his Jurisdiccions and to reform the abuse of prohibicions." In repeating that "the Court of Comon Please ought not to awarde any Prohibition especially upon a Suggestion," Magna Carta chapter 11 is interpreted as limiting, not magnifying, the jurisdiction of the Bench. A refutation of eight various "suggestions" or grounds upon which prohibitions had been issued includes arguments similar to Cosin's: chapter 29 applies only to the proceedings of temporal judges in temporal causes, standing, as it does, *after* the sweeping confirmation of ecclesiastical liberties in chapter 1; furthermore (rather inconsistently), "law of the land" must apply to and reinforce the statute of 1 Elizabeth! [87]

The outcome of course was inconclusive. Puritans and lawyers had to wait for the Long Parliament to relieve them of High Commission. For the time being its most powerful opponent was silenced by Coke's dismissal in 1616. In 1611 James had issued a new commission in which he made two minor concessions, but the ex officio oath was retained, as was the power to suppress unlawful conventicles and to enforce penal laws against the Catholics.[88] Usher characterizes these letters patent of 1611 as

[85] Under the fourth head, "In what cases the King's Court of Comon pleas may graunt prohibicions." Cott. MSS Cleopatra F I, fols. 220–21 (209–10).

[86] Coke's answer dated Easter, 1611, to a petition signed by the most prominent civilians and presented to James, was later incorporated into his *Fourth Institute*, "Of Ecclesiastical Courts," of which pp. 324–35 treat "of the High Commission in Causes Ecclesiastical." This is a detailed exposition of the statute of 1 Eliz. to prove that it does not authorize the High Commission to fine and imprison, except in special cases—that is, where authorized by parliament. It concludes "And these were the resolutions of the whole Court of Common Pleas, Pasch. 9. Jacobi Regis, upon often conference and mature deliberation, and accordingly they proceeded."

[87] Cott. MSS Cleopatra F II, fols. 305–6 (298–99). Cf. "Copy of the information delivered to his Majesty by Mr. Serse his proctor, touching the many prohibitions sent to the High Commissioners Ecclesiasticall from the Court of Common Pleas, 1611." Lansd. MSS 161, no. 105.

[88] Tanner, *Constitutional Documents*, pp. 146–47. Coke and six other judges were placed on the new commission but declined to serve and "rejoiced that they did not sit by force of it."

"rather a statement of what the Commission had become than a remodeling of the Court, an express authorization rather than a radical change of its jurisdiction and practice." [89] Wigmore concludes that some restraint on use of the oath resulted from the conflicts of the years 1606–16.[90]

High Commission was only one of the prerogative courts with which Sir Edward came in conflict in these years. Although at the time of his dismissal James taxed him with hostility to Star Chamber, I have found little evidence of conflict here. Coke, as attorney general, had lodged informations before it and had served as judge there. One of the alleged virtues of his *Reports* was that they familiarized the common lawyers with the new ideas originating in this and other courts.[91] Even in his *Fourth Institute,* probably completed about 1628, he is no less laudatory of "the Honourable Court of Star Chamber" than was Lambarde in his *Archeion.*

It is the most honourable Court (our Parliament excepted) that is in the Christian world, both in respect of the judges of the Court and of their honourable proceeding to their just jurisdiction and the ancient and just orders of the Court. . . . And it is truly said, *Curia Camerae Stellatae, si vetustatem spectemus est antiquissima. si dignitatem, honoratissima.* This Court, the right institution and ancient orders thereof being observed, doth keep all England in quiet.[92]

Of course, Coke could not appropriately, and did not, use Magna Carta as a major "precedent" in all instances. Rival interpretations of recent statutes and letters patent (commissions) loomed large in some disputes.[93] In the dispute over the jurisdiction of the Council of Wales and the Marches which went on intermittently for several years, the main issue was whether the president and council "hath jurisdiction, according to his instructions, over the four shires, by the true construction of the statute of 34 H. VIII." [94] The privy council naturally supported the presi-

[89] For a detailed discussion of this and later commissions, see Usher, *Rise and Fall,* Chap. XI.

[90] In his *Evidence,* IV, 805–6, he concludes that what had been settled by 1616 "was (in effect) that the ecclesiastical Courts (including that of High Commission) could not as a matter of jurisdiction and procedure, put laymen to answer 'ex officio' to penal charges."

[91] Holdsworth, *Makers of English Law,* p. 128: "Thirdly, the information which his reports gave of the doings of the courts outside the sphere of the common law, such as the court of Chancery, the Star Chamber, and the Court of Admiralty, familiarized common lawyers with the new ideas originating in those courts, which were giving rise to new legal developments."

[92] *Fourth Institute,* chap. v.

[93] In line with the thesis he had developed in the conferences of 1611 and in the preface to his *Eighth Report,* published the same year, Coke may have issued prohibitions based on Magna Carta ca. 11 to prerogative courts encroaching on common pleas (as had his predecessors to the Court of Requests in the nineties), but I have not found such actual writs quoted in the sources examined.

[94] The four border shires of Hereford, Worcester, Shropshire, and Gloucestershire. This whole dispute is worked out in detail with the pertinent sources in Spedding, *Life and Letters,* III, 368–82. For the council, its history, and the turbulent areas it was set to govern, see Skeel, *The Council in the Marches of Wales,* chaps. iv, v.

dent and council with considerable help from Bacon who, as solicitor general, won the reputation of one that "had laboured much against the shires." On the other hand, King's Bench and Common Pleas encouraged and aided by prohibitions the local gentry of the four shires. Although the statute of 34 Henry VIII was most debated, evidently the common lawyers had urged that subjects within the four shires were deprived of the common law as assured by Magna Carta, for Bacon retorted:

And whereas the freedom and birthright of the subject is so much urged, your Honour may be pleased to consider whether in all *Magna Charta* there be any greater benefit than this—to have near and cheap justice: and whether the Attorneys of the Courts of Common Law inhabiting those shires, from whom all this business springeth, do seek their own or the people's good, when they would draw them an hundred miles and make them spend twenty nobles and a twelvemonth's time to recover forty shillings: and whether as the administration of justice in particular men's causes is necessarily delegated to men of law, so the provincial and equal distribution thereof doth not in all countries belong unto men of state, as a chief branch of the King's prerogative; who as *Pater patriae,* and the source of all laws, will ever be more wise for his people than they are for themselves; though in this case every one will be sensible enough of his own interest and ease, and of the great difference of charge and expedition betwixt the Council and the Courts above.[95]

The Council of the North had come to resemble a modern county court, including in its jurisdiction Common Pleas, Equity, and a "measure of probate jurisdiction."[96] Coke questioned the legality of the commission that had established it: instructions so vague and secret that defendants could not "plead to the jurisdiction of the court"; the entertaining of suits on penal laws, writs of error, and real actions.[97]

The proceedings before the President and Councell are by absolute power, their decrees uncontrollable and finall. . . . but these sentences are unreversible, which makes them adventure and presume too much upon their authority, and tends to the great oppression and grievance of the Subject.

Here Coke used neither chapter 11 nor 29 but a rather far-fetched application of chapter 12 (reinforced by Westminster II, chapter 30). He

[95] Spedding, *Life and Letters,* III, 384. In his *Fourth Institute,* chap. xlviii, Coke repeats that the four shires are included in the commission, but ought not to be: "For a Commission without an Act of Parliament cannot raise a Court of Equity as often hath been said before . . . These four shires were ancient English shires, and governed by the laws of England, and not by discretion of the President and Councell; and this were to bring their inheritances, goods, etc. *ad aliud examen.*"

[96] Reid, *Council of the North,* Pt. III, chap. iv, describes its jurisdiction and sphere of usefulness, and "the validity of the commission"; Pt. IV, chap. iii, deals with "The Fall of the Council of the North."

[97] Its receiving of bills of equity for widows' thirds was one form of "meddling with freehold" mentioned by Miss Reid. According to her account, cases involving "tenant's right" were the most numerous, and justifiable.

seems to say that since by these two statutes it is prescribed that such actions as *novel disseisin* must be held in their counties, *ergo* the king, except by statute, cannot assign any common pleas to a particular court or district, or in other words, give power by commission to determine causes between party and party.[98]

According to the version of the *Twelfth Report,* Coke used this same chapter 12 as an example of a lawful commission, in contrast to certain unlawful commissions of inquiry.[99] This report was used against the Council of the North in the Long Parliament. Much of it was quoted verbatim in conference with the Lords, but it is Magna Carta chapter 29, not 12, which Hyde quotes here.[100]

[98] The decision of the judges in Trinity term, 1609, as recorded in Coke, *Reports,* XII, 31–32. Coke quotes this decision in his *Fourth Institute,* chap. xlix, and concludes that though the council still exists, it is illegal.

[99] T. 5 Jac. Coke, *Reports,* XII, 31–33. The commissioners were assigned to inquire in certain counties "of depopulation of houses, converting of arrable land into pasture," and so on. "It was resolved . . . that the said Commissions were against Law for three causes. . . .
"3. For this, that it was only to enquire, which is against Law, for by this a man may be unjustly accused by Perjury, and he shall not have any remedy . . ."

[100] " 'Whether his Majesty,' he said, 'may cantonize out a part of his kingdom to be tried by commission, though according to the rules of law, since the whole kingdom is under the laws and government of the courts established at Westminster, and by this reason the several parts of the kingdom may be deprived of that privilege, will not be now the question; that his Majesty cannot by commission erect a new Court of Chancery, or a proceeding according to the rules of the Star Chamber, is most clear to all who have read the Magna Carta, which allowed no proceedings, *nisi per legale judicium parium et per legem terrae!* ' " Quoted, Reid, *Council of the North,* p. 443.

❦ CHAPTER X ❦

Chapter 29 in Courts and Inns of Court

Yet finding how obvious this law was upon all occasions insomuch that noe ordinary accion could be brought importing violence and wrong, but it had his foundation from hence; no extraordinary writ of prohibition was granted to restreyne the swelling and exhorbitant power of Ecclesiastiques or of any other Jurisdiction which by way of encrochment seeked to impeach the vigor of the municipall law, but had this Law for their warrant. And finding farther that no execution, oppression, violence or grievance in the Common wealth could be named but every vulgar understanding could have recourse to Nullus liber homo, I suppose I could not imploy my Labors upon a more worthy subiect or more profitable and therefore resolved farther to informe myself concerning this Law so usefull, so behoofull: And by that occasion have therein found both liberty and safety, Liberty to the persons and safety to the Lyves and Estates. And in breif I found that it was bought to[o] dear to be sold to[o] cheap. (ASHLEY'S READING)

APART from these major disputes there were a number of individual cases, some grave, some trivial, which may have contributed to Ashley's "finding how obvious this law was on all occasions." Before turning to chapter 29 we may note briefly other clauses of the Charter which received some practical application, sometimes positive, sometimes negative. For instance, in *Sir Drue Drury's case,* Magna Carta chapter 3 construed as to what it did *not* contain, served to secure to a guardian the value of the marriage of a young ward, knighted by the king while under age. This was an important case which received considerable publicity. It was referred to Chief Justices Popham and Coke and Chief Baron Fleming and argued at Serjeants Inn in Hillary and Easter terms, 4 Jacobi. The judges announced their decision publicly in the Court of Wards in the presence of the Earl of Salisbury, master of the court. It was to the effect that the defendant, young Sir Drue, must pay the value of his marriage and that his creation as knight did not discharge him of it.[1]

---

[1] The question was whether the knighting by the king of the ward of another (the effect of which is equivalent to declaring the youth of age) also discharges him of the value of the

Nothing was too local or humble for the privy council or judges to consider. "The old mill of Chester on the River Dee" was saved from a breach by the commissioners of sewers by its great age: it was not within the terms of Magna Carta chapter 23 (which related only to fish weirs); pertinent statutes related only to mills and "causyes" "much enhanced," or erected in Edward I's reign or after. "And the statute of 12 E. 4 ca. 7 confirms all the said acts" and through them "the generality of the said act of *Magna Charta* is restrained, as by the acts themselves appear." [2] In 1605 and again in 1606 purveyors and their deputies were fined and imprisoned by Star Chamber for wrongful taking of growing trees "for they are parcell of a man's enherytaunce and thereunto fyxed." [3] Here chapter 21 of the Charter was cited, and in this instance clearly by Coke who informed against the offenders. Still in the role of the loyal and vigorous attorney general, he took occasion to deplore abuse of the king's prerogative, as did Lord Chancellor Ellesmere himself on the second occasion.

The Lord Chauncellor did likewyse delyver that before Magna charta was, the prerogative was; for Magna Charta is but a declaracyon or manyfestacyon thereof . . . For as withoute the prerogative the kinge's crowne and dignitie can not be mainteyned, so he can not be more dishonered then under shadow of his prerogative, his subiects be oppressed and burdened; for his greateste care in the worlde, nexte to the service of all mightye god, is the welfare and prosperous libertie of his subiectes and no greater griefe unto him then to have them oppressed and burdened.

In 9 Jacobi the right to action on the case for scandalous words ("Tirlot the plaintiff is a Bankrupt") was upheld by the judges even though

marriage. But by the old common law (before Magna Carta) when a ward was knighted, though under age, his land was out of wardship. "And therefore it was provided by the statute of Magna Charta cap. 3 *Ita tamen quod si ipse dum infra etatem fuerit, fiat miles, nihilominous terra remaneant in custodia dominorum suorum* . . ." Thus the land remained in the custody of the lord, "and if the law had not been clear on the value of the marriage, for the cause and for the reason aforesaid, no doubt the makers of the act would have made provision for that as for the land."

[2] P. 7 Jac., Coke, *Reports*, X, 137v–38v, one of a group of cases on the Commissions of Sewers. The question was referred by the lords of the council to the two chief justices and chief baron, and argued by learned counsel, with "good consideration" of all the statutes on sewers.

[3] Hawarde, *Les Reports del Cases*, pp. 193–95, 278–79; *Attorney general v. Stokes*, 1605; *Attorney general v. Graves and others*, 1606.

According to Coke here, the prerogative is necessary for the provision of the king's household, "but the abusinge thereof is dishonor to ye kinge, greevance and oppression to the subiecte, and the kinge would not in any wyse have his prerogative rackte or strechte, but used tenderlye and withall possible Favoure as might be . . . and therefore Commaunded his Atturnie Generall to attende of all the Judges for there [*sic*] opinion in this takings of trees, whether his prerogative doe warrante it: for the aunciente and greate Charter of Englande, 22 [*sic*] times Confyrmed by ye Kinges of this realme, saythe, 'nec nos, nec ballivi nostri, nec alii, capiemus boscum alienum ad castra vel ad alia agenda nostra, nisi per voluntatem illius cuius boscus ille fuerit.' " This case was cited in parliamentary debates on purveyance, 1626; see below, p. 323.

Tirlot was "an alien born and a merchant stranger, and out of the allegeance of the King." Said Yelverton at the bar:

If these words had been spoken of an English Merchant, the words are scandalous, and the Action by such a one well maintenable; *a fortiori*, in the case of Merchants strangers, for that they, by the Laws of *England*, are enabled to trade here, and this is also to them strengthened by the Statute of Magna charta cap. 30 *Omnes mercatores* . . . [quoted in full].[4]

Appeals to chapter 9, so much used by the Londoners in earlier years, are noticeable for their absence. In coming parliaments the city was to contribute through its representatives to the causes of freedom of trade and "liberty of the subject" (as per Magna Carta chapters 30 and 29) on the national scale. When it came to some real challenge of a civic custom it was now the statute of 7 Richard II[5] upon which the citizens relied. Evidence of definite parliamentary sanction was essential, for the lawyers had developed the theory that the customs of a city or borough, even those of London, could not stand if in conflict with the common law, unless those customs had been confirmed by act of parliament. On the other hand, even a custom of London could be "defeated" if expressly abrogated by statute.[6] To be sure, Magna Carta was commonly accepted as a statute, and chapter 9 had been cited as a potent *parliamentary* confirmation of their customs by the Londoners in cases of 7 Henry VI and 8 Henry VII described above, and by the author of the *Little Discourse* as late as 1584. The superior value placed on the act of 7 Richard II, as brought out in contemporary cases, was not only that it was a statute, but the latest parliamentary confirmation which the city could cite, some 175 years after Magna Carta.[7] Typical was the famous *Case of the City of London* brought into King's Bench on a habeas corpus in 1610. "And in this case," remarks Coke, "both the serjeants and the judges had much to say of the antiquity of the City." The writ was directed to the mayor, aldermen, and sheriffs for the body of one James Wagner, arrested and in their custody for violating a cus-

---

[4] P. 9 Jac. *Tirlot v. Morris* (or Morrison), Bulstrode, *Reports*, Pt. I, pp. 134–35. Similarly, Heath for the plaintiff.

[5] See above, Chap. IV.

[6] Chrimes, *English Constitutional Ideas*, p. 285, note 4: "According to Viner, however, the customs of London were of such strength that they prevailed even against statutes in the negative . . . But apparently as early as Henry VII's reign the lawyers held a different view. A number of serjeants held in 1505–6 that the 'prescription' enjoyed by the citizens of London that no attaint lay against any servant in the city was defeated by statute."

[7] In 1578–79, for instance, the custom by which a freeman might alienate in mortmain "in spite of the statute" (Quia Emptores) was upheld because the usage in question was confirmed *after the making of the statute*. "And thus a man maie see yt a playne case that the Customes Liberties and usages of Cities Boroughes and Townes are revyved by the foresaid Confirmacions." Lansd. MSS 27, no. 67; a brief entry rehearsing a case in which a London citizen claimed it was lawful to grant a tenement to a vicar.

tom, namely practising the art of tallow chandler although not free of the city. The return, an able defense of the city's customs in general, including the right to "rectify and amend" customs, stressed this parliamentary confirmation of 7 Richard II.[8]

The same conception appears in data collected for Sir Julius Caesar on The Liberties franchises and Customes of the Citie of London," [9] introduced with the statement "All the Liberties usages and customes hereafter followinge are confirmed by an especiall act of Parliament made at Westminster Anno 7⁰ Regni Regis Ricardi secundi. . . ." and in the collection of "cases concerning the Customes of the Citty of London by Sir H. Calthrop Kt. Recorder thereof." [10] In one of these (the *Case of the Cittizens of London concerning payment of Prisage*) Coke, Yelverton, Williams, and Dodderidge are quoted as arguing that merchants should not be disheartened by a strict construction of charters, "for the advancement and good of Merchandizinge and tradeing which are as it were the blood which giveth norishment unto the whole bodie of the kingdome is to have a favourable and benigne construccion . . ." In another,[11] while the defendant emphasizes 7 Richard II, Magna Carta chapter 9 is quoted on his behalf in the judgment, one is tempted to suspect by Sir Edward.

In 14 Jacobi even 7 Richard II was cited to no avail. This was the *Case of the Custome of London in not removing the Bodie and Cause upon habeas corpus directed unto them.*[12] Such defiance of King's Bench by

---

[8] Coke, *Reports*, VIII, 121–30. " 'It was resolved that there is a difference between such a custom (that no foreigner shall keep a shop or use a trade in London) within a city, and a charter granted to a city to such effect; for it is good by way of custom, but not by grant; and therefore no corporation made within time of memory can have such privilege unless it be by act of Parliament.' " Holdsworth, IV, 346, note 3.

[9] Lansd. MSS 170, 171. Items from charters of Henry VI, Edward IV, and Henry VII are followed by a note to the effect that these were not confirmed by act of parliament as other charters were.

Under the title *Forraine bought & forraine sold*, that troublesome old statute of 9 Ed. III is eliminated as far as London is concerned: "The Sta. of A⁰ 9 E. 3. . . . is forasmuche as concernethe London both expounded and repelled [*sic*] and the liberties of MAGNA CARTA as touchinge London are revived, and the entent of the Lawe makers declared that there meaninge was not to touche London nor yet to infringe the liberties of the great charter. . . . The foresaid Statute of A⁰ 9 Ed. 3 hathe ben verie often obiected againste the Citie of London in Parliamentes by such as are ignorant of our chartres and statutes."

[10] Lansd. MSS 1075, marked "These are Sir H. Calthrop's Reports." There are ten cases (7 to 14 Jac. I) all in King's Bench. In each, some custom of the city is claimed and, with a few exceptions, allowed.

[11] *Allen v. Talley*, "The Case of the Cittizens of London concerninge theire Custome for leaving of the trade they have been Apprentice to by the space of 7 yeares and betaking themselves to another trade." In a case H. 1 Car. chapter 9 was cited in support of 1 Ed. III, discharging London citizens from payment of *prisage*, but the case was complicated by the fact that the defendant, a widow, while conceded to be a citizen, as *executrix* for her husband, was not *owner* of the ships unloaded after his death. The judges of King's Bench were divided, two and two. Bulstrode, *Reports*, Pt. III, pp. 1–26.

[12] The city officials had returned ". . . that London is an auncient Cittie, that time out of minde of man, the Maior, Aldermen and Cittizens have the Conuzance of all manner of

the city officials was neither customary nor tolerable, so ruled the judges in taking emphatic exception to the sufficiency of the return. They even turned the tables on the Londoners by quoting a clause of the Charter in their own support. Surely, they said, justice could be done to London citizens in King's Bench, a higher court than theirs, and one where the king is supposed to sit in person, "and the Judges of the kinge do say nulli negabimus nulli vendamus aut differemus Justiciam, and the reteyning of theise Causes [by London officials] would be a denying of Justice."

Sir Edward, at the time he wrote his *Fourth Institute,*[13] could not quite ignore Magna Carta, but was forced to the same conclusion as to the pre-eminence of 7 Richard II.

Now to treat of the great and notable Franchises, Liberties, and Customes of the City of London, would require a whole Volume of itself. But there is a most beneficiall statute made for the strengthening and preservation of the same which I know no other Corporation hath. It is enacted that the Citizens of London shall enjoy all their whole liberties whatsoever with this Clause, *Licet usi non fuerunt vel abusi fuerunt,* and notwithstanding any Statute to the contrary, tc. *Lege statutum,* for by this Act the City may claim liberties by prescription, Charter, or Parliament, notwithstanding any statute made before 7 R. 2. And this is the statute mentioned in our Books. . . .

Albeit by the statute of *Magna Carta* and other Acts of Parliament, the liberties, priviledges, and franchises of the City of London be confirmed; yet the most beneficiall of them all is that of 7 R. 2 before mentioned; whereby it is enacted, that the Citizens of London shall enjoy the same with this clause Licet usi non fuerint vel abusi fuerint, and notwithstanding any statute to the contrary.

These notable, rare, and special liberties we have attempted to remember: but whether herein we have done that good to the City that we intended, we know not, for we have omitted many more of no small number and great rarity and consequence too long to be remembered.

Local Officials and the Rule of Law

A WELL-RECOGNIZED feature of this period was the tendency of Star Chamber to become an administrative court developing administrative law, where officials were both supported and disciplined. Equally characteristic was the careful supervision and correction of local officials by the

pleas both reall and personall . . . and doe shewe a Confirmacion made by R. 2 in the seaventh yeare of his raigne of all their Customes, and so for this Cause had not the Bodie heere nor the Cause . . ."

The judges pointed out that if the cause returned is one which "will beare an accion onely by the Custome and not at Common Lawe" the court will grant a *procedendo* and send it back to London, lest there be a failing of justice—"Wherefore they do grant a procedendo and remand it."

[13] *Fourth Institute*, Chap. L.

privy council, central courts, or justices of assize. Within this system, even in Star Chamber, the older conception of the rule of law prevailed. Before chapter 29 of Magna Carta figured in the great case of the prerogative (the *five knights case*) affecting council and crown itself, it had played an increasing role as a defense against over-exercise of authority, including arbitrary arrest and imprisonment, undue or excessive fines, and other penalties. These cases involve offenses by local officials, and by the lesser prerogative courts, the Marshalsea, the Greencloth (purveyors), the Stanneries. It was a different matter when special commissions composed of privy councilors or such a court as Chancery was involved. The following cases nearly all involve the ubiquitous chapter 29, which was the "statute" Ashley had in mind.

Cases involving city and borough corporations and their officials carry us back a few years to 1696, *Clarke's case,* an action of false imprisonment in Common Pleas. Here St. Albans was the offender. An ordinance passed by the corporation assessing the burgesses for the erection of housing for the law courts (removed thither from London to escape the plague), with penalty of imprisonment for failure to pay, was adjudged illegal on the grounds that it was contrary to Magna Carta chapter 29.[14] It was ruled that the corporation might have had recourse to distress or an action of debt, but not imprisonment. A few years later a London goldsmith was implicated in complicity with two minor city officials, a sergeant and the *secondary* of the Counter in Woodstreete. This, an information brought by Attorney General Coke in Star Chamber against the three defendants for arresting the Dowager Countess of Rutland, involved not only the privilege of a peeress (exemption from liability to arrest for debt) but also the principle that a feigned suit as excuse for arrest is contrary to Magna Carta.[15] The penalties imposed upon the offenders, and still more the censures expressed by the lords in Star Chamber, afford an excellent example of the responsibility put upon local officials, the assumption that they are subject to the law and may not plead the orders of superiors:

and for a sheriff secondarye, it was sayde that he ys bounde and sworne to execute all suche wryttes as shall come to him. The kinges sealle is his warrante, and he is not to examine whether it be good, or whether it will lye, or whether it be againste a person arrestable or no; he is not to dispute it, but to execute his office. Which seemed reasonable, and warranted by good

---

[14] This, to be sure, as reported by Coke, *Reports*, V, 64, but the wording seems to indicate that this was actually the basis for the judgment. Following the mayor's attempted justification, we read: "et fuit adiudge nul plea, Car cest ordinance est encounter lestatut de magna Charta cap. 29. Nullus liber homo imprisonetur: Quel act ad estre confirme, et establie oustre 30 foits, et lassent ne poit alter le ley in tiel case." The thirty confirmations may well have been Coke's contribution!

[15] Hawarde, *Les Reports del Cases*, pp. 237–41; October 23, 1605.

aucthoritie, to some of ye benche and barre; Yet the Judges were of another opinion, and delyvered that an officer oughte to be learned, and furnished with sufficiente iudgement and knowledge to understande what he oughte to doe, and ye sherife one [sic] his perill ought to make choyce of such a one; and therefore yf Stone, ye secondarye yt made ye warrante, and Dies, the atturnie that sued out the execution, th'one had bene charged in ye bill, th'other made a partie in the bill, the Courte woulde have censured them bothe; and for suche a faulte compleyned of in the kinges benche of an Atturnie, he showlde have bene hurled out of ye Courte.

For the en[t]ringe of feigned Actions in London and arrestinge upon them, a Custome prescribed and used there, but resolved now by the Judges to be an ill Custome and against lawe, and mischievous, and hathe undone many a man; and therefore hereafter not to be used, for it is against ye free-dome of ye greate Charter: For ye Sergeaunte, he was much condemned for his craftie and violent Caryage, havinge heretofore bene allso censured in this Courte.

Although the countess was allowed her privilege, she did not escape her share of censure, *noblesse oblige,* for "the Lord Chancellor delivered that it was a good course that great ladies and Countesses should pay their debts, so they would have no use for this privilege; and so to do is honorable."

On another occasion one of the sheriffs of London, defendant in an action of false imprisonment, was supported by all the judges, although *Clarke's case,* including Magna Carta chapter 29 and the thirty confir-mations, was cited for the plaintiff.[16] "The whole Court clear of opinion that the Defendant had done well here, that the Imprisonment was just and lawfull; and the plea in Barre, by way of justification, good."

Even Sir Walter Raleigh, as Lord of the Stanneries, was taken to task by a motion in Star Chamber (May 24, 1598) "because he had directed a warrant to imprison two men who had sued divers Tinners of the Stan-neryes and had [obtained] judgment and execution against them, and after this he granted his warrant. Which was disallowed and disliked by the Court, and a day was given [him] to answer it." Two days later the same being moved again and referred to the judges, the practice was con-demned as "contrary to the Great Charter (*quod nullus liber homo im-prisonetur*) and the common law is the surest and best inheritance that any subject hath, *et perde ceo et perde tout.*" [17]

[16] *Chune v. Piott,* H. 12 Jac. Bulstrode, *Reports,* Pt. II, pp. 328–31. The sheriff, in search of a prisoner, escaped from the Counter in Woodstreet, "did meet with the Plaintiffe *in nocturno tempore, circa horam nonam,* wandring, who used him undecently," giving him uncivil words and pushing him against a wall; "therefore he did take him and for this did imprison him."

[17] Hawarde, *Les Reports del Cases,* pp. 94–96. Present on the twenty-sixth were Egerton, Sir John Fortescue, Chancellor of the Exchequer, Sir Tho. Sackville, Francis Gawdy, J. of Q. B., Sir Wm. Knollys, Controller of the Household, Whitgift, and Sir John Popham. Coke was, of course, attorney general at this time but is not mentioned as in the case of purveyors.

Some years later one Hodges, a burgess of Liskerret, was released on habeas corpus by King's Bench. The mayor had imposed a penalty out of proportion to the offense (insulting words and threats to himself), a "malicious kind of Imprisonment." Here it is not Coke but Justice Croke who makes an extension of Magna Carta chapter 14 to cover any disproportionate penalty, and works in a characteristic reproof for the mayor, but also for his unruly victim, thus upholding the dignity of officialdom.[18]

Most of these instances involve some application of the phrase *per legem terrae,* or of *pares* interpreted as equals or a jury. As we have seen, the right to trial by peers had become too well established to need support from Magna Carta, yet chapter 29 remained the standard "statute" on the subject. For instance, Lord Vaux, indicted on a *praemunire* in King's Bench "upon the new Statute, for the refusing the Oath of Allegeance," "prayed that he might be tryed *Per pares.*"

But it was resolved, that he shall not in this case be tryed by his Peers for the Statute of *Magna Charta, cap.* 29. *Nec super eum ibimus, nec super eum mittemus, nisi per legale judicium parium suorum* is only to be understood of Treason, Misprision of Treason, Petit Treason and Felony, and of Accessories to them, &c. But Premunire is but a Contempt, and Pardon of all Contempts pardons it; and for this cause it shall not be *Per pares.*[19]

In London the phrase *per judicium parium* received a rather surprising application. In the *Case of the Custome of London concerning orphans' portions* the custom was upheld on behalf of the widow of a freeman of the city. One of the exceptions had been "it appeareth by the return that the devisor was a woman and alsoe onely the wife of a freeman and not a free woman." This was met by an ingenious extension of Magna Carta chapter 29 and 20 Henry VI chapter 9:

[18] M. 11 Jac., *Hodges against Humkin, the Maior of Liskerret.* Bulstrode, Pt. II, pp. 139–40. "*Croke Justice.* This Return is not good, but altogether uncertain and insufficient here, both the Maior and Hodges ought to learn how to behave themselves: Here the speeches used by Hodges are very unseemly speeches, and unfit to be used by him to any one, much less to such a person as the Maior was, being a person in authority and an Officer of the King; but yet, for such words thus used, the Maior ought not to use a malicious kind of Imprisonment, in regard of the time of it, when the same was, being so long time after the offence, as in August, for an offense in June before; and also in regard of the manner of this Imprisonment, and of the place where, he being to be thrown into a Dungeon, and so to be there kept, without any Bed to lie on, or any bread or meat to eat, and for all these Causes, the Imprisonment was unlawful; Imprisonment ought always to be according to the quality of the offense, and so is the Statute of *Magna Charta* cap. 14 and of *Marlbridge,* cap. 1 *secundum magnitudinem, et qualitatem delicti* the punishment ought to be, and correspondent to the same, the which is not here in this Case . . ."

[19] 10 Jac. Coke, *Reports,* XII, 93. Similarly, H. 1 Car. in an action upon the case for a promise including payment of relief, in King's Bench, Dodderidge, J. says, "The Statute of Magna Charta is in part *Introductivum novi juris,* for the Barons' relief before this Statute was at the King's pleasure, as appears by Glanvile tit. Relief; but the Statute of Magna Charta hath now made this certain." Bulstrode, *Reports,* Pt. III, p. 325.

A woman beinge a freeman within the Statute of Magna Charta Cap. 19 [*sic* for 29] which enacteth that noe freeman shalbe taken or imprisoned &c. but by the lawfull Judgment of his peeres, so that shee beinge a baronesse or a Countesse shalbe tryed by her peeres upon an indictment preferred against her, she shalbe also reputed a freeman in the Custom.

Thus by the happy device of "extension of the words of the statute" a privilege designed for baronesses was made to aid a mere commoner, a citizeness of London. To be sure there was a second, more routine argument to the effect that "the wife of a freeman havinge the libertie to trade in the Cittie and so able to take benefitt by it, shee shall alsoe be bound by the Customes of it."

The reader must have observed in these episodes the pervasive presence of Sir Edward Coke as prosecuting attorney, judge, or reporter. In the following instances he occupied both the last-named roles. The first, which must have been argued in Common Pleas just before his unwelcome promotion, afforded one more opportunity to vindicate that court and the common law and, more particularly, to oppose arrest and imprisonment by "usurped" jurisdiction. The second, shortly before his dismissal from King's Bench, led to a glorification of that court, its supereminent authority and obligation to maintain the rule of law.

In the first, the *Case of the Marshalsea* (Court of the Steward and Marshal) 10 Jacobi,[20] one Richard Hall brought an action of trespass— assault, battery, and wounding—and false imprisonment against officials of the court. Hall, a pledge for debt, was on a *capias ad satisfaciendum* arrested within the verge by Stanley and delivered to Richardson the marshal, who detained him in prison three months. The defendants pleaded not guilty to all but the assault and detainer in prison, and defended the latter on the grounds that the Court of the Marshalsea had jurisdiction in pleas of trespass and trespass on the case within the household and within the verge. "And much was said by those who were counsell for the court of the marshalsea for the antiquity, honour and jurisdiction of the court. . . . But on solemn argument at the bench it was unanimously resolved that judgment be given against the defendants."

The jurisdiction of the court, it was argued, had been defined by the *Articuli super cartas,* chapter 3, and these were but "explanations on the Charters," namely the Great Charter and Charter of the Forest.

But then it will be asked in what part of Magna Charta can one find anything concerning the court of the marshalsea: to this it was replied, that the

---

[20] Coke, *Reports*, X, 68v–77. The case was several times argued at the bar, and on the two principal issues raised it was ruled that the jurisdiction of the court extended to trespass only (*al transgressione simpliciter, s. vi et armis*), not to trespass on the case (*assumpsit*), and that the defendants were liable to an action for false imprisonment.

twenty-ninth chapter of Magna Charta extends to this, for there it is provided *quod nullus liber homo capiatur, vel imprisonetur, aut disseisietur de libero tenemento suo, vel de libertatibus, vel liberis consuetudinibus suis, aut utlagetur, aut exuletur, aut aliquo modo destruatur, nec super eum ibimus, nec super eum mittimus nisi per legale iudicium parium suorum aut per legem terrae*: by which act each arrest or imprisonment, and each oppression *contra legem terrae* is prohibited, therefore if anyone against law usurp any jurisdiction, and by color of the same arrest or imprison a man, or in any manner by color of an usurped authoritie oppress any man (which is a kind of destruction) against the law, he could be punished by this statute . . .[21]

The second in King's Bench, 13 Jacobi, was another instance of official name-calling.[22] The corporation of Plymouth was taken to task for unjustifiably disfranchising one of its citizens. Bagge, the plaintiff, one of the "chief" or "capital" burgesses and magistrates of Plymouth, had been accused of calling the mayor and his fellow burgesses names and of criticizing their official acts. On failure to reform when warned, he was removed from office and from the freedom. It is easy to appreciate the feelings of the offended magistrates as we read the official record. Interspersed through the court clerk's formal Latin phrases appear Bagge's good round English epithets: "haec falsa, opprobriosa, et scandalosa Anglicana verba sequentia, viz. 'Master Maior carrieth himselfe foolishly in his place; and if you will join with me, wee will turne him out of his Mayoralty, and choose a wiser man in his place.'" And further, "You are a cozening knave," "an insolent fellow"; "I will make thy necke cracke."

Even so, the cause of removal was ruled insufficient. Bagge might have been punished for contempt and made to give sureties to keep the peace, but "mere words" were not enough to warrant disfranchisement. "Otherwise the best citizen or burgess would be disfranchised some time or other." A freeman may not be disfranchised by the corporation unless it has express authority by express words of its charter or by prescription. Where such is lacking, he must be convicted by the course of the law before he can be removed,

and this appears by Magna Carta cap. 29 *Nullus liber homo capiatur vel imprisonetur, aut disseisetur de libero tenemento suo, vel libertatibus vel liberis consuetudinibus suis &c. nisi per legale iudicium parium suorum, vel per legem terrae.* And if the corporation has power by charter or prescription to remove him for reasonable cause, that will be *per legem terrae,* but if they have not such power, he must be convicted per iudicium suorum &c. . . .

---

[21] This was one of five points: the others were its jurisdiction at common law before 28 Ed. I; reasons why the common law assigns to the Marshalsea such a particular and limited jurisdiction; authorities of the law in all ages since that act; the nature of this action on the case on *assumpsit.*

[22] Coke, *Reports,* XI, 93v–100.

But Bagge, like Hodges, did not escape a scolding. As Coke informs his readers in a *Nota Lecteur*, much was said urging burgesses to give obedience and reverence to their magistrates, who derive authority of the king. Furthermore this case afforded an irresistible opportunity to assert the authority of the court:

And in this case it was resolved, "that to this Court of King's Bench belongs authority not only to correct errors in judicial errors and misdemeanors, tending to the breach of the peace, or oppression of the subjects, or to raising of faction, controversy, debate, or to any other manner of misgovernment, so that no wrong or injury, either public or private, can be done, but that this shall be reformed or punished through due course of law."

No wonder that when Coke was dismissed from the bench and commanded to revise his reports this was one of the cases singled out for special criticism.[23]

Profound indeed was the impression made upon the king by these and similar episodes in which his chief justice figured. According to James' complaint, possibly framed for him by Bacon—"Remembrances of his Majesty's Declaration touching the Lord Coke"— [24]

That for things passed, his majesty had noted in him a perpetual turbulent carriage, first towards the liberties of his church and estate ecclesiastical; towards his prerogative royal, and the branches thereof; and likewise towards all the settled jurisdictions of all his other courts, the high commission, the star-chamber, the chancery, the provincial councils, the admiralty, the duchy, the court of requests, the commission of inquiries, the new boroughs of Ireland; in all which he has raised troubles and new questions; and lastly in that, which might concern the safety of his royal person by his exposition of the laws in cases of high treason.

The indictment does not stop here. The uncourtier-like demeanor of the chief justice, and his refusal to be won over elicit further caustic comment:

That besides the actions themselves, his majesty in his princely wisdom hath made two special observations of him; the one, that he having in his nature

[23] "Observations on the Lord Coke's Reports" attributed to Ellesmere. After quoting the offending passage in which the reporter "digresseth from his matter," this critic comments: "Herein (giving Excess of Authority to the King's Bench) he doth as much as insinuate, that this Court is all-sufficient in it self to manage the State; for if the Kings-Bench may reform any manner of Misgovernment (as the Words are) it seemeth that there is little or no Use, either of the King's Royal Care and Authority exercised in his Person, and by his Proclamations, Ordinances, and immediate Direction, nor of the Council Table, which under the King is the chief Watch-Tower for all Points of Government, nor of the Star-Chamber, which hath ever been esteemed the highest Court, for Extinguishment of all Ryots and publick Disorders and Enormities; and besides the Words do import, as if the Kings-Bench had a Superintendence over the Government itself and to judge wherein any of them do misgovern."

For this tract, a collection of cases entitled, "Lord Chancellor Egerton's Observations on the Lord Coke's Reports," and questions of authorship, see Holdsworth, V, 478, note 1.

[24] Bacon, *Works*, VII, 350–51. (Not dated—c. October 1616.)

not one part of those things which are popular in men, being neither civil, nor affable, nor magnificent, he hath made himself popular by design only, in pulling down government. The other, that whereas his majesty might have expected a change in him, when he made him his own, by taking him to be of his council, it made no change at all, but to the worse, he holding on all his former channel, and running separate courses from the rest of his council; and rather busying himself in casting fears before his council, concerning what they could not do, than joining his advice what they should do.

King and Council Have Their Way

THIS citing of Magna Carta was distinctly a lawyers' game. Few laymen participated. The writer eagerly examined, in the manuscript *State Papers Domestic,* scores of petitions indicated in the calendars as coming to the privy council or an individual councilor or lord from persons in prison. Disappointingly few of those examined made any appeal to the Great Charter. Most petitioners sought to invoke a great person rather than a great principle, pardon or pity rather than justice, or even more modestly, merely to ask transfer to another prison. Of the exceptions, an obscure "poor orator," one Henry Jekin of St. Thomas Hospital, imprisoned by the mayor of a Kentish town for "his yll cariage and misbehaviour towarde the said Maior," received scant courtesy for his pains. The mayor, defending himself against the petitioner's complaints *seriatim,* remarks dryly, "And as touchinge his learninge in Magna Carta wee passe it over." [25]

Equally futile were the pleas of Legate, St. John, and Whitelocke. Here the authority of king and councilors was involved. Yet these cases were notable enough on the one hand, to publicize chapter 29, and on the other, to afford king's counsel an opportunity to appropriate and interpret the Great Charter.

Appeal to the Charter failed to save Bartholomew Legate from prosecution by the Bishop of London and his consistory, and ultimately from the fate of an heretic. Legate was not a Puritan or Brownist but was accused of Arian heresies, summed up in the charge against him in some thirteen propositions, "his damnable tenets," as Fuller calls them. [26] As

[25] State Papers, 14/86, nos. 97, 98, 1616. The petitioner claims that he "was and is seised of the said hospitall in fee" (whereas the mayor denies that any burgess of the hospital of St. Thomas "was ever seised thereof," but received an allowance from the governors), and that by "the old custom of the Realme no man shalbe taken imprisoned, disseised, nor otherwise distraned, but that he be put to answeare by the lawe of the land magna Charta cap. 26 [*sic*]."

[26] Particularly the denial of the divinity of Christ and of the Trinity. State Trials, II, 727-34, no. 90. "The cases of Bartholomew Legatt and Edward Wightman, for Heresy: 10 Jacobi I a.d. 1612"; an extract from Fuller's Church History, "A True Relation of the Commission and Warrants for the Condemnation and Burning of Bartholomew Legatt and Edward Wightman; the former at West Smithfield, the latter at Lichfield," with

described by the latter in his *Church History,* Legate seems to have been a rather striking individual: "native of county Essex, person comely, complexion black, age of about 40 years: of a bold spirit, confident carriage, fluent tongue, excellently skilled in the Scriptures . . . His conversation (for ought I can learn to the contrary) very unblamable." Legate was accorded the unusual distinction of attempted conversion by the king himself, but successfully evaded the subtleties of the royal theologian.[27] Although John King, Bishop of London, confuted him so effectively that it "happily unproselited some inclinable to his opinions," Legate himself remained "pertinacious." His final condemnation came in a consistory afforced by Bishop King with "many reverend bishops, able divines, and learned lawyers to assist him. So that the consistory so replenished for the time being, seemed not so much a large court, as a little convocation." Even so, it was not a convocation. It was in connection with this case that Coke followed Fitzherbert in contending that the writ *de haeretico comburendo* could be issued only against one who had been judged an heretic in convocation. But let Legate speak for himself. Whether he was as well versed in the law as the scriptures or relied on "learned counsel," he presented an able petition, protesting the whole treatment accorded him for several years past. It charges illegality in process; arrest without proper warrant; long imprisonment "in ye most lothsome Limbo of Newgate"; denial of a copy of the charge (the warrant "with Cause of Arianisme therein, as they say"); "neither hath he bene duly accused or presented much lesse lawfully convicted of such Cryme." [28] Submitted with the petition, "the Reasons within written" include principles based on the scriptures and Roman law, the law of England (Magna Carta chapter 29), and recent statutes (25 Henry VIII, chapter 14, and 1 Elizabeth, chapter 1):

Doth our Lawe Judge a man before it heare him and know what he hath done? Jo. 7.15

The Lawe of God sayth that for any synn or fault a man offendeth in, the matter shalbe established by two or three witnesses. Deut. 19.15

documents such as the king's warrant and the writ *de haeretico comburendo.* The editor adds in a note, "Very diligent efforts were made, but unsuccessfully, to discover any records of the Trials of these two persons."

[27] "King James caused this Legate often to be brought to him, and seriously dealt with him to endeavour his conversion. One time the king had a design to surprize him into a confession of Christ's Deity, as his majesty afterwards declared to a right reverend prelate, by asking him, Whether or no he did not daily pray to Jesus Christ, Which, had he acknowledged, the king would infallibly have inferred, that Legate tacitly consented to Christ's divinity as a searcher of the hearts. But herein his Majesty failed of his expectation, Legate returning That indeed he had prayed to Christ in the days of his ignorance, but not for these last seven years. Hereupon the king in choler spurned him with his foot; 'away, base fellow (said he) it shall never be said that one stayeth in my presence, that hath never prayed to our Saviour for seven years together.' "

[28] Harl. MSS 6803, fols. 123–24.

It was not the maner of the Romans for favor to deliver any man to death till his Accusers were before him and he had place to defend himself concerning the Cryme obiected against him.

To which agreeth the lawe of England which saith: no freeman shalbe taken imprisoned outlawed &c but by lawfull Judgment of his Peeres and according to the lawe of the land. Also that Justice and Right should not be sould denied or deferred to any subiect . . . 9 H. 3.

Neither did success attend Oliver St. John in his well-known protest against benevolences. Writes Chamberlain to Carlton, January 5, 1615: "there is a gentleman of Wiltshire commonly called the blacke Oliver St. John committed for writing a letter to the towne of Marleborow (where he was a neighbour) wherein he dissuaded them from giving a benevolence." [29] St. John's letter is headed "As I thinke this kind of benevolence is against Law, reason, and religion." Then, "The Lawe is in the Statute called Magna Charta 9 H. 3 Cap: 29 that no free man be any way destroyed, but by the Lawes of the Land." This Charter, he notes, has been confirmed by all princes since, and supplemented by 25 Edward I (on aids and prises) and 1 Richard III (on benevolences). It is against reason that the commons "in their severalls and particulars" should be asked to do what the better informed and advised parliament has refused. It is against religion, for the king commits perjury in thus violating his coronation oath, his subjects abetting, and such policy may pave the way for another Henry IV. His subjects incur the "several curses and sentences of excommunication," and here he cites the two great sentences of Archbishops Boniface and Winchelsea, quoting the latter.

St. John was arrested and tried. The charge made by Bacon makes no specific answer to the statutes cited, but rather indulges in a eulogy and defense of King James as the protector, not violator, of the laws:

Is it so that King James shall be said to be a violator of the liberties, laws, and customs of his kingdoms? Or is he not rather a noble and constant protector and conservator of them all? . . . "For the maintaining of the Laws, which is the hedge and fence about the liberty of the subject, I may truly affirm it was never in better repair. He doth concur with the votes of the nobles; *Nolumus leges Angliae mutare.*"

[29] State Papers, 14/80, no. 1. St. John's letter, State Papers, 14/78, no. 23, is quoted by Spedding, *Life and Letters*, V, 132–34, along with Bacon's charge, pp. 136–46, and St. John's submission, 147–48.

Spedding, p. 131, identifies him as "the second son of John St. John of Lydiard Tregoze near relation of Lord Grandison," and says that the letter was written at the mayor's request, as from a "man of good family and a person of importance in the place"; that St. John "forbore to give any answer in private, but the next day, when the Justices were to meet, sent a letter to the Mayor, with authority to lay it before them if he thought fit." This man was no relation to the St. John M. P. in 1593.

Whitelocke's protest against the commissioners of inquiry for the navy, like Coke's last tilt with Chancery, is too well known to need much description here.[30] Both are of interest for the rival interpretations they elicited from the crown lawyers who sought not to repudiate but rather to appropriate the Great Charter. Few detractors appear until the days of Eliot's troublesome fellow Cornishman and enemy Bagg, Bishop Laud himself, and finally freeborn John Lilburne and his like. Just as Cosin, Whitgift, and Bancroft had claimed that the *lex terrae* of Magna Carta included ecclesiastical law, so now Hobart and Bacon did the same for "his Majesty's Prerogative and his absolute power incident to his sovereignty," and Ellesmere for the "matters of conscience and equity" of Chancery.

The commission to inquire into abuses in the management of the navy was to consist of the Lord Chancellor, Lord Privy Seal, Lord Admiral, Lord Chamberlain "and divers other great councellors and other persons of eminent qualitie." They were to discover deceipts and abuses,

and upon the discoverie of them as well to give order for the due punishment of the offenders for the time past as likewise to sett downe fitt ordinances and rules for the well governing and ordering the navye and all the incidents thereof for the tyme to come, with reasonable pains to be inflicted upon the offenders, provided that all should be aggreable to lawe . . .

According to Gardiner, it was Nottingham, the Lord High Admiral, who prompted Sir Robert Mansell, treasurer of the navy, to obtain Whitelocke's opinion on the commission. We do not have the text of his opinion, but have to rely on the charges made against him before the council. The "several great contempts" included misrepresentation of the nature of the commission (that punishment of offenses was left to the discretion of the commissioners), the presuming "in a verie strange and unfitt manner to make an excursion into general censure and defyinge of his Majesties power and prerogative," and comparison with the ill-famed commission of 42 Edward III "mencioned in the yeare bookes."

The charge against Whitelocke was opened by Attorney General Hobart and concluded by Bacon, while that against Mansell was left to the recorder. Spedding thinks that the version which he uses was drawn up by Bacon.

And for the second contempt, it was opened by his Majestys said Counsel that the said Whitlocke had affirmed and maintained by the said writing that the King cannot, neither by commission nor in his own person, meddle with

<hr />

[30] Detailed accounts are given in Gardiner, II, 187–91 and Spedding, IV, 346–57. Whitelocke had been committed to the Fleet May 18, 1613. He made his submission June 12, and on the next day he and Mansell were released after "grave admonitions" for their future behavior.

the body, goods, or lands of his subjects, but only by indictment, arraignment, and trial, or by legal proceedings in his ordinary Courts of Justice, laying for his ground the statute of *Magna Charta, Nullus liber homo capiatur,* etc. which position in that general and indefinite manner was set forth by his Majestys said Counsel to be not only grossly erroneous and contrary to the rules of law, but dangerous and tending to the dissolving of Government.

First, for that *Lex Terrae* mentioned in the said Statute, is not to be understood only of the proceedings in the ordinary Courts of Justice, but that his Majestys Prerogative and his absolute power incident to his sovereignty is also *lex terrae,* and is invested and exercised by the law of the land, and is part thereof; and it was thereupon observed and urged that the opinion broached by the said Whitlocke did manifestly (by consequence) overthrow the King's martial power and the authority of the Council Table, and the force of his Majestyes proclamations, and other actions and directions of State and Policy applied to the necessity of times [and] occasions which fall not many times within the remedies of ordinary justice, nor cannot be tied to the formalities of a legal proceeding, *propter tarda legum auxilia;* neither could he the said Whitlocke be so blind (except he would wilfully mistake) but that he must needs discern that this present Commission was mixed with matter of State and martial defence, tending to the conservation of the Navy which is the walls of this island, and a principal portion of the surety, greatness, and renown of king and kingdom, and therefore not like unto a Commission of oyer and determiner, or other such ordinary Commissions. . . .

Thirdly, it was enforced by his Majestys said Counsel, that if the Statute of *Magna Charta* in the point of *nullus liber homo capiatur,* etc. should receive the construction that the said Whitlocke giveth unto it, it doth manifestly impeach all imprisonment either for causes of State or common justice before trial, whereas the general practice of the realm is and hath ever been that not only the Council of the estate [*sic*], but Justice of Assizes and Justice of Peace do commit offenders capital upon pregnant presumptions, before either trial or indictment; and common reason teacheth that if the persons of malefactors were not secured by safe custody before indictment, there would be nothing but escapes and general impunity; and therefore that assertion of the said Whitlockes every way pernicious; whereupon the King's learned Counsel concluded upon both parts as well for the slander of his Majestys Commission as for the clipping and impeaching of his Majestys prerogative and power, the said Whitlocke's contempts were very great and deserved sharp punishment; neither were anyways to be defended by the privilege of a Counsellor at Law . . .[31]

In his contest with Chancery, Coke relied on two groups of statutes. These the lord chancellor in his defense enumerates and answers as "the statutes which he [Coke] now urged and stood upon against Chancery."

[31] At Whitehall, in the queen's Chamber of Presence, on Saturday, June 12, 1613. Spedding, IV, 350–51, based on a manuscript in the British Museum which he says belonged to D'Ewes and is more correct than the text in the appendix of the *Liber Famelicus.*

Ellesmere had little difficulty in demonstrating that the first statute of *praemunire* and 4 Henry IV, chapter 23, had no bearing on his court.[32] As to the other group, Magna Carta and some of its fourteenth-century interpretations, including three of the *six statutes,* he appropriated rather than repudiated them, interpreting *law of the land* as comprehending "matters of conscience and equity." [33] As to Magna Carta:

where the words be *nisi per Legale iudicium parium suorum vel per Legem terrae.* It is *lex terre* that as the Iudges of the Common Law shall determine questions in lawe and *pares et Iurors* to try matters in fact, soe the Chancery is to order and decree matters of Conscience and Equitie which cannot be remedied by the strict rules of the Common Law . . .

"The same rule serveth for understanding of 25 Edward III ca. 4," he said, and in fact of the others, for the statutes Coke cited either prescribe due process of law—and such is the proceeding in Chancery—or are intended to correct faulty proceedings in common law. As to the statute of 2 Edward III, chapter 8, which forbids disturbance or delay of common right by commands under the great or little seal:

The ordinary Iudiciall proceedings by the Chancery, according to conscience and equitie is not any disturbance or delay of comon right, but is the doing of right and Justice in cases which the common Lawe cannot helpe, for common right standeth not onely in the strict rigour and extremity of the law (for often *summum ius est summa iniuria*) but rather in the doing of right according to equity and conscience. And the Judges of the common Law themselves doe almost every daye extend their discretion to stay and mittigate the rigour and strictnesse of the common Law: and in so doing they doe well, notwithstanding the strict word of their oath.

Sir Francis Ashley's Law Lectures on the Liberty of the Subject

THOSE familiar with debates in committee of both houses on "liberty of the subject" in 1628 will recall Serjeant Ashley's speech on behalf of the crown. Few perhaps will realize the import of his introductory statement:

It is well known to many that know me how much I have laboured in this Law of the Subjects Liberty very many Years before I was in the King's Service, and had no Cause then but to speak ex Animo; yet did I then maintain and publish the same Opinion which now I have declared, con-

---

[32] The statute of 1403 was more difficult to explain away than *praemunire*. Cf. Holdsworth, I, 462–63.

[33] "Some notes and observacions upon the Statute of Magna Carta Chap. (29) and other Statutes concerning the proceedinge in the Chancery in cases of Equitie and Conscience (collected by the Lord Ellesmere for the Kings learned Councells direccion, the month of September 1615. Anno 13 Jacobi."

cerning the King's supreme Power in Matters of State; and therefore cannot justly be censured to speak at this present only to the merit of my Master.[34]

His allusion was undoubtedly to the reading on the "statute" of Magna Carta chapter 29 which he gave in his Inn of Court, as autumn reader, 1616. What appears to be Ashley's own, or at least a "fair copy," has been preserved in the Harleian Manuscripts.[35]

Middle Temple Hall, the scene of the reading, is rich in traditions. It was there on February 2, 1601, that *Twelfth Night* "that most delightful of farces was performed . . . by Shakespeare's own Company." [36] The "glorious hall" for the building of which Edmund Plowden was mainly responsible during his treasurership is more than a hundred feet long, forty feet wide, and nearly sixty feet high, with roof of the architectural type known as the "open double hammer." "Tradition says the floor was formerly composed not of planks and supports but of trees sawn in half. . . . On a dais at the western end is the Bencher's table. It is nearly thirty feet long, and made from four planks sawn from a single oak grown in Windsor Forest. It was presented by the Society's royal patron Queen Elizabeth and was floated down the Thames to the old Temple Stairs or Bridge." Below the dais is "a priceless piece of furniture" a table which is thus described by a modern Reader:

The "Cupboard," at which I am now delivering my Reading and at which our Readers have always stood while similarly engaged, and at which our students after call to the Bar enter their names on the roll of members of this Inn, is said to be made from timber of the "Golden Hind," the famous ship in which Drake made his great voyage round the world between 1577 and 1580.[37]

[34] See below, pp. 343–45.
[35] Harl. MSS 4841, catalogued as "Sir Francis Ashley's Law Lectures on the Liberty of the Subject 1616, In 8 divisions fairly written." There is no title, as the top of the page is torn away, but fol. 4 is headed, "The Account of my Reading given at the Terme Michaelmas 14 Jacobi 1616."
  Divisions 1, 5, 6, 7, 8, and 9 have the lecturer's exposition of a clause or phrase of the "statute" but no hypothetical cases and discussion thereof; divisions 2 and 3 have the reading plus cases and discussion; division 4, cases but no discussion. As was customary, the introductory lecture is in English, the others in law French, which I translate or paraphrase.
[36] Gover's Reading, pp. 8–9.
[37] Blackham, *Story of the Temple*, pp. 152–55. In modern times the cupboard "is provided with a cover to protect the precious relic, and more venerated perhaps than any other piece of timber in the Temple. This priceless link with the 'wooden walls of England' was used as the Reader's lectern when he delivered his discourses in by-gone days. It was, and still is, generally used as a centre of ceremonial observance.
  "Here proclamation was formerly made of matters of importance affecting members of the House, and at this table in the present day newly-called barristers enter their names on the Society's Roll.
  "It is styled the 'Cupboard,' or *Abacus*, a term which Cicero used signifying a sideboard, and in addition to its employment as a reading desk, the table is used appropriately enough on great occasions for displaying some of the Inn's plate, of which the Honourable

In fact, Drake had been a member of the Society. On August 4, 1586, while the members were at dinner, the great adventurer, "just seven days returned from the West Indies, after capturing from the Spaniards the cities of San Domingo and Cartagena and other places, came into the hall and was received enthusiastically by his fellow members."

For the traditions and ceremonies observed in connection with a reading, we turn again to Bagshawe's description:

Readers of the Law, during the time of their Reading, do hold up the ancient honor and dignity of a Reader, on whom, for that time is devolved the Government of the House. They have four Cubbard men, ancient Barristers of the House to attend them in their Reading, and four Stewards to attend them in their Feasting, for the inviting their Guests of Noble Ranck, and ten or twelve men of his own to attend his person. . . .

And Readers, if they do amiss, are answerable to the Governours of that Society at their next Parliament, where the Reader and his Assistants (being alwayes Benchers) do give an account of that Reading as I did . . . and had thanks from them all. And such acceptation my Reading found with the Gentlemen of that Society (which I shall with thankfulness ever acknowledge) that scarce any Reader before was ever attended out of Town with such a number of Gentlemen of the same House.

A similar honor was accorded Sir Edward Coke in 1592: "he tells us that he delivered only five lectures as the presence of the plague made it necessary to leave London; that there were present 160 'socii,' and that nine of the Bench and forty of the Bar escorted him as far as Romford on his way home to Huntingfield." [38]

According to Middle Temple records "Mr. Francis, third son of Antony Ashley of Dameram, Wilts, eq." was admitted to the Inn at a "parliament" held November 21, 1589. We know that he was an utter barrister in 1597 for his name is entered with eighteen others of that rank and thirteen inner barristers "fined 20s each for absence and being out of commons in Lent last during Master Shurley's reading." Ashley served his colleagues in the customary roles described above, with three others: in 1609 "to provide the Readers' feast"; and in 1614 and 1615 "to stand at the cupboard," with Richard Martin and Nicholas Hyde. Finally "at the Parliament holden 27th Oct., 1615, Mr. R. Martin was chosen Reader for next Lent, and Mr. F. Ashley for next autumn." [39] Owing to the

Society has a goodly store. The old oak almost groans under the load of precious metal which it has to support on Grand Nights, when the Benchers entertain Royalty and other distinguished visitors."

[38] Holdsworth, V, 460, note 2.

[39] And again, at the May 1616 parliament, "Mr. Francis Ashley was chosen reader for next autumn." June 1616, "Mr. R. Martin was chosen Assistant to Mr. Fr. Ashley, Reader next Autumn. The two preceding Readers shall in future be assistants to the Reader." *Middle Temple Records*, I, 310, 375, 503, 592, 596, 608, 610.

Middle Temple Hall

From Hugh H. L. Bellot's *The Inner and Middle Temple Hall* (Methuen and Company Ltd.)

custom of fining, it is easier to ascertain the absentees than the actual hearers of the reading; fourteen utter barristers and nine inner barristers are listed as "vacationers" fined for "absence and being out of commons during Mr. Ashley's reading."

In his introductory lecture Ashley admits that he has chosen a dangerous subject, a theme "whereby it is impossible I should gaine any opinion unless it be an opinion of foolhardiness" since he thus puts forth in a perilous sea with the Superior bodies threatening storms. "The Subiect of my labours" he says, "was such as you heard, a theme deep enough I confes for some profound Ploden to dive into and dangerous enough for some daring Hercules to undertake that could as well goe through dangers as adventure on them. Yet finding how obvious this law was upon all occasions . . ." He continues in the words quoted at the first of this chapter, and concludes, "In which nevertheles I did proceed with such moderation that I hope none could justly take offence." Evidently he succeeded in this aim, since he was made king's serjeant not long after.

As to the historical origin of the Great Charter, the Reader does not do as well as his Elizabethan predecessor. He does not know, or at least does not follow, the current popular chronicles like Holinshed, or even Coke's *Eighth Report* (which he uses in other connections). According to Ashley, it was Duke William's Norman sword which established absolutism in England with the result that "the government in this kingdome was rather arbitrary then legall until the tyme of king Henry 3."

At which tyme the state being better setled and the tymes more peaceable the Barons and Commons then became more sensible of the losse of the benefit of those antient Lawes of which the power of a Conqueror had deprived them. And thereupon (making happily some advantage of the tendernes of the kinges yeares) by Parliament in 9 H. 3 obtayned restitution of those Lawes which had sustayned so long a suspension, which statutes are styled the kings Great Charter and the Charter of the forest, though enacted by Parlement, because they could not passe but by his Royall assent. . . . the Subiect not regarding quo nomine theyr Libertye came so they might enjoy it.

Whether or not the Charter "be a Statute de novo, or be but a declaration of the auncient common law," Ashley inclines with *Doctor and Student* to the latter view, for "it conteyned the some and substance of all those Lawes which were in use in the tyme of that king Edward who had the addition of holy." Yet it may well be that

these Lawes having new life put into them by parlement after so long disusage may well be called and accounted Statutes . . . And it is most usuall at this day in an action brought upon this law to conclude contra formam statuti, which I mention to this purpose that a man that imployes his travayles to the exposition of this Law may as well be sayd to reade on a Statute as he which reades on the Statute of 25 E. 3 of Treasons, and many others which I could instance which are agreed to be but declarations of the Common Law, yet have often ben taken as Statutes by those which have taken up the place wherein I now sit.

Here Ashley launches into a eulogy obviously inspired by Coke, but which fairly outdoes his great mentor:

But if it be the Common Law, it is the Law of Lawes for as the L.[ord] Coke sayth in his preface to his 8th Report the old Statutes which were the auntient Common Lawes are the body and the text, and all Records and Reports are but comentaryes and Expositions upon them, and so is this Law in effect the ground, and the rest subsequent but flourishes upon it, this the base and others the descent. But if it be a meer Statute, it is the Statute of Statutes, for it hath begotten many of the lyke kind [40] . . . And the L. Coke sayth in his 5 Report it hath bene confirmed 30 tymes, and 30 times more I suppose it would if it lay in the power of the Subiect to give any strength unto it. And no marvayle if we consider eyther the worth or extent of it: for it is as much worth as our Lyves or estates are worth, and the extent is as large as anything we have which we hold pretious.

For if we love our Libertye *Nullus capietur vel imprisonetur.* If we would enjoy our Lands without uniust disturbance *Nullus disseisietur de libero tenemento suo.* If we regard fredomes franchises royaltes and priviledges *Nullus disseisietur de Libertatibus.* If we esteem our antient free Customes by which we have gained tytle in our Lands property in our goods or interest in our priviledges *Nullus disseisietur de liberis Consuetudinibus.* If we would enjoy the benefit of the Lawes in generall *Nullus utlagetur,* or if we reioyce in the ayre of our own Countrey *Nullus exuletur.* Or if we would be delivered from any kind of oppression *Nullus aliquo modo destruatur.* Nay if lyves themselves be dear unto us and that we would be protected against the mischeifes of power and art *Nec super eum ibimus Nec super eum mittemus nisi per legale iudicium Parium vel per legem terre.*

In brief by vertue of this statute we have property in our goods tytle to our Lands Libertye for our persons and safety for our Lyves. . . . It is farther added and that iustly, That by force of this Statute every free Subiect may have remedy for every wrong don to his person, Landes or goods. And not only so for that would but give recompense for a wrong don, but this Statute also prevents wrongs, for by vertue hereof no man shalbe punished before he be condempned and no man shalbe condempned before he be heard and none shalbe heard but his iust deffence shalbe allowed.

These last sentences constitute the key to all that follows, the theme that pervades the infinite details and intricacies of Ashley's reading. They

[40] His "statutes of lyke kind" include four of the *six statutes*; 2 Ed. III, ca. 8, and 11 Rich. II, ca. 10.

are strikingly similar and very likely inspired by Coke's pronouncements in the recent *Case of the Marshalsea.*

Yet Ashley's reading is not a mere series of "thou shalt nots." All the proper and necessary powers which may and should be exercised within the rule of law, whether pertaining to the king and council or to the mayor of a borough or a village constable, receive their due definition. As he puts it in another passage of his introduction, "the Statute you may perceive proclaymes Libertie for the Subiect, but it must not be conceyved to be a lawles libertie whereby men may live like libertines, but a liberty bounded by the lymites of Law and reason . . ."

As was customary, each lecture raises a major question or proposition: *Divisio Secunda, Quel sera dit arrest ou imprisonment deins cel statut.* Here the Reader begins with a careful exception of the powers of king and council which must have contributed not a little to the "offenseless conclusion" for which he hoped. This statute, he says, so privileges the person of a free subject that he need not suffer wrong in his person, and the law has so much regard for liberty that no one may deprive a man of it without lawful conviction following answer (*responce*) and sentence thereupon. Nor may the king himself nor his patentee "by express terms nor by inference or consequence nor general custom justify the arrest or imprisonment of a free subject, but *by special custom or direct commandment the king himself or his council may imprison lawfully, without trial or judgement.*" [41] Then follows his "evidence," including Westminster I, chapter 15, "which declares in what cases men are replevisable and bailable and in what not," and practice as revealed by the Register and Fitzherbert. After further exposition of the powers of commitment accorded privy council, chancellor, and judges, he continues to this effect:

The King himself cannot arrest for suspicion of felony or treason, for if it were wrongful (*tortious*) the party could not have action against him [the king] as he could against a subject. . . . But when the king commands a man to prison of his absolute authority, the law would rather suppose that it was for good cause, as for contempt in his presence or other good cause than to suppose that the king who is the fountain of justice would do wrong; and the same is true if a judge commit.

What Reader Ashley says here accords with the ruling in Judge Anderson's reports, 1591, and with the practice in privy council and Star Chamber. It is exactly the stand which Serjeant Ashley and the other crown lawyers took in 1627–28.

After these reservations, "In the next place," continues the Reader, "let

[41] So underlined in the manuscript, possibly by Ashley himself in the day of need, 1627–28.

us see what will constitute an offence against this statute by color of office, for that is the greater oppression." Here he defines in most meticulous detail (some twenty items) the precise powers of arrest and imprisonment proper to local officials and officials connected with special jurisdictions. In the first group are included sheriffs, justices of the peace, constables, forest officials, and even "mine host" the innkeeper. The second group includes officials connected with the Marshalsea, ecclesiastical courts, officers of the Greencloth, the lord Admiral, and in general "courts which proceed by discretion without limited rules of law." [42]

The third division deals with disseisin of free tenement,[43] the fourth with disseisin of "liberties." The liberties intended within this statute are not only *fraunchises et royalties* but every immunity and freedom to which an Englishman is heir. Here are discussed disseisins such as are involved in lawful and unlawful monopolies and patents, use by corporations of their power to make bylaws, enforced enclosure of commons, dispensations, and others. Rules limiting the dispensing power are justified on the ground that the king is the *preserver* of the law.[44] The people look to him for the execution and maintenance of law and justice, therefore he can not *change* the laws.

The customs intended by this statute (*Divisio quinta*) are one of the principal grounds of the law of the realm, as set forth by St. Germain and by Fortescue, and indeed, the king at his coronation is sworn to observe the ancient customs of the realm. General customs, local customs, and particular customs are discussed, and "how a man might be disseised of such customs" is instanced by twelve illustrations.

The outlawry and exile prohibited by this statute are any not warranted by the law of the land, be it in respect of the person against whom it is pronounced, the matter for which it is adjudged, or the manner in which it is accomplished.[45] The "destruction" intended by this statute is any

---

[42] For examples, see Appendix I.

[43] *Divisio tertia—Quel sera dit disseisement de. franktenement et quel sera accompte franktenement.* Here are recited instances in which the king may lawfully seize the land of a subject, the temporalities of a bishop, the land of alien priories in wartime, lands alienated without license, and so on. More emphasis is placed on what may *not* lawfully be done, the taking of growing trees by purveyors, disseisin of free tenement by ecclesiastical courts, holding of an office granted to another. In all these the subject would have redress by this statute.

[44] The king may not grant the burgesses of Dorchester that none be impleaded outside for some act done within the borough, for each subject is heir to the right to sue in the bench. Dispensation of a law for a subject is disseisin of others; and the right to dispense may not be granted to a subject, for that is prerogative and pertains to the king's person alone.

[45] After citing several examples, he concludes, "In all these cases the outlawry is not *per legem terre.* And by force of this Statute *action on the case* lies for the party outlawed against him who procured it." As to exile, "our law" does not use it "nisi soit par Parlement ou par Judgment sur le Statute." That originator of despotism, the Conqueror, exiled several who would not obey his orders, "and so that practice continued at the

oppression, extortion and unjust exaction, or wrong made by authority or color of authority "whether it be against the body or the goods." Here again the examples afford full play to the penchant of the age for holding local officials within bounds. Possible offenders include local courts, public and private, commissioners of sewers, clerks of the market, and justices of the peace. The "destructions" they may commit are all sorts of unreasonable and excessive fines, amercements, fees, "taxes," tolls, distresses, and sureties for good abearing, as indeed, any other imaginable exaction, oppression, or extortion. The rights of the "little fellow" are not overlooked: excessive fines on copy-holders are ruled out, for here the court and "not the hard conscience of the lord" should prevail.

Divisio septima—nec super eum ibimus nec super eum mittemus quel est translate—

*neither shall any passe or sitt in Judgment upon him—*Pulton *accusacion*

nor we shall not passe upon hym nor condempne hym—Statutes at Large

Quel sera dit triall Judgement ou condempnacion d'un home prohibit per cel Ley.

Here Ashley accepts without question the translations in the most reputable editions of the printed statutes of his day, and comments accordingly. By this statute are prohibited all judgments without hearing and the response of the party, and without trial, all unlawful trials, and all judgments by judges not lawfully authorized and all manner of unlawful proceedings to judgment, and all unlawful executions. Even the king or a judge who saw a man commit murder could not adjudge him to be hung, for it is upon his "judicial knowledge" only that he may act.[46] The intent of this statute is clear for it has been expressly clarified by subsequent acts as 25 Edward III, chapter 4, and 28 Edward III, chapter 3 (two of the ubiquitous *six statutes*). The various forms of *lawful* trial Ashley dismisses with a mere listing. *Unlawful* practices are enlarged upon.[47]

Although Ashley follows the judges in *Cawdry's case* in comprehending ecclesiastical law within the "law of the land," and lists offenses properly within its jurisdiction, he takes occasion in almost every lecture to make strictures on court christian and its procedure. Here he follows

pleasure of the king until this Statute was made to avoid it, and thenceforth only by parliament." Early examples of parliamentary exile are those of Gaveston and Mortimer in Edward II's time, Richard Belknap and the other judges in Richard II's.

[46] Quoting Gascoigne, 7 Hen. IV, to the effect that a judge has private knowledge and judicial knowledge; granting that in his private knowledge he knows that a crime worthy of death has been committed, still in his judicial knowledge he cannot take cognizance of it.

[47] For these, see Appendix I.

Sir Edward wholeheartedly and speaks with more asperity than in his comments on any of the other non-common-law courts. It had evidently been those writs "to restreyne the swelling and exhorbitant power" of ecclesiastical jurisdiction, prohibitions based on Magna Carta, that had served to make that law "so obvious" to him. He questions its jurisdiction, its process and procedure as exercised in recent years; doubts the validity of the *new canons*; and emphatically condemns use of the oath ex officio in cases other than matrimonial and testamentary as an unlawful "passing upon a man."

Incidentally this Reader makes much of that favorite of the lawyers, Fortescue's admonition to the young prince that while the king is the fountain of justice, sits, or is assumed to sit in his courts, and has judgments pronounced in his name, still these are actually pronounced by his judges who alone are sufficiently learned in the law. This theme leads him into a digression based on Bracton and Britton, quite sound historically, on the early days when king in council judged matters "according to natural equity and reason," a jurisdiction since distributed to the courts of Chancery, Requests, and Star Chamber.

The eighth division, on the famous *nisi per legale judicium parium suorum*, is all quite routine, just what any lecturer might have learned from Staunford, the statutes, and current cases. He quotes Coke on the *Lord Norris' case* and refers to that of the Duke of Somerset as *en nostre fresh experience*. He includes the accepted dual definition of *pares*, "peers of the realm" and "equals," already employed by Lambarde, Selden, and others.

Finally, ninth, *Quel sera dit le Ley del terre deins l'intencion de cel Statute*, Ashley strikes a happy medium. He does not confine the *lex terrae* of Magna Carta to the common law, as had Morice and Fuller earlier, and as Littleton was to do in 1627–28. To be sure, the phrase refers primarily to the common law, statute law, and customs of the realm, as all that he has said in his previous lectures goes to prove, "and if a man be annoyed in his person, lands, or goods against any of these laws it is prohibited." On the other hand he does not go as far as the civilians, Hobart, Bacon, and Ellesmere, in comprehending other bodies of law. Divers other laws there are within the realm, but they are defined and bounded by the common law. They include ecclesiastical law, the law of the Admiralty, martial law, the law merchant, the law of the Marshalsea, the Green Cloth, Star Chamber, Chancery and Requests.[48]

---

[48] Each is elaborated in turn: canon law is not *lex terrae* unless confirmed by act of parliament. In time of invasion, martial law is *lex terrae mes contra en temps de peace*. The law merchant is *lex terrae*—it is lawful for a merchant stranger to sue before the council instead of delaying for trial by twelve men.

A proclamation is not *lex terrae,* for it cannot make or declare law. Still it is much to be respected as the command of king and council. In conclusion he repeats, "But of all these courts it is intended that they must not exceed their proper jurisdiction for then the trial, passing, and judgment there given is not *per legem terrae.*"

✤ CHAPTER XI ✤

A Decade of Parliaments, 1621-1629

I do thinke your Maiestie shall exsedingelie please your people if you shall be graciouslie pleased to take Sir Edward Cooke in to your highnes prinslie favour for we do all of us thinke him to be as good A Common welthes man as anie you have in all your kindomes, and we doo knowe him to bee a sounde protestant . . . (A PETITIONER)[1]

IN THE decade from 1620 to 1630 the main interest in Magna Carta history shifts from councils and court to parliament—the third and fourth of James and the three short parliaments of Charles I, 1625, 1626, 1628–29. Even so, the chief protagonists and their opponents, in constitutional issues turning on the Charter, were not the ordinary country gentlemen or merchants but "all the lawyers in the House" in general and Sir Edward Coke in particular. Their arguments were a reflection of what had already been worked out in councils and courts. Selden drew on his own learned treatises, Coke on the cases and "conceits" in his reports, Ashley on his Reading, and so on. But there were these differences: the issues were now thrashed out on a broader stage with a wider audience; the principles of the Charter were pressed ever nearer home, no longer excepting privy council and crown. Rules of law recently applied to the sheriffs of London, the burgesses of Plymouth, or a mayor of Liskeratt, were now to be extended to privy councilors and royal favorites.

These parliamentary episodes are essential to complete the story. They may be dealt with briefly, as familiar to most readers through the works of Gardiner, Trevelyan, recent monographs and articles, and the sources which have been long in print. As will appear, however, while most of the precedents and arguments are not novel, we may learn much more about their use and their users through the wealth of new source material—the parliamentary diaries recently published or transcribed.

There is little to be said for the years 1616 to 1621, naturally perhaps

---

[1] *State Papers*, 16, vol. 132, no. 35. Endorsed, "Januar. 18. 1628. Robert Triplet Beerebrewer at Islington delivered this to his Maiestye concerninge ye parlament which was to beginne to sitt Janua. 20." It consists of three octavo sheets written on both sides: professions of loyalty, a Puritan harangue on how to receive God's blessing and avoid his wrath by suppressing the papists, and advice on the coming parliament.

with no parliaments in session, Coke under a shadow, and Buckingham's star in the ascendant. Still the Charter continued to be cited in the courts, and very likely in petitions and tracts which I have not spotted. As to the courts, for instance, we find Dodderidge in King's Bench, 14 Jacobi, citing chapter 14 in connection with a "rule of law." [2] In the Lord Treasurer Suffolk's case in Star Chamber, it was Coke who had proposed a fine of 100,000 pounds and Hobart who brought it down to 30,000 pounds, "*salvo contenemento* (a phrase of Magna Carta)," as Chamberlain wrote to Carleton. [3]

The Parliament of 1621

AFTER an interval of six years of no parliaments, indeed, of ten years since a parliament had passed laws or granted a subsidy, there was at last summoned what has been termed "a parliament of necessity." Although there was a certain willingness to proceed with caution, " 'to make his majesty in love with parliaments,' " the Commons set themselves an ambitious program. What was attempted and what was accomplished is effectively summarized by the editors of the *Commons Debates*:

A good many things which members of parliament had on their minds had been waiting since the later years of Elizabeth. Many of the bills introduced had long been on the Commons' schedule in one form or another and now seemed about to become laws. Abuses in the law, especially those that were obnoxious to country gentlemen, were to be remedied, some of them by bills of grace. Procedure in courts and the administration of justice were not what they should have been and timely rectification by legislation was planned. Fees in courts and new offices had roused the wrath of those who resorted to courts frequently and who were now ready with bills to regulate officers and their compensation. It was proposed to define the jurisdiction of courts in some important details. Chancery in particular was the target of the stalwarts of the common law who could think of a number of bills to settle the old score with the keeper of the king's conscience. Informers had been careless to their own profit, and needed to have their activities curtailed by specifically stated legal limitations. Ecclesiastical courts had their critics and bills were put through the House to remove abuses in the administration of wills. Even

---

[2] In connection with the finding of pledges at common law: "For the rule of Law is, That every Declaration or Writ, ought to contain certainty and verity, and for default herein, Amercements grievous were imposed upon the Plaintiffs, until the Statute of *Magna Charta* cap. 14. which doth enact, that Amerciaments shall be *secundum modum delicti, salvo contenemento suo* . . ." Bulstrode, *Reports*, Pt. III, p. 279.

[3] "But the Lord Hobart did so antagonize the cause, as my Lord Chancellor termed it, and gave so good reasons for every particular, that he brought down the one fine to L30,000, and the other to L2000; adding, withal, that the institution of that court was not to ruin men and their families; that it might fine, but not ransom so far as that *salvo contenemento* (a phrase of Magna Carta). a man should not have means to uphold his degree, which being approved by all, without exception . . ." F. Williams, ed., *Court and Times of James I*, II, 193–94. Gardiner, III, 208–10.

justices of the peace were scolded and escaped the reformers only by the intervention of the King. Obsolete statutes had long been a serious problem. A comprehensive weeding out of such statutes was now at last about to be realized in the bill for continuance and repeal. The long standing grievance of monopolies, for the first time since the days of Elizabeth, seemed destined to undergo successful investigation. While the King looked on with misgivings, projectors of every description were put through a parliamentary inquisition that was uncomfortable. To smite the first of projectors the Commons revived in the form of impeachment that "judgment which hath been asleep these 300 years." With impeachment they went on to sweep the Lord Chancellor out of office and wakened apprehensions in other officials. With more dispatch than discretion they pronounced judgment on Floyd, and smarted under royal reprimand and the polite chiding of the Lords. But this bold bid for power of judicature, abortive at the moment, proved the beginning and not the end of that question. The revelations of the Committee for Courts about Bacon and Bennett resulted in the bill against bribery. One of the leading grievances, of course, was the decay of money and the decline of trade." [4]

Several of these grievances might seem of a nature to evoke appeals to Magna Carta. Actually, as far as the recorded debates reveal, chapter 29 was again "the most obvious," primarily in connection with the abuses of the patentees for monopolies, and in the autumn session rather broadly as a guarantee of the privileges of the Commons.

Among the available sources for this parliament the diaries are outstanding. The *Lords Journals* have effective official statements of the charges against the patentees and such offenders as Bacon and Bennett, and the judgments pronounced. As was customary, no individual speeches were recorded but the king's. "The peers allowed, indeed, their Journal Book to tell us what were their official acts, what bills were read, what messages were sent to the Commons, what reports were brought up from Committees. But nothing said by a peer in his individual capacity was ever set down." [5] The *Commons Journals* give us the ordered sequence of events and speeches, the reading of bills, the membership of committees, and the substance of some of the speeches, albeit in compressed and intentionally discreet form.[6] In addition the present-day researcher

[4] A number of economic problems were debated and remedies proposed, laws against papists revived, and bills "proposed for the regulation of the clergy and for their relief." *Commons Debates*, 1621, I, 3–5.

There were two sessions: the first, January 30 to April 13, and after the Easter recess, April 17 to June 4; the second in the autumn, November 20 to December 19.

[5] While Gardiner's edition of *Notes of Debates in the House of Lords* does something to supply this lack, the book contributes little to this subject.

[6] "Speeches of such different character by men of such varied mannerisms of speech and thought become in the hands of the Clerk a good deal the same." Speeches "against the government were likely to lose a little of their pungency and spice in the course of transmission to the Journal." The editors summarize "other things he [the clerk] fails to tell us," such as irritation at the rulings of the speaker, exciting passages in the House "where there was tension or a sharp set-to between members," excitement on certain days. *Commons Debates*, 1621, I, 104–9.

has what Gardiner lacked, the remarkable collection of diaries (*Commons* *Debates*) in the admirable edition of Notestein, Relf, and Simpson. These are valuable for the present studies in two important respects: (1) some of the diarists succeed in catching the flavor and idiom of speeches, in including quotations, illustrations, "precedents," and stories which the clerk ignored; (2) they report at length what went on in committees, including summaries or attempted verbatim reports of the debates.

Fortunately two of the diarists, Holland and Belasye, were partial to recording the speeches of Sir Edward Coke, though it would be hard indeed to avoid them, his personality and influence so pervaded this parliament. He it was who was largely responsible for the linking of Magna Carta first to the grievances against the patentees, then to the charges against Sir John Bennett, and finally to the privileges of the House. To be sure, his arguments were not always cogent or his historical precedents apt or accurate. As to certain precedents we are told, "Of this he shewed a manuscripte, because he was suspected by some malevolent persons to have devised them of his owne head." [7]

Certain episodes suggest that his age may have begun to tell upon him, [8] though even in the 1628 parliament his activity and vigor were extraordinary and his speeches still "packed a punch." The distinguished editors of the diaries are not enthusiastic about Sir Edward, feeling, no doubt rightly, that he has been overrated at the expense of abler parliamentarians like Alford, Phelips, and Sandys, yet the very character of their criticism is a tribute to his influence over his colleagues. For instance, of the diarist Holland they say:

His judgments of men were probably those of his fellow members. Sir Edward Coke was the idol of the average member who seldom knew enough law and enough of the personal egoism of Coke to appraise him as other than he seemed. Holland was likely to give a good deal of space to Sir Edward, more than to any others. It is to be said for him, however, that he did not neglect Sir Edwin Sandys and Phelips. [9]

As to Coke's "style of talking and writing," to which the editors also take exception, it seems likely that he was just too much for the diarists and lost by their faulty recording. While they were struggling with some learned Latin phrase or quotation, he got away from them, and hence the

[7] March 13, *ibid.* V, 36 (Belasye).
[8] The editors of the *Commons Debates, 1621* (II, 272, note 15) cite an occasion, March 27, on which Sandys reproaches Coke for having made a report of conference with the Lords "because he had no direction from the House to make the report." They quote a letter from Chamberlain to Carleton, perhaps due to this incident, showing that " 'Sir Edward Cooke doth not altogether hold the great applause he had . . .' "
[9] *Ibid.* I, 94. Cf. p. 66 on Belasye: "With speakers all through the diary he is given to playing favorites, Coke in particular, Edwin Sandys, Phelips, Nathaniel Rich, Crew, Alford, Calvert, Noy, Hakewill, Sir Thomas Wentworth, and a few others are the men he prefers to quote, and in that choice he cannot be regarded as undiscriminating."

choppy and sometimes incoherent effect. Belasye, who was "sharper on legal points than some of the other diarists," [10] does rather well with Sir Edward's Latin, and if his notes may be trusted, many of Sir Edward's speeches began in this disconcerting fashion.

In this and subsequent parliaments Coke was decidedly *persona grata* with the Lords, active in conferences, reporting back to the Commons, repeatedly conveying bills and messages. In the Commons he was active on committees, serving as chairman of the important committee of grievances.[11] The length of his speeches in committee and in the House, or at least the space accorded them by the diarists, is impressive, and their number is so great it takes six columns of index to record them all.[12]

There were few subjects with which he did not deal, but naturally he was at his best in the legal field—correction of faults in courts of justice such as Chancery and the Court of Wards; informers and concealments; points of procedure and privilege. In these last respects he did much to help the House of Commons to acquire something of the dignity and formalism of a court of law.

Sir John Eliot once aptly referred to Coke, "that great Father of the Lawe," as "having consulted with his memorie of the proceedings in like cases." [13] In this instance it was "presidents of the Antients" which Eliot had in mind, but there were a number of occasions on which Sir Edward "consulted with his memorie" for precedents in his own living experience. His rich political and official career extended over forty years, under two (and after 1625, three) sovereigns, in parliament, privy council, and courts. Few had held as many successive posts as he who could say "when I was speaker"; "and because I had served as attorney and so conversant in every court." [14] "He said, he was once a Judge of the King's Bench, and did wonder how the Judges of these times did interpret that Statute." [15]

Belasye caught the pat phrases[16] and the enlivening anecdote as well as

[10] *Ibid.*, p. 65. Perhaps this legal interest was one source of his devotion to Coke. Where Sir Edward had time for careful preparation and there was good reporting, as in some of the conferences with the Lords (for instance, his part in the charges against Middlesex in 1624), his arguments have coherence and organization. *L. J.* III, 307–9.

[11] For an effective summary of his work see Willson, *Privy Councillors*, pp. 89–91, 153–54.

[12] This, of course, includes references to one speech as recorded by several diarists. For August 2, 1625, it is recorded that "Sir Ed(ward) Cooke (havinge spoken before, yet beinge permitted contrary to the orders of the House to speake agayne . . ." *Commons Debates, 1625*, p. 71 (Pym)—the debate on Mountague.

[13] *Negotium Posterorum*, II, 39.

[14] *Commons Debates, 1621*, VI, 127–28 (Holland); II, 307 (Diary X). Similar instances, V, 38, 97–98 (Belasye). The first of these reads, "Sole importacion is a Monopolie, and I beinge Atturney general brought *Quo Warrantes* against such . . . and over threw them all."

[15] *L. J.* III, 729a (1628). Coke's speech in conference with the Lords, referring to Westminster I.

[16] "Commonly when yow followe two hares you lose bothe." "I would never take breviate of one syde, unless I might have of bothe. Ile keepe my eares open for bothe parties, I love to come even." "It would be too great an Almanie Leape betwixt this and alhalloutide, the bills would take winde." *Commons Debates, 1621*, V, 67, 88, 184.

the learned citation, and has passed on to us some of the stories that led Prince Charles to delight in Sir Edward's speeches.

A Pattent to marchaunt Taylours that should putt cloathe to none but of ther companye adiudged voyde, for they can not restrayne the libertie of the subiect without common consent. A lawe that he that puts out one eye of another shall loose one of his owne. It happened that a Monoculus had his eye putt out and it was adiudged reasonable that he that putt it out should loose both. Amongst the Locrenses he that propounds a new lawe was to come in with a halter about his neck, and if reiected to be hanged. A Fitt Lawe for new proiectours . . ." [17]

Even more impressive were his recollections of actual historical events. Fellow members listened with respect to one who could ridicule Buckingham's inefficiency by comparison with the Lords Admiral of the Elizabethan age—"It was never heard that Q[ueen] Eliz[abeth's] navy did daunce a paven" [18] and who could vividly recall the plots against the queen such as that of William Parry: "I myself have seen him walking with the Queen when' he had his stilleto in his pocket (as he confessed afterwards) and the Lord preserved her." [19] One more, too choice to omit, comes from Coke as chief justice of King's Bench:

When I was the Queen's Attorney, she said unto me, I understand that my Counsel will strongly urge, *Praerogativa Reginae,* but my will is, that they stand, *pro domina veritate* rather than *pro domina Regina,* unless that *domina Regina* hath *veritatem* on her side: And she also used to give this in charge many times, when any one was called to any Office by her, that they should ever stand *pro veritate,* rather than *pro Regina.* [20]

In the great case of monopolies in Elizabeth's reign the main issue had been unlawful restraint on freedom of trade. Now, after several years of experience with James' patentees, that was still an issue, but was aggravated by the abuses committed by monopolists in the exercise of their patents, and their connection with persons in high places—Attorney General Yelverton and protégés of Buckingham such as Edward Villiers and Mompesson. The patents, their history and character, have been fully described. [21] Some were of long standing and worthy of continuance such as that for the manufacture of glass. This had been issued to a Venetia Versellini, as early as 1574, and to other native patentees, 1606 and 1611.

---

[17] *Ibid.* V, 58. Cf. Diary X, *ibid.* II, 250–51.

[18] Speech of August 5, 1625, *Commons Debates,* 1625, p. 85.

[19] *Commons Debates,* 1621, II, 457 (Diary X). And again, "he heard Queen *Eliz.* say that her Father, King *Henry* the Eighth, did hope to live so long till he saw his Face in Brass, i. e. in Brass Money." *L. J.* III, 761 (1628).

[20] *Tr.* 13 *Jac., Banco Regis,* Bulstrode, *Reports,* Pt. III, p. 44. This in a case of writ of error upon a judgment on a *quare impedit.* The original judgment was upheld. Although some errors were admitted, Coke concluded, "in this Case there appears no title for the King."

[21] *Commons Debates,* I (intro.) and VII, app. B. Gardiner Vol. IV, cap. xxxiii.

Then in 1615 two courtiers, the Earl of Montgomery and Sir Robert Mansell, were included among the patentees and foreign imports prohibited. This patent and others of its kind were exempted from the statute of 1624. Most of the patents objected to in parliament had been newly issued within the last ten years. They were numerous (seventeen were condemned by James in his proclamation) and varied enough to affect persons in many walks of life and social strata. For instance, two patentees, Bassano and Vaudry, backed by the Company of Fishmongers, had a method of keeping salmon and lobsters alive in boats from Ireland to the London market, but in practice the monopoly deteriorated into plundering poor fishermen. Another group of humble station were the *Wharfingers* of London. The patents for licensing inns and alehouses offended justices of the peace by encroaching on their jurisdiction. Said Crew before the Lords, "justices are made servants to him [Mompesson]. . . . He hath vexted ancient inns . . ." [22] Sir Robert Floyde's patent for "the sole ingrossing of all wills and inventories" must have affected persons of property, denying them "the right which the subject hath," the "liberty by law to ingross his own will," or if intestate, to write his own inventory or employ whom he would to do it.

It was the grants which empowered patentees to arrest and imprison infringers[23] that aroused the greatest indignation, and which were alleged to be contrary to Magna Carta chapter 29. There were several such, but most conspicuous among them was the patent for gold and silver thread. This, like the patent for glass, had begun promisingly enough with the importation of a foreign craftsman, or rather craftswoman, when in 1611 Lady Bedford had a certain Madame Turatta brought over from France. Four men under Lady Bedford's patronage were granted the monopoly of the sole making of gold and silver thread. A second patent was issued in 1616 in which Sir Edward Villiers invested four thousand pounds.

[22] The patent for inns, an idea of Sir Giles Mompesson, kinsman of Buckingham, was issued to Mompesson and two others, 1617. They made out licenses to inns, which were then to be validated by the justices of assize. At the time of its issue, this patent was considered valid by Bacon, Coke, and others. Crew called Mompesson "a principal projector, one that had gotten a plurality of patents." As to this of licensing, "But the common law did ever allow free trade. If statutes then have not restrained the innkeeper he needs not to have a licence more than a shipmaster or carrier, etc. . . ." *Commons Debates*, II, 180–84 (Diary X).

[23] On April 18, 1621, Sir Edward Coke, reporting to the House from committee, ten of the lesser, but also obnoxious monopolies, names seven, and then three others as "The Patents of new Invention, when have Clauses of giving Oath, and Imprisonment, against *Magna Charta*, 32 times confirmed.

"1. Sir Geor. Douglasse, a Patent to dispense with the hot Press. a Way to spoil our Cloth. —This a Proclamation.

"2. *Innocent Lamyer*, the Power of Conservation of the *Thames* to take away Shelves, and take Balance.—The Life of the City, the Navigableness of the *Thames*.

"3. A Patent to Sir A. Apseley, and Sir Jo. Keyes, a Grant of the penal Law for Cask against a Statute 23 H. VIII." *C. J.* I, 580a.

"Sir Edward Coke's report from the Committee of Grievances" concludes "To minister oaths and to commit by virtue of a patent is against the Great Charter." Diary X, p. 298.

When the goldsmiths continued to protest and infringe on the monopoly, the patentees received support from the king through Attorney General Yelverton. Eventually (1618) the manufacture was taken into the king's hands, new commissioners, including Mompesson and Michell added, and their powers increased. Matters came to a crisis in the spring of 1619 with fresh imprisonments, houses broken into, tools and "engines" seized. Bonds were forced on the goldsmiths and silkmen obliging them not to sell their wares to unlicensed persons. It was alleged that Mompesson and Michell had threatened five silk mercers that if they refused to seal bonds "all the prisons in London should be filled, and thousands should rot in prison." The city was in an uproar. Four aldermen offered to stand bail for the prisoners for one hundred thousand pounds. When a deputation protested to the king he ordered the prisoners set free, yet a fresh proclamation authorized continuance of the system.

Disaffection was widespread. The revelations on this patent in the Commons aroused many interests:

The champions of the common law were justly dissatisfied with the creation of an arbitrary tribunal which sent men to prison without the interference of a jury. The advocates or those who thought themselves advocates of liberty of trade were displeased by the restriction placed upon the freedom of labour, whilst those whose great commercial doctrine was the preservation of the precious metals were horrified when they heard of the treatment to which the coin had been subjected.[24]

The formal charges against the chief offenders, Mompesson, Michell, and Yelverton, are best set forth in the *Lords Journals*.[25] The Lords followed the cue given by their committee (on Mompesson's offenses) to deal "chiefly with the Execution, not with the Legality of those Patents." The king himself had conceded (in his speech of March 26) "That of Gold and Silver Thread was most vilely executed, both for Wrongs done to Mens Persons as also for Abuse in the Stuff; for it was a kind of false Coin. I have already freed the Persons, that were in Prison. I will now also damn the Patent; and this may seem instead of a Pardon." He urged

[24] Gardiner, IV, 48.

[25] *L. J.* III, 62, 69–70, 89, 109a. The Lords found "in the Execution thereof, that the Authority given by the Letters Patents (which ought to be used rarely) was used by them familiarly, to the Undoing of Thousands. That the Warrants Dormants, to seize and imprison, &c. exceed all Kind of Warrants; whereof there be Three, and one of them is without Date, and razed, and the other hath a Date with a new Hand. That Sir *Gyles Mompesson* committed divers to Prison without Examination, which they could not do by that Warrant. That divers were threatened to be imprisoned. That *Fowles* did locke up divers in his own House. That divers Houses were violently broken up, and the Parties Goods seized. That divers were compelled to enter into Bonds not to exercise their own trade, and to stand to their Orders, and to make Oath what Quantity of Gold and Silver Thread they sold, and to whom. . . ." Similar charges of illegal commitments were made against Sir Francis Michell, and further: "That he erected an Office, kept a Court, made Officers, and divers unwarrantable Orders, and exacted Bonds for the Observance of the same."

the Lords to "proceed judicially, and spare none, where you find just cause to punish; but let your Proceedings be according to Law." Fitting the penalty to the crime, the Lords included in their sentence of Michell "that he shall be imprisoned during the King's Pleasure, in *Finsbury Gaol,* in the same Chamber there, where he provided for others, *The Tower,* where he now remains, being a Prison too worthy of him."

But it is in the speeches of the gentlemen of the Commons that indignation is most effectively voiced, and charges of illegality supported by Magna Carta. On March 3 the Commons took up the patent for gold and silver thread. Two days later their committee which had examined Michell and Yelverton in the Tower (Mompesson had fled) reported to the House through Sir Robert Phelips. Immediately following the report, Sir Edward Coke set the key for what was to follow. His speech evidently impressed his hearers, for there are four versions of it, all of which include Coke's "32 confirmations" and three include explanations of the name:

The Statute of *Magna Charta* 29° *Cap.* confirmed 32 Times:—None to be imprisoned, Ec.—Called *Magna Charta,* not for the Largeness, but for the Weight.—If this suffered, no Man shall live in Safely.—42 *Ass.* a Commission granted to this Purpose as now: The Justices of Assise took away his Patent, and informed the King, that this against the Great Charter of *England.* A grant by Queen *Eliz.* to make By-Laws: They made a By-law to imprison; therefore adjudged, against the Law. All the old writers called *Magna Charta Chartam Libertatis.*—Sorry, the Attorney-general should be a Commissioner, or this be countenanced by greater Persons.[26]

Next day Hakewill reported to the House the plans for the conference with the Lords to be handled by a formidable array of legal talent. Following Digges' introduction Crew, Finch, and Hakewill, with equally able assistants, were to handle the body of the conference; Sir Edwin Sandys "to aggravate the whole"; "lastly for matter of precedents to justify our proceedings for punishment for the offences and remedies to prevent the like in time to come and so to conclude, and this is referred to Sir Edward Coke, who hath been a father of the law."

On March 8, "After dinner, the Lords being sat in the Painted Chamber (the Prince also being present and sitting at the end of the table,) Sir Dudley Digges made an eloquent introduction to the business (so that he did, as Sir Edward Coke often said, orator like, *aperte, distincte, ornateque, dicere perspicue et breviter*) shewing first our joy for this kind concurrence of their Lordships with us in these matters of grievances . . ."[27]

[26] *C. J.* I, 538b. Also three of the diarists, Belayse, Pym, and Diary X, (*Commons Debates,* V, 25; IV, 124; II, 167). This last is evidently a mis-hearing or misreading when it quotes Coke as saying "And it is called Magna Charta not for the voluminousness of it but for the *delight.*" It is *weight* in his reports and earlier speeches. Three mention the precedent from the *Liber Assisarum* and three *Clarke's case.*

[27] *Commons Debates,* 1621, II, 179–88 (Diary X).

Although Digges' introduction and Sandys "aggravation" were the more eloquent, it is only Finch's part that need concern us here, for

Mr. Recorder Finch spake next concerning the patent of gold thread, which he said was as weighty a grievance to the King and kingdom as ever any. . . . To strengthen all they got a commission which was thought fit by the Lord Chancellor and Lord Treasurer and Sir Henry Yelverton, whereby they had power to examine delinquents upon oath, to punish offenders by discretion, and any two to commit such to prison as they shall suspect to offend. Divers great men were put in the commission, as . . . Now to put in great men's names and base ones only to execute it is an ill course. This was a commission of a very large extent. Gives power to imprison men, which is contrary to the statute of Magna Charta which hath been 32 times confirmed, which sayeth *nullus liber homo imprisonetur*. Their meetings upon this commission they called Commission Courts; and if the parliament had not come, I think they would have called them High Commission Courts.

All this while was little done, but now you see comes in Sir Giles Mompesson as one that would be loath there should be any ill in a commonwealth wherein he would not have a finger.

After a description of the resulting evils experienced by the various craftsmen, how some were warned to appear before the attorney general, and refusing to enter into bonds were sent to the Fleet by Mr. Attorney "at the instance of Sir Edward Villiers," Finch continues:

There was 100,000 li bail of 4 Aldermen refused. My Lord Chancellor upon entreaty confirmed the commitment, and they lay four or five weeks and then were brought before the Lord Chancellor and counsel heard. And they continuing obstinate were sent back to the Fleet. The Citizens hearing of it, the Lord Mayor petitioned the King for them, who graciously caused them to be released, saying he would not govern his subjects by bonds. So you see it's best going to the fountain. But what, stayed they here. No, they went on . . .[28]

Next afternoon Crew and Finch were sent back to the Lords where they "repayred their former omissions, touchinge ther taskes of Innes and gold thread." These included censure of the referees, and as Coke insisted, Magna Carta and imprisonment.[29] The same day after dinner in committee of the whole House, the "warrant dormant" was produced and read.[30] "It was ordered that this should be delivered to the Lords together

[28] *Ibid.*, pp. 184–88. Further, "where they found resistance they brake open houses, shops, and chambers and seized poor men's goods. . . . Moore, Symons and Underwood (Underhill?) were committed by Sir Francis Michell alone, 17 days, which was contrary to their commission. For by it two were to join in the committing of any person. A poor maid was committed because she would not take an oath to accuse her mistress who was suspected to have spun gold thread. So divers were committed 20 days, only upon suspicion when nothing was found. . . ."

[29] *Commons Debates, 1621*, VI, 47 (Holland). Cf. II, 201 (Diary X).

[30] *Ibid.* IV, 139–40 (Pym): "In th'afternoone, the Speaker beinge appoynted to attend, the Warrant Dormant was produced whereby authoritie was given to the bearers thereof (1) to

with the opinion of the House That it was against Lawe and the Great Charters Priviledges." [31]

Two patents of a different character, not involving arrest and imprisonment, nevertheless were condemned by Coke as contrary to Magna Carta. These were Floyde's patent for the "sole ingrossing of wills and inventories," and Lepton's patent "for making all bills at York" (that is, for drawing bills for the parties in the "Court of York"). [32] Sir Edward's speeches do not define the measure of offense against the Charter explicitly, but imply some undue curtailment of "liberty of the subject," in the first to make his own will or inventory, in the second, to have his bill drawn by a competent and unbiased clerk. Both patents were condemned by the House as a "grievance in the creation and the execution."

In addition to presenting the most obnoxious patents to the Lords as grievances, the Commons introduced a bill "for renewing of Magna Carta," or more fully, "for the better Securing of the Subjects from wrongfull Imprisonment, and Deprivation of Trades and Occupations, contrary to the 29th Chapter of *Magna Charta*." [33] Although it did not reach the Lords, it is significant as a true forerunner of the various measures introduced in 1628 culminating in the Petition of Right, and because of the publicity given chapter 29 both in committee and in the House. Morice's and Fuller's bills had been directed against High Commission and other ecclesiastical courts and was of interest mainly

search, Arrest, and attache such as showld worke or be suspected to worke, (2) to enter into any suspected howse and to apprehend the bodies of such as should hinder or delaye the execution of that warrant, (3) to seaze Instruments, tooles, and other materialls, and them to keepe till further warrant. Signed: Fra. Bacon, Tho. Suffolke, Tho. Lake, Rob. Nawnton, H. Yelverton, Allen Apsly, Tho. Coventree, Fra. Michell, Ed. Twedye." Say the editors, "The description is accurate. A copy of the warrant without date, is printed in *Archaeologia*, 41:253–254."

[31] "To Mr. Finch referred to deliver the referrees, Chancelor, Tresorer, and Yelverton, dobly. . . . Proclamation 15 Jac. to touch the commyttment therupon contrary to magna charta. Commission, the commission court, Warrant Dormant ordered to bee read at the conference, Extortions, Imprysonments, hindrances of 11 trades . . .
"*Post meridiem*. Conference with the lords, wherin Thomas Crewe and the Recorder Finch repayred their former omissions, touchinge ther taskes of Innes and gold thread." *Commons Debates*, 1621, V, 287–88 (Smyth).

[32] *Ibid*. II, 250–51, 363–64 (Diary X), gives a good idea of both patents. Nichôlas (II, 65) has the best version of Coke's report on the nature of Lepton's patent. For the passages citing the Charter we must turn to *C. J.* I, 565b–66a, 620a; Belayse; and Barrington, which last reads as follows: "Sir Edward Coke's report of Leptons Patent. He gave 900 *li.* for his Patent to the Lord Sheffield. Sir E. Coke drew the Patent. He had the Kings warrant for it; and, though it is not fitt for him to enioye it as unskillfull and against magna Charta (*Ne patris onoretur plus solito*), and which he doth by imposing new charges on them by virtu of his office and Pattent for every writt, bill, Letter." Pym, as was characteristic, gives brief summary statements. *Commons Debates*, 1621, V, 59–60; III, 244; IV, 177–79, 335–37 respectively.

[33] *C. J.* I, 596b; nearly identical in Holland; slightly different wording in Belasye, Diary X, and Pym. *Commons Debates*, 1621, VI, 111; V, 113; II, 332; IV, 274.
Whenever the bill is referred to briefly, it is the point of wrongful imprisonment that is sure to be named, as in Smyth, V, 355: "Bill to restrayn the imprisonment of the subiect contrary to the statute of magna carta *cap.* 29 I *lectio*," and others. I have not succeeded in finding the text of this bill, but neither did the editors of the diaries, who include in their appendix A all pertinent bills found.

to a minority, the Puritan nonconformists. The practices of the patentees were more flagrant and affected more varied interests. Here mere individuals were exercising judicial powers—"he erected an office, kept a court"—and effecting commitments that by no stretch of the imagination or reasoning could be claimed to be *per legem terrae*. Although both Lords and Commons made studied efforts to exempt king and council from any blame, a few of the privy councilors, the "referees," Attorney General Yelverton, and indirectly Buckingham, were implicated. The bill attempted to define, albeit still generously, the powers of commitment by the council. "Put in by that Abell man Sir Will Fletwood," it received its first reading in the Commons, April 30. Only one of the diarists, Belasye, attempts a summary of its contents:

The penaltie 10 times so much as the partie damnified by beinge imprisoned or dispossessed of his trade, the iudge offendinge to forfeit his place, the cause of the committement to be expressed in the *mittimus* unless it be in open Courte, not to extend to high treason or suspition therof. This bill committed.

The debate following the second reading, May 5, indicated a general consensus of opinion that some such bill was needed, and that it should cover corporations imprisoning for infringement of their bylaws, imprisonment by monopolists, and proclamations enforcing execution of a monopoly. The privy councilors in the House questioned the clause providing that the cause of commitment be expressed in the *mittimus*, a rule extending even to matters of state other than high treason or suspicion of treason. Sir Edward Coke agreed with Serjeant Ashley here that "matters of state ought not to be inserted in a *mittimus*." Penalties for offending judges ("the judge offending to forfeit his place") were also opposed as dangerously severe, affecting even the usual powers of justices of the peace. Here Ashley, quite in line with his reading as to what practices were properly *per legem terrae*, assured the House that "Justices of peace and corporations need not feare, if the imprisonment be lawfull 'tis not against magna charta, which is *per legem terrae*." [34]

[34] There are a number of accounts of this debate. Barrington, pp. 172–73; Pym, pp. 307–8; Belasye, pp. 143–44; Nicholas, II, 25–26. The clerk's record gives the best idea of the sequence of speakers, and their import, albeit briefly and choppily. Some of the diarists do better by parts of Ashley's and Coke's statements.

According to Pym: "It was desired that Corporacions and Justices of Peace might be excepted. To which was answere(d) That the Lawfull authoritye of both was preserved, for the Words of Magna Carta were That noe man should be imprisoned *Contra Legem terrae*.

"Sir Edward Cooke. Yf there be a Charter to make By-Lawes, with a power to imprison for not performing of them, theis Charters are voyde in Lawe. Soe is a Proclamacion for a Commission for the Execution of a Monopolye and those that advise such Proclamations and Commissions are to be punish't. Yet herein is a defect in the Bill, That Treasons onelye are to be Excepted. 33 H. 6. Yf a man be Committed by the bodye of the Counsell he is not to be bayled, neither are they to set downe the Cause in the *Mittimus*. There are divers matters of State that are not high Treason."

The bill was assigned to an able committee, including privy councilors and lawyers especially capable of dealing with the vexed subject of commitment, specialists in economic interests such as Sir Edwin Sandys, representatives of injured groups such as the members for London and York. The lawyers included Sir Edward Coke, Sir Edward Mountague, Noy, of course Sir William Fleetwood "to take care of this bill," and notably, Francis Ashley. Others who were increasingly to assume leadership in coming parliaments were Sir Robert Phelips, Sir William Spencer, and Nathaniel Rich.[35]

Monday, May 28, Fleetwood reported the bill with amendments.[36] These included (1) a provision for the "saving of the Lords of the Councell's authority," which Calvert in the ensuing debate refers to as "the Clause binding 6 of the Councell within sixe daies after the comittment of any two of them"; (2) a modification of the penalty for offending judges which Mr. Solicitor refers to as the "Clause of questioning the Judges in Parliament, for refusing, upon the first Motion, to deliver the Party." Recalcitrant justices of the peace were to be removed from the commission for the peace for one year. Again the opposition of the privy councilors led to the bill's recommitment. Secretary Calvert pointed out the danger of discovering the cause "when upon matters of state there is cause of secrecy." Mr. Solicitor indicated the likelihood of injustice to judges and justices of the peace "if an error in judgment be questioned." [37] Here again Sir Edward concurred with his fellow privy councilors that restrictions on councilors went too far. Commitment by "two hands of the council" was sanctioned by practice. "Therfor t'is not fit to inlarge it to a necessyty of 6 hands now." According to the clerk's version, "Mr. Secretary" had urged that commitment by the king or *one* of the privy council was valid, but Coke had insisted on two, citing as precedents 33 Henry VI and the ruling of the judges in Queen Elizabeth's reign.[38]

And in part as per Nicholas: "He saith further, that a Man committed by the Body of the Privy Council may not be bailed, as hath been resolved by all the Judges of the Kingdom:— That it is inconvenient and may be dangerous to have in a Business of State the Reason expressed in the *Mittimus.*"

[35] *C. J.* I, 610a. The members for London were Sir Thomas Lowe, knight; Robert Bateman, skinner; William Towerson, skinner; and, notably, Robert Heath, at this time London's recorder. York sent Sir Robert Askwith, knight and alderman, and Christopher Brooke.

[36] *Ibid.* I, 628b.

[37] *Commons Debates,* 1621, VI, 172 (Holland). Cf. *ibid.* II, 397 (Diary X).

[38] *Ibid.* III, 323-24 (Barrington). Cf. *ibid.* II, 397, and IV, 382 (Diary X and Pym). The others are very brief. Also *C. J.* I, 628b.

Pym does not quote separate speeches, but with his faculty for pithy extractions of the substance of a debate, summarizes the objections as follows:

"(1) The saveinge of the authoritye to the Counsell too shorte. 36 H. 6 one was Committed by two of the Counsell, procured a Habeas Corpus. The Writt was returned *pro rebus ipsum Regem tangentibus.* And the Judges did forbeare to meddle anie further. 34 *Eliz.* It was resolved that Committment by two of the Counsell was good in Lawe.

November 20, the first day of the fall session, the Commons attempted to resume where they had left off. Bills were taken up again, and times appointed for the sittings of their respective committees, including "Imprisonment against *Magna Charta.—Friday* next, in the House." Tuesday, the 27th, Fleetwood reported the bill with amendments. It had its third reading and was passed on Friday, November 30. In its final form it made exceptions in the direction urged by the privy councilors: its limitations were not to extend to commitments for treason, or commitments by six privy councilors "wherein they must likewise signifie that is for matter of State not fitt to be revealed." "If judges do wrongfully commit any to prison, then to be censured by Lords of the next parliament."[39] But on December 18, at the king's instance, came the adjournment till February 8 next.

Characteristically here in the Commons, as in the courts, it is usually not the injured parties in their petitions and depositions who cite the Great Charter, but "the lawyers in the House." One of the few exceptions comes from the *Wharfingers*, "keepers of Wharfs for stoage of wood and cole upon the River of Thames in or neere London." After rehearsing at length the history, nature, and operations of the patent to the Woodmongers, they point out that the

said Grant (accompanied with ordinances as aforesaid) is not onely a Monopoly, but the execution thereof tends to deprive his Maiesties subiects of their libertie, by unlawfull imprisonment, contrary to the great Charter of the Liberties of England, and to the hinderance of Legall proceedings and stop of Iustice for their goods uniustly and against law taken from them, and to the destruction of their trade, and is otherwise enormous and extreme grievous to the petitioners and others his Maiesties subiects, and may with the like colour be put in execution against Brewers, Scavingers, and divers other trades; and for that the petitioners are ready to make good each of the said generals, with divers particulars of every sort.[40]

"(2) That it is very dangerous to the Judges if uppon mistakeinge in not graunting Habeas Corpus they showld bee subiect to the Censure of Parliament.

"(3) The Limittacon *sine Judicio parium* Extends to a Committment for a Contempt in open Courte, Committment by the high-Commission and Ecclesiasticall Judges, which is never done by a Jurie. It is likewise dangerous to Justices of Peace if they showld be subiect to prove the Lawfullnes of Imprisonment perchance two yeares after when the witnesses be dead."

[39] A clause in Belasye's version seems to indicate that the penalty for justices of the peace remained the same, one year's suspension from office "if anie doe, to forfeit ten times so much in damages to be recovered in anye of the kings Courts of record, and the offendour to be disabled for one yeare to exercise the office by colour wherof Committed." Cf. Diary X for an attempt, not very clear, to indicate the amendments. *Commons Debates*, 1621, V, 226, II, 477–78. C. J. I, 640b, 647a, 653a, 661b.

[40] According to the petition, the wharfingers and their servants have at several times "beene (by colour of the said Letters patents) committed to prison by the Master and Wardens of the said Companie, and there detained sometimes 7 or 8 dayes; at other times their Carres have beene by the said Companie or their ministers taken from them; and when they endeavoured by course of law to relieve themselves, they have beene unduly staid." *Commons Debates*, 1621, VII, 98–100.

Another such instance, although in quite a different connection, is found "At the Committee for the cause betweene my Ladie Stafford and her copihoulders of the Mannour of Thornburie and Ouldburie in Glostershire."

The tenants exhibite ther bill in parliament to reverse a decree in the Chancerie wherby ther fines were reduced to a resonable certaintie, as a yeare and a halfes value for land not harriotable and a yeares value for land harriotable. And they pretended it to have bene obtayned by surreption, that not above 8 were made parties to the Bill and yet all were bound by the decree; that ther customes ought to be tried at the common Lawe and that it is against Magna Charta, chap. 29, to trie them elswhere.

But "the opinion of the committee was that was no iniustice in the Decree for anie thinge appearinge to them, and therfor no cause to reverse it." The very able defense of Chancery which led the committee to this conclusion and which is reported in great detail by Belasye begins, "The Lord Chancellour Elsmer never did anie thinge better for the common wealth then by orderinge the differences betweene the tenants copiholders and ther Lords; and the Chancerie entertained those causes for these reasons . . ." As to the point of jurisdiction, "These proceedings are not against magna Charta, for that the Lawe of the chancerie is *Lex terrae*. The Statute speakes onelie of *Liberae consuetudines,* which these are not." [41]

It was the Commons' committee for abuses in courts of justice that dealt with Bacon and Bennett. Oddly enough in all the charges and proceedings against the chancellor I have found no instance of his being accused of "sale of justice" contrary to Magna Carta. In charges of bribery against Sir John Bennett, judge of the Prerogative Court, however, Coke does bring his favorite *nulli vendemus* clause into more than one speech as recorded by the diarists.[42] A similar opportunity was afforded Sir

The draft of a proposed remedial act (*ibid.*, pp. 91–95) describes the monopoly as a corporation for "the rule, oversight and government of the Carrs, Carts, Carters and Carmen of all persons workinge any Carrs or Carts within the said Citty and liberties," resulting in unfair discrimination, high prices of carriage and consequently of wood and coal, and the danger that the patentees may engross the whole "fewell" supply of the city.

[41] This diarist, "sharper on legal points" than some of the others, was evidently interested in the able defense of Sir John Walter, an M.P. and attorney, who explains in great detail the exact procedure in Chancery in such cases and the reasons for it. *Commons Debates,* 1621, V, 178–80. The petition and "Briefe hereunto annexed," VII, 184–85.

[42] For Bennett's case, see *L. J.* III, 87–88, 144–48, 152–53. As per Barrington (*Commons Debates,* 1621, III, 13): "*Apr. 18, post prandium* [*Committee for Courts*] Sir Edward Sackvill the Chayre." Mr. Newman examined, described one transaction in which Sir J. Bennett secured the value of goods worth over 1000 pounds. Then, "Mr. Pimm. That we may see whyther he bought his right or an ill cause. Sir Edward Cooke. That it is against magna Charta, which runns *nulli vendemus,* and therfor a bribe howsoever." (Cf. Smyth, V, 334.) It was on April 23 that Coke made a long speech in which he gives precedents of medieval judges who took bribes and what happened to them. *Ibid.* II, 313–14; III, 16–17; *C. J.* I, 587.

Edward in his opening of the charge against the lord treasurer in 1624.[43] It was Coke again, in the committee concerning the Cinque Ports, who cited Magna Carta chapter 9 on their behalf, although their petition refers only to their individual charters.[44]

In the autumn session there occurred a rather unwonted use of the Charter, the extension of the "liberties" of chapter 29 to cover the privileges of the Commons. Although little was made of it as a precedent in the future, it offers one more example of the possibilities of this elastic clause. The question of freedom of speech had been raised immediately upon parliament's reassembling in November, first by Williams' speech urging the Houses to vote supplies for the recovery of the Palatinate, all other business to be left until a promised February session; second, by the fact of Sir Edwin Sandys' detention, although Calvert insisted that it was not for anything said or done in the House. Alford brought up Sandys' case November 23. Consternation was increased by James' letter, read on the 4th, claiming that he could punish members either during or after sessions if he chose, and again December 14 by the king's answer to the Commons' explanatory petition. The more conciliatory answer of the 17th did not go far enough to satisfy the House, which proceeded to frame the Protestation suggested by Coke. The session was abruptly terminated on the 19th.

The first allusion to the Charter comes rather incidentally toward the conclusion of the debate of December 1, and not from Coke, but from Sir Guido Palmes, who "comended the great Care of our Ancestours in preservinge the privileges of this Land by magna Carta and many laws since. And desiered Sir Edwin Sandys to be sent for . . ."[45] This application was elaborated by Crew on the 15th. There are several versions of his speech. Most concisely in Belasye:

Crew would have the protestation of 1° *Jacobi* veiwed, for then it was sayd by the kinge that our liberties were but of grace, upon which a protestation was entered of the right of them. The liberties of all confirmed in Magna charta. *Vide* 8 H. 4; 21 E. 4, 44; 49 *assis*.[46]

[43] L. J. III, 307–9. Cf. debate in the committee of grievances, April 16, as per Harl. MSS 159; "Sir Edward Coke put a case: Sir Robert (William) Thorpe, one of the king's justices sitting at Lincoln, there were divers young gentlemen brought before him for a robbery done by them. Upon a gift of 80 li. made amongst them he deferred their trial till the next assizes. He himself was hanged, *ob munus corruptionis et felonice acceptum*. And that is all the word the law hath for a bribe, for the great canon of the law is *nulli de negabimus ius, nulli vendemus, nulli differemus* [sic]." Cf. Gurney Diary, p. 104.

[44] *Commons Debates*, 1621, II, 375–76: "By the common law it is lawful for all men to trade, much more for the Cinque Ports, the gates of this kingdom. Magna Carta, *cap*. 9° sheweth the possession." For the petition, *ibid*. VII, 593–96.

[45] *Commons Debates*, 1621, VI, 219 (Diary Z).

[46] *Commons Debates*, 1621, V, 239; cf. Diary X, II, 525–26. C. J. I, 665–66, reads in part as follows: "Our Inheritance; not Matter of Grace, nor Toleration. . . . This of that importance to us, that if we should yield our Liberties to be but of Grace, these Walls, That have known

According to Diary Z, after his statement that "we hould our privileges as our Inheritance and by Lawe," Crew "read Magna Carta to prove our privileges to be then renewed and Confirmed." The fullest report is that of the clerk, who is evidently trying to give the substance of what Crew read. Others followed Crew, and then Sir Edward put in his word with one of his favorite Charter maxims: "The libertie of everie Court is the Lawe of the Court. Magna Charta is called *Charta libertatis quia liberos facit*."

Better proof of the right of the Commons to discuss matters of state was to be found in the exercise of such powers in past reigns, the various specific incidents which were produced in plenty by various participants in the debates. These legitimate precedents ranged from matters of diplomacy and war in the parliaments of Edward II and III and the Lancastrians, culled from the parliament rolls, to episodes of Elizabeth's parliaments actually within the memory of old-timers like Coke and Sir Thomas Hoby.[47] On December 5 Wentworth moved "that a committee be chosen to draw up a remonstrance of precedents," and Phelips urged that discussion of the match with Spain be justified by "reason and precedent and that is seasonable for a committee." For the privileges of the Commons there were no historical precedents based on Magna Carta such as the lawyers were able to produce from their "books" for "liberty of the subject." Still the application is not too farfetched if we recall that few, not even the more scholarly, of this generation doubted the antiquity of parliament; it was coequal, if indeed, it did not antedate Magna Carta. Coke furnished a cue when he spoke of the "liberties of this House" as "the laws of this Court." This was a parliament in which much emphasis was being placed on the House of Commons as a court. Although they had overstepped their authority in *Floyd's case,* as they were forced to admit, they were recognized as a "court of record" and as having jurisdiction over their own members. Magna Carta had long been used to protect the common-law courts in their jurisdiction and procedure, why not this "high court of parliament"?

the holding them thus many many Years, would blush. *Magna Charta* above Thirty times confirmed, beginning *a Jove.*—Confirmeth all our Liberties, which but a Confirmation of the Common Law.—Confirmation to *London,* Cinque Ports, and after general, to all Men;—Concludeth with 'renew.'—So as Liberties of Subjects, confirmed, and renewed, to be perpetual."

[47] For instance, in the debates of December 3, as reported in Diary X, the speeches of Wentworth, Brooke, Crew, Phelips, Coke; December 5, Hakewill; and December 10, Coke again. *Commons Debates,* II, 489–509 *passim.*

Wentworth says: "Methinks then it should be suitable to petition God's lieutenant. There have been two things spoken against: first war; second, marriage. For war, in Hen. 5 his time it was moved in parliament to make war in France. 35 Hen. 8 mentioneth making of war with France and it's treated of by Vapo of his alliance with the Turk. . . .

"For the matter of the marriage 25 E. 3; 33 Hen. 8, 21 *cap.* expressly we have a case touching the Prince's wife.—So likewise 25 Hen. 8 the commons beseech his Majesty for a match, etc. saying . . ."

It was after the dissolution following the stormy scenes connected with the Commons' Protestation that several of their leaders, including Coke, were sequestered or imprisoned. Even this treatment did not immediately change Sir Edward's views as to the Magna Carta bill. In the next session, as we shall see, he still maintained that "matters of state" could not be included in a *mittimus*, the view not only of the typical privy councilor, but of the Elizabethan statesman who well remembered the plots against the queen. By 1628 however, circumstances had changed, and in the debates on the Commons' bill he recalled to his colleagues his experience of 1621 in these words:

I was committed to the Tower, and all my bookes and studdie searched and 37 manuscrips were taken away and 34 were restored and I would give 300 l. for the other 3. I was inquired after what I had doone, soe then there may bee cause found out after the commitment, and this commitment is fearefull all mens mouths are open against the partie.[48]

The Parliament of 1624

IN JAMES' fourth parliament both the program and the personnel of the Commons were similar to those of 1621: "the parliament of 1624 is in reality but the conclusion of the 1621 parliament; almost the same schedule of bills was carried through in 1624, the same grievances were reviewed and even the final chapter of the argument over foreign affairs is recorded then." [49] Coke and Sandys were present in spite of James' desire to exclude them.[50] It was in this parliament, according to one of the diarists (Erle, May 29), that the King was to declare frankly: "The lawyers of all the people in the world are the greatest grievance to my subjects, for when the cause is good for neither party, yet it proves good and beneficial himself [for themselves?]." Yet there were differences. Affairs moved rather more smoothly owing to what Gardiner calls the temporary "league which appeared to be springing up between the Prince of Wales and the English nation": the universal joy at Charles' return from Spain "alive, a Protestant, and a bachelor," and at the ultimate breaking off of the Spanish treaties. Freedom of speech was, temporarily at least, not an issue, for James' opening speech had invited counsel in foreign affairs—"I assure you ye may freely advise me." To be sure Eliot urged the House not to

[48] Mass. MSS, p. 221. "Coke was the first to be sent for. That a Privy Councillor should have done what he had done was a special cause for irritation. On December 27 he was committed a close prisoner to the Tower, and Sir Robert Cotton and two other persons were commissioned to search his papers. It was given out at first that he was not questioned for anything done in Parliament, but it was impossible long to keep up the deception." Phelips and Mallory followed Coke to the Tower, Pym was sequestered, and Digges and one or two others named on a commission for Ireland. Gardiner, IV, 267.

[49] *Commons Debates*, 1621, I, 5.

[50] Gardiner, V, 182.

forget in their new interests to vindicate the privileges threatened in the last parliament. Alford concurred with a reminder of Magna Carta and its thirty confirmations, but no action was taken.[51]

The pages of the *Lords Journals* are filled with great matters: how to advise the king on vital issues of war and diplomacy; the recovery of the Palatinate; the Prince's marriage; and nearer home, the impeachment of the Lord Treasurer Middlesex, all involving frequent conferences with the Commons and the maintenance of "good correspondency" between the Houses. Here again, for the purpose of these studies, an invaluable supplement to the *Commons Journals* are the diaries.[52] Debates recorded there reveal that there were still in operation patents which conferred powers of arrest, and that patentees were being supported by royal proclamations and by "the great officers of the kingdome."[53]

Frequent entries give testimony to the zeal of the Commons to expedite bills, many of them left over from 1621, and even 1610 and 1614.[54] Nicholas records for Monday, February 23, that Sir Thomas Hoby

moveth that all those good general bills that passed the last convention, or

[51] "Mr. Alford:—When Time serves, will concur with this Gentleman, to leave this Place as free to our Successors, as they to us.—Magna *Charta* confirmed Thirty Times.—*Opus hujus diei*. Many Rocks will here fall out.—To have a select Committee to draw a Bill . . ." *C. J.* I, 719b.

Cf. Holles, fol. 83v: "Mr. Alford said Magna Charta was confirmed 30 times, 12 times by one king. It is our duty to leave the parliament as free in privileges to our successors as our predecessors left it to us."

"Sir John Eliot moved for a petition to the King to confirm our privileges."

[52] I am indebted to Professors Notestein and Simpson for the use of their transcripts of the diaries. For 1624: D'Ewes (Harl. MSS 159), Erle, the Gurney Diary, Holland, Holles, Nicholas, and Pym.

[53] For instance, Sandys' report from the committee of trade (May 24, 1624) indicates that the patent of the Eastland Company was a grant "to impose on Persons of Traders, to fine, and imprison"; that for "Ginny and Binny" had a "Clause of Imprisonment and Confiscation of Goods . . ." *C. J.* I, 793b.

The *Gurney Diary* (same date) says the merchants from Eastland, Guinea, Turkey, and Spain "have a grant to impose upon their company, to imprison, to attach and imprison without bail persons offending . . ." Erle (May 26): "Sir Edward Coke presents a grievance of the Staplers who by virtue of a proclamation were threatened and imprisoned etc. . . ." As to Sir Robert Mansel's patent "for the sole making and melting of all manner of Glasse," with Sea-coale, Pit-coale, and Scotch-coale," an elaborate indictment is to be found in *State Papers*, vol. 162, no. 64, April 16, 1624, "Reasons proposed unto the Honourable Assembly of the House of Commons, why the Patent . . . should be voyd." As to powers of arrest, it is charged that:

"8. The great Officers of the Kingdome, as the Lo: Treasurer and Chancellor of the Exchequer, the Iudges of the Realme, the Barons of the Exchequer, and the Officers of Iustice have all commandment given them by this Patent, to assist Sir Robert and his Agents in the granting of writs for searches to bee made in apprehending of such as shall offend against this Patent, and in making of entry into mens houses whereby his actions are countenanced uner the colour of Iustice by Officers of Iustice.

"9. Since the last order in Parliament, some have had their Glasse seized and taken away from them, others have beene imprisoned untill Sir Robert gave way for their liberty; others not being suffered to worke in their lawfull trade, have starved and perished, and their children doe beg their bread."

[54] For the numerous entries of groups of bills sent up to the Lords, *L. J.* III, 248b, 271b–72a, 293b, 315b, 340, 393, 405, 412.

were ready to pass, may be first read according to the order as they were prepared last convention, vizt., those that passed both Houses first, next those that
passed one our House only, then those that were most forward for passing in
our House, and that no bills may be read till these are all dispatched thus.[55]

It was so ordered, but with the two reservations offered by Pym, that the
order was not "to bar any other good bills" nor hinder the reading of
private bills.

The Magna Carta bill, one of Sir Thomas' category of those that "passed
one our House only," again sponsored by Fleetwood, had its first reading
February 25.[56] On the second reading March 9, it was assigned to a committee which included several of the same members as that of 1621.[57]
Nicholas gives the clearest statement of the contents of the bill, indicating
that it was virtually in the form adopted in the November session, 1621:

> By this the party that hindereth any man from his lawful trade shall for-
> feit 10 times as much as they shall hinder any such person and no essoin, pro-
> tection, privilege or injunction shall be allowed to the offender in this case.
> Proviso that this shall not extend to any commitment made by his Majesty or
> 6 of the Privy Council.[58]

Sir George Moore spoke, then Mr. Coryton, who oddly enough found the
terms of the bill contrary to the very statute it was designed to enforce:
"This is contrary to the statute of Magna Carta and against Edward I
chapter 6. A greater amerciament than the quality of the offence." [59]

On March 17 the bill was reported from committee and "the alterations
twice read." Only one diarist, Holland, gives any hint as to the amendments: "That in every court upon commitment the cause shall be set
down. That 4 of the Privy Council or more do commit anyone and do
certify that it is for matter of state not fit to be revealed, it is sufficient." [60]
This time opposition came not merely from the privy councilors in general, using arguments based on "matters of state," but from the prerogative
courts. Objections were effectively voiced by Dr. Arthur Ducke, a distinguished civilian, who had served as chancellor in two dioceses, as

---

[55] Nicholas, fol. 2v.

[56] "Feb. 25, Wed. L. 1a An Act to secure the Subiect from wrongful Imprisonment, and
Deprivation of their Trades and Occupations, contrary to the 29th Chapter of the Statute of
Magna Charta." *C. J.* I, 673b.

[57] Namely, "Mr. Treasurer," Sir Edward Coke, Sir William Fleetwood, Sir George Moore,
Sir G. Jerrard (Gerard), Sir Henry Poole, Sir George Manners, Sir William Spencer. *C. J.* I,
680. London was represented by its recorder, now Sir Heneage Finch, knight and serjeant-at-
law.

[58] Nicholas, fol. 20v; the first reading is recorded by all the diarists but one (Holles), the
second reading by all.

[59] Erle, fol. 62v; also Nicholas, fol. 60: "Mr. Coryton thinketh this bill crosseth the 14
chapter of Magna Carta. Would therefore have this bill committed."

[60] Holland, fol. 58v; the Gurney Diary and Holles have nothing on the bill for this date,
and Erle nothing at all for March 14–18; for Pym, see below.

master in Chancery, and now was "king's advocate" in the Earl Marshal's court.

Dr. *Ducke:*—Made Two Objections at the Committee:—Will cross the Power of Two great Officers: Lord Admiral and Lord Marshal. Lord Admiral imprisons by Course of the Civil Law. 2. Lord Marshal his Jurisdiction in Matter of Arms: His Power, by the Law of Honour and Arms. This will not come under the Words *legem terrae*. These will stop the Bill above. A third Objection the King's Power in Causes ecclesiastical; where Commissioners Power to imprison. This will take away their Power. Mr. *Fanshaw:*—In all these Courts nothing more usual, than to have *Habeas Corpus.*[61] To have the Bill recommitted.

The bill was recommitted to the same committee, but now afforced by such able opponents as Dr. Ducke, Mr. Fanshawe, and others, where it apparently remained until the end of the session.[62]

Another subject, impositions, which had been uppermost in the parliaments of 1610 and 1614, was raised again on April 9 when Sir Edwin Sandys reported from the committee for trade "The over-burthening of Trade."[63] It was the first speaker to follow Sandys' report, Richard Spencer, who condemned the new impositions as contrary to Magna Carta chapter 30. The diarists were particularly impressed by his comment on the "taking away the propriety of men's goods which distinguish a freeman from a slave," and his precedents as to "what our ancestors had done in like case." Three diarists and the clerk record his citation of the Charter. As usual Pym affords the most clear-cut and intelligible summary of the speech:

[61] Apparently meaning that since the persons committed by these courts would resort to writs of habeas corpus, the judges would not want to be subject to these restrictions. *C. J.* I, 738; cf. Nicholas, fol. 84v, and Pym, fol. 30, as follows: "To which Dr. Duck objected that it was like to be opposed in the Upper House as restraining the power of the Lord Admiral, Lord Marshal, and High Commission. The proceedings in the Admiralty be according to the civil law, in the Marshal's court neither according to the civil law nor common law, but by the law of honor and arms. The High Commission is granted upon statute, but their proceedings are by instructions under the great seal."

[62] "The Bill, upon Question, to be re-committed to the same Committee: Doctor *Ducke,* Mr. *Fanshawe,* Mr. Recorder, Sir *Wal. Pye,* Mr. *Olesworth;—Friday,* Court of wards." *C. J.* I, 738b. Sir Thomas Fanshawe was Remembrancer of the Exchequer.

We learn from one account only, Pym, fol. 43v, under the date of March 25: "It was moved by some that all committees might be dissolved but the committee for the continuance and repeal of statutes. By others it was desired a new committee might be appointed for the bill concerning our liberty and confirmation of Magna Carta. But Mr. Brooke informed the House that bill could hardly be made a good bill, there were many exceptions to it, that it was unfit for a new committee that were ignorant of them."

And from another, Nicholas only, fol. 114v, April 6: "Saturday in the afternoon is appointed for the Committee touching the bill against imprisonment contrary to the 29 chapter of Magna Carta."

[63] Detailed accounts of Sandys' report are given by the clerk, *C. J.* I, 759b, and by D'Ewes (Harl. MSS 159), fols. 96–96v. The "burthens" he presented were the "great imposition of the Merchant Adventurers"; the "pretermitted customs"; and "some new Impositions by reason of a new Book of Rates . . ."

Mr. Spencer insisted upon 4 points: (1) that these impositions were offensive to all the subjects; (2) to inquire who was the procurer of them; (3) what our ancestors had done in like case; (4) touching our proceeding in this complaint. For the first point he gave these reasons (1) that it was against the law of Magna Carta, and of Ed. 1 whereby it was expressed that nothing should be taken without the good will of the Commons. (2) It did overthrow the very essence of a subject, took away his property, and made him a slave, for by the civil law a slave hath no property. . . . For the third he alleged 21 E. 3, that no impositions should be set but by common consent. 50 Ed. 3 the Commons prayed it might be a capital offence to lay any new impositions, and in the same year Richard Lyons was adjudged to perpetual imprisonment, fine and ransom, to which he added the judgment against the Lord Latimer.[64]

Nicholas, evidently attempting to quote, is more colorful and emphatic, while another includes the effective clause, "this offence is against the laws of [the] Kingdom, and against the essence of a freeman and subject and against the ancient charter of England, Magna Carta, which provides for freedom in buying and traffic . . ."

Coke's contribution to this debate included the first practical use of John's Charter, anticipating Selden's in 1628 though less accurate and precise. Sir Edward does not actually quote chapters 12 and 14, but evidently has them in mind, quotes chroniclers, comments on their omission, and assumes that 25 Edward I (the *Confirmatio Cartarum*) practically reinstated them in the law. His speech evidently made an impression, for six diarists gave it considerable space, though with varying degrees of success in the reporting. The most reasonable versions are those of Nicholas and the *Commons Journals.*

Sir Edward Coke that the clause against the setting of impositions and taxes is in the great charter Magna Carta and though E. 1 would not confirm that charter till that clause were left out, but this taketh it not away, for kings before and since confirmed that charter with that clause. By 25° E. 1 in old Magna Carta, parte 2a, folio 25, no taking nor taxing shall be made.

. . . Plain that the Clause, against Impositions to be set, unless by Parliament, Parcel of *Magna Charta. Edw.* I would not exemplify the great Charter, unless this left out. So says *Walsingham* and *Wendover.* Custom came by Act of Parliament.—One in print, Stat. 25 *Edw.* I. In old *Magna Charta,* "No Aid, nor Taking, nor Mise, nor any other Thing taken, unless Wools, Woolfells, and Leather, which was granted to us by the Commons." Which must needs be in Parliament.

These reports taken together become understandable if we assume that by *Old Magna Carta, parte 2a fol. 25,* Coke was not referring to a text of

---

[64] Pym, fol. 55v; cf. *C. J.* I, 760; the Gurney Diary, fols. 194–95; Nicholas, fol. 130. The clerk is most accurate in quoting Spencer's precedents. Nicholas records more of the details, laying blame on the Lord Treasurer.

Sir Edward Coke

John's Charter but to the *Vetera Statuta*, which as we have seen was commonly called "The Book of Magna Carta," and which contained 25 Edward I, quoted here in the clerk's version. Of course, there was much more to the speech: other precedents such as the establishing of the old customs in 3 Edward I, the resolution of the judges on impositions at the beginning of Elizabeth's reign, and of course Latimer and Lyons, concluding, picturesquely, as per Holles' version:

Color upon color and metal upon metal is ill armory, so imposition upon imposition is damnable. The principal article against the Duke of Suffolk in Henry the 6 time was for procuring some grants against the common law of England. The Lord Latimer was the abettor, Lyons was the projector, for all these great Lords have a projector or polypragmon; this was meant by Sir Arthur Ingram.[65]

Purveyance was still a grievance, descending from the major burden of "horses, carts and carriages for his Majesty's service" to such a minor annoyance as "hawks' meat." Now, as on an earlier occasion, Coke seems to conceive of Magna Carta (chapters 19 and 20) as authorizing, rather than limiting, this aspect of the prerogative.[66]

The committee for abuses in courts of justice did not have occasion to deal with such great personages as Bacon and Bennett. One interesting case which came before them was that of Lady Darcy. Through the influence of the lord keeper she had been refused a writ of *quare impedit* for making claim to an advowson.[67] In addition to the various issues of right and inheritance, the propriety of the action of the master of the wards in granting the advowson to the lady (as guardian) in the first place, and that of the lord keeper in presenting the king's chaplain to the living, the denial of the writ was challenged as against Magna Carta and the king's coronation oath.

Mr. Stone, for my Lady: My Lord Keeper's first presentation was *ratione minoris aetatis,* but since he hath made another *ratione minoris aetatis seu per lapsum temporis aut quocunque alio modo.* That she might have a *quare impedit* to recover damages but never to remove the clerk. If he had any war-

[65] Nicholas, fols. 130v–31; *C. J.* I, 759–60; Holles, fols. 125v–26; Pym, fol. 56.

[66] "Sir *Edward Coke.* This is a high point. It appears by Magna Carta that the king had right. Fit to go by precedent. An act of parliament in point of purveyance, concerning the price 25 and 36 E. 3, the Constable and 4 good men of the town, *ergo a fortiori* justices of the peace may be trusted with setting the price.—This bill passed to engrossing." Erle, March 13, 1624. Cf. *C. J.* I, 685a. What Coke appears to say is that Magna Carta sanctions the king's prerogative; hence we cannot touch it without precedent, but we have precedents of acts of parliament on purveyance—which he proceeds to give.

[67] In the cryptic account of the journal, the lady "sued to the King.—Desires of this Assembly to have Relief. This Petition retained by the Committee. Parties on both Sides appeared, and Council. Came into Question, whether an original Writ might be stayed. Lawyers vouched some Precedents for it in Chancery. Committee concluded, these were not proper in the Cause, and not to be followed. Desired an Accomodation of this Business between the Lady and the Doctor." *C. J.* I, 785a.

rant from the King, it was verbal, and not under the great seal; and the denial was against the King's oath, my Lord Keeper's oath, and Magna Carta. In all the precedents vouched, the suit was betwixt two other parties; here he was a party himself, for which there is no precedent.[68]

After counsel retired, the issues were debated by the committee. Coke called the lord keeper's presentment "a plain usurpation." Glanvill expressed the opinion that Lady Darcy must be relieved by bill, and added, "The subject ought not to be denied originals." In defense of the lord keeper for the denial of the *quare impedit*, precedents were cited. Serjeant Hedly

acknowledged it to be against the law the statute of Magna Carta, and against the statute of 2 E. 3. Those general rules have particular exceptions. In some cases the king may command the stay of a writ under the great seal, where he hath a right, not proceed *rege inconsulto*.

Or in another version: "He confesseth that the Lord Keeper did deny the quare impedit. He acknowledgeth that the law is *nulli differemus nulli negamus iusticiam* but there is no rule so general but that there are some exceptions . . ." The Commons concluded that a bill was necessary to restore to the lady and the heir their rights, and such a bill was passed.[69]

The Parliaments of 1625 and 1626

CHARLES' ill-fated first parliament is of interest here only indirectly in introducing the problems and grievances of the early years of the reign. In the two brief and troubled sessions—at plague-infested Westminster from June 18 to July 11, and at Oxford August 1 to 12—the Houses were hardly ready or able to descend to particulars. The first impression made by the young king was favorable, but fears were aroused by the government's seeming Catholic leanings. There was the French marriage, the loan of ships to reduce La Rochelle, the leniency to recusants at home. Something was known of the miserable fiasco of Mansfield's expedition. Neither king nor councilors gave any adequate information as to plans for the future prosecution of the war—would it be the desired sea war against Spain? Through it all was the growing distrust of the favorite. The Commons did little more than formulate a broad plan of action summed up in Rich's "five propositions" adopted August 6.[70] A meager

---

[68] Pym, p. 76. Cf. Nicholas, fol. 166: "That the denial of the writ is an offence to the King who is to do *aequum et iustum*, which power the King hath committed to the Lord Keeper. . . . but the question of presentment is between the Lord Keeper and the Lady, but his lordship in denying the writ of *quare impedit* maketh himself both judge and party."

[69] Pym, p. 76; Erle, fol. 155; Nicholas, fols. 165–65v. *C. J.* I, 789a (May 14).

[70] "Sir Nath. Rich. Not to refuse to give; but first to represent to the King our wants. 1. For religion: to have his Majesty's answer in full Parliament, and enrolled, which then of the force of an Act of Parliament. 2. To know the enemy against whom our war is to be made. 3. The

two subsidies were granted as a token of good will. Tonnage and pound-age were voted for one year only, instead of the customary life grant, to permit examination of the whole question of impositions. The petition on religion framed early in the Westminster session was answered by the king at Oxford. In the July session the Commons did not appoint their usual committee for grievances, but resolved to seek an answer to the grievances framed in James' last parliament.

Relatively few bills were introduced. That for Magna Carta was not revived. Indeed there was little occasion for even casual allusion to the Charter in debate. To be sure, Sir Thomas Crew, on being presented to the king as speaker, made much of the last parliament as "justly accounted happy." There passed then, he said, "more flowers of the Crowne, more Bills of Grace then in Magna Charta . . ." [71] Seymour, Phelips, and Eliot were leaders of the opposition. Coke was still active, frequently employed by the House in carrying messages to the Lords, and putting in his word in every debate. As the session proceeded, members inclined more and more to innuendoes directed at the duke. It was easy to produce unpalat-able precedents of evil counselors of past ages, their misdeeds and fates. Particularly bitter was the debate on August 10. Seymour struck at the sale of offices and honors: "Who will bringe up his sonne in learning when mony is the way to preferment. The price of a sergeant is as knowen as the price of a calfe; and they which buy deare must certainelye sell deare." Sir Guy Palmes reminded the House that "For the disorders in Henry 7ths tyme, Empson and Dudley were hang'd in H. the 8th's tyme." [72] Sir Edward's choice of a precedent, if not strictly accurate, was suggestive when with impressive Latin maxims he introduced Hubert de Burgo, chief justice, who advised Henry III "*Magna Charta* was not to hold," and was disgraced from his earldom of Kent. [73]

This was not only a parliament of many precedents but of comments on the validity of precedents bandied back and forth between the privy councilors in the House and the opposition leaders. In 1621, in connection with *Floyd's case*, James had said to the Commons, "Reason is too large. Find me a precedent and I will accept it." But now precedents were prov-

---

necessity of an advised Council, for government of the great affairs of the Kingdom. 4. The necessity of looking into the King's estate. 5. To have his Majesty's answer concerning im-positions. To have a Committee for these. Though this time not fit for the decision on all these points, yet to set down the heads of them, and then to have the King's answer in Parliament unto them. This no capitulating with the King, but an ordinary Parliamentary course, as 22° Ed. III, and that without which the Commonwealth can neither supply the King, nor subsist." Quoted by Gardiner, *Commons Debates*, 1625, p. xiii.

[71] *Commons Debates*, 1625, p. 3. Cf. Eliot's version, *Negotium Posterorum*, I, 47–48.
[72] *Ibid.*, pp. 111, 112.
[73] "Two Leaks to drown any Ship: 1. a bottomless Sieve: 2. *Solum et malum Con-silium* . . . 15 H. III. Hubert de Burgo, Chief Justice, advised the King, *Magna Charta* was not to hold, because the King under age at the Time of the Act. Created Earl of Kent 13 H. III. disgraded for this 15 H. III." *C. J.* I, 814b.

ing inconveniently numerous and damaging. On July 7 in the debate on Mountague, warned "Mr. Chancellor of the Duchy" (Maye), "Ill presedents are noe where so dangerous as in Parliaments"; and again August 10, urging supply, "Let no man despise ancient president(s); no man adore them. Examples are powerfull arguments, if they be proper, but tyme(s) alter; every parliament must be wise with his owne wisdome; hee valewes more a dram of wisdome fit for the present, then a mountaine of wisdome that was fitted for 500 yeares past." In the same debate Sir George More advised "Precedents have always changed with the Times." On the other hand, Phelips reminded the House, "We are the last monarchy in Christendome that retayne our originall rights and constitutions . . . Hee added the safty of keepinge to our presidents, the meannes of the some required, the unfortunate counsell that brought us hither . . ."[74]

Eliot later was to write scathingly of one Mallet, a lawyer who

did appear reasoning by presidents against presidents . . . that presidents were at the discretion of all times. . . . which I observe the sooner for the qualitie of the man, that he whose profession was the Lawe, & on which ground he built all the good hopes he had, should argue against presidents, which are the tables of the Lawe, & soe unlawlike terme everie act a president, making noe differenc[e] betweene examples & their rules.[75]

Several of the ardent spirits of the 1625 parliament were missing from the Commons in 1626. Pricked for sheriffs intentionally to exclude them were Coke, Seymour, Phelips, Alford, Sir Guy Palmes, Wentworth, and Fleetwood. But with Sir John Eliot to lead them there was still a considerable group of "countrymen" and lawyers ready to carry on. These included such able parliamentarians as Sandys, Rich, Spencer, and Pym; and among the lawyers Glanvill, Noy, Selden, Bulstrode, Whitelocke, and Sir Henry Martin. Others less notable, but to figure in debates of special interest, were Sherland, Whitby, Wilde, and Browne. Sir Heneage Finch, recorder of London, was elected speaker. In the upper House there was a distinct group of opposition lords in sympathy with the leaders in the Commons, among them Archbishop Abbot, Lord Keeper Williams, the Earl of Arundel, Pembroke, and Bristol. The exclusion of Arundel and Bristol from the House increased the friction between the king and the duke on the one hand and the whole body of peers on the other. Although the treatment accorded the two earls led to persistent assertions of privilege and searching of precedents, the Great Charter was not one of them.[76]

---

[74] *Commons Debates*, 1625, pp. 52, 110–11 (Pym).
[75] *Negotium Posterorum*, II, 75–76.
[76] To be sure *trial by peers* was not the issue, and there were too many specific precedents to need the vague *per legem terrae* phrase. For Arundel and Bristol, see *L. J.* III, 526–681 *passim*.

Eliot's speech of February 10 set the program which was followed, and it was Eliot who kept the Commons steadfast to this course whenever the privy councilors tried to divert them from it. Supply was to be generous but redress of grievances must *precede* supply. They were to inquire into the war account (the expenditure of the moneys voted by the last parliament) and the king's estate. The usual committee of grievances was appointed, with Mr. Whitby as chairman. Subcommittees of inquiry were to report to it under special heads. In addition there was appointed a committee for secret affairs headed by Mr. Wandesford to deal with "evils, causes and remedies," to be "separately taken and reported," including the "condition of the subject in his freedom." [77] As the session wore on, from each subcommittee came "day by day, to the grand committee for evils, causes, and remedies, its quota of wrongs under one or other of the four divisions . . . To one delinquent each report pointed as the cause, and there only could lie the remedy." In the formal impeachment of Buckingham which thus became the focus of action, the Great Charter was cited and appropriately in only one of the twelve charges, the *sale of justice*. In connection with commitment, chapter 29 was evoked on behalf both of the duke himself and of his accusers, Digges and Eliot. This and a few other clauses (liberties of the church, purveyance, free trade) were used pertinently in connection with various grievances and bills not so directly connected with the duke. Here again we have the diarists to thank for their reports of debates in committees and subcommittees.[78] Although Sir Edward was absent, his penchant for quoting the Charter as well as the debates on the confirmation bill had evidently left their influence on his colleagues.

The impeachment of the duke took the form of twelve articles of charges, two or three each presented by the five "managers" and their assistants, with a prologue by Digges, and what proved to be a scathing epilogue by Eliot. The ninth and tenth charges had originally been assigned to Mr. Whitby, the able recorder and member for Chester, but owing to his illness, Mr. Sherland, recorder of Northampton, with Noy to assist him, was substituted.[79]

Said Mr. Sherland, as reported to the Lords by the Earl of Devonshire,[80] "the particular Articles which fall to my Lot are concerning Honour and Judicature, Two Prime Flowers of the Crown." After a long, flowery discourse drawing on both the philosophers and the civilians, and calculated to appeal to their lordships' pride of birth and place, specific

---

[77] Forster, *Eliot*, I, 489, 496–97.

[78] Here again I am indebted to Professors Notestein and Simpson for the use of their transcripts of the diaries of Grosvenor, Rich, and Whitelocke.

[79] *C. J.* I, 858.

[80] *L. J.* III, 610–12. Article 10 itself does not cite Magna Carta. The other charges, several of them relating to foreign policy, were hardly of a nature to invoke it.

instances of the duke's sale of honors were adduced. After reading the tenth article and protesting that no reflections on persons at present in seats of justice were intended, Sherland launched vigorously into his attack:

For the Things charged in the last Article; *videlicet*, the Sale or Procurement of Judicial Places, and other Offices of Trust, for Money; that this is an Offence, is so clear, that to spend Time in Proof of it were all one as to go about to make Glass more transparent by painting it.

I will take the Ground of what I shall say upon this Subject from Magna Charta, Cap. 29. These Words, *Nulli vendemus, nulli negabimus, nulli differemus Justitiam*; this, as you may see, is spoken in the Person of the King, in the Behalf of Him and His Successors. He therefore that abuses his Favour and Power with his Majesty, to procure Places of Judicature unto others for Money, doth as much as in him lies to make the King break his Word with his People. This will appear more clearly by looking into the other Parts of that Clause. If any should procure the King to leave the Seats of Justice empty, and make no Judges or to delay the Supply of vacant Rooms of Judges, when their service might be requisite for the Administration of Justice, I think therein no Man but would say Magna Charta were infringed; so is it certainly in the other Part too, when those through whose Lips and Hands Justice is to run are put to buy their Places; for it cannot but follow, and it must be expected, that they that buy must and will sell again, to make their own up with Advantage.[81]

Sherland then names six "ill consequences that must needs follow," and supports these with the "especial caveats" which "Moral Heathens" (Aristotle and others) have made against this offense. Further, "I may well bring in the Popes next to the Pagans, a Generation none the purest (I may say safely) from Corruption; yet have they shewed their Dislike and Detestation of this foul and hateful Offence." And finally, "now to come nearer Home, to the Judgements of former Parliaments, which I imagine will cheifly sway with your Lordships."

A few miscellaneous allusions to the Charter may be briefly noted. February 25, in a debate on the "Bill against scandalous Ministers," Mr. Spencer, while proposing another title, maintained that the bill was "not against the great Charter Eccles[ia] Anglicana et libera."[82] According

---

[81] Specific instances as recorded in the *Commons Journals* and the diaries are not numerous. Whitelocke records (for April 24) "Resolved that the buying of the place of warden of the Sinque Portes by Lord Admiral and of the office of Treasurership by the Lord Maunchester are to be fixed uppon the person of the Duke of Buckingham under the head of the sale of offices of Judicature." The duke had admitted this, but denied others: "I am charged to have sold Byshopricks, which I utterly deny ever to have done; and the like for Judges." Whitelocke, fol. 114v; L. J. III, 656–57.

There were various general sweeping charges such as Eliot's speech of March 27, quoted Forster, *Eliot*, I, 519–20.

[82] The diaries give no evidence that any one had claimed the bill *was* against Magna Carta. Sir Henry Martin, now Dean of the Arches and judge of the Prerogative Court, had

to Whitelocke, at the committee for purveyance, June 13, a copy of a report was produced which quoted Coke's information against purveyors brought in Star Chamber when he was attorney general.[83] In spite of the proclamation of 1621 and the statute of 1624, there were still some monopolies to be quashed. One such, "Mr. More's patent for salt," was condemned "as a grievance both in the creacion and execution thereof." Although the bill to prevent imprisonment and restraint of trades contrary to Magna Carta had not been reintroduced, this patent, like several of those condemned in 1621 and 1624, was said to confer powers "very unusual and unfitt." It was finally branded as "beeing graunted upoon a false suggestion, and a grievance in that it is agaynst the liberty of the subject by Magna Charta." The speech thus damning it was from that very lawyer, Mr. Mallet, scorned by Eliot in 1625 for "unlawlike" arguing against precedents.[84]

On two occasions the privy councilors in the House turned the tables by citing the Charter as a defense against commitment first of the duke himself, and then of a certain witness summoned for questioning. As to the duke, it will be remembered that eight of the charges against him were presented before the Lords on May 8, with the accused himself present, outfacing his accusers, indeed, according to the letter writers, even jeering and laughing. So incensed were the Commons that the following day was spent in debate for and against commitment of the duke during impeachment proceedings.[85] Among proponents of the favorite "There arose a lawyer, one Mr. Dyott, one that hath often spoken for the duke," and "spoke some unseemly words of the House." His defense was so warm that he was charged with having been "hired" to make it, and was sequestered.

opposed it on first reading, in spite of the rule against debate at that time: "That there is an Ecclesiastical Court which lookes carefully to it." Others opposed it "because it putts the triall of Clergie men to lay men"; and sanctioned juries "medling with their (the clergy's) freeholds." Selden, while approving the change of title, held that "for the Jurisdictions of lay men over the Clergie it stand with the lawes of England," but would "have the Jurors of better ranck."

See Rich for February 13 and 25, fols. 9, 39; Whitelocke, February 13 and 15, fols. 87v–84v. C. J., p. 825a.

[83] Whitelocke, fol. 238. "In the Starre chamber 36 Eliz." here, but evidently the same that Hawarde reports for 1605 and 1606. See above, p. 269.

[84] Whitelocke, fol. 180v. Another version, Grosvenor, fol. 50. Mr. Whitby, reporting this patent from the committee of grievances March 28, described the powers of the patentees thus: "in which patent power was given to punish false weights, measures, and selling on Sundays, and to command officers to search for delinquents, and other power given them very unusuall and unfitt."

[85] Some felt that the charges brought against him by Bristol constituted treason, and hence warranted commitment. Others questioned whether the Commons could take account of these. Those most bitter against the duke claimed that some of the charges were at least felony. The fullest account, including the speech quoted in the text, is Grosvenor's, fols. 62–70. Cf. Whitelocke, fols. 183–87; C. J. I, 858. After the vote, 225 to 105 for committing, Selden's suggestion was followed, to move the Lords for a commitment, but the request was not to be delivered until Thursday after the charges were completed. The duke absented himself on the 10th.

But it was not he, but a Mr. Whitacre who stole the opposition's thunder by quoting chapter 29:

Among the Romans noe thinge conduced to make there iustice Levell as when the greatest man in there estate might be questioned. In Magna Charta: *Nullus liber homo imprisonetur nisi pro* [*sic*] *Iudicium parium aut pro legem terrae*; the Duke yet a free man: ought to be free till he have passed the Iudgment of his peers: and law is now agaynst him: presidents that have bene alledged . . . 3 presidents in our tymes: Sir Albans: Middlesex: B. of Norwich: his charg as great as the Dukes: but noe imprisonment of him: that noe mocion for commitment be made.

Harrison was one of several witnesses questioned by the House in regard to a letter of Sir John Savile's. His answers to the interrogatories proving unsatisfactory, Mr. Bish "moves that for the uncertain answears and abuses offered to the house, and that he may the better recollect himselfe, Harrison may be committed close prisoner till tomorrow morning." It was Sir Humphrey May that put in "Magna Charta should be remembered here. If this man be restrayned he must pay fees." Brooke defended him as "a substantiall man, an honest man, of good credit in his country." Others, including Glanvill and Littleton, opposed his commitment, and these moderate counsels prevailed. He was given until Monday to give "a cleare and full answear." [86]

In the end it was not the duke who was committed but the orators, Digges and Eliot, whose eloquence had introduced and concluded the charges. The reader need only be reminded that Eliot's was the famous speech made familiar by Gardiner and Forster in which literally the speaker may be said to have "aggravated" what went before. The invectives against which particular offense was taken included the classical epithet *stellionatus* and the detailed comparison to Sejanus which led Charles to exclaim, "implicitly he must intend me for Tiberius." [87] It was on Thursday the eleventh that the House was stunned by the news that Eliot and Digges had been taken to the Tower. They rose until next day, and on reassembling insisted there be "no business till we are righted in our liberties."

The House "sate long silent." It was Mr. Wilde who first ventured to speak, urging the House to petition the king for the restoration of the missing members and the preservation of their liberties, and reminding

---

[86] Whitelocke, fols. 205–6, 223–25 (May 22, June 8); cf. Grosvenor, fols. 170–76.

[87] "And first, his collusion and deceit; crimes in themselves so odious and uncertain that the ancients, knowing not by what name to term them, expressed them in a metaphor calling them *stellionatus,* from a discoloured beast so doubtful in appearance that they knew not what to make of it. And thus in this man's practice, we find it here . . .

"Of all the precedents I can find, none so near resembles him as doth Sejanus, and him Tacitus describes thus . . . My lords, I have done. You see the Man. What have been his actions, whom he is like,. you know. I leave him to your judgments." Forster, *Eliot,* I, 541–52. (Cf. *L. J.* III, 618.)

them of the "Goad charter of our great inheritance, gayned with soe great cost, so often confirmed, we ought with al care to convey the same to our posterity as our Ancestors have done to us." May 17, the House having resolved itself into a grand committee with Mr. Rolles in the chair, the Chancellor of the Exchequer tried to satisfy the Commons as to the term *extra judicial*, "which is that the offences are high crimes done to his Majesty out of this house for which Sir John Eliot is committed." The ensuing debate is reported at length by the diarists, Whitelocke, Grosvenor, and Rich.[88] Wilde's contribution here is significant as a fore-runner of the arguments in the *five knights case*, and the parliament of 1628, for he now ventured to broach directly the royal power of commit-ment. Cautiously he admits that there is in the prerogative something for imprisoning subjects, at least outside parliament:

I will not tuch upon his Majestys prerogative it is a poynt to high for me: but the Kings prerogative and the Subiects liberty must have a reciprocall abidinge: there is a certayne duty owing as well from the imperiall crowne to the lawes as a loyalty from the Subiects to the prince. In this prerogative something for imprisoning subiects I will not disput it; but we have some resolucions in our books that the King may in some cases committ a man without shewinge the Cause; but this is in cases out of parlament: but in parlament I find noe case or president that there is any warrant for it; here is a committment of our members; wherein we must know there is a liberty of fredome of spech belonging to every member of this house to declare him-self and this is soe ancient: and without this the fredome used of parlament is gone: [89]

The Chancellor of the Duchy moved that "we may goe on with the buisnes of the house to give the king satisfaction," but two more mem-bers, Browne and Mason, rose to contribute their views on the prerogative of commitment and its limitations. Browne's speech, as reported by Rich, is significant as the first instance I have found of a specific statement that the writ of habeas corpus is based on Magna Carta.

Mr. Browne: The prerogative of the king great so is libertie of the Subiect and the king tyed by his Oath to governe according to law this an honor to the king: the question how the king may by law imprison: the king can doe no wrong but he doth by misinformacion; we may appeale from Philip sleep-ing to Philip waking. The king did no wrong in committing Sir D. Diggs but missinformed. The rule of the law is not because the king did it therefore well done but we must inquire into the cause—Magna Charta, No man com-mitted but *per legale Iudicium* and this the ground of the writt *Habeas Corpus*: 34 Eliz. a Resolution of all the Iudges of England that the Queen nor

[88] Including speeches by Spencer, Rich, Carleton, and Hoby. Digges had been liberated May 13, and on the 16th resumed his seat in the House, which at once "turned themselves into a grand committee concerning Sir John Eliot." Wilde's speech, Grosvenor, fol. 78.
[89] Grosvenor, fols. 101–2; cf. Whitelocke, fols. 197–98.

Counsell can committ above 24 howres but the cause must be rendred and this was reported to the Queen.[90]

On May 18 Eliot was examined in the Tower on questions drawn up by the lord keeper, but nothing was elicited to justify the charge of "extra judicial crimes." Next day the order for his release was signed. On the 20th he returned to the House where Carleton repeated the charges, and the House had the opportunity to enjoy Eliot's·spirited defense, even to his justification of calling the duke "that man." Said Eliot, "That there should be offense taken that I should call him that man, truly I do yett beleeve he is no God." It was "resolved by question that Sir John Eliot had not exceeded his Commission which he had from his house in any thinge that he spake at the Conference with the Lords concerning the impeachment of the Duke of Bucks, *nullo negative*." [91]

The *Five Knights Case*

THE interval between Charles' second and third parliaments witnessed no lessening of incompetence. Abroad there was the futile expedition to the Island of Rhé to relieve the Rochellois, this time led by Buckingham himself. At home the need for funds to prosecute the war, still conceived on a grand scale, was but scantily met by mortgage or sale of crown lands and a loan from London. Other devices were proposed only to be abandoned—an excise, a standing army, privy seals again, and ship money. In July 1626 the justices of the peace were asked to solicit a "free gift." In September the government substituted for this benevolence a forced loan at the rate at which tax payers would be assessed had parliament voted five subsidies. Although collections were fairly successful in some areas, opposition was voiced by high and low: the judges, several peers, Archbishop Abbot, some of the local commissioners themselves, a number of the country gentry, as well as some of the poorer classes. Several gentlemen were bound over to appear before the privy council or committed, often being sent into places of confinement as far distant from their homes as possible. Lesser persons were pressed for military service. As funds were still lacking to pay the soldiers, they were billeted in private homes. Indignation was aroused by the outrages of these unwelcome guests and

[90] Rich, fol. 90. According to Whitelocke, "Mr. Browne. A king cann doe no wrong because wee thinke he will doe noe wrong, and if wrong be done it is through misinformation. We must not say, bicause the king had done it therefore it is no wrong, but wee must examine it. 34 El.—by the Judges resolved that if the Queene committed ony one and the Judges send an *habeas corpus* for him, the cause of the Committement must be showen. And the king cannot deteine any one in prison above twenty-four howers without showing the cause of his emprisonment if it be demaunded. Magna Charta." Grosvenor's fol. 109 is long, but less clear.

[91] Whitelocke's version, fols. 202–3.

by the continued detention of the gentlemen who had resisted the loan. Finally, on January 2, 1628, orders were given that the prison doors be opened. "Seventy-six persons in all, some imprisoned, some in banishment in different counties, were permitted to return home . . ." On January 30 Charles authorized the issue of writs for a parliament.[92]

Some of the recalcitrants had tried to veil their opposition to the loan in the guise of economic disability, alleging poverty, hard times, large families, and so on. Bolder spirits frankly refused on grounds of unconstitutionality, agreeing that they would gladly pay "in a parliamentary way." [93] Few, perhaps, had the learning to cite medieval statutes as precedents. In this respect Eliot's petition, which seems to have served as a model for several others, was an exception. But Eliot was not a lawyer. His "precedents" were usually drawn from his own rich knowledge of the classics, or from historical episodes such as were furnished him by his friend, Sir Robert Cotton. Even in this petition he does not *cite* his acts as a lawyer would have done but quotes pertinent clauses. His petition "offers up the reasons that induced him, and which he conceives, necessity of his duty to religion, justice, and your majesty, did enforce." He explains that "he had recourse unto the laws, to be informed by them; and now in all humility he submits to your most sacred view, these collections following." His choice of precedents is discriminating. He does not use Magna Carta as a defense against arbitrary taxation. That aim is more properly served by five other "laws," ranging from Edward I's *Confirmatio cartarum*, chapter 7, to Richard III's act against benevolences.[94] Besides the laws, other reasons that induced him to resist are conceived "in the action itself": the element of coercion, the danger that it might serve as a precedent to future rulers, the violation of the subject's liberties through imprisonment. Only in this last connection does he cite the Charter, much as he must have observed its application in recent parliaments.[95]

It was Eliot's petition which led to one of the few early instances of

[92] For details, see Gardiner, VI, cas. lix, lx.

[93] These statements are based on the examination of the many pertinent petitions in the manuscript *State Papers*.

[94] The five acts he uses are 25 Ed. I, ca. 7; the "statute" *de tallagio non concedendo*; 14 Ed. III, stat. 1, ca. 21; 25 Ed. III, *Rot. Parl.*, no. 16; 1 Rich. III, ca. 2. According to Adair (see below, pp. 329–30), Eliot used one of the two alternatives available—a petition to the king, the writ of habeas corpus as employed by the five knights. He had been summoned before the council in May, and committed to the Gate House in June.

[95] "He could not, therefore, as he feared, without pressure to those immunities, become an actor in this loan; which by imprisonment and restraint has been urged, contrary to the grants of the Great Charter, by so many glorious and victorious kings so many times confirmed." The entire petition is quoted by Forster, *Eliot*, II, 87–92.

" 'I could be content to lend,' said John Hampden, who had appeared in discharge of his bond, 'as well as others: but I fear to draw upon myself that curse in Magna Charta which should be read twice a year against those who infringe it.' " *Ibid*. I, 407–8 (1626).

an attempt to discredit the Charter by an account of its origin as the product of baronial revolt under John and Henry III: "the Magna Charta! Which though Eliot so magnifies, yet we shall find it abortive in the birth and growth." Forster was the first to discover and publicize the letter written to Buckingham by James Bagg of Cornwall, a sycophant of the duke and bitter enemy of Eliot. "I met this Petition," writes Bagg, "wandering amongst the subjects, directed to, or rather against, my sovereign; not repenting, but justifying, an offence . . ." Charging that Eliot "forgets that law without circumstances observed, is no law," he disposes of each of the precedents cited in the petition. More particularly, of the origin and history of the Charter he writes:

> But the excommunication and curses denounced against all that violate these laws is a terrible thunderbolt to the petitioner's conscience! Why rather fears he not the curses of Pope Innocent, in conscience of the royal wrongs, denounced against all the procurers of such laws, and especially the Magna Charta! which, though Eliot so magnifies yet we find it abortive in the birth and growth!
>
> For it was not originally freely and regally granted, nor (if the petitioner would have dealt candidly in his allegation) so voluntarily confirmed. The beginning was in Henry the First's time, who was but an usurper upon the right of Robert, his elder brother; and to establish himself in that usurpation did by it curry favour with the nobles and smooth the people—a low thing in a king! Wherein he granted away, peradventure, some of his regality to them, lest they should assist in taking away all from him. And for the confirmation of this Magna Charta, King John, having as crackt a title as Henry the First, had used the same policy in selling his regality. For, being environed with a rebellious army in the meadows of Staines, he was forced by a strong hand to grant the Magna Charta de Foresta; which grants as aforesaid were admitted by Pope Innocent. Nor yet was the Magna Charta, thus extorted, a law, till the 52nd year of Henry the Third. Neither was it then so freely enacted by the royal assent (which is the form and life of a law) as wrung out by the long, bloody, and civil wars of those never-to-be-honoured barons! Yet was posterity loth to forego the price of so much blood, by them called liberty; as it feared (through due revenge) that every act of their prince, whom they had justly provoked, would lead to their bondage. Yet, sithence, have many pious princes suffered them to enjoy an equal liberty under it; preserving to every man his own vine. But it never was, as now, especially by a single brain, made a chain to bind the king from doing anything and a key to admit the vassal to everything! [96]

Much the same story had been presented by Sir Walter Raleigh in his "Prerogatives of Parliaments," though with the aim of pointing quite a

[96] Quoted in full by Forster, *Eliot*, II, 87–93. Forster devotes many pages to Bagg, the "duke's man," for whom this ardent biographer of Eliot can hardly find words scathing enough. He blames Bagg for Eliot's arrest.

different moral. The arguments were suggested by a similar episode, the proceedings against Oliver St. John in Star Chamber, 1615, though not published until 1628. Very likely the two writers had used the same type of chronicle. In Raleigh's dialogue, a justice of the peace defends the Charter in spite of its origin: confirmations by parliament have conferred upon it authenticity and legal status. The counselor of state emphasizes the "beginning of the Great Charter, which had first an obscure Birth from usurpation, and was secondly fostered and shewed to the world by Rebellion." He does not deny its ultimate legitimation, but recognizes in it only a modest limitation on crown and prerogative. The justice of the peace blames the counselor and his like for St. John's imprisonment contrary to the "law of the land." [97] The sentence quoted ("The beginning of the Great Charter . . .") was used by Bishop Laud, citing "Rauly," in his observations on the Charter, March 1628.[98]

The five knights made of themselves a test case to question not merely the illegality of the loan but, more fundamental, the power of king and council to exercise arbitrary imprisonment. They applied for a writ of habeas corpus. The hearing was held before King's Bench November 22, with Hyde, the newly appointed chief justice, presiding; his associates were Whitelocke, Jones, and Dodderidge. Able counsel pleaded to the insufficiency of the return: "The gentlemen's counsel for Habeas Corpus, Mr. Noy, Sergeant Bramston, Mr. Selden, Mr. Calthorp, pleaded yesterday with wonderful applause, even of shouting and clapping of hands which is unusual in that place." [99] Attorney General Heath was counsel for the crown. This famous case, rather misunderstood by earlier constitutional historians such as Hallam and even Gardiner, has been more effectively treated by Jenks in his essay on habeas corpus, and in detail by Miss Helen Relf in *The Petition of Right*.[100] Under the same title E. R. Adair

[97] "The Prerogatives of Parliament in England, Proved in a Dialogue between a Counsellor of State, and a Justice of Peace," *Harleian Miscellany* (1809 ed.), IV, 304–46. It was published in 1628 with a dedication to James I and to parliament, and in 1657 with a dedication to parliament. *D.N.B.*
Like Bagg, the "counsellor" identifies Magna Carta with the charter of Henry I, but notes additions and changes in John's time. Both kings are called usurpers, needing support against better claimants. The justice of the peace cites later confirmations in support of his views. The passage quoted above is noted by McIlwain, *High Court of Parliament*, p. 56.

[98] *State Papers*, 16, vol. 96, no. 31. In the calendar this is dated March 17, 1628, and called a "list of Parliaments, from the time of Henry II to this day; with Notes by Bishop Laud of the several grants and subsidies voted by them. . . . Under the last head occur the observations on Magna Charta . . . which have been quoted against the Bishop. . . . the Bishop's principal authorities are the Statute Book and 'Rauly.' "

[99] November 23, a letter from London. Father Cyprien de Gamache, *Court and Times of Charles I*, I, 292. Noy pleaded for Sir Walter Erle, Calthorp for Sir John Corbet, Selden for Sir Edmund Hampden, and Serjeant Bramston for Sir John Heveningham. Although the case sometimes bears his name, the fifth, Darnel, did not plead. According to Miss Relf, he was "too staggered by the return."

[100] Edward Jenks, "Habeas Corpus," in *Select Essays in Anglo-American Legal History*, II, 531–48; Frances Helen Relf, *The Petition of Right*; E. R. Adair, in *History*, V, 99–103, 1920.

gives the best concise statement of just what was involved and what actually happened:

There was no question of the complete discharge of the prisoners; they merely sued to be released on bail; to this the judges returned judgment that they should be remanded—not until they should be tried according to the law, which would have meant a definite refusal of bail—but simply remanded; this was not a final judgment, and merely implied a remand while the judges consulted together or until they received information from the Crown as to the real cause of commitment. As the knights made no further application to the court, no further final judgment was given, and the matter was left undecided.

But in order to understand the intense feeling which the case aroused both at the time and in the succeeding parliament, this statement needs to be supplemented by two points brought out in Miss Relf's account. First, the immediate contemporary understanding of the award was that it *was* a final judgment. Explanation as to the real nature of the award came from Solicitor Shelton in parliament and was cleared up by the subcommittee appointed to search for records and precedents. They inspected the entry for the case and found only a *remittitur*, with a space left for the entry of the final judgment. Second, apprehension was further aroused by the discovery by Selden (a member of this subcommittee) of a draft of an entry for a final judgment. This, it was finally revealed, had been drawn by a clerk at Heath's insistence and in an unprecedented form. Coke and Eliot believed that only the meeting of parliament had prevented the entry of the judgment. Selden went farther: "I do believe that it will be recorded yet so soone as the Parliament arises, if it be not prevented." On April 14, when the judges were called before the Lords to explain their award, it was made clear that they had not supported Heath. The nature of their award was finally made clear. "Never again would the men of that time consider it as a final judgment." [101]

Counsel for the five knights used chapter 29 of Magna Carta in two ways. First there was the general interpretation that no free man should suffer imprisonment without having first been condemned by due process of law.[102] The effect, if not the intent, of the government's present policy, they argued, might well be just such unlawful and indeterminate im-

Cf. Miss Relf, p. 3: "These men made the issue very plain. They maintained that according to the law any person committed by the King or Council without cause shown should be bailed. Attorney Heath was equally positive that the law showed he should be kept in prison until the King was ready to bring him to trial."

[101] Relf, *Petition of Right*, pp. 4–9.

[102] This and the following quotes are from Howell's *State Trials*, III, 1–59. "'If the law be, that upon this return this gentleman should be remanded . . . then his imprisonment shall not continue on for a time, but for ever . . . and by law there can be no remedy for the subject: and therefore this return cannot stand with the laws of the realm

prisonment. Heath agreed in principle,[103] but maintained that because there was this possible consequence of commitment without cause shown, that did not make the commitment illegal. It must be assumed that the sovereign would exercise this, like other prerogative powers, with discretion. Each side sought to ridicule the other's arguments by pushing them to extremes. In the second place, they emphasized the technical meaning of the *per legem terrae*, as it had long been interpreted in "our books"; law of the land meant due process of law; process of law included not only trial but some lawful initial process such as indictment, presentment, original writ; commitment "by special command" did not fall within this regular procedure.

The four lawyers had evidently worked out together their plan of attack. Before proceeding to the "matter and content" of the writ, each dealt with technicalities, the "manner and form": the return was indirect; it expressed only the "cause of a cause"; it ought to have specified the cause and time of the caption as well as of the detention.[104] Here Noy and Calthorp made considerable use of precedents to point parallels—rules of law not directly pertinent to the case in hand but which indicated the spirit and intent of the common law. Calthorp, for instance, used the Register, Fitzherbert, Plowden, and Dyer to prove that in pleading there must be direct affirmation. "And if in pleading there must be direct affirmation of the matter alleged then *a fortiori* in a return, which must be more precise than in pleading."

As to their technical interpretation of the *per legem terrae*, they were obviously relying on the fourteenth-century statutes in the printed editions such as Rastell's under the title *accusation*. This is borne out by Heath's proceedings. He elected to discuss his opponents' objections as to matter under five heads, the fourth being "Acts of parliament in print." The clerk of the court, Keeling, stood by with the volume and read each in turn before Heath commented on it. The attorney introduced Richard II, chapter 12, as "the last act of parliament in print the counsel on the other side produced" and concluded "these were all the printed Statutes cited by the counsel on the other side. But because I would not mis-

or that of Magna Charta. . . . And if they sue out a writ of Habeas Corpus, it is but making a new warrant, and they shall be remanded and never have the advantage of the laws which are the best inheritance of every subject.' "

"Justice Jones. Mr. Attorney, if it be so that the law of Magna Charta and other statutes be now in force, and the gentlemen be not delivered by this court, how shall they be delivered? Apply yourself to shew us any other way to deliver them.

"Doderidge. Yea, or else they shall have a perpetual imprisonment."

[103] "My lord, this Statute is intended to' be a final prosecution; for if a man shall be imprisoned without due process and never be brought to answer, that is unjust and forbidden by this statute."

[104] "The return, which ought to be certain, and punctual, and affirmative, and not by the way of information out of another man's mouth, may not be good, as appeareth by the several books of our law."

interpret these Statutes, I thought it equal to desire your Lordship that they might be read." We are not left in any doubt as to how seriously these statutes were taken. Said Selden of 42 Edward III:

The answer there is, that as this is an article of the Great Charter this should be granted. So that it seems the statute is not taken to be an explanation of that of Magna Charta, but the very words of the statute of Magna Charta.

Said Noy:

What "lex terrae" should be, I will not taken upon me to expound, otherwise than I find them to be expounded by acts of parliament; and this is, that they are understood to be the process of the law, sometimes by writ, sometimes by attachment of the person . . .

In the basing of arguments on these printed statutes there was a division of labor. It was for Bramston, who appeared first, to maintain that the return should show the cause at least in general, and that it ought to appear that commitment was upon presentment or indictment, and not upon petition or suggestion made to the king or lords, "which is against the statute made in the 25 E. 3, ca. 4; 42 E. 3, ca. 3." This return "cannot stand with the laws of the realm, or that of Magna Charta; nor with the statute of 28 E. 3, ca. 3. for if a man be not bailable upon this return, they cannot have the benefit of these two laws, which are the inheritance of the subject." [105]

It was for Noy to meet the possible argument that *speciale mandatum Domini Regis* was one form of due process of law. This he did with the help of another of the printed statutes, 37 Edward III, chapter 18, which excludes "false suggestion to ye king himselfe" from due process, and actually uses the phrase "by special command." It was the presence of this phrase which led Noy to make the mistake of including from the parliament rolls not only 36 Edward III, chapter 20, but the quite inapplicable number 9, which, in spite of Heath's correction, was to become one of the *six statutes*.[106]

[105] "By the statute 25 E. 3, c. 4, it is ordained and established 'That no man from henceforth, shall be taken by petition or suggestion made to the king or his council, but by indictment or course of law'; and accordingly it was enacted 42 E. 3, c. 3, the title of which statute is, 'None shall be put to answer an accusation made to the king without. presentment.' "

[106] See above, p. 93. "For these words 'per legem terrae,' what 'Lex terrae' should be I will not take upon me to expound, otherwise than I find them- to be expounded by acts of parliament; and this is, that they are understood to be process of the law, sometimes by writ, sometimes by attachment of the person: but whether, 'speciale mandatum Domini Regis' be intended by that or no, I leave it to your lordship's exposition upon two Petitions of the commons, and Answer of the king, in 36 E. 3, No. 9 and No. 20.

"In the first of these the commons complain that the Great Charter, the Charter of the Forest, and other statutes were broken, and they desire that for the good of himself and of his people, they might be kept and put in execution, and that they might not be infringed *by making an arrest by special command*, or otherwise; and the answer was, that the assent of the lords established and ordained, that the said charter and the other statutes

Selden modestly undertook to "add a little to that which hath been said" on the statutes.

The statute of Magna Charta, cap. 29, that statute if it were fully executed as it ought to be, every man would enjoy his liberty better than he doth. The law saith expressly, "No freeman shall be imprisoned without due process of the law"; out of the very body of this act of parliament, besides the explanation of other statutes, it appears "Nullus liber homo capiatur vel imprisonatur nisi per legem terrae." My lord, I know these words "legem terrae," do leave the question where it was, if the interpretation of the statute were not. But I think under your lordship's favour there it must be intended by due course of law, to be either by presentment or indictment.

He continues with an ingenious argument to demonstrate that if *per legem terrae* meant no more than the king's counsel took it to mean—a general "according to the laws"—and *per speciale mandatum* be within the meaning of these words, "this act would extend to villeins as well as freemen." [107] He concludes "with a little observation upon these words, 'nec super eum mittimus.'" Noy had made "bold to inform your lordship" that in this statute these words *in carcerem* are omitted out of the printed books: for it should be "nec eum in carcerem mittimus." To account for the correction, Selden had only to draw on his own scholarly little tract, the *Epinomis*. Though Coke had first introduced John's Charter into the debates in 1624, and Bagg had tried to discredit it by a sinister origin, Selden's, as a more accurate and formal public introduction to John's Charter merits quotation:

But my lord, in the 7th [*sic* for 17] king John, there was a Great Charter, by which this statute in the 9th H. 3, whereby we are now regulated, was framed, and there the words are, "nec eum in carcerem mittimus." We will not commit him to prison; that is, the king himself will not; and to justify this, there is a story of that time in Matthew Paris, and in that Book this Charter of king John is set down at large, which book is very authentic, and there it is entered: and in the 9th of Hen. 3, he saith, that the statute was renewed in the same words with the Charter of king John. And my lord, he

should be put in execution according to the petition, and that is without any disturbance by arrest by special command or otherwise; for it was granted, as it was petitioned.

"In the same year, for they were very careful of this matter and it was necessary it should be so, for it was then an usual thing, to take men by writs 'quibusdam de causis,' and many of these words caused many acts of parliament . . ." Here follows his comment on no. 20.

Calthorp, too, demonstrating that certain forms of "special command" are unlawful, cites 25 Ed. III, ca. 4, and 37 Ed. III, ca. 10. His argument includes a famous passage from Bracton to prove that the judges, "which are indifferent between the king and his subjects," must be given the opportunity to judge "whether his commitment be against the laws of this realm, or not."

[107] That is, "the freman shall have no privilege above the villein" who may lawfully be imprisoned by his lord: "the lords and the king, for then they both had villeins, might imprison them, and the villein could have no remedy."

might know it better than others, for he was the king's chronologer in those times: and therefore, my lord, since there be so many reasons, and so many precedents, and so many statutes, which declare that no freeman whatsoever ought to be imprisoned but according to the laws of the land; and that the Liberty of the Subject is the highest inheritance that he hath, my humble request is, that according to the ancient laws and privileges of this realm this gentleman, my client may be bailed.

Heath tried to belittle the phrase as of no account. "I know not why we should contend about these words, seeing the first part of this statute saith 'Nemo imprisonetur,' why then may not I say as well, 'nec eum in carcerem mittimus'? I see no difference in the words . . ." But Selden had a real point. In the current printed statutes the English translation for *mittimus* was always "pass upon" ("we shall not pass upon him nor condemn him but by lawful judgment of his peers or by the law of the land"). Thus the phrase *per legem terrae* might be construed as relating only to the *pass upon and condemn*, that is *trial* and *judgment*. Selden's reading would relate it to preliminary *commitment* also.

Attorney General Heath answered all objections as to form to his own satisfaction at least. As to matter, the question resolved itself in his mind to one issue, were they replevisable or remandable? He dealt with his opponents' arguments under five heads.[108] Their cases, "precedents of divers times, wherein men committed by the king had been bailed," he eliminated as not analogous: some were routine, involving no matters of state, again the judges had other information, and so on. Their "petitions of the Commons" and "acts of parliament in print" he dismissed as irrelevant by putting a different interpretation upon them.

[108] "Inconveniences to liberty if not so. Authorities out of law-books. The Petition of the Commons answered by several kings in parliament. Acts of parliament in print. Precedents of divers times, wherein men committed by the king had been bailed." According to his interpretation, Magna Carta ca. 29 and the statutes of 28 Ed. III, ca. 3, and 25 Ed. III, ca. 4, were to the effect "that none should be *condemned* but he be brought to answer and be tried." They had no bearing on preliminary commitment or delay of trial. 37 and 38 Ed. III related only to private suggestions made to king or council. Rich. II, ca. 12, contained an exception favoring his thesis: "the scope of this Statute is against the Wardens of the Fleet, for some miscarriages in them; but there is one thing in this Statute which I shall desire your lordship to observe; and that is, for these misdemeanors he shall forfeit his office, *except it be by writ from the king or his commandment* so that it was no new doctrine in those times, that the king might then give such commandment for committing." He showed correctly that the petition from the parliament roll (no. 9) was merely a confirmation: "The commons then petitioned the king that all the statutes made in exposition of Magna Charta and of the Forest, may be kept and observed; the king makes Answer, that it shall be done. And in one of the Answers it is said, If any man be grieved he may complain. But what is all this to the point in question?"

As to Westminster I, ca. 15, his opponents had gone too far in assuming that it restricted bail as used by the sheriff only, and did not extend to the judges such as those of King's Bench. According to Heath it forbids bail absolutely in the four cases specified. He characterizes it as "a full expression to the purpose of Magna Charta," made near the time of the Charter. "If they had understood the Statute of Magna Charta in another sense, would they not have expressed it so in this statute?"

And now my lord, we are where we were, to find out the true meaning of Magna Charta, for there is the foundation of our case; all this that had been said concerneth other things and is nothing to the thing in question. There is not a word either of commitment of the king, or commandment of the council, in all the Statutes and Records.

Heath did not go as far in exalting the prerogative as Serjeant Ashley was to do in 1628, but he does describe that "*absoluta potestas* that a sovereign hath":

. . . the king cannot command your lordship, or any other court of justice, to proceed otherwise than according to the laws of this kingdom; for it is part of your lordships' oath, to judge according to the law of the kingdom. But my lord, there is a great difference between those legal commands, and that *absoluta potestas* that a sovereign hath, by which a king commands; but when I call it *absoluta potestas* I do not mean that the king may do what he pleaseth, for he hath rules to govern himself as well as your lordships, who are subordinate judges under him. The difference is the king is the head of the same fountain of justice which your lordship administers to all his subjects; all justice is derived from him, and what he doth, he doth not as a private person, but as head of the commonwealth, as *justiciarius regni*,—yea, the very essence of justice under God upon earth is in him . . .

He concluded that the only recourse of the gentlemen was to a petition of right (even this would require the royal warrant for the words *Soit droit fait al partie*). "And this may answer a perpetual imprisonment, and God forbid that this should be so." [109]

The Parliament of 1628–29: First Session

For my own part, I shall be very glad to see that good, old decrepit Law of Magna Charta which hath been so long kept in and lain bed-rid as it were; I shall be glad I say to see it walk abroad again, with new Vigour and Lustre, attended by the other Six Statutes: For questionless, it will be a general heartening to all. (BENJAMIN RUDYERD)

ON JANUARY 30 Charles finally gave the order for writs for a parliament. As sheriffs were chosen in November, it was too late to exclude unwanted members by the device employed in 1626. Says Gardiner, quoting Contarini, "It is even said that it was proposed to issue a proclamation excluding all lawyers from sitting, and it was decided that any attempt to touch the Duke should be followed by an immediate dissolution. In that case the King would consider himself no longer bound by the laws and customs of the realm." Actually all the active leaders and opponents of

[109] And so ruled Chief Justice Hyde: "If in justice we ought to deliver you, we would do it; but upon these grounds, and these Records, and the Precedents and Resolutions, we cannot deliver you, but you must be remanded."

the duke were elected: Wentworth, Eliot, and Phelips; the lawyers Selden, Noy, Littleton, Whitby, and Sir Edward Coke, now in his seventy-sixth year. A few days before the opening of the parliament (March 17) a meeting of the leading members of the House of Commons was held at Sir Robert Cotton's.

There was a general feeling that the attack upon Buckingham should not be repeated, and Eliot, who was of the contrary opinion, withdrew his opposition in the face of the general sentiment, reserving his right to revert to his original position at some future time. To the others it was becoming clear . . . that the main struggle was with the King and not with Buckingham. . . . Coke and Phelips, Wentworth and Selden, concurred in the opinion that the violated rights of the subject must first be vindicated.[110]

The contest in parliament, then, was to center around principles rather than persons.

The religious issue was still keenly felt by many. Eliot, early in the session, coupled, as he had done before, the two great causes of religion and liberty. The government's leniency toward recusants was protested by joint petition of the Houses in this first session; the dangers of "popery and Arminianism" were voiced in the well-known "Eliot's resolutions" of the second session. But uppermost in most men's minds was the threat to liberty of the subject in the four respects eventually set forth in the Petition of Right: the forced loans, arbitrary arrest and imprisonment, the billeting of soldiers, and martial law. Of these the second seemed most dangerous, its free exercise by king and council threatening not only individual liberty, but indeed all liberties, the very existence of parliament itself. In the words of Eliot:

It has been well propounded for a generall overture to our worke, that the manie points of consideration in this P(arliament) are to be the matters of relig(ion) & our lib(erties) whose necessities require a present aid & succor, & whose safties comprehend all our happiness & hopes. . . .
In the lib(erties) the invasions have beene made upon that sacred relicke of our ancestors; the attempts upon our goods, the attempts upon our persons; our monies taken, our wares & marchandises seisd; loanes, benevolences, contributions, impositions levied, & exacted; our bodies hurried & imprisoned, & the power & execution of the Lawes vilified and contemnd . . . but that which is more than lives, more then the lives and liberties of thousands, then all our goods, all our interests & faculties, the life, the libertie of the p(arliament) the privilidges & immunities of this h(ouse) which are the basses & support of all the rest what preiudice has it suffered? [111]

The immediate practical question, then, was how best to protect and

110 Gardiner, VI, 226, 230–31.
111 *Negotium Posterorum*, I, 164–65 (supplement).

guarantee these liberties. The Petition of Right was the last of a series of possible solutions, actually six in number, proffered by Commons, Lords, and king in the course of the session. These were: (1) the bill offered by Sir Edward Coke, March 21; (2) the four resolutions of the Commons presented to the Lords, April 7; (3) the counter resolutions of the Lords sent to the Commons, April 25;[112] (4) the king's offer to confirm Magna Carta and the *six statutes*; (5) the Commons bill; and (6) the Petition of Right. Gardiner and, in more detail, Miss Relf, have traced the course and character of these successively proposed solutions. It is Adair again, however, who gives the most effective answer to the questions, just what was the Petition of Right? Why was it substituted for the Commons resolutions and their bill? The Commons abandoned their resolutions because they were too sweeping to be accepted by the Lords. They rejected the latter's resolutions because of their too great "saving" of the royal power. They abandoned their bill on intimation that Charles would never let it pass, but refused the king's offered confirmation on the grounds that definition rather than confirmation was needed. The Petition of Right, then, was more limited and less satisfactory than the original Commons resolutions, since it substituted certain particulars for broad general principles, but was the only practicable (passable) solution at the time. Adair goes so far as to call it a *pis aller*, a makeshift, and not the all-conquering statute that Hallam believed it. Yet its value was "to place on record the statement that certain definite grievances were illegal according to the already existing laws, to gain the King's assent to this view, and consequently to secure that this statement would be binding on the judges, while at the same time there was no attempt to infringe the royal prerogative by an enlargement of the law." [113] The "already existing laws" thus formally defined, of course included Magna Carta chapter 29, and actually quoted only one of the *six statutes*, 28 Edward III, chapter 3. At last they were to mean beyond dispute what the common lawyers had long contended.

Neither the Commons resolutions nor Coke's bill cites the Charter.[114] According to one of the newswriters, however, besides this bill "Sir Edward Coke hath also ready drawn into the form of an act of parliament an explanation of the Magna Charta, which he means ere long to present

[112] *State Papers*, 16, no. 14, marked in Laud's hand, "The 5 propositions sent to the Lower house about accommodation in ye busines concerninge ye Libertye of ye subiect, penned bye D. Harsnet Bp. of Norwich," comments, as to the first: "The good old Lawe called Magna Charta—That Charter is a Collection of many Lawes, and cannot bee fittly termed a Lawe, in the singular number. The request to have these stand still in force, beeing in force allreddy and unrepealed, seems to be a vaine & superfluous Request."

[113] Adair, *History*, V, pp. 101–2.

[114] Sir Edward's "act against long and unjust detaining in prison" provided that any person detained untried must be released on bail at the end of two months; even one who could not find sureties must be released after three months. Harl. MSS 4771, fol. 15.

to the House, to the end that every man may know how far he may be touched in life, liberty, lands, or goods." [115] No such bill seems to have been introduced at this time, but Coke was a member (Adair calls him the most influential member) of the Commons' committee which brought in its bill April 29. Next day, March 22, in speaking for supply but against forced loans, the old reporter succeeded in packing into one speech all his favorite clichés culled from the records: the many confirmations (thirty-three here!), the *sententias latas super Chartas,* the *charta libertatis quia liberos facit,* the statute of 42 Edward III—"that all laws against Magna Charta are voyd," the *confirmatio Chartarum,* and the *Statutum de tallagio non concedendo.*[116] In this same debate Eliot mentions the Charter as one among various statutes prescribing that "the subject is not to be burthened with loanes tallages or benevolences."

The Commons bill began by declaring that Magna Carta and the "acts of explanation" "bee putt in due execucion," then added defining clauses on commitments and loans. "At the Committee of lawyers about the bill for Magna Charta and the liberties of the Subjects" [117] Selden argued that though Magna Carta was a statute and had been recognized as such, it should now be definitely re-enacted. Coke seems to have been responsible for the formidable list of "precedents"—the old interpretive statutes to be included and confirmed along with Magna Carta. Modern historians who conceive of the Great Charter as public law directed against the crown may well ponder the debate which followed Coke's report. When the bill was criticized for its wording—the explicit way in which it named the king—three of its supporters felt it necessary to point out that Magna Carta too had actually extended to the king for "is not the king named in Magna Carta at least by way of implication?" [118] The Lords' resolutions, like the king's promised confirmation, agreed that Magna Carta and the *six statutes* were in force, but they availed little as definition. The Commons found the first four too vague, and the fifth,

[115] Probably from Mr. Pory, March 21, 1628, de Gamache, *Court and Times of Charles I,* I, 333.

[116] Harl. MSS 4771, fols. 21–22. Here this follows as if part of Phelips' speech, but other versions indicate that it is Coke's. This text is less corrupt than the Mass. MS.

[117] Under this caption the *True Relation* (Harl. MSS 4771) has a rather garbled version of Selden's speech, and one by Coke in which he offers "precedents" on loans to be included in the bill. The version of the bill based on the *True Relation* (printed in Relf, *The Petition of Right,* App. B; Gardiner, VI, 264–65), as Miss Relf points out, seems sketchy and incomplete when compared with Coke's report from the committee on the 29th, which names the three "heads" of the bill and a long list of precedents.

[118] Coke—"Objection: Shall wee doe that to the King now that never was before?

Answer: Why was there ever such violacions and is not the King named in Magna Charta at least by way of implicacion and 36 E. 3 and 25 E. 3 names the King and his counsell."

Noy—"It was answered Magna Charta is nec eum in carcere etc."

Shervill: "Others object it is not the language of Parliament to bind kings and the Counsell by express words. I answer it is the language of Magna Charta non super eum ibimus aut etc."

Harl. MSS 124, 125, 126, 127.

the saving "His Majesty's Royal Prerogative," intrinsical to his Sovereignty, and entrusted to him from God, *ad communem totius Populi Salutem, et non ad Destructionem,* dangerous.

In the debates on these successive solutions many members spoke on some phase of liberty of the subject—too many to bear quoting, or even citing here. Magna Carta was on every tongue. It was debated pro and con whether the king's promised confirmation would avail aught; whether the now famous document was a statute *ab initio* or as a result of repeated parliamentary confirmations.

Rival interpretations of its meaning were aired again and again, and various formulas offered for some infallible definition. The main arguments are well-known, the most striking speeches often quoted. Hence all that will be attempted here is to remind the reader of the most notable debates and telling thrusts, with emphasis on the occasional new contribution to Charter history or interpretation.

LEX TERRAE AND "ARREST WITHOUT CAUSE SHOWN"

The arguments which carried most weight with the Lords were those which the Commons presented in conference with the upper House April 7, and again on the 17th. Several of the ablest lawyers in the House were chosen to confer with the Lords "concerning certain ancient and fundamental Liberties of England." Each of the principals was assigned two assistants.[119] In the words of the lord president reporting to his fellow lords:

The Subject of all was about the Liberty of the Subjects. To set this forth, they employed Four Speakers. The First was Sir *Dudley Dygges,* a man of Volubility and Elegancy of Speech. His part was but the Induction. The second was Mr. *Littleton* a Grave and Learned Lawyer, whose part was to represent the Resolution of the House, and their Grounds whereupon they went. The third was Mr. *Selden,* a great Antiquary and a pregnant Man; his Part was to shew the Law and Precedents in the Point. The Fourth was Sir *Edward Cooke,* that famous Reporter of the Law, whose Part was to shew the Reasons of all that the others had said; and that all which was said, was but in Affirmance of the Common Law.

Now to report the First Man, Sir *Dudley;* how his Words will come off from my Tongue, I cannot tell . . .[120]

[119] Digges was to make the introduction. "Mr. Littleton to justify the Declaration of this House by Acts of Parliament, and to answer all Objections to the contrary. Matter of Record, and judicial Precedents, committed to Mr. Selden; and the Remedy of Law by *Habeas Corpus.* The Draught of the Judgment, produced by Mr. Solicitor, to be specially mentioned. Sir Edw. Coke to shew these Acts of Parliament, and Precedents, to be but Affirmations of the Common Law; To shew the Reasons hereof; and that the Shewing of Cause of Imprisonment not against Reason of State." Digges was to be assisted by Rudyerd and Pym; Coke by Rolles and Hakewill; Selden by Herberte and Whitby; Littleton by Sir Robert Phelips and Mr. Charles Jones. *C. J.* I, 880a.

[120] *L. J.* III, 717b–18a.

All this really amounted to a re-arguing of the *five knights case* with some amplification of the evidence, a rather more effective division of labor, and more publicity. The conference was not only reported to both Houses, as was usual, but the conferees were instructed as follows by the House on April 14: "Sir Edward Coke, Sir D. Digges, Mr. Littleton, Mr. Selden, which argued the Case of the Liberty of the Persons of the Subjects from Imprisonment, to bring in, by Thursday next, their several Arguments, fair written; as also the Copies of the Records, produced by them; And the Clerk to insert the Arguments into the Journal, and to have Liberty to give out Copies of them." [121]

It now fell to Littleton to expound Magna Carta and all the interpretive evidence of printed statutes and parliament rolls. His accomplishment could not be more perfectly characterized than it was by Sir John Eliot:

... the understanding of the former and latter times of the scope of Magna Charta, soe exquisitly retrivd out of the most hidden & obstruse corners of antiquitie by my most learned frind, & the exposition of those other lawes that were descendants from that great mother & made onlie in explanations of the same . . . [122]

Littleton's arguments, as reported to the Lords by the Earl of Hertford, reveal that neither time nor all the efforts of king's counsel had abated a whit the faith of the common lawyers in Magna Carta and the *six statutes*. "Leaving the Reasons of Law and Precedents for others," he says, "they have charged me particularly

to give your Lordships Satisfaction, that this Liberty is established and confirmed by the whole State, the King, the Lords Spiritual and Temporal, and the Commons, by several Acts of Parliament; the Authority whereof is so great, that it can receive no Answer, save by Interpretation, or Repeal by future Statutes; and those that I shall mind your Lordships of, are so direct to the Point, that they can bear no other Exposition at all; and sure I am they are still in Force: The First of them is the Grand Charter of the Liberties of England, first granted in the seventeenth Year of King *John,* and then renewed in the Ninth Year of King *Henry* the Third, and since confirmed in Parliament above Thirty Times. The Words are thus: Cap. 29. *Nullus . . .*"

After quoting the chapter in full, he introduces the "historical evidence" used by Selden before King's Bench in 1627. He finds it expedient to

[121] *C. J.* I, 883a. And April 21: Report to the House from the conference with the Lords by Digges, Littleton, Selden, Coke. "And Serjeant *Ashley* his Argument and Speech particularly reported by Sir *Edw. Coke.*" *Ibid.,* p. 886b. April 23: "Mr. Littleton delivereth in, in Writing, his Arguments, and the objections and Answers at the Conference. And any member of the House may have copies of this or any other Parts of Mr. Selden's, Sir Edward Coke's, or Sir D. Digges."

[122] *Negotium Posterorum,* II, 119, introduced by the editor thus: "A short but pungent Speech succeeds this upon close of the Lawyers' arguments on behalf of Liberty of the Person." For Littleton's arguments, *L. J.* III, 718b–22a.

emphasize and illustrate the fact that the words of the Charter extend to the king's suit, again drawing on history (the circumstances of its origin in 1215) and his great namesake's interpretation of the chapter (Littleton in 10 Edward IV).

And though the Words of this Grand Charter be spoken in the Third Person, yet they are not to be understood of Suits betwixt Party and Party, at least not of them alone, but even of the King's Suits against his Subjects, as will appear by the Occasion of the getting of that Charter, which was by reason of the Differences betwixt those Kings and Their People; and therefore properly to be applied unto their Power over them, and not to ordinary Questions betwixt Subject and Subject; and the Words *per legale Judicium Parium suorum*, immediately preceding the others of *per Legem Terrae*, are meant of Trials at the King's Suit, and not at the Prosecution of a Subject. And therefore, if a Peer of the Realm be arraigned at the Suit of the King upon an Indictment of Murder, he shall be tried by his Peers (that is, Nobles). But if he be appealed of Murder by a Subject, his Trial shall be by an ordinary Jury of Twelve Freeholders, as appeareth in 10 E. IV. 6.; 33 H. VIII. *Brooke*, Title Trials, 142 . . .

Then follows his interpretation of each of the *six statutes* and Westminster I, concluding, "Thus your Lordships have heard Acts of Parliament in the Point."

Selden, dealing with the technicalities of procedure, emphatically upheld the writ *corpus cum causa* (not an individual petition of right) as the proper remedy on commitment by king and council without cause shown:

I shall first observe the Remedy that every Freeman is to use for the regaining of his Liberty, when he is against Law imprisoned . . . But that Writ of *Habeas Corpus* or *Corpus cum Causa*, is the chiefest Remedy in Law for any Man that is imprisoned, and the only Remedy in Law for him that is imprisoned by the special Command of the King, or of the Lords of the Council, without shewing Cause of the Commitment. Neither is there in the Law any such Thing, nor ever was there Mention of any Thing in the Laws of this Land, as a Petition of Right to be used in such Cases for Liberty of the Person . . .[123]

Sir Edward Coke, assigned to show "the reasons of all the others had said; and that all that which was said was but in affirmance of the Common Law," naturally contributed little that was new. However, he was in rare good form, and his pungent phrases served as an exclamation

---

[123] He makes a telling point in answer to Heath's objection to the precedent of Sir Thomas Monson's case, 14 Jac.: "That everybody knew by common Fame that this gentleman was committed for suspicion of the Death of a gentleman in *The Tower*, and that he was therefore bailable . . . Was there not as much a Fame why the Gentlemen that were remanded in the late Judgement were committed? and might not the self-same reason have served to enlarge them; their offence (whatsoever it were) being much less, I think, than that for which this Gentleman was suspected."

point to all that had gone before. As reported by the Bishop of Lincoln: ". . . there had been procured Twelve Precedents, *in Terminis terminatibus*, a whole Jury of Precedents, all in Point . . ." Again, of four "Book Cases and Authorities all in the Point," he said "that if the Learned Counsel on the other Side could produce but one against the Liberties so pat and pertinent, oh! how they would hug and cull it."

And then he made a Recapitulation of all that had been offered unto your Lordships: That generally your Lordships had been advised by the most faithful Counsellors that can be, dead Men: These cannot be daunted for Fear, nor misled by Affection, Reward, or Hope of Preferment, and therefore your Lordships might safely believe them . . .

Equally felicitous was Coke's conclusion to the second conference with the Lords.[124]

He agreed with Mr. Attorney, he said, in the Enumeration of all the Kinds of *Habeas Corpus*; and if they Two were alone, he did not doubt but they should agree in all Things; only he said that to be a Tenant at Will for Liberty he could never agree to: It was a Tenure could not be found in all *Littleton*.

This Imprisoning destroys all Endeavours; if he were young, he durst not be a Soldier, Lawyer, or Merchant, if Tenant at will for Liberty, for that would make him desperate; for a Tenant at Will never keeps any Thing in Reparation, etc.

And finally, following Heath and Ashley:

He put your Lordships in Mind that you had the greatest Cause in Hand that ever came in the Hall of *West*[*minster*] or indeed in any Parliament. My Lords (saith he), your Noble Ancestors, whose Places you hold, were Parties to *Magna Charta,* so called for Weight and Substane, for otherwise many other Statutes are greater in Bulk, as *Alexander*, a little Man, called *Magnus* for his Courage; and you my Lords the Bishops (saith he) are commanded *fulminare,* to thunder out, your Execrations against all Infringers of *Magna Charta, Sententia lata super Chartam.* And all worthy Judges, that were worthy of their Places, have had *Magna Charta* in Great Estimation. Now, as Justice hath a Sword, so hath it a Balance; *ponderat haec Causas, percutit ille reos.* Put therefore (saith he) my Noble Lords, in the one Balance Seven Acts of Parliament, Records, Precedents, Reasons, all that we speak, and that of 18 *Ed.* III, wherto I found no Answer; and in God's Name, put into the other Balance what Mr. Attorney said, his Wit, Learning, and great Endowments of Nature. And, if he be weighty, let him have it; if no, then conclude with us; you are involved in the same Danger with us, and therefore we desire you, in the Name of the Commons of *England,* represented in us, that we may have Cause to give God and the King Thanks for your Justice in complying with us.

And here rested Sir *Edward Coke.*

[124] For the first conference, L. *J.* III, 727–31; for the second (April 17, reported on the 19th), pp. 761–62.

On April 14 the judges who had been concerned in the *five knights case* appeared before the Lords to explain the stand they had taken: "We are here to deliver, before your Lordships, what judgment was given by us concerning the *Habeas Corpus*; to which I answer, no Judgment was given . . ." Their respect for the old statutes was apparent. They readily conceded that Magna Carta was in force and that some of 'the other acts were commentaries upon it. Said Mr. Justice Jones:

I have now served seven Years Judge in this Court, and my Conscience beareth me witness that I have not wronged the same; I have been thought sometimes too forward for the Liberty of the Subject. I am myself *liber Homo,* and my Ancestors gave their Voice with *Magna Charta.* I enjoy that House still which they did; I do not, now, mean to draw down God's Wrath upon my Posterity; and therefore I will neither advance the King's Prerogative, nor lessen the Liberty of the Subject, to the Danger of either King or People. This is my Profession before God and your Lordships.

Again it was a question of interpretation. As Chief Justice Hyde concluded, "I know not any Statute that goeth so far, that the King may not commit." [125]

It was the evident inclination of the Lords to accept the judges' explanation and let the matter drop that led the Commons to ask a further conference, which was held on April 17. Littleton, Selden, and Coke for the Commons, Heath and Ashley for the crown, went over much the same ground, but there was more real debate. [126] It was on this occasion that Heath called to the attention of the Lords the proposed bill of 18 Jacobi, "An Act for the better securing the Subject from wrongful Imprisonment contrary to Magna Charta cap. 29," and quoted Sir Edward's speech condemning it. "I have a note of the very words," said Heath. [127] The Lords were interested enough to request the clerk of the Commons to produce the journal book of that parliament, but times had changed. Neither the bill as then framed, nor the speeches in the debate on it would suit the purpose of the Commons now. Coke and Hakewill spoke against submitting the record, and the House returned an evasive answer. [128]

Heath was ably seconded by Serjeant Ashley. Surely no one might more appropriately have argued in this great cause than he who had so thor-

---

[125] *State Trials,* III. Cf. Dodderidge: ". . . upon Consideration of the Statutes and Records, we found some of them to be according to the good old Law of *Magna Charta;* but we thought, that they did not come so close to this Case, as that Bail should be thereupon presently, granted."

[126] *L. J.* III, 746–62. Reported April 19.

[127] "Upon this Occasion Sir Edward Coke stood 'up and said thus: (I have a Note of the Very Words:) 'There are divers Matters of State, which are not to be comprehended in the Warrant; for they may be disclosed: One committed by the Body of the Council not bailable by Law resolved so by all the Judges in Wraye's Time (that, my Lords, is the Resolution of 34 Eliz. when Wraye was Chief Justice,) upon the Commitment of the King or the Body of the Council: For this is out of the Statute of Magna Charta.' "

[128] *C. J.* I, 885.

oughly expounded the "statute" to the students of the Middle Temple in 1616. He now recalled that occasion, and spoke truly on the whole in claiming that he had not altered his opinion.

> It is well known to many that know me how much I have laboured in this Law of the Subjects Liberty very many Years before I was in the King's Service, and had no Cause then but to speak *ex Animo*; yet did I then maintain and publish the same Opinion which now I have declared, concerning the King's supreme Power in Matters of State; and therefore cannot justly be censured to speak at this present only to the merit of my Master.

But Ashley's speech, as it proceeded, was *plus royaliste que le roy*. The Lords felt obliged to apologize for it to the gentlemen of the Commons, and the too zealous serjeant, upon motion of the Earl of Warwick, was taken into custody, shortly to be released on making his submission.[129] The Journals do not make clear which passage of the speech, whether one more than another, proved most distasteful to their lordships. Several features are worthy of comment. His description of the customary practices of officials was just such as he had used in his reading—"And various are the Cases that may be instanced, where there may be a lawful Commitment without Process." The common lawyers had never denied this, but it had pleased the king's counsel to push their position to absurd lengths. His definition of the prerogative is as grandiloquent a statement of the divine right of kings as ever Charles or his father could have wished for or devised.

> And Divine Truth informs us, that Kings have Their Power from God, and are Representative Gods; the Psalmist calling Them *the Children of the Most High,* which is in a more special Manner understood than of other Men; for all the Sons of *Adame* are, by Creation, the Children of God, and all the Sons of *Abraham* are, by Recreation or Regeneration, the Children of the Most High, But it is said of Kings, They are the Children of the Most High, in respect of the Power that is committed unto Them, who hath also furnished Them with Ornaments and Arms fit for the exercising of that Power, and given them Scepters, Swords, and Crowns; Scepters to institute, and Swords to execute Laws, and Crowns as Ensigns of that Power and Dignity with which They are invested. Shall we then conceive that our King hath so far transmitted the Power of his Sword to Inferior Magistrates that He hath not reserved so much supreme Power, as to commit an Offender to Prison?

In conclusion Ashley presented a gloomy but acute evaluation of the dilemma—a clear-cut victory for either side would be a calamity.

> I conceive it to be a Question to high to be determined by any legal Decision;

---

129 The lord president said to the gentlemen of the Commons, "That though at this free Conference, Liberty was given by the Lords to the King's Counsel to speak what they thought fit for his Majesty's Service, yet Mr. Serjeant *Ashley* had no Authority nor Direction from them to speak in the Manner he hath now done."

for it must needs be a hard Case of Contention when the Conqueror must sit down with irreparable Loss; as in this Case, if the Subject prevail, Liberty but loses the Benefit of that State Government, without which a Monarchy may too soon become an Anarchy; or, if the State prevail, it gains absolute Sovereignty, but loses the Subjects not their Subjection, for Obedience we must yield, though nothing be left us but Prayers and Tears; but it loses the best Part of them, which is their Affections, whereby Sovereignty is established, and the Crown firmly fixed on his Royal Head.

His broad interpretation of *lex terrae* was only a comprehensive statement of what had been claimed in past years by Bacon, Ellesmere, the civilians, and even by the judges of King's Bench in *Cawdry's case,* but it was not the interpretation of "our books." The gentlemen of the Commons were unconvinced. Littleton, in a ringing rebuttal, showed that "their Intent was not to call in Question the Power of the King, as well to commit as to bail, but to regulate it." Further, that

Mr. Sergeant understood *per Legem Terrae,* many Laws in England: Martial, Admiral, Ecclesiastical, and that 9. *Edward* III called *Merchant Law*; to this Mr. Littleton replied, with some Animosity, and a Challenge to any Man living to shew, That *Lex Terrae* should be spoken of any but the Common Law, in any Law Books, Statutes, or antient Records: And so he closed up his Discourse.[130]

In the conference with the Lords on their saving to the Petition of Right, Marten and Glanvill were commended for their able handling of their assignment.[131] John Glanvill, "that pregnant westerne lawier," as Eliot calls him, was recorder of Plymouth. His arguments merit attention for his exposition of the law as to the dispensing power, and for his use of historical sources. As to the first, he grants that the king may dispense with laws which forbid matters merely as *mala prohibita,* but the Petition of Right is grounded upon statutes of another nature.

---

[130] Meanwhile another instance of wrongful imprisonment by local authorities had come before the committee of grievances. On December 17, 1627 the City of London had reluctantly agreed "to pay 120,000 l. by installments on the security of the King's rents from landed property." Clegatt, for refusing to lend, was imprisoned by the corporation. Coke reported from the committee its opinion "that *Clegatt* in this Case, for not agreeing to lend towards the late Contract, with his Majesty, for Lands, was unlawfully imprisoned." The House concurred and resolved to petition the king for Clegatt's enlargement. This is all we learn from the *Journal,* but the *True Relation* gives us the arguments of "Mr. White of Councell for Clegatt" before the committee April 9. White follows the arguments used in Clark's case which he cites from Coke's report, as well as other cases and "precedents" used there, including Magna Carta and 28 Ed. III, ca. 3. *C. J.* I, 891b. Harl. MSS 4771, fol. 73. Gardiner, VI, 220.

[131] "A Report from the Conference, that both the Gentlemen that spake, have deserved especial Thanks from this House, for performing the Service enjoined them by the House, to the Honour thereof. Whereupon a general Expression of Thanks to them with Acclamations and putting off Hats." Afternoon. "Sir H. *Martyn* and Mr. *Glanvyle* to bring in their Arguments, and leave them with the Clerk; that every man that will, may have Copies thereof." *C. J.* I, 903.

There shall your Lordships find us to rely upon the good old Statute called *Magna Charta,* which declareth and confirmeth the ancient Common Laws of the Liberties of *England.* There shall your Lordships find us also to insist upon divers other most material Statutes, made in the Times of King *E.* I, and King *E.* III, and other Famous Kings, for the Explication and Ratification of the lawful Rights and Privileges belonging to the Subjects of this Realm . . . Statutes incorporate into the Body of the Common Law, over which (with Reverence be it spoken) there is no Trust reposed in the King's Sovereign Power, or Prerogative Royal, to dispense with them, or to take from his Subjects that Birth-Right and Inheritance which they have in their Liberties, by virtue of the Common Law and of these Statutes.

In ruling out the particular historical "savings" cited by the Lords as precedents, Glanvill relies on his knowledge of the evolution of parliamentary procedure. Up to 2 Henry V, he says, legislation was by petition. "To these Petitions the Kings made Answer as they pleased; sometimes to Part, sometimes to the Whole, sometimes by Denial, sometimes by Assent, sometimes absolutely, and sometimes by Qualifications." But in 2 Henry V, as established by parliament, "Ever since then the Use hath been as the Right was before, that the King taketh the whole, or leaveth the Whole, of all Bills or Petitions exhibited for the obtaining of Laws." As to 28 Edward I, with its general saving "for the right and seignory of the Crown in all things," "it gave distaste from the Beginning, and wrought no good effects." [132] Subsequent acts "restored Magna Charta to the original Purity wherein it was first moulded."

I beseech your Lordships, therefore, to observe the Circumstance of Time wherein we offer this Petition to be presented, by your Lordships and by us, unto His Majesty.

Do we offer it when *Magna Charta* stands clogged with a Saving? No, my Lords, but at this Day, when latter and better Confirmations have vindicated and set free that Law from all Exceptions: And shall we now annex another and worse Saving to it, by an unnecessary Clause in that Petition, which we expect should have the Fruits and Effects of a Law? Shall we ourselves relinquish or adulterate that which cost our Ancestors so much Care and Labour to purchase and refine?

---

[132] As to 25 Ed. I, "saving the ancient aids and prises due and accustomed," this was explicit. For proof Glanvill interprets 25 Ed. I by John's ca. 12, as Coke had already done: "And that these were the only Aids intended to be saved to the Crown by that Statute, appeareth in some Clearness by the Charter of King *John,* dated at *Rumnemeade,* the Fifteenth of *June,* in the Seventeenth Year of His Reign, wherein they are enumerated, with an Examination [*sic*] of all other Aids whatsoever. Of this Charter I have here One of the Originals, whereon I beseech your Lordships to cast your Eyes, and give me Leave to read the very Words which concern this Point." What his "one of the originals" was may only be conjectured. Neither 42 Ed. III nor any of the other explanatory statutes, he points out, had savings annexed.

May 23. *L. J.* III, 813–18. This follows his rehearsal of the Lords' defense of their saving, and his effective application of the saving to each item of the Petition in turn: "In a Word, this Clause, if it should be admitted, would take away the Effect of every Part of the Petition, and become destructive of the whole."

It was Rudyerd's speech of April 28, urging acceptance of the king's promised confirmation which included the famous passage quoted above.[133] "That great artist," as Eliot dubbed him, admitted that "out of all question the very Point, Scope and Drift of Magna Charta was, to reduce the Regal to a Legal Power, in Matters of Imprisonment, or else it had not been worth so much contending for." But his concession was unconvincing when coupled with the courtier's advice that "as for intrinsical Power and Reasons of State, they are Matters in the Clouds; where I desire we may leave them and not meddle in them at all"; and the blunt "certainly there is no Court of justice in *England,* that will discharge a Prisoner committed by the King, *Rege inconsulto,* i. e. without acquainting the King . . ."

Eloquence had not been confined to the Commons. On April 21 (following Serjeant Ashley's submission) the Lords went into committee on liberty of the subject. The Earl of Warwick rehearsed some of the precedents—Coke's "37 acts of parliament" and Littleton's petitions from the parliament roll. He ridiculed Heath's interpretation—"Truly I wonder how any Man can think that this House (tho' no Lawyers) can admit of such a Gloss upon a plain Text, as should overthrow the very End and Design of the Law"—and corrected Ashley's symbolism:

Mr. Sergeant Ashley, the other Day, told your Lordships of the Emblem of a King; but, by his Leave, he made a wrong Use of it: For the King holds in one Hand the Globe, and in the other the Sceptre, the Types of Sovereignty and Mercy, but his Sword of Justice is ever carried before him by a Minister of Justice; which shews that Subjects may have their Remedies for Injustice done, and that Appeals lie to higher Powers; for the Laws of England are so favourable to their Princes, as to declare that they themselves can do no Injustice. Therefore I will conclude, as all Disputes should do, *Magna est Veritas & prevalebit:* And I make no Doubt, we living under so good and just a Prince as we do, when this is represented unto him, he will answer us, *Magna est Charta, & prevalebit.*[134]

LEX TERRAE AND MARTIAL LAW

Grievances connected with the billeting of soldiers were debated in the Commons April 4 and again on April 8, when it was resolved: "The grand Committee for Billeting of Soldiers, to have Power to debate the Matter concerning the Commissions for martial Law, and the Clerk of the Crown to bring the Commission for martial Law, and the Instructions for the same unto the Committee." [135]

[133] See p. 335. This last is in the version in *Parl. Hist.* VIII, 81–84, not in that in Rushworth, I, 551–52.

[134] *Parl. Hist.* VIII, 69–70.

[135] *C. J.* I, 880. There is nothing on this subject in the *Journal* for April 15, 16, 18 and 22, dates for which the diarists record debates in committee. Gardiner recounts several of the episodes involving abuses which indignant members reported from their home counties. (VI, 247–48, 253–54; cf. 219).

Martial law, administered in the Court of the Constable and Marshal included (1) discipline of the army, and (2) heraldry and slanders upon men of noble blood (the *scandalum magnatum* of the law books). As the court grew in importance and prestige in the course of the fourteenth century, it tended to encroach on the common law and conflicts arose. Regulatory statutes to define and limit its jurisdiction were passed in the reigns of Richard II and Henry IV. Their effect was to establish that in matters both civil and criminal pertaining to war outside the realm the court had unlimited jurisdiction. Within the realm its jurisdiction was limited to alien enemies, matters arising out of some past war, such as prisoners or prize, and "war within the realm," such as a state of rebellion.[136]

Edward IV boldly extended the powers of the court, enabling it to try all cases of treason (by acts of 1462 and 1467). The Tudors used it more guardedly, but were inclined to extend its jurisdiction not only to actual war but to "a time of merely apprehended disturbance"; not only to soldiers, but to citizens liable to serve as soldiers. While the commissions for martial law issued from 1626 to 1628 were intended primarily for the discipline of soldiers being mustered for foreign service, in the words of the commission, there was included "those who join with them." In practice the deputy lieutenants found it necessary to discipline the whole countryside.

In debates in the "grand committee" and committee of the whole House, the same difference of viewpoint appeared as in respect to the other special jurisdictions. The privy councilors included martial law within the *lex terrae* of Magna Carta, but separate from and coequal with the common law. For the first point of view, Secretary Coke, at the committee of the whole house, April 22, argued as follows:

There is no man that desires to live under this law, and wee all hold the common law our inheritance that doth preserve us, we are in the government of a state. The Martiall law toucheth Kings highlie, it is their very originall, they are God's captaines and leaders of his people, the name of king is sacred and the foundacion of the Commonwealth depends on them. All civill government may passe well and have happie success but Armes and the conducting of Armies it can admitt of noe formall law. I must tell you that Martiall lawe is an essentiall law of the Kingdome and the whole government consists not in the Common law but in others . . . We all admitt and subscribe to the Ecclesiasticall lawe, wee have the Martiall lawe . . .

The common lawyers admitted the existence of a body of martial law, derived from the civil law, the *ius gentium*, but insisted that it was sub-

[136] 8 Rich. II, ca. 5; 13 Rich. II, stat. 1, ca. 2; 1 Hen. IV, ca. 14; Holdsworth, I, 573–80. See above, pp. 89–90.

ordinate to, and limited and bounded by, the common law. Prohibitions might be, and indeed, had been issued to the court of the Constable and Marshal when it exceeded its jurisdiction.[137]

More specifically the common lawyers conceded that martial law pertained to the matters enumerated in the medieval statutes: war abroad and the pursuit of rebels at home, the trial and execution of an alien enemy. They, the lawyers, differed among themselves as to the legitimate extent of its use for troops billeted in England. Selden argued that the common law was adequate even for military discipline. Rolles admitted the use of martial law for discipline, but not to the extent of capital punishment. Bankes complained that martial law took a man's life "without jury or trial," and "made even small offences capital." All united, of course, in opposing its extension to civilians. This was the major grievance.[138]

Naturally Magna Carta and the most pertinent of the interpretive statutes (5 Edward III, chapter 9, 25 Edward III, chapter 4, and 8 Edward III, chapter 3) were used as they had been against the other special jurisdictions. Martial law was not *lex terrae,* the procedure of the court was not *due process of law*; by it a man might be deprived not only of his liberty but of his very life. As Mr. Ball put it, "where the Common law may take place wee are not to bee governed by the Civill law. Magna charta to this poynt is most cleare. *Nullus liber homo destruatur nisi per legem terre.*" [139]

Selden was undoubtedly responsible for the more novel use of precedents which appears in his and Rolles' arguments. Again he had only to draw on his own past research. In compiling his *Privileges of the Baronage* for the Lords, he had culled from the parliament rolls those dramatic

---

[137] For this second, Selden: ". . . in England wee have the common law, and the Martiall lawe all in due time and place, as the canon and civill law, we have from Rome and out of the Empire, soe is this Martiall lawe out of the lawe of the Emperour in the title of the civill lawe, they have tytles de re militari these lawes were at the pleasure of the Emperour or Generall of the Armie." After this admission Selden goes on to indicate the martial law's limitations as per the statutes of 13 Rich. II and 1 Hen. IV.

Similarly Mr. Bankes, April 16: "the Common law regulates in what case Commissions ought to bee awarded . . . the Common lawe is the Judge of other Courts to keepe them in their due bounds, this wee doe in the daylie course in prohibicions . . ." And of course, Sir Edward Coke, April 18: ". . . this question must bee determined by the lawe of England, and the Martiall lawe is bounded by it . . ." Harl. MSS 4771, fols. 103, 87–88, 91v.

[138] Selden, April 15: "The Commission gives power to proceed against Soldiers or Marriners or *anie that joyne with them,* and to proceed according to martiall lawe."

Bankes, April 16: "But this Commission for Martiall lawe alters the Common law, for it extends to all that joyne with souldiers. It is noe dash of a pen that dashes and takes away a man's life. In that course a man shall suffer death without a Jurie and tryall, and soe against the laws, and allsoe small offences are made capittall, which are not by the Common law."

[139] April 18 at the committee for martial law, following Sir Henry Martin's and Nethersole's defense of its use at least for soldiers, in a speech beginning: "What the Civill law is or the practice of the Low Countreys the language of England never knew. Our ancestors sayd Nolumus leges Angliae mutare. The Constable and Martiall must proceed according to the Comon law. . . ."

episodes of alleged injustice to "peers of the realm," for instance, the successful plea of Henry of Lancaster (1 Edward III) for reversal of the judgment against his brother, the great Earl Thomas. In the arbitrary procedure of Edward II and his favorites in putting to death Earl Thomas without trial by peers "in a time of peace when the courts were sitting," Selden saw a parallel to the use of martial law in his own day. Indeed, Henry of Lancaster's plea evidently suggested the criterion as to what constitutes "a time of peace":

The error is assigned in the record that in time of peace every subject ought to bee arraigned according to the lawe of the land, and hee sett forth that it was in time of peace, for dureing the rebellion and conviccion the Chancerie and the other Courts were open and soe hee ought to bee adjudged by the law of the land and not otherwise. Also the said Earle of Lancaster was a Peere of the land and hee was not tryed by his Peares, which was contrarie to the lawe and the tenour of the great Charter and therefore it was considered by the King, the Lords and Commons that Judicium fuit nullum et vacuum in lege.[140]

The Petition of Right did not abolish legitimate jurisdiction over soldiers in time of war. It was considered a declaratory act. It did declare extensions of the court's jurisdiction illegal—under no circumstances did it have jurisdiction over anyone within the realm in time of peace. "It should be noted also that the question what was a time of peace was clearly settled. It was a time of peace if the central courts were open, and the sheriff could execute the king's writ." [141] The issue was not closed. The crown lawyers put a strained construction on the Petition of Right, claiming that as it was merely declaratory, it did *not* condemn the recent extensions of the court's jurisdiction. Special codes were found necessary during the civil war and interregnum, and such were also issued by Charles II (1666, 1672) and James II (1686). The problem was finally solved by the passing of the mutiny act, 1689, and the successive "army acts." As the effect of these acts was to legalize courts martial, what jurisdiction there was passed from the Court of the Constable and Marshal to the army officers. Holdsworth concludes that the Petition of Right did play some part in the outcome: "their victory over the Constable and Marshal's Court has left the case of riot or rebellion to the Common law, and has caused the state of siege to be practically unknown in England."

The Parliament of 1628–29: Second Session

THE first act of the Commons in the ill-fated session of 1629 was to order

---

140 Rolles uses the plea of the son of John Mountague, Earl of Salisbury, for reversal of the judgment against his father. For a discussion of these medieval episodes as factors in Charter history, see above, Chap. III.
141 This and the following are based on Holdsworth, I, 578.

that "a Committee should be appointed to examine what innovation hath been made upon the liberty of the subject against the Petition of Right since the end of the last Session of Parliament." [142] In the course of this first day's debate (January 21) Selden charged:

For this Petition of Right, it is known to some how it hath been lately violated since our last meeting; the liberties for life, person, and freehold, how have they been invaded? Have not some been committed contrary to that Petition? Now we, knowing this invasion, must take notice of it. For liberties in estate, we know of an order made in the Exchequer, that a sheriff was commanded not to execute a replevin; and mens goods are taken away, and must not be restored; and also no man ought to lose life or limb, but by the law, and hath not one lately lost his ears (meaning Savage that was censured in the Star Chamber by an arbitrary judgment and sentence)? Next they will take our arms, and then our legs, and so our lives. Let all see that we are sensible of these customs creeping upon us. Let us make a just representation here of to his Majesty.[143]

In this and succeeding debates it was natural that the Petition be cited rather than the Charter which it defined. The major invasion of "liberty of the subject" was now conceived to be the levy of tunnage and poundage without parliamentary sanction and the treatment accorded merchants who refused to pay, centering on *Chambers case* and "Mr. Rolles' business." This last involved parliamentary privilege also. The strict censorship of the press aroused protests. It was charged that divers printers had been "pursuivanted for printing of orthodox books; and that the licensing of books is now only restrained to the Bishop of London [Laud] and his chaplains." Again in the words of Selden:

The refusing of licensing of books is no crime, but the licensing of bad books is a crime, or the refusing to license books because they write against Popery or Arminianism is a crime. There is no law to prevent the printing of any book in England, only a decree in the Star Chamber. Therefore that a man should be fined, and imprisoned, and his goods taken from him is a great invasion on the liberty of the subject. Therefore he moved that a law may be made on this.[144]

The religious grievances—"Popery and Arminianism"—evoked theological rather than legal arguments. Much space in the diaries is devoted to the recording of scathing Puritan harangues in which Old Testament epithets served more adequately than laws and statutes to express the

[142] *Commons Debates,* 1629, p. 4 (*True Relation*). C. J. I, 921a. The *Journal* for this session contains very few speeches. It is effectively supplemented by the *Commons Debates* (edited by Notestein and Relf and containing "The True Relation," "Nicholas's Notes," and "Grosvenor's Diary"). None of the speeches as recorded in these sources cites Magna Carta, but speakers defending "liberty of the subject" no doubt had it in mind.

[143] *Ibid.,* p. 5.

[144] February 11, at the Committee for Religion. *Ibid.,* pp. 58–59.

speakers' scorn. Characteristic of such was Mr. Rouse's speech of January 26, which passes quickly from "liberty of the subject" to "right of an higher nature":

Mr. Speaker, We have of late entered into consideration of the Petition of Right, and the violation of it, and upon good reason, for it concerns our goods, liberties, and lives; but there is a right of an higher nature that preserves for us far greater things, eternal life, our souls, yea our God himself; a right of Religion derived to us from the King of Kings, conferred upon us by the King of this Kingdom, enacted by laws in this place, streaming down to us in the blood of the martyrs, and witnessed from Heaven by miracles, even by miraculous deliverances. . . .

Particularly vehement, nay, virulent, is the passage:

. . . For an Arminian is the spawn of a Papist; and if there come the warmth of favour upon him, you shall see him turn into one of those frogs that rise out of the bottomless pit. And if you mark it well, you shall see an Arminian reaching out his hand to a Papist, a Papist to a Jesuit, a Jesuit gives one hand to the Pope and the other to the King of Spain; And these men having kindled a fire in our neighbour country, now they have brought over some of it hither, to set on flame this Kingdom also.[145]

The abrupt dissolution of this parliament on March 2, 1629, did not entirely silence appeals to the two "liberty documents." The case, or "cases" of the nine members arrested and imprisoned after the dissolution was conceived to be a violation of the Petition of Right. Their application for habeas corpus was not denied, but the cause alleged in the *mittimus* was colored to satisfy Charles, and the question whether persons so charged were bailable was left to the judges, again under royal pressure.[146] Others took their cue from the parliament men. Michael Sparke, London stationer, questioned before High Commission (April 20, 1629) for his printing and publishing of unlicensed Puritan books, protested that the Star Chamber decree of 28 Elizabeth, on which the censorship proceedings were based,

doth directly intrench upon the hereditary liberty of the subiects persons and goodes subiecting them one to Imprisonment without bayle or Mainprise the other to forfeiture contrary to Magna Charta, the petition of right and other Statutes of this kingdome which noe private Decrees of any corte of Justice but only an expresse Act of Parliament can controule . . .[147]

[145] January 26, *ibid.*, pp. 12–14.
[146] Discussed at length by Gardiner, VII, ca. lxviii. *State Trials,* III.
[147] *State Papers*, 16, 141/17. Described in *Cal. S. P.*, 1628–29, p. 525, as "Articles objected by the Ecclesiastical Commissioners against William Jones and Augustine Matthewes, printers, and Nathaniel Butter and Michael Sparke, stationers, for printing and publishing various books without the same being licensed by the Archbishop of Canterbury or Bishop of London, according to the Decree in the Star Chamber of the 28th year of Queen Elizabeth . . ." Sparke was charged with printing Henry Burton's "Babel no Bethel" and publishing William Prynne's "The Antithesis of the Church of England."

The Puritan preachers were not yet entirely silenced. In May certain "notes of Mr. Salisbury's sermon" were sent to Chief Justice Hyde by Laud for his advice. These contain a lament "to see the famous lawes and auncient Charters of this kingdome to ly in contempt . . ." [148]

[148] *State Papers*, 16, 142/94. May 17, 1629.

❊ CHAPTER XII ❊

Coke's Commentaries: Summation of Three Centuries

". . . and so ended his argumente with greate admyration of the better and wyser sorte, infinite commendacyon of all, and good satysfaction of verye manye . . ." (HAWARDE, LES REPORTES)

IT is not easy to find a good stopping place in Magna Carta history. Yet as some point must be set to terminate these studies, the year chosen is 1629, and the last topic to receive intensive treatment, appropriately, Sir Edward Coke's commentary on Magna Carta, the *Second Institute*. Here was put into definitive form by an authoritative pen all the current knowledge and understanding of the great document, both routine and controversial, to date. To be sure, in one sense, 1629—the eve of the eleven years of no parliaments and King Charles' seemingly successful bid for absolutism—is a low ebb in Charter history. The practical victory was yet to be won, first by the statutes of the Long Parliament, and ultimately by the sword. In the century and more between Coke and Blackstone, the Great Charter was still to figure in many a case and parliamentary debate. There were to be further interpretations, novel uses and novel abuses. Some of the most characteristic of these will be briefly suggested in conclusion, but no intensive study has been made of the sources for this period. In these same years, as Professor A. B. White reminds us, in the American colonies Magna Carta "was influencing the 'fundamentals,' 'bodies of liberties' and charters which determined the trend of the new governments and was becoming a generic term for documents fundamental to or protective of liberties. It was much cited at the time of the revolution and in connection with the constitution and its adoption." As far as the present writer is concerned, all this is really "another story."

"The first of our English textbooks upon the modern common law," Coke's *Institutes* in four books, are designedly interdependent and supplement each other, as the author himself makes clear by numerous cross references. The *First Institute*—"Coke upon Littleton"—says Holdsworth "is very different in character to all the others. It is very much more full and more elaborate . . ." It was in fact a veritable encyclopedia of legal knowledge and lore which served as a basis for the succeeding books. In the *First* "every word, every doctrine, every legal institution is explained. When necessary its history is given, and changes and developments which have occurred since Littleton are noted. All Coke's reading in the older text books, in the Year Books, abridgments, and records, in modern legal writers, in general literature, and all his experience as counsel and as judge, are pressed into this service." [1]

The *Second Institute* "deals mainly with public law,[2] and with the additions which statutes had made to that common law which had been more or less described in the preceding book." Twenty-six are medieval. The remaining "modern" statutes are selected from acts of Henry VIII, Elizabeth, and James I which introduced new branches of law. The commentaries on these last are "historically very valuable, because they often give us the contemporary view of the reasons for passing them, and first hand information of the results of their working."

The commentary on Magna Carta is not as long as that on the great Edwardian statutes (or aggregates of many laws) Westminster I and II.[3] Even so, it would be impracticable to give the reader a complete exposition, and indeed, in view of all that has gone before in these studies, quite unnecessary. What will be attempted is to indicate the character and value of Coke's work. It is notable: (1) for its completeness—the first treatise dealing with the entire document, and collecting historical and interpretive data hitherto widely scattered in treatises, dictionaries, Year Books,

---

[1] " 'I have termed them Institutes because my desire is, they should institute and instruct the studious, and guide him in a ready way to knowledge of the national laws of England.' Co. Litt. Pref. Perhaps it was Camden who suggested the title to him, as he quotes him, 10 Co. Rep. Pref. XVII, XVIII, as saying that Littleton's Tenures were no less useful to the students of the common law than Justinian's Institutes to the civilians." Holdsworth, V, 465, note 10, 466–67.

The *First Institute* was published in 1628; the *Second* (the commentary on Magna Carta and other statutes, 39 in all) and the *Third,* on the criminal law (beginning with high treason, and expounding "in a hundred chapters all kinds of offences new and old") were completed in 1628 but not published until 1641, as was the *Fourth,* on the jurisdiction of courts, finished in the last years of Coke's life.

[2] "Round the commentary on Magna Carta, the Confirmatio Cartarum, the De Tallagio non concedendo, and the Articuli super Cartas, is grouped much learning on those constitutional doctrines which Coke spent his later years in asserting; and round the commentary on Circumspecte Agatis, De Asportatis Religiosorum, and Articuli Cleri, is to be found the learning as to the relations of the ecclesiastical to the common law. Throughout the commentaries on these statutes we hear echoes of the great political controversies of the day—the questions of impositions, of monopolies, of prohibitions, of the right to release on bail, of the right of the king to stay proceedings in an action. . . . Certain sixteenth century statutes, which introduced new branches of the law, are noted. They comprise the statute of enrolments, certain statutes of Henry VIII's reign relating to procedure, to the repair of bridges, and to printers; and certain statutes of Elizabeth's and James I's reigns relating to hospitals, houses of correction, rogues, and the building of cottages." Holdsworth, V, 468–69.

[3] In the large quarto edition of 1669, there are 78 pages devoted to Magna Carta, 107 on Westminster I, 155 on Westminster II. Of course, the mere quoting of these longer texts accounts for part of the difference.

and reports; (2) for its learned, but clear-cut and readable style; (3) for the voice of finality and authority it gave on certain keenly controversial issues. But let us hear what Coke himself advances for the *Second Institute* as a whole in his "Proeme."

Upon the Text of the Civill Law, there be so many glosses and interpretations, and again upon those so many Commentaries, and all these written by Doctors of equall degree and authority, and therein so many diversities of opinions, as they do rather increase then resolve doubts, and incertainties, and the professors of that noble Science say, That it is like a sea full of waves. The difference then between those glosses and Commentaries, and this which we publish is, that their glosses and Commentaries are written by Doctors, which be Advocates, and so in a manner private interpretations: and our Expositions or Commentaries upon *Magna Charta* and other Statutes are the resolutions of Judges in Courts of Justice in judiciall courses of proceeding, either related and reported in our Books, or extant in judiciall Records, or in both, and therefore being collected together, shall (as we conceive) produce certainty, the Mother and Nurse of repose and quietnesse, and are not like to the waves of the Sea, but *Statio bene fida peritis*: for *Judicia sunt tanquam Juris dicta*.

It is hardly to be expected that he who had been accused of putting too much of himself into his works (*de propris suo*, as Bacon said of the *Reports*) would now avoid that spirit of advocacy ("private interpretations") with which he taxes the civilians. On the other hand, he is substantially correct in his claim that his expositions "are the resolutions of Judges in Courts of Justice." There is relatively little that is entirely novel or due to his own invention. Again, he is correct in assuming that the result would be to "produce certainty, the Mother and Nurse of repose and quietnesse." This certainty, however, would be due not so much to the mere "being collected together" as to the extraordinary prestige and accepted authority of the collector.

Much of the material was quite routine. Virtually all the feudal clauses relative to tenures and obligations had been dealt with by Littleton and more exhaustively by "Coke on Littleton." In his discussion of Chapters 2 to 7, parts of 14, and 27, 29, 37, and others, he frequently refers the reader to his *First Institute* for both definition and exposition.[4] *Common*

---

[4] Definitions of *ecclesiastica persona*; *beneficium*, "a large word"; *scutagium* (*escuage*) and others. The commentary on ca. 2, for instance, though fairly long (5½ pages) leans heavily on the *First Institute*: "*Per Servitium militare*. For this see the first part of the *Institutes* . . . Whereunto you may add this Record following . . ."

Ca. 27, after a definition or two, is dismissed with the curt "This Act, as well concerning tenures in fee farm, socage, and burgage, as by little serjeanty, is declaratory of the Common Law, and constantly in use to this day, and needeth no further explanation."

In connection with the *rationabilia servitia* of ca. 4, after quoting Glanvill, he adds: "But it may be demanded, How and by whom shall the said reasonableness in the cases aforesaid be tried? This you may read in the first part of the Institutes, Sect. 69."

pleas (chapter 11), *tourn,* and *leet* (chapter 35) naturally permit of cross reference to the *Fourth Institute*; *trial by peers* (chapter 29) to *treason* in the *Third Institute,* and *crown pleas* (chapter 17) to the same treatise. But back of these, of course, were "our books," the treatises of Stamford and Lambarde, the handbooks for justices of the peace, Fitzherbert, and the Register.[5]

In the process of collection, of course, Coke's own *Reports* also had much to offer: the historical data of the prefaces, the "scattered conceits" of the *Nota lecteur* inserts, and the reports of famous cases in which principles of the Charter were applied by Coke's distinguished predecessors of bench and bar, his colleagues, and himself.[6]

Of course, he proceeds chapter by chapter. No other treatment was conceivable. The result is like a collection of miniature "Readings" in the Inns of Court, except for reasons indicated above, he need not be complete, nor include the hypothetical cases—the "posers"—which Readers introduced to tax the wits of the apprentices of the law. Sir Edward informs his readers in the "Proeme" what his method, necessitated by the "quality" of the document, is to be:

It was for the most part declaratory of the principall grounds of the fundamentall Laws of *England,* and for the residue it is additionall to supply some defects of the Common Law . . .

We in this second part of the *Institutes,* treating of the ancient and other Statutes, have been inforced almost of necessity to cite our ancient Authors, *Bracton, Britton,* the *Mirror, Fleta,* and many Records, never before published in print, to the end the prudent Reader may discerne what the Common Law was before the making of every of those Statutes, which we handle in this work, and thereby know whether the Statute be introductory of a new Law, or declaratory of the old, which will conduce much to the true understanding of the Text it selfe.

Thus, wherever possible, he quotes Glanvill to indicate the old common

---

[5] Of course, in his comment on the medieval statutes such as Marleborough, and Westminster I and II, Coke finds occasion to refer back to the Charter, and sometimes adds to his exposition of the latter. This is particularly true of the *Confirmatio Cartarum, De tallagio non concedendo,* and the *Articuli super cartas.* Of this last he says "and justly are they called Articuli super Chartas, meaning Magna Charta and Charta de Foresta, for that they contain the substance of all that is contained in these Articles."

Of Marleborough, ca. 5, he writes: "This as hath been said, was one of the principal causes of the summons of this Parliament, and after this ensued great and constant peace and tranquillity. And where some have thought, that Magna Charta had not the strength of a Parliament before this Act, how they mistake it, you may, read before in Magna Charta, Cap. 32 and 38."

[6] See above, Chap. IX. The "Proeme" of the commentary, for instance, contains much the same data as the *ad lectorem* of the Eighth Report: origin and significance of the various titles: *Magna Charta (magnum in parvo), Charta libertatium Regni (Quia liberos facit);* the grants by John and Henry III; the notable confirmations, and so on. Cases cited in the text or margin of the Commentary include *Sir Drue Drury's, Greyslies, Clarke's, Darcy's, Bate's,* the *case of the Marshalsea,* and others.

law which the "statute" was to declare. Bracton, Britton, Fleta (and the *Mirror*!) serve variously for evidence of the perpetuation of a rule, or for further elucidation.

There are errors, of course, of the same kind that we have seen in Coke's reports and speeches. These include his implicit reliance on Lambarde's Latin translation of the Anglo-Saxon laws, his acceptance of the *Mirror of Justices* as an authority comparable to Bracton and Fleta, the odd etymologies,[7] and the far too ancient lineage assigned to the Court of Common Pleas, the possessory assizes, the coroners, and especially to parliament.[8] On the other hand some of his historical illustrations are not only cleverly phrased, but apt and accurate. For instance, there is his account (chapter 4) of William Rufus' "chaplain," Ranulph Flambard, "a man *subacto ingenio* and *profunda nequitia*," who was "a factor for the King in making merchandize of Church livings," for "oftentimes no profession receives a greater blow, then by one of their own coat." Henry I, having remedied the evil by his charter: "He committed the said Ranulph then Bishop of Durham to prison for his intolerable misdeeds, and injuries to the Church, where he lived without love, and died without pity, saving of those, that thought it pity, he lived so long."

Again, in pointing out the penchant of the framers of Magna Carta to revert to the good customs of Henry II's reign in contrast to that of his sons, Coke gives us as nice a tribute to that king as one could wish:

Here it is to be observed, that in the raign of King John, and of his elder brother King Richard, which were troublesome and irregular times, divers oppressions, exactions, and injuries, were incroached upon the Subject in these Kings names, for making of Bulwarks, Fortresses, Bridges, and Banks, contrary to Law and right.

But the raigne of King H. 2. is commended for three things, first that his privy Counsell were wise, and expert in the Laws of the Realme. Secondly, that he was a great defender and maintainer of the rights of his Crown, and of the Laws of his Realme. Thirdly, that he had learned and upright Judges, who executed Justice according to his Laws.

Therefore for his great and never dying honor, this and many other Acts made in the raigne of H. 3. do referre to his raign, that matters should be put in ure, as they were of right accustomed in his time, so as this Chapter is a declaration of the common Law, and so in the raignes of H. 4. and H. 5. the Parliaments referre to the raigne of King E. 1. who was a Prince of great fortitude, wisedome and justice.

[7] As, for castle, *estoverium* (ca. 6), *contenemento, wanagio* (ca. 14), and others.

[8] It is not surprising that a medieval chronicler's description of a great council sounded like parliament, but in one instance Coke's bias leads him to emphasize such flimsy "evidence" as a mere adverb: (*nisi publice antea prohibiti fuerent*, ca. 30): "the prohibition intended by this Act, must be by the common or publique Council of the Realm, that is, by act of Parliament, for that it concerneth the whole Realm, and is implied by this word (*publice*)."

He is not always awry on chronology and can do a good bit of dating by "internal criticism." [9] In pointing out that the *salvae sint archiepiscopis* of chapter 37 is not properly a *saving*, he concludes "and therefore the English Translation, both in this and many other places of this great Charter, is very vicious." [10]

He can range from the lofty to the lowly as when he quotes the "Law of God" (Deuteronomy 25:13, 14) as the basis for the law on weights and measures, or describes the pitiable state of the poor villein deprived of his cart (*wainagium*).

The kind of anecdotes that enlivened Sir Edward's speeches in the Commons, of course, could hardly find place in a learned treatise, but there was plenty of opportunity to gratify his penchant for Latin maxims. Economic clauses (chapters 25, 30, and others) permit of asides in praise of Britain's trade and traffic, "the life of the Common wealth," of the merchant "the good Bailiffe of the Realm," and of woolen cloths: "And this is the worthiest and richest commodity of this Kingdom, for divide our native Commodities exported into ten parts, and that which comes from the Sheeps back is nine parts in value of the ten, and setteth great numbers of people on work."

Dearest to his heart, the virtues of the common law and its professors were readily introduced. Of the coroner, he writes:

By the ancient Law, he ought to be a Knight, honest, loyal, and sage, *Et qui melius sciat, et possit officio illi intendere.* For this was the policy of prudent antiquity, that officers did ever give a grace to the place, and not the place only to grace the officer.

Of the law itself:

The ancient law of England had great regard of honour and order. . . .

So dangerous a thing it is to shake or alter any of the rules or fundamental points of the Common law, which in truth are the main pillars and supportes of the fabrick of the Common wealth as elsewhere I have noted more at large, and yet not so largely as the weight of the matter deserveth.[11]

[9] In determining when the prerogative of guardianship of the lands of idiots, a kind of lifelong wardship, came to the crown: "At the making of this statute, the King had not any prerogative in the Custody of the lands of Idiots during the life of the Idiot . . . but at this time the gardianship of Idiots tc. was to the Lords and others according to the Course of the Common Law. . . . But then it is demanded, when was this prerogative given to the King? Certain it is, that the King had it before the Statute of 17 E. 2. *de praerogativa Regis,* for it appeareth in our Books, that the King had this prerogative, Anno 3 E. 2. And before that, it is manifest that the King had it before *Britton* wrote in the raigne of E. 1. as you may read in this book. And it is as clear, that when *Bracton* wrote (who wrote about the end of the reign of H. 3.) that the King had not then this prerogative. And therefore . . ."

[10] Though, as we have seen, neither Coke nor any of his contemporaries questioned the current translation of *ibimus* and *mittimus,* already traditional as "pass upon" and "condemn."

[11] And again: "To conclude this point, with two of the *maximes* of the Common Law. 1. *Le common ley ad rielment admeasure les prerogatives le Roy, que ilz ne tolleront, ne*

But now to turn to the more fundamental elements of his commentary, chapter by chapter. If we exclude the great controversial clauses (chapters 29 and 30), there are few major misinterpretations. It is evidently his own idea that two provisions (chapters 22 and 26) were temporarily annulled, only to be restored by force of the great confirmation of 42 Edward III.[12] He was wrong in assuming that by chapter 22 the king was accorded "year and day" *instead of* "waste." As to chapter 28, he was dealing with a provision obscure by Edward I's day, and recently misdirected by the Puritan lawyers against the oath *ex officio*. He was no doubt indebted to Selden for calling attention to chapter 12 of John's Charter, but was himself responsible for reinstating it with the help of the "statute" *De tallagio non concedendo*.[13]

Occasionally, no doubt, Sir Edward is also responsible for reading "modern" ideas into medieval words, as when he explains the *Nos vero* of chapter 8: "These words being spoken in the politique capacity do extend to the successors, for in judgment of Law the King in his politique capacity dieth not." But on the whole, as he says, his exposition is that of "our books." He is bringing this part of the medieval law up to date as he did other parts of it.[14] There is seeming inconsistency between his insistence on Magna Carta as fundamental law and his admission that certain chapters have been annulled, amended, or modified. We come out with a sort of compromise—the Charter is fundamental law, but within the scope and meaning which judges and parliament have given it.

The following examples may serve as illustrations of Coke's recognition of change and modification. He indicates that the procedure prescribed for collecting debts due the crown (chapter 18) was modified by the statute of 33 Henry VIII, chapter 39; that chapter 32 was altered by *Quia*

prejudiceront le inheritance dascun, the Common law hath so admeasured the prerogatives of the King, that they should not take away, nor prejudice the inheritance of any: and the best inheritance that the Subject hath, is the Law of the Realm. 2. *Nihil tam proprium est imperii, quam legibus vivere.*"

[12] Earlier, in his reports, he was content merely to note that the writ *de odio et atia* was taken away by 28 Ed. III, ca. 9, but by 1628 he was eager to include this writ as one of the means by which the common law insures "liberty of the subject" and so he reinstates it! As to *Prerogativa regis*, which sanctions waste, he says, "But if this act of 17 E. 2. be against this branch of Magna Charta, then it is repealed by the said Act of 42 E. 3. cap. 1." Of another (ca. 16) he is content to note, "This Statute, saith the Mirror, is out of use."

[13] At the end of his comment on ca. 8 we read: "Note here is a chapter omitted, viz., *nullum scutagium vel auxilium ponam in regno nostro nisi per commune concilium regni nostri,* which clause was in the Charter, anno 17, *Regis Johannes,* and was omitted in the exemplification of this great Charter by *Ed.* 1. *vide* Cap. 30."

[14] Cf. Holdsworth, V, 489–90, on "five very considerable merits" of Coke's writings in general. His first, third, and fifth points are: "They cover the whole field of English law and restate it from the point of view of the sixteenth century . . ." "His writings not only brought the Year Books into line with the modern reports, they brought the medieval litera-ture of the common law into line with the modern literature." "As a result his writings ensured the continuity of the development of the common law amidst all the vast changes of this century of Renaissance, Reformation, and Reception."

Emptores;[15] that a clause of chapter 35 was amended by 2 Edward VI, chapter 25.[16] The defects of chapter 12, brought to light by time, "all these are holpen by the Statute of W. 2. cap. 30 as shall appear when we come thereunto." Chapter 36 was the first of a series designed to check the granting of too much land in *mortmain*—"and the foundation of all these Statutes was this chapter of Magna Carta." He includes, of course, the commonplace that 20 Henry VI, chapter 9 extends trial by peers to peeresses.[17]

Other changes are indicated as due to usage; to judicial interpretation— by the "equity of the statute" or by being "excepted out of the statute." These are based on Year Books and reports. A widow, tenant of a mesne lord, he says, need not "at this day" have the consent of her lord to remarry, as was "used of ancient time," and so prescribed in Glanvill, Magna Carta chapter 7, and Bracton.[18] As to the amercement of peers (chapter 14): "Although the statute be in the negative, yet long usage hath prevailed against it, for the amerciament of the Nobility is reduced to a certainty, viz. a Duke 10 L, an Earl 5 L, a Bishop, who hath a Barony, 5 L &c. . . ."

In his interpretation of chapters 11 and 12 Coke is merely following the rulings of his early predecessors on the bench. Though "common pleas shall not follow our court," "divers special cases are out of this Statute." [19]

Albeit originally the Kings Bench be restrained by this Act to hold plea of

[15] "Many excellent things are enacted by this Statute [*Quia Emptores*] and all the doubts upon this Chapter of *Magna Charta* were cleered, both Statutes having both one end, (that is to say) for the upholding and preservation of the tenures, whereby the lands were holden; this Act of E. 1. being enacted *ad instantiam magnatum Regni*.

1. First this Statute of 18 Ed. 1. doth begin with a *de caetero liceat*, which proveth that before it was not lawful to alien any part, unless sufficient were left, and this approveth the aforesaid common opinion, that in that case, the heire might enter, otherwise this Chapter of *Magna Charta*, had been in vaine and this *de caetero liceat*, had not needed." And so on, with three other points of contrast.

[16] *Et ubi major terminus*. "This is altered by the Statute of 2 E. 6. [ca. 25] whereby it is provided that no County Court shall be longer deferred, but one moneth from Court to Court, and so the said Court shall be kept every moneth, and none otherwise. By which Act every County of England, concerning the time of the keeping of the County Court is governed by one and the same Law." As to the view of frankpledge, he quotes a ruling on this clause of the Charter in 24 Hen. VIII.

[17] "It is provided by the Statute of 20 H. 6. That Dutchesses, Countesses, and Baronesses shall be tried by such Peers as a Noble man, being a Peer of the Realm ought to be; which act was made in declaration, and affirmation of the Common Law; for Marquesses and Viscountesses not named in the Act shall be also tried by their Peers, and the Queen being the Kings consort, or dowager, shall also be tried, in case of treason, *per Pares*, as Queen *Anne*, the Wife of King *Henry* the eight was *Termino Pasch. anno* 28. H. 8. in the Towre of London before the Duke of *Norff*. then high Steward."

[18] "Hereby you may see what had been used of ancient time in these cases: But at this day widows are presently after the decease of their husbands without any difficulty to have their marriage (that is, to marry where they will without any licence, or assent of their lords) and their inheritance, without any thing to be given to them . . ." (Ca. 7.)

[19] He lists six exceptions, including, "The King may sue any action for any Common plea in the King's Bench, for this general act doth not extend to the King."

any real action, tc. yet by a mean they may. . . . lest any party that hath right should be without remedy or that there should be a failer of Justice, and therefore Statutes are alwaies to be expounded, that there should be no failer of Justice, but rather then that should fall out, that case (by construction) should be excepted out of the Statute, whether the Statute be in the negative, or affirmative.

Similarly, of the "elsewhere in their itinerary" (*alibi in itinere suo*) of chapter 12, he says

This is taken largely and beneficially, for they may not only make adjournment before the same justices in their circuit, but also to Westminster or to Serjeants' Inne, or any other place out of their Circuit, by the equity of this Statute, and according as it had been alwayes used: For constant allowance in many cases doth make law.[20]

And again, concluding his exposition of chapter 12:

Hereby it appeareth (that I may observe it once for all) that the best expositors of this and all other Statutes are our books and use or experience.

Coke's contribution was not merely one of completeness and application of the "statute" in routine matters. More significant for constitutional progress was the absolute assurance of his pronouncements on controversial issues. At the time he wrote these were still undecided. The crown had in no wise conceded the popular view on impositions and tunnage and poundage. The Petition of Right was to be evaded in the next few years. But there was not the least doubt in Coke's mind on certain propositions, and assuredly none conveyed in his dogmatic statements. As to *Bate's case* "the common opinion was that that judgment was against law." "Rightful customs are those granted by Parliament." An English subject cannot be sent against his will to serve in Ireland.[21] "By the law of the land" (that is, to speak at once for all) means "by the due course and process of the Law." That the cause must be expressed in a *mittimus*. That the issues as to habeas corpus were settled for all time by the Petition of Right. That in the Great Charter "that here is not any saving at all for the King, his heires, or Successors . . ."

Naturally, then, as we might expect, the lengthiest commentaries are those on the two chapters that had figured so prominently in the recent controversies. Seven pages are devoted to chapter 30. The arguments here are those already used in courts and parliament. Coke is sure that the "old customs" did not exist at common law, but were granted by parlia-

[20] It is here that he records the exception in the case of the Lord Marcher, who "though he had *jura Regalia*, yet could not he do justice in his own case . . ."

[21] "This is a beneficial Law, and is construed benignly, and therefore the king cannot send any subject of England against his will to serve him out of this Realm, for that should be an exile, and he should *perdere patriam*; no, he cannot be sent against his will into Ireland, to serve the King as his Deputy there, because it is out of the Realm of England."

ment. Rejecting the "evil," he advances the "good precedents," and particularly the "statute" *De tallagio non concedendo* which has restored to Magna Carta a vital clause.[22] Furthermore:

Upon this Chapter, as by the said particulars may appear, this conclusion is necessary gathered, that all Monopolies concerning trade and traffique, are against the liberty and freedome, declared and granted by this great Charter, and against divers other Acts of Parliament, which are good commentaries upon this Charter. . . .

Eleven and a half pages are devoted to chapter 29.

Upon this Chapter, as out of a root, many fruitful branches of the Law of England have sprung. . . .

As the Goldfiner will not out of the dust, threds, or shreds of Gold, let pass the least crum, in respect of the excellency of the metal: so ought not the learned Reader to let pass any syllable of this Law in respect of the excellency of the matter.

"This chapter," he says, "containeth nine several branches," [23] and upon these he bases his discussion. "The genuine sense being distinctly understood, we shall proceed in order to unfold how the same have been declared, and interpreted. 1. By authority of Parliament. 2. By our books. 3. By precedent." Most reminiscent of parts of Ashley's reading is Coke's exposition of *per legale judicium* both as to what is *legale* in trial by peers[24] and enumeration of the many acts of process and procedure by

---

[22] "By the Statute *De tallagio non concedendo* (which is but an explanation of this branch of the Statute of *Magna Charta*) it is provided: *Nullum tallagium vel auxilium per nos vel haeredes nostros in Regno nostro ponatur, seu levetur sine voluntate, & assensu Archiepiscoporum, Episcoporum, Comitum, Baronum, Militum, Burgensium, & aliorum liberorum Comit' de Regno nostro*; So as E. 1. in conclusion added the effect of the clause concerning this matter, which in his exemplification he had omitted out of *Magna Charta*."

[23] The nine are:

1. That no man be taken or imprisoned . . . 2. No man shall be disseised . . . 3. No man shall be outlawed . . . 4. No man shall be exiled, or banished out of his country . . . 5. No man shall be in any sort destroyed . . . 6. No man shall be condemned at the King's suit, either before the King in his Bench, where the Pleas are *Coram Rege*, (and so are the words, *Nec super eum ibimus*, to be understood) nor before any other Commissioner, or Judge whatsoever, and so are the words, *Nec super eum mittimus*, to be understood, by the judgement of his Peers, that is equals, or according to the Law of the Land. 7. We shall sell to no man Justice or Right. 8. We shall deny to no man Justice or Right. 9. We shall defer to no man Justice or Right.

He gives a short explanation of each of the first six; says the last three are obvious.

[24] "*Per legale judicium*. By this word *legale*, amongst others, three things are implied. 1. That this manner of trial was by Law, before this Statute. 2. That their verdict must be legally given, wherein principally it is to be observed. 1. That the Lords ought to hear no evidence, but in the presence, and hearing of the Prisoner. 2. After the Lords be gone together to consider of the evidence, they cannot send to the high Steward to ask the Judges any question of Law, but in the hearing of the Prisoner, that he may hear, whether the case be rightly put, for *de facto jus oritur*; neither can the Lords, when they are gone together, send for the Judges to know any opinion in Law, but the high Steward ought to demand it in Court in the hearing of the Prisoner. 3. When all the evidence is given by the Kings learned Council, the high Steward cannot collect the evidence against the Prisoner, or in any sort conferre with the Lords touching their evidence, in the absence of the Prisoner, but he ought to be called to it; and all this is implied in this word, *legale*. . . ."

various grades of officials which are *per legem terrae*. This phrase, of course, is construed by the now traditional "divers acts of parliament," three of which are quoted, "for the true sense and exposition of these words." [25]

"Now seeing that no man can be taken, arrested, attached, or imprisoned but by due processe of Law, and according to the Law of the Land, these conclusions hereupon do follow." Thus Coke introduces a precise formula for lawful arrest: the lawful warrant or *mittimus* containing specific cause and lawful conclusion "him safely to keep, until he be delivered by law." Sample writs of habeas corpus are quoted,[26] and the later statutory rules for their availability anticipated:

The like Writ is to be granted out of the Chancery, either in the time of the Term, (as in the Kings Bench) or in the Vacation; for the Court of Chancery is *officina justitiae,* and is ever open, and never adjourned, so as the Subject being wrongfully imprisoned may have justice for the liberty of his person as well in the Vacation time, as in the Term.

The rule that certain cause be shown accords with Scripture: "And this doth agree with that which is said in the holy History, *Sine ratione mihi videtur, mittere vinctum in carcerem, & causas ejus non significare*." But why should he elaborate?

But since we wrote these things, and passed over to many other Acts of Parliament; see now the Petition of Right, *Anno Tertio Caroli Regis*, resolved in full Parliament by the King, the Lords Spiritual and Temporal, and the Commons, which hath made an end of this question, if any were.

The *nulli negabimus* clause, long a favorite of Coke's, is not neglected. It offers him an opportunity to define right (*rectum*) and the qualities of justice,[27] to quote again the famous passage originally derived from the

---

[25] "For the true sense and exposition of these words, see the Statute of 37 E. 3. cap. 8 where the words, by the Law of the Land, are rendered, without due process of Law, for there it is said, though it be contained in the Great Charter, that no man be taken, imprisoned, or put out of his free-hold without proces of the Law, that is, by indictment or presentment of good and lawful men, where such deeds be done in due manner, or by writ original of the Common Law.

"Without being brought in to answer but by due Proces of the Common Law.

"No man be put to answer without presentment before Justices, or thing of record, or by due proces, or by writ original, according to the old Law of the Land.

"Wherein it is to be observed, that this Chapter is but declaratory of the old Law of England."

In another passage, p. 46, he says: "This branch and divers other parts of this Act have been notably explained by divers Acts of Parliament, &c. quoted in the margent." Here are listed the series under Rastell's title, *Accusacion*.

[26] In another passage, six remedies for one taken or committed *contra legem terrae* are rehearsed. P. 55.

[27] "The law is called *rectum*, because it discovereth that which is tort, crooked, or wrong, for as right signifieth law, so tort, crooked or wrong, signifieth injury, and *injuria est contra jus*, against right . . . it is called Right, because it is the best birth right the Subject hath, for thereby his goods, lands, wife, children, his body, life, honour and estimation are protected from injury and wrong: *major haereditas venit unicuique nostrum a jure, & legibus quam a parentibus* . . ."

Year Books of Henry IV, and to conclude with the picturesque "shreds of gold" figure quoted above.

Nulli vendemus, &c. This is spoken in the person of the King, who in judgment of Law, in all his Courts of Justice is present, and repeating these words, *Nulli vendemus, &c.*

And therefore every Subject of this Realm, for injury done to him in *bonis, terris, vel persona,* by any other Subject, be he Ecclesiastical, or Temporal, Free or Bond, Man or Woman, Old or Young, or be he outlawed, excommunicated, or any other without exception, may take his remedy by the course of the Law, and have justice and right for the injury done to him, freely without sale, fully without any denial, and speedily without delay.

Hereby it appeareth, that Justice must have three qualities, it must be *Libera, quia nihil iniquius venali Justitia; Plena, quia Justitia non debet claudicare; & Celeris, quia dilatio est quaedam negatio;* and then it is both Justice and Right.

It was only natural that the popular leaders of the Long Parliament should have set as one of their early aims the recovery and publication of Coke's commentary on Magna Carta. It constituted a perfect justification in principle of their current policies and legislation. According to Sir Simonds D'Ewes, as early as December 5, 1640, "a motion was made to recover Sir Edward Coke's written books or other bookes being 19 in number which were taken from him during his last sicknes: etc. and ·a Committee appointed to search for them, of which I was one." As we might expect, with Sir Simonds on the committee, the *Journal* contains several entries on progress in the matter. It was on December 21 that

Sir Thomas Roe brought a message from the King touching Sir Edward Cokes bookes which were in Secretarie Windebankes hande should bee delivered before Christmas Eve into the hands of Sir Randolph Crew one of his executors: which message gave the Howse great content. The same Sir Thomas Roe added that the saied Sir Edward Cokes comment on Magna Charta was in Sir John Cokes hande.[28]

On May 12, 1641, Coke's heir was authorized to publish the commentary on Magna Carta according to the intentions of the author. It actually appeared in 1642. With characteristic antiquarian zeal D'Ewes had moved "that some well skilled in Records [himself, perhaps?] might have the overviewing of the said comment. But ther was nothing ordered therin."

[28] *The Journal of Sir Simonds D'Ewes,* p. 174. "Mr. Cooke said, That when his father (Sir Edward Coke) was on his death bed, his Study was broken and searched and his bookes carried away, among others three bookes of his owne Labour, 1. Pleas of the Crowne. 2. Jurisdiction of Courtes. 3. Explanation of Magna Charta." (Supplied by the editor.) *Ibid.,* p. 108, note 3.
  Saturday, February 13. "Sir Thomas Roe shewed that all the bookes which had been taken out of Sir Edward Cokes librarie weere now restored to his executors who would deliver them to Sir Robert Coke sonne and heir of the saied Sir Edward. Then it was moved that those three bookes of his viz. His Jurisdiction of Courts, The Pleas of the Crowne; and his Comment on Magna Charta might bee printed." *Ibid.,* p. 358.

It is interesting to find Sir Simonds calling attention to the fact that the "Charter itselfe is now misprinted in divers places," but a bit ludicrous is his fear that the author (Coke of all persons) through lack of access to the old records, may not have been aware that "the subject enioied the greatest parte of [those liberties] before the Charter at Common Law." [29]

Next year, 1643, also by order of the Commons, there appeared the work of another distinguished lawyer-scholar, Prynne's *Soveraigne Power of Parliaments and Kingdoms.*

Prynne quotes with approval Coke's views of Magna Charta expressed in the preface to his Second Institute as "a clear resolution, that the Principal Liberties, Customs, Laws, contained in these great Charters and ratified by them, are both FUNDAMENTAL, PERPETUAL, & UNALTERABLE." Along the same lines Prynne argues in his Soveraigne Power of Parliaments and Kingdoms . . . against the King's right to withhold his assent to a bill that has passed the Houses of Parliament, "because it is point blanke against the very letter of *Magna Charta* (the ancient fundamental Law of the Realm, confirmed in at least 60 Parliaments) ch. 29. WE SHALL DENY, WE SHALL DEFERRE (both in the future tense) TO NO MAN (much lesse to the whole Parliament and Kingdome, in denying or deferring to passe such necessary publike Bills) JUSTICE OR RIGHT, a law which *in terminis* takes cleane away the King's pretended absolute negative Voyce to these Bills we now dispute of." [30]

An intensive search in state papers, plea rolls, and reports for the eleven years of no parliaments (1629–40) would no doubt reveal instances similar to those of Michael Sparkes and "Mr. Salisbury" described above, but it remained for *Hampden's case* and then the Long Parliament in its first year of feverish activity, to bring "liberty of the subject" once more into the open. These episodes and others suggesting the turns in Magna Carta history in the second half of the century will be merely suggested here.

The feat performed by Oliver St. John in Exchequer Chamber as counsel for Hampden was to give to chapter 12 of John's Charter legal application, to put it into the statute book, as it were. Coke had insisted

[29] ". . . But for his comment on Magna Charta: ther was great necessitie that the old Great Pipe Rolls from the first yeare of H. 2 to the end of King Johns raigne; And the old Plea Rolls temp. R. 1 and King John should be viewed; without the knowledge of which it was impossible to make an exact comment on the same Magna Charta. For howsoever the preface of it, by the cunning contrivence of Hubert de Burgo seems to implie that all those liberties weere newly granted by H. 3 yet I durst boldlie averre that the subject enioied the greatest parte of them before the Charter at Common law.

"Besides the Charter itselfe is now misprinted in divers places as for instance in that place about exemption of cartes it is putt in the carte of anye knight or Lorde. The wordes of the Charter are *militis* and *domine*: and it should bee printed knight or Lady. And by this false printing, many Ladies being widowes had ther cartes taken from them against the expresse libertie of Magna Charta." *Ibid.*, p. 358.

[30] McIlwain, *High Court of Parliament*, pp. 65–66. Cf. *ibid.*, pp. 154–55, where McIlwain quotes another passage in which Prynne "cites the King's promise in Magna Charta not to deny nor defer justice and right, as an argument for frequent sessions of Parliament . . ."

that it was virtually reinstated as law by the "statute" *De tallagio non concedendo,* and had thus made it cover *prises* and customs. St. John seized on the significance of *scutagium* as a levy for military purposes to relate it to ship money and the "defense of the realm." Attorney general Bankes repudiated this chapter of the spurious *Carta de Runnymede,* extorted

when the Banners were displayed, when there was War or Rebellion, between the Barons, Commonalty, and the King. It was not assented unto the King sitting in Parliament; for Parliaments are not called with Arms, and in the Field. It was in truth an inforced Act from a Distressed King; shall this bind the Crown?

Bankes held, as well he might, to the officially correct text of the statute 9 Henry III, current for four centuries. Hampden "lost his case before the judges but gained it in public opinion." [31] Neither the judgment against him nor the *dicta* of the judges deterred other conscientious objectors from justifying resistance to ship money by Magna Carta, as did Sir Richard Strode in 1639. It appears from a letter written to Laud by Finch, C. J.:

that Sir Richard Strode had had one of his cows distrained for non-payment of ship-money. He thereupon drew up and delivered to the grand jury for Devon a paper "in the nature of a presentment; in which Magna Carta and the other medieval statutes against taxation without the consent of Parliament were recited, to prove that this distraint was illegal. One of the grand jury informed Finch of this. Finch thereupon directed that nothing should be done in the matter without acquainting him—'which I did lest they might be induced to find the presentment, which I thought might be of ill consequence.'" [32]

As to St. John himself, his speech in *Hampden's case* "gained him an immense reputation, and though hitherto he had had little practice in Westminster Hall, henceforward he was called 'into all courts and to all causes where the King's prerogative was most contested.'" St. John was elected to the Short and the Long Parliaments as member for Totnes. In the second he appropriately led the attack on ship money. "He was 'in firm and entire conjunction' with Pym and Hampden, and 'of intimate trust' with the Earl of Bedford, being thus one of the half dozen opposition politicians who made up 'the engine which moved all the rest.'" [33]

Another episode, less well known than *Hampden's case,* must have been equally significant in its implications. Although the complexion of the bench had been altered by Charles' removals, in the congenial atmos-

---

[31] Rushworth, II, 509, 517–18. Bémont, *Chartes,* pp. lii–liii.

[32] Holdsworth, VI, 65, based on a letter, Finch's own account, of the manner in which he had dealt with an objector at the Exeter assizes.

[33] C. H. Firth, in *D.N.B.,* quoting Clarendon.

phere of the Inns of Court barristers and students still venerated the common law and pursued their studies with the usual moots and readings. Yet not even these academic halls proved beyond the reach of Laud, as appeared when Edward Bagshaw, Lent Reader of the Middle Temple, 1639, lectured on the *Statutum pro Clero* (25 Edward III, chapter 7). His material was prepared, he later explained, two years before, but he saw no cause to alter it; it had no reference to the quarrel with Scotland then in progress. It was in the division of the lectures to which Laud took particular exception, and which would have delighted James Morice and Nicholas Fuller, that Magna Carta was made to figure.

I held, that a Beneficed Clark Imprisoned, Deprived and Excommunicated by the High Commission for enormous offences (not naming the particular offence) that this Clark, notwithstanding, was such a possessor of a Church as might Plead, Counterplead and Defend his Right within my Law. . . .

Whether the fine, Imprisonment, Deprivation and Excommunication of a Clerk for Enormous offences, (and no offence named) be good or void in Law? And I think the sentence to be void and against Law.

This is a great and high question, and much concerns the Liberty of the Subject (a most precious thing). *Libertas est res inestimabilis* was the Motto of the Emperor *Justin* upon the reverse of his Coyn. And in this point Magna Charta is broken in two Chapters, cap. 1 *Habeat* &c. *Ecclesia Anglicana libertates suas illaesas,* and here is an English Clergy-man undone: And cap. 29 *Nullus liber homo imprisonetur nisi per legem terrae,* and here is a free Subject quite destroyed in his Goods by his Fine; in his Land and Living by his Deprivation; in his Body by his Imprisonment, Take him Gaoler; in his Soul by his Excommunication, Take him Devil; For this is the meaning of that sentence *Tradatur Satanae.*

As we listen to his "divers reasons" for choice of a statute it is as if the voice of Coke were speaking again: "The Honour I bare to my Profession of the Common Law, by advancing it above the Civil and Canon Laws, and all other Ecclesiastical law exercised within this Kingdome, from which they all have their being and Foundation . . ." Again, "The Common Law of England speaking to all those Courts in the Language of the supreme Lawgiver, *Hither shall you pass and no further and here shall you stay your proud waves*."

As Bagshaw tells the story,[34] an *accusator fratrum* misreported his reading to Laud, who complained to king and council that he "read against the Bishops." Questioned by Lord Keeper Finch, defended before the

[34] "Just Vindication of the Questioned Part of the Reading of Edward Bagshawe, Esq. an Apprentice of the Common Law. Had in the Middle Temple Hall the 24th day of February, being Munday, Anno Dom. 1639, upon the Statute of 25 E. 3. called, Statutum pro Clero, from all Scandalous Aspersions whatsoever. With a True Narrative of the Cause of Silencing the Reader by the then Archbishop of Canterbury: With the Arguments at large of those Points in his Reading, for which he was Questioned at the Council-Board. London, Printed in the Year 1660. And to be sold in Westminster-Hall and Fleetstreet."

council by the Earl of Manchester, a former Middle Temple Reader, Bagshaw was eventually summoned to Lambeth. He went by barge, attended by Mr. Roger Pepys "the next summer Reader, and other my Cubbard men, with my servants." This was an unwonted service. "Readers, if they do amiss, are answerable to the Governors of that Society at their next Parliament, where the Reader and his assistants (being alwayes Benchers) do give an account of that Reading as I did." But Laud was no more impressed than if his guests had been humble country preachers. "Mr. Reader, had you nothing else to do but to read against the Clergy? My Lord, my Statute was *pro Clero*, and I read not at all against them but for them." [35] "Well, you shall answer it in the High Commission. Had you no other time to do it but in such a time? Farewell, Mr. Reader, and much good do it you with your fine [?] friends."

The incident did not pass unnoticed. Laud's act, says Bagshaw, "made a loud noise throughout the Cities of London and Westminster." A peer merrily told him "that he had often heard of a silenc't preacher but never of a silenc't Reader before." As a result, the next year the people of Southwark elected him one of their burgesses, and tried to get him to prefer the *Root and Branch Petition,* but in spite of his alleged "reading against the bishops," he favored reform rather than abolition, and ultimately espoused the royalist cause.

The Long Parliament in its first year made two definitive contributions. First, as we have seen, it authorized the publication of Coke's *Second Institute* and of Prynne's *Soveraigne Power of Parliaments and Kingdoms.* By its authorization or tacit approval, various tracts and speeches of earlier days were now printed or reprinted, among them Fuller's "tract" of 1607, Hakewill's speech against impositions in the session of 1610, and Sir Robert Cotton's *A Short View of the Long Raign of King Henry the third* and *The Dangers wherein the Kingdom now Standeth.* Second, it passed the group of well-known statutes, not repudiated at the restoration, which put into unmistakable terms what had earlier been claimed for Magna Carta and other medieval laws as bars to non-parliamentary taxation and the prerogative courts. The act of 16 Charles I, chapter 14, prescribes that all points of the Petition of Right are to be in force, and declares that the writs for ship money, the judgment against Hampden and the opinion of the judges "were and are contrary to and against the laws and statutes of this realm, the right of property, the liberty of the

---

[35] "I thought I should deserve thanks from the Clergy by the discovery to them of the favours and priviledges they received cheifly and principally by the Common Law, to which Law, above all men in the Kingdome, they are the most beholden. . . . four of the nearest and dearest things Clergy men have at this day, viz. The Blessing and happiness of true Religion: The enjoyment of their Lives and Liberties: The Society of their Wives, and the benefit of their Church livings in Glebe and Tythes . . . they have, hold, and enjoy them all by, from, and under the Comon Law."

subjects, former resolutions in Parliament, and the Petition of Right . . ."
The act abolishing the Court of High Commission condemns its use of
fine and imprisonment and the oath ex officio. The act abolishing Star
Chamber and other prerogative courts quotes Magna Carta chapter 29
and four of the *six statutes* (5, 25, 28, and 42 Edward III) in the familiar
words of the current printed editions of the statutes.

Debates, of course, reveal that the Charter was in men's minds and on
their tongues not only in the framing of these statutes but in connection
with other grievances. For instance, the new canons were condemned
as unlawful and void "and in many parts of them directlie to crosse
Magna Charta." D'Ewes tells us how he himself opposed a motion "that
wee should make an order to receive noe petitions" but "I spake against
it and dashed it, shewing that, though we dispatched little and men complained of it, yet to make an order heere to refuse petitions would be a
iust grievance. It was expresselie against Magna Charta, *Nulli negabimus
iusticiam*." [36]

As the more radical elements increased in numbers and strength, the
tone changed. To be sure, Lilburne, in the Tower, was making his
"collection of the marrow and soule of Magna Charta," but the position
of the extremists has been well put by Professor McIlwain:

In reality, however, while the extreme republicans might make use of the
idea of fundamental law on occasion,—especially as a protection when in
danger,—there was nothing in the old law to which they could appeal as a
basis for their constructive programme. It was only the negative aspect of the
fundamental law that they accepted,—a limitation of the powers of a king or
a parliament; their republicanism could find no precedent in the English constitution. Lilburne might talk of fundamental law at the time of his trial,
but his real feeling is better expressed when he says: "The greatest mischief of
all and the oppressing bondage of England ever since the Norman yoke is a
law called the common law." And again: "Magna Charta itself being but a
beggarly thing, containing many marks of intolerable bondage, and the laws
that have been made since by Parliaments in very. many particulars made our
government more oppressive and intolerable." [37]

From another pen, directed against the new tyranny of parliament and
army came a satiric parody: [38]

A new Magna Charta enacted and confirmed by the High and Mighty
States, the Remainder of the Lords and Commons, now sitting at Westminster

[36] *The Journal of Sir Simonds D'Ewes*, p. 415.
[37] McIlwain, *High Court of Parliament*, pp. 90–91.
[38] "The people's prerogative and priviledges asserted and vindicated (against all tyranny
whatsoever), by law and reason. Being a collection of the marrow and soule of Magna Charta
and of all the most principall Statutes made ever since to this present year 1647; for the
preservation of the peoples liberties and properties . . ." Printed 1647 o.s. Bémont, *Chartes*,
p. liii, comments on this.

in Empty Parliament, under the command and wardship of Sir Thomas Fairfax, lieutenant-general Cromwell (our present soveraigne lord the king, now residing at his royal pallace at White hall) and prince Ireton his sonne, and the army under their command. Containing the many new, large and ample Liberties, Customes and Franchises, of late freely granted and confirmed to our Soveraigne lord King Charles, his Heirs and Successors; the Church and State of England and Ireland, and all the Freemen, and Freeborne People of the same.

New Magna Charta, Cap. 20.

Omni vendemus, omni negabimus, aut differemus Iustitiam vel rectum.[39]

Against the "new despotism" of Cromwell the Charter was cited only to be met with the Protector's contemptuous ridicule of such a "precedent." Several historians have described one such episode. According to Firth, during the rule of the major generals, "A merchant named Cony refused to pay customs duties not imposed by act of Parliament, and his counsel, Serjeant Twysden, asserted that their levy by Cromwell's ordinance was contrary to Magna Carta. Chief Justice Rolle, before whom the case came, resigned his place to avoid determining the question." McIlwain reminds us that Hobbes "makes his philosopher in the dialogue ask the lawyer: 'When their new republic returned into monarchy by Oliver, who durst deny him money upon any pretence of Magna Charta, or of these other Acts of Parliament which you have cited?' "[40]

After 1660 the scene again changes. A modern historian has characterized the restoration as "essentially a return to government by law. . . . Arbitrary rule was no longer possible to a king who could neither legislate nor tax out of Parliament, nor do justice outside the courts of Common Law and of Chancery."[41] A natural accompaniment was a return to the traditional views of Magna Carta, those of 1628, 1637, and 1641. To be sure, as Bémont reminds us, the abolition of the feudal tenures must have had the effect of annulling a number of provisions of the Charter, but not those which were currently of the greatest political interest.[42] Its sponsors were now of a relatively conservative stamp, members of the Cavalier parliament, the recently restored Anglican Church and the Inns of Court. In 1667 "even a Chief Justice of the King's Bench was called

[39] British Museum printed tracts. It consists of about twelve items, the first, for instance: "That the Church of England shall be free to deny the perpetuall Ordinances of Jesus Christ, to countenance spreading heresies . . ."

[40] Firth, Cromwell, p. 418. According to Bémont, Chartes, p. liv and note 3: "Cromwell ne s'en émut guere et ne dissimula pas son dédain pour l'acte de Runnymead quand il parut le gener. . . . Quand les juges alleguerent 'humblement' la Grande Charte et la Petition des droits, il tourna ces lois en ridicule en termes trop grossur et scandaleux pour que l'histoire les rapporte." The story comes originally from Clarendon.

[41] Keir, Constitutional History of Modern Britain, pp. 230–31.

[42] Bémont, Chartes, pp. liv–lv. "Un des premiers actes du roi restauré fut d'abolir ce qui subsistait encore du régime féodal. Cet acte . . . annulait un grand nombre d'articles de la Grande Charte mais sans toucher a ceux qui presentaient le plus d'intéret politique . . ."

to the bar of the Commons and forced to a humble apology for a contemptuous expression let fall concerning it in a moment of anger . . ."[43]

As early as 1661 it had been drawn into the service of the Church in the harangue of "Pen. Whalley Esq. one of his Majesties Justices of the Peace," and promptly printed under the title: "The Civil Rights and Conveniences of Episcopacy with the Inconveniences of Presbytery asserted; as it was delivered in a charge to the Grand Jury, at the General Quarter Sessions, held at Nottingham, April 22, 1661." The zealous justice quotes entire chapter 1 of the Charter, reminds his hearers of the sentence of excommunication, and characterizes events of the past decade as "that great violation of Magna Charta, the disfranchisement of the Clergy." He refers to the Charter as "the first of that we call Statute Law." "If Magna Charta," he says, "be as most of us are apt to incline to believe, it is, like the Laws of the Medes and Persians unalterable, as to the main, it is so in every Part . . ."[44]

Late in the reign as parties developed and political agitation became acute, Whigs and Tories drew the Charter into service for their polemical tracts. Such for instance was William Pettyt's "The ancient right of the Commons of England asserted," and such Doctor Robert Brady's reply denying to the document any such role as "the principal foundation of the laws of England," but rather as designed for a little group of selfish Norman Barons and prelates.[45]

Naturally the most effective restoration of Magna Carta came through the Inns of Court. Sir Edward Coke "spoke" again through new editions of his *Institutes* and Spelman through his *Glossary*. Bagshaw was now able to print a vindication of his Reading and thus of academic freedom in the Inns of Court. Readers chose as their "statute" Magna Carta or the Petition of Right. A Reading on chapter 1 of the Charter is prefaced with a eulogy based on Coke, and a historical introduction describing it as "usher'd in and attested by a numberous train of the prime nobility of the nation both clergy and laity."[46] It was Prynne as Lent Reader, February 1662, who seems to have revived the custom of Readings so long out of use. Although his statute was the Petition of Right, in his first

---

[43] McIlwain, *High Court of Parliament*, p. 13.

[44] A printed tract of 13 pages, based on *State Papers*, 29, 34, no. 79.

[45] According to Bémont, *Chartes*, lv–lvi, Brady, "garde des archives de la Tour de Londres et royaliste déclaré," "s'éforcea de prouver que toutes les libertés dont jouissait le peuple anglais étaient un pur don de la royauté, que la Grande Charte ne saurait, comme l'avait avancé Coke, passer pour etre 'le foundement principal des lois d'Angleterre,' car ce n'était pas pour les Anglais qu'elle avait été faite, mais seulement pour un petit nombre de barons normands desireux d'affaiblir la rigueur des obligations féodales, et de quelques prélats, aussi d'origine normande, empressés a secouer le joug de pouvoir séculier."

Bémont also points out that it was left for Burnet, Bishop of Salisbury, to use the insurrection at Runnymead and chapter 61 of John's Charter to justify to contemporaries the events of 1688–89.

[46] Rawlinson MSS D, 836, fols. 7–63.

lecture he treats at length of the origin and early history of Magna Carta, the texts of John and Henry III and the various confirmations. He calls the barons' petition to John "one of the first petitions of right." Through his vast knowledge of the records he is able to correct Coke on a number of points. His Reading is a memorial not only to the two liberty documents, but to the great spirits of the past generation who revived the one and framed the other. He chose that statute, he tells us, because of its great value, its violation "in the late years of usurpation," and furthermore

Because it unanimously passed both Houses of Parliament after more learned solumne studied Arguments Debates Conferences between and in both Houses, by the Learnedest Lawyers Antiquaries England ever bred (Sir Robert Cotton, Mr. Selden, Sir Edward Cooke, Mr. Noy, Mr. Littleton, Sir Henry Martyn, Mr. Glanvill, Mr. Mason, Mr. Banks and divers others) then eny Act of Parliament ever did.[47]

IT IS hoped that these studies have served to fill out the well-known but hitherto sketchy and episodic history of the Great Charter, and also to correct some misconceptions. The truth seems to strike at a golden mean between the extravagant eulogy of the old-time historian and the extreme depreciation of the ultra-critical modernists—the "myth of Magna Carta" school. The famous document meant many things to many groups, varying greatly from age to age in actual content (meaning) and realistic value. Originally, to be sure, it was primarily of interest to such as Laud's and Doctor Brady's "selfish Norman barons and prelates," but even from the first it contained provisions of value to humbler elements in medieval society. While some chapters became obsolete or were virtually annulled, others remained in use throughout the centuries here under discussion. Although the number of provisions actually enforceable decreased, the number of persons qualified to profit by such increased. Both chance and design played a part in the Charter's transformation: chance in its mere placement as first in the statute book, and in its convenience to the lawyers as an "academic reference"; design in the studied interpretations of a Morice or a Coke. Thus the Charter of *liberties* became a Charter of *liberty*. Whatever historical errors may have been committed by the gentlemen of the Inns of Court, currently the law was what they made it.

Any study of this kind easily lends itself to charges of exaggeration. The document was only one of many promises to the English Church, only one of London's civic charters. It embodied but a small part of feudal law. Even as to "liberty of the subject" it might have availed little "*un*attended by the six statutes" and the Petition of Right. But granting that the Charter was often only one of many precedents advanced in a

[47] Inner Temple Library MSS 538. 16. i. Another copy, 538. 32. ii, is said to be in Prynne's hand.

given cause, what a precedent it was! No other had the name and fame which made it, as Coke said, "the law of laws." No other had quite the fundamental character which forced even the ablest of king's counsel to interpret, but never dare to impugn or repudiate it.

To be sure, the subject could have been handled in an abstract and concise form, but the writer must confess to having enjoyed the tale more than the moral, the proponents of the Charter more than the theories they propounded. It is hoped that the reader too has enjoyed meeting in these pages these sometime stubborn and often illogical, but nevertheless choice exemplars of the English character, creators of the "myth of Magna Carta" if you like, but also the real "makers of the English constitution."

APPENDIXES, BIBLIOGRAPHY, AND INDEX

❧ APPENDIXES ❧

APPENDIX A

1. The Great Charter of Henry III[1]

(Third revision, issued February 11, 1225)

Henricus Dei gratia rex Anglie, dominus Hibernie, dux Normannie, Aquitanie, et comes Andegavie, archiepiscopis, episcopis, abbatibus, *prioribus,* comitibus, baronibus, vicecomitibus, prepositis, ministris et omnibus ballivis et fidelibus suis *presentem cartam inspecturis,* salutem. Sciatis quod nos, intuitu Dei et pro salute anime nostre et *animarum* antecessorum et successorum nostrorum, ad exaltationem sancte ecclesie et emendationem regni nostri, *spontanea et bona voluntate nostra, dedimus et concessimus archiepiscopis, episcopis, abbatibus, prioribus, comitibus, baronibus et omnibus de regno nostro has libertates subscriptas tenendas in regno nostro Anglie in perpetuum.*

1 (1). In primis *concessimus* Deo et hac presenti carta nostra *confirmavimus* pro nobis et heredibus nostris in perpetuum quod anglicana ecclesia libera sit, et habeat *omnia* jura sua integra et libertates suas illesas. Concessimus etiam omnibus liberis hominibus regni nostri pro nobis et heredibus nostris in perpetuum omnes libertates subscriptas, habendas et tenendas eis et heredibus suis de nobis et heredibus nostris *in perpetuum.*

2 (2). Si quis comitum vel baronum nostrorum sive aliorum tenencium de nobis in capite per servicium militare mortuus fuerit, et, cum decesserit, heres *ejus* plene etatis fuerit et relevium debeat, habeat hereditatem suam per antiquum relevium, scilicet heres vel heredes comitis de baronia comitis integra per centum libras, heres vel heredes baronis de baronia integra per centum libras, heres vel heredes militis de feodo militis integro per centum solidos ad plus; et qui minus debuerit minus det secundum antiquam consuetudinem feodorum.

3 (3). Si autem heres alicujus talium fuerit infra etatem, *dominus ejus non habeat custodiam ejus nec terre sue antequam homagium ejus ceperit; et, postquam talis heres* fuerit in custodia, cum ad etatem pervenerit, *scilicet viginti et unius anni,* habeat hereditatem suam sine relevio et sine fine, *ita tamen quod, si ipse, dum infra etatem fuerit, fiat miles, nichilominus terra remaneat in custodia dominorum suorum usque ad terminum predictum.*

4 (4). Custos terre hujusmodi heredis qui infra etatem fuerit non capiat de

---

[1] The following text (that of *S. R.* I:22–25) is Professor McKechnie's arrangement as given in his *Magna Carta,* pp. 497–508. Words in italics indicate those passages not to be found in the Charter of 1215, but introduced in 1216, 1217, or 1225. Numbers in parentheses refer to corresponding articles of John's Charter. For variations, 1216, 1217, and 1225, see footnotes given by Professor McKechnie, pp. 497–508, or Bémont, *Chartes,* where a similar arrangement is given.

terra heredis nisi rationabiles exitus et rationabiles consuetudines et rationabilia servicia, et hoc sine destructione et vasto hominum vel rerum; et si nos commiserimus custodiam alicujus talis terre vicecomiti vel alicui alii qui de exitibus *terre* illius nobis debeat respondere, et ille destructionem de custodia fecerit vel vastum, nos ab illo capiemus emendam, et terra committetur duobus legalibus et discretis hominibus de feodo illo qui de exitibus nobis respondeant vel ei cui eos assignaverimus; et si dederimus vel vendiderimus alicui custodiam alicujus talis terre, et ille destructionem inde fecerit vel vastum, amittat ipsam custodiam et tradatur duobus legalibus et discretis hominibus de feodo illo qui similiter nobis respondeant, .sicut predictum est.

5 (5). Custos autem, quamdiu custodiam terre habuerit, sustentet domos, parcos, vivaria, stagna, molendina et cetera ad terram illam pertinencia de exitibus terre ejusdem, et reddat heredi, cum ad plenam etatem pervenerit, terram suam totam instauratam de carucis *et omnibus aliis rebus, ad minus secundum quod illam recepit. Hec omnia observentur de custodiis archiepiscopatuum, e₂ iscopatuum, abbatiarum, prioratuum, ecclesiarum et dignitatum vacancium que ad nos pertinent, excepto quod hujusmodi custodie vendi non debent.*

6 (6). Heredes maritentur absque disparagatione.

7 (7). Vidua post mortem mariti sui statim et sine difficultate *aliqua* habeat maritagium suum et hereditatem suam, nec aliquid det pro dote sua vel pro maritagio suo vel pro hereditate sua, quam hereditatum maritus suus et ipsa tenuerunt die obitus ipsius mariti, et maneat in capitali mesagio mariti sui per quadraginta dies post obitum ipsius mariti sui, infra quos assignetur ei dos sua, *nisi prius ei fuerit assignata, vel nisi domus illa sit castrum; et si de castro recesserit, statim provideatur ei domus competens in qua possit honeste morari, quousque dos sua ei assignetur secundum quod predictum est, et habeat rationabile estoverium suum interim de communi. Assignetur autem ei pro dote sua tercia pars tocius terre mariti sui que sua fuit in vita sua, nisi de minori dotata fuerit ad hostium ecclesie.*

(8). Nulla vidua distringatur ad se maritandam, dum vivere voluerit sine marito, ita tamen quod securitatem faciet quod se non maritabit sine assensu nostro, si de nobis tenuerit, vel sine assensu domini sui, si de aliquo tenuerit.

8 (9). Nos vero vel ballivi nostri non seisiemus terram aliquam nec redditum pro debito aliquo quamdiu catalla debitoris *presencia* sufficiant ad debitum reddendum *et ipse debitor paratus sit inde satisfacere;* nec plegii ipsius debitoris distringantur quamdiu ipse capitalis debitor sufficiat ad solutionem debiti; et, si capitalis debitor defecerit in solutione debiti, non habens unde reddat *aut reddere nolit cum possit,* plegii respondeant pro debito; et, si voluerint, habeant terras et redditus debitoris quousque sit eis satisfactum de debito quod ante pro eo solverunt, nisi capitalis debitor monstraverit se inde esse quietum versus eosdem plegios.

9 (13). Civitas Londonie habeat omnes antiquas libertates et liberas consuetudines suas. Preterea volumus et concedimus quod omnes alie civitates, et burgi, et ville, *et barones de quinque portubus,* et *omnes* portus, habeant omnes libertates et liberas consuetudines suas.

10 (16). Nullus distringatur ad faciendum majus servicium de feodo militis nec de alio libero tenemento quam inde debetur.

11 (17). Communia placita non sequantur curiam nostram, set teneantur in aliquo loco certo.

12 (18). Recognitiones de nova disseisina *et* de morte antecessoris non capiantur nisi in suis comitatibus, et hoc modo: nos, vel si extra regnum fuerimus, capitalis justiciarius noster, mittemus justiciarios per unumquemque comitatum *semel in anno,* qui cum militibus comitatuum capiant in comitatibus assisas predictas. *Et ea que in illo adventu suo in comitatu per justiciarios predictos ad dictas assisas capiendas missos terminari non possunt, per eosdem terminentur alibi in itinere suo; et ea que per eosem propter difficultatem aliquorum articulorum terminari non possunt, referantur ad justiciarios, nostros de banco, et ibi terminentur.*

13. *Assise de ultima presentatione semper capiantur coram justiciariis nostris de banco et ibi terminentur.*

14 (20). Liber homo non amercietur pro parvo delicto nisi secundum modum *ipsius* delicti, et pro magno delicto, secundum magnitudinem delicti, salvo contenemento suo; et mercator eodem modo salva mercandisa sua; et villanus *alterius quam noster* eodem modo amercietur salvo wainagio suo, si inciderit in misericordiam nostram; et nulla predictarum misericordiarum ponatur nisi per sacramentum proborum *et legalium* hominum de visneto.

(21). Comites et barones non amercientur nisi per pares suos, et non nisi secundum modum delicti.

(22). *Nulla ecclesiastica persona amercietur secundum quantitatem beneficii sui ecclesiastici, set secundum laicum tenementum suum, et secundum quantitatem delicti.*

15 (23). Nec villa, nec homo, distringatur facere pontes ad riparias nisi que ex antiquo et de jure facere debet.

16. *Nulla riparia decetero defendatur, nisi ille que fuerunt in defenso tempore regis Henrici avi nostri, per eadem loca et eosdem terminos sicut esse consueverunt tempore suo.*

17 (24). Nullus vicecomes, constabularius, coronatores vel alii ballivi nostri teneant placita corone nostre.

18 (26). Si aliquis tenens de nobis laicum feodum moriatur, et vicecomes vel ballivus noster ostendat litteras nostras patentes de summonitione nostra de debito quod defunctus nobis debuit, liceat vicecomiti vel ballivo nostro attachiare et imbreviare catalla defuncti inventa in laico feodo ad valenciam illius debiti per visum legalium hominum, ita tamen quod nichil inde amoveatur donec persolvatur nobis debitum quod clarum fuerit, et residuum relinquatur executoribus ad faciendum testamentum defuncti; et si nichil nobis debeatur ab ipso, omnia catalla cedant defuncto, salvis uxori ipsius et pueris suis rationabilibus partibus suis.

19 (28). Nullus constabularius vel ejus ballivus capiat blada vel alia catalla alicujus *qui non sit de villa ubi castrum situm est,* nisi statim inde reddat denarios aut respectum inde habere possit de voluntate venditoris; *si autem de villa ipsa fuerit, infra quadraginta dies precium reddat.*

20 (29). Nullus constabularius distringat aliquem militem ad dandum denarios pro custodia castri, si *ipse eam* facere voluerit in propria persona sua, vel per alium probum hominem, si ipse eam facere non possit propter rationabilem causam, et, si nos duxerimus eum vel miserimus in exercitum, erit quietus de custodia secundum quantitatem temporis quo per nos fuerit in exercitu *de feodo pro quo fecit servicium in exercitu.*

21 (30). Nullus vicecomes, vel ballivus noster, vel alius capiat equos vel carettas alicujus pro cariagio faciendo, nisi *reddat liberationem antiquitus statutam, scilicet pro caretta ad duos equos decem denarios per diem, et pro caretta ad tres equos quatuordecim denarios per diem. Nulla caretta dominica alicujus ecclesiastice persone vel militis vel alicujus domine capiatur per ballivos predictos.*

(31). Nec nos nec ballivi nostri *nec alii* capiemus alienum boscum ad castra vel alia agenda nostra, nisi per voluntatem illius cujus boscus ille fuerit.

22 (32). Nos non tenebimus terras eorum qui convicti fuerint de felonia, nisi per unum annum et unum diem; et tunc reddantur terre dominis feodorum.

23 (33). Omnes kidelli decetero deponantur penitus per Tamisiam et Medeweiam et per totam Angliam, nisi per costeram maris.

24 (34). Breve quod vocatur Precipe decetero non fiat alicui de aliquo tenemento, unde liber homo *perdat* curiam suam.

25 (35). Una mensura vini sit per totum regnum nostrum, et una mensura cervisie, et una mensura bladi, scilicet quarterium London., et una latitudo pannorum tinctorum et russettorum et haubergettorum, scilicet due ulne infra listas; de ponderibus *vero* sit ut de mensuris.

26 (36). Nichil detur de cetero pro brevi inquisitionis *ab eo qui inquisitionem petit* de vita vel membris, set gratis concedatur et non negetur.

27 (37). Si aliquis teneat de nobis per feodifirmam vel soccagium, vel per burgagium, et de alio terram teneat per servicium militare, nos non habebimus custodiam heredis nec terre sue que est de feodo alterius, occasione illius feodifirme, vel soccagii, vel burgagii, nec habebimus custodiam illius feodifirme vel soccagii vel burgagii, nisi ipsa feodifirma debeat servicium militare. Nos non habebimus custodiam heredis *nec* terre alicujus quam tenet de alio per servicium militare, occasione alicujus parve serjanterie quam tenet de nobis per servicium reddendi nobis cultellos, vel sagittas, vel hujusmodi.

28 (38). Nullus ballivus ponat decetero aliquem ad legem *manifestam vel ad juramentum* simplici loquela sua, sine testibus fidelibus ad hoc inductis.

29 (39). Nullus liber homo *decetero* capiatur vel imprisonetur aut disseisiatur *de aliquo libero tenemento suo vel libertatibus vel liberis consuetudinibus suis,* aut utlagetur, aut exuletur aut aliquo *alio* modo destruatur, nec super eum ibimus, nec super eum mittemus, nisi per legale judicium parium suorum, vel per legem terre.

(40). Nulli vendemus, nulli negabimus aut differemus rectum vel justiciam.

30 (41). Omnes mercatores, *nisi publice antea prohibiti fuerint,* habeant salvum et securum exire de Anglia, et venire in Angliam, et morari, et ire

per Angliam tam per terram quam per aquam ad emendum *vel* vendendum sine omnibus toltis malis per antiquas et rectas consuetudines, preterquam in tempore gwerre, et si sint de terra contra nos gwerrina; et si tales inveniantur in terra nostra in principio gwerre, attachientur sine dampno corporum vel rerum, donec sciatur a nobis vel *a* capitali justiciario nostro quomodo mercatores terre nostre tractentur, qui tunc invenientur in terra contra nos gwerrina; et, si nostri salvi sint ibi, alii salvi sint in terra nostra.

31 (43). Si quis tenuerit de aliqua escaeta, sicut de honore Wallingefordie, Bolonie, Notingeham, Lancastrie, vel de aliis que sunt in manu nostra, et sint baronie, et obierit, heres ejus non det aliud relevium nec fiat nobis aliud servicium quam faceret baroni, si *ipsa* esset in manu baronis; et nos eodem modo eam tenebimus quo baro eam tenuit, *nec nos, occasione talis baronie vel escaete, habebimus aliquam escaetam vel custodiam aliquorum hominum nostrorum, nisi alibi tenuerit de nobis in capite ille qui tenuit baroniam vel escaetam.*

32. *Nullus liber homo decetero det amplius alicui vel vendat de terra sua quam ut de residuo terre sue possit sufficienter fieri domino feodi servicium ei debitum quod pertinet ad feodum illud.*

33 (46). Omnes *patroni abbatiarum* qui habent cartas regum Anglie *de advocatione,* vel antiquam tenuram *vel possessionem,* habeant earum custodiam cum vacaverint, sicut habere debent, *et sicut supra declaratum est.*

34 (54). Nullus capiatur vel imprisonetur propter appellum femine de morte alterius quam viri sui.

35. *Nullus comitatus decetero teneatur, nisi de mense in mensem; et, ubi major terminus esse solebat, major sit. Nec aliquis vicecomes vel ballivus faciat turnum suum per hundredum nisi bis in anno et non nisi in loco debito et consueto, videlicet semel post Pascha et iterum post festum sancti Michaelis. Et visus de franco plegio tunc fiat ad illum terminum sancti Michalis sine occasione, ita scilicet quod quilibet habeat libertates suas quas habuit et habere consuevit tempore regis Henrici avi nostri, vel quas postea perquisivit. Fiat autem visus de franco plegio sic, videlicet quod pax nostra teneatur, et quod tethinga integra sit sicut esse consuevit, et quod vicecomes non querat occasiones, et quod contentus sit eo quod vicecomes habere consuevit de visu suo faciendo tempore regis Henrici avi nostri.*

36. *Non liceat alicui decetero dare terram suam alicui domui religiose, ita quod eam resumat tenendam de eadem domo, nec liceat alicui domui religiose terram alicujus sic accipere quod tradat illam ei a quo ipsam recepit tenendam. Si quis autem de cetero terram suam alicui domui religiose sic dederit, et super hoc convincatur, donum suum penitus cassetur, et terra illa domino suo illius feodi incurratur.*

37. *Scutagium decetero capiatur 'sicut capi solebat tempore regis Henrici avi nostri. Et salve sint archiepiscopis, episcopis, abbatibus, prioribus, templariis, hospitalariis, comitibus, baronibus et omnibus aliis tam ecclesiasticis quam secularibus personis libertates et libere consuetudines quas prius habuerunt.*

(60). Omnes autem istas consuetudines predictas et libertates quas concessimus in regno nostro tenendas quantum ad nos pertinet erga nostros, omnes de regno nostro tam clerici quam laici observent quantum ad se pertinet erga suos. *Pro hac autem concessione et donatione libertatum istarum et aliarum libertatum contentarum in carta nostra de libertatibus foreste, archiepiscopi, episcopi, abbates, priores, comites, barones, milites, libere tenentes, et omnes de regno nostro dederunt nobis quintam decimam partem omnium mobilium suorum. Concessimus etiam eisdem pro nobis et heredibus nostris quod nec nos nec heredes nostri aliquid perquiremus per quod libertates in hac carta contente infringantur vel infirmentur; et, si de aliquo aliquid contra hoc perquisitum fuerit, nichil valeat et pro nullo habeatur.*

His testibus domino Stephano Cantuariensi archiepiscopo, Eustachio Lundoniensi, Jocelino Bathoniensi, Petro Wintoniensi, Hugoni Lincolniensi, Ricardo Sarrisberiensi, Benedicto Roffensi, Willelmo Wigorniensi, Johanne Eliensi, Hugone Herefordiensi, Radulpho Cicestriensi, Willelmo Exoniensi episcopis, abbate sancti Albani, abbate sancti Edmundi, abbate de Bello, abbate sancti Augustini Cantuariensis, abbate de Eveshamia, abbate de Westmonasterio, abbate de Burgo sancti Petri, abbate Radingensi, abbate Abbendoniensi, abbate de Maumeburia, abbate de Winchecomba, abbate de Hida, abbate de Certeseia, abbate de Sireburnia, abbate de Cerne, abbate de Abbotebiria, abbate de Middletonia, abbate de Seleby, abbate de Wyteby, abbate de Cirencestria, Huberto de Burgo justiciario, Ranulfo comite Cestrie et Lincolnie, Willelmo comite Sarrisberie, Willelmo comite Warennie, Gilberto de Clara comite Gloucestrie et Hertfordie, Willelmo de Ferrariis comite Derbeie, Willelmo de Mandevilla comite Essexie, Hugone Le Bigod comite Norfolcie, Willelmo comite Aubemarle, Hunfrido comite Herefordie, Johanne constabulario Cestrie, Roberto de Ros, Roberto filio Walteri, Roberto de Veteri ponte, Willielmo Brigwerre, Ricardo de Munfichet, Petro filio Herberti, Matheo filio Herberti, Willielmo de Albiniaco, Roberto Gresley, Reginaldo de Brahus, Johanne de Munemutha, Johanne filio Alani, Hugone de Mortuomari, Waltero de Bellocampo, Willielmo de sancto Johanne, Petro de Malalacu, Briano de Insula, Thoma de Muletonia, Ricardo de Argentein., Gaufrido de Nevilla, Willielmo Mauduit, Johanne de Baalun.

Datum apud Westmonasterium undecimo die februarii anno regni nostri nono.

2. Comparison of Texts of 1215 and 1225[2]

The final revision of 1225,[3] the definitive text of the Great Charter, resembled that of 1215 in its legal form; in the predominance of feudal liberties among its provisions; in its injunction that barons, lay and ecclesiastical, observe toward their feudal dependents the rights granted them by the king;

---

[2] See above, pp. 4–6.

[3] The revision of 1225 differs but slightly from that of 1217. For comparison of changes in successive issues, see McKechnie, pp. 139–55; *Select Charters*, pp. 335–39, 349–51; Bémont, *Chartes*, pp. xxvi–xxx; Norgate, *The Minority of Henry III*, pp. 10–15, 78–81.

One subsequent change is noted by McKechnie: the relief of a barony reduced from 100 pounds to 100 marks. "The date of this change, if we may rely on Madox, lies between the twenty-first and thirty-fifth years of Edward I." P. 198.

in granting the liberties in perpetuity. Although the text of the revisions gives evidence of more careful consideration and greater precision of language, lack of any logical grouping or arrangement is as marked as in the original grant.

The text of 1225 differed from all previous issues in the following particulars. It contained the clause *spontanea et bona voluntate nostra, dedimus et concessimus*. It recognized the grant of the fifteenth paid for the reissue of the liberties. It reserved to archbishops, bishops, abbots, priors, templars, hospitallers, earls, barons, and all other persons, ecclesiastical as well as secular, the liberties and free customs which they had formerly enjoyed. The binding force of the grant in perpetuity was now strengthened by the declaration that any policy or enactment contrary to the terms of the Charter was to be held invalid. Here in the text of the document itself was suggested the conception of the Great Charter as a sort of fundamental law, a conception to be strengthened in succeeding years and to be emphasized in the confirmations of 1253 and 1297.

3. Notes on the Forest Charter[4]

The character and history of the royal forests in England have been well treated, in brief by McKechnie and in detail by Turner and Petit-Dutaillis.[5] In my *First Century of Magna Carta* (Chapter VI) I emphasized the close connection between the Great Charter and the Charter of the Forest. Originally an offshoot of the greater document—an expansion of chapters 44, 47, and 48 of John's text—the Forest Charter was constantly associated with it. The two were confirmed together. Orders for publication and enforcement, sentences of excommunication, the "buying" of the liberties at a price applied to both. All this continued to be true for a time in the fourteenth century. All that will be done here is to indicate briefly the character of this interest and how long it persisted.

Chapter 1 offered great expectations—the disafforestment of certain districts, a hope long deferred by royal reluctance. Other chapters (2–17) were of immediate practical value in checking abuses of officials within the areas permanently royal preserves. "It was principally the struggle for disafforestment which connected the history of the Forest with the history of the English constitution." (Petit-Dutaillis, p. 210.) The struggle over disafforestment was still keen in the reign of Edward I. It was only at the Lincoln parliament, January 1301, that the king was finally forced by the barons to confirm the results of recent perambulations. On February 14 letters were issued authorizing the disafforestments, but it was these concessions from which Edward was released by papal bull in 1305. The *Ordinatio Forestae* (May 27, 1306) undid the work of 1301. In the reign of Edward II, especially in the years when the barons dominated the government, disafforestment proceeded on the lines laid down by the Charter and by the perambulations of the preceding reign. The

---

[4] See above, pp. 4–6.

[5] McKechnie, pp. 414–31, 435–40, and for the text of the Forest Charter, pp. 508–12. G. J. Turner, *Introduction to Select Pleas of the Forest* (S. S.). Petit-Dutaillis, *Studies*, Vol. II, chaps. 6, 7, and 8.

settlement was completed and confirmed by statute in the first year of Edward III, and that king "failed in all attempts to escape from its provisions." (McKechnie, p. 438 and note 2.)

"We think, therefore, that if a precise date is to be assigned to the end of the long struggle for disafforestment, it is not the reign of Edward II, but the beginning of the reign of Edward III that must be chosen. In later times, notably in 1347 and during the first years of the reign of Richard II, the commons are found complaining because the royal officers 'of their malice have afforested, and strive from day to day to afforest, what had been disafforested,' and the king replies that he wishes the Charter to be respected. Officially, as the records of these incidents prove, the dispute was settled." (Petit-Dutaillis, p. 232.) In some of these instances, however, the petitioners complain of the violation of local district charters—it is only the official reply which confirms the Forest Charter. In the 1370's we find protests that forest officials prosecute those who hunt beasts that have wandered into the *purlieu* (districts adjacent to the forest, and disafforested regions). "In 1372, 1376 and 1377 parliament protested and demanded 'that every man might hunt in the purlieu without hindrance.' The king each time replied that the Charter of the Forest should be observed, an answer which meant nothing, since the charter made no provision for such cases." (*Ibid.*, pp. 236–37.)

McKechnie dismisses the further history of the forest boundaries in a few sentences. "No changes were made until the sixteenth century. When Henry VIII afforested the districts surrounding Hampton Court in 1540, he did so by consent of Parliament, and on condition of compensating all who suffered damage. The same course was followed by Charles I in creating the Forest of Richmond in 1634. Finally, as a result of attempts of the Stewarts to revive obsolete rights, a statute of the Long Parliament, reciting the Act of 1327, 'ordained that the old perambulation of the forest in the time of King Edward the First should be thenceforth holden in like form as it was then ridden and bounded.'"

The Forest law continued in force throughout the fourteenth century. The administrative machinery remained about the same. The king's writs still referred to the assize of the Forest and to the Charter of 1217. Offenses against the assize continued to be punished but with diminished severity. At his accession Edward III "gave permission to landowners to take from their woods within the Forest whatever they needed for their houses or fences." General inquisitions took the place of the inquisition by, and the fining of, the four nearest townships. Trespasses against vert and venison were leniently treated by the king. To complaints the king replies that he means to observe the Forest Charter. M. Petit-Dutaillis cites a number of examples of such complaints against Forest officials, ranging in time from 1325 to 1381, but concludes that nevertheless in the fourteenth century "the Forest was no longer one of the chief grievances of the nation." He considers it significant that the peasants in their rising of 1381 "demanded the abolition of hunting privileges but not the abolition of prosecutions for assart, purpresture, and waste, though these were an essential feature of the forest code in England."

Both before and after the revolt, poaching was on the increase. Edward III had hardly sailed for France at the beginning of the Hundred Years War when "a general attack was made on the game in the forests, parks, and chases belonging to the crown." As time went on, king, barons, and other wealthy landowners with chases and warrens combined in defending their privileges against peasants, artisans, and the lower clergy. Complaints of landowners in the parliament of 1390 were answered by a statute limiting the right to hunt to those with landed property worth forty shillings a year and to clerks with an income of ten pounds and over. In 1417 while Henry V was busy in Normandy "parliament complained that armed bands laid waste the chases of lords, beating and wounding the keepers. During the wars of the Roses, disguised and masked brigands stole deer and committed murders in forests and game preserves."

APPENDIX B

The Early Manuscript Volumes of Statutes[6]

For a description and list of the early manuscript volumes of statutes as given by the Record Commissioners, see *S. R.* I, xxxviii–xxxix, and their Appendix C, especially pp. lxi–lxii, "Books and Manuscripts not of Record." These lists, however, do not distinguish between volumes containing Magna Carta and the other *antiqua statuta* (before Edward III) and those containing only the *nova statuta* (Edward III to Henry VII). The collections noted are in Lincoln's Inn Library, Inner Temple Library, the Bodleian, University and some college libraries of Cambridge, Lambeth, and especially the Cottonian, Harleian, Royal, Donative, and Lansdowne manuscripts in the British Museum. Bémont, *Chartes,* p. lxx, comments on these "recueils manuscrits des statuts qui ont été si souvent copiés au xiv et au xve siecle, et dont les exemplaires abondent aujourd'hui encore dans les biblioteques anglaises, sans oublier celles du continent."

While no attempt has been made to examine them all, enough has been done to warrant conclusions as to their character and variety. The description above in the text (Chapter II) and the following are based on selections from the British Museum collections, as follows: Harleian MSS 79, 395, 408, 409, 489, 493, 867, 1317, 1335, 1807, 3817, 3818, 3819, 3937, 3942, 3994, 4975, 5022, 5430, 6644; Lansdowne MSS 471, 475, 652, 1174.

The following types may serve by way of illustration. Lansdowne 1174 is an elegant little volume in a fourteenth-century hand, neatly written on vellum. Initial letters are ornamented with figures, and some pages with grotesques. The Great Charter, the *inspeximus* of 25 Edward I, is divided into chapters numbered to twenty-two by the original copyist and continued to forty-one in

[6] See above, pp. 5 and 39.

a later hand. Harleian 867 is a rather large, thick quarto nicely written on vellum, with red and blue capital letters and an illuminated first capital for each statute, from Henry III to Richard II, some ninety-three items in all. Here the Charter is divided into thirty-seven (though not quite the modern thirty-seven) chapters, numbered in the margin, and introduced in the text by a red or blue capital letter. The compiler gives marginal cross-references from Magna Carta to related statutes, and vice versa.[7] Harleian 395 and 408 include a table of the chapters of the Charter and some other statutes.[8] Harleian 1807, a thick quarto in a fifteenth-century hand (Henry V or later) contains such substantial items as the *Old Tenures, Curia Baronis,* and *Natura Brevium,* as well as the *antiqua statuta,* with a table only of the *nova statuta.* Again anticipating a feature of the later printed editions, there is an alphabetical table of matters, citing under each the appropriate chapters of statutes in chronological order. Thirty-six chapters of Magna Carta are thus listed under one title or another, but the job is rather carelessly done.[9]

Harleian 1317[10] (late fifteenth century) anticipates the sixteenth-century printed abridgments. Short summaries of the chapters of statutes are distributed under the appropriate alphabetical titles. Sixteen chapters of Magna Carta are thus dealt with under thirteen titles.[11] A few short chapters are quoted verbatim in Latin; others, long and short, are paraphrased in law French.[12] This treatment seems to be the final step in the process by which the legal profession had reduced the Charter to a "mere statute," indeed fragmentized it into many separate enactments as of 9 Henry III.

[7] For instance, from Magna Carta ca. 4 (wardship) to Gloucester, ca. 6, West. I, ca. 23, West. II, cas. 25 and 32, 14 Ed. III, cas. 15 and 16; from Gloucester, ca. 6 to Magna Carta ca. 4; from Merton, ca. 1 to Magna Carta ca. 7. Such cross-references follow some 13 chapters of the Charter, with references back to the Charter from 22 chapters of later statutes.

[8] *Harl.* 395: Incipiunt Capitula magne carte de Libertatibus Angliae. Cap. i. De libertatibus ecclesie et Regni. Cap. ii. De releviis capiendis. Cap. viii. De libertatibus Civitatum. Cap. xiii. De amerciamentis capiendis. Cap. xxvi. Quod iusticia non negatur.

[9] For instance:

Comen plees   Magna Carta ca. xi
Dower   Magna Carta ca. vii
Libertas et Jura Ecclesie Magna carta ca. primo
Libertates et consuetudines Civitatum Burgorum et villarum Magna carta ca. ix
Merchauntz aliens c xxvii
Ne iniuste vexes Magna Carta cap. x
Precipe in Capite Magna Carta cap. xxii

[10] The catalogue calls this "An Old Book written on Paper in very large 4to" and part I "An Abridgment of our Statute Laws, since Magna Carta, to the latter end of the Reign of Henry VI., reduced under proper heads and these entered in alphabetical order."

[11] The chapters are 2, 4 (5 used, though not listed), 11, 13, 17, 20, 22, 24, 25, 27, 28, 29, 30, 31, 35 (I substitute modern numbers here); under *Exchequer* the chapters of the *Articuli super cartas* forbidding the holding of common pleas in the Exchequer, and under *Forest* a number of clauses of the Forest Charter. The headings are: *Comen plees, Darreyn presentment, Droit, Eschete, Garde, Ley, Mesures, Marque, Purveours, Piers de Realm, Relief, Tourne de Vic., Waste.*

[12] "Breve quod vocatur precipe in capite de cetero non fiat alicui de libero tenemento unde liber homo perdat Curiam suam tc."

"Nullus liber homo capiatur aut imprisonetur nec super eum ibimus nisi per legale iudicium parium suorum tc."

"Comen plees serront tenne in certen lieu tc."

"Assise de Darreyn presentement soit toutz foitz prise en Banke."

APPENDIX C

Sources of Chapter II

For the reign of Edward I several cases in which the Charter is cited appear in the brief printed *Placitorum Abbreviatio*. These are discussed in my *First Century of Magna Carta*. These and others, an impressive number, are to be found in the recent *Select Cases in the Court of King's Bench*, edited by Sayles (Selden Society, vols. 55, 57, 58). For the latter part of the reign, cases citing Magna Carta cas. 7, 11, 12, 29, and 34 are in vol. 57, pp. 67–68, 11–12, 58–59, 94, and 24–25 respectively; cas. 7 and 29, 11, 27 (?), and 34 in vol. 58, pp. 90–91, 20–21, 73, 114, 218, and 148 respectively. Some are described above.

The examination of three centuries of manuscript plea rolls would have been an impossible task. It would be the kind of thing that groups or indeed generations of researchers might do on the side while engaged in editing or examining the rolls for other purposes. With the aid of a competent research assistant a generous sampling of the *coram rege* rolls was made — some 80 rolls in the reign of Edward II and early reign of Edward III. The instances in which Magna Carta was cited or quoted were so few as to discourage further search.

It is interesting evidence of the prevailing conception that the Great Charter was concerned with *public* law that fellow researchers advised me to consult the *coram rege* rolls rather than the *de banco* rolls, and to consult the *rex* portion of the former only. Their assumption was that only where the king's interests were involved, and royal encroachments or acts of injustice were to be corrected would the Charter be invoked. As a matter of fact the *justice* part of the *coram rege* rolls and the *de banco* rolls proved more fruitful. Here in pleas between party and party are cited chapters of the Charter like any other parts of the private common law.

I examined only one of the *de banco* rolls, roll 255, H. 18 Edward II. A valuable supplement, however, are the recent volumes of the Year Books (Selden Society) in which the editor supplies the corresponding record from the roll whenever it can be identified. No doubt examination of the manuscript rolls would yield additional examples of "actions on the statute."

Miss Neilson (introduction to Year Book 10 Edward IV) speaks of the great bulk of the fifteenth-century plea rolls, 4000 cases for Easter term 1470, and nearly 6000 in the roll for the following year, though it is hard to distinguish between litigants appearing for the first time and later stages of cases. Many entries are mere brief recordings of the appearance of the plaintiff or his attorney, the failure of the defendant to come, and further instructions to the sheriff. In the trespass cases of the *coram rege* rolls I was impressed with the oft-repeated *non est inventus*, which runs through the membranes like a refrain!

Miss Neilson comes to the conclusion that "the Year Book reports hardly touch the surface of the great mine of material contained in the roll, that cases of much intrinsic interest and historic importance are passed over in silence."

However, for the purpose of these studies the Year Books were chosen as most worthy of careful examination. While omitting much routine data and often neglecting to record the judgment, the reporters do include the pleadings, arguments on points of law, advice and *obiter dicta* of the justices. I have used the printed Year Books only, preferably, of course, the excellent texts of the Selden Society; for the many years which these do not yet cover, the older Rolls Series edition, and for the later Middle Ages the black-letter editions of Tottell, and in some instances, the seventeenth-century *Les Reports des Cases*.

Naturally the black-letter Year Books are looked at askance by the able editors of the Selden Society past and present, but in spite of the corruptions of text, they are reasonably satisfactory for the limited purposes of this study. They have recently been used extensively by Professor Chrimes without arousing adverse criticism. After all, it was these very volumes of Tottell's which the Tudor and Stuart lawyers used, and which contributed to *their* conception of Magna Carta.

I have examined the Year Books in the Selden Society and Rolls Series editions; for the later Middle Ages, pretty completely through 20 Henry VI; then selected years from this and succeeding reigns (Edward IV to Henry VIII).

Statham's *Abridgement* and Fitzherbert's *Grand Abridgement* were standbys of the lawyers in the Tudor and early Stuart periods, but abridgment meant omission of much of the pleading. Under the more promising of Fitzherbert's titles, I have found a few Magna Carta citations. Further search might reveal others. The following may serve as examples.

Title *Accion sur lestatut*. M. 10 Ed. II, no. 34. "Un briefe fuit port vs. le bailiff de L'evesque de W. foundu sur lestatut de Magna Carta de moderata misericordia."

Title *Droite*. P. 6 Ed. III, no. 15. "Briefe de droit precipe in capite vers Thomas del maner de F. . . . Scott dit que xx acres de mesne le maner sont tenus d'un William qe est icy et diomus que le graund Charte voit que precipe in capite ne serra graunte dount franke home pardra son courte et nous vous maundomus quod si Ita vobis constare poterit secundum legem et consuetudinem. Parnyng. Le graunde Charte voit."

Also under titles *Error* (M. 14 Ed. III, no. 6, chapter 11) and *Prerogative* (H. 5 Ed. III, no. 4, chapter 31).

APPENDIX D

1. Actions Founded on the Statute: *Brevia de Statuto*[13]

The *Old Natura Brevium* indicates that *ne iniuste vexes* and *de moderata misericordia* are based on Magna Carta; the author also connects the Charter with the writs of *admeasurement of dower, waste, ravishment of ward, escheat, novel disseisin,* and *writ of right, precipe in capite.*

The following writs, according to the Register, are "founded on Magna

13 See above, p. 43.

Carta," and in the 1553 and later editions are grouped under the caption
Brevia de statuto:

Ne iniuste vexes. Et est done per Magnam cartam cap. x come il semble.

De plegiis acquietandis in comitatu, Magna carta, ca. viii — Aliter de acquie-tando plegio quia principalis debitor sufficit, Magna Carta, ca. viii.

Quod communia placita non teneantur in scaccario, Magna carta, ca. xi. Articuli super cartas ca. iiii, Statutum de Roteland, ca. ultimo.

Quod mulieres habeant rationabiles partes suas de bonis virorum suorum. Regula. In quibusdam brevibus breve istud fundatur super Magnam cartam, sed non valet pur ceo que forpris de statute nest pas statuit.

The following have some connection with the Charter indicated in the *regula* following the writ:

De recto de advocatione et assisa ultimae presentationis. Nota quod datur per magnam cartam ca. xii, quod assise ultime presentationis et quare impedit semper capiantur coram iusticiariis de banco et ibi terminentur et non debent indorsari per magistrum nec aliter.

De eiectione custodie prioratus . . .

De Odio et Atia . . .

.2. Examples of Actions Founded on the Statute, as Described by Fitzherbert

"The Writ of Quarentina habenda lieth where a Man dieth seised of any Messuage and Lands, &c and immediately after the Death of the Husband, the Heir or he who ought to have the Lands after his Death, will put the Wife out of the Messuage, &c. Then the Wife shall have this Writ; for by the Statute of *Magna Charta*, ca. 7 the Wife shall remain in the capital Messuage after the Death of her Husband by forty Days, if it be not a Castle; and that Writ is Vicontiel, and shall be directed unto the Sheriff, and he shall hold Plea thereof; and the Writ is such:

"*Rex. Vic' &c vel ballivis suis S. salutem. Ex querel' B. que fuit uxor D. accepimus, quod cum in Magna Charta de libertatibus Angl' contineatur, quod vidua maneant in capitali Messuag' maritorum suorum I. de C. ipsam B. statim post mortem praed' viri sui de capitali Messu' quod fuit ejusdem D. in H. licet castrum non sit, nec dos ei assign' fuer', violenter ejecit & ipsam estoverium suum de bonis eorund' com' percipere non permitt', in ipsius B. damnum non modic' & gravamen, & contra tenorem Chartae predict. . . .*

"And upon that Writ the Sheriff shall award Process against the Party to come, and answer the same, and shall not stay until the County-Court be holden; for this Writ is a Commission unto him, and upon the Same he shall immediately make Process against the Party, for to answer &c. in two or three Days, according to his Discretion, and thereupon to proceed as justices shall do upon a commission of oyer and terminer, &c."

"The writ of moderata misericordia lieth in case where a man is amerced in a court baron, or other court which is not a court of record, outragiously for trespass or other offence; then he may sue this writ directed unto the lord of the court or unto his bailiffs, commanding them, that they moderately amerce the party according to the quantity of the trespass, &c. And this writ is founded upon the statute of magna charta, cap. 14 Quod nullus liber homo amercietur nisi secundum quantitatem delicti, &c. And the process upon this writ is alias and pluries, and attachment, and the attachment shall be awarded against him against whom the original writ was sued; and the form of the writ is such:

"The king to the bailiff of I. of S. greeting: C. hath shewed unto us, that whereas he was lately amerced in the court of your aforesaid lord of I. for a small fault into which he fell; you require from him a grievous ransom contrary to the tenor of the great charter of the liberties of England, wherein it is contained that no freeman shall be amerced but according to the greatness of his fault, and this saving to him his contenement, and saving to villains their wainage; And therefore we command you, that you take a moderate amercement from the said C. according to the measure of his fault, that no repeated clamour thereupon may come to us, Witness &c."

The extent to which the plea rolls were being used in "search of records" is illustrated by the following odd entry in the Close Rolls for 39 Henry VI:

"To the chief clerk of the Common Bench, otherwise called keeper of writs there, or to his deputy. Order, at his peril, upon petition of the prior and convent of St. Bartholomew in 'Westsmythfeld,' London of the foundation of the king's forefathers and of his patronage, as he would avoid the king's displeasure and will answer for it, to put off delay and remove out of the priory to the Tower of London, or some other place convenient to put them, the chests and records hereinafter mentioned; as the petition shews that aginst their will and the will of their predecessors their church is much encumbered with divers great chests containing records of the said Bench, to the disturbance of those ministering divine service by searches of the records at inconvenient times, and of the convent in their religion, in procession and otherwise, the disfigurement of the church and the chapels therein, and to perils unknown, praying their discharge from custody of the same. By K." (*Cal. Close Rolls*, 1454–61, p. 468.)

APPENDIX E

Judicium Parium in the Later Middle Ages[14]

1398. In the Shrewsbury parliament, Thomas Despenser, newly created Earl of Gloucester, secured the reversal of the judgments against his ancestors, Edward II's favorites. Although Thomas' petition enumerates some of the errors alleged by them in 1322, it cites the Charter only indirectly by quoting their petition. More in keeping with the Shrewsbury parliament and its despotic master, the Earl plays up the idea that the judgment of 1321 was the work of the barons not the king, in prejudice to the royal power: "*et a cause qe la*

---

[14] See above, p. 85.

dite Agarde feust fait soulement par les Contes, Barons, Piers du Roialme, &
nient par vostre dit tres noble besaiel, quel feust emblemissement & prejudice
de sa Corone & de sa Dignitee Roiale, & de ses heires Roys d' Engleterre."
(*Rot. Parl.* III, 360–61, no. 55.)

1405. As to Mowbray, Vernon-Harcourt argues that both he and Scrope had
lawful trial, not in parliament, but with some peers present. He rejects the
popular contemporary view (which Oman adopts). "That Gascoigne was told
as chief justice to try and sentence Scrope and that he very properly declined
to do so, and thereupon Scrope was subjected to a mock trial by a few laymen, is
a complete travesty of the facts." Tait (*Scrope*, in the *D.N.B.*) shows that Henry
V appointed a commission composed of Chief Justice Gascoigne, the Earl of
Arundel, and five other peers, Arundel and Beaufort to act as deputies for
the absent constable and marshal. Actually the prisoners were brought before
Fulthorpe ("learned in the law," though not a judge), Arundel, Beaufort, and
Sir Ralph Euer. "Fulthorpe at once declared them guilty of treason, and by
the royal order sentenced them to death." Early in the morning on this very
day, June 8, Archbishop Arundel arrived on the scene, as Tait puts it, "to
deprecate any summary treatment of a great prelate of the church." Henry
misled him into believing that no action would be taken without his concurrence, but while the king and his distinguished guest breakfasted, judgment
and sentence were imposed.

1415. Henry, Lord Scrope, nephew of the archbishop, Richard of York, and
the Earl of Cambridge were arraigned before commissioners for high treason
in plotting against Henry V. Lord Scrope claimed his privilege as a peer:
"*Et cum hoc dicit, quod ipse est Dominus & unius Parium Regni Anglie, &*
petit quod ipse per Pares suos Regni Anglie, prout moris est, trietur & judice-
tur." (*Rot. Parl.* IV, 66.) The king then appointed his brother Thomas, Duke
of Clarence, to summon some peers and to pronounce judgment *per vestrum*
eorundem parium communem assensum. (For the above and the following, see
the accounts in Vernon-Harcourt, pp. 372–85.)

1450. Lord Say (James Fiennes, Lord Say and Sele) claimed his peerage, but
to no avail. "Than upon the morne, being the third daye of July and Frydaye,
the sayd capitayne entered agayne the cytie, and causyd the lorde Saye to be
fette from the Tower and ladde unto the Guyldhall, where he was arreygned
before the mayre and other of the kynges justyces . . . Then the lorde Saye
. . . desyred that he myghte be juged by his pyers. Wherof herynge, the
capitayne sent a company of his unto the halle, the whiche perforce toke hym
from his offycers, and so brought hym into the standarde in Chepe, where, or
he were halfe shryven they strake of his hede." (Fabyan, p. 624. Cf. *Chronicles*
of London, p. 161—"desired to be demyd by his perys." See *Fiennes* in the
D.N.B.)

1450. The Duke of Suffolk, when impeached, waived his right to trial by
peers, and "submitted wholly to the king's rule and governance." On his second appearance before the king and lords the chancellor reminded him of the
charges, "and how, at that time ye put you not upon your peerage." (*Rot.*
Parl. V, 182–83.) "The indictment against the duchess appears to have been

removed into parliament in due course. The peers tried and acquitted her."
"In eodem parliamento ducissa Suffolciae acquietata est per pares suos."

1441. The statute extending trial by peers to peeresses as a result of the famous case of Eleanor, Duchess of Gloucester, quotes Magna Carta: *"Item come contenue soit en la graunde chartre entre autres en la fourme qensuyt: Nullus liber homo . . . En quele estatuit nest mencion fait coment femmes Dames de grande estate . . . qe quelle il est ambiguite & doute en la ley . . ."* (20 Hen. VI, ca. 9; *S. R.* II, 321–22.)

APPENDIX F

Matthew Paris' Text of Magna Carta[15]

Matthew Paris' chronicle, whether used in manuscript or in the first printed edition (Parker's), must have been responsible for the misconceptions which scholars in the reigns of Elizabeth and James entertained—that is, that the text of Henry III's charter (1225) and that of John's were identical. As McKechnie reminds us, "Much of the blame must be borne by Roger of Wendover, who, in his account of the transactions at Runnymede, incorporated in place of John's Charter, the text of the two charters granted by Henry." Actually then, as a result, Wendover's statement appears true: *"Istarum autem chartarum superius habetur expressius, ubi historia agitur de rege Johanne; ita quod cartae utrorumque regum in nulle inveniuntur dissimiles."*

Matthew Paris repeats verbatim Wendover's statement as to the identity of the texts, but the version which he gives is not the same. It is a strange hybrid, whether of his own composition, or something he found in the archives at St. Albans. Here Luard's description is good as far as it goes. "The copy of Magna Charta as given by Paris is nominally John's; it bears John's salutation at the beginning, and is given under his reign in the year 1215; moreover the names at the beginning are those which are given in John's charter. But in the charter itself will be found all the additions peculiar to the charters of the 2nd and 9th years of Henry III. At the same time it contains many of the passages peculiar to John's Charter (not of course the forest clauses) which were omitted in those of Henry III." Not only are the forest clauses omitted, but all those of a temporary nature (relating to John's mercenaries, hostages, etc.). It looks as if the compiler of this hybrid was trying to hold fast to anything of constructive value in either text!

These chroniclers were also responsible for the belief that a separate Forest Charter was issued in 1215. As Luard points out: "John issued no forest charter. Wendover (and Paris after him), having omitted the forest clauses in the great charter, has inserted this from the copy at St. Albans, and put John's name instead of Henry's at the beginning; though immediately below he is made to call Henry II his grandfather, this being left unaltered."

Luard hardly gives the correct idea of Wendover's text when he calls it "a

15 See above. p. 161.

charter made up in the same way from those of John and Henry III." For
the texts of the Charters, Roger of Wendover, II, 119–27 (R. S.); Matthew
Paris, II, 589–98; and for Luard's comments *ibid.*, II, xxxiii–xxxv, and III,
598–99, n. 4 (R. S.).

APPENDIX G

Extracts from the "Treatisours" [16]

THESE PASSAGES FROM DOCTOR COSIN'S APOLOGIE ILLUSTRATE HIS LINE OF
ARGUMENT AND "HISTORICAL METHOD."

"They are pretended both by the *Treatiser* and the *Note-gatherer* to be
grounded upon these words of *Magna charta*, viz. *No free man shall be taken
or imprisoned, or be disseised of his freehold or liberties, or free customes, or
be outlawed, or exiled, or any otherwise destroyed, nor we shal not passe upon
him nor condemne him, but by lawfull iudgement of his peeres, or by the lawe
of the land.* Whereupon the *Notegatherer* also doeth collect that none may be
attached, but such as be first indited. But the end why this law was made, and
the time when it was made are needfull to be considered. The ende was this,
that the *Kings* of this realme should not chalenge an infinite and absolute
power to themselves (as some kings elsewhere did, & yet do) without iudgement and lawful proceeding, to take away any mans *libertie, life, country,
goods* or *lands.* And it was at time when the kings themselves thought, that
Iurisdiction ecclesiasticall, was not (in right) no more than it was in fact at
that time belonging to the crowne: therefore in that it is here sayd, *Wee will
not passe upon him, nor condemne him, but by lawfull iudgement of his
peeres, or by the lawe of the lande*; it is manifest, that the wordes have no
relation to Iurisdiction ecclesiasticall: for that which was done by that Iurisdiction, was not (at that time) taken to be done by the *King* or by his
authoritie: and the lawes that *ecclesiasticall* Iudges practised were not then
holden to be the *Lawes of the Land,* or the *Kings* lawes; as (since the lawfull
restitution of the ancient right in that behalfe to the crowne) they be often
called The *Kings or the Queenes ecclesiastical lawes. . . .*"

"Furthermore, it is well and notoriously knowen, that proceedings and con-
demnations Ecclesiasticall in ordinarie Courts were never made by *the iudgment of a mans peeres,* viz. by a *Iurie*: and therefore those words, rehearsed,
can not be so farre extended, as to include that iurisdiction."

After discussing institution unto a benefice and deprivation from a benefice,
both before and after Magna Carta, he concludes:

"And this (by the way) may also shew, how unsound a collection the
Notegatherer maketh, out of those words of *Magna Charta*; where, because
a *benefice is a freeholde,* he would inferre that a Clerke may not be deprived of
his *benefice,* but by a iudgement at the *Common* law."

[16] See above, pp. 223, 225, 226.

THIS PASSAGE OF MORICE'S SPEECH, FOLLOWS HIS DENUNCIATION OF THE OATH, AND THE PASSAGE QUOTED IN THE TEXT ON THE GREAT CHARTER. HERE HE IS SETTING FORTH HIS IDEAL OF HIS COUNTRY'S GOVERNMENT.

"Many Reasons there are to stirre us upp to be carefull, earnest, and diligent in this behalfe. Fyrst the Sacred Majestie and Honour of Almighty God, which all good Christians ought at all times to the uttermost of their power Religious-lie to regard and mayntaine. Next the preservation and maintenance of our Estate and Pollicie exquisitlie planted and established in great wisdome. For amonge all sorts and kindes of Government, the Monarchie is preferred as the best, and worthelie as I thinke. Behold with us the Sovereigne Authoritie of one, an absolute Prince, Greate in Majestie, rulinge and reiginge, yet guyded and directed by Principles and precepts of Reason, which wee terme the lawe. No Spartane King or Venetian Duke, but free from accompt and cohercion of anye, eyther equall or Superiour, yet firmelie bound to the Comon wealth by the faithfull Oathe of a Christian Prince, bearinge alone the sharpe sworde of Justice and Correction, yet tempered with mercy and compassion, requiring Tax(e) and Tribute of the people, yet not causeless, nor without common assent.

"Wee agayne the Subjects of this Kingdome are borne and brought upp in due obedience butt farre from Servitude and bondage, subject to lawfull author-itye and commaundement, but freed from licentious will and tyrannie, en-joyinge by lymitts of lawe and Justice oure liefs, lands, goods, and liberties in greate peace and security, this our happy and blessed estate yf wee maie continue the same dearlie purchased in a greate part not manye years paste by our Auncestours, yea even with the effusion of their bloud, and losses of their liefes . . ." (From Mrs. Maguire's transcript.)

AN ACTE CONFIRMINGE A BRANCHE OF MAGNA CHARTA. (MORICE'S BILL?)

"Whereas the bodies of sundrie her Maties subiects without anie suite, or Lawfull proces or Arrest or without sufficient warrant or ordinary and due course and proceedinge in Lawe onlie uppon some sinister and uniust accusa-cion or informacion and by the procurement of some malitious persons have bene committed to prison and ther remaine to their grevous and intollerable vexacion and contrary to the great Charter and auncient good Lawes and statutes of this realme. For remedy whereof be it enacted &c. That the pro-visions and prohibicions of the said great Charter and other Lawes in that behalfe made be dulie and inviolatelie observed. And that no person or persons be hereafter committed to prison but yt be by sufficient warrant and Authoritie and by due course and proceedings in Lawe uppon paine that he or thei that shall so procur anie person to be comitted or imprisoned contrarie to the Lawes aforsaid and the true meaninge of this Acte shall forfeite to the partie so imprisoned his treble damage susteyned by reason of anie suche imprison-ment the said damages to be recovered by action uppon the Case in anie Courte of Record at the common Lawe of this realme wherein no wager of Lawe proteccion or essoyne shalbe admitted or allowed. And that the Justice of anie the Queenes Maties Courts of Recorde at the common Lawe maie

awarde a writt of habeas Corpus for the deliverye of anye person so imprisoned
and yf the keeper of the prison or his deputie shall after notice of such writt
deteyne the bodie of such person so committed he shall forfeit and loose to
the partie so greaved xl li of Lawfull englishe money and shall also answear to
the said partie Treble damages to be recovered by accion uppon the case Bill
pleint or Informaccion in anie of the Queenes Ma^tiea Courtes of Recorde
wherein no essoyne proteccion or wager of Lawe shalbe admitted." (Harl. MS
6847, fols. 64–65.)

APPENDIX H

1. Selden's *Privilege of the Baronage*[17]

THE MEANING OF JUDICIUM PARIUM AND AMERCEMENT BY PEERS, AS MODIFIED
IN PRACTICE.

"That which may be here objected out of the statute of the grand charter,
whereby every man ought to be tried by his peers, *id est, per judicium parium
suorum,* or out of the statute of 25 Ed. III by which all treasons are to be
tried by men of the same condition of which the offender is, may easily be
answered. For both these antient statutes are now to be interpreted, as it is
clearly taken in continual practice, and in the books, according to the known
use of the legal proceedings, and not by literal interpretation of words, as it
is plainly seen in both of them. For all gentlemen, esquires, knights, bachelors
or bannerets, and at this day baronets, are accounted peers, not only amongst
themselves, but to all other men of the lowest condition, which yet cannot be
out of the force of the word only. The like appeareth in that *non amercientur
comites, vel barones, nisi per pares suos,*—as it is shewed in the title of the
amerciaments, wherein that which the statute refers to peers is done solely
by judges. And this of bishops referred to those statutes is only to be judged
according to use and practice, which is the best interpreter of the statutes, and
not by the meer interpretation of the word peers. . . .

"In case of amerciaments of barons of parliaments upon nonsuits, or other
judgments, ending in *misericordia,* there is a special course, both for the sum
and the way of ascertaining of it, which differs from the amerciaments of
common persons.

"For the sum. The amerciaments of an earl, or spiritual or temporal baron
is equal, that is 5 l. of a duke, 10 l. and the sessing of this is by the king's
justices, before whom the action dependeth, the justices in this place supplying
the room of peers, by which according to the grand charter they are to be
amerced, as expressly it is affirmed in the judgment under H. VI against the
earl of Northumberland, where the words of the justices are, *Pur ce que le
conte est un pair de roiaume il sera amercy par ses pairs solonque le statute,
& pur ceo nous ne mettons le mercement en certain.*

"And thence and thus is the statute of the grand charter to be understood,

[17] See above, p. 242.

that saith, *Comites & barones non amercientur, nisi per pares suos.* But continual usage hath thus (as is before is shewed) interpreted that privilege, and so hath the practice been."

2. Coke's Reports: *Nota Lecteur*[18]

In a *replegiare* the *Nota Lecteur* adds an interpretation of the action of *ne iniuste vexes* based on Magna Carta ca. 10, which is quoted to the effect that this action extends only to "true lord and tenant." Another *replegiare* affords opportunity for further interpretation of the same chapter: "by construction" it "extends to right and never to possession." *Davenport's case* affords Sir Edward an opportunity to instruct the reader on the origin of the Court of Common Pleas. This bit of historical digression has nothing to do with the case, but is suggested by one of the Year Book cases cited. The *Poulters case* in which the court upheld an action for conspiracy, leads to a miniature "treatise" on the various safeguards of the common law to protect against false accusation. These include, of course, the old writ *de odio et atia* founded on Magna Carta ca. 26. At this writing Coke was content to accept the authority of the Register and Staunford that the writ was extinguished by 28 Ed. III, ca. 9. In another case involving the fine imposed by a court leet, Magna Carta is cited to prove that excessive amercement is against law. Introduced after a *vide*, it would be hard to tell whether this was part of the case reported, or Coke's addition. (Coke's *Reports*, VIII, 64–65; IX, 33v; VIII, 145v; IX, 55v–57; VI, 42–46; respectively.)

The following may serve as an example: "Nota Lecteur, lessee pur vie ou donnee en taile naver' *Ne iniuste vexes* vs. le doner, car entant que le reservation est le title, nul encrochment serra eux noier', mes ils avoider' ce en avowrie, et lestatut de Magna Charta ca. 10 sur que le breve *Ne iniuste vexes* est foundue, *s. quod nullus distringatur ad faciendum maius servicium de libero tenemento quam inde debetur,* n'extend al donee en taile, lessee pur vie ou grantee de rent charge, que est entend par ceux parols *maius servitium,* que est entend inter veray Seigniour et veray tenant."

APPENDIX I

Ashley's Reading[19]

DIVISIO SECUNDA: EXAMPLES OF "OPPRESSION BY COLOR OF OFFICE"

If a person be imprisoned for lawful cause and then detained by the sheriff after release, that is *"caption et imprisonment prohibit par cel loy."* If a sheriff refuses sufficient bail *sur capias* for one lawfully bailable, that is *"caption et tortious imprisonment."* If a justice of the peace commits to prison an offender who offers sureties to appear and answer, this is *"tortious imprisonment contra cel Statut, contra si soit par Justice en Sessions."* On the other hand a justice of

---

[18] See above, p. 243.
[19] See above, pp. 290, 291.

the peace may, at his discretion, commit a man to prison if he will not find sureties for good abearing, for the law of necessity must refer many particulars to the discretion of the judge, but he may not use unlimited discretion.

Officers of the Greencloth may imprison for resistance to lawful, but not to unlawful purveyance. Imprisonment by a privy councilor of one offending against a patent of monopoly is not lawful. Imprisonment by the lord admiral for detaining the goods of a pirate is against this statute yet frequent in use! Courts which proceed by discretion without limited rules of law can imprison a man until he perform the order of the court. Imprisonment by the privy council for contempt against a proclamation is lawful. A proclamation shall be said to be lawful if it adds force to the execution of the law that was in being before; or if it commands or prohibits anything that is not against any law. But if it is against any law and prohibits that which the law requires or commands that which the law prohibits, it is not lawful.

DIVISIO SEPTIMA: EXAMPLES OF LAWFUL AND UNLAWFUL
TRIAL AND CONDEMNATION.

He condemns the use of the oath *ex officio* by court christian in causes not matrimonial or testamentary, justifies the oath used in Star Chamber, and the oath in Chancery to discover secret matter as in trusts and frauds. Trial by wager of law (*loy gager*) is lawful "passing on a man" in civil causes, though not in criminal. Indictment is lawful as a means to bring the party to answer. To deny the party his reasonable challenges of jurors is "passing upon a man" not *per legem terrae*, for the *venire facias* calls for twelve *liberos et legales homines*. The word *mittemus* extends to the execution as well as to the judgment. If lawful trial be followed by unlawful execution, it is against this statute, for instance, if a sheriff should behead one adjudged to be hung, *et in similibus*. *Peine forte et dure* is justifiable for one who stands mute, as is the procedure used by Chancery and Star Chamber against persons who refuse to answer to a bill or continue obstinate after commitment.

❖ BIBLIOGRAPHY ❖

MANUSCRIPTS

Selections from the following collections. (Specific classifications are indicated in footnotes, *passim*.)

LONDON. British Museum: Cottonian, Harleian, Lansdowne.
       Public Record Office: Ancient Petitions; Charter, Close and Patent Rolls; Plea Rolls; and others.
       Inner Temple Library.
CAMBRIDGE. University Library
OXFORD. Bodleian Library, General Bodleian.

Parliamentary diaries, used in transcript only
For 1624. Anonymous (Gurney MS), Sir Walter Erle, Sir Simon D'Ewes, Sir Thomas Holland, John Holles, Edward Nicholas, Sir Nathaniel Rich, John Pym.
For 1626. Sir Richard Grosvenor, Sir Nathaniel Rich, Sir Bulstrode Whitelocke.
For 1628. Sir Richard Grosvenor, the Massachusetts MS (a copy of "The True Relation"), Edward Nicholas.

COLLECTIONS OF PLEAS, REPORTS, STATE TRIALS,
AND LEGAL TREATISES AND HANDBOOKS

BEALE, ROBERT. *A Collection Shewinge what Jurisdiction the Clergie Hathe Heretofore Lawfully Used.* c. 1590.
The Boke for a Iustice of the Peace. Berthelet, 1534.
BULSTRODE, E. *The Reports of Edward Bulstrode* (cases in King's Bench, 1609–26). 3 parts in 1 vol. London, 1688. 1st ed., 1657–59.
COKE, SIR EDWARD. *Institutes of the Laws of England.* Part I, "Coke on Littleton," 1628. Parts II, III, IV, 1641.
————. *Reports.* Parts I–XI, 1600–15, in French. Cases from the courts of King's Bench, Common Pleas, Exchequer Chamber, Star Chamber, Court of Wards, 1572–1615. Parts XII and XIII in English. 1655, 1658.
COSIN, RICHARD. *An Apologie for Sundrie Proceedings by Iurisdiction Ecclesiastical . . .* 1593.
COWELL, JOHN. *The Interpreter.* 1607.
CROMPTON, RICHARD. *L'Office et Aucthoritie de Iustices de peace . . .* Tottell, 1583.
DYER, JAMES. [Reports.] *Cy ensuont ascuns novel cases, collectes per le iades tres-reverend Iudge, Mounsieur Iasques Dyer, chiefe Iustice del common banke . . .* Tottell, 1585.
FITZHERBERT, ANTHONY. *La Graunde Abridgement.* Tottell, 1565, 1577, etc.
————. *La Nouvelle Natura Brevium.* Tottell, 1553.
————. *The Newe Booke of Iustyces of the Peas, made by Anthony Fitzherbard, Judge, lately translated out of Frenche into Englyshe.* Petyt, 1541.
FORTESCUE, SIR JOHN. *De Laudibus Legum Angliae* (and Hengham) with notes on Fortescue and Hengham by that famous and learned Antiquarie John Selden Esq. London, 1672.
————. *De Laudibus Legum Angliae, a treatise in commendation of the law of England . . .* with translation by Francis Gregor, notes by Andrew Ames, and a life of the author by Thomas (Fortescue) Lord Clermont. 1874. Edited and translated with introduction and notes by S. B. Chrimes. Cambridge University Press, 1942.
————. *The Governance of England.* Ed. Charles Plummer. Oxford, 1885.
HARGRAVE, FRANCIS. *A Collection of Tracts relative to the Law of England.* Dublin, 1787.
HAWARDE, JOHN. *Les Reports del Cases in Camera Stellata, 1593–1609.* Ed. W. P. Baildon of Lincoln's Inn. Privately printed, 1894.
HOWELL, T. B. AND T. J. *Complete Collection of State Trials.* 1809–28.
LAMBARDE, WILLIAM. *Archeion, or A Discourse upon the High Courts of Iustice in England.* London, 1635.
————. *Eirenarcha, or of the Office of the Iustices of Peace.* London, 1582.
————. *A Perambulation of Kent.* London, 1576, 1596, etc.
LEONARD, WILLIAM. *Reports and cases of law: argued and adjudged in the courts at West-*

minster, in the times of the late Queen Elizabeth and King James I. In 4 parts. 4 vols. in 2, 1686–87. 1st eds., 1658, 1659, 1666, 1675.

LITTLETON, THOMAS. *Treatise of Tenures.* Many editions and reprints in English and in French. 1st ed., 1581 or 1582. Others such as: *Les Tenures du Monsieur Littleton,* Tottell, 1569; *Littleton tenures in Englishe Imprinted at London in Fletestrete within Temple Barre, at the signe of the hand and starre,* Tottell, 1568.

Middle Temple Records. Ed. C. H. Hopwood, K. C. 4 vols. London, 1904.

MORE, SIR THOMAS. *Apologye of Syr Thomas More Knyght.* (Early English Text Society.) 1930.

————. *Workes.* London, 1557.

MORICE, JAMES. *A Briefe Treatise of Oathes exacted by Ordinaries and Ecclesiastical Judges . . .* 1598.

Natura Brevium newly and moost trewly corrected. Redman, 1529, 1531.

Natura brevium newly corrected in Englisshe. Redman, 1532.

Placitorum Abbreviatio, Richard I to Edward II. (Record Commission.) 1811.

PLOWDEN, EDMUND. *Les Commentaries ou Reportes de Edmund Plowden un Apprentice de le Common Ley.* 1594, 1599. 1st ed., 1571.

Proceedings before the Justices of the Peace in the Fourteenth and Fifteenth Centuries, Edward III to Richard III. Ed. Bertha H. Putnam. 2 vols. (Ames Foundation.) 1938.

Registrum Omnium Brevium tam originalium quam iudicialium. Rastell, 1531. Tottell, 1553, etc.

Reports of Cases in the Courts of Star Chamber and High Commission. Ed. S. R. Gardiner. (Camden Society.) 1886.

ST. GERMAIN, CHRISTOPHER. *A Treatise concernynge the division betwene the spiritualitie and the temporalitie.* Berthelet, n.d.

————. *The Dialogue in English, betweene a Doctor of Divinitie, and a Student in the Lawes of England.* 1613. 1st extant ed., first dialogue, Latin 1528, English 1531; second dialogue, English 1530.

Select Bills in Eyre, 1292–1333. Ed. W. C. Bolland. (Selden Society.) 1914.

Select Cases before the King's Council, 1243–1482. Ed. I. S. Leadam and J. F. Baldwin. (Selden Society.) 1918

SELDEN, JOHN. *Opera Omnia.* 3 vols. in 6. 1726.

Select Cases in Chancery, 1364–1471. Ed. W. P. Baildon. (Selden Society.) 1896.

Select Cases in Exchequer Chamber before all the Justices of England, 1377–1461. Ed. M. Hemmant. (Selden Society.) 1933.

Select Cases in the Court of King's Bench. Ed. George Sayles. 3 vols. (Selden Society.) 1936, 1938, 1939.

Select Cases in the Court of Requests, 1497–1569. Ed. I. S. Leadam. (Selden Society.) 1898.

Select Cases in the Star Chamber, 1477–1509, 1509–1544. Ed. I. S. Leadam. 2 vols. (Selden Society.) 1902, 1910.

Select Pleas in the Admiralty Court, 1527–1545, 1547–1602. Ed. R. G. Marsden. 2 vols. (Selden Society.) 1892, 1897.

SMITH, SIR THOMAS. *De Republica Anglorum—The Maner of Government or Policie of the Realme of England.* 1584. Published as *The Commonwealthe of England,* London, 1640.

SPELMAN, HENRY. *Archaeologus in modum Glassarii.* Part I, 1626. Pts. I and II, 1664.

STAUNFORD, WILLIAM. *Les Plees del Corone.* London, 1607. 1st ed., Tottell, 1557.

————. *[Prerogativa Regis] An Exposicion of the Kinges Prerogative collected out of the great abridgement of Iustice Fitzherbert and other olde writers of the lawes of Englande . . . whereunto is annexted the Proces to the same Prerogative appertaining.* Tottell, 1567.

Year Books of the Reign of Edward I. Ed. A. J. Horwood and L. O. Pike. (Rolls Series.) 1863–1901.

Year Book Series, Edward II, Henry VI, Edward IV. Various editors. (Selden Society.) 1903–42.

Year Books of Richard II. Various editors. (Ames Foundation.) 1914, 1929, 1937.

Year Books. Early printed editions, Tottell. Late 17th century ed., *Les Reports des Cases,* 11 parts, London, 1678–80.

STATE PAPERS, PARLIAMENTARY RECORDS AND
DIARIES, LETTERS AND MEMOIRS

BIRCH, THOMAS. *Court and Times of James I.* Ed. R. F. Williams. 2 vols. London, 1849.

BOWYER, ROBERT. *The Parliamentary Diary of Robert Bowyer, 1606–1607.* Ed. D. H. Willson. Minneapolis, 1931.

Cabala, Mysteries of State, in Letters of the Great Ministers of King James and King Charles. London, 1654.

COLE, SIR HENRY. *Documents Illustrative of English History Selected from the Records of the Exchequer*. London, 1884.

Commons Debates, 1621. Ed. W. Notestein, F. H. Relf, and H. Simpson. 7 vols. New Haven, 1935.

Commons Debates for 1629. Ed. W. Notestein and F. H. Relf. Minneapolis, 1921.

Calendar of Close Rolls. (1272–1422 and after.) Rolls Series.

Calendar of Patent Rolls. (1232–1374, 1377–1485.) Rolls Series.

Calendar of State Papers, Domestic.

Debates in the House of Commons in 1625. Ed. S. R. Gardiner. (Camden Society.) 1873.

DE GAMACHE, FATHER CYPRIEN. *The Court and Times of Charles I*. 2 vols. London, 1848.

D'EWES, SIR SIMONDS. *The Journal of Sir Simonds D'Ewes from the beginning of the Long Parliament to the opening of the Trial of the Earl of Strafford*. Ed. Wallace Notestein. New Haven, 1923.

————. *The Journals of all the Parliaments during the Reign of Queen Elizabeth*. London, 1682.

ELIOT, SIR JOHN. *Negotium Posterorum*. Ed. A. B. Grosart. 2 vols. London, 1881.

Journals of the House of Commons. Vol. I, 1547–1629.

Journals of the House of Lords. Vol. III.

Letters and Papers . . . of the Reign of Henry VIII. Ed. J. S. Brewer, J. Gairdner, *et al.* London, 1862, etc.

NICHOLAS, EDWARD. *Proceedings and Debates in the House of Commons in 1620 and 1621*. 2 vols. Oxford, 1766.

Notes of the Debates in the House of Lords . . . 1621. Ed. S. R. Gardiner. (Camden Society.) 1870.

Notes of the Debates in the House of Lords . . . 1624 and 1626. Ed. S. R. Gardiner. (Camden Society.) 1879.

Notes of the Debates in the House of Lords . . . 1621, 1625, 1628. Ed. F. H. Relf. (Royal Historical Society.) 1929.

Parliamentary Debates in 1610. Ed. S. R. Gardiner. (Camden Society.) 1862.

The Parliamentary or Constitutional History of England from the Earliest Times to the Restoration of King Charles II. 24 vols. London, 1751–62.

Rotuli Parliamentorum. (1278–1503.) 6 vols. 1832.

Rotuli Parliamentorum Anglie hactenus inedit mcclxxix–mcccxxiii. Ed. H. G. Richardson and George Sayles. (Royal Historical Society.) 1935.

RUSHWORTH, JOHN. *Historical Collections*. 8 vols. London, 1721–22.

RYMER, THOMAS. *Foedera, Conventiones, Litterae, et cujuscunque generis acta publica*. 4th ed. (Record Commission.) 1816–69.

Statutes of the Realm. (Record Commission.) 1810–28.

WHITELOCKE, SIR JAMES. *Liber Famelicus*. Ed. John Bruce. (Camden Society.) 1858.

EARLY PRINTED STATUTES

Antiqua Statuta.

[*Magna Charta*] Pynson, London, 1508, 1514.

Magna Carta in f[olio] whereunto is added more statutz than ever was imprynted in any one boke before this tyme, with an Alminacke & a Calendar to know the mootes. Necessarye for all yong studiers of the lawe. "Printed at London in Flete street by me Robert Redman dwellynge at the synge of the George nexte to Saynt Dunstones Churche." 1529.

Magna Carta cum aliis antiquis statutis, quorum catalogum in fine operis reperies. Berthelet, 1532.

The boke of Magna Carta with divers other statutes whose names appere in the nexte lefe folowynge, translated into Englyshe by George Ferrers. Redman, 1534.

The great Charter called in latyn Magna Carta with divers olde statutes whose titles appere in the nexte leafe newly correctyd. 1540.

Magna Charta cum statutis quae Antiqua vocantur iam recens excusa, & summa fide emendata, iuxta vetusta exemplaria ad Parliamenti rotulos examinata . . . Tottell, 1556, 1576, 1587, etc.

Secunda pars veterum Statutorum. Tottell, 1556.

Statutes at Large and Abridgments

The Great boke of statutes conteyning all the statutes made in the parliamentes from the begynnyng of the fyrst yere of kyng Edward the thyrd tyll the begynnyng of the xxv yere of the moste gracyous reigne of our soueraigne lord kyng Henry the VIII. Redman, c. 1530.

The Whole Volume of Statutes at Large, which at anie time heeretofore have beene extant in print, since Magna Charta, untill the xxix yeere . . . *Elizabeth.* Barker, 1587.

[Rastell's Statutes]. *A colleccion of all the Statutes from the begynning of Magna Carta unto the yere of our Lorde, 1557.* Tottell.

————. *A colleccion in English of the Statutes nowe in force, continued from the beginning of Magna Charta, made in the 9. yeere of the reigne of King H. 3 untill the ende of the Session of Parliament holden in the 23 yeere of the Reigne of our gratious Queen Elizabeth* . . . "Imprinted at London by Christopher Barker, Printer of the Queen's most excellent Maiestie." 1583, 1588, 1591, etc.

An Abridgment of the Statutes in English Enprinted by John Rastell. 1527.

An Abstract of all the Penall Statutes which be generally in force and use . . . "Collected by Fardinando Pulton of Lincolne Inne Gentleman." Tottell, 1577.

ECCLESIASTICAL TREATISES AND TRACTS AND BISHOPS' REGISTERS

CARDWELL, EDWARD, D.D. *Synodalia.* Oxford, 1842.

Concilia Magnae Britanniae et Hiberniae. Ed. David Wilkins. 4 vols. London, 1737.

FOXE, JOHN. *The Actes and Monuments.* Ed. S. R. Cattley. 8 vols. London, 1837–41.

HOOKER, RICHARD. *Ecclesiastical Polity.* Books I–IV with intro. by Ronald Bayne. (Everyman's Library.) 1927.

————. *The Works of that learned and judicious Divine Mr. Richard Hooker.* "With an account of his Life and Death by Isaac Walton." 2 vols. Oxford, 1845.

ISLIP, SIMON. *De Speculo Regis Edwardi III seu tractatu de mala regni administratione conscripsit Simon Islip.* Ed. Joseph Moisant. Paris, 1891.

JOHN DE BURGH. *Pupilla Occuli.* 1514, 1518.

LYNWOOD, WILLIAM. *Constitutions Provincialles, and of Otho and Octhobone.* Redman, 1534.

————. *Provinciale, (seu constitutiones Anglie) continens Constitutiones Provinciales quatuordecim Archiepiscopum Cantuariensium, viz.* . . . . First printed at Oxford, c. 1470–80; then 1496 with Caxton's cipher and Wynkeyn de Word's colophon; reprinted 1499, 1508, 1517, and 1529.

The Marprelate Tracts. Ed. William Pierce. London, 1911.

Puritan Manifestoes. Ed. W. H. Frere and C. E. Douglas. London, 1907.

The Seconde Parte of a Register. Ed. Albert Peel. 2 vols. Cambridge, 1915.

Tracts on Liberty of Conscience and Persecution, 1614–1661. Ed. E. B. Underhill. (Hanserd Knollys Society.) 1846.

BATH AND WELLS. Register of Ralph of Shrewsbury, 1329–63; of Thomas Bekynton, 1443–65. (Somerset Record Society, vols. 9, 10, 49.) 1896, 1934.

CANTERBURY. *Litterae Cantuarienses.* 3 vols. (Rolls Series.) 1887.

CHICHESTER. Register of Bishop Robert Rede, 1397–1415. (Sussex Record Society, vol. xi.) 1910.

COVENTRY AND LICHFIELD. Registers of Roger de Norbury, 1322–1358; of Robert de Stretton, 1358–85. (Wm. Salt Arch. Society.) 1880, 1907.

DURHAM. *Registrum Palatinum Dunelmense.* 4 vols. (Rolls Series.) 1873, 1875.

EXETER. Registers of the following bishops, all in *Episcopal Registers, Diocese of Exeter,* ed. F. C. Hingeston-Randolph: Walter de Stapleton, 1307–27; John de Grandison, 1327–69; Thomas de Brantyngham, 1370–94; Edmund Stafford, 1395–1419; Edmund Lacy, 1420–55.

HEREFORD. Published by the Cantilupe Society, registers of the following bishops: Richard de Swinfield, 1283–1317; Adam of Orleton, 1317–27; Thomas de Charlton, 1327–44; John de Trillek, 1344–61; Lewis de Charlton, 1361–67; William de Courtenay, 1370–75; John Gilbert, 1375–89.

LONDON. Registers of Ralph Baldock, Gilbert Segrave, Richard Newport, and Stephen Gravesend, 1304–38; Simon of Sudbury, 1362–75. (Canterbury and York Society, vols. vii, xxxiv.) 1911, 1927.

SALISBURY. The Register of Simon of Ghent, 1297–1315. (Canterbury and York Society, vols. xl–xli.)

WINCHESTER. Registers of John de Sandale, 1316–18; Rigaud of Assier, 1320–23; William of Wykeham, 1367–1404. (Hampshire Record Society.)

CHRONICLES, CITY AND BOROUGH CHRONICLES, AND OTHER RECORDS

The Anonimale Chronicle of St. Mary's Abbey, York, 1333 to 1381. Ed. C. H. Galbraith. Manchester, 1927.

Arnold's Chronicle or *The Customs of London*. 1st ed., 1502; 2nd ed., c. 1520–21.
AVESBURY, ROBERT OF. *De Gestis Mirabilibus Regis Edwardi Tertii*. (To 1356.) Ed. E. M. Thompson. (Rolls Series.) 1889.
GEOFFREY LE BAKER DE SWYNBROKE. *Chronicon*. Ed. E. M. Thompson. Oxford, 1889.
The Brut, or *The Chronicles of England*. Ed. F. W. D. Brie. (Early English Text Society.) 1906.
A Briefe Discourse, declaring and approving the necessarie and inviolable Customes of London. London, 1584.
BURTON, THOMAS OF. *Chronicon Monasterii de Melsa*. (1150–1396, with continuation to 1406.) Ed. E. A. Bond. 3 vols. (Rolls Series.) 1866–68.
Calendar of Letter Books of the City of London. Ed. R. S. Sharpe. 12 vols., A–L. London, 1899–1912.
Calendar of Plea and Memoranda Rolls preserved among the Archives of the City of London at the Guildhall. Ed. A. H. Thomas. 3 vols., 1323–64, 1364–81, 1381–1412. 1926, 1929, 1932.
CAPGRAVE, JOHN. *The Chronicle of England*. Ed. F. C. Hingeston. (Rolls Series.) 1858.
CAXTON, WILLIAM. *The Chronicles of England* or *Caxton's Chronicle*. Westminster 1480, 1482, etc.
Chronica Monasterii S. Albani. Johannis de Trokelowe et Henrici de Blaneford, Chronica et Annales; and Annales Ricardi Secundi et Henrici Quarti regum Angliae, 1392–1406. Ed. H. T. Riley. (Rolls Series.) 1866.
Chronicle of London, 1089–1483. Ed. Edward Tyrrell and N. H. Nicolas. London, 1827.
Chronicles of the Reigns of Edward I and Edward II. Ed. William Stubbs. 2 vols. (Rolls Series.) 1883. (Contains *Annales Londonienses, Annales Paulini, Gesta Edwardi de Carnarvan auctore canonico Bridlingtoniensi cum continuatione to 1377, Vita Edwardi II, et al.*)
Chronicon Angliae ab anno Domini 1328 ad annum 1388 auctore monacho quodam Sancti Albani. Ed. E. M. Thompson. (Rolls Series.) 1874.
Chronicon de Lanercost, 1201–1346. Ed. Joseph Stevenson. (Bannatyne Club.) Edinburgh, 1839.
Chronique de la Traison et Mort de Richart II Roi d'Engleterre. (1397–1400.) Ed. Benjamin Williams. (English Historical Society.) 1846.
The Coventry Leet Book (or Mayor's Register), 1420–1555. (Early English Text Society.) 1907–13.
CRETON, JEAN. "Histoire du roy d'Angleterre Richard II . . . 1399." Ed. John Webb. *Archaeologia*, XX, 1–423. London, 1824.
Croniques de London. (44 Henry III to 17 Edward III.) Ed. G. J. Aungier. (Camden Society.) 1844. In translation, H. T. Riley, *The French Chronicle of London, 1259–1343*. London, 1863.
De Legibus Angliae Municipalibus Liber. London, 1583.
De Antiquis Legibus Liber. Ed. T. Stapleton. (Camden Society.) 1846.
An English Chronicle of the Reigns of Richard II, Henry IV, Henry V, and Henry VI. Ed. J. S. Davies. (Camden Society.) 1856.
Eulogium Historiarum . . . Ed. F. S. Haydon. 3 vols. (Rolls Series.) 1863.
FABYAN, ROBERT. *The New Chronicles of England and France*. Ed. Henry Ellis. London, 1811.
FAVENT, THOMAS. *Historia sive narracio de modo et forma mirabilis parliamenti apud West. . . .* (1386.) Ed. May McKisack. (Camden Miscellany vol. xiv.) 1926.
Flores Historiarum. Ed. H. R. Luard. 3 vols. (Rolls Series.) 1890.
FROISSART, JEAN. *The Chronicle of Jean Froissart*. "Translated out of French by Sir John Bourchier, Lord Berners, annis 1523–25 with intro. by W. P. Ker."
GRAFTON, RICHARD. *Chronicle at Large and meere History of the Affayres Englande and Kinges of the same*. 1569.
————. *Grafton's Chronicle or History of England*. (1189–1558.) London, 1809.
The Great And Ancient Charter of the Cinque Ports and its Members. From the First granted by King Edward the 1st. To the Last Charter granted by King Charles the 2nd. "Printed from an ancient copy dated 1668. . . ." Dover, 1807.
GREGORY, WILLIAM. *Gregory's Chronicle, 1189–1469*. Ed. James Gairdner. (Camden Society.) 1876.
Grey Friars of London Chronicle. (1189–1556.) Ed. J. G. Nichols. (Camden Society.) 1852.
HALL, EDWARD. *Hall's Chronicle*. (1399–1547.) Ed. Henry Ellis. London, 1809.
HARDYNG, JOHN. *Chronicle*. "From the earliest period of English history [to 1461], together with the continuation by Richard Grafton to 34 Henry VIII." Ed. Sir Henry Ellis. London, 1812.

HEMINGBURGH, WALTER OF. *Chronicon de Gestis Regum Angliae.* Ed. H. C. Hamilton. (English Historical Society.) 1848–49.

HEREFORD. *The Ancient Customs of the City of Hereford, with translations of the Earlier City Charters and Grants by Richard Johnson late town clerk.* 2nd ed. London, 1882.

HIGDEN, RALPH. *Polychronicon.* Ed. J. R. Lumby. 9 vols. (Rolls Series.) 1865–86.

Historia Vitae et Regni Ricardi II [1377–1402] *a monacho quodam Evesham consignata.* Ed. Thomas Hearne. Oxford, 1729.

HOLINSHED, RAPHAEL. *Chronicles of England, Scotlande, and Ireland. . . . Until this present time 1577.* 2 vols. 1577. Modern ed., 1807–8, in 6 vols.

Holinshed's Chronicle as used in Shakespeare's Plays. Ed. Allardyce and Josephine Nicoll. Based on W. G. Boswell-Stone, *Shakespeare's Holinshed: The Chronicle and the Historical Plays Compared.* (Everyman's Library.) 1927.

JEAKES, S. *Charters of the Cinque Ports.* London, 1728.

KNIGHTON, HENRY. *Chronicon, monachi Lycestrensis.* (959–1366 with continuation 1377–95.) Ed. J. R. Lumby. 2 vols. (Rolls Series.) 1889–95.

LE BEAU, JEAN. *Chronique de Richard II, 1377–99.* Ed. J. A. Buchon. (Collection des Chroniques Francaises.) Paris, 1826.

LEICESTER. *Records of the Borough of Leicester.* Ed. Mary Bateson. 2 vols. London, 1899; Cambridge, 1901.

Le Livere de Reis de Brittanie e Le Livere de Reis de Engletere (to 1274), with continuation, *Chroniques de Sempringham* (1280–1326). Ed. John Glover. (Rolls Series.) 1865.

MATTHEW PARIS. *Chronica Majora.* Ed. H. R. Luard. 7 vols. (Rolls Series.) 1872–83.

Memorials of Henry the Fifth King of England. Ed. C. A. Cole. (Rolls Series.) 1858.

Munimenta Gildhallae Londoniensis: Liber Albus, Liber Custumarum et Liber Horn. Ed. H. T. Riley. 3 vols. (Rolls Series.) 1859–62.

MURIMUTH, ADAM OF. *Continuatio Chronicarum.* (1328–88.) Ed. E. M. Thompson. (Rolls Series.) 1869.

NORTHAMPTON. *The Records of the Borough of Northampton.* 2 vols. Vol. I, ed. by C. A. Markham. Northampton, 1898.

NOTTINGHAM. *Records of the Borough of Nottingham.* 5 vols. Ed. W. H. Stevenson. London, 1882–1900. Vols. I–III.

OTTERBOURNE, THOMAS. *Chronica regum Angliae.* (From Brutus to 1420.) Ed. Thomas Hearne. Oxford, 1732.

RASTELL, JOHN. *The Pastime of People,* or *the Chronicles . . .* 1529. "Now first reprinted, and systematically arranged, with fac-simile woodcuts of portraits of popes, emperors, &c. and the kings of England." 1811.

READING, JOHN OF. *Chronica* [et anonymi Cantuariensis, 1346–67]. Ed. James Tait. Manchester, 1914.

Six Town Chronicles of England. Ed. Ralph Flenley. Oxford, 1911.

STOW, JOHN. *The Annales of England faithfully collected out of the most Authenticall authors, Records and other monuments of Antiquitie . . .* 1590. 1st ed., 1580.

———. *Summarie of Englyshe Chronicles 1565.* Frequently reissued, with additions bringing the information up to date, 1567–1607.

Three Fifteenth Century Chronicles. Ed. James Gairdner. (Camden Society.) 1880.

TREVET, NICHOLAS. *Annales sex regum Angliae, 1135–1307.* Ed. Anthony Hall. Oxford, 1719.

VERGIL, POLYDORE. *Three Books of Polydore Vergil's English History, comprising the reigns of Henry VI, Edward IV, and Richard III.* Ed. Sir Henry Ellis. (Camden Society.) 1844.

———. *Polydori Vergilii Urbinatus Anglicae historiae libri vigintisex.* 1546.

USK, ADAM OF. *Chronicon.* Ed. with transl. E. M. Thompson. (Royal Society of Literature.) 1904.

WALSINGHAM, THOMAS. *Historia Anglicana.* Ed. H. T. Riley. 2 vols. (Rolls Series.) 1863–64.

WHETHAMSTEDE, JOHN. *Registrum . . .* Ed. H. T. Riley. (Rolls Series.)

WRIOTHESLEY, CHARLES. *Chronicle of England.* (1485–1559.) Camden Society.

PRINTED SECONDARY ACCOUNTS

ADAIR, E. R. "The Petition of Right." *History,* V, 99–103. 1921.

ADAMS, G. B. *The Origin of the English Constitution.* New York, 1912.

BEALE, J. H. *A Bibliography of Early English Law Books.* (Ames Foundation.) 1926.

BÉMONT, CHARLES. *Chartes des Libertés Anglaises, 1100–1305.* Paris, 1892.

BLACKHAM, R. J. *Wig and Gown, The Story of the Temple, Gray's and Lincoln's Inn.* London, n.d.

BURDICK, W. L. *Bench and Bar of Other Lands*. Brooklyn, 1939.

BURRAGE, CHAMPLIN. *The Early English Dissenters in the Light of Recent Research*. (1550–1641.) 2 vols. Cambridge, 1912.

CHAMBERS, R. W. *Thomas More*. London, 1935.

CHRIMES, S. B. *English Constitutional Ideas of the Fifteenth Century*. Cambridge, 1936.

CLARKE, M. V. "The Origin of Impeachment," in *Oxford Essays in Medieval History, presented to H. E. Salter*. Oxford, 1934.

DAVIES, J. C. *The Baronial Opposition to Edward II, Its Character and Policy, a Study in Administrative History*. Cambridge, 1918.

The Dictionary of National Biography. Ed. Sidney Lee and Leslie Stephen. 1885, etc.

DUFF, E. GORDON. *A Century of the English Book Trade*. London, 1905.

———. *The Printers, Stationers and Bookbinders of London and Westminster in the Fifteenth Century*. Cambridge, 1899.

EHRLICH, LUDWIG. *Proceedings against the Crown, 1216–1377*. (Oxford Studies in Social and Legal History.) 1921.

FORSTER, JOHN. *Sir John Eliot, A Biography, 1592–1632*. 2 vols. London, 1872.

GARDINER, S. R. *History of England from the Accession of James I to the Outbreak of the Civil War. 1603–1642*. 10 vols. London, 1883–84.

GOVER, J. M. *Literary Associations with the Middle Temple*. A Reading delivered before the Honourable Society of the Middle Temple. 1935.

GRAY, H. L. *The Influence of the Commons on Early Legislation*. (Harvard Historical Studies.) 1932.

GROSS, CHARLES. *The Sources and Literature of English History*. 1915.

HOLDSWORTH, SIR WILLIAM S. *A History of English Law*. 9 vols. London, 1922–26.

———. *Some Makers of English Law*. Cambridge, 1938.

HUGHES, DOROTHY. *A Study of Social and Constitutional Tendencies in the Early Years of Edward III*. London, 1915.

JENKS, EDWARD. "The Story of the Habeas Corpus" in *Select Essays in Anglo-American Legal History*, II, 531–48.

KNAPPEN, M. M. *Tudor Puritanism, A Chapter in the History of Idealism*. Chicago, 1939.

LAPSLEY, G. T. "Archbishop Stratford and the Parliamentary Crisis of 1341." *English Historical Review*, XXX, 6–18, 193–215. 1915.

MACASSEY, SIR LYNDEN LIVINGSTON. *The Middle Temple's Contribution to the National Life*. A Reading delivered before the Honourable Society of the Middle Temple. 1930.

MAGUIRE, MARY HUME. "The Attack of the Common Lawyers on the Oath *ex Officio* as administered in the Ecclesiastical Courts in England" in *Essays in History and Political Theory in honor of C. H. McIlwain*, pp. 199–229. Harvard University Press, 1936.

———. "The History of the *Ex Officio* Oath in England." Radcliffe College dissertation, 1923. (Unpublished.)

Magna Carta Commemoration Essays. Ed. H. E. Malden. (Royal Historical Society.) 1917.

MAITLAND, F. W. *The Constitutional History of England*. Cambridge, 1908.

———. *English Law and the Renaissance*. Cambridge, 1901.

———. *Roman Canon Law in the Church of England*. London, 1898.

MCILWAIN, C. H. *Constitutionalism, Ancient and Modern*. Ithaca, 1940.

———. *The High Court of Parliament and its Supremacy*. New Haven, 1910.

MCKECHNIE, WILLIAM SHARP. *Magna Carta, A Commentary on the Great Charter of King John*. (With a historical introduction.) 2nd rev. ed. Glasgow, 1914.

MOORE, W. HARRISON. "Executive Commissions of Inquiry." *Columbia Law Review*, XIII, 500–523. 1913.

NORTON, GEORGE. *The City of London, its History, Constitution and Franchises*. 3rd rev. ed. London, 1869.

PEARSON, A. F. SCOTT. *Thomas Cartwright and Elizabethan Puritanism, 1535–1603*. London, 1925.

PENDRILL, CHARLES. *London Life in the Fourteenth Century*. London, 1925.

PETIT-DUTAILLIS, CHARLES. *Studies and Notes supplementary to Stubbs Constitutional History*. Vol. II ("The Forest"). Manchester, 1914.

PIERCE, WILLIAM. *An Historical Introduction to the Marprelate Tracts*. London, 1908.

———. *John Penry, His Life, Times and Writings*. London, 1923.

PIKE, L. O. *A Constitutional History of the House of Lords*. London, 1894.

PLUCKNETT, T. F. T. "The Lancastrian Constitution" in *Tudor Studies Presented . . . to Albert Frederick Pollard*. Ed. R. W. Seton-Watson. London and New York, 1924.

————. *Statutes and their Interpretation in the First Half of the Fourteenth Century.* (Cambridge Studies in Legal History.) 1922.

POLLARD, A. F. *The Evolution of Parliament.* London, 1926.

POLLOCK, SIR FREDERICK, AND F. W. MAITLAND. *The History of English Law before the Time of Edward I.* 2 vols. 2nd ed. Cambridge, 1898

REID, RACHEL R. *The King's Council in the North.* London, 1921.

RELF, FRANCES HELEN. *The Petition of Right.* Minneapolis, 1917.

SKEEL, CAROLINE A. J. *The Council in the Marches of Wales, a Study in Local Government during the Sixteenth and Seventeenth Century.* London, 1904.

SPEDDING, JAMES. *The Letters and Life of Francis Bacon, Including All His Occasional Works.* 7 vols. London, 1861–74.

STRYPE, JOHN. *Annals of the Reformation under Elizabeth.* 4 vols. in 7. Oxford, 1824.

————. *Ecclesiastical Memorials.* 3 vols. in 6. Oxford, 1822.

————. *The Life and Acts of John Whitgift.* 3 vols. Oxford, 1822.

————. *Matthew Parker.* 3 vols. Oxford, 1821.

THOMPSON, FAITH. *The First Century of Magna Carta: Why It Persisted as a Document.* Minneapolis, 1925.

TOUT, T. F. *Chapters in the Administrative History of Medieval England.* 4 vols. Manchester, 1928.

————. *The Place of Edward II in English History.* Manchester, 1914.

TREVELYAN, G. M. *England in the Age of Wycliffe.*

————. *England under the Stuarts.* (Oman Series.) London, 1916.

————. *English Social History, a Survey of Six Centuries, Chaucer to Queen Victoria.* London, 1943.

UNWIN, GEORGE (ed.). *Finance and Trade under Edward III.* (Publications of the University of Manchester, Historical Series.) Manchester, 1918.

USHER, R. G. *The Reconstruction of the English Church.* 2 vols. New York, 1910.

————. *The Rise and Fall of the High Commission.* Oxford, 1913.

VERNON-HARCOURT, L. W. *His Grace the Steward and Trial of Peers.* London and New York, 1907.

WHITE, A. B. "Magna Carta" in *Encyclopedia of the Social Sciences,* X, 44–46.

————. *The Making of the English Constitution.* New York and London, 1925.

WIGMORE, J. H. *A Treatise on the Anglo-American System of Evidence, in Trials at Common Law.* 5 vols. 2nd ed. 1923.

WILLSON, D. H. *The Privy Councillors in the House of Commons, 1604–1629.* Minneapolis, 1940.

WOOD-LEGH, K. L. *Studies in Church Life in England under Edward III.* Cambridge, 1934.

WRIGHT, LOUIS B. "The Elizabethan Middle Class Taste for History." *Journal of Modern History,* III, 175–197. 1931.

❊ INDEX ❊

Abbot, George, 326
Abstract of all the Penal Statutes, 153
Alford, Edward, 297, 309, 312, 320
Anderson's Reports, 289, 306, 326
Antiqua statuta (Vetera statuta), 10; manuscript editions, 37–39; sentence of excommunication in, 125; printed editions, 144, 146, 148–49, 150, 152, 317
Antiquaries, Society of, 162, 216, 245
"Antiquities," cult of, 160–61
Apologie for Sundrie Proceedings Ecclesiastical, 218
Archaionomia, 183
Archeion, 186–90
Articuli super cartas, 5, 19; on purveyance, 21–23; quoted, 43, 57; on Court of Steward and Marshal, 62, 276; cited in later times, 89, 172, 174
Arundel, Thomas, Archbishop of Canterbury, 18, 130–32
Arundel, Earl of (Thomas Howard), 320
Ashley, Sir Francis, 286–87, 294, 306, 343–44, 347; reading, 191, 234, 255, 268, 286–93

Bacon, Sir Francis, rates Charter as fundamental law, 16; and *Briefe Discourse,* 203–4; plans for law revision, 234; speaks in Commons, 247, 248, 254–55; defends Council of Wales and Marches, 266; frames James' denunciation of Coke, 278–79; defends king as protector of laws, 281; defends crown's power of commitment, 283; impeachment, 296, 308, 354, 356
Bagg, Sir James, 166, 328
Bagshawe, Edward, 191, 286, 367–69, 372
Bancroft, Richard, 207
Bankes, John, 349, 366–67
Bate's case, 249–50, 302
Beale, Robert, 216–17, 217–18, 219, 224, 260
Bennett, Sir John, 97, 296, 297, 308
Berthelet, Thomas, 146, 148
Bloxham, 120
Boke of Magna Carta, 148–49, 159, 317. See also *Antiqua statuta*
Boniface, Archbishop of Canterbury, 125–26, 130
Bonner, Edmund, 142–43
Bracton, Henry de, on trial by peers, 72; cited in later treatises and reports, 179, 193, 236, 357–58, 361
Bramston, John, 329, 332
Briefe Discourse . . . of the Laudable Customs of London, 195

Brief Notes, 217–18
Briefe Treatise of Oathes, 218
Bristol, Earl of (John Digby), 320
Browne, ———, 325–26
Brownists, 226–27
Buckingham, Duke of (George Villiers), 318–19, 323–24, 326, 328
Burghley, Lord (William Cecil), 183; quoted in Star Chamber, 204; protests use of oath ex officio, 212; petition from Cartwright, 214; and the Brownists, 226–27

Calthrop, Sir Henry, 271–72, 329, 331
Calvert, Sir George, 306–9
Camden, William, 161, 162, 182, 200, 245
Cartwright, Thomas, 209, 213–16
Cases. See by name.
Cawdry's case, 206, 213, 216, 291, 345
Caxton, William, 145, 155
Caxton's Chronicle, 156–58
Chambers case, 351
Chancery, court of, 283–84, 295, 364
Charles I, 311, 318, 335, 354
Chaucer, Geoffrey, quoted, 102, 143
Chicheley, Henry, 132–33
Chronicles of England, Scotland, and Ireland, 163
Cinque Ports, 118–19, 309
Clarke's case, 273, 274
Coke, Sir Edward, count of parliamentary confirmations, 9–10; interpretation of *praemunire,* 134; anticipated by Lambarde, Puritan lawyers, Fuller, 186, 209, 244–45, 257, 261–62; on origin of Court of Common Pleas, 200; on *Cawdry's case,* 213; and Morice's bill, 224–25; in *Darcy v. Allen,* 229; *Reports,* 242–45; mediator at time of *Fuller's case,* 261–62; and High Commission, 262–63, 263–64; praises Star Chamber, 265; attacks Council of Wales and Marches and Council of the North, 265–67; informations in Star Chamber, 269, 273–74; cases affecting London, 270–71; as judge and reporter, 276–78; removed from bench, 278–79; conflict with Ellesmere, 283–84; reading, 286; influence on Ashley, 291–92; in 1621 parliament, 294, 297–99; on monopolists, 302–4; and Magna Carta bill, 305–6; charges Bennett with sale of justice, 308; cites Magna Carta for Cinque Ports, 309; plays up Commons as court, 310; and 1624 parliament, 315–17, 319; and 1626 parliament, 320, 323; and 1628 parliament, 337–41; *Institutes,* 354–65, 373

Coke, Sir John, quoted on martial law, 348
Collection Shewinge what Jurisdiction the Clergie Hathe heretofore Lawfully Used, 217–18
Commissions, arbitrary methods in fourteenth century, 88, 94–95; executive commissions of inquiry, 93; Coke on unlawful commissions, 266–67
Common Pleas, court of, 57, 187, 200–3, 238, 264, 266
Confirmatio Cartarum, 5, 42–43; on excommunication, 126; cited in sixteenth and seventeenth centuries, 187, 252, 315–17, 327, 338
Constable and Marshal, court of, 87, 89–90, 94, 95, 347–50
Cosin, Doctor Richard, 218, 222–23, 223–24
Council of the North, 266
Council of Wales and the Marches, 265
Cowell, Doctor John, on origin of Court of Common Pleas, 200, 234; career, 235–36; *Institutiones*, 236; *Interpreter*, 236–38
Crompton, William, 175, 178–79, 236

Darcy, Lord, 141
Darcy v. Allen, 228, 260, 299
Dering, Sir Edward, 246
D'Ewes, Sir Simonds, 365–66, 370
de Burgh, John, 130
De tallagio non concendo, statute of, 253, 338, 363, 367
Dialogue of the Doctor and Student, 175–77
Digges, Sir Dudley, and impeachment of monopolists, 302–3; and impeachment of Buckingham, 321; committed, 324–26; in conference with Lords, 339–40
Despenser, Hugh, father and son, 41, 73–75, 77–78, 98, 127
Dodderidge, Sir John, 229, 250–51, 254, 295
Ducke, Doctor Arthur, 313–14
Dyer, Sir James, 168, 173–74, 174–75, 197, 331

Ecclesia anglicana, 121–25, 135, 140, 142, 151, 322
Edward I, 4–5
Edward II, and confirmations of Charter, 11–12; and purveyance, 21–22; and *judicium parium*, 72–77; quotes ca. 29, 84; and alien merchants, 111
Edward III, and confirmations of Charter, 10; first parliament, 15; grievances in minority, 21; character of reign, 79; crisis of 1340–41, 80–84; and London, 108–10; and alien merchants, 111–12; warned by Meopham, 128–29
Edward IV, ca. 23 cited, 26; and Cinque Ports, 119; and Magna Carta, 134–35
Eirenarcha, 184–85
Eliot, Sir John, comment on Coke, 298; in 1624 parliament, 311–12; in 1625 and 1626 parliaments, 319–20; commitment protested by Commons, 323–26; letter against forced loans, 327; in 1628 parliament, 336, 338, 340
Elizabeth, 199; relations with Whitgift, 210–

11; praised by Coke, 243–44; patroness of Middle Temple, 285; Coke reminisces on, 299
Ellesmere, Earl of (Thomas Egerton), 243, 269, 274, 284, 308
England's Epinomis, 239–41
Exchequer, court of, 89, 249–50
Exchequer Chamber, 65–66, 366–67
Excommunication, in thirteenth century, 125–26; in fourteenth century, 126–28; in fifteenth and early sixteenth centuries, 135–36, 195; in sixteenth and early seventeenth centuries, 211, 223, 252, 281, 327, 338

Fabyan, Robert, 155, 158, 166
Fanshawe, Sir Thomas, 314
Ferrers, George, 147, 150–51
Finch, Sir Heneage, 303, 309–10, 320
Finch, Henry, 224n
Fitzherbert, Sir Anthony, *Natura Brevium*, 43–48; tract on justices of the peace, 178–79; *Grand Abridgement*, 86, 178–79; reading, 191; works used by others, 180, 184, 220, 236, 280, 357
Five knights case, 68, 329–35, 339–47
Fleetwood, Sir William, member of parliament, 305–7, 313, 320
Fleetwood, Sir William, recorder of London, 162, 198
Fleta, 56n; on trial by peers, 72; used by Cowell, 236; and Coke, 357–58
Forced loans, 326–27. See also Petition of Right
Forest Charter, 9–19; in *antiqua statuta*, 39; in later Middle Ages, 383–85
Fortescue, Sir John, 65–66, 67, 197, 242, 244, 290, 292
Fuller, Nicholas, 144, 203, 209; counsel for Cartwright, 215; in *Darcy v. Allen*, 228–30; *Fuller's case*, 259–62

Gardiner, Stephen, 142–43
Gaveston, Peter, 73–74, 80
Glanvill, Ranulf, 46, 61, 172; on pleas in Exchequer, 172, 200–1; quoted in sixteenth and seventeenth centuries, 172, 179, 197, 236, 357–59; edited by Staunford, 179
Glanvill, John, recorder of Plymouth, 318, 320, 345–46, 373
Gloucester, Eleanor, Duchess of, 85, 392
Grafton, Richard, 139, 155, 165–66, 220
Grand Abridgement, 178–79
Gray's Inn, 169. See also Inns of Court.
Great Abridgement, 149–50
Great Boke of Statutes, 152
Great Yarmouth, 116–18

Habeas corpus, writ of, 68, 86–87, 262, 266, 271, 325–26, 329–30, 339, 341–43, 362
Hakewill, William, 112, 251–54, 302, 343, 369
Hampden, Edmund, see *Five knights case*
Hampden, John, 6, 327n
Hampden's case, 249, 366–67, 369–70

Hastings, 119
Heath, Sir Robert, 93; in *five knights case,* 329–31, 334–35, 343, 347
Henry III, Great Charter of, 5–6; described by Tudor chroniclers, 156–59
Henry IV, 115, 130–31
Henry VII, 30, 149
Henry VIII, 146, 149, 159, 165, 167, 205–6
Hereford, 146
High Commission, court of, 205–15, 218–19; defended by bishops, 256; challenged by Fuller, 259; new commission issued, 263–65; against Puritans, 352; abolished, 370
Hobart, Sir Henry, 263, 281–82, 295
Holinshed, Raphael, 6, 155, 162–64, 166, 237
Hyde, Nicholas, 329, 335, 343, 353

Impeachment, origin, 90–91; revival in 1621, 296; of the monopolists, 301–4; of Middlesex, 308–9; of Buckingham, 321–23
Impositions, 110–12, 314–15, 315–17
Inner Temple, 169, 175, 192. See also Inns of Court
Inns of Court, 144, 167, 168, 169; readings in, 135–36, 190–95, 284–93, 367–68
Inspeximus of Edward I, 5, 39, 148
Ireland, 92

James I, 168; attitude toward courts, 206; scholarship and love of argument, 233–34; destroys notes and papers of Addled Parliament, 256; defends oath ex officio, 256; and High Commission, 263–65; denounces Coke, 278–79; attempts to convert Legate, 280; condemns some of patents, 301–2; and 1624 parliament, 311; asks for "precedent," 319
John, 156–59, 165–66, 194–95; Great Charter of, 37, 240–41, 246–47, 328–29, 366–67, 370–71, 372
Johnson, Francis, 227–28
Jonson, Ben, quoted, 168, 233, 245
Judicium parium, in fourteenth and fifteenth centuries, 72–86, 390–92; in trial by peers, 180, 292, 357; Littleton's ruling on, 85–86; cited, 273, 275; and trial by jury, 185–86, 238n, 242

Kalendar or Table of all the Statutes, 234–35
King's Bench, court of, 271–72, 277–78, 298, 329–30

Lambarde, William, 70, 182–90, 204, 233; works used by others, 237, 239, 357–58
Lancaster, Duke of (John of Gaunt), 101
Lancaster, Thomas, Earl of, 72, 75–76, 350
Langton, Stephen, 125–26
Langton, Walter, 79–80
Laud, William, 329, 353, 367, 368–69, 373
Legate, Bartholomew, 279–81
Leicester, 116n
Leland, John, 159–60
Lettou, John, 145

Lilburne, John, 370
Lincoln's Inn, 146, 147, 154, 169, 182–83. See also Inns of Court
Little Treatise concerning Writs of Subpoena, 177–78
Littleton, Sir Thomas, 13; cases in Exchequer Chamber, 65–66; ruling on how Magna Carta became statute, 66; interpretation of *judicium parium,* 85–86; quoted on "law of the land," 87; *Tenures,* 67, 145; reading on De Donis, 191; quoted, 341, 354–57
Littleton, Edward, 339–41, 343, 345, 347, 373
London, 12, 13; control of Thames and Medway, 23–24; cites *ca. 9,* 63–64; part in winning the Charter, 100–1; in later Middle Ages, 100–4; *ca. 9* used as guarantee for economic and political liberties, 104–10; and alien traders, 110–16; subsequent charters, 113–15; and other towns, 116–20; in early Stuart period, 270–72; notable cases, 270–72
Long Parliament, 365, 369–70
Lords Appellant, 95
Lords Ordainers, see *New Ordinances*
Lyndwood, William, 132

Machlinea, William de, 145
Magna Carta, *ca. 1,* 82, 121–25, 130–36, 140–41, 221–23, 227–28, 258, 368, 372; *ca. 2,* 40, 176, 200; *ca. 3,* 42, 66, 198, 268; *ca. 4,* 42, 52, 61; *ca. 5,* 64–65; *ca. 7,* 53n, 59, 174–75, 181, 199, 361; *ca. 8,* 42, 173, 200, 360; *ca. 9,* 63–64, 104–10, 116–20, 196, 309; *ca. 10,* 54–55, 173; *ca. 11,* 41, 57–58, 62, 171, 173, 187–88, 200–3, 238, 245, 264, 361–62; *ca. 12,* 58–59, 62, 171, 174, 266–67, 360, 361–62; *ca. 13,* 60; *ca. 14,* 34, 44–46, 63, 179, 184–85, 198, 221, 237, 242, 261, 275, 295, 361; *ca. 16,* 40n; *ca. 17,* 171, 178–79, 191; *ca. 18,* 46, 360; *ca. 19,* 21, 247, 317; *ca. 21,* 21, 247; *ca. 22,* 180, 182, 199, 360; *ca. 23,* 23–27, 135, 269; *ca. 24,* 49–51; *ca. 25,* 27–30, 40, 133, 238n; *ca. 26,* 223, 360; *ca. 27,* 39, 181; *ca. 28,* 56–57, 191, 221–22, 223–24, 238n, 261, 360; *ca. 29,* 68–69; *ca. 30,* 110–12, 185, 249–50, 250–55, 269–70, 362–63; *ca. 31,* 19–20, 39n, 41, 181, 238n; *ca. 34,* 55, 171, 174, 179n; *ca. 35,* 30–31, 48, 63, 64, 175, 178–79, 361; *ca. 36,* 199, 361; *ca. 37,* 34, 41. See also *Per legem terrae, Judicium parium,* and *Nulli negabimus*
Marshalsea, case of, 276–77, 289
Martial law, and Court of Constable and Marshal, 89–90, 348; and *lex terrae,* 347–50; effect of Petition of Right, 350
Martin, Sir Henry, 345, 349n, 373
Matthew Paris, 5, 161, 162, 163, 187, 239, 245, 392–93
May, Sir Humphrey, 320, 324, 325
Meopham, Simon, 22, 78; *Speculum,* 127–29
Middle Temple, 168, 169, 174, 190, 285, 286. See also Inns of Court

Middlesex, Earl of (Lionel Cranfield), 308–9, 312

Mirror of Justices, 40, 70, 98, 358

Monopolies, in Tudor period, 228; criticized in 1597 and 1601 parliaments, 228–29, 255; abuses in reign of James I, 296, 299–301; chief offenders dealt with by Lords, 301–2; patentees' powers declared against Magna Carta, 302–4, 307, 312, 323

More, Sir Thomas, 140, 146, 147

Morice, Sir James, 213, 215, 218, 219–20, 224–26, 257, 304

Mortimer and Isabella, 76–78, 90, 101, 108

Natura Brevium, 43–48

New canons, 257–58, 292

New Ordinances, confirm and supplement Charters, 11–12, 15, 22; cited in petitions, 40, 72–76, 80, 104–6

New Year's Gift, 159–60

Northampton, *Records,* 116

Norwich, 116

Nova statuta, 38, 148, 197

Nowell, Lawrence, 183n

Noy, William, 87, 306, 320–21, 329, 331–32, 336

Nulli negabimus, 41, 97–99, 244, 247, 318, 321–22, 364–65

Oath *ex officio,* 208–9, 213–16, 219–20, 222–23, 256

Old Natura Brevium, 43–51

Ottobone, the Legate, 125–26

Owen, Sir Roger, 244, 248, 251

Palmes, Sir Guy, 310, 319, 320

Parker, Matthew, 160–61, 183, 239

Penry, John, 227–28

Per legem terrae, in later Middle Ages, 86–97; rival interpretations of, 263–64, 242, 283, 284, 292–93, 332, 368

Petition of Right, 86–87, 336–39, 345, 350, 362, 369, 372–73

Phelips, Sir Robert, 306, 320

Pilgrimage of Grace, 141

Plea Rolls, 33–36; compared with Year Books, 53–54

Plowden, Edmund, 167, 168; career, 169–70; *Reports,* 170–73; and Middle Temple Hall, 285; cited in *five knights case,* 331

Plymouth, 277–78

Popham, Sir John, 268

Praerogativa Regis, 180–82

Prerogatives of Parliaments, 328–29

Priviledges of the Baronage, 241–42, 349–50

Prynne, William, 366, 369, 373

Pulton, Ferdinando, 153–55, 234–35

Pupilla Oculi, 130

Puritans and puritanism, 142; in Elizabeth's reign, 209–10; resistance to Whitgift's regime, 212–13; Magna Carta bill, 257–58

Purveyance and purveyors, 21–23, 247–48, 317, 323

Pym, John, 313, 320

Pynson, Richard, 145–46, 148

Raleigh, Sir Walter, 169; in Star Chamber, 274–75; *Prerogatives of Parliaments,* 328–29

Rastell, John, 146–50; *Great Abridgement,* 149–50; *The Pastyme of People,* 158

Rastell, William, 147; editions of statutes, 152–53; later reprints, 160; used by legal profession, 189, 222, 331–32, 364n; *Exposicions of the Termes of the Lawes of England,* 237n

Redman, Robert, 146, 152

Register of Writs, "actions founded on the statute," 43–51, 171, 173, 217, 331, 357

Replication of a Serjaunte of the Laws of England, 177

Requests, court of, 202–3

Rich, Nathaniel, 306, 318, 320

Richard II, 16, 18, 84–85

Rolles, John, 349, 350–51

Rudyerd, Benjamin, 86, 347

St. Albans, 273

St. Germain, Christopher, on abuses of excommunication, 136; *Doctor and Student,* 175–77; dispute over writ of subpoena, 177–78; quoted by Ashley, 290

St. John, Oliver (Viscount Grandison and Baron Tregoz), 224

St. John, Oliver (of Marleborough in Wiltshire), 279, 281

St. John, Oliver, counsel in *ship-money case,* 366–67

Sandwich, 119

Sandys, Sir Edwin, 248, 306, 309, 312n, 314, 320

Scrope, Richard, 132

Selden, John, 6, 68, 70, 233, 239–42; *Privilege of the Baronage,* 241–42, 349–50; in conference with Lords, 339–41, 343; on martial law, 349–50; in 1629 parliament, 351–52

Seymour, Sir Francis, 319, 320

Shakespeare, William, 133, 139, 164–65, 285

Sherland, Christopher, 321–22

Six statutes, 87–90, 90–94; cited under title *accusacion,* 153, 155; cited in sixteenth and seventeenth centuries, 189–90, 209, 220, 222, 225n, 258, 284, 291, 332, 335, 337, 370

Skinner's and Catcher's case, 204–5

Speculum, 22, 127–29

Spelman, Sir Henry, 238, 372

Spencer, Richard, 314

Spencer, Sir William, 313n, 320, 322

Stafford, John de, 134

Star Chamber, bill for reorganization, 189, 204–5; and Cartwright, 215–16; informations put in by Coke, 269, 273–74, 289; *Suffolk's case,* 295; as administrative court, 272; on censorship, 351–52; abolished, 370

Statutes at Large, 235

Staunford, Sir William, 168, 175; *Pleas of the Crown,* 179–80; *Praerogativa Regis,* 180–82; used by others, 236

Steward and Marshal, court of, 89, 106–7, 276–77, 290

Stow, John, 155, 162–63, 166, 200

Stratford, John de, 22, 81–84, 101, 123, 127

Suffolk, Duke of, 85n, 391–92

Summarie of Englyshe Chronicles, 162–63

Survey of London, 162–63

Tottell, Richard, 152

Vergil, Polydore, 158–59, 237

Vetera statuta, see Antiqua statuta

Warham, William, 140

Wendover, Roger, 5

Wentworth, Thomas, 310, 320, 336

Westminster, 100–2

Whitby, Edward, 320, 336

Whitelocke, Sir James, 190–91, 254, 282–83

Whitgift, John, 207, 210–11, 212, 217, 243

Wilde, John, 324–25

Williams, Sir Thomas, 192

Winchelsea, John de, 123, 126

Wolsey, Thomas, 142

Wycliff, John, 122, 129–30

Wyems, Humphrey, 246

Year Books, 38, 60–61, 385–86